GENERALIST PRACTICE
WITH
ORGANIZATIONS
AND
COMMUNITIES

GENERALIST PRACTICE
WITH
ORGANIZATIONS
AND
COMMUNITIES

Karen K. Kirst-Ashman
University of Wisconsin–Whitewater

and

Grafton H. Hull, Jr.
Indiana University Northwest

Nelson–Hall Publishers
Chicago

Project Editor: Dorothy Anderson
Typesetter: Precision Typographers
Printer: The Courier Companies
Illustrator: Don Baumgart
Cover Painting: Bill Moran, *Daydreaming II*

Library of Congress Cataloging-in-Publication Data

Kirst-Ashman, Karen Kay.
    Generalist practice with organizations and communities / Karen K.
Kirst-Ashman and Grafton H. Hull, Jr.
       p.   cm.
    Includes bibliographical references and indexes.
    ISBN 0-8304-1400-2
    1. Social service.   2. Social case work.   3. Community
organization.   I. Hull, Grafton H.   II. Title.
HV40.K464   1997
361.3′2—dc20   96-34766
                                             CIP

Manufactured in the United States of America

10 9 8 7 6 5 4 3 2 1

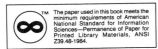

The paper used in this book meets the
minimum requirements of American
National Standard for Information
Sciences—Permanence of Paper for
Printed Library Materials, ANSI
Z39.48-1984.

To Gary A. Kirst, Ruth Kirst, and Jannah Mather

CONTENTS IN BRIEF

CONTENTS

CHAPTER 2
Using Micro Skills in the Macro Environment 45

Introduction 46

CHAPTER 5
PREPARE—Decision Making for Organizational Change 165

CHAPTER 6
IMAGINE How to Implement Macro Intervention: Changing Agency Policy   201

CHAPTER 7
IMAGINE Project Implementation and Program Development   227

CHAPTER 11
Advocacy and Social Action with Populations-at-Risk 355

CHAPTER 12
Ethics and Ethical Dilemmas in Macro Practice   389

CHAPTER 13
Working with the Courts   433
Patricia M. Christopherson

PREFACE

This book is a guide to generalist social work practice with organizations and communities. The three adjectives that best describe this text are *relevant, practical,* and *readable*. Generalist practice is clearly defined. Specific macro practice skills are presented in a straightforward and interesting manner. Applications to actual macro practice situations are emphasized throughout, as is the importance of client system strengths. The content is geared to either the undergraduate or graduate generalist practice sequence.

This text aims to fulfill five major goals. First, it provides a *readable and practical guide* to working in and with organizations and communities (macro practice). A major concern in social work education today is the strong tendency for students to veer away from thinking about helping communities and organizations to seek and achieve social change. Instead, students are frequently drawn to the perceived psychological drama and intensity of more clinically oriented practice with individuals, families, and small groups. This text emphasizes the importance of macro practice for practitioners working in direct service or lower level supervisory positions. (An assumption is that practitioners cannot always assume administrators will do the effective, efficient, or even the right thing. In these cases, the burden of change may fall on the practitioner.) Numerous case examples are presented to make the material interesting and relevant. Organizational and community theories are examined and linked to practice applications.

Second, the text proposes a *generalist perspective* that emphasizes how micro, mezzo, and macro skills can be interlinked. This generalist approach assumes that group (i.e., mezzo) skills are built on a firm foundation of individual (i.e., micro) skills. Likewise, skills involved in working with organizations and communities (i.e., macro skills) rest on a solid base of both micro and mezzo skills. This text links the three levels of practice—micro, mezzo, and macro—so that students can clearly see how all three skill levels are used in everyday practice situations. On the one hand, whole chapters and numerous examples throughout illustrate how micro and mezzo skills can be applied to macro practice situations. On the other hand, the text aims to structure how students think about clients and their problems so that they automatically explore alternatives beyond the individual and small group levels.

The text's third basic goal is to provide clearly defined, *step-by-step frameworks* for thinking about and initiating macro change in organizations and communities. A model for decision making concerning whether or not to pursue macro intervention is proposed. Additionally, a procedure for pursuing the macro intervention process is described.

The text's fourth goal is to identify, explain, and examine *specific skills* useful in macro practice and address significant issues relevant to this practice. Skills include working with the media, using new technological advances, fund-raising, grant writing, working within court macro settings, evaluating macro practice effectiveness, resolving ethical dilemmas in macro contexts, advocating for populations-at-risk, and managing time and stress within macro environments.

The fifth basic goal concerns presenting material to students that is not only relevant and interesting, but also *consistent with new accreditation standards*. This

xix

material targets social work values and ethics, human diversity, the promotion of social and economic justice, and the empowerment of populations-at-risk. The text adopts a generalist perspective, emphasizes evaluation of practice, focuses on the differential use of communication skills with colleagues and community members, demonstrates the appropriate use of supervision, and examines practitioner functioning within organizational structures.

Many generalist curriculums structure their practice sequences so that courses oriented toward macro practice with organizations and communities follow practice courses concerned with micro and mezzo systems, respectively. An assumption is that students will use the content of this book close to the point at which they seek employment. Therefore, chapters on constructing resumés and finding jobs, in addition to stress and time management, are included. This content is covered here because it is vital to students, yet it is not necessarily covered elsewhere in the curriculum.

An *Instructor's Manual and Test Bank* is available to assist instructors in presenting material and students in implementing practice skills. A student workbook entitled *The Macro Skills Workbook: Social Work Practice with Organizations and Communities* is also available on a complimentary basis for instructors adopting this book and for student purchase. This workbook provides a broad range of activities focusing on macro practice applications. These include problematic situations for students to address, role plays, and practice exercises directly related to the text's content.

This text is the third of a triad. The first text in the triad is *Understanding Generalist Practice*, which focuses on micro skills. The second of the triad, focusing on mezzo skills, is in press. All three texts stress the generalist approach. However, each focuses on the specific skills necessary for its level of practice. Each stresses the linkages among all three practice levels to maintain the generalist perspective. On the one hand, the three texts can be used in sequence, as one builds on another. On the other hand, each of the three texts can be used independently in conjunction with other practice texts. Each can be used to integrate a generalist perspective at any point in the practice sequence. A student workbook complete with classroom exercises and assignments, in addition to an instructor's manual and test bank will be available for all three.

ACKNOWLEDGMENTS

We wish to express sincere thanks to illustrator Don Baumgart whose drawings capture the heart of this book. Many thanks to Pat Christopherson who wrote chapter 13, ''Working with the Courts.'' We wish to express our sincere gratitude to Vicki Vogel for her exceptional technical assistance and support. Our heartfelt appreciation goes to Gary A. Kirst who provided steadfast consultation and expert feedback as we wrote. We convey many thanks to Robert E. Duea, president and CEO of Lutheran Social Services of Wisconsin and Upper Michigan, Milwaukee, Wisconsin, and Fern Behlke, director of administration, Family Service, Madison, Wisconsin, for their help and consultation regarding content on social service organizations. We express our genuine indebtedness and appreciation to Steve Ferrara, president of Nelson–Hall, who encouraged us to pursue this endeavor and provided invaluable assistance and advice throughout the project. Sincere gratitude is extended to Libby Rubenstein, senior college editor, whose helpful feedback and organized direction guided us through the publication process. Many thanks to Richard Meade, general manager, and Tamra Campbell-Phelps, production manager and designer, whose help and creative consultation greatly facilitated our writing. We extend our earnest thanks to Nick Ashman who provided support, encouragement, and patience in addition to many hours of cooking and other domestic sustenance while Karen Kirst-Ashman wrote. We extend genuine appreciation to H. Wayne Johnson and James Wahlberg for their conscientious, constructive critiques and helpful suggestions as they reviewed the text.

CHAPTER ONE

Introduction to Generalist Practice with Organizations and Communities

What is generalist practice anyway?

Why do you need to know what generalist practice is? Social work is social work, isn't it?

Why do you need to understand *organizations and communities* if you will be working primarily with individual clients and families?

Aren't *supervisors and administrators* supposed to take care of all those agency and policy matters?

What is *agency life* like?

Why Do You Need the Content in This Book?

Most social workers first entering professional practice view their jobs as work that deals mostly with individuals and families. Obviously, work takes place within an agency and community context. You usually need an agency to employ you in order to have an arena in which to practice your social work skills. Practice takes place within an agency environment. Similarly, the agency functions within a community milieu. Agencies provide resources and services to communities through their workers' performance. The point is that both agencies and communities are extremely significant factors in your ability to practice social work. However, it is probably easy for you to focus on the individual clients sitting right in front of you and give little if any thought to the larger picture, namely, that of the agency and the community. It is tempting to think in terms of administrators and politicians assuming responsibility for any administrative and political matters that arise within agencies and communities.

Yet, a much broader approach to social work practice exists, one that emphasizes the importance of the many systems engulfing and having an impact on large numbers of individual clients. Inevitably, you will work within some agency or organization context. Therefore, the agency's rules and policies will have a monumental impact on what you can and cannot do for your clients.

For example, your agency policy might limit the hours you can see your clients to a traditional eight to five time structure. What if most of your clients are readily available only during evening hours? What if

you decide that your agency should be more responsive to meeting clients' real needs? Your job description will probably have *nothing* to do with changing agency policy. However, what if you feel the most ethical thing to do is to implement an agency policy change on your clients' behalf? How would you go about planning such an endeavor? What specific skills would you need to "pull it off"?

Consider another example. Suppose you discover that many of your clients, suffering from severe poverty, have little if any money to buy their children food, let alone gifts, during the upcoming Christmas holiday season. You feel this is sad and unfair. Giving clients additional resources may have nothing to do with your job description. However, you feel that pursuing such a goal would mean very much to them. How might you go about raising the funds or getting the resources? Whom would you go to for help? What skills might be useful in this project? How might you establish a plan for accomplishing this goal?

Think about still another instance where you might be working in an agency serving survivors of domestic violence. The agency supports a shelter for temporary residential respite in addition to providing financial and emotional counseling for survivors. The agency also use an extensive referral network for services ranging from vocational testing to day care services. Suppose after careful thought you determine that the agency really needs to start providing help for abusers, too. You become fully convinced of this necessity when you begin seeing second and third wives of the same abuser visit the agency because of his continued battering. You would like to develop an educational, self-awareness group for batterers. You think that this tack would substantially impact the violence problem. How might you go about initiating and developing such a program? Who would you talk to about it? Where might you get the required resources?

The three preceding examples concern internal agency issues that affect clients. Just as you function professionally within an agency context, so do you, your clients, and your agency carry out activities and responsibilities within a community context. Community issues also have major impacts upon your and your agency's ability to perform.

First of all, virtually every community is subject to social, economic, and political forces. For example, a community's social conditions might involve extreme racial segregation resulting in serious racist activity. "Skin heads" and "neo-Nazis" frequently burn crosses on the lawns of African-American residents. Racial slurs are commonly hurled back and forth between white and African-American groups. Race-related gang activity is prevalent. Under such social conditions, how well do you think you would be able to function as a social worker? How could you effectively practice with your clients? How could you simply ignore these conditions and go about your business? What is the ethical thing to do? Could you try to implement changes within your community that would, in turn, have massive impacts upon your clients' quality of life?

Likewise, a community may experience extreme economic hardships when a large corporation, the community's primary employer, moves to another state where taxes are significantly lower. Unemployment climbs sky high. Subsequently, smaller businesses dry up and close as people have no money for purchases. Along with others in the community, your clients may lose the employment they have. You may even eventually lose your job if public funding or private purchasing power can no longer support social services. What kinds of things could you do in response to such economic pressure? What social work skills might help you address such a serious problem at the community level?

Political forces also drastically affect community functioning. Suppose the state legislature or Congress decides to discontinue subsidizing public transportation in your state's major urban areas? Without such subsidies, public transportation can no longer operate. What if most of your clients depend on this transportation in order to get to work, shopping areas, and school. Essentially, most clients use public transportation to satisfy many of their travel needs. Your agency job description will probably not include anything about mobilizing and trying to change political forces. However, regardless of what specific social service you provide to your clients (for example, counseling or financial assistance), what if an issue like transportation suddenly supersedes all these other problems? What if you can't effectively do your own job because you can't see your clients when they don't have any transportation? Do you just ignore the political decision to cease subsidizing public transportation? Can you ethically just sit back and do so?

One of this text's major assumptions is that generalist practitioners require a wide range of skills for helping individuals, groups, families, organizations, and communities in a wide variety of situations. Generalists thus require a sound understanding of the organizational environments in which they practice. They need to know what goes on in organizations and how such organizations function within the community and larger macro (large scale) environments in which organizations exist.

The intent of this book is to explore the larger systems such as organizations and communities within which you will strive to provide services and resources to your clients. We will examine a wide range of approaches to intervention on the macro (that is, organizational and community) level. Our assumption is that you as a worker will probably begin your professional life providing some form of direct service or, perhaps, even serving in a lower level administrative position. However, we also assume that you will probably have chances to effect much broader changes on your clients' behalf by seeking and implementing changes in your clients' larger (macro) environments.

You might now be asking yourself the questions, "What about agency administration? Isn't it supposed to be responsible for such macro problems and issues?" Usually, agency administrators implement changes as part of their administrative responsibility, or agency authority figures solicit help and advice from outside consultants (Holloway, 1987). In both instances, formal authority figures (such as an agency director, unit service director, chief executive officer, or board of directors) initiate and control the change process. In an ideal world, administrators would automatically initiate and implement all the changes necessary for the most effective and efficient service provision to clients. However, in the real world, people in power often have multiple pressures and distractions. In reality, they either choose not to make macro changes or fail to see a valid need for such changes.

As a social work practitioner you will likely have to face community problems and gaps in services. As a generalist practitioner you will likely encounter times when your agency is accomplishing tasks ineffectively, is not doing something it should do, or is simply doing the wrong thing. Holloway (1987) describes how some problems facing human service organizations are "profound," while others are very "subtle"; specific problems include how "the agency does not reach out to potential clients, the agency is insensitive to clients' definitions of problems, it serves those for whom public sympathy is high and refuses to serve others, it makes referrals for its own rather than the client's convenience, or it offers one kind of service to meet all needs" (p. 731). When such community or organizational problems exist, it is the practitioner's professional and ethical responsibility to consider helping the agency improve its service provision to clients.

This chapter will:

- Introduce the Generalist Intervention Model.
- Define generalist practice and explain each component of this definition including professional knowledge, skills, and values.
- Introduce a wide range of professional roles practitioners may assume in macro practice.
- Discuss and explain the problem-solving process within the macro practice context.
- Provide a brief history of practice with organizations and communities within a professional context.
- Introduce content covered in the remainder of the book.

The Generalist Intervention Model

Social workers are generalists (Johnson, 1989). That is, they need to have a wide array of skills at their disposal. Social workers don't pick and choose what problems and issues they would like to address. They see a problem, even a very difficult problem, and try to help people solve it. They must prepare themselves to help people with individualized personal problems on the one hand and very broad problems that affect whole organizations and communities on the other.

This book is about generalist practice in organizations and communities. There is a multitude of ways to describe what generalist social workers do. They work with individuals, families, groups, organizations, communities, and social systems. This work is based on a body of knowledge, practice skills, and professional values. They perform their work in a wide variety of settings focusing on children and families, health, justice, education, economic status, and many more too numerous to list.

The social work profession has been struggling with the concept of generalist practice for many years. Historically, there was a tendency to educate new practitioners so that they were tracked into emphasizing only one area of skills—for example, work with individuals, groups, or communities—or one area of practice—for instance, children and families, or administration.

(Highlight 1.2 explains this in greater depth.) Much the opposite, a generalist practitioner needs competency in a wide variety of areas instead of being limited to such a single track.

Generalist practice as described here is based upon a Generalist Intervention Model (GIM)[1] characterized by a least three major features. First, this generalist perspective is founded on a definition of generalist practice that, in turn, is supported by the knowledge, skills, and values characterizing the unique nature of the social work profession. This definition is reviewed and explained in depth later in the chapter.

Second, this generalist perspective uses a specific problem-solving method involving seven major steps. This method is infinitely flexible in its application. As illustrated in figure 1.1, the seven steps include engagement, assessment, planning, implementation (or intervention), evaluation, termination, and follow-up. Each step will be addressed in this chapter.

The third feature of the generalist perspective proposed here is oriented toward solving problems at multiple levels of intervention. That is, such problems may involve individuals, families, groups, organizations, and communities. In other words, the model involves micro, mezzo, and macro systems as targets of change. Micro systems are individuals. Mezzo systems are small groups. Families, because of their intimate nature, arbitrarily lie somewhere between micro and mezzo systems. Finally, macro systems are any large systems, including organizations and communities. In effect, this generalist approach means that virtually any problem may be analyzed and addressed from a wide range of perspectives that could potentially involve any size system.

Figure 1.2 illustrates how you as a generalist practitioner might choose any of the three levels of intervention to address a particular problem. First, you must use micro skills to engage the individual or individuals with whom you are talking about the problem. This involves using your micro skills to establish a relation-

---

1. The Generalist Intervention Model was first proposed in *Understanding Generalist Practice* by K. Kirst-Ashman and G. Hull (Chicago: Nelson-Hall, 1993). This book is considered the first in a trilogy addressing generalist practice and emphasizing specific skills necessary for the micro, mezzo, and macro levels. *Generalist Practice with Organizations and Communities* is the third of this trilogy. The second, *Generalist Practice with Groups and Families* is forthcoming.

Figure 1.1
Problem-Solving Steps in the
Generalist Intervention Model

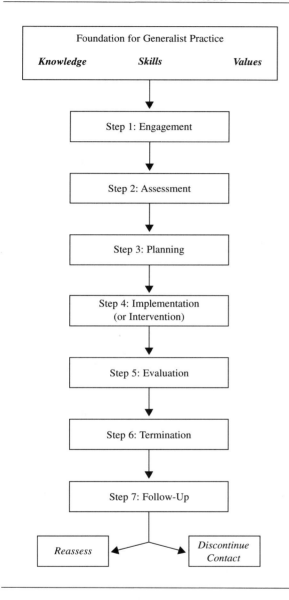

planning, implementation (or intervention), evaluation, termination, and follow-up process regardless of which level of intervention you choose to pursue.

For example, suppose you are a generalist practitioner for a rural midwest county. Your job entails receiving referrals from your supervisor (who has received them from an intake worker). You then establish initial connections with clients and other referral persons by engaging them in the problem-solving process, familiarize clients with the agency and supply them with information, solicit necessary data to assist in service provision, provide short-term counseling when needed, and make appropriate referrals to agency units and other community resources as appropriate.

You receive a referral involving an elderly individual, Murray Strewynskowski. The person who calls, Duke Earl, is one of Mr. Strewynskowski's concerned neighbors. Mr. Earl expresses concern because Mr. Strewynskowski has twice fallen down on his icy sidewalk and been unable to get back up and into the house. Both times Mr. Earl happened to notice the fall and was able to assist Mr. Strewynskowski into the house. While inside, Mr. Earl noticed extremely chaotic conditions. Rotting garbage was strewn all around the kitchen and about a dozen cats leisurely wandered around at will. Mr. Earl noticed that a black cat with a white patch over her left eye was eating what seemed to be canned creamed corn mixed with ketchup from a plate on the table that looked as if it might have been Mr. Strewynskowski's lunch. Mr. Earl also expresses concerns about Mr. Strewynskowski's diet in a general sense. Mr. Earl wonders whether Mr. Strewynskowski is able to shop or cook adequately, as he looks gauntly thin.

Initially, you call Mr. Earl to clarify any questions you might have and to thank him for his interest and help. This means that you have engaged Mr. Earl in the problem-solving process. Engagement is the initial period when a practitioner becomes oriented to the problem at hand and begins to establish communication and a relationship with the other individual or individuals addressing the problem. Subsequently, you proceed to figure out what to do about Mr. Strewynskowski. You must also engage him as the client in the problem-solving process. Of course, as a generalist practitioner you must work with the client to establish what he needs and wants.

During the assessment phase of the problem-solving process, you may decide to pursue planning and

ship and begin effective communication. Second, you assess the problem. This entails seeking information about various aspects of the issues surrounding the problem. At this stage, you might choose to pursue a micro, mezzo, or macro approach to solving the problem. Figure 1.2 depicts how you might progress through the

Figure 1.2
Steps in the Problem-Solving Process—Initiating Macro Change

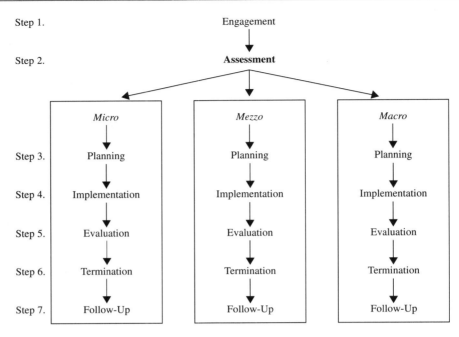

implementation at either the micro, mezzo, or macro level. You might also decide that intervention at more than one level would be appropriate.

A Micro Approach

A micro level plan that focuses upon the individual might be to refer Mr. Strewynskowski to the appropriate services and oversee service provision. You might then continue Mr. Strewynskowski's assessment and arranges for services such as traveling homemaker and daily hot meal delivery. You might also provide supportive services as needed, such as assisting Mr. Strewynskowski with paying his bills, attaining medical assistance, or making arrangements to get groceries and other needed items.

A Mezzo Approach

Assuming another perspective, however, you might choose to focus on a mezzo or group/family-oriented approach. Suppose that there are no services for traveling homemakers or hot meal delivery in Mr. Strewynskowski's immediate area. Perhaps the county in which you work is neither very populated nor very wealthy. In fact, suppose that the county is downright poor. Without all the services and resources you would like to have, what would you do?

For one thing, you might decide to investigate the possible help and support of Mr. Strewynskowski's friends, neighbors, and family. Upon further investigation, you find out that Mr. Strewynskowski has two sons and a daughter living in the county. You decide to explore the extent to which they are aware of their father's situation and can provide some of the help he needs. This would involve engaging his relatives in the helping process. Additionally, you decide to look into whether Mr. Strewynskowski has any friends or neighbors who might be willing to help him out. You already know that Mr. Earl is concerned about Mr. Strewynskowski's well-being.

Thus, this approach using a mezzo perspective involves people and family who are close to Mr. Strewynskowski. You might also purse the mezzo approach of getting Mr. Strewynskowski into some type of social or support group to minimize his isolation. Perhaps, Mr. Strewynskowski belongs to a church that could serve some of his needs, such as having volunteers take him shopping or involve him in both religious and social activities.

A Macro Approach

Finally, in addition to thinking purely in micro or mezzo terms, you might decide to pursue a macro approach. Once again, suppose that there are not services that offer traveling homemakers, meal delivery, elderly protection, or supportive workers in your county. Perhaps, you discover that you have a number of elderly clients who are experiencing difficulty maintaining themselves in their own homes. You find that on a regular basis you are having difficulty helping such clients. This issue extends beyond the simple provision of help to one individual client. Similarly, this issue encompasses more than the solicitation of family or group involvement at the mezzo level.

Rather, you determine that services are needed at the macro level. Perhaps, your county agency should develop a new program to serve these clients. Maybe you should approach agency administrators to explore the possibility of funneling funds and resources away from other less critical needs to these elderly clients who are in what you consider grave need. Possibly, your own agency's policy should be changed in order to make such elderly clients eligible to receive services or resources already available in the agency, but accessible only client's falling into some other client category (for example, people who have specific types of physical or developmental disability). Such changes in agency service provision, policy, or distribution of resources is what macro practice and this book are all about.

What Is Generalist Practice?

Johnson (1992) speaks of the "generalist approach" as requiring "that the social worker assess the situation with the client and decide which system is the appropriate unit of attention of focus of the work, for the change effort" (p. 1). She explains that this means a generalist practitioner's attention could be devoted to

"an individual, a family, a small group, an agency or organization, or a community."

Sheafor and Landon (1987) describe the generalist perspective as one where "the social worker has an eclectic theoretical base for practice, . . .is grounded in a systems framework suitable for assessing multiple points for potential intervention, . . .perceives that productive intervention occurs at every practice level (individual to community) and that frequently the most effective and beneficial changes occur through multilevel interventions," and "a central responsibility of social work practice is the guidance of the planned change or problem-solving process" (p. 666). Although this definition is a mouthful, there are major themes involved. First, generalist social workers need to be infinitely flexible. Second, they require a solid knowledge base about many things. Third, they need to master a wide range of skills and have these skills at their disposal.

The current *Encyclopedia of Social Work* (Landon, 1995) states that no precise "agreed-on definition of generalist practice" exists (p. 1102). However, it continues to summarize some common areas of agreement in addition to domains where the definitions vary substantially: "There appears to be definitional agreement on the centrality of the multimethod and multilevel approaches, based on an eclectic choice of theory base and the necessity for incorporating the dual vision of the profession on private issues and social justice concerns. Differences lie in emphases placed on the use of the planned change process, the ecosystem base, and the various central philosophical concepts such as empowerment; the centrality of context; and the definition of specific knowledge and skills needed, which depend a great deal on the theoretical stance of those who write the definitions" (Landon, 1995, p. 1103).

Generalist social work practice may involve almost any helping process. A generalist practitioner may be called upon to help a homeless family, a sexually abused child, a pregnant teenager, an elderly person who's sick and unable to care for herself any longer, an alcoholic parent, a community that's trying to address its drug abuse problem, or a public assistance agency that's struggling to amend it policies in order to conform to new federal regulations. Therefore, generalist practitioners must be well prepared to address many kinds of difficult situations.

For our purposes, we will define generalist practice as follows: Generalist practice is the application of an

HIGHLIGHT 1.1

AN OUTLINE OF DIMENSIONS INVOLVED IN THE DEFINITION OF GENERALIST PRACTICE

1. Acquisition of an eclectic knowledge base
   A. Theoretical foundation: Systems theory
   B. Human behavior and the social environment
   C. Social welfare policy and services
   D. Social work practice
   E. Social work research
   F. Human diversity
   G. Promotion of social and economic justice
   H. Populations-at-risk

2. Acquisition of professional values
   A. National Association of Social Workers Code of Ethics
   B. Awareness of personal values
   C. Clarification of conflicting ethical dilemmas
   D. Understanding of oppression
   E. Respect for diverse populations

3. Use of a wide range of practice skills
   A. Micro
   B. Mezzo
   C. Macro

4. Orientation to target any size system
   A. Micro
   B. Mezzo
   C. Macro

5. Effective work within an organizational structure

6. Appropriate use of supervision

7. Assumption of a wide range of professional roles
   A. Enabler
   B. Mediator
   C. Integrator/Coordinator
   D. General manager
   E. Educator
   F. Analyst/Evaluator
   G. Broker
   H. Facilitator
   I. Initiator
   J. Negotiator
   K. Mobilizer
   L. Advocate

8. Employment of critical thinking skills

9. Use of a problem-solving process
   A. Engagement
   B. Assessment
      1. Defining issues
      2. Collecting and assessing data
   C. Planning
      1. Identifying alternative interventions
      2. Selecting appropriate courses of action
      3. Contracting
   D. Implementation of appropriate courses of action (Intervention)
   E. Evaluation
      1. Using appropriate research to monitor and evaluate outcomes
      2. Applying appropriate research-based knowledge and technological advances
   F. Termination
   G. Follow-Up

eclectic knowledge base, *professional values*, and a *wide range of skills* to *target any size system* for change within the context of three primary processes. First, generalist practice involves working effectively within an *organizational structure* and doing so *under supervision*. Second, it requires the assumption of a *wide range of professional roles*. Third, generalist practice involves the application of *critical thinking skills* to the *problem-solving process*.

There are nine key concepts inherent in that defini-tion that this chapter will address. The order in which they are presented does not imply that one concept is more important than another. Each is significant. The concepts include: (1) an eclectic knowledge base; (2) professional values; (3) a wide range of skills; (4) targeting any size system; (5) organizational structure; (6) use of supervision; (7) professional roles; (8) critical thinking skills; and (9) the problem-solving process. For the sake of clarification, highlight 1.1 summarizes these concepts in outline form.

Figure 1.3 illustrates how the various concepts fit together. The large square in the top half of the figure portrays the organizational structure. An organization (or agency) will employ you to do a social work job. As chapter 4, "Understanding Organizations," will discuss in detail, organizational structure involves the operation of lines of authority and communication within an agency. It entails how the administration runs the organization and what the agency environment is like. As a generalist practitioner you will work in this environment with all its constraints, requirements, and rules. Thus, figure 1.3 pictures you, the generalist practitioner, as a small rectangle within this large square.

Figure 1.3
The Definition of Generalist Practice—
A Pictorial View

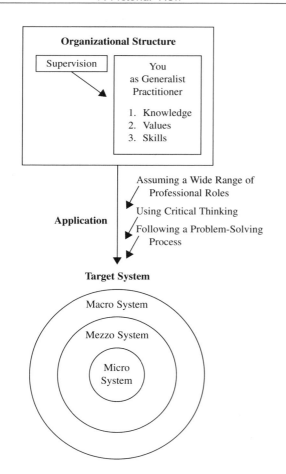

In that same square you see the terms *knowledge*, *values*, and *skills*. These illustrate that you bring to your job a broad knowledge base, professional values, and a wide range of skills so that you can do your work effectively. Also in the large upper square is another rectangle labeled *supervision*. An arrow runs from the supervision rectangle to the rectangle representing you. Part of working as a generalist practitioner involves receiving and using supervisory input appropriately. Chapter 2, "Using Micro Skills in Macro Practice," will more thoroughly address how to use supervision.

The large square at the bottom of figure 1.3 illustrates your potential *target systems*. As we have established, generalist practitioners may choose to work with a micro, mezzo, or macro system as the target of their change efforts. These three systems are arbitrarily portrayed in concentric squares to reflect their respective sizes.

An arrow flows from the organizational structure square down to the target system square. This shows that you as an generalist practitioner will apply your knowledge, skills, and values to help change a micro, mezzo, or macro system. Likewise, there are three smaller, curved arrows leading from concepts listed to the right of the application arrow into the application process. This depicts how you as a generalist practitioner will use a wide range of professional roles, critical thinking skills, and the problem-solving process as you work to help a system improve its functioning.

Each concept portrayed in figure 1.3 requires further definition and explanation. Before we begin, highlight 1.1 introduces in greater detail some facets of each of the nine major concepts used in the definition of generalist practice.

Note that some of the more specific concepts are arbitrarily divided among these nine major dimensions. Sometimes, a concept could easily fit under a number of dimensions. For example, consider the concept "promotion of social and economic justice." It involves the dimensions of professional knowledge, skills, and values. However, it is arbitrarily placed under the first dimension, the "acquisition of a professional knowledge base." This is done simply because knowledge is the first dimension cited. Listing "promotion of social and economic justice" under each of the dimensions of knowledge, skills, and values would be redundant and complicated. The intent here is to present a definition of generalist practice that you can remember.

Defining Generalist Practice: Acquisition of an Eclectic Knowledge Base

The acquisition of an eclectic knowledge base is the first dimension involved in the definition of generalist practice. Such a base requires selection ''of what appears to be best in various doctrines, methods, or styles,'' deriving this selection ''from various sources'' (*Webster's Ninth New Collegiate Dictionary*, 1991, p. 395). Knowledge entails understanding the dynamics of people's situations and determining what skills work best under particular circumstances. We have emphasized that generalist social workers need a broad knowledge base because they are called upon to help solve such a variety of problems.

Social work has a growing and progressive groundwork of knowledge. More and more is being researched and written about how social workers can become increasingly effective in helping people solve problems. Additionally, the field has borrowed much knowledge from other fields such as psychology and sociology. Social work then applies this knowledge to practice situations.

Therefore, generalist practitioners must know much about many things. Look at the vagueness inherent in that last sentence. As a generalist, you are supposed to know much about many things. What does this mean, specifically? On the one hand, it's difficult to be specific about how much you need to know. The point is that your knowledge base must be broad so that you can select from a wide range of theoretical approaches and skills in order to apply them to your own practice. Arbitrarily, we will introduce one significant perspective—systems theory—for you to adopt as part of your knowledge base. Systems theory provides a strong part of the theoretical foundation upon which this book is based.

However, on the other hand, there are some areas of knowledge that the social work profession considers necessary for you to assimilate. These include content on human behavior and the social environment, social welfare policy and services, social work practice, social work research, human diversity, the promotion of social and economic justice, and populations-at-risk (Council on Social Work Education [CSWE], 1992a, 1992b). After explaining systems theory and its application to generalist practice, each other content area is addressed briefly below.

Knowledge Base for Generalist Practice: Systems Theory

Social work focuses on the interactions between individuals and various systems in the environment. A system is a set of elements that are orderly and inter-related to make a functional whole. You, your class, your family, and your college or university are all systems. Each involves many components that work together in order to function.

Systems theories provide social workers with a conceptual perspective that guides them regarding how to view the world. Such theories involve concepts that emphasize interactions among various systems. They stress ''the relationships among individuals, groups, organizations, or communities,'' and ''they focus on the interrelationships of elements in nature, encompassing physics, chemistry, biology, and social relationships'' (Barker, 1991, p. 233). In other words, systems theories provide a very broad approach for understanding the world that can be applied to a multitude of settings.

Understanding systems theory is especially important because generalist practice targets virtually any size system for change. As a generalist you will evaluate any confronting problem from multiple perspectives. You will determine whether change is best pursued by individual, family, group, organizational, or community avenues. You might determine that any of these systems should be the target of your problem-solving and change efforts.

Conceptualizing Systems in Macro Practice

To better understand the macro change process, it is helpful to conceptualize a number of systems interacting within the environment. As we discussed earlier, systems theory implies dynamic, connected interactions among any number of systems and subsystems. These systems are of various sizes. Our intent is to give you a clear picture of what the general macro change process involves. Specifically, we will discuss four types of systems critical to the change process. They include the client, target, change agent, and action systems (Pincus & Minahan, 1973; Resnick, 1980b, 1980c). Chapter 6, "IMAGINE How to Implement Macro Intervention: Changing Agency Policy," reviews these four concepts within an organizational context.

The Macro Client System

A *client system* is any individual, family, group, organization, or community who will ultimately benefit from social work intervention. For our purposes, the *macro client system* is some number of clients, families, or groups of clients with some similar characteristic or qualification for receiving resources or services, or an agency or community that will be the beneficiary of the macro intervention process. For example, you as a generalist practitioner may work to develop and imple-ment a job placement program that will eventually affect dozens or perhaps even thousands of individual unemployed people. Likewise, developing an internal agency training program on new treatment techniques is intended to benefit the agency by improving its service provision.

The point is that macro change benefits larger groups of people, whether the group involves some client population, agency personnel, or community residents. In a different way, micro and mezzo changes benefit a *single* individual, family or group.

The Target System

The *target system* is "the individual, group, or community to be changed or influenced to achieve the social work goals" (Barker, 1991, p. 234). In macro practice this usually involves an organization or community. It might be that the agency in which you work needs to

Macro social work practice is concerned with many problems including unemployment. Generalist social workers can target community conditions that contribute to unemployment and support social programs that aid those who have lost their jobs.

improve some of its policies or services. Likewise, your community may need to provide some new service that citizens really need (for example, a drug rehabilitation program or a crime prevention effort).

The concepts of organization and community are broad. On the one hand, they can refer to very small organizations or communities. On the other hand, they can include systems that are huge entities. The concept of organization can be used to include very large organizations such as city, county, state, or federal government units. Similarly, a community in its broad sense might be the citizens of an entire state. We know that systems can be of virtually any size. Therefore, the target system is any system that macro intervention intends to change.

The Change Agent System

Within a macro practice perspective, the *change agent* is the individual who initiates the macro change process. In our context *you* are the change agent because this book intends to teach you how to implement macro level change. You might seek changes such as improving agency effectiveness or enhancing a community's quality of life. Later on, you might gain the support of, and join in coalitions with, others who also believe in the proposed macro change. Then you as a single change agent might become part of a larger system. Whether you undertake macro change by yourself or join with others, you are part of the action system described below.

The Action System

The *action system* includes those people who agree and are committed to working together in order to attain the proposed macro change. We have established that sometimes, you alone will be the action system for the change effort. Other times, it will be more useful to band together with others to help implement a macro change. As a change agent, you need to select supporters for your action system very carefully. It is best to muster support from staff who are well respected and competent (Resnick, 1980c). Additionally, people in the action system should intend to work together toward mutual ends or goals.

For example, you might work together with influential community residents such as local politicians, business people, and clergy to initiate and develop an activity center for teens. Another example involves working with colleagues and designated agency administrators to initiate and implement a crisis intervention program in your agency.

Figure 1.4 illustrates the relationships among the change agent, action, target, and macro client systems. As you know, this book assumes that you are the change-agent system because you are the one who initiates the macro change idea. However, at that point you may choose one of three options depicted in figure 1.4. First, you might decide to pursue the macro intervention process by yourself. The arrow leading from you, the worker, as the change agent system to you as the action system portrays this scenario. Here you are both the change agent and action systems because you both initiate the change effort and are going to implement the change by yourself.

The second option is to join with others to implement the change process. Figure 1.4 depicts this by the arrow leading from you as the change agent system to the circle encompassing both you and other individuals and/or groups. This illustrates how you can be part of a larger action system. That circle arbitrarily portrays you in addition to three other individuals or groups. In reality the action system could encompass any number of people or groups.

The third scenario illustrated in figure 1.4 indicates how you, as the change agent system, may initiate the idea, but then hand it over to some other action system to implement the changes. The arrow to the right leading from you as the change-agent system to the action system composed of other individuals portrays this. You don't necessarily have to be part of the action system as long as the macro change process keeps going.

For example, state budget cuts abruptly ceased reimbursement for the special transportation of children with multiple physical and mental disabilities to and from a large private agency providing a variety of services. These included a range of therapies (speech, physical, occupational, and medical) in addition to psychological and social work services. The children, most of whom were poverty-stricken, required transportation in specially equipped vans in order to accommodate wheel chairs and crutches. Thus, riding on public busses

Figure 1.4
The Change Agent, Action, Target, and Macro Client Systems

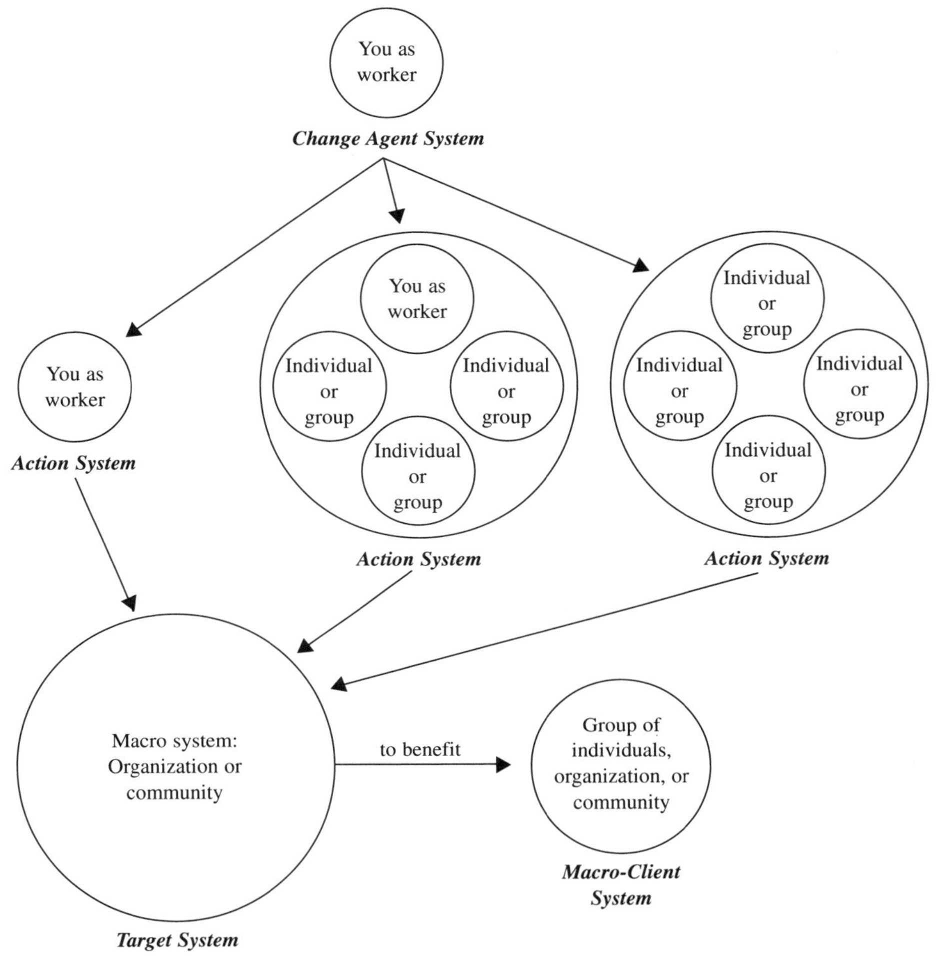

was not a viable option. The social worker at the agency providing treatment decided that something must be done immediately. The children needed their treatment and the agency needed to provide its services. The worker subsequently called members of the County Board of Supervisors responsible for monitoring the county's budget and administering funds. She explained the vulnerability of these children and pleaded on their behalf. As a result, during its next bimonthly meeting, the board decided that the county would pay for the

necessary transportation. The worker initiated the idea as the change-agent system but was unable to participate in its implementation. The board, then, became the action system. It implemented the necessary macro changes affecting hundreds of children with disabilities.

The final system illustrated in figure 1.4 is the client system, in the macro context, the macro-client system. After the action system energizes the target system (an agency or a community) into action, the intended beneficiary is the macro-client system. Figure 1.4 depicts this with an arrow leading from the target system to the macro-client system.

Knowledge Base for Generalist Practice: Human Behavior and the Social Environment (HBSE)

One way of classifying what bodies of knowledge generalist social workers must have involves the educational content provided in social work education programs. The Council on Social Work Education (CSWE) is the organization that accredits social work programs throughout the country and specifies required content. Human behavior and the social environment (HBSE) is one required dimension of content. Other dimensions discussed later on are social welfare policy and services, social work practice, research, human diversity, promotion of social and economic justice, and populations-at-risk.

Knowledge about HBSE is essential as a foundation on which to build practice skills. After engagement the second step in the problem-solving process is accurate assessment of the person, problem, and situation. The environment is vitally important in the analysis and understanding of human behavior. As social work has a person-in-environment focus (Johnson, 1989, p. 30), the interaction among individuals, systems, and the environment are critical. Such a conceptual perspective provides social workers with a symbolic representation of how to view the world. It provides ideas for how to assess clients' situations and identify alternative solutions involving various levels of practice.

The Curriculum Policy Statement (CSWE, 1992, p. 7) summarizes necessary HBSE content as follows:

> Programs of social work education must provide content about theories and knowledge of human bio-psycho-social development, including theories and knowledge about the range of social systems in which individuals live (families, groups, organizations, institutions, and communities). The human behavior and the social environment curriculum must provide an understanding of the psychological, and cultural systems as they affect and are affected by human behavior. The impact of social and economic forces on individuals and social systems must be presented. Content must be provided about the

ways in which systems promote or deter people in the maintenance or attainment of optimal health and well-being. Content about values and ethical issues related to bio-psycho-social theories must be included. Students must be taught to evaluate theory and apply theory to client situations.

Knowledge Base for Generalist Practice: Social Welfare Policy and Services

Social welfare policy and services entail another major dimension of the knowledge base for generalist social work practice. Policy, in its simplest portrayal, might be thought of as rules. Our lives and those of our clients are governed by rules. There are rules about how we're supposed to drive our cars. There are rules about when we're supposed to go to school. There are rules about how we're supposed to talk or write our sentences.

Policies, in essence, are rules that tell us which actions among a multitude of actions we may take and which we may not. Policies guide our work and our decisions. Social welfare policies tell us what resources are available to our clients and what kinds of things we may do for our clients. Generalist practitioners require the ability to analyze policy and undertake implementation of change when it is needed.

Policy might be divided into two major categories, social policy and agency policy. Social policy includes the laws and regulations that govern which social programs exist, what categories of clients are served, and who qualifies for a given program. It also sets standards regarding the type of services to be provided, the qualifications of the service provider and other rules.

Social policy involves "decisions of various levels of the government, especially the federal government, as expressed in budgetary expenditures, congressional appropriations, and approved programs" (Morris, 1987, p. 664). In other words, it involves the rules for how money can be spent to help people and how these people will be treated. There are policies that determine who is eligible for public assistance and who is not. Likewise, there are policies which specify what social workers can do for sexually abused children and what they cannot.

In addition to social policies, there are agency policies. Agency policies include those standards adopted by the individual organizations and programs that provide services (for example, a family service agency, a Department of Human Services, or a nursing home). Such standards may specify how the agency is structured, what qualifications supervisors and workers are required to have, which rules governing what a worker may or may not do, and what the proper procedures are for completing a family assessment, among many other aspects of agency life.

The point is that knowledge about policy is vitally important. An organization's policy can dictate how much vacation an employee can have and how she can earn raises in salary. An adoption agency's policy can determine who is eligible to adopt a child and who isn't. A social program's policies determine who is able to get needed services and resources and who will be left without them.

One more thing should be said concerning social workers and social policy. Sometimes, for whatever reasons, social policies are unfair or oppressive to clients. A social worker may conclude that a policy is ethically or morally intolerable. In such a case, the worker may decide to advocate on the behalf of clients to try to change the policy. Later chapters will say much more about making changes in larger systems and their policies.

Additionally, generalist practitioners need a sound foundation of knowledge concerning social services. This includes a historical perspective about how services have been developed. This also involves an analytical perspective concerning the effects of social services on the maintenance of people's "optimal health and well-being" (CSWE, 1992a, p.7; 1992b, p. 9).

Knowledge Base for Generalist Practice: Social Work Practice

Still another curricular area that forms the foundation for generalist practice is that of practice itself. Social work practice is the *doing* of social work. If knowledge is the *what* of social work, then practice is the *how*. It involves identifying and choosing among a range of intervention alternatives and undertaking the problem-solving process to achieve the intervention's goals. (The problem-solving process will be described in greater detail later in this chapter.)

Practice involves working with individuals, families, groups, organizations (both large and small), communities, and large social and governmental structures.

The social work knowledge base includes knowledge about skills in addition to knowledge about problems and services. A social worker needs to evaluate and determine what skills will be most effective in what situations.

For example, Norman, age fourteen, approaches his school social worker Melba and states softly, "I think I'm going to kill myself." Melba then must determine what is the best practice alternative to pursue in order to help Norman. What counseling approach would be most effective? What crisis intervention skills would best apply? Does the problem extend even beyond Norman? Is Melba seeing an excessively large number of students expressing similar thoughts? Should Melba initiate and develop new preventive programs within the school context in order to combat this larger problem? Must Melba pursue agency and political policy changes in order to provide funding to more effectively help Norman and other students in similar situations?

Knowledge Base for Generalist Practice: Social Work Research

Research is yet another major dimension of curriculum content required in social work programs. It accompanies HBSE; social welfare policy, services, and practice; human diversity; promotion of social and economic justice; and populations-at-risk as necessary components of the knowledge base for generalist practice.

Knowledge about social work research is important for three basic reasons (Reid, 1987). First, it can guide social workers to become more effective in their practice. It can help them get better and clearer results. Framing social work interventions so that they can be evaluated through research provides information about which specific techniques work best with which specific problems. When work with a client is clearly evaluated, social workers can determine whether they are really helping a client with his or her problem; additionally, practitioners can monitor their progress during the actual implementation process (Hudson & Thyer, 1987). Similarly, whole agencies can use research to evaluate their programs' effectiveness.

There is a second reason why knowledge about research is important for generalist practice. Namely, accumulated research helps to build a foundation for understanding situations and planning effective interventions. Knowledge about what has worked best in the past provides guidelines for which approaches and techniques should be used in the present and in the future. Research forms the basis for the development of whole programs and policies that affect large numbers of people. Such knowledge can also be used to generate new theories and ideas to further enhance the effectiveness of social work.

The third reason for research's importance is that it "serves the practical function of providing situation-specific data to inform such actions as practice decisions, program operations, or efforts at social change" (Reid, 1987, p. 474). In other words, at any point in the problem-solving intervention process, it can provide guidelines for what to do. It gives information about what has worked in the past and clues about how to proceed.

The content of social work research tends to fall within four major categories (Reid, 1987). First, many studies involve the behavior of individual clients and their interactions with others close to them, including families and small groups. Second, much research focuses on how services are provided to clients, what specifically such services involve, and how successful they are in accomplishing their goals. Third, many studies address social workers' attitudes and educational backgrounds, in addition to what's occurring in the entire social work profession itself. The fourth research category involves the study of organizations, communities, and social policy" (p. 478). This latter category emphasizes the importance of the larger social environment upon the behavior and conditions of clients.

Thus, research is important to generalist practice. Research informs and supports intervention approaches. It identifies theories and programs which are more likely to be effective. Finally, it helps the worker to ensure that the client system is being helped, rather than hurt, by what workers do.

Knowledge Base for Generalist Practice: Human Diversity

Human diversity is still another pillar in the knowledge base for generalist practice. Any time a person can be identified as belonging to a group that differs in some respect from the majority of others in society, that person is subject to the effects of human diversity. People

meriting special attention "include, but are not limited to groups distinguished by race, ethnicity, culture, class, gender, sexual orientation, religion, physical or mental ability, age, and national origin" (CSWE, 1992a, p. 6; 1992b, pp. 7–8).

Membership in groups that differ from the young white male heterosexual mainstream can place people at increased risk of discrimination and oppression. Discrimination concerns "the prejudgment and negative treatment of people based on identifiable characteristics such as race, gender, religion, or ethnicity" (Barker, 1991, p. 64). Oppression involves putting extreme limitations and constraints on some "group or institution" (Barker, 1991, p. 162). Discrimination and oppression often result from stereotypes. A stereotype is "a standardized mental picture" that may be held about members of some designated group, usually on the basis of some characteristic or set of characteristics that represents an oversimplified opinion of group members and fails to take into account individual differences (*Webster's Ninth Collegiate Dictionary*, 1991, p. 1156).

One might envision a number of relevant scenarios. For instance, picture being a woman in an all-male business establishment. Think of a sixty-two-year-old person applying for a sales job in a department store where everyone else is under forty. Or consider an African-American person applying for membership in an all-white country club.

Membership in any diverse group provides a different set of environmental circumstances. A Chicano adolescent from a Mexican-American inner city neighborhood has a different social environment than an upper middle-class adolescent of Jewish descent living in the well-to-do suburbs of the same city.

The critical thing is for social workers to be integrally aware of the awesome variety of human diversity. In order to work effectively with various groups, social workers must constantly strive to gain understanding about cultural and situational differences. Such understanding is necessary for effective communication that, in turn, is a requirement for effective generalist practice.

Knowledge Base for Generalist Practice: Promotion of Social and Economic Justice

Another requirement for your generalist knowledge base is information about the promotion of social and economic justice. Social justice involves the idea that in a perfect world, all citizens would have identical "rights, protection, opportunities, obligations, and social benefits" (Barker, 1991, p. 219). Similarly, economic justice concerns the distribution of resources in a fair and equitable manner. Social work education programs are required to provide "an understanding of the dynamics and consequences of social and economic injustice, including all forms of human oppression and discrimination" (CSWE, 1992a, p. 6; 1992b, p. 8).

In real life, social and economic justice are hard goals to attain. Rarely are rights and resources fairly and equitably distributed. Even the definitions of "fair" and "equitable" are widely debated. What does "fair" mean? Does it mean that all people should receive the same income regardless of what work they do or even whether or not they have jobs at all? The point is that social workers must be vigilantly aware of the existence of injustice. It is our ethical responsibility to combat injustice whenever it is necessary and possible to do so.

When we speak of ethical responsibility, we are really referring to the application of professional values. In addition to knowledge about the promotion of social and economic justice, generalist practitioners must understand that such promotion is a basic professional value. We as social workers must make practice decisions with this value in mind. Likewise, we must learn practice skills that work on the behalf of the promotion of social and economic justice. Thus, although the promotion of social and economic justice requires knowledge, it also requires the acquisition of professional values and practice skills.

Knowledge Base for Generalist Practice: Populations-at-Risk

Clearly related to the concepts of human diversity and the promotion of social and economic justice is the notion of populations-at-risk. This is the final portion of the knowledge base for generalist practice that we will address here. Certain populations or groups of people, based on some identified characteristics, are at greater risk of social and economic deprivation than the general mainstream of society. Because our job as social workers involves getting people resources and helping people

solve their problems, we will likely work primarily with populations-at-risk of such deprivations. These populations include "people of color, women, and gay and lesbian persons"; additional at-risk groups "include but are not limited to, those distinguished by age, ethnicity, culture, class, religion, and physical or mental ability" (CSWE, 1992b, pp. 7–8). It follows that we need information and insight concerning these populations' special issues and needs. As social workers, you need both "theoretical and practice content about patterns, dynamics, and consequences of discrimination, economic deprivation, and oppression" (CSWE, 1992a, p.7; 1992b, p.8). Chapter 11 ("Advocacy and Social Action for Populations-at-Risk") stresses the importance of knowledge concerning at-risk populations, the promotion of social and economic justice, and human diversity in addition to investigating each in detail.

Defining Generalist Practice: Assimilation of Professional Values and Ethics

We have reviewed the first concept inherent in the definition of generalist practice, namely, the acquisition of an *eclectic knowledge base*. The definition's second critical dimension involves the integration of *professional values* and *ethics*. Not only must generalist practitioners have substantial and diverse knowledge at their disposal, but they must also have assimilated professional values.

Values are principles, qualities, and practices that a designated group, individual, or culture deems inherently desirable (*Webster's Ninth New Collegiate Dictionary*, 1991, pp. 1302–3). Values, then, give direction concerning what is considered right and wrong. Subsequently, values provide guidelines for behavior. Ideally, one should behave in accordance with the values in which one believes. *Ethics*, then, are principles based on a set of values that serve to guide one's behavior. Values reflect what you consider to be right and wrong. Ethics involve how you behave based on these values. Generalist practitioners must have a sound basis for making ethical decisions that accord with social work values. Aspects of professional values and ethics we will discuss here include: the National Association of Social Workers (NASW) Code of Ethics; awareness of personal values; clarification of conflicting ethical dilemmas; understanding of oppression; and respect for diverse populations.

NASW Code of Ethics

Social work has a clearly delineated set of professional values reflected in the National Association of Social Workers Code of Ethics (National Association of Social Workers [NASW], 1993). The following ten basic values serve as the foundation for ethical behavior (Barker, 1991; NASW, 1983).

1. *Each person is uniquely and deservedly important in her or his own right.*
2. *Each person has the right to privacy and confidentiality.* Confidentiality is the ethical principle that workers should not share information provided by a client or about a client unless that worker has the client's explicit permission to do so (Barker, 1991, p. 46).
3. *Modification of social policy and conditions may be necessary in order to meet people's rightful needs.* In other words, sometimes interventions targeting macro systems are necessary in order to serve people's best interest.
4. *It is important to distinguish between professional values and those values one holds personally.* Personal values should not interfere with one's ability to perform professional practice.
5. *It is important to willingly share information and practice wisdom* (e.g., knowledge about skills) *with other people who need and can use them.*
6. *Both individual and group uniqueness and differences should be held in high regard.*
7. *Clients should be able to make their own decisions and plans to benefit themselves with as much assistance as they might need or as workers are able to offer.*
8. *Helpful interventions should be pursued for clients despite defeats and frustration.*
9. *The pursuit of "social justice and the economic, physical, and mental well-being of all members of society" should be held in high regard* (Barker, 1991, p. 246).
10. *Professional social workers should maintain professional integrity and consistently behave in a professional manner.*

The Code of Ethics applies these values in a series of ethical standards. These standards focus on six primary contexts including the social worker's "conduct and comportment as a social worker, . . .ethical responsibility to clients, . . .ethical responsibility to col-

leagues, . . .ethical responsibility to employers and employing organizations, . . .ethical responsibility to the social work profession, . . .[and] ethical responsibility to society" in general (NASW, 1993, pp. 1–2). Chapter 12, "Ethics and Ethical Dilemmas in Macro Practice," elaborates upon each of these areas.

Awareness of Personal Values

Before you are able to prevent personal values from interfering with ethical professional practice, you must clearly identify those personal values. This proposition stems directly from the fourth value cited above. You certainly have the right to maintain personal values and opinions. However, a generalist practitioner is professionally obligated to prevent personal values that conflict with professional values from interfering with practice.

The abortion controversy provides an excellent example of the potential clash of personal and professional values. Professional values emphasize an individual's right to self-determination. Additionally, NASW has put forth a policy statement concerning abortion. It states each person has the right to make her own decision concerning whether or not to pursue the abortion alternative. This may seriously conflict with a worker's personal values. For instance, you may feel that you would never consider an abortion for yourself under any circumstances. However, this position is totally distinct from how you should ethically behave in your professional practice. You would be ethically obligated to help a client pursue an abortion if she'd made that decision.

On the other hand, your personal values may be clearly pro-choice. You may feel that women have an absolute right to abortion. Indeed, you may feel that abortion is definitely the route of choice in certain circumstances. These conditions might include: when the pregnancy results from rape or incest; when carrying the pregnancy to term would endanger the mother's life; when it has been established that the fetus is abnormal or seriously damaged; or when the pregnant woman simply does not want to have a baby. In these instances, you may find it very difficult when a client decides to have the baby anyway. You may personally feel this decision is a *big* mistake. However, you are professionally obligated not only to abide by your client's decision, but also to assist her to the best of your ability in attaining her goal. Sometimes, separating personal and professional values is very difficult.

Clarification of Ethical Dilemmas

An ethical dilemma is a problematic situation in which ethical standards are in conflict. In other words, sometimes it is not possible to make a perfect choice and abide by all ethical guidelines. For example, consider a client who tells you he plans to murder his girlfriend, yet forbids you to tell anybody. You cannot maintain the primary ethical standard of protecting human life (namely, your client's girlfriend) and confidentiality at the same time. Hence, you are in the midst of an ethical quandary.

Generalist practitioners must be vigilant and prepared to address such ethical dilemmas, as they occur regularly. Yet each such dilemma is unique. Chapter 12 addresses a wide range of ethical dilemmas occurring within organizational and community settings and discusses how practitioners might make decisions about what to do.

Understanding Oppression

We have established that oppression involves putting extreme limitations and constraints on some "group or institution" (Barker, 1991, p. 162). By implication the concept of oppression involves unfairness. Somebody is being more limited, in terms of rights or access to services, than somebody else. Oppression is usually based on some characteristics of a particular population or on some particular group's subjection to an unfair practice, an unbalanced relationship, or unequal treatment by an organization.

Earlier we discussed the importance of knowledge about oppression in order to understand people's rights and where such rights are being abused. The assumption here is that we also comply with the professional value that oppression is unjust and, therefore, should be fought.

Respect for Diverse Populations

As with learning about oppression, it is crucial to establish a firm knowledge base about diverse populations.

We discussed this concept earlier in the context of the essential knowledge base for generalist practitioners. It follows, then, that practitioners should assume a professional value stance that human diversity will be respected, appreciated, and promoted. Such a value stance leads to ethical professional practice working to achieve these ends.

Defining Generalist Practice: Mastery of a Wide Range of Practice Skills to Target Any Size System

The first two components of the definition of generalist practice include acquisition of, first, an eclectic knowledge base and, second, professional values. The definition's third and fourth aspects involve the need for a wide range of practice skills to target any size system for change. These dimensions are so intertwined that we will address them here together. There are different and specific skills used respectively with micro, mezzo, or macro systems.

Historically, social work skills were clustered into three major categories. First, *casework* involved working primarily on a direct level with individual clients and their families. This resembles in some ways the micro level of practice. Second, *group work* involved organizing and running a wide variety of groups (for example, therapeutic groups or support groups). The mezzo level of practice might be said to correspond to this skill cluster. Third, *community organization* involved working with organizations and communities. This in some ways is similar to the macro level of social work practice.

Under this old model of practice, social workers usually concentrated on developing an expertise in one particular approach. They were either caseworkers, group workers, or community organizers. They did not necessarily see themselves as having a sound basis of skills in more than one arena.

In contrast, the generalist perspective assumes a multiple level approach to intervention. That is, for any particular problem or situation, a generalist practitioner might have to intervene with individuals, families, groups, organizations, or communities. Therefore, social workers must master and have readily available skills involved in working with any of these entities.

Micro practice is generalist social work practice focusing on problem solving with and for individuals. The context is usually "intervention on a case-by-case basis or in a clinical setting" (Barker, 1991, p. 144). The focus of attention is the individual and how to communicate and work on a one-to-one basis.

Mezzo practice is generalist social work practice with small groups. Understanding group dynamics and communication patterns among several different people is important. Working with families lies somewhere between micro and mezzo practice. Because of the intimacy and intensity of family relationships and the importance of the family context to individuals, families deserve special status and attention.

Finally, *macro practice* is generalist social work practice intending to affect change in large systems including organizations and communities (Barker, 1991, p. 136). Skills involved include changing agency and social policies, planning and implementing programs, and initiating and conducting projects within agency and community contexts.

However, regardless of what system is the focus of attention, a generalist practitioner always keeps in mind the possibility of moving to other levels of intervention. The intent of generalist practice is to provide a solid base of skills in working at the micro, mezzo, and macro levels of practice. Social workers are no longer divided and channeled into one of the three methods and directed to specialize in that method. The assumption is that generalist social workers must be prepared to approach a problem from a wide variety of perspectives. You can learn to view most problems from many levels.

Additionally, as we will see, mezzo skills are based to a great extent on micro level skills. In order for workers to work with small groups of people, they must thoroughly understand the communication and interaction occurring between individuals. They must know how to listen effectively, provide information, make plans, and follow through on these plans.

Likewise, macro level skills have a basis both in mezzo and micro skills. Macro interventions can involve both working with individuals within a macro context (for example, a colleague, an administrator, or a resident representing her community) and with small groups of people (for instance, a community group oriented toward the task of abolishing neighborhood drug houses or a group of agency staff charged with evaluat-

ing program effectiveness). Later chapters will explore a range of macro skills for you to use in practice.

Defining Generalist Practice: Effective Work Within an Organizational Structure

We have reviewed the knowledge, the values, the wide range of skills, and the orientation to any size system that form part of the generalist practice definition. The fifth component involves the ability to work effectively within an organizational structure. *Organizational structure* is the formal and informal manner in which tasks and responsibilities, line of authority, channels of communication, and dimensions of power are established and coordinated within an organization.

Tasks and responsibilities, of course, involve what you and other staff are supposed to accomplish during your workday. Lines of authority concern who supervises whom. You might think of them as the chain of command. For example, who has the responsibility for overseeing your work performance? Channels of communication entail who communicates with whom. Dimensions of power delineate whose opinions carry the most weight in agency decision making. To whom do staff listen most attentively during staff meetings? Who has the most control over agency policy?

Agency structure may be either formal—that is, by the book and according to the rules—and/or informal—that is, based on the way the agency really works. Consider channels of communication, for example. On the one hand, they may follow formal lines of authority. On the other, they may follow very informal routes. How information really gets circulated within an agency may be very different from what formal charts specify.

The following is an example of an informal agency structure, very different from what formal charts would indicate. Here the agency director's brother-in-law is a direct service worker within an agency that has several levels of authority. That is, designated supervisors oversee supervisees, managers are responsible for supervisors, assistant directors supervise managers, and the agency director oversees the assistant directors. Each level is responsible for the employees on the level below.

In our example, the agency director's brother-in-law has the agency director's ear whenever he wants it. Thus, the channel of communication flows directly from the bottom level to the very top, from the director's brother-in-law to the director. This is the informal reality that does not coincide with the formal structure. The brother-in-law also has greater power than other staff at his level and at higher levels because of his special influence with the agency director. Therefore, the dimensions of real power vary quite drastically from those portrayed in the formal lines of authority.

It is very important for generalist practitioners to examine, evaluate, and understand their agency's formal and informal structure in order to do their jobs effectively. Chapter 4, "Understanding Organizations," will address these and other similar issues much more thoroughly.

Defining Generalist Practice: Use of Supervision

Following the concept of working effectively within an organizational structure, the sixth concept involved in the definition of generalist practice is the use of effective supervision. The Curriculum Policy Statement prescribing what graduates of social work education programs must be able to do includes using "supervision appropriate to generalist practice" (CSWE, 1992a, p. 4). What does this mean? We propose that the appropriate use of professional supervision involves one very important and specific aspect of working effectively within an organizational structure. Chapter 2, "Using Micro Practice Skills in Macro Practice," discusses the following factors that we feel are involved in using supervision appropriately: practitioners' general expectations of supervisors; understanding the administrative, educational, and other functions of supervisors; using supervision as effectively as possible; addressing problems commonly occurring in supervisory relationships; and adapting specific techniques to assist supervisors in the supervisory process.

Defining Generalist Practice: A Wide Range of Roles

The seventh major concept involved in the definition of generalist practice concerns the fact that generalist

practitioners assume a wide range of professional roles. A role is "a socially expected behavior pattern usually determined by an individual's status in a particular society" or unit of society (*Webster's Ninth Collegiate Dictionary*, 1991, p. 1021). For example, people have certain expectations regarding how social workers are supposed to act. There are certain activities in which social workers are expected to participate.

In order to best understand the various roles generalist practitioners play, it is useful to recall the four types of systems involved in generalist practice. These include the client system, target system, change-agent system, and action system. As we discussed, the *client system* includes those people who will ultimately benefit from the change process. In micro practice, the client system is usually an individual and in mezzo practice a small group. (Because of their intimate nature, families lie somewhere between micro and mezzo practice.) A *macro-client system* usually involves larger numbers of people (such as clients with similar problems for whom the macro intervention process was initiated), an agency, or an entire community. Macro practice's intent is to benefit larger numbers of people. Therefore, when we talk about macro practice roles, the client system is almost always a macro-client system.

The *change agent system* is the individual who initiates the macro change process. From our perspective this is you. The diagrams in figures 1.5 through 1.16 refer to the worker. For our purposes, this is the same as the change-agent system.

The *action system* includes those people who agree to and will work together to attain the proposed macro change. You alone can be the action system or you can work with others who also compose such a system. It depends on who expends effort to affect change based upon mutual change goals.

Finally, the *target system* is "the individual, group, or community to be changed or influenced to achieve the social work goals" (Barker, 1991, p. 234). We have already indicated that frequently our own agency, some subsystem within our agency, or the community becomes the target system, or the system at which we direct our intervention efforts.

Figures 1.5 through 1.16 illustrate a variety of possible social work roles characteristic of macro generalist practice. They include: enabler, mediator, integrator/coordinator, general manager, educator, analyst/evaluator, broker, facilitator, initiator, negotiator, mobilizer, and advocate. Although these figures represent macro practice roles, remember that many of the roles can also characterize interventions in micro or mezzo practice.

Figures depicting common macro roles use circles to represent worker, client macro systems, and organizational or community macro systems. Lines and arrows depict how systems relate to each other. Note that, unless specified otherwise, a macro system can illustrate interaction with either an organization or a community. Macro-client systems can encompass, on the one hand, some number of individuals, families, or small groups, or, on the other hand, communities or organizations. In any particular practice instance, it simply depends on who is the intended beneficiary of the intervention process.

Enabler

The enabler role involves providing support, encouragement, and suggestions to members of a macro client system so that the system may proceed more easily and successfully in completing tasks or solving problems. In the enabler role, a worker helps a client system ''become capable of coping with situational or transitional stress. Specific skills used in achieving this objective include conveying hope, reducing resistance and ambivalence, recognizing and managing feelings, identifying and supporting personal strengths and social assets, breaking down problems into parts that can be solved more readily [partialization], and maintaining a focus on goals and the means of achieving them'' (Barker, 1991, p. 74). Enablers, then, are helpers. Practitioners can function in the role of enabler for micro, mezzo, or macro systems.

It should be noted that this definition of *enabler* is very different from the definition used in the topic area of substance abuse. There the term refers to a family member or friend who facilitates the substance abuser in continuing to use and abuse the drug of his or her choice.

Figure 1.5 illustrates the enabler role in macro practice. Arrows point from the worker system both to the organizational or community macro system circle and to the macro-client system. These portray the support provided by the worker that assists either macro system in undertaking some action. The latter is depicted by

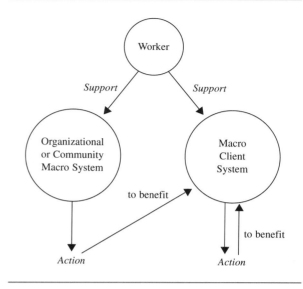

Figure 1.5
The Enabler Role in Generalist Macro Practice

arrows leading from both macro systems to the word *action*. This action, in turn, is intended to result in some benefit for the macro-client system. Thus, arrows also lead from the word *action* back to the macro client system.

Mediator

The mediator resolves arguments or disagreements among micro, mezzo, or macro systems in disagreement (Yessian & Broskowski, 1983, pp. 183–84). At the macro level, mediation involves helping various factions (subsystems) within a community—or helping a community system and some other system (such as another community)—work out their differences. For example, a community (or neighborhood) and a social services organization may require mediation over the placement of a substance abuse treatment center. In this case, the social services organization might have selected a prime spot, but the community or neighborhood might balk at having such a center within its boundaries.

The role may involve improving communication among dissident individuals or groups, or helping those involved come to a compromise. A mediator remains

Figure 1.6
The Mediator Role in Generalist Macro Practice

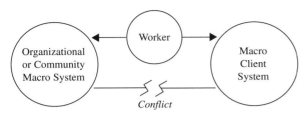

Figure 1.7
The Integrator/Coordinator Role
in Generalist Macro Practice

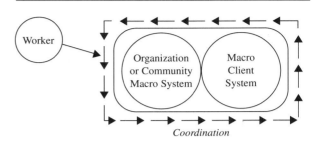

neutral, not siding with either party in the dispute. Mediators make sure they understand the positions of both parties. They may help to clarify positions, recognize miscommunication about differences, and help those involved present their cases clearly.

Figure 1.6 illustrates the mediator role. The worker circle is placed between the organizational or community macro system circle and the macro client system circle. This reflects the worker's neutral stance requiring that she or he take neither of the involved parties' sides. The broken line beneath the worker circle depicts the two parties' broken lines of communication and their inability to settle differences. This particular diagram depicts a worker mediating between an organizational or community macro system, on the one hand, and a macro client system, on the other. However, mediation can occur between or among virtually any size systems.

Integrator/Coordinator

Integration is "the process of bringing together components into a unified whole" (Barker, 1991, p. 116). Coordination involves bringing components together in some kind of organized manner. The integrator/coordinator role, therefore, brings people involved in various systems together and organizes their performance (Yessian & Broskowski, 1983, pp. 183–84). A generalist social worker can function as an integrator/coordinator "in many ways, ranging from . . . advocacy and identification of coordination opportunities, to provision of technical assistance, to direct involvement in the development and implementation of service linkages" (Yessian & Broskowski, 1983, p. 184).

Figure 1.7 depicts an organizational or community macro system and a macro client system located right next to each other. They are then enclosed in a box to illustrate that they are working together. The arrow pointing from the worker to the box enclosing the two circles portrays the worker's active leadership in bringing together and coordinating the two systems' performances. The arrows circulating around the box reflect the coordination process.

General Manager

The general manager role in social work involves assuming some level of administrative responsibility for a social services agency or some other organizational system (Yessian & Broskowski, 1983, pp. 183–84). Administrators "determine organizational goals; acquire resources and allocate them to carry out programs; coordinate activities toward the achievement of selected goals; and monitor, assess, and make necessary changes in processes and structure to improve effectiveness and efficiency" (Barker, 1991, p. 5). Management involves a number of tasks including planning programs, getting and distributing resources, developing and establishing organizational structures and processes, evaluating programs, and implementing program changes when needed (Patti, 1983).

Figure 1.8 portrays the general manager role. We assume that the organization employs both social workers and other staff members including other social workers, other professionals, and support staff. The worker circle is located above two staff circles with arrows

Figure 1.8
The General Manager Role
in Generalist Macro Practice

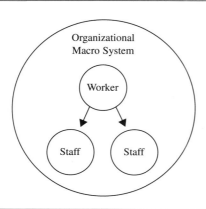

directed down from the worker circle to both staff circles. This diagram indicates that the worker, having administrative status, has authority over the staff. All three circles are located within the larger organizational environment circle. This indicates that the general manager role usually occurs within an organizational context.

Educator

The educator gives information and teaching skills to other systems (Yessian & Broskowski, 1983, pp. 183–84). To be an effective educator, the worker must, first, be knowledgeable. Additionally, the worker must be

Figure 1.9
The Educator Role in Generalist
Macro Practice

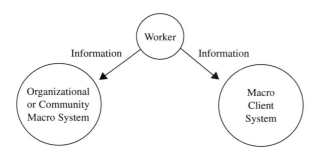

a good communicator so that information is conveyed clearly and is readily understood by the receivers.

Figure 1.9 illustrates the educator role in macro practice. Arrows run from the worker circle both to the organizational or community macro system circle and to the macro client system circle. This depicts that a worker conveys information to these other systems.

Analyst/Evaluator

The analyst/evaluatior role involves analyzing or evaluating effectiveness (Yessian & Broskowsky, 1983, pp. 183–84). An analyst can determine the effectiveness of a program or even of an entire agency. This can occur in an organizational or community context. Generalist social workers with a broad knowledge base of how various sized systems function can analyze or evaluate how well programs and systems work. Likewise, they can evaluate the effectiveness of their own interventions.

Figure 1.10 reflects how an analyst/evaluator functions. One arrow points from the worker circle to an organizational or community macro system circle. This illustrates how a worker in an analyst/evaluator role can evaluate either a program's or an agency's effectiveness. A second arrow points from the worker circle to another worker circle and a macro client system circle joined together by a line. The connecting line illustrates the worker's professional problem-solving relationship

Figure 1.10
The Analyst/Evaluator Role
in Generalist Macro Practice

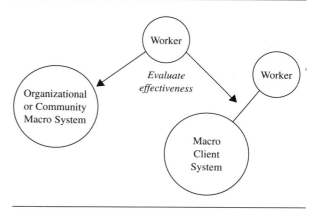

with his clients. The arrow illustrates how workers can and indeed are responsible for evaluating their own practice with clients.

Broker

The broker links any size system (individuals, groups, organizations, or communities) with community resources and services. A broker also helps put "various segments of the community in touch with one another to enhance their mutual interests" (Barker, 1991, p. 27). Getting resources for client systems is the key concept in the broker role.

In figure 1.11, the line from the worker circle to the arrow leading from the macro system to the macro client system portrays the worker's role. It illustrates the worker's active involvement in obtaining resources for the organization or community client system. The arrow points from the organizational or community macro system circle that provides resources to the client system circle that receives these resources.

Facilitator

A facilitator is "one who serves as a leader for some group experience" (Barker, 1991, p. 80). Facilitators lead groups. Although the facilitator role is very common in mezzo practice, workers also frequently assume it in macro practice. In the macro context a facilitator assumes "the responsibility to expedite the change effort by bringing together people and lines of communication, channeling their activities and resources, and

Figure 1.11
The Broker Role in Generalist Macro Practice

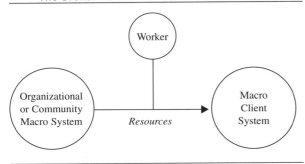

Figure 1.12
The Facilitator Role in Generalist Macro Practice

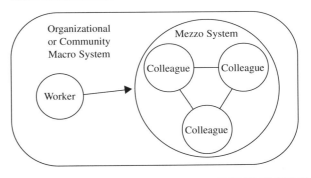

providing them with access to expertise" (Barker, 1991, p. 80).

Figure 1.12 depicts three circles labeled "colleague" that are connected with each other by lines. These lines represent group interaction and communication. Additionally, the linking lines illustrate how colleagues working together form a mezzo system. These three colleague circles are enclosed by a larger circle. This larger circle, a mezzo system, could be a task or planning group within an organization or a community. The arrow pointing from the worker circle to the mezzo system circle depicts the worker's leadership in the mezzo system. Hence, the larger circle, entitled macro system, encompasses all of the interaction. The worker facilitates whatever interaction occurs within the mezzo system that, in turn, occurs within the macro context. Note that, due to lack of space, figure 1.12 arbitrarily depicts three colleagues. In reality, any number of colleagues, clients, community residents, administrators, or politicians could be involved.

Initiator

Kettner, Daley, and Nichols (1985) define the initiator as the person or persons who call attention to an issue. The issue in the community may be a problem, a need, or simply a situation that can be improved. It is important to recognize that a problem does not have to exist before a situation can be dealt with. Often preventing future problems or enhancing existing services is a satisfactory reason for creating a change effort. Thus, a social worker may recognize that a

Figure 1.13
The Initiator Role in
Generalist Macro Practice

Figure 1.14
The Negotiator Role in
Generalist Macro Practice

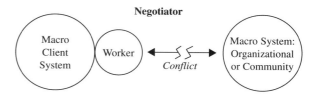

policy is creating problems for particular clients and bring this to the attention of her supervisor. Likewise, a client may identify ways that service could be improved. In each case, the worker is playing the role of initiator. Usually, this role must be followed up by other kinds of work because pointing out problems does not-guarantee they will be solved.

Figure 1.13 portrays an arrow leading from the worker circle on the far left of the diagram to the macro system circle in the middle. This arrow represents the worker's activities directed at improving service provision. Another arrow leads from the macro system to the macro client system on the far right. This arrow reflects the benefits that the macro system is supposed to provide for the macro client system as the ultimate result of the initiator's efforts.

Negotiator

A negotiator is an intermediary who acts to settle disputes and/or resolve disagreements. However, unlike mediators, negotiators clearly take the side of one of the parties involved.

The macro client system circle and the worker circle illustrated in figure 1.14 are located together on the left-hand side of the figure. This indicates that the worker is negotiating on behalf of the macro client system. Two jagged lines with arrows pointing away from them in opposing directions characterize the conflict that has arisen. The macro system circle on the right-hand side of the conflict represents an organization or community engulfed in conflict with the macro client system and the worker/negotiator on the opposing side. The worker/negotiator seeks to resolve the conflict but

does so on behalf of one side of the conflict, namely, the macro client system.

Mobilizer

The mobilizer identifies and convenes community people and resources and makes them "responsive to unmet community need" (Halley, Kopp, & Austin, 1992, p. 256). The mobilizer's purpose is to match resources to needs within the community context. Sometimes, a mobilizer's goal involves making services more accessible to citizens who need them. Other times, a goal concerns initiating and developing services to meet needs that heretofore were unmet.

Figure 1.15 illustrates the mobilizer role in generalist macro practice. The worker circle on the left depicts a worker assuming a mobilizer role in a macro practice context. The large central circle represents a community macro system. The citizen circles within the community macro system circle depict a number of community residents. (Six citizen circles are arbitrarily portrayed.) There might be fewer citizens involved, or there might be thousands of community residents who are part of the mobilization process. Ideally, an entire community with virtually all of its residents could be congregated to participate in the macro intervention process. The arrow leading from the worker (mobilizer) to the community macro system represents the worker's efforts directed toward the mobilization process. The arrows inside the community macro system circle leading from the citizen circles to "action" represent the resultant efforts of citizens as they participate in the process of meeting the community's unmet needs. The larger arrow leading from the community macro system circle to "action" represents the process of pooling all the citizens' efforts into some coordinated action.

Figure 1.15
The Mobilizer Role in Generalist Macro Practice

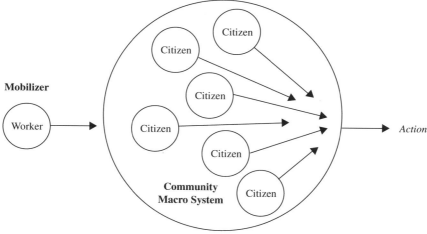

Note that, unlike most of the other roles illustrated in these figures, the mobilizer role occurs only in the context of a community. By our definition, it applies to communities and not to organizations.

Advocate

Advocacy is ''the process of working with and/or on behalf of clients (1) to obtain services or resources for clients that would not otherwise be provided, (2) to modify extant [currently operating] policies, procedures, or practices that adversely affect clients, or (3) to promote new legislation or policies that will result in the provision of needed resources or services'' (Hepworth & Larsen, 1990, p. 459). In other words, the advocate is one who steps forward and speaks out on the behalf of the client system in order to promote fair and equitable treatment or gain needed resources. In macro practice, of course, it would be on the behalf of some macro client system. This may be especially appropriate when a macro client system has little power to get what it needs. Advocacy often involves expending more effort than is absolutely necessary to accomplish your job. It also often involves taking risks, especially when advocating on a client's behalf in the face of a larger, more powerful system.

The advocate role is one of the most important roles a generalist social worker can assume, despite its potential difficulties. To emphasize its importance it is the last macro practice role to be discussed here. It is one of the practice dimensions that makes generalist social work practice unique (Kirst-Ashman & Hull, 1993). It is part of a generalist social worker's ethical responsibility to expend more effort than is minimally necessary in working on behalf of a client system when that client system is in desperate need of help or resources.

Figure 1.16 depicts a macro client system circle and a worker circle standing together. This reflects the worker's alliance with the macro client system during the advocacy process. The bold arrow leading from the worker to the macro system is exceptionally thick. This represents the significant amount of energy it often takes to have an impact on a larger, more powerful system.

Figure 1.16
The Advocate Role in Generalist Macro Practice

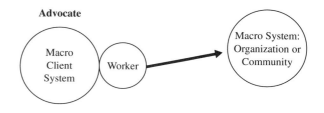

The elevated status of the macro system above the worker and macro client system illustrates the former's greater power.

Defining Generalist Practice: Critical Thinking Skills

Not only do generalists have an eclectic knowledge base, professional values, many different practice skills to work with various sized systems, and the ability to assume a wide range of roles, but they must also have the ability to think critically as they engage in the problem-solving process. The eighth component, then, in the definition of generalist practice is critical thinking skills.

Critical thinking is the ability to use intellectual and "affective processes which evaluate statements, arguments, and experiences by judging the validity and/or worth of those statements, arguments, and experiences" (Lindsay, 1995, p. 20). In other words, critical thinking entails the ability to carefully evaluate the validity of an assumption and even of a so-called "fact."

Gibbs et al. (1994) state that critical thinking in social work practice involves:

> (1) a predisposition to question conclusions that concern client care and welfare; (2) asking "does it work?" and "how do you know?" when confronted with claims that a method helps clients, and also questioning generalizations about treatment methods and clients; (3) weighing evidence for and against assertions in a logical, rational, systematic, data-based way, and (4) analyzing arguments to see what is being argued, spotting and explaining common fallacies in reasoning, and applying basic methodological principles of scientific reasoning. (Pp. 11–12)

For example, if a colleague tells you that bubble-blowing therapy is the best thing since forty-calorie-a-slice bread (compared to the usual seventy-to-eighty-calorie kind), you would critically evaluate the validity of that statement. What research does the colleague have to back up the remark? What are the theoretical underpinnings of bubble-blowing therapy. Of course, we are being facetious when talking about bubble-blowing therapy. The point is that critical thinking means not necessarily accepting situations or stories at face value.

Rather, it entails using your own judgment to seriously consider their worth and relevance.

Gibbs and Gambrill (in press) cite a number of practice fallacies that can trick practitioners into false beliefs. A fallacy is a false or erroneous idea, often hidden behind what appears to be a sound argument or presentation (*Webster's Ninth New Collegiate Dictionary*, 1991). A fallacy or mistaken assumption can trick you into believing what is not true. Fallacies often appear to be true, but really are not.

One fallacy involves charisma, charm, and possibly even glamour (Gibbs & Gambrill, in press). For example, a new agency director of a private family services agency assumes his post. He is a charming, charismatic character who has lots of new and exciting ideas for massive changes within the agency. Staff are taken by his striking presence and awed by his massive accumulation of experience. However, they are just as stupefied when he loses one-third of the agency's funding because of an arrogant personal dispute with the administrators of one of the agency's primary funding sources. Likewise, they are shocked when his wife sues him for adultery (this is still legal in some states) for having an affair with the same agency's public relations director. Agency staff, other administrators, and board members are mortified at the negative publicity this brings to the agency. The director abruptly leaves the agency after a devastating eighteen months to manifest his charisma at some other eager organization. Critical thinking would encourage staff to review performance before forming an opinion of the director. They would scrutinize the apparently wonderful exterior appearance and wait to see what characteristics and qualities really lay underneath.

Two other fallacies involved in this particular example include those of "newness" and of "experience" (Gibbs & Gambrill, in press). The director came to the agency with bright new ideas. A person using critical thinking would not assume that because these ideas are new and popular elsewhere, they must be good. The other fallacy involves the director's supposed extensive experience. Was his experience really good? Was it relevant to what this particular agency needed? Were his interpersonal skills really effective or were they based on his pumped up ego?

Still another fallacy concerns the "fact" that if it is written down (for example, in a book like this), then it must be true. Beware. One of the reasons that you are required to take a research course is so you can evaluate for yourself the quality of the research backing up any ''facts'' you read in books and journals. Critical thinking urges you to consider the rationale and proof for anything you read.

You can use critical thinking throughout generalist practice. This includes the evaluation of client records, agency policy, administrators' directives, the effectiveness of treatment modalities, or recommendations for problem solving with clients. It is not that you should distrust everything you see or hear, but rather that you be on the lookout for possible fallacies that seem to be true.

Defining Generalist Practice: The Problem-Solving Process

The ninth major concept involved in the definition of generalist practice is application of the problem-solving process. As you know, this process arbitrarily entails seven basic steps. Illustrated earlier in figure 1.1, they include engagement, assessment, planning, implementation (or intervention), evaluation, termination, and follow-up. Because of its significance in generalist practice, we will spend some time here discussing each step.

Engagement

Engagement is the initial period in which a practitioner orients herself to the problem at hand and begins to establish communication and a relationship with the individual or individuals also addressing the problem. Brill (1995) states that during the engagement process practitioners should pursue the following four goals: ''(1) to involve themselves in the situation, (2) to establish communication with everyone concerned, (3) to begin to define the parameters within which the worker and the client(s) will work, and (4) to create an initial working structure'' (p. 113).

Engagement marks the beginning of the problem-solving process. It ''may be as simple as walking into a crowded waiting room, receiving a letter, a card, a phone call, or as complicated as attending a board meeting involving differences about a major company decision, or going into a neighborhood that is in a state of crisis over some loaded issue such as school busing'' (Brill, 1995, p. 113).

The outcomes of engagement should be fourfold (Brill, 1995). First, the practitioner should become an integral facet of the problematic situation. Thus, the worker becomes engaged in the problem-solving process. Second, those involved in the engagement process should establish communication among themselves. Third, the practitioner and the client system should establish some agreement concerning the problematic issue and how to go about addressing it. Fourth, they should develop an understanding about what to do next.

Assessment: Defining Issues and Collecting Data

According to Siporin (1975, p. 224), assessment is the ''differential, individualized, and accurate identification and evaluation of problems, people, and situations and of their interrelations, to serve as a sound basis for differential helping intervention.'' Sheafor, Horesji, and Horesji (1988, p. 222) define assessment as ''the process of interpreting or giving meaning and conceptual order to data; it is an attempt to make sense out of the data that have been collected.'' They continue that assessment ''is an activity directed toward understanding the client's problem or situation and developing a plan of action'' (p. 224). In other words, assessment refers to gathering relevant information about a problem so that decisions can be made about what to do to solve it.

Generalist practitioners are oriented to choose from a wide range of alternatives and skills when confronted with any particular problem. They have a solid foundation in intervention approaches at the micro, mezzo, and macro levels.

During the assessment process you continue to use your micro skills in relationship-building and interviewing to work with individual clients or others. You then go about defining the issues and collecting data. Essentially, four steps are involved in this process. They include: identifying your client; assessing the client-insituation from the micro, mezzo, and macro perspectives in addition to that of diversity; citing information about client problems and needs; and, finally, making certain to identify client strengths.

Figure 1.17 illustrates the assessment process in generalist intervention. Remember the assumption, is

Figure 1.17
Assessment in the Generalist Intervention Model

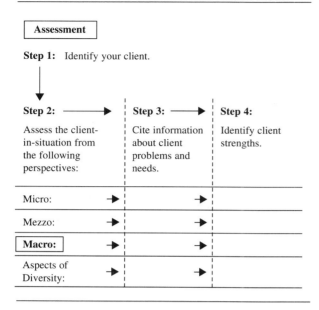

that your role is that of a direct practitioner or lower level supervisor with no real designated responsibilities for undertaking macro level interventions. However, generalist practice means that at any time in the intervention process you might choose either a micro, mezzo, or macro approach. Figure 1.17 emphasizes the macro potential for assessment because this text stresses generalist practice with organizations and communities.

Identify Your Client

Who exactly is your client? On whose behalf are you working? The first step in assessment is to determine who your client is. This may not be as easy as it sounds. It seems logical to say your clients are those people who are cited on your client list (or, you might say, your caseload). However, people, their lives, and their problems are often very perplexing. The designation of who is really your client and who is not may become blurred and vague. Even assuming a micro perspective in a direct service position, the issue may be complicated. For example, you may be a social worker at a group home for delinquent female adolescents. Your prescribed job role might involve individual, group, and family counseling. So who is your client system? Is it each individual

female resident? Is it the entire group of eight residents? Is it each resident within her family system? Or, is it all the residents and all their family systems?

Essentially, you must decide who your client is in each particular practice situation. It is helpful to think in terms of a "client system" (Pincus & Minahan, 1973; Lippitt, Watson, & Westley, 1958). We have defined a client system as any individual, family, group, organization, or community who will ultimately benefit from social work intervention. Furthermore, we have established that a macro client system may involve any of a number of entities. It may be an identified number of clients, families, or groups of clients with some similar characteristic or qualification for receiving resources or services. Similarly, a macro client system may be an agency. Finally, it may be a community that will be the beneficiary of the macro intervention process.

In the group home setting described above, your client system will sometimes be an individual teen. At other times, the client system may be a teen and her family as part of one mezzo client system. Still other times, your client system may be the mezzo system of all eight residents as you run group counseling. Finally, your client system may be a macro client system, namely, the agency or the community, depending on who is supposed to benefit from the intervention process.

Assess the Client-in-Situation and Cite Information about Problems and Needs

The second step in the generalist intervention assessment process involves examining the client-in-situation and citing information about the client's problems and needs. Consider an agency serving homeless men. Many of the male clients also have substance abuse problems. However, agency staff really are not trained and prepared to deal with these issues. Suppose you are a social worker for this agency. You think about the clients' situation (illustrated as step 2 in figure 1.17). Most clients currently involved with the agency temporarily live in the homeless shelter. They are served by social work and other staff providing various types of counseling. Likewise, you think about clients' problems and needs (depicted as step 3 in figure 1.17). Common problems involve unemployment, lack of self-esteem, poor planning skills, and substance addiction. Subsequently, typical needs include planning for vocational training or job placement, gaining self-confidence, learning planning and problem-solving skills, and, as it turns out, controlling addiction. Clients are already involved with the agency at the micro level. Many are also involved in group counseling at the mezzo level. You cannot think of specific ways to address this situation further at either the micro or mezzo levels.

Figure 1.17 emphasizes the macro alternative in bold type because macro intervention is what this book is about. You know that the clients are already readily accessible as most live in the shelter. Additionally, most are already involved in counseling with the agency's staff. Therefore, you decide that the agency itself looks like a good target of intervention. You begin to define the need for personnel more adequately trained in dealing with substance abuse problems.

You start thinking about the need to establish an in-service training program where the agency brings in a series of experts to train staff concerning this issue.[2] We have established that the client system in this case would be all agency clients with substance abuse problems who would eventually benefit from this training. The client system is made up of these *agency clients* despite the fact that *agency staff* would participate in and hopefully benefit from the training.

At this stage you have come up with an idea involving macro intervention. You would like to establish a time-limited training program for agency staff on substance abuse. This is one type of macro intervention, namely, project implementation, within an agency setting that chapter 7, "IMAGINE Project Implementation and Program Development," will address in much greater detail. The other two primary macro interventions within agency settings that we will explore are program development and changing agency policy.

Along with assessing the client-in-situation from micro, mezzo, and macro perspectives, you also must assess aspects of diversity. In this case many clients are Hispanic. Therefore, you consider how important it might be to include trainers with an expertise in the needs of Hispanic clients who have substance abuse problems.

---

2. In-service training is "an educational program provided by an employer and usually carried out by a supervisor or specialist to help [an employee] become more productive and effective in accomplishing a specific task or meeting the overall objectives of the organization" (Barker, 1995, p. 188).

Identify Client Strengths

Finally, it is critically important to incorporate client strengths into your assessment (portrayed as step 4 in figure 1.17). From a micro perspective, many individual clients are highly motivated to improve their life conditions. Most are penniless and feel hopeless. They have "hit bottom" and sincerely desire positive change for themselves. Additionally, we have noted that these clients are readily available, since they reside in the agency's shelter.

Strengths from a mezzo perspective are a bit more difficult to pinpoint. On the one hand, most clients are severed from close family relationships. On the other hand, potential goals for these clients might include rebuilding some of their family relationships. Thus, with at least some clients there are possibilities of establishing familial support at this mezzo level. Additionally, clients frequently participate in support and educational groups run by the agency, thereby establishing an additional strength at the mezzo level.

Finally, you examine strengths at the macro level. First, you verify that the agency probably has adequate funds to provide the required in-service training. Second, you think that you very likely could convince the agency administration to support the proposed project on the basis of its benefits. Third, you feel that staff would be very receptive to participation in the project because it would enhance their skills in an area of need.

Assessment and Planning in Macro Practice: The PREPARE Process

Because macro practice involves many more people, variables, contexts, and circumstances than micro and mezzo practice usually do, the planning process, too, is much more complicated. Many more variables merit consideration. At the micro and mezzo levels of intervention, the possibility of macro level change must always be considered a possibility. Yet, in most cases, generalist practitioners will address their clients' problems from the micro and mezzo perspectives as these workers' job descriptions probably dictate.

Once you seriously consider the possibility of pursuing macro level change, there are a number of additional issues to think about and steps to follow. Once again, this is because macro change is usually much

Figure 1.18
Macro Practice Problem Solving

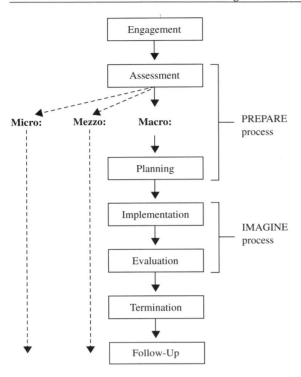

indicate that micro or mezzo approaches might be employed any time during the problem-solving process.

Figure 1.18 also identifies how the problem-solving process differs in macro practice from that in micro and mezzo practice. Namely, when generalist practitioners consider macro intervention, they can implement a seven-phase decision-making process. This process entitled PREPARE evaluates whether a macro change effort within a particular organizational setting is worthwhile. Brager and Holloway (1978) term this phase "initial assessment" within a macro context. The practitioner first acknowledges that a problem exists and then judges whether or not the potential resources to pursue change are available.

Due to the extensiveness of macro level assessment, planning essentially becomes an extension of the assessment process. Figure 1.18 indicates how both assessment and planning are aspects of the PREPARE process.

Figure 1.19 summarizes the PREPARE decision-making model for macro practice. Each step is explained briefly below. (Chapter 5, "PREPARE—Decision Making for Organizational Change," will explore each aspect of this model much more thoroughly.) Although the steps involved in PREPARE are presented in a designated order, it should be noted that in practice, workers

Figure 1.19
PREPARE—An Assessment of Organizational or
Community Change Potential

1. P   Identify **PROBLEMS** to address

2. R   Review your macro **REALITY**

3. E   **ESTABLISH** primary goals

4. P   Identify **PEOPLE** of influence

5. A   **ASSESS** potential financial costs and benefits to clients and agency

6. R   Evaluate professional and personal **RISK**

7. E   **EVALUATE** the potential success of a macro change process

more complex and affects many more people than micro or mezzo interventions. When considering a macro intervention, additional assessment steps are necessary. Because macro practice assessment and planning are so complicated, the inherent assessment and planning steps often blend to some degree. Possible alternatives usually stretch further beyond the worker's control than when that worker is assessing micro or mezzo problems and planning their solutions.

Figure 1.18 illustrates the problem-solving process in macro practice. It portrays how you might undertake micro, mezzo, or macro level intervention at any time during the assessment phase in generalist intervention. Assessment is always an ongoing process. Likewise, flexibility is invariably a necessity. Therefore, figure 1.18 illustrates dotted lines running from "assessment" to "micro" and "mezzo." These lines continue down along the seven step problem-solving process (engagement, assessment, planning, implementation, evaluation, termination, and follow-up). These dotted lines may apply the steps in whatever order they think is most effective.

PREPARE poses a pivotal concept for the approach to macro intervention proposed here. We have established that new practitioners are likely to obtain agency jobs that do not include responsibility for macro intervention. Goals such as changing agency policy or developing new programs require thought and effort beyond their regular daily routines. Therefore, the decision to pursue macro change is a serious one. Practitioners have to solemnly consider both their own status in the agency and any potential risks. Chapter 5, "PREPARE—Decision Making for Organizational Change," will examine these risks more closely and provide a formula for evaluating whether the pursuit of macro change is worth your effort or not. Each of PREPARE's steps is reviewed next. (Note that figure 1.18 illustrates how implementation and evaluation in macro practice are addressed using another process entitled IMAGINE. This process is summarized and its concepts briefly explained in figure 1.20.)

PREPARE Step 1—Identify *Problems* to Address

The first step in the process for organizational changes is the identification of which *problems* you feel are the most significant to address. You, thus, might ask yourself a number of questions. For example, what problem or problems are most severe and in need of attention? What do clients perceive as the most pressing problem? About which problems are you most seriously concerned? Can you ethically live with the problems despite inconveniences, or do you feel you must address them directly at the macro level? Finally, how can you most concisely identify the problems requiring macro level intervention?

PREPARE Step 2—Review Your Macro and Personal *Reality*

A major task in the decision-making process concerning whether or not to pursue a macro level intervention involves a serious recognition of the practitioner's reality. *Reality* as it is used here refers to the actual conditions, both in the working environment and with respect to personal characteristics, that may affect the macro change process.

Macro reality is the macro environment in which social workers practice. In PREPARE's step 2, you as a worker must begin to identify what aspects in your macro environment might affect your change effort. What organizational and other macro variables will potentially work for or against you? Are resources and funding available? Will regulations or laws constrain your flexibility? What is the political climate within your agency? Is it supportively creative or conservatively restrictive?

Personal reality involves each practitioner's own personal strengths and weaknesses that might affect your ability to implement a macro intervention within the macro environment. Many issues and questions are involved. For example, have you established positive interpersonal relationships with other staff, your immediate supervisor, or other administrators who could help you in the macro change process? How dedicated are you to the agency and its performance? What is your general reputation within the agency? Do you have confidence in your own skills to effect macro changes? How confident are you that you can achieve your macro change goals?

PREPARE Step 3—*Establish* Primary Goals

What does a practitioner need to fulfill identified needs? What does the practitioner see as the ultimate goal that will fulfill the need and solve the problem? What goals does the worker think might be possible to accomplish within the reality of his own macro environment? PREPARE's step 3 concerns the *establishment* of primary goals. This step comes too early in the PREPARE process to allow for detailed, specific objectives. However, you as a practitioner should be able to set your sights on some distant target. Establishing primary goals can provide general direction as you evaluate macro intervention potential and establish plans.

Resnick (1980, p. 212) describes goals as follows:

> Examples of goals may range from the establishment of regular meeting times for physicians, social workers, and nurses in a hospital to discuss cases, to the shifting of the program focus of a social work unit from individual services to a group or community service. A goal may be as minute as designing a new face sheet on a case record or as major as establishing a workshop to improve administration-staff relationships.

PREPARE Step 4—Identify Relevant *People* of Influence

Whom do you know that might be available to help you make the proposed macro changes? PREPARE's step 4 involves the identification of relevant *people of influence*. Potential action systems might include specific individuals or groups within either the organization, the enveloping community, or other agencies. People with access to influence or power within the agency or community are probably the most significant. Are there any others that you as the worker could go to for help? It is important to consider all potential assets including influential and potentially helpful individuals both inside and outside the agency.

PREPARE Step 5—*Assess* Potential Costs and Benefits to Clients and Agency

Any macro change requires some new input. Therefore, PREPARE's step 5 concerns the *assessment* of potential financial costs and potential benefits to clients and the agency or community. Input can be in the form of actual money spent, or it can involve worker's time and efforts. In pursuit of macro change, workers can miss out on other good opportunities where their time would be better spent. This is often referred to as *opportunity cost* (Rubin & Rubin, 1992). Practitioners can also lose political and social influence with respect to those who disagree with the proposed change (Rubin & Rubin, 1992). For example, if you as a practitioner are constantly asking for extra funds for one project or another, administrators may simply get sick of you and ignore your requests. You would then lose some of your potential power or influence. Colleagues might resent the fact that you appear to be using your own agenda which, in turn, might erode your social interaction with these colleagues.

Rubin and Rubin (1992, p. 391) suggest asking three basic questions before pursuing a new project. First, will the results be "worth the effort"? Second, might "alternative solutions produce more benefits at less cost"? Third, "who gets the benefits and who pays the costs"?

PREPARE Step 6—Evaluate Professional and Personal *Risk*

PREPARE's sixth step addresses the evaluation of professional and person *risk*. You as a practitioner should ask yourself three questions involving risk before seriously undertaking macro change in an organization (Resnick & Patti, 1980). You should then evaluate the potential jeopardy for each. First, to what extent are you in danger of losing your job? Do you perceive no, some, moderate, or serious danger? Second, to what extent will such macro change efforts decrease your potential for upward mobility within the agency? Might you make enemies who could stand the way of your future promotions? Third, to what extent would your efforts for macro change seriously strain your interpersonal relationships at work?

Note, however, that there may be another side of this coin. Involvement in macro activity may enhance your standing within an agency if decision-makers interpret your actions as demonstrating initiatives and a sense of responsibility.

PREPAR*E* Step 7—*Evaluate* the Potential Success of a Macro Change Process

This final step in the PREPARE process involves the worker's overall *evaluation* of the potential success of a macro change process. You as the worker must conclusively determine whether to continue with the change effort or stop it right here. First, the pros and cons of proceeding with the macro change process as evaluated in earlier steps must be weighed. You might subsequently determine that a macro change effort would not be worth it. However, if you decide macro intervention is the preferred course of action, then you need to identify the possible macro approaches to use, roughly estimate the effectiveness of each, and select the most appropriate one to pursue. This final PREPARE step reflects the traditional stage between *deciding* to pursue a macro change effort and actually *doing* it.

Implementation and Evaluation in Macro Practice: The IMAGINE Process

We have established that any macro change process will probably involve many more people, circumstances, and details than will micro or mezzo changes. Therefore, a special process is proposed for pursuing both the implementation and the evaluation steps in macro-level problem solving. These, of course, follow generalist intervention's assessment and planning steps demonstrated by the PREPARE process.

Figure 1.20 summarizes the seven major steps of the implementation and evaluation process entitled IMAGINE. A worker can implement any of three major types of organizational and community change using IMAGINE. The three include undertaking specific projects, developing programs, and changing policies (Kettner, Daley, & Nichols, 1985; Netting, Kettner, & McMurty, 1993).

We have established that chapter 5, "PREPARE: Decision Making for Organizational Change," will describe the decision-making process as it concerns whether to pursue macro change or not. Likewise, chapter 6, "IMAGINE How to Implement Macro Intervention: Changing Agency Policy," will explain the IMAGINE process in great detail. Subsequently, chapter 6 will present an example of IMAGINE's application concerning agency policy change. Chapter 7, "IMAGINE Project Implementation and Program Development," will subsequently apply PREPARE to project implementation and program development, the other two primary types of macro change, within an agency setting. Finally, chapter 9, "Macro Practice in Neighborhoods and Communities," will discuss the application of both PREPARE and IMAGINE to macro practice within the community context.

IMAGINE Step 1: Start with an Innovative *Idea*

The first step in the IMAGINE process it to identify and start with an innovative *idea*. At this point in the process, we assume that a worker has already expended some time and effort thinking about the potential macro change by completing the PREPARE process.

IMAGINE Step 2: *Muster* Support and Formulate an Action System

The second step in the IMAGINE macro change process involves *mustering* support from others. It is assumed that the practitioner has no or very little agency-designated power within his or her job role to initiate macro change. Therefore, regardless of the type of macro change chosen, the practitioner needs help. In PREPARE, he or she would already have identified relevant people of influence who can be targeted for support.

IMAGINE Step 3: Identify *Assets*

Regardless of the type of macro level change, step 3 in the IMAGINE process determines what *assets* are available to implement the change. Assets involve any resources and advantages that will help the worker to undertake and complete the proposed change process. Assets can include funding that is readily available, personnel who are able and willing to devote their time to implementing the change, and office space where the change activities can occur.

IMAGINE Step 4: Specify *Goals* and Objectives

IMAGINE's fourth step concerns specifying *goals* and *objectives*. At this stage in problem solving, the worker would already have identified primary goals during the PREPARE process. Additionally, here the worker can begin to formulate the necessary objectives or action steps for achieving the proposed goals. Objectives or action steps are the smaller steps necessary for achieving some broader goal.

Figure 1.20
IMAGINE—A Process for Initiating and Implementing Macro Change

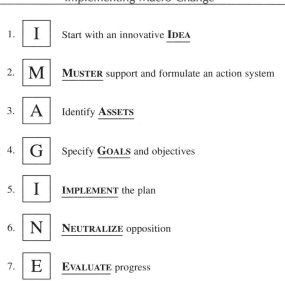

1. **I**   Start with an innovative **IDEA**

2. **M**   **MUSTER** support and formulate an action system

3. **A**   Identify **ASSETS**

4. **G**   Specify **GOALS** and objectives

5. **I**   **IMPLEMENT** the plan

6. **N**   **NEUTRALIZE** opposition

7. **E**   **EVALUATE** progress

IMAGINE Step 5: *Implement* the Plan

IMAGINE's fifth step involves *implementing* the established plan. All macro changes require a plan. What decision-makers need to be contacted as part of the target system? In what order should they be contacted? What should they be told? What recommendations should such decision-makers be given? Implementation is the actual doing of the plan. The plan's goal or end result is to establish the macro change.

IMAGINE Step 6: *Neutralize* Opposition

IMAGINE's sixth step concerns *neutralizing* any possible opposition to the macro plan. The macro change process does not usually involve a direct linear thrust in which all objectives proceed perfectly as planned. Rather, the process usually follows a twisting path chock-full of surprises. Goals, objectives, and plans often need modification in view of vacillations in the macro environment. People change their minds. New elements such as funding cuts enter the scene seemingly out of nowhere. The change agent worker may be assigned to a new supervisor. The larger the target of change and the agency environment, the more likely that new factors will develop to influence the change process. The continuous influence of decision-makers remains important. Significant facets of such influence involve elements to consider before talking to administrators, anticipation of their logical reactions, anticipated phases of administrative resistance, and the use of collaborative and adversarial strategies.

IMAGINE Step 7: *Evalute* Progress

The final step in the IMAGINE macro change process involves *evaluating* the intervention's progress and effectiveness. In all such processes there is an ongoing need to evaluate progress made toward the worker's goal. Is the worker progressing as planned? Or is she or he "stopped dead in the water?" If the latter is true, what can she or he do to get going again?

Because of the importance of evaluation in macro practice, chapter 10, "Evaluating Macro Practice," elaborates on the following issues and skills: purposes of evaluation; key concepts; problems and barriers; types of evaluation; possible evaluative designs; specific steps addressed; and ethics concerning the evaluation process.

Termination in Macro Practice

After an intervention has been evaluated, one of two things usually occurs. On the one hand, the problem-solving process in the macro context can simply be terminated. In this case, either goals have been achieved to an adequate extent or the worker determines that continuation of the macro pursuit is pointless. On the other hand, a practitioner may decide that goals have not been adequately achieved and problems still exist. In this case the worker may decide to continue the problem-solving process, beginning once again with assessment. Therefore, step 7 in the IMAGINE process, the evaluation of progress, can determine whether or not goals have been adequately achieved. This information allows a worker to decide whether to terminate the process or to begin addressing the problematic issue once again.

Follow-Up in Macro Practice

Follow-up is the last step in the generalist intervention model's problem-solving process. Following formal termination, follow-up involves checking on whether the macro intervention process has, indeed, succeeded or whether the same old problems have resurfaced in another form. Many times this is the most difficult step to follow. Caseloads may be too heavy and filled with crises. The worker may be distracted by other issues and demands. Follow-up information might be hard to get. However, most often, substantial effort must be expended to pursue a macro change effort. Follow-up can establish whether the entire process produced lasting, effective changes, or whether problems have surfaced again and merit renewed attention.

Brief Summaries of the Remaining Chapters

We have defined generalist practice and alluded to what some of the forthcoming chapters contain. Following on page 40 is a brief summary of each chapter's content and a rationale for its inclusion in this book.

HIGHLIGHT 1.2

THE HISTORY OF GENERALIST PRACTICE WITH ORGANIZATIONS AND COMMUNITIES IN THE PROFESSIONAL CONTEXT

Social work practice has evolved significantly over the past 130 years. It has responded to vast social changes. It has struggled with the concept of generalist practice and with ways to integrate micro, mezzo, and macro levels of practice. The following will review some of the major facets of this evolution of generalist practice with organizations and communities.

Between the Civil War and World War I, three major economic and social changes occurred in the United States (Garvin & Fox, 1995). The first was industrialization. Mammoth growth in manufacturing and technology brought with it a "wide range of social problems" including "problems of working hours and conditions, safety, and child labor" (Garvin & Fox, 1995, p. 65). The second primary change was urbanization. Concurrent with the centralization of industry in urban settings came the tremendous growth of urban populations. Masses of people moved from rural to urban areas on a quest for work and prosperity. Unfortunately, most were forced into the oldest, most crowded, and least sanitary portions of the cities. The third major change during this period was explosive immigration primarily from Europe. Immigrants brought with them their own problems. Many came from poor rural environments and had little with which to start their lives in this country. Many became ill during the immigration process. As a result of these conditions, most immigrants lived in very poor conditions and accepted whatever work they could find.

In response to these rapidly expanding social problems, two social and ideological movements became the foundation for social work practice in the 1880s (Lewis & Suarez, 1995). They were the Settlement House Movement and the Charity Organization Societies.

Settlement houses were "places where minis-

Between the Civil War and World War I, immigrants such as this family came to America in large numbers. The Settlement House movement was one response to this influx of people.

ters, students, or humanitarians 'settled' (hence the name) to interact with poor slum dwellers with the

(continued)

HIGHLIGHT 1.2—(Continued)

---

purpose of alleviating the conditions of capitalism'' (Smith, 1995, p. 2130). Settlement houses ''wanted to be 'neighbors' to the poor and to help communities solve self-identified problems, such as day care, literacy, and citizenship'' (Popple, 1995, p. 2282). Additionally, they and the people developing them ''advocated for child labor laws, urban parks, women's suffrage, public housing, and public health'' (Smith, 1995, p. 2130).

Settlement houses formed a strong partial foundation for generalist social work practice. Smith (1995) summarizes the settlement house approach: ''Characteristics of the settlement house movement include having a holistic rather than a specialization approach, advocating for social reform while giving services, bridging various groups and classes of people, identifying people as neighbors rather than as needy clients, transforming people from victims of outside forces to participants who are responsible for their own lives, exercising a large and flexible range of activities that are governed by a volunteer community board, and having an orientation to family and neighborhood strengths rather than to individual pathologies'' (p. 2130).

Settlement houses emphasized the empowerment of people. At its most basic level, empowerment involves providing people with authority or power. Settlements focused on social issues and improving living conditions, especially for those who were poorer or less fortunate than others. They provided the background for generalist practice within communities. People were viewed not as helpless victims, but as capable people who could gain power to improve the conditions in which they lived. The concept of community organization and group work developed within the Settlement House context. Jane Addams and Ellen Gates Starr began perhaps the most famous settlement house, Hull House, in Chicago in 1889.

The settlement perspective contrasted strikingly with that of the Charity Organization Societies (COS). According to Lewis and Suarez (1995), ''COS em-

phasis was not on lay communal expertise but on scientific practice and expert knowledge'' (p. 1769). They continue, '' . . .the underlying assumption was that individual need was a result of moral turpitude and that moral teaching combined with minimal assistance, would support people in taking care of themselves'' (p. 1769). Initially, COS used ''friendly visitors'' who tried to help people figure out how to solve their problems (Brieland, 1995, p. 2247). As time passed, COS sought to establish a base of scientific knowledge and apply it to the helping process. The scientific emphasis in fields such as medicine and engineering inspired this process. COS ''wanted to study the problem of dependence, gather data, test theories, systematize administration, and develop techniques that would lead to a cure'' (Popple, 1995, p. 2283). The beginning struggle toward social work professionalism began when COS recognized that friendly visitors needed more education and training to perform their tasks effectively (Brieland, 1995; Popple, 1995).

COS focused on curing individuals rather than on empowering communities. Traditional social casework developed from this approach. Additionally, because of the emphasis on expert knowledge, the significance of administration and supervised practice was incorporated into the casework concept. This emphasis on expertise contrasted sharply with the settlement approach that emphasized the empowerment and self-sufficiency of all.

Despite the different paths taken by the Settlement Houses and the COS, ''social work pioneers were clear about the primary commitment owed to the poorest and most oppressed and disenfranchised members of our population'' (Landon, 1995, p. 1101). In the early twentieth century, social work continued to seek a professional identity regarding what social work practice involved. The emphasis on scientific advances and the new, enticing therapeutic approaches being introduced during the first half of this century (such as psychodynamic and social learning theories) strengthened the profession's commitment to social casework (Landon, 1995). Social casework stressed therapeutically helping individuals and families solve their particular problems. Thus, the target of change was the individual or the family.

The divergence between the settlement orientation (emphasizing group and community work) and the COS approach oriented to individuals remained strong. Thus, three method tracks (casework, group work, and community organization) characterized social work through the 1950s. Casework was further fortified by the developing fields of practice, or specializations, that were generally incorporated under its umbrella. These included medical social work, psychiatric social work, child welfare, and school social work (Brieland, 1995).

The Great Depression of the 1930s and the Social Security Act switched many aspects of service provision from the private to the public sector. Thus, the type of social work jobs available and the characteristics of people getting them shifted. Popple (1995) describes the change. Prior to the depression, social work was close to becoming a profession strictly for those with graduate degrees. Popple explains (1995), "The nature of the social worker's task was coming to be defined as . . . providing skilled casework services based on a thorough understanding of psychotherapy" (p. 2286). Many clients were not poor but suffered from other problems, such as mental health. Working to change communities and social policies was most often overlooked.

The Depression changed all this, however, with the massive growth of new social work jobs created by the Social Security Act. The majority "of the new jobs involved helping basically well-adjusted people deal with problems brought about by unemployment" (Popple, 1995, p. 2287). Essentially, these jobs required skills other than the ability to facilitate therapy—as many master's degrees social workers (MSWs) were doing. Thus, numerous baccalaureate degree social workers (BSWs) were hired for these jobs because of the different skills required. However, MSWs refused to accept BSWs as professional social workers, not even allowing BSWs to join professional social work organizations (Popple, 1995).

The economy saw rapid growth during World War II and after with the increased demand for production of needed goods. The resulting relative affluence of the 1940s and 1950s once again encouraged social workers to turn to psychotherapy and casework (Popple, 1995). During the 1950s, 85 percent of social work students selected casework as their orientation of choice (Popple, 1995). MSWs dominated the scene.

The 1960s produced a new focus on social change versus individual pathology. Many began to realize that poverty and other vast social problems still existed in the United States. A series of federal administrations began implementing antipoverty programs. At first, these programs generally disregarded social workers because their intent was to empower the poor themselves (Popple, 1995). However, it soon became clear that expertise was needed "in community organization, administration, and direct service with clients" in order to run them effectively (Popple, 1995, p. 2288). As a result, most social work schools added "policy, planning, and administration specialties to their curricula" (Popple, 1995, p. 2289). This probably initiated the move toward working with and within organizations as a major facet of generalist practice.

"Accountability" became a key word when talking about social service provision (Popple, 1995, p. 2289). Taxpayers and government officials did not want to waste their money. They demanded to see results.

At this point, the social work professional faced a serious problem. More than three quarters of all people holding social work jobs were not considered to be professional social workers by major social work organizations. That is, most workers did not hold the MSW degree (Popple, 1995). Needless to say, this did not enhance the profession's accountability—the vast majority of the people doing social work were not considered social workers. The logical move was to recognize the BSW as the practical requirement for an entry level job in the social work profession. People performing social work jobs should be social workers.

In 1955, seven separate professional organiza-

(continued)

HIGHLIGHT 2.1—(Continued)

tions came together to form the National Association of Social Workers (Brieland, 1995). The need for a unifying generalist approach motivated this union. Many social work leaders and educators became increasingly concerned about the profession's commitment to rectifying social injustice and advocating for positive social change.

The Council of Social Work Education (CSWE), the field's accrediting body, was born in 1952 when several predecessor organizations merged; at this time the first Curriculum Policy Statement and accreditation standards were issued (Brieland, 1995). Such a statement and standards guide curriculum content and structure. Additionally, this initial statement required that students "develop a social philosophy rooted in an appreciation of the essential dignity of human beings" (Brieland, 1995, p. 2255). Such a broad goal implied that social work should be more than just casework. Rather, social work should seek to benefit society generally and oppressed populations specifically.

Many social work leaders began calling for a unified foundation for social work practice (Bartlett, 1970; Boehm, 1959) and referring to levels of social work practice among various sized systems (Pincus & Minahan, 1973; Schwartz, 1961; Siporin, 1975). Social workers needed a broad base of skills to work with individuals, families, groups, organizations, and communities. The prolific development of BSW programs in the late 1960s and early 1970s emphasized the need for a generalist foundation for social work practice (Landon, 1995). Baccalaureate and Master's programs required differentiation of purpose. In 1974 CSWE "stipulated generalist education as appropriate for the baccalaureate level of practice" and in 1984 "declared that the required foundation material on both undergraduate and graduate levels should consist of the knowledge, values, and skills essential to generalist practice" (Landon, 1995, p. 1102).

Currently, "the BSW is considered the entry-level degree and [that] the MSW provides advanced, specialized training" (Popple, 1995, p. 2290). Landon (1995) concludes that "generalist programming is embedded in the profession, both in practice and education" (p. 1106).

Chapter 2: Using Micro Skills in the Macro Environment

A premise of generalist practice is that micro skills form the foundation for mezzo skills, both of which are necessary for developing effective macro practice skills. Thus, we have a continuum where one level of practice is a prerequisite for mastering the next practice level. Another premise is that practicing from a generalist perspective might require the application of micro, mezzo, or macro skills at a particular point in the intervention process.

Chapter 2 applies to a range of micro-skill dimensions to macro practice contexts. These include: beginning relationships with colleagues, administrators, politicians, community residents, and the like; using both verbal and nonverbal behavior for effective communication in macro contexts; applying appropriate assertiveness; addressing and resolving conflict; and working under supervisors.

Chapter 3: Using Mezzo Skills in the Macro Environment

Just as mastery of basic micro skills is necessary for both effective mezzo and macro practice, so are mezzo skills necessary for effective macro practice. A wide range of mezzo skills can apply directly to macro settings, including those in organizations and communities. Chapter 3 describes and examines the following applications of mezzo skills to macro contexts: networking with other individuals and systems; working in and with teams; planning and conducting meetings;

using parliamentary procedure correctly; and managing conflict within a wide range of non-client groups.

Chapter 4: Understanding Organizations

In order to work effectively within an organizational structure, it is critical to understand what that structure involves. Therefore, we propose here that such effective work requires understanding of the organizational dimensions and issues discussed in chapter 4. This includes: definition of and differences among organizations, social services, and social agencies; organizational theories; social agencies as systems; the nature of organizations, including settings, goals, macro contexts, and structure; methods of management; bureaucracy and potential alternatives; the exceptional problems of social service organizations; and other common problems encountered in organizations.

Chapter 5: PREPARE—Decision Making for Organizational Change

The decision on whether or not to pursue a macro practice goal is a critical one. Chapter 5 introduces the types of change that are possible in organizations. These include undertaking specific projects, initiating and developing programs, and changing agency policies. The majority of the chapter focuses on the decision-making process, PREPARE, that was introduced earlier in the discussion of the problem-solving process. An extensive case example is used to illustrate PREPARE.

Chapter 6: IMAGINE How to Implement Macro Intervention— Changing Agency Policy

Chapter 6 applied the problem-solving process to organizational change. A process for initiating and implementing macro change, IMAGINE, is thoroughly discussed. IMAGINE was introduced earlier during our discussion of the problem-solving process. The case example initiated in chapter 5 is continued here to portray each state in the IMAGINE process.

Chapter 7: IMAGINE Project Implementation and Program Development

Chapter 7 applies the IMAGINE process to both project implementation and program development. The specification of goals and objectives is emphasized. Program Evaluation and Review Technique (PERT) charts are explained as useful tools for setting forth a timeline to accomplish goals. An extensive case example of developing an sexual harassment awareness program for employees of a large social services agency is examined.

Chapter 8: Understanding Neighborhoods and Communities

Agencies employing generalist practitioners function within the context of neighborhoods and communities. Therefore, we propose that community content is absolutely essential in order to perform generalist practice effectively. Chapter 8 explains the following aspects of work within the community macro context: social work role; definitions of community and neighborhood; application of the systems perspective to communities; viewing the community from ecological, social system, and other perspectives; community resource systems; demographic development of communities; social stratification; community economic and political systems; power in communities; and the significance of neighborhoods.

Chapter 9: Macro Practice in Communities

Chapter 9 identifies several perspectives on communities, including a philosophical view of the change process within communities. How to begin the change process is emphasized. PREPARE is applied to the assessment and planning of community change and IMAGINE to the implementation and evaluation of such change.

Chapter 10: Evaluating Macro Practice

Evaluation of practice effectiveness is critically important in all levels of practice. Generalist practitioners must be accountable. You must be able to prove that your work is effective and valuable in order to validate the existence of your job. Chapter 10 defines evaluation and elaborates on its purposes. Key concepts in evaluation are explained. Problems and barriers often encountered in evaluation are explored. Different kinds of evaluation, evaluation designs, and stages in evaluations are discussed.

Chapter 11: Advocacy and Social Action with Populations-at-Risk

Chapter 11 discusses advocacy and social action skills at length. Advocacy involves stepping forward on the behalf of others, usually going beyond the minimal requirements for accomplishing one's job. Social action involves targeting a "disadvantaged segment of the population that needs to be organized, perhaps in alliance with others, in order to make adequate demands on the larger community for increased resources of treatment more in accordance with social justice or democracy" (Cox, Erlich, Rothman, & Tropman, 1987, p. 6).

Chapter 11 also identifies and discusses populations-at-risk. Advocacy and social action on their behalf are explained. The importance of empowerment is emphasized. Legislative advocacy is explored and steps in its process are delineated.

Chapter 12: Ethics and Ethical Dilemmas in Macro Practice

You know by now how important professional values are in the social work curriculum and profession. Values dictate what is right and what is wrong. Ethics provide guidelines for how to behave. Chapter 12 discusses the NASW Code of Ethics, segment by segment. The significance of personal values and their relationships to professional performance is examined. The type of ethical issues confronting agency workers and the dilemmas involved in macro settings are introduced. Decision-making steps for resolving ethical dilemmas are identified and explained. Guides to ethical decision making are reviewed. A range of possible ethical dilemmas is appraised. They include: distributing limited resources; lack of community support for service provision; problematic relationships with colleagues; conforming to agency policy; breaching confidentiality; co-optation versus cooperation; fraud and illegal behavior; conflict of interest; potential harm to participants; and stigmatization tactics.

Chapter 13: Working with the Courts

It is not news that this country's courts are massively powerful. There is a wide range of potential situations generalist practitioners may find themselves in with relationship to the courts. For example, courts might call upon a practitioner to write up a family assessment recommending the most appropriate placement for a child, testify concerning alleged child maltreatment, or submit progress notes involving a client who committed a felony. Therefore, we propose that effective work within an organizational structure should include a basic understanding of the courts and the legal system in addition to skills for working effectively with the courts. Chapter 13 describes and examines the following issues and skills: terms commonly used in courts and by lawyers; general differences between social work practice and courtroom protocol; preparation for testimony in court; and potential ploys used by lawyers.

Chapter 14: Developing and Managing Agency Resources

Chapter 14 describes a variety of activities associated with developing and managing agency resources. Specific skills stressed include: working with the media to help ensure that your agency receives positive treatment; using technology to manage agency resources, facilitate service delivery, and evaluate agency effectiveness; and raising funds to pursue a wide range of goals. A substantial portion of the chapter addresses various facets of grant writing, such as where to find grants in the first place, how to follow the application process, and what to cover in your grant proposal.

Chapter 15: Stress and Time Management

It is easy for hard work and problematic situations in agency and community contexts to cause undue stress.

Therefore we propose that effective work in organizational settings requires the appropriate use of stress ad time management skills. Chapter 15 addresses the following issues and suggests the following techniques: understanding stress within the agency context; perceptions of stress; confronting stress; specific techniques for managing stress; the relationship between poor time management and increased stress; styles in dealing with time; planning your time; gaining control of your own behavior in regard to time; and combating procrastination.

Chapter 16: Resumés, Interviewing, and Getting the Job

Before closing this chapter, one other aspect related to macro practice merits mentioning. In order to function effectively in an agency setting that exists in the larger community context, you must get the job in the first place. Therefore, we include a chapter on resumés, interviewing, and getting the job. This chapter is offered because of our assumption that macro skills are built upon mezzo skills which, in turn, are built upon micro skills. By the end of this book, you will approach the end of your acquisition of the skills involved in generalist practice. Therefore, we assume you will also be approaching the job-seeking process.

Specifically, chapter 16 addresses the following issues: assessing your own capabilities and interests within a job-finding context; investigating actual job possibilities by using newspapers, state merit system lists, NASW publications, networking, and consulting your college resources; preparing your resumé; writing application letters; and preparing for job interviews, including finding out about the agency and preparing to answer tough questions.

Chapter Summary

This chapter introduces generalist practice and stresses the integration of micro, mezzo, and macro perspectives in any intervention process. Generalist intervention is defined. The definition involves nine primary concepts including: the acquisition of an eclectic knowledge base; the assimilation of professional values; mastery of a wide range of practice skills targeting any size system for change; effective work within an organizational structure; use of appropriate supervision; assumption of a wide range of professional roles; employment of critical thinking skills; and the application of a problem-solving process.

Two major processes in macro intervention are introduced. The first, PREPARE, represents a model for assessing the potential for macro change. It coincides with the assessment and planning steps in the generalist intervention problem-solving process. The second process, IMAGINE, concerns the implementation and evaluation of macro change. Hence, IMAGINE corresponds to the implementation and evaluation steps of the problem-solving process. Later chapters address both processes in detail.

Content covered in succeeding chapters is introduced. Such content includes: using micro skills in macro settings; using mezzo skills in macro settings; understanding the nature or working of organizations; decision making for organizational change; changing agency policy; project implementation and program development; understanding neighborhoods and communities; macro practice in communities; evaluating macro practice; advocating on behalf of populations-at-risk; ethics and ethical dilemmas in macro practice; working with the courts; using specific macro skills, such as grant-writing and fundraising; implementing stress and time management techniques; and issues concerning resumés, interviewing, and getting the job.

CHAPTER TWO

Using Micro Skills in the Macro Environment

A colleague approaches you and says, "You know, you're really intimidating." How do you respond?

Your supervisor asks you, "Have you finished your special assignment yet?" You think, "Special assignment? What the heck is she talking about?" What should you say to your supervisor at this point?

You work for a private agency that runs a dozen homes throughout your state for adults with developmental disabilities. The agency's board of directors (the body responsible for establishing basic agency policy) suddenly decides to combine the homes into two campuses instead of twelve individual homes. You think this would be a terrible mistake. Most clients would be moved far from their family support systems. Maintaining such familial contact was a major reason for selection of the twelve homes' location in the first place. How do you approach the board's chairperson about your concerns?

You think your agency needs to establish a Personnel and Policy Committee to review and revise the agency's policy manual, which is twenty years out of date. Sick leave, vacation time, procedures for admitting clients, and an almost endless array of other matters need clarification and definition. What should you say when you approach the appropriate supervisors and administrators?

You applied for a grant to develop a series of training sessions for your agency's workers. The grant is not actually denied, but the grant review committee raises a variety of serious concerns. The committee encourages you to contact members to address the issues. How do you approach these people?

A legislative committee abruptly cuts off your agency's funding. That means your job. What do you say when you contact the relevant legislators?

A worker from another social service agency in the community walks into your office and confidently says, "Hi! I thought I'd stop by and tell you to complete the summary of our meeting last week. Send me a copy when you're finished. Be cool. See you later." He catches you off guard. You don't know what to say. You think to yourself, "What does he mean by ordering me to do some totally pointless summary report? He's not my boss. Who does he think he is? Why didn't I think faster and tell him what he can do with his report!!!" Okay, you weren't fast enough on your feet. What do you do now?

These are among the vast range of interpersonal scenarios you may encounter in the macro environment.

We assume that you have acquired an assortment of skills for working with clients in micro and mezzo practice. However, how do you apply these skills in macro practice contexts? How can you use them to interact effectively with colleagues, supervisors, other staff, high-ranking administrators, community leaders, and politicians? How do you maintain pleasant relationships with such people? How do you resolve conflicts? How do you gauge how assertive, nonassertive, or aggressive you should be? Such issues are what this chapter is all about.

Introduction

The concept of doing macro practice can be threatening. You might think "What in the world can I do in my lowly direct service position to influence what goes on in a whole agency, let alone a large bureaucracy, let alone a state government?"

The answer arises from that fact that agencies, mammoth bureaucracies, state governments, and even national arenas are made up of individuals, all operating within their own unique contexts. Each powerful decision-maker, including directors of large agencies and prestigious politicians, is a human being just like you. Although their behavior and decisions affect many layers of people beneath them in whatever power structure they oversee, they may have *direct* contact with relatively few others. These few, in turn, influence the people below them in the hierarchy, and so on. The point is that each person, no matter how *theoretically* important he or she is, interacts and communicates in order to get things done. They do this in much the same way you will interact and communicate in your own work setting.

This chapter focuses on the techniques necessary for communicating with other people in macro practice contexts. It first reviews basic communication techniques which are similar to those used in direct practice with clients. However, they are presented in the context of communication with colleagues, supervisors, other agency staff, community leaders, and government representatives. We have established that such basic micro techniques form the foundation for learning and applying mezzo skills (working with groups) and macro skills (working with agencies, organizations, communities, and social systems). Learning how to communicate well and work with individuals is an absolute necessity for any type of generalist social work practice. Subsequently, this chapter explores two common interactional issues in the macro environment. They include assertiveness and conflict resolution.

There are times when you will need to become more assertive within your work setting. A supervisor may ask you to take some work home to complete on unpaid overtime on the weekend you're getting married or attending your uncle's funeral. A colleague may borrow your files without asking and simply forget to return them. You may need to urge a local politician to support the building of new public housing your clients desperately need. You may feel a strong need to initiate a sex education program for your teenage clients in view of soaring pregnancy rates, even though scarce resources plague your agency. In any of these cases, and in an infinite number of other instances, you will require well-developed assertiveness skills.

Likewise, you may often encounter conflict in your work environment. Conflicts involve differences of ideas, opinions, and goals. For example, you may think that your agency should adopt a polity of enhanced worker discretion, encouraging practitioners to make their own practice decisions. You might feel that such freedom would allow you to respond more effectively to each client's unique situation. A colleague of yours, on the other hand, might think that your agency should establish stronger centralized control. This colleague feels that specific regulations and procedures for handling various client-related issues make decision making easier. Likewise, this colleague believes such structure helps workers avoid making mistakes. What policy should the agency adopt?

In another example, you may feel it is extremely important to initiate a clothing drive for your poor clients as winter approaches in your cold northern climate. Your agency's assistant director, on the other hand, may consider such an endeavor frivolous and beneath a professional social worker's role. How will you resolve these differences?

Any kind of conflict resolution requires, first, that you thoroughly understand the dynamics of conflict and, second, that you can implement conflict resolution techniques. Hence, this chapter addresses both these needs within the macro practice context. Note that conflict is such an important aspect of interpersonal dynamics in virtually any practice setting that the next chapter ("Us-

ing Mezzo Skills in the Macro Environment") examines its impacts in mezzo contexts.

Finally, this chapter explains how you can facilitate the supervisory process. The supervisory relationship can significantly benefit from use of your micro skills. Because of the importance of supervision and of your relationship with your supervisor, we will examine the issues involved in supervision and potential problems that can arise. Ultimately, we will propose suggestions for how to use supervision most effectively.

This chapter will:

- Explore how to establish rapport and build a relationship with others in the macro environment.
- Describe a variety of interviewing techniques and apply them to macro practice situations.
- Discuss assertiveness and its application in a macro context.
- Investigate the pros and cons of conflict, and suggest procedures for conflict resolution.
- Examine the supervisory relationships and some of its inherent problems.
- Formulate suggestions for maximizing your supervisory relationships and enhancing the communication process.

Beginning Relationships in Macro Practice

Communication with other people in macro practice is obviously necessary to get anything done. We assume here that you have already had the opportunity to learn and practice some interviewing skills within micro and mezzo practice contexts. That is, you have learned some basic skills for working with individual clients and groups. As we have discussed, we assume that macro practice skills are built upon mezzo practice skills that, in turn, are built upon skills necessary in micro practice. In other words, you need to know how to work with people as individuals in order to work with them in groups. Likewise, you need both these skill levels to work with people as members of organizations, communities, and political decision-making bodies.

Working with individuals within macro settings is very much like working with clients in your social work practice. Interviewing, of course, is considered one of the core skills for micro practice. An interview involves "interpersonal verbal and nonverbal communications" and is characterized by three attributes (Kadushin, 1995,

p. 1527). First, it includes a structured purpose and goal. Second, an interview is conducted in a context where the participants have certain roles (such as practitioner and client). The interview's context also includes prescribed time limits and an assigned location. The interview's third characteristic is that it follows a number of sequential steps, including "a beginning, a middle, and a termination" (Kadushin, 1995, pp. 1527–28). In micro practice, the interview is more than having a pleasant conversation with a client. The interview's purpose is to "exchange information in order to illuminate and solve problems, promote growth, and plan strategies or actions aimed at improving people's quality of life" (Hepworth & Larsen, 1987, p. 996).

Your intent in macro practice is very similar in that it usually involves communicating and problem-solving. However, instead of working with individual clients, you are communicating and problem solving with groups of clients, agency administrators, your colleagues, politicians, community residents, and professionals from various other community agencies. Figure 2.1 conceptualizes macro systems as consisting of *individuals* who all are, in effect, potential targets of change or helpers in the change process. The macro environments in which you work—including agency, community, and political entity—all consist of people with individual personalities, qualities, and quirks. Each individual can be part of a macro intervention.

In learning how to communicate and work with other people, it's wise to start by examining how to establish good relationships in general. Some people are naturally popular. Others are not. Certain basic behaviors and characteristics usually make a person more appealing to others. Likewise, in interpersonal dynamics, certain behaviors and personal qualities tend to nurture relationships. Exhibiting these traits and behaviors tends to put others at ease. This chapter begins by discussing how verbal and nonverbal behavior, in addition to certain other human characteristics demonstrated through such behavior, can enhance relationships within macro practice contexts.

At this point we assume your thinking about micro skills has focused primarily on their application to client situations. Therefore, this chapter and this book address a wide range of situations that can occur in macro settings, including those involving your initiation and pursuit of a macro change process. For example, you might want to fight for a group of your clients' rights, change

Figure 2.1
The Worker in the Organizational, Community, and Political Macro Environments

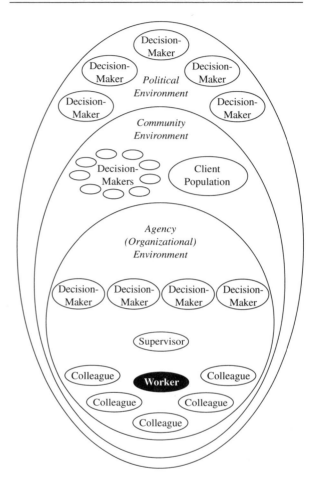

an agency policy, help start a community program, or implement a special project. We also examine everyday interactions with colleagues and administrators in macro environments. Our assumption is that part of understanding macro practice involves cooperating with colleagues and supervisors in agency settings. Such interactions may not be addressed elsewhere in the practice curriculum. Everyday activities might include responding to a colleague's criticism of your work. Likewise, they might involve making an effective request to a supervisor for help with an exceptionally difficult client. We consider any type of interaction in the macro environment where micro skills are used as an aspect of macro practice.

A Review of Basic Micro Skills

Macro practice always involves human interaction. Any interpersonal interaction involves an intricate web of communication. Many of the same skills you use to communicate with and help clients can be applied directly to macro situations. For example, you might be initiating the development of a needle exchange program for drug addicts in a deteriorating urban neighborhood to prevent the spread of HIV through contaminated needles. You would first need to establish rapport and positive relationships with community residents and decision-makers (involving micro and mezzo aspects of practice) in order to get such a program (an aspect of macro practice) off the ground.

Or, suppose you work in a protective services agency and want to initiate an in-service training program focusing on new child abuse assessment techniques. In-service training involves "an educational program provided by an employer and usually carried out by a supervisor or specialist to help an employee become more productive and effective in accomplishing a specific task or meeting the overall objectives of the organization" (Barker, 1994, p. 188). You would need the help of your immediate supervisor or other agency administrators to get the project off the ground. How likely would you be to receive assistance from those people whom you had already antagonized or alienated? Not every likely. Instead, you would need to have established, open, positive relationships with the people who can help you. You might also need to display appropriate assertiveness when approaching those who could help you and proposing your idea to them. If an interpersonal conflict should arise, you should know how to handle and resolve it. The following sections will review verbal and nonverbal behavior, significant personal qualities involved in communication, and types of verbal responses.

Verbal and Nonverbal Behavior

As we know, the most basic level of human communication involves both verbal and nonverbal behavior. Verbal behavior is what is said. Nonverbal behavior is what is communicated in other ways than through spoken words. People communicate by the expressions on their faces, the movements of their hands, the relaxed or tense manner in which they sit, the amount of eye contact they maintain, and by how close they stand to you. Any aspect of a person's presence that conveys unspoken ideas or information is an element of nonverbal communication.

For example, Monica, a county social services worker, initiates a meeting with a variety of community residents to help them talk about starting a crime prevention program. She is concerned about one resident, Jorgé Cordoba, forty-one. Jorgé has agreed that the program is important. Yet during each of the meetings, he sits in the back of the room and closes his eyes, almost as if he were asleep. Monica happens to know that Jorgé has a sixteen-year-old son whom she thinks may be a member of a local gang, the Toros Machos. This gang is particularly renowned for its drug trafficking and gun sales. Monica's hunch is that Mr. Cordoba is very ambivalent regarding the crime prevention program. On the one hand, he wants to curb crime in his neighborhood and community. On the other, he wants to protect his son. How might Monica approach Mr. Cordoba? What might she say? How should she act toward him? The answer is to master relevant micro practice skills and apply them to this particular macro practice situation.

There are many aspects of nonverbal behavior. Here we will focus on four of them—eye contact, attentive listening, facial expressions, and body positioning.

Eye Contact

It is important to look another person directly in the eye as you communicate. Direct eye contact means that you face the other person and make visual contact with the other person's eyes. This establishes a rapport between you and conveys that you are attending to what the other is saying.

You must know people who have difficulty "looking you in the eye." This can convey that they are afraid or insecure. Appearing afraid is not advantageous. For example, consider a colleague who confronts you by telling you that your writing style is exceedingly dull and overly complicated. Surprised, you feel this criticism is unwarranted and unfair. Which would be more effec-

Having good micro skills in the macro environment is critical. The professionals pictured here have established good eye contact to enhance communication.

tive—to look sheepishly down at your feet and mumble a response or to hold your head high, look him in the eye, and state, "I'm surprised at that feedback. I don't agree with you, but I wonder what your reasons are for saying that." In the first instance, probably no matter what words you used, your lack of eye contact would make you appear afraid or timid. It would be difficult for your critic to take seriously whatever you were saying. On the other hand, providing appropriate eye contact in addition to a straightforward response would probably convey your intent much more clearly.

Of course, this example shows that appropriate eye contact is only one channel of communication. Facial expression, content clarity, tone of voice, and a range of other behaviors contribute to the effectiveness or lack of effectiveness of your message.

Failing to look people directly in the eye may also imply disinterest or dishonesty. A cartoon of a "guy with shifty eyes" comes to mind. On the other hand, maintaining continuous eye contact may make the other person uncomfortable. Additionally, it can be tedious— as if you were in a who-can-hold-out-and-not-blink-the-longest contest. Eye contact is a complex nonverbal behavior. Moderate eye contact that is somewhere between no eye contact and constant eye contact seems to put people the most at ease (Epstein, 1985, p. 29). Thus, direct eye contact with an occasional glance away—at your hands, at a bookcase, or simply at nothing—is probably most appropriate.

It should be noted, however, that you must maintain a sensitivity to cultural differences concerning any aspect of nonverbal behavior including eye contact. People with different cultural backgrounds may have different expectations in terms of appropriate nonverbal behaviors. For example, for American Indians, "eye contact [on your part] may indicate lack of respect" (Devore & Schlesinger, 1991, p. 199).

Attentive Listening

You always listen carefully to a person who is talking to you, right? Or, in reality, might you drift off for just a moment to think about what you are going to make for dinner or wear on Friday night. Just as in micro practice, listening in macro practice settings is not as simple as it sounds. First, the distinction needs to be made between *hearing* and *listening*. Listening implies more than just audio perception of spoken words. Listening means that you try both to hear and to understand most of what another person is saying. It focuses on comprehending the meaning of what is said.

There are a number of barriers to attentive listening. They involve three aspects of communication. First, the person sends a message with some *intent*, some meaning he or she wishes to convey. Second, the receiver of the message tries to decipher the meaning of what has been said. Thus, the message has some *impact* on the receiver. This impact arises from what the receiver thinks the sender said. What the receiver actually hears may or may not be what the sender intended the receiver to hear. Third, there may be environmental barriers that impede communication of the message (see figure 2.2).

The first cluster of communication barriers involves the sender, in this case, the person who is talking to you. This individual might be using words, phrases, or concepts that are unclear to you. The person may say something very vague or may wrongly assume that the receiver already knows something basic to understanding the message. The sender's *intent*, then, may not be the same as the *impact* on the receiver.

Figure 2.2
Barriers to Attentive Listening

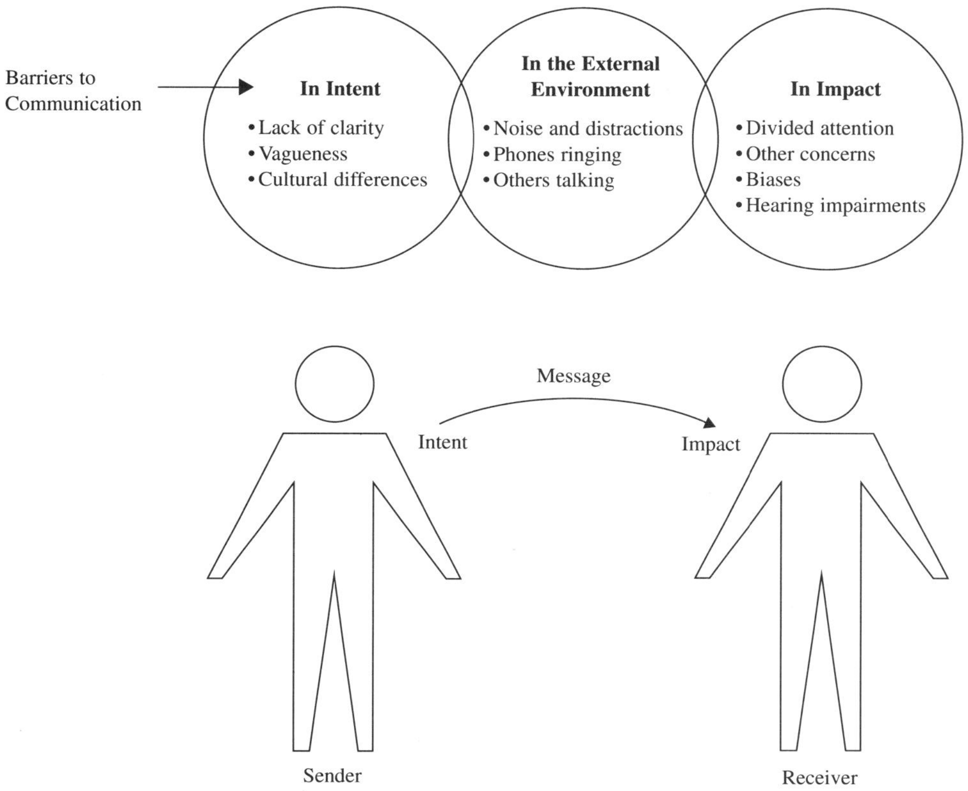

Source: The concepts of "intent" and "impact" were taken from the film *Behavioral Interviewing with Couples*, available from Research Press, Dept. 95, P.O. Box 9177, Champaign, IL 61826.

For example, consider a situation where you are working for a YMCA Center for Youth Alternatives.[1] You are in the process of developing a crisis intervention program that involves a telephone crisis hotline, a series of temporary placements, and referral services. Clients include "runaways, homeless youths, and troubled youths, all of whom are vulnerable to injury and exploitation in the streets (Morrow, 1987, p. 138). Setting up a new program is difficult, but in the long run you feel it will be much more effective and efficient than working with clients referred in the more traditional way by other community agencies.

You are embroiled in getting the project going and have been working closely with your supervisor. As you busily pass each other in the hallway, she asks you, "Can you get it done by Monday?" Your supervisor here has a specified *intent*. You hear her say "it" and then interpret "it" to mean finishing your list of temporary placements for clients, along with addresses, phone numbers, and contact persons. This, then, is the *impact* of her statement.

However, what if this is not what your supervisor really means by "it"? Suppose her real intent is to ask you if you can get the plan for publicizing the crisis hotline to her by Monday. If people don't know that the hotline exists, it will be useless. Your supervisor's

_____

1. This example is based on a description of Project "Safe Place," Louisville, KY, in C.A. Morrow, "Child and Family Homelessness," in *Children, Families and Cities: Programs That Work at the Local Level*, J. E. Kyle (Ed.) (Washington DC: National League of Cities, 1987), pp. 137–40.

intent (what she wants you to do) is very different from what you think she means. In essence, "it" is vague. You hear that you need to get your list of temporary placements completed (impact). Her intent, on the other hand, is that you are supposed to submit your plan for publicizing the hotline to her (intent). With such a misunderstanding you would complete the wrong thing and find yourself up a creek without a paddle.

The second type of communication barrier involves the receiver, in this case, you as the social worker. Your attention may be divided between what the other person is saying and what you want to say next. You might be preoccupied. You might be focusing on what direction the interaction should take in the future. Thus, it is easy not to pay full attention to the sender and listen to all that is said. Refer to the earlier example of misunderstanding between you and your supervisor. The list of temporary placements was the last thing you remember talking to your supervisor about. Additionally, it was the primary thing on your mind when you passed each other in the hall and she made her comment.

The third cluster of communication barriers to attentive listening involves the external environment and its potential noise and distractions. For example, a telephone might ring, another staff member might approach you and start talking, a group might arrive early, or somebody might have turned the air conditioning up to frigid levels.

In summary, listening is not always easy. It demands concentration, perceptiveness, and the use of a range of interpersonal and communication skills. This chapter will describe a number of these skills.

Facial Expressions

Facial movements and expressions provide an excellent means of communicating. A furrowed brow may convey intense concentration, uncertainty, or concern. A casual smile can indicate pleasure and, many times, warmth. Raising the eyebrows may portray surprise or sudden interest. In contrast, a blank, deadpan expression conveys little or no information about what you mean or what you think.

Facial expressions can be used to reinforce what is said verbally and to corroborate the fact that you mean what you say. However, two aspects about using facial expressions should be noted. First, be aware of your

facial responses so that you know how you are communicating. Second, make certain that your facial expressions correspond with both your other nonverbal and your verbal behavior. It is not helpful to give others mixed messages. That is, to say one thing and look as if you mean another only confuses people. It can generate doubt that you're being truthful.

For instance, you might be a practitioner working for a large public social services agency. You have been laboring on the behalf of agency employees who desperately need good child care. Specifically, you have been working with a Child Care Committee of other interested employees to propose changing agency policy so that employees can redirect up to $5,000 of their annual salary to cover child care expenses.[2] There are a number of advantages to this plan: "Since the earned salary has been redirected before the employee receives it, employees do not have to pay taxes on the part of their incomes that [is] redirected to child care. Therefore, child care purchased in this fashion is more affordable. The city also saves dollars through this plan because it does not pay social security or withholding taxes on the money which is redirected for child care expenses (Smith, 1987, p. 54)."

You and the others on the Child Care Committee decide that the easiest way to implement this policy would be to gain the support of the agency's assistant director. The committee designates you to meet with him and propose the change.

During the meeting, you make your proposal. In response, he states simply that it is a terrible plan. He questions why you would waste your paid work time pursuing something that he considers the employees', not the agency's, business. Subsequently, with a huge, Cheshire-cat grin reaching from ear to ear, the assistant director says, "Of course, I'm terribly sorry that your plan is unworkable." Obviously, this administrator is anything but sorry. His facial expression clearly indicates his personal satisfaction about trashing your idea. He may have made the "I'm sorry" comment to try to terminate your generally negative meeting with him on a more positive note. Or perhaps he always says he's sorry when he disagrees with employees. Nonetheless,

---

2. This example is based on a description of the Office of Child Care Initiatives, Denver, CO, in *Children, Families and Cities: Programs That Work at the Local Level*, J. E. Kyle (Ed.) (Washington, DC: National League of Cities, 1987), pp. 53–55.

the lack of consistency between verbal and nonverbal behavior clearly indicates that he does not mean what he is saying.

The postscript will involve going back to the Child Care Committee and the drawing board concerning your plan to implement the policy change. The assistant director is obviously not going to provide any support. The community needs to propose an alternative tactic to pursue its policy change. Perhaps going directly to the agency's executive director is now in order.

Body Positioning

The way people position their bodies and move their extremities also provides information to others. Two continuums are especially important. These are the tense/relaxed and formal/informal continuums. The amount of space you allow between you and others is another aspect of body positioning.

Tense/Relaxed Continuum

Body tension involves how rigid or tense your muscles appear as you position yourself. Such tension most often coincides with emotional tension. If you look up tight, you probably feel up tight inside. Such tension can be demonstrated by sitting rigidly straight and allowing minimal movement of extremities. Tension is also apparent when you make quick, nervous movements, such as continuously tapping a foot or finger, or jingling loose change in your pocket.

The opposite of a tense stance is a relaxed one. Relaxation can be portrayed by slow, loose movements and a decidedly casual, informal presentation of self. The most extreme relaxed stance is probably lying down. The term "laid back" is often used to refer to such a relaxed approach.

When trying to communicate with another person, it is important to be aware of how you present yourself nonverbally. Extreme tension may convey lack of confidence in yourself or excessive nervousness. It may put distance between yourself and the other. Likewise, it may make it difficult for that other to feel comfortable with and trust you.

On the other hand, an extremely relaxed stance may convey to the other person that you do not care very

much about what happens. It may also eat away at your credibility as a professional if you appear too lax, disinterested, and informal.

Ideally, it's best to present yourself somewhere between the two extremes. To some extent it is a matter of personal style. You need to appear genuine, that is, reflecting to the other person aspects of your true individual personality. The important thing is to be aware of your body positioning and how it affects your interaction with others in the macro environment.

Formal/Informal Continuum

The second continuum, formal/informal, relates to some extent to the tense/relaxed continuum. Being more rigid and tense suggests formality while being relaxed is associated with informality. Formality implies greater structure. It also implies less warmth. To the extent that you are more formal with someone, you are less personal. You allow less of your true personality to show through the professional facade. On the other hand, complete informality or relaxed lack of structure impedes getting anything done. Relationships with others in the macro practice context are not usually friendships. The interpersonal relationship exists for the purpose of solving a problem, initiating a plan, or attaining a goal. This implies some degree of formality and structure.

As with the tense/relaxed continuum, the extent of formality often relates to personal style. The best approach lies somewhere between being the extremes. The important thing is to be aware of how you're presenting yourself, how you feel most comfortable, and how others react and relate to you. Ask questions in the way and in the tone of voice you feel at ease with. Smile when you feel like smiling. Use the gestures and personal presentation that reflect your true personality.

Personal Space

One other part of body positioning involves the use of personal space. This is the actual space or distance between you and other people as you interact. Hall (1969) identifies four distances or zones that we set in our daily interactions. These include the intimate zone, the personal zone, the social zone, and the public zone. Each zone respectively demonstrates more formal and less intimate relationships. The *intimate zone* is just that. It ranges from skin contact to about eighteen inches. It obviously is reserved for very close personal relationships. The *personal zone* ranges from about eighteen inches to approximately four feet, the *social zone* from four to twelve feet, and the *public zone* outward from twelve feet. Contact with other people in a macro context should generally occur in the closer half of the social zone. This allows for comfortable discussion, but it provides an adequate degree of personal space so that other people do not feel restricted or pressured.

However, note that there are exceptions to this rule. For example, during intense negotiations it might be advantageous to place yourself either closer or farther than the closer half of the social zone. Positioning yourself closer may emphasize your strong interest in and commitment to the issues at hand. You may also need to be closer when sharing documents that are at issue. On the other hand, you may choose to position yourself further than the closer half of the social zone during times of intense conflict. This could emphasize the fact that conflict is occurring.

Warmth, Empathy, and Genuineness

In generalist social work practice a variety of relationship-enhancing characteristics can be defined and learned. Demonstrating these characteristics involves employing the appropriate corresponding verbal and nonverbal behavior. Three specific such relationships-enhancing traits are warmth, empathy, and genuineness. These attributes are characterized in the social work literature as among the most basic and important in developing relationships (Austin, Kopp, & Smith, 1986; Fischer & Gochros, 1975; Hepworth & Larsen, 1987, 1990). This is true for relationships with clients, colleagues, administrators, and anyone else with whom you interact.

Warmth

Displaying warmth involves conveying a feeling of interest, concern, well-being, and liking to another individual. It is often difficult to find specific, accurate English words for feelings. For example, *Webster's Ninth New Collegiate Dictionary* (1991, p. 1329) defines warmth as "the quality or state of being warm in feeling" such as "a child needing human warmth and family life." We do have a tendency to define a word by using the same word in the definition (referred to as a tautology). There's often no exact synonym available. Conveying warmth, however, does involve enhancing the positive feelings of one person toward another. Warmth promotes a sense of comfort and well-being in that other person.

Warmth can be communicated to another person verbally and nonverbally. Such behaviors can be defined, practiced, and learned. The following are examples of verbally communicating warmth:

Hello. It's good to meet you.
I'm glad we have the chance to talk about this.
It's pleasant talking with you.
It's good to see you again.
Please sit down. Can I get you a cup of coffee?
You are really a good listener.
I really appreciate your efforts and your help.

These are just a few of the many statements you can make to convey the feeling that you respect the individual with whom you are talking. Such statements help to convey a sense of concern for others and for other's well-being. There are also many ways to communicate warmth nonverbally. We've discussed how eye contact, attentive listening, and body positioning can all be used to a worker's advantage.

Empathy

Empathy is a second basic worker characteristic that enhances relationships. Empathy involves not only being in tune with how the other people feel, but also conveying to people both verbally and nonverbally that you understand how they feel. It does not necessarily mean that you think another individual's feelings are positive or negative. Nor does empathy mean that you are having the same feelings yourself. It purely means that you acknowledge and understand the other person's situation. For instance, Sly is a social worker for a private,[3]

---

3. Private social agencies generally provide some targeted group of clients, such as a specific community's residents or a specified age group, with personal social services such as counseling or services for children. These are distinguished from public institutional services such as financial assistance or education (Barker, 1995).

nonprofit[4] agency called Jobs for Youth (JFY) in a large midwestern city.[5] JFY helps impoverished youth ages sixteen to twenty who are not currently in school "become self-reliant, independent, and self-supporting adults . . . by helping them prepare for, find, and keep jobs in local businesses and industry (Cohen, 1987, p. 83). JFY emphasizes remedial education and job readiness skills in addition to actual initial job placement. The intent is to prepare young people for a lifetime of self-reliance through work ability and potential. Sly functions both as a counselor and as an employer services representative. The latter role involves seeking appropriate jobs for clients and working with employers to place clients in suitable positions.

Sly likes and respects his supervisor, Rhonda, who is also JFY's director. Sly approaches Rhonda with a problem. Recently, he has been experiencing difficulty with the personnel director, Barry Helafonte, in one of the local industrial plants where JFY places some clients. Sly explains the situation to Rhonda: "Okay, here's the problem. On a number of occasions, I contacted Barry about a potential job placement candidate. He tells me, 'Oh, sure, there's a great job available.' Then he stalls for weeks, sometimes even months. You know how that kind of behavior eats away at our clients' motivation and commitment to our program. I am just about at my wit's end. Barry's driving me nuts. I know we need to keep up good relationships with employing organizations, but I just do not like this guy."

Rhonda, using her nonverbal empathic skills, leans toward Sly and looks at him seriously. She then responds, "Sly, I know how hard it can be to work with some employers day after day. You're trying to do your very best and they just don't seem to be cooperating. Why don't you avoid him for a few days and let your feelings settle down? Sometimes, it helps just to let it go for a while. I'll take up the slack temporarily."

This response conveys that Rhonda understands the situation and Sly's feelings. However, it does not condone Sly's desire to stop working with Barry. Rhonda

empathizes with Sly, thereby communicating that she is on his side. She understands. Once Sly feels that she listens to how he feels and that she's not against him, he will more likely work with her toward a solution. Additionally, Rhonda here proposes a solution that is satisfactory to Sly in view of Rhonda's understanding attitude.

On the other hand, Rhonda could have jumped at Sly in an abrupt, tense manner with a scowl on her face. She could have responded by saying something like, "How unprofessional! Get your act together! You are responsible for doing the job you're getting paid for. I do not want to hear another thing about it!" This reaction would blame Sly for doing something wrong. It would clearly communicate to him that Rhonda did not understand his feelings or his situation. It totally lacks empathy. Sly could easily view Rhonda as the enemy, someone to be fought with and avoided.

By taking the pressure off Sly for a few days and by empathizing with him, Rhonda significantly improved the situation. Sly was able to think about the situation more objectively. He continued to talk about the problem with Rhonda. She encouraged him to empathize with Barry's situation. In view of the huge size of Barry's organization, Barry had loads of iron in the fire. Barry's heart was probably in the right place, that is, he probably wanted to help out JFY's clients, all of whom really needed a job. However, Barry had many others onerous responsibilities in his own job as well. Sometimes, Barry was just overwhelmed and unable "to get his act together."

Together, Sly and Rhonda decided on a new approach to Barry. It was critical for JFY to maintain good relationships with community employers. However, Barry's behavior was not helpful to clients. Sly dealt with his own anger toward Barry and decided he needed to get control of the situation. He determined to continue referring clients when appropriate. He also would continue being courteous to Barry. However, Sly established a two-week deadline. If Barry failed to come through with a specific job possibility within two weeks of being contacted, Sly would simply look elsewhere for his client's employment. Sly would also thank Barry for his efforts and explain why he needed to move on in his client's best interests. Sly maintained his contact with Barry so that he did not alienate Barry and, thus, totally cut off this potential job source.

---

4. Nonprofit agencies and organizations are established for motives other than profit; they are generally run by a board of directors and receive funding from a variety of sources including client fees, donations, public contributions, and grants (Barker, 1995).

5. This example is based on a description of Jobs for Youth, in M. I. Cohen, "Youth Employment," in *Children, Families and Cities: Programs That Work at the Local Level*, J. E. Kyle (Ed.) (Washington, DC: National League of Cities, 1987), pp. 83–86.

As a worker you can use empathy to help establish an initial rapport. You can also use it to elicit feelings and talk about issues that might never be broached had feelings not been mentioned. Empathy, thus, can provide you with a means of getting at other people's feelings that are not expressed out loud.

For example, Bill is a social worker at a health-care center for the elderly. He notices that Brenda, a new colleague, avoided having eye contact with him throughout the monthly staff meeting in which they both participated. After the meeting, Bill says, "Brenda, I noticed you weren't giving me much eye contact during our meeting. That bothers me. Is something wrong? Let's talk about it." In this way Bill empathetically provides an opportunity for Brenda to talk to him about what was bothering her, if anything. As it turns out in this particular instance, Brenda is furious. During the meeting she thought she heard Bill say he had completed one of her job responsibilities for a particular case. She took this as a total put-down. Bill's subsequent empathic comments to Brenda give her the opportunity to confront him with her anger. After Bill approaches her about it, they work it out. Bill apologizes and convinces Brenda that is certainly was not his intent to take credit for her work.

Yet another use of empathy involves "making confrontations more palatable" (Hepworth & Larsen, 1990, p. 105). Empathy can be used to disperse hostility. For example, Laura, a protective services worker, is helping neighborhood residents at a fundraiser for school recreation equipment. The old equipment is rusty and decrepit, but there is no money for new things in the available budget. A community resident, Lucky, is also volunteering at the fundraiser. He stomps up to Laura, breathing shallowly and rapidly. His face is red, and his vocal tone is loud, gruff, and hostile. He states, "I'm sick of you taking over this whole shebang! All you ever do is tell other people what to do. I've had it. Go to blazes!"

Laura chooses not to respond to what Lucky has said. She does not react with something lacking in empathy like, "You have your nerve talking to me like that. If you can't talk to me courteously, don't talk to me at all!"

Rather, Laura uses empathy by stating, "You sound like you're really angry at me. I'm sorry you feel like that. Please tell me your reasons. I apologize for giving you the wrong impression." This latter response is much more likely to help Lucky calm down and talk about what's wrong. Laura's response diffuses his anger momentarily so that they are able to sit down and work out what Lucky sees as problems.

Nonverbal communication can also be used to enhance empathy. A worker's gestures can reflect or mirror how another person is feeling. For instance, furrowing the brow can convey a serious focusing of attention and reflect another person's grave concerns over some issue. Nonverbal communication can emphasize or enhance verbal empathic responses. For example, consider a coworker who appears exceptionally happy one day. Smiling broadly, you empathetically state, "You look simply radiant when you're so happy. What's up?" In this example, smiling while making an empathic verbal response may indicate more convincingly to the coworker that you really understand how she feels. However, be careful. Sometimes, smiling when addressing a serious issue may imply lack of sincerity or sarcasm. The important thing is to attend to your own nonverbal communication and be sensitive to other's reactions.

Concerning empathy in general, we have established that using it can act as a significant tool. However, as with most other techniques and approaches, it does not always work.

Genuineness

The third quality that has been found to enhance relationships is genuineness. This involves the "sharing of self by relating in a natural, sincere, spontaneous, open and genuine manner" (Hepworth and Larsen, 1987, p. 998). Genuineness simply means that you continue to be yourself, despite the fact that your are working to accomplish goals in your professional role.

Personality refers to the unique configuration of qualities and attributes that make you an individual. Some people have effervescent, bubbly, and outgoing personalities. Others have more subdued, quiet temperaments. Some people relate to others by using their sense of humor. Others prefer to relate more seriously. The point is that there is no one type of personality that is best in a professional role. Rather, it is important that you be yourself. Don't pretend to be something or someone that you're not. Genuineness portrays a sense of honesty to others and gener-

HIGHLIGHT 2.1

PRACTICING EMPATHIC RESPONSES IN MACRO PRACTICE CONTEXTS

There are a number of leading phrases that you can use to begin an empathic statement. Following are some examples:

- My impression is that . . . .
- It appears to me that . . . .
- Is what you're saying that . . . ?
- Do I understand you correctly that . . . ?
- I'm hearing you say that . . . .
- Do you mean that . . . ?
- Do you feel that . . . ?
- I feel that you . . . .
- I'm getting the message that . . . .
- You seem to be . . . .
- When you sat that, I think you . . . .
- You look like you . . . .
- You sound so _____. Can we talk more about it?
- You look _____. What's been happening?

Following are several vignettes illustrating macro situations. For each one formulate empathic responses in your own words and practice them. The first vignette offers an example.

Example

You are a school social worker in an urban neighborhood. Residents find out that a vacant lot two houses away from the school was used to dump dangerous chemicals between ten and twenty years ago. One dozen children attending the neighborhood school have gotten cancer within the past fifteen years.

It is not part of your job description to address this issue. However, you feel it is your professional and ethical responsibility to help the neighborhood resident formulate a plan concerning what to do. One potential idea is a class action law suit against the companies that dumped chemicals. The intent would be to prove that the companies are at fault and hold them responsible for their actions.

The mother of one child, Eric, who is fourteen and has leukemia, makes an appointment to see you. When she enters your office, she breaks out in tears. She states, ''I am so angry! How could people do this to little children? They must have known that dumping those wastes so close to children was dangerous.''

Possible empathic responses include:

- ''You sound really angry. I don't blame you. What are your thoughts about what to do?''
- ''I'm hearing you say that you are furious about this situation. I'm also very upset. What can I do to help you?''
- ''It appears that this whole situation has been a horror story for you. I, too, feel terrible about it. Where do you think we can go from here?''

Vignette 1

You are a social worker in a health-care facility for the elderly. You are very interested in starting a visitation program for middle-school children to visit your elderly clients. You feel that such interactions with the respective age groups would be mutually beneficial for both our clients and the children. Kimberly is the other social worker in the facility. You have approached her with this idea. She has responded only hesitantly and, in your opinion, negatively. You think that she is worried that this proposed project would result in a lot more work for her than she is ready or willing to undertake.

In actuality, you feel you have pretty much paved the way for the plan already. You have contacted school administrators and teachers to obtain their permission and support. You have established a transpor-

(continued)

HIGHLIGHT 2.1—(Continued)

tation plan and a proposed form for students' parents to sign, giving students permission to participate. Before you have the chance to approach Kimberly one more time, she initiates a conversation with you. She states, "I know you're trying to do the right thing with this student visitation project [*which is an empathic response on Kimberly's part*]. However, you're pushing me into it. I don't have enough time to do my own work, let alone get involved in some petty little program you propose."

You empathetically respond . . . . (Remember that you *do not* have to solve the problem right now. You only need to let Kimberly know that you understand how she feels.)

Vignette 2

You are a social worker at a diagnostic and treatment center for children with multiple physical disabilities. Your primary function is to work with parents, helping them to cope with the pressures they are under and connecting them with resources they need. The Center's staff includes a wide range of disciplines such as occupational therapy,[a] physical therapy,[b] speech therapy, psychology, and nursing. A problem you sometimes encounter involves professionals from other disciplines asking you to keep parents from asking these professionals questions. This is true especially when children have conditions that are sadly getting worse. One day a physical therapist approaches you and asks, "Do you think you could talk to Mrs. Harris? She keeps asking me these uncomfortable ques-

tions about Sally [Mrs. Harris's daughter]. Sally's condition is deteriorating. I don't know what to say."

You empathetically respond . . . .

Vignette 3

You are an intake worker at a social services agency in a rural area. Your job is to take telephone calls, assess problems, and refer clients to the most appropriate services. You identify a gap in service for people who have developmental disabilities. You think that development of a social activities center is a wonderful idea. You talk with administrators in your agency who, you determine, generally support the idea but don't know where funding will come from. They suggest you talk with some of the local politicians to get their reactions. You make an appointment with the chairperson of the County Board to share your suggestion and get feedback about possible funding for such a workshop. The chairperson responds, "Yeah, it sounds good, but who's going to pay for it and run it?"

You empathetically respond . . . .

Notes

a. Occupational therapy is "a profession for helping physically disabled people use their bodies more effectively and mentally impaired people overcome emotional problems through specially designed work activity" (Barker, 1991, p. 160).
b. Physical therapy is "the treatment of disease by physical and mechanical means (as massage, regulated exercise, water, light, heat, and electricity)" (*Webster's Ninth New Collegiate Dictionary*, 1991, p. 887).

---

ally makes them feel that you're someone they can trust.

Communicating with Other People in Macro Contexts

We have established that communication is the core of interpersonal interactions in macro settings. Communication, of course, involves exchange of information. A

variety of specific skills and techniques can facilitate the exchange of information. Using these techniques helps to maximize the chances that your *intent* will match your *impact* for another person, and vice versa.

Most of these techniques are much the same as those used in your micro and mezzo interventions with clients. They involve ways to initiate communication, solicit information, encourage responses, and respond appropriately to something some other individual says. Here we will define and explain a number of verbal responses.

They include simple encouragement, rephrasing, reflective responding, clarification, interpretation, providing information, emphasizing other people's strengths, summarization, and eliciting information. Some hesitations about using the word "why" are also examined.

Simple Encouragement

Many times a simple one word response or nonverbal head nod while maintaining eye contact is enough to encourage the other person to continue. Verbal clues such as "mm-mm," "I see," and "uh-huh" help convey that the communication's receiver really is listening and following what the sender is saying. For example, a worker at another agency might say to you, "I've been meaning to talk to you about your agency's policy concerning the treatment of clients who are poor." You might simply encourage the worker to continue by saying, "I see. Please go on" or "Mm-mm, tell me more."

Rephrasing

Rephrasing involves stating what the other person is saying, but using different words. Rephrasing has a variety of purposes. On the one hand, it can communicate to another person that you are really trying to listen to what she's saying. On the other hand, it can let her know you did not understand her real intent so she can clarify her meaning. Rephrasing can also help the other person take time out and reflect on what she has just said.

Rephrasing does not involve interpreting what the other person has said. It simply repeats a statement by using other words. For example, a colleague might state, "I'm so furious with my supervisor. He never gives me any credit for anything!" You might then reply by rephrasing his statement, "You're mad at your boss because you don't think he appreciates all the work you do."

Reflective Responding

Reflective responding is translating into words what you think the other person is feeling. It is a verbal means of displaying empathy. Such responding conveys that you understand both what the other is going through

and how he feels about it. A typical scenario involves a person who *talks* about his problems, but doesn't really articulate how he *feels* about his problems. In this situation, you might help the other identify and express his feelings. Only then is he likely to do something about them. Both verbal and nonverbal behavior can be used as cues for reflective responding. For example, a colleague approaches you and says, "I can't seem to keep up with all that *%#&*#! paperwork!" A reflective response might be, "Wow, you really sound mad. I guess this load of paperwork is getting to you."

Clarification

Clarification involves making certain that what another person says is understood. Its intent is to make the communication more understandable. Clarification is typically used in one of two ways (Benjamin, 1974). First, you can help another person articulate or say more clearly what she really means by providing the words for it. This is clarification for the other person's benefit. A second reason for using a clarifying statement is to explain what the other person is saying for your own benefit. Many times clarification will serve to benefit both sender and receiver. For example, the director of another agency's vocational rehabilitation unit might say to you, "I think your agency should maintain more involvement with my program,"[6]

To clarify what the director said, you might respond, "You mean that you would like to have representatives from my agency visit your staff." In this situation you are attempting to clarify for both yourself and the director exactly what "more involvement" means.

In summary, clarification, restatement, and reflective responding have a number of differences. Clarification is used when there is a question about what another person means. Restatement, on the other hand, paraphrases exactly what the other person has said. This paraphrasing assumes that you already understand the communication. Finally, reflective responding expands on another person's statements to include the dimension of emotion.

---

6. Vocational rehabilitation involves training people who have physical or mental disabilities so they can do useful work, become more self-sufficient, and be less reliant on public financial assistance (Barker, 1991, p. 248).

Interpretation

Interpretation involves seeking meaning beyond that of clarification. To interpret means to help bring to a conclusion, to enlighten, to seek a meaning of greater depth than that which has been stated. Interpretation helps lead another person to look deeper into the meaning of what she said. The intent is to enhance another person's perception of the meaning of her own words.

For instance, one colleague might state to another, "I like Samson, but he always seems to get the most interesting cases. It's just not fair, that's all there is to it." The second colleague might respond by interpreting this statement, "It seems you have some conflicting feelings toward Samson. On the one hand, you like him. On the other, you seem to resent the fact he's getting more challenging cases than you are."

To interpret means to take a statement a step beyond its basic meaning. In the above example, the second colleague went beyond the first colleague's feelings of anger and resentment. He focused on the motivations behind the first colleague's feelings by trying to provide some insight into the source of such feelings.

Providing Information

Many times it is appropriate to provide information to another person. That person may ask you a direct question, such as what should he do in a specific situation? Where in the agency policy manual is sick leave explained? Sometimes another person is misinformed or has inaccurate information. You might then need to identify the inaccuracy and provide accurate information. The circumstances for providing information are infinite. The important thing is to give information straightforwardly and humbly. Other people will likely bristle at being told what to do in a condescending manner.

Emphasizing People's Strengths

Your instructors have probably drilled into you the importance of emphasizing your clients' strengths. It is also important to emphasize the strengths of colleagues, administrators, and others. Each individual in the macro environment has personal strengths, weaknesses, concerns, and defenses. It is critically important to tune

into these dimensions throughout your interactions and communication with others.

Even when you feel you must give another a constructive suggestion or criticism, a strengths perspective implies that it is still important to carefully support that person's ego. You want to convey to that person that you are on her side. By emphasizing that person's strengths, you can try to get the point across that you are not the enemy. You value that person's opinions and respect her right to make her own decisions. Two ways to do this include emphasizing accomplishments and stressing personal qualities. Often, prefacing a communication, even one that involves criticism, with positive feedback helps to provide a *constructive* versus *destructive* context for that communication.

An example of emphasizing accomplishments is to say, "I know you have worked with in-service training programs like this numerous times in the past. Would you mind if I made a minor suggestion concerning potential resources?"

An example of emphasizing personal qualities might be, "I appreciate how easy you are to talk to. You're a good listener. I feel comfortable talking over issues with you. However, I have some concerns about the policy you've implemented. Might you have some time to talk to me about it?"

Summarization

Summarization involves briefly and concisely covering the main points of a discussion or series of communications. Summarizing information can be done periodically throughout a discussion. This helps the other person focus in on the main points covered during a portion of the interaction. It also helps to keep communication on track. It can be used "as a transition to new topics, or to review complex issues" (Whittaker & Tracy, 1989, p. 135). Summarization is difficult in that you must carefully select only the most important facts, issues, and themes. Exclude less essential detail. Condense and emphasize only the most salient points.

You can also use summarization to bring a discussion to a close. Emphasizing the major points made during a discussion can send a cue to the other discussant that the communication is ending. Summarization focuses on what has already been said. It is past- versus future-oriented. Summarizing what has been accomplished during communication or discussion allows participants to leave on a positive note. For example, at the end of a staff meeting, summarizing recommendations about who is to do what before the next meeting crystallizes the plans that have been made in all participants' minds.

Eliciting Information

Just as sometimes you will be in the position of providing information, at other times you will need to elicit information. One way of doing this is simply to ask questions. There are two basic types of questions, open-ended and closed-ended. Closed-ended questions include those which seek simple yes or no answers. The following are examples:

Are you coming to tomorrow's boring staff meeting?
Did you have a nice time in Cudahy?
Do you want to run for the NASW state president?
Has the attorney seen the grievance yet?
Do you have a bachelor's degree in social work from an accredited program?

Closed-ended questions may also be asked when there are a number of clearly defined answers to choose from. Such questions do not encourage or even allow an explanation of why the answer was chosen, or an elaboration of thoughts or feelings about the answer. For example, consider these questions:

Do you prefer orange or chartreuse name tags for the conference?
What time does our policy committee meet?
What color suit are you going to wear to the hearing?
When do you expect the Senator to return?
How old are you?

In each of the above instances, a simple response is required. The choices for the response are established ahead of time and have a closed number of options. Your job is simply to choose one. For example, your age is probably between 19 and 107 years.

Unlike closed-ended questions that require simple, established answers from a predetermined selection, open-ended questions seek more extensive thoughts, ideas, and explanations for answers. They encourage elaboration and specifics about answers unique to the person answering them. For instance, the following illustrates open-ended questions:

How do you think our country should go about solving the homelessness problem?
What are your feelings and opinions about affirmative action?
What changes would you most like to see in the social work program at your school?
What types of qualities do you value most in your relationships with people?
What would make you more comfortable with this bill, Representative Schlenekinsy?
How would you define macro practice?

Each of these questions allows for a more detailed explanation as an answer. Any individual in any particular situation would provide a unique answer. For example, how you would describe what you like about your favorite activity would be a unique response, unlike anyone else's.

The Use of "Why?"

It is easy and common to use the word *why* when asking questions. However, it is important to remember that "why" can be a threatening term. It can put people on the spot. In other words, it often implies that the person to whom it's directed is at fault.

For example, a practitioner enters a staff meeting three minutes late. The supervisor asks in front of all the worker's colleagues, "Why are you late?" This question places a demand on the worker to explain his reasons for doing something wrong by not being on time.

The following are other examples:

Why did you skip out of that meeting?
Why are you always complaining about that policy?
Why are you so bossy?
Why aren't you married yet?

The word "why" also can put the burden of seeking a solution on the individual to whom it is directed. The solution often involves recalling facts, organizing your thoughts and ideas, and presenting them in an understandable form right then and there. The following questions illustrate this:

Why did the director reject our petition?

Why are public assistance and social security so complicated?

Why did you vote as you did in the last national election?

Why did you choose social work as your profession?

In summary, it's best to be cautious in using the word "why."

Overlap of Techniques

Sometimes it's difficult to label a technique specifically as "clarification" or "interpretation." Some responses fulfill only one purpose and thus will obviously fit into one of the categories. Others will combine two or more techniques as they fulfill two or more functions, because there is an endless variety of words, expressed emotions, ideas, and any combination thereof. The important thing is to master a variety of techniques and thereby become more flexible and more effective in your communication with others.

Appropriate Assertiveness in the Macro Environment

Most people have times when they wish they had been more assertive. Yet at those moments they feel very uncomfortable doing so. At other times they feel they were caught off guard.

For example, Caitlin works as a foster care placement specialist for a public social services agency in a major metropolitan area on the east coast. She has also been appointed by her agency's administration as a member of the city's Interagency Council on Adolescent Pregnancy.[7] This council, strongly supported by city government, has representatives from a dozen major social service agencies within the city. Each participating agency provides one or two council members, depending on the agency's size.

The council's task is to undertake a major assessment of the city's adolescent pregnancy problem, recommend solutions, and develop a coordinated strategy

_____

7. This example is based on a description of Adolescent Pregnancy and Parenting Services, New York, *Children, Families and Cities: Programs That Work at the Local Level*, by J. E. Kyle (Ed.) (Washington, DC: National League of Cities, 1987), pp. 157–194.

for the recommendations' implementation. Thus far, the council has gathered facts and examined the issues. It has also established a strategy that "emphasizes efforts to reduce the incidence of first pregnancies, early and continuing services to help teen parents become independent adults and enhance their children's growth and development, and special efforts to prevent repeat pregnancies and births to teens" (Pittman, Adams-Taylor, & Morich, 1987, p. 167). The council continues to work on the task of specifying its strategy to implement the plan.

Caitlin is getting out of her car, about to attend one of the council's biweekly meetings. Suddenly, Harvey, one of her colleagues and her agency's other council representative, drives up and parks next to her. He says, "Oh, hi. Would you mind writing out that announcement we talked about and circulate it to the other council members?" The announcement involves a fundraising dinner that a council subcommittee, including both Caitlin and Harvey, have planned. He continues, "I have a court appearance scheduled downtown today so can't make the council meeting. I'm glad I caught you because I have to get going."

He catches Caitlin off guard. Then he jumps in his car and drives away. Harvey typically "leeches" time, energy, and money from people he works with including other council members. It may entail just asking for a cigarette from the few remaining colleagues who smoke. Or it might be a request that Caitlin or someone else write up the results of one of the meetings because he doesn't have time (even though it was his turn to function as the meeting's secretary). Sometimes, he asks Caitlin to pick him up the next morning because his son needs the car (even though he lives twenty-five miles out of her way). Another of his favorite ploys is to sheepishly request that Caitlin or some other colleague "catch the check" for lunch because he forgot his checkbook and didn't have any cash (he typically says he will pay the lender back later, but never does—at least, not without being badgered a half dozen times). In other words, Harvey is fairly inconsiderate about others' rights. In essence, he is pretty downright self-centered.

When he asks Caitlin to do this favor, she doesn't have much time to think and almost automatically says, "Oh, yeah, sure." Then, thirty seconds after he's disappeared and it's too late, she thinks, "What did I do that for? I know better than to get sucked in by his requests. Rats!"

The problem is that he surprises Caitlin when she least expects it. She has other things on her mind. For one thing, she's thinking about the idea she wants to present at today's council meeting. It involves developing a program for providing "vocational/employment training and parent responsibility counseling for eighteen- to twenty-five-year-old fathers on relief who are not currently supporting their children" (Pittman, Adams-Taylor, & Morich, 1987, p. 169). Caitlin has also been wondering whether the meeting will be over in time for her to make her appointment to change her car's oil.

Caitlin would never impose upon people as Harvey does. In his view, not only should she automatically agree to circulate the dinner announcement, but she should also *write* it! She thinks, "Oh, come on. That is his responsibility." She's not certain about all the details for the dinner. She wonders why he didn't call her earlier about the announcement or drop off a note. Not expecting his sudden request, she is unprepared to respond. She never really thought about such a situation before.

Over the next half hour Caitlin remains preoccupied about what she *should* have said. For example, "No." Or, maybe she should have compromised and replied, "Sure. You write the announcement and I'll be happy to circulate it to the council." She continues to stew about her mistake and Harvey's inconsiderate behavior for quite a while.

But it's too late to do anything about it after the fact. Now Caitlin has already agreed to do it. She's stuck. She has simply been too unassertive in response to Harvey's request.

In other situations people allow their frustration at their own nonassertiveness to build until they can't stand it anymore and subsequently "lose it." All their emotions explode in a burst of anger. This can readily happen to nonassertive people who allow their discomfort to build until they erupt in rage. This display of temper and anger reflects one aspect of the other end of the continuum—aggressiveness.

For example, Shelia just got her first social work position in a sheltered workshop for adults with developmental disabilities three months ago. One of her male colleagues, a speech therapist also employed by the agency, regularly makes what Shelia considers extremely rude, sexist comments about his female colleagues and even some of the female clients. She feels his behavior made others so uncomfortable that they find it difficult to work effectively with him in the macro environment.

Shelia considers herself a fairly confident, straightforward person. Yet she just started this job and does not want to "make any waves" or be labeled a trouble maker or a complainer. Shelia knows that this man's behavior is inappropriate, derogatory, and simply wrong. Every time she runs into him at work, he makes one off-color comment or another. Meanwhile, her feelings continue to simmer . . . and simmer . . . and simmer. Finally, something snaps and she screams, "I can't stand it anymore! I think you're a disgusting sexist! Just shut up!" This outburst does little for their relationship or to improve his behavior.

Appropriate assertiveness is a necessity in micro, mezzo, and macro practice. Assertiveness involves expressing yourself without hurting others or stepping on their rights. Being assertive means considering both *your own rights* and *the rights of others*. When interacting with colleagues, supervisors, administrators, staff from other agencies, politicians, or community residents, it is critical to use your assertiveness skills. The following sections will discuss the assertiveness continuum, the advantages of assertiveness, assertiveness training, and assertiveness as a special issue for women.

Nonassertive, Assertive, and Aggressive Communication

On an assertiveness continuum, communication can be rated as nonassertive, assertive, or aggressive. *Assertive* communication includes verbal and nonverbal behavior that permits a speaker to get her points across clearly and straightforwardly. A speaker who is assertive takes into consideration both her own value and the values of whomever is receiving her message. She considers her own points important, but she also considers the points and reactions of the receiver important.

Nonassertive communication comes from a speaker who devalues herself completely. She feels the other person and what that person thinks are much more important than her own thoughts. People who have difficulty being assertive can experience a range of problems. On the one hand, they can be very shy and withdrawn. Nonassertive persons are often afraid to express their real feelings. While they may become increasingly uncomfortable about their failure to be assertive and protect their rights, they rarely can respond assertively.

For example, Pete has a problem. Information is commonly routed through him and the other workers in his unit. In other words, Pete's unit supervisor receives some piece of information, such as an announcement about an upcoming conference, a minor change in agency policy, a potential grant application, or similar information. She staples a form with Pete's and his other unit colleagues' names on it to the paper that is to be circulated. This routing sheet requires each recipient to check off her or his name and then send it on to another person listed on the sheet. Pete's supervisor, therefore, places the paper arbitrarily into one of the staff members' mailboxes.

Pete's problem is that Gerri, one of his colleagues, typically holds on to the information so long that it doesn't get to Pete until it's too late. The conference is already over or a grant application deadline has already passed. Unit staff usually deal with this nonassertively by giving it to Gerri last. Then it really doesn't matter how long she keeps it. However, sometimes—for whatever reason—this process doesn't work. Gerri gets her hands on some critical announcement and loses it amongst the towering skyscrapers of paper and files on the floor of her office. This infuriates Pete, especially when the information concerns something he is particularly interested in. However, Pete considers himself a relatively shy person. He hates to confront other people, especially people like Gerri who have exceptionally outgoing and vibrant personalities. Thus, Pete leaves the situation as it is. He maintains his nonassertive position and allows his underlying anger to seethe.

We have indicated that *aggresiveness* lies on the opposite end of the assertiveness continuum for nonassertiveness. It engenders bold and dominating verbal and nonverbal behavior whereby a speaker presses his point of view as taking precedence above all other points of view. An aggressive speaker considers only his views important and devalues what the receiver has to say. Aggressive behaviors are demanding and often annoying. Figure 2.3 depicts the assertiveness continuum.

One example of aggressive behavior would be a fellow worker who consistently talks and occasionally raises his voice during staff meetings so that other staff

Figure 2.3
The Assertiveness Continuum

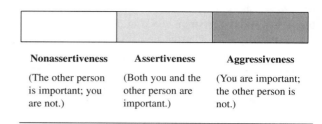

have little or no opportunity to "get their two cents in." This worker pays attention only to his own needs with no consideration for the needs and wants of others. Another instance of aggressive behavior is the employee who consistently makes it a point to get the agency's best vehicle to make home visits. On the one hand, she feels it is supremely important for her to get the best available. On the other, she blocks any thoughts about how consistently getting the best means that other workers are left with the worst on a regular basis.

One form of aggressiveness is passive-aggressiveness. Here, an individual is really aggressive, but secretly or covertly so (Barker, 1991). Often, such a person dislikes confrontation and tries to avoid it at all costs. However, to get his own way, a passive-aggressive individual will go behind others' backs to get what he really wants. For example, Donald, a chemical dependency counselor, thinks Herschel, a colleague with the same job status, is lazy. Donald would like Herschel to be reprimanded by their supervisor Maria and, thereby, be forced to assume more of the workload. Donald does not want to confront Herschel himself. Therefore, Donald passive-aggressively meets with Maria behind closed doors (literally) to complain about Herschel's laziness and work performance. He encourages Maria to reprimand Herschel. Donald is being passive in that he doesn't confront Herschel. However, Donald is also be aggressive in that he tries to manipulate the situation so that Herschel receives his reprimand. Donald, however, appears (on the outside) to remain uninvolved and blameless.

There's no perfect recipe for what to say when you are trying to be assertive. The important thing is to take into consideration both your own rights and the rights of the person with whom you are interacting. Following are a few examples.

Situation 1

Amorette is a social worker at a residential treatment center for adolescents with severe emotional and behavioral problems. She completes the draft of a grant application for funds to start a sex education program in the center. The proposal involves the sponsorship of experts to provide both educational programming and contraceptives. Agency policy requires that all grant proposal drafts be reviewed by an agency Grants Committee before being submitted outside the agency. Prunella, one of the center's teachers, is a member of the Grants Committee.

When Prunella sees the proposal, she flies through the roof. She feels that for this population, talking about sex in such explicit terms will only encourage them to engage in it. She cannot believe that the proposal also includes providing contraceptives directly to the girls. "Why not show them pornographic movies, too?" she thinks to herself.

Prunella approaches Amorette and declares, "That grant proposal you wrote is totally inappropriate. Under no circumstances will I condone it!" How should Amorette reply?

Nonassertive response: "You're probably right. I'll just forget about it."

Aggressive response: "What's wrong with you? Are you still living in the dark ages or something? Maybe what you need is a little action yourself."

Assertive response: "I understand your concerns. However, I still think this is an important issue to address. Let's talk further about it."

Situation 2

Gigette is a social worker for a public agency providing supportive home-based services for the elderly. The agency's intent is to help people maintain their independence and reside in their own homes as long as possible. A county policy states that clients may receive a maximum of eight service hours from Gigette's agency or others like it each month. Gigette works with numerous clients who require more help than this. She understands that the rationale for the policy is to cut costs. However, she feels that changing the policy to increase potential service to a maximum of sixteen instead of eight hours would allow many clients to remain in their own homes much longer. Providing or subsidizing the nursing-home care clients subsequently need is monstrously expensive.

Gigette works through her agency's administration and gains its support. With the agency's sanction, she approaches Biff Bunslinger, the County Board chairperson, and shares with him her proposal and its rationale. She has determined that his support would be the most beneficial in changing the county's restrictive policy. Biff responds, "It's a good idea, but where will you get the money for it? What else do you want to cut? Do you have any idea what repercussions such a major policy change would have?" How can Gigette respond?

Nonassertive response: "I don't know. I'm sorry. Let's forget it."

Aggressive response: "You haven't heard a word I've said. Get off your butt, Biff, and start thinking about those people out there who really need help!"

Assertive response: "I know funding is tight and that you have many financial needs you're trying to balance right now. Let me show you why I think in the long run this plan will both save the county money and help your elderly constituents."

Situation 3

Bo, an outreach worker for urban homeless people, is on the board of directors of another agency called the AIDS Support Network. A board of directors is "a group of people empowered to establish an organization's objectives and policies and to oversee the activities of the personnel responsible for day-to-day implementation of those policies" (Barker, 1991, p. 25). Another board member, Eleni, a local lawyer, bluntly states to Bo, "I wish you would be more specific when you make your comments during meetings. I can never understand what you're talking about." What can Bo reply?

Nonassertive response: "Yes, you're right. I'll try to speak more clearly in the future."

Aggressive response: "I'm not nearly as unclear as you are, nor, by the way, as arrogant!"

Assertive response: "I'm sorry you feel that way. Perhaps, you could speak up when you don't understand something during a board meeting. Your feedback will help us communicate better."

The Advantages of Assertiveness

There are many benefits to developing assertiveness skills (Lewinsohn et al., 1978; Sundel & Sundel, 1980). For one thing, you can gain more control over your work and other interpersonal environments. Assertiveness may help you avoid uncomfortable or hostile interactions with colleagues, administrators, other agency personnel, politicians, and community residents. You will probably feel that other people understand you better then they did before. You can enhance your self-concept and interpersonal effectiveness as the result of this increased control. In the past, bottled up feelings may have resulted in psychosomatic problems like piercing headaches or painful stomach upsets. Appropriate assertiveness helps to alleviate the build-up of undue tension and stress. As a result, such psychosomatic reactions will probably subside and eventually cease.

Finally, other people may gain respect for you, your strength, and your own demonstration of respect for others. People may even begin to use you as a role model for their own development of assertive behavior.

Assertiveness Training

Assertiveness training leads people to realize, feel, and act on the assumption that they have the right to be themselves and express their feelings freely. Assertive responses differ from aggressive responses. The distinction between these two types of interactions is important. For example, consider a woman who has an excessively critical colleague. She can intentionally and aggressively do things that will bother him (bringing up topics which she knows will upset him such as the lack of support for his pet project, reminding him that some uncomfortable deadline is fast approaching, or criticizing his behavior). She can purposely goad him into arguments with her. This would be considered aggressive behavior.

On the other hand, she can respond more assertively and counter his criticism by saying, ''When you offer such excessive criticism, I think you lose some of the value of your points. Perhaps making positive suggestions for changing the system would be more useful.''

As we know, social work is practical. Therefore, you can use the suggestions provided to enhance your own assertiveness in a wide range of macro settings. Alberti and Emmons (1976) developed the following thirteen steps to help establish assertive behavior:

1. Scrutinize your own actions and evaluate how effective you are according to the assertiveness continuum.
2. Make a record of situations in which you feel you could have been more effective, either more assertive or less aggressive.
3. Select and focus on some specific instance when you felt you could have been more appropriately assertive.
4. Analyze how you reacted in this situation. Critically examine your verbal and nonverbal behavior.
5. Select a role model and examine how she handled a similar situation requiring assertiveness.
6. Identify a range of other new assertive verbal and nonverbal responses that could address the original problem situation you targeted.
7. Picture yourself in the identified problematic situation.
8. Practice the way you've envisioned yourself being more assertive.
9. Once again, review your new assertive responses. Emphasize your strong points and try to remedy your flaws.
10. Continue practicing steps 7, 8, and 9 until your newly developed assertive approach feels comfortable and natural to you.
11. Try out your assertiveness in a real-life situation.
12. Continue to expand your assertive behavior repertoire until assertiveness becomes a part of your personal interactive style.
13. Give yourself a pat on the back when you succeed in becoming more assertive. It's not easy changing long-standing patterns of behavior.

A Final Note on Assertiveness Training

You need to recognize that you must choose whether or not to be assertive in any given situation. You always have a choice. Making an assertive response to a boss who fires people for speaking up may not be the best plan. You must make a decision about how to respond. No one else can make it for you. Also, recognize that as with any other solution to human problems, being assertive may not always work. Some people don't respond to assertiveness. They may get angry or continue to make inappropriate requests. When assertiveness does not work for you, accept this fact, praise yourself for your progress, and identify areas where you can still improve.

HIGHLIGHT 2.2

EACH OF US HAS CERTAIN ASSERTIVE RIGHTS

Part of becoming assertive requires figuring out and believing that we are valuable and worthwhile people. It's easy to criticize ourselves for our mistakes and imperfections. It's easy to hold our feelings in because we're afraid that we will hurt someone else's feelings or that someone will reject us. Sometimes feelings that are held in too long will burst in an aggressive tirade. This is so not only in micro and mezzo but also in macro contexts.

A basic principle in social work is that each individual is a valuable human being. Everyone, there-

fore, has certain basic rights. The following are eight of your assertive rights:

1. *You have the right to express your ideas and opinions openly and honestly.* For example, Manuéla, a nursing home social worker, attends a meeting at another agency also attended by workers from a range of community social service agencies. The meeting's purpose is to discuss the possibility of conducting a fundraiser to acquire Christmas presents for the poverty-stricken children in the community.

The women at this pro-choice rally commemorating the twenty-second anniversary of the *Roe v. Wade* decision are demonstrating a basic right—the right to behave assertively.

(continued)

HIGHLIGHT 2.2—(Continued)

Each other participant has already stated a preference for collecting money from community residents, businesses, schools, and social service agencies. Manuéla, however, feels that they would get more if the group asked for donations of *toys* and *clothing* instead of *money*. Even though Manuéla is going against the flow, so to speak, she still has the right to voice her opinion straightforwardly and honestly. The final consensus regarding strategy may or may not agree with her proposal. However, she has the right to be heard.

2. *You have the right to be wrong. Everyone makes mistakes.* For example, Mohammed is a school social worker who applies for a state grant to start a summer neighborhood activity program for adolescents in an urban neighborhood. He works on the grant every night for two weeks, thinking that such an activity program will keep scores of children off the streets and out of trouble for at least part of the time the following summer. In a way it is like trying to compose three twenty-page research papers that you've put off until the final two weeks of the semester. This work is *tedious*. Mohammed finally gets the document off and postmarked on the day he thinks it is due. The key word in the previous sentence, of course, is thinks. Unfortunately, he has read the due date as December 8. He has probably read that grant application form twenty-five times. Each time in his mind he saw 8 instead of 5.

Unfortunately, the state grant evaluators are strict regarding the timeliness of grant applications. Any submitted even one day late are immediately returned to sender. This is similar to the practice of most graduate schools concerning application dates. One day late and you're out of luck. Needless to say, Mohammed is disappointed and disgusted with himself. He has bragged about his plan to his supervisor and fellow workers. Now he has to face the music. What a bummer.

However, Mohammed has the right to make a mistake, even an apparently careless one like this. The cliché is that we all make mistakes. That's exactly

right. We all have the right to make mistakes, because even when we try our best we *do* make mistakes.

It is in Mohammed's best assertive interest to chalk his endeavor up as an "experience" and learn from it. On the brighter side, first, he has his proposal written up and ready for the next grant opportunity. So all that work has not really been wasted. Second, there may be other opportunities for adolescents' summer activities. He can look into other programs and other possibilities. Third, he can learn a specific axiom from the experience. *Always* make certain you know what the deadline is for *any* application. Note that chapter 14, "Developing and Managing Agency Resources," will discuss grant writing in substantial detail.

3. *You have the right to direct and govern your own life. In other words, you have the right to be responsible for yourself.* For example, Audrey directs a group home for adults with physical disabilities, run by a conservative religious organization. This organization has publicly declared its anti-abortion stance. Her direct supervisor, the organization's director, is also personally strongly anti-abortion. Audrey, however, maintains a solid pro-choice stance on the issue.

A pro-choice rally is being held on an upcoming weekend. Audrey plans to attend and participate. She even expects to hold a pro-choice banner and march in a procession through the main area of town. Audrey knows that such behavior will annoy her supervisor and the agency. However, she feels she has the right to participate in the activity on her own time. This option *is* her right. She is prepared to take responsibility for her behavior and deal assertively with any potential consequences. (Chapter 12, "Ethics and Ethical Dilemmas in Macro Practice," will discuss a range of ethical issues in greater depth.)

4. *You have the right to stand up for yourself without unwarranted anxiety and make choices that are good for you.* For example, Helena works for a child abuse and protection unit with three other workers in a rural social services agency serving sev-

eral counties. The agency, like many others, is tormented by serious financial problems. Staffing is short. Funding is severely limited. Therefore, worker activities outside of essential job duties are extremely restricted.

A friend and fellow social worker at an agency in another county calls Helena and excitedly describes an upcoming workshop on new identification techniques for child neglect. Helena thinks it sounds wonderful. She knows that the agency's money is tight, but thinks what a beneficial investment it would be if she and her other unit colleagues could attend the workshop. The workshop would cost the agency $600 at $150 per attendant.

Helena talks to the other workers who agree that the conference was a great idea. They tell Helena if she can muster agency support, they would love to go. Helena decides to request support from the agency, despite the fact she knows her own supervisor will bristle at the thought of spending a penny more on anything than the agency absolutely has to. Helena determines that she has the right to stand up for herself, and, in effect, for her unit colleagues and ask to attend this workshop. She develops a detailed rationale concerning why and how the workshop will benefit workers and enhance agency effectiveness.

Additionally, Helena prioritizes what the agency can potentially do for her and her colleagues. She starts with her first priority and then works down to her last. First, the agency can pick up the entire workshop cost and give her and her unit colleagues the two days off with pay. Second, the agency can pick up part of the cost for each worker and allow them all to take the two days off without pay. (In this case, Helena and the others will have to pay the remaining costs themselves.) Third, the agency can allow Helena and her colleagues to attend with pay, but require them to cover the entire workshop cost themselves. Finally, Helena decides that if she has to, she will take the two days off without pay and also pay the entire workshop fee herself. She is uncertain what her colleagues will choose to do in this instance of last resort. Helena assertively proceeds with her request. What do you think will happen?

5. *You have the right not to be liked by everyone. (Do you like everyone you know?)* For example, Hiroko is a public assistance worker for a large county bureaucracy. She is very dedicated to her job and often works overtime with clients to make certain that they receive all the benefits possible. Her colleague, Bill, holding the same job title, thinks this is utterly stupid. He resents it that she seems to stand out as a star worker. Bill is not all that much into work himself. He feels he is "tenured," meaning permanently implanted in his position. He is not interested in doing any more work than he has to. He often refers to Hiroko as a "drudge."

Hiroko really doesn't care. She knows that effective performance of her job on the behalf of clients is important to her. Frankly (she asserts), it really doesn't matter to Hiroko whether Bill likes her or not. She has the right not to be liked by everybody. By the way, Hiroko doesn't much like Bill either.

6. *You have the right, on the one hand, to make requests and, on the other, to refuse them without feeling guilty.* For example, Merle is a case manager for veterans who suffer from posttraumatic stress disorder.[a] Part of the job requires that he take turns with four other staff members to wear a beeper—that is, to be on call in case of emergency for one week out of every month.

Merle's large family is staging a reunion at a ranch resort in Colorado. It happens to be set for a week when Merle is supposed to be on call, and would not ordinarily take his vacation time. Merle has the right to assertively ask one of the other three staff members on call to switch weeks (assuming that agency policy allows this practice). His colleagues, on the other hand, also have the right to refuse. From another perspective, consider what would happen if the situation were reversed. Merle then would have the right either to accept or to refuse a request to switch on-call weeks in a similar manner.

7. *You have the right to ask for information if you need it.* For example, Louise is a financial counselor at a private mental health agency. She is aware that the agency has access to special funding for persons "with special needs." She knows this only informally via the agency grapevine. Therefore, she

(continued)

HIGHLIGHT 2.2—*(Continued)*

---

is not certain that the term ''special needs'' means the same to her as it does to agency administrators. Since the agency is privately run, it is not subject to the same requirements concerning revelations of funding sources as are similar public agencies. (The public, who pays for public agencies, has the right to scrutinize budgets and spending.)

Louise is working with several families whom she feels are in excellent need of special help. Problems in the families include unemployment, depression, mental illness, poverty, unwanted pregnancy, and truancy. Louise knows that her agency administration discourages its workers from seeking this relatively secret special funding. Available amounts are probably very limited, so the administration must disperse these funds with discretion. Although Louise knows that the administration will not look kindly on her request, she decides to approach the agency's executive director to seek funding for the families in need. She decides she needs to know what requirements make clients eligible for this special funding. She feels she has the right to ask for this information, even though the agency administration would rather she did not.

8. *You have the right to decide not to exercise your assertive rights.* In other words, you have the right to choose not to be assertive if you don't want to. For example, Horace, a state probation and parole agent, is a member of a task force to curb substance abuse in his state.[b] He attends the last of a series of meetings aimed at facilitating a range of educational prevention and treatment thrusts to obliterate substance abuse among youth, especially delinquents. Horace feels that the task force has made great strides. It established goals, developed plans, carried out initiatives, and evaluated its results. Throughout the process, however, he felt that the task force chairperson Tobin, who happens to be an administrator in Horace's own state Division of Probation and Parole, was being much too pushy. Horace thinks Tobin frequently tried to coerce the group into following Tobin's own agenda. Although the group frequently ignored Tobin's ploys, Horace thinks Tobin's actions were inappropriate and perhaps even unethical.

After careful deliberation, Horace decides that it is not worth it to assertively confront Tobin about his behavior. Horace decides not to be assertive. After all, Tobin as task force chairperson has led the group to achieve great things. The moral here is that you don't have to be assertive every single time the opportunity presents itself.

Notes

Most of these rights have been adapted from those identified in *The New Assertive Woman* by Lynn Z. Bloom, Karen Coburn, and Joan Pearlman (New York: Dell, 1976) and in *Four One-Day Workshops* by Kathryn Apgar and Betsy Nicholson Callaghan (Boston: Resource Communications Inc. and Family Service Association of Greater Boston, 1980).

a. Posttraumatic stress disorder (PTSD) is ''a psychological reaction to experiencing an event that is outside the range of usual human experience'' such as military combat or a natural disaster. The disorder is characterized by a number of symptoms including inability to concentrate, severe nervousness, and extreme lack of emotion (Barker, 1995, p. 288).

b. A task force is ''a temporary group, usually within an organization, brought together to achieve some previously specified function or goal'' (Barker, 1991, p. 235).

Women: A Population-at-Risk

A special note should be made here with respect to women, including professional social workers. Because of traditional gender-role stereotypes, women continue to manifest a number of problems related to lack of assertion. Collier (1982, p. 65) states it well:

The culture teaches women that they are mediators and conciliators, not direct parties to conflict; they are to be gentle, nurturing, soft-spoken, and unaggressive. But this suppression of the ability to confront frustration, disappointment, conflicts or interest, anger, and even minor irritation demands a high price. Most women need to learn how to improve the direct expression of their needs, wants, and feelings. This need is so widespread that it accounts for the instant popularity of what is called "assertiveness training," which gives women the tools for expressing themselves. The need of many women, however, is deeper; they need to learn that their emotions are valid, that they have a right to express them, and that other people have the obligation to respond.

For many women, assertiveness training leads down a long road of practice before they become spontaneously and naturally assertive. A major problem for women is lack of self-confidence. Slipman (1986) suggests: "To think positively means that you must see yourself as a person with rights in the situation you are in at any specific time. The first stage is to turn your negative feelings about your abilities into a positive goals to be practiced and attained" (p. 65).

Conflict and Its Resolution

An *interpersonal conflict* occurs "whenever an action by one person prevents, obstructs, or interferes with the actions of another person" (Johnson, 1986, p. 199). Words commonly associated with conflict include fighting, competition, incompatibility, open warfare, antagonism, "divergent ideas," opposition, and "mental struggle" (*Webster's Ninth New Collegiate Dictionary*, 1991, p. 276).

Conflict can occur in an infinite number of ways in an unending array of contexts. As in micro and mezzo, conflict frequently occurs in macro situations. This chapter will focus on conflict between individuals in macro contexts. Chapter 3 ("Using Mezzo Skills in the Macro Environment") will address specific types of conflict and conflict management guidelines for group (mezzo) situations in macro environments.

The Pros of Conflict

Conflicts in macro situations are difficult for many people. It is easy to view conflict and confrontation as being very negative, something to avoid at all costs. This is not necessarily the case. Conflict has some positive aspects, including the following (Johnson, 1986, p. 200):

1. Conflict can help us explore a situation more thoroughly. It can force us to more extensively evaluate issues and problems involved in interpersonal communication, such as identification of what problems are, who are participants in the conflict, and what can be done to achieve resolution.
2. Conflict can cause us to make improvements in our behavior and communication. Change is frequently avoided because it requires some energy to accomplish it. When a conflict arises, you may be forced to address an issue and make changes—whether you like them or not.
3. Conflict can generate new energy to solve a problem. Conflict increases our awareness of issues and, thus, may motivate us to make changes in our behavior.
4. Conflict can simply make daily routines more exciting. Disagreements can stimulate creative thinking to develop new solutions. Argument and debate can spawn new, sometimes exciting ideas that we might never have thought of had the conflict not occurred.
5. Conflict can improve the quality of problem resolution and decision making. Conflict encourages exploration of ideas and options as well as more critical evaluation of these options.
6. Conflict can release emotional "steam." Pent-up feelings simmer and build. Release and resolution through conflict can be constructive in maintaining interpersonal relationships.
7. Conflict can enhance our own self awareness. What issues bother us the most? How do we respond to conflict? Can we identify what "buttons" people can press in us to get us going?
8. Conflict can be fun when it is not taken too seriously. Many people enjoy hearty discussion and debate. Games are often based on conflict that is supposed to be fun. The game of "Risk" comes to mind. It is a board game in which the world is divided up into forty-two countries or regions. To win, one player must conquer all the others. Explaining the details would take too much space here. However, even though no actual blood is spilled, emotions are heightened as one player slaughters another. This author has been known to violently hurl the board in the air when feeling betrayed by another player who has methodically and unemotionally triumphed. Yet such conflict is *fun* (although it tends to be more fun when you win).
9. Conflict can actually facilitate the development and depth of relationships. Working through conflicts provides opportunities to get to know another person in a deeper, sometimes very meaningful way. What things are the most important to the other person? How does that person feel about and react to these important issues? What is that person really like in situations that are not entirely positive? Additionally, conflict can dispel negative feelings when conflict resolution is achieved.

The Cons of Conflict

On the other hand, when considering confrontation as a response to some conflict, it is important to weigh at least three potential losses in the context of macro practice (Daft, 1992). First, conflict takes energy. Energy and resources are always limited. You have just so much time, enthusiasm, effort, and initiative. What you expend in one endeavor, you will not have available to use for some other task. Therefore, you must make certain that the targeted conflict is significant enough to merit your efforts.

The second potential negative impact of conflict involves the possibility of having winners and losers. Adequate compromise might not be possible or realistic. One opponent in the conflict may feel downtrodden and unfairly treated by the resolution. Research suggests that losers of conflicts often become uncooperative and cease to concern themselves with colleagues' rights and wants (Daft, 1992).

A third possible result of conflict is decreased collaboration and teamwork. Extreme conflict may end in almost total lack of communication. Concern for the opponents' welfare may vanish. When a worker is totally immersed in intense conflict, her anger might prevent her from working toward compromise. Preoccupation with conflict can even obstruct her ability to do her job.

In summary, it is very important to consider both the potential positive and negative consequences of conflict. Results can range from extraordinarily positive to absolutely destructive.

Personal Styles for Addressing Conflict

Just as each of us has a unique personality, so also does each have an individualized style for approaching conflict. Johnson (1986, pp. 208–11) describes five personal styles for managing conflict; these include "the turtle," "the shark," "the teddy bear," "the fox," and "the owl." Of course, these are relatively simplistic categories. However, they graphically reflect the general types of behaviors people display when conflict occurs.

The turtle describes the style of people "who *withdraw* into their shells to avoid conflicts" (p. 208). For them it is easier to avoid conflict than to muster up the initiative and energy it takes to address it. Turtles typically have relatively poor self-concepts. They do not have faith in their ability to resolve a conflict. They are nonassertive, valuing the views and needs of others above their own. We have already said that whenever you allow frustration, disappointment, or hostility to build without dealing with it, your emotions may erupt in an explosion you cannot control.

The shark is an *aggressor*. The shark moves into a conflict boldly, pushing opponents aside. Sharks are bullies. The shark wants to win and has little interest in nurturing his relationship with an opponent. A shark approaches any situation from a win/lose perspective. He considers neither negotiation nor compromise. Sharks like power. To get it and win, they will do just about anything, including threatening, intimidating, and attacking opponents.

The teddy bear's style is the direct opposite of the shark's. The teddy bear *values the relationship* with the opponent much more than the achievement of his own goals. The teddy bear is a bit more assertive than the turtle because he does value his own ideas. However, teddy bears will put their own goals aside in deference to their opponents' whenever they feel their relations might be threatened.

The fox is a *compromiser*. Slyly, the fox works to reach some agreement acceptable to both herself and her opponent. The fox's orientation dictates that both parties should relinquish some of their demands in order to come to a reasonable compromise. Foxes are adept at figuring a way to work things out to the satisfaction of most.

Finally, the owl, like the fox, believes in each party making compromises. However, the owl is much more assertive in conflictual interactions. The owl's approach is based on *confrontation*, which the owl welcomes. The owl values conflict and sees it as an opportunity for brainstorming solutions, attacking problems, and enhancing relationships. The owl places exceptional value on conflict's positive potential as described earlier. Owls encourage the assertive expression of opposing ideas and the venting of feelings and frustrations in order to achieve the most ideal solution possible.

One theme that recurs throughout this book is the importance of getting to know yourself and your own reactions better and better. How do you address conflict? How will you react to conflict in macro situations? Are you a turtle, shrinking into your shell for safety? Or are you a shark, savagely eager to devour your opponents (albeit, this is a bit on the dramatic side)? On the other hand, do you tend to approach conflict somewhere in between, like the teddy bear, fox, or owl? Identifying both your own style of conflict and that of your opponents is important in planning the most effective approach to conflict and confrontation. Generally, it is more effective to take both your needs and those of your opponents into consideration. In addition, both your goals and your relationships with your opponents merit your attention.

Steps in Conflict Resolution

Johnson (1986) proposes seven steps for conflict resolution. Although it is not always possible to go through each one, it is important to keep them in mind. Emphases are on both communication and coordination with the opponent. It should be noted that chapter 3, "Using Mezzo Skills in the Macro Environment," will also discuss conflict management guidelines, especially in mezzo situations. The steps presented here are among the many approaches to dealing with conflict.

For the purposes of illustration, a case involving the process of conflict resolution will be presented and discussed. Highlights 2.3 through 2.9 will examine the case concurrently with each step.

Step 1: The Confrontation

The first step in resolving any kind of conflict is to confront the opponent. A confrontation is "the act of bringing together opposing ideas, impulses, or groups for the purpose of systematic examination or comparison" (Barker, 1991, p. 47). Confrontation entails activity intended to resolve or combat some conflictual situation. To confront means to disagree with another person and make a point of stating that disagreement. This, of course, involves risking a negative or hostile reaction by the person you're confronting.

People handle conflict and confrontation very differently. They have widely varied interpersonal styles and skills. Usually, when engaging in a confrontation, it is wise to keep two major issues in mind (Hooyman, 1973; Johnson, 1986; Weissman, Epstein, & Savage, 1983). First, clearly identify and examine your personal goals. Conflicts can arise because of differences, often concerning goals or perceptions of goals. How important to you are these goals? Are they very important or only minimally so?

The second major issue to keep in mind when beginning a confrontation is the nurturance of your interpersonal relationship with the other person. Nunnally and Moy (1989) maintain that "the key to maintaining relationships when in disagreement is to show respect" (p. 97). This includes both respect for yourself and for the other person. Yes, you have a disagreement and you feel some degree of intensity about your position. However, to what extent are you willing to jeopardize your relationship with this person in order to win the conflict? To what extent will you be able to compromise? How can you balance conflict resolution with maintaining a positive a relationship with your opponent? You do not need any more enemies than you absolutely have to have. One theme of this book is the need to muster support from others in order to achieve your specified goals. Therefore, the more strongly you can sustain your various relationships with others in the macro environment, the better off you are in terms of performing your job and achieving your intervention goals.

Step 2: Establish Common Ground

Establish an acceptable common definition of the problem. Such a definition should make neither you nor your opponent defensive or resistant to working out a mutually agreeable compromise. Emphasize how important the conflictual issue is to both of you. Be as clear and specific about your concerns as possible. Express and clarify your own feelings, while drawing out those of your opponent. Most important, keep trying to empathize with your opponent's position.

Step 3: Emphasize the Importance of Communication

When pursuing conflict resolution, it is crucial for you to establish and nurture communication channels between you and the person(s) with whom you are in conflict. Many of the communication techniques already discussed can be put to excellent use in communicating with an opponent throughout the conflict resolution process. Additionally, Sheafor, Horejsi, and Horejsi (1991, pp. 337–38) propose the following seven general communication guidelines to keep in mind:

HIGHLIGHT 2.3

STEP 1—THE CONFRONTATION

Brainard supervises a ten-person unit serving AFDC[a] clients in an urban county's social services department. Brainard's problem is Cheryl, one of his ten supervisees. Essentially, Cheryl is incompetent. She consistently makes decisions that negatively affect clients, fails to complete her paperwork, and effectively disrupts any unit meetings and projects in which she participates. Scores of clients have complained pointedly about her work and her treatment of them.

Brainard, who is newly hired as unit supervisor, inherited Cheryl from the unit's former supervisor Charlie who had originally hired her. Cheryl is not only incompetent, she is also a bitter fighter. Two years earlier when Charlie began to notice Cheryl's difficulties in completing her work adequately, he tried to help Cheryl solve her problems and improve her performance. However, she bristled defensively and fought him every step of the way. The agency has a strong union of which Cheryl, of course, is a member. Once employees pass their probationary period of one year, they essentially gain tenure. It is extremely difficult, if not impossible, to terminate their employment after that point. During Cheryl's probationary period, she accused Charlie of harassment and hired legal counsel to represent her. At the time, the agency was suffering some severe public criticism and resulting budget cuts. Therefore, higher administration commanded Charlie to leave Cheryl alone and not cause any trouble. Charlie, who was not renowned for his strength of character or ability to pursue open conflict anyway, backed down and soon thereafter transferred to another agency unit.

Now Brainard, stuck with Cheryl, continues to see the problem more clearly as the months pass.

Brainard prides himself on his commitment to advocate on the behalf of clients and consistently work in their best interest. He feels it is his responsibility to do something about Cheryl and her incompetence. He, too, initially tried to help her through her difficulties, making numerous specific recommendations for how she might improve her job performance.

Every one of the other nine unit members has similar concerns about Cheryl. They all feel that Cheryl is a blight on their unit. However, she is tenured and hostile. Colleagues are at a loss about what to do.

Brainard, a competent supervisor, begins to clearly document his efforts at helping Cheryl and her failures to perform her job adequately. After several dozen incidents are noted, Brainard brings the situation to the attention of higher administration. The agency administration has a history of disagreement and conflict with the agency's union. Therefore, the administration feels their wisest alternative is to bring in a neutral trained mediator from outside the agency. Such mediation involves "intervention in disputes between parties to help them reconcile differences, find compromises, or reach mutually satisfactory agreements" (Barker, 1995, p. 228). Obviously, there is quite a dispute between Cheryl and Brainard.

Note

a. AFDC, Aid to Families with Dependent Children, was "a public assistance program, originating in the Social Security Act as Aid to Dependent Children, funded by the federal and state governments to provide financial aid for needy children who are deprived of parental support because of death, incapacitation, or absence" (Barker, 1995, p. 14).

---

1. Do not begin a confrontation when you are angry. Anger makes you lose your objectivity. You may lose sight of both your goals and the welfare of your opponent and focus instead on punishing or beating your opponent.
2. Do not enter into a conflict unless you have a clearly established reason for doing so. Unless you are willing to try to resolve the conflict, do not bother confronting your opponent. Such confrontation will only waste both your and your opponent's time and energy.
3. If you absolutely despise your opponent or have immense difficulty reaching for any positive, empathic feelings about him, do not confront him. If you do not respect

---

HIGHLIGHT 2.4

STEP 2—ESTABLISH COMMON GROUND

The mediator, Jimmy Hoffa, interviews each of the ten unit personnel including Cheryl. He also talks extensively to Brainard. He carefully scrutinizes and begins to bring together the evidence. Jimmy is able to establish a common ground between Cheryl and the rest of the unit. All involved staff including Cheryl are unhappy with the conflictual situation. They all feel both their individual performance and that of the unit in general suffers significantly because of it.

---

your opponent, a confrontation will only waste your and your opponent's time and energy. Rather, explore other ways of addressing the conflict (such as calling upon the support of others) or drop the matter completely.

4. Include positive statements and feedback along with the negative aspects of confrontation. For example, you might emphasize your opponent's strengths before beginning the confrontation, thereby minimizing her perception of being attacked. You might say, ''I know you are very knowledgeable and have strong ideas on this subject. I would like to discuss with you some alternative thoughts I've had about it. I know you're busy, but might you have some time to talk?''

   This particular example first gives the opponent a compliment (''I know you are very knowledgeable and have strong ideas on this subject.''). Compliments by the way, should be honest, believable ones so that you do not sound insincere. Next, the example above introduces the issue in a general way (''I would like to discuss with you some alternative thoughts I've had about it.''). Finally, it implies respect for the opponent's time and work efforts (''I know you're busy, but might you have some time to talk?'').

   In some ways, giving your opponent positive feedback or complimenting her is similar to confrontation (Nunnally & Moy, 1989). Both complimenting and confrontation provide people with feedback or information about their behavior. Confrontation, of course, incorporates negative feedback, while compliments involve positive feedback. It makes sense to provide some of both during the conflict resolution process.

5. Be certain to explain your concerns regarding the conflict in a ''descriptive and nonjudgmental'' manner (Sheafor, Horesji, & Horesji, 1991, p. 338). Prepare details in your head beforehand in order to explain and clarify the issues and behaviors involved. In the same way, try to present your stance objectively and factually. Avoid overly emotional appeals. If your opponent hears your emotions talking instead of you, she may react to your emotions instead of to what you are intending to say.

6. Supply relevant data in support of your stance. Articulate your position clearly. Describe the issue straightforwardly. In other words, make sure you know what you're talking about. Have your facts straight. Have both your ideal solution and some potential compromises clearly established in your mind.

7. Use ''I-messages'' frequently. Simply rephrasing your thoughts to include the word ''I'' enhances the quality of personal caring and empathy. This technique can emphasize the fact that you are trying to address a conflictual issue and are seeking a mutually agreeable solution, instead of criticizing or blaming. For example, you might say, ''*I* would like to share with you some inconsistencies in my perception of what you've been saying and what you've actually been doing.'' This is far more personal and far less blaming than a statement such as, ''*You* have been saying one thing and doing another.''

What about when someone confronts you? Much of this discussion involves initiating a confrontation with a colleague, supervisor, agency, administrator, some other agency representative, community leader, or the like. What about your own feelings, communication, and behavior when someone confronts you? In these cases your opponent may or may not have well-developed conflict resolution skills. Nunnally and Moy (1989, pp. 135–36) make at least five suggestions for how to respond.

1. Pay very close attention to what the confronter is telling you. Make certain you understand exactly what the confronter intends to say. Concentrating on the specifics helps you listen and comprehend what is being said. Is it clear or vague?

   For example, suppose a colleague approaches you

HIGHLIGHT 2.5

STEP 3—EMPHASIZE COMMUNICATION

Jimmy helps people on both sides of the conflict begin to talk about their feelings and think about suggestions for improvement. By the time Jimmy arrives, the situation is so tense and threatening that communication between Cheryl and Brainard has basically stopped. Cheryl has also ceased to communicate with her other unit colleagues. A typical comment by other workers at unit meetings reveals that they hesitate to say anything, because of Cheryl's threats to

sue them. It has been very difficult to get anything accomplished in the unit for a long time.

Jimmy's approach is to use positive feedback as much as possible. He talks of how committed Cheryl is to maintaining her job at the agency. Likewise, he emphasizes that Brainard and the other workers want to function as well as they can in providing services to clients.

and flatly states, ''You really are pretty intimidating.'' Focusing on the specific words being said can improve your understanding. Likewise, if the statement is vague, you can ask for clarification. To ''intimidate'' means either ''to make timid or fearful,'' or ''to deter as if by threats'' (*Webster's Ninth New Collegiate Dictionary*, 1991, p. 634). The confronter's accusation is pretty imprecise. Exactly whom do you intimidate? This person who is confronting you? Other agency staff? Agency administration? Everybody? Similarly, do you make some unidentified other(s) fearful or are you making threats? In either case, in what way? What verbal and/or nonverbal behaviors does your confronter feel elicit an intimidating reaction? In what contexts does intimidation occur? The point here is that by listening you can clarify the negative feedback while the confrontation is occurring.

Another reason for paying close attention to the words involves your own emotional reactions to the negative feedback. Paying attention to exactly what the confronter says can divert your attention from your own reactions of anger or resentment. Becoming overly emotional and losing track of your objectivity does not help you evaluate the situation or help resolve the conflict.

2. Explain to the confronter exactly how you will respond to his feedback. In the example above, you might tell the confronter that you will approach the people who feel intimidated and help resolve their negative feelings. You can elaborate upon what you will do to correct the problem. Think about what else you will say and do. In what contexts will you make the changes? Staff meetings? Interviews with community leaders? Casual lunchtime interactions with colleagues?

Sometimes, you can be caught off guard when someone confronts you. Under these circumstances, you might not be able to think quickly enough to respond immediately. Then it's no problem simply to say something like, ''Oh, that surprises me. Give me some time to think about it and I'll give you a call later.''

3. Tell your confronter that you appreciate his effort and his feedback. This is not an easy suggestion to follow. Being criticized can be hard to take. It's really easy to get defensive: ''What do you men I'm intimidating? You have your nerve! You have a pretty noxious personality yourself!''

In reality, feedback can almost always be helpful. Even if you don't agree with what the confronter says, at least you know how he feels. In the worst case, the interaction gives you some information concerning how to operate with the confronter in the future. In the best case, you can receive some constructive feedback that may help in your future communications and interactions.

4. Approach your confronter later, and tell him how you have responded to his feedback. Explain how you have changed your behavior or attitude. You might thank him once again for his effort.

Most people are hesitant about this particular suggestion. It is important to consider carefully and as objectively as possible and evaluate the confronter's feedback. However, if you decide in good conscience that he is inaccurate, you obviously will not alter your behavior in future situations. In effect, you will not believe your behavior requires change (at least not the behavior he criticized). In that case, you can choose either to confront him about the inappropriateness of his remarks or simply

---

HIGHLIGHT 2.6

STEP 4—EMPHASIZE YOUR WILLINGNESS TO COOPERATE

Jimmy encourages Cheryl and the rest of the staff to work toward some solution. He has already established the common ground of a miserable working environment. This motivates participants to cooperate and work toward a mutually satisfying decision about what to do.

---

let the matter drop. It might not be worth your effort to extend the confrontation.

Also, be careful of the multi-confronter, the person who regularly tells you all the things that are wrong with you. He might do this only in his interactions with you, or he might interact in this manner with almost everyone. In any case, depending on your own motivation, you may decide to confront him about his own overly confrontational behavior. As our discussion illustrates, the possibilities for confrontation are endless.

5. At the time of the confrontation, *do not* reproach the confronter with a criticism of your own. That type of response is usually petty and inappropriate. Address the issue at hand first. Settle that. Then, as we discussed in suggestion number four above, you might decide to confront the person about his own behavior at another time.

Step 4: Emphasize Your Willingness to Cooperate

Emphasize your willingness to work with your opponent to find some mutually satisfactory solution. By definition, conflict is staged in the context of disagreement. In order to minimize the disagreement or, at least, to develop a viable, agreeable plan of action, stress the commonalities you have with your opponent.

Step 5: Empathize with Your Opponent's Perspective

Work to understand why your opponent feels the way she does. What are her motivation for taking the stand she does? How does the conflict affect her feelings and her work? How can you express to her that you are sincerely trying to understand her side of the conflictual issue?

Step 6: Evaluate Both Your Own and Your Opponent's Motivation to Address the Conflict

You and your opponent may view a conflict very differently. For instance, you may feel the conflict is of extraordinary importance. Your opponent, on the other hand, may think that it's silly to even bring up the issue because it's so minor. Essentially, evaluate whether or not it is worthwhile to expend the energy to resolve the conflict. Maybe it would simply be easier to maintain the status quo and leave the whole thing alone.

For example, the chairperson of a social work department in an undergraduate program felt it was infinitely important to emphasize that each of the six faculty members could teach any course in the program. This chairperson typically spent fifteen minutes to an hour at each faculty meeting chit-chatting about how important such flexibility was. One faculty member in particular thought the whole issue was blatantly absurd. Different faculty had specified areas of interest in which they both studied and published. Why should faculty be forced to teach in areas they knew very little about instead of in areas in which they had established some degree of expertise? Would it be good for students to be taught by people who knew little of what they were talking about? Of course not. However, the faculty member chose to let the entire issue rest. In reality, all the faculty taught the same classes each semester anyway, so the point was moot. The faculty member acknowledged the chairperson's strong feelings and decided that confront-

---

HIGHLIGHT 2.7

STEP 5—EMPATHIZE WITH YOUR OPPONENT'S PERSPECTIVE

As participants become motivated to cooperate and begin to discuss their feelings, Jimmy helps each side see the other's point of view. He holds several meetings with all unit staff present and gives everyone the opportunity to air their views. On the one hand, Brainard and the unit staff are terribly frus-trated with Cheryl's inability to work up to the unit's standards. On the other hand, Cheryl has become so ostracized that Jimmy has some concern that she might jump off the eight-story building in which the agency is housed. Cheryl is isolated, lonely, and un-happy.

---

ing the chairperson on this issue would simply not be worth the effort. The faculty member didn't think he could win anyway. Besides, the worst thing that actually occurred was wasted time at faculty meetings.

Note that in many situations it is possible to change the degree of motivation on your or your opponent's part (Johnson, 1986). In the above situation, the department chairperson might have begun to implement what the faculty member termed the "absurd idea" of forcing faculty to teach outside their respective areas. Subsequently, the concerned faculty members might be extremely motivated to address the conflict and pursue some resolution.

Step 7: Come to Some Mutually Satisfactory Agreement

The final step in conflict resolution is to come to some mutually satisfactory agreement. To do this, follow these five suggestions (Johnson, 1986). First, articulate exactly what your agreement entails. Second, indicate how you will behave toward the other person in the future as compared to the past. Third, identify how the other person will behave toward you. Fourth, indicate ways of addressing any future mistakes (that is, if you or the other behaves differently than you have agreed to). Fifth, establish how and when you and the other

---

HIGHLIGHT 2.8

STEP 6—EVALUATE BOTH YOUR OWN AND YOUR OPPONENT'S MOTIVATION TO ADDRESS THE CONFLICT

As both sides air their feelings and frustrations, Jimmy helps them verbalize their motivation for change. Both express sincere interest in halting the conflict. All unit members are getting tired. There-fore, Jimmy determines that both parties are eager to pursue a viable alternative if the group can come up with one.

HIGHLIGHT 2.9

STEP 7—COME TO SOME MUTUALLY SATISFACTORY AGREEMENT

It looks to Jimmy as if no agreement can be reached to resolve the situation if Cheryl remains in the unit. Feelings are so strongly directed against her that it is unlikely they would change. Major supervisory efforts to help Cheryl improve her work performance have hopelessly failed. Therefore, it does not look as if a change in Cheryl's behavior is a viable alternative.

Cheryl has the equivalent of tenure and refuses to leave the agency without a major battle. Thus, the only remaining alternative is to transfer her to another position. Cheryl, Brainard, and the other unit workers first breathe a sigh of relief and then are ready to cheer when they examine this alternative. Jimmy works with Brainard and the agency's administration to implement this plan. The administration

arranges for the necessary retraining Cheryl needs to assume her new position.

Cheryl happily transfers to another unit. She retains a job in the agency and no longer has to deal with colleagues whom she considers irascible, irritable, faultfinding, and backbiting. Likewise, relative peace descends upon the AFDC unit and workers can once again focus their energies on their jobs.

Cheryl is virtually not heard from by anyone in the unit again except when her name occasionally appears in an agency newsletter, as all agency staff names do at one time or another. Brainard, despite his immense relief at Cheryl's departure, soon becomes bored at the lack of challenge and leaves the agency for a higher paying, more demanding job.

---

will meet in the future to continue your cooperative behavior and minimization of conflict.

As we stated at the beginning of this section, conflict is natural and predictable. Anticipating it, learning the various types of conflict, and considering ahead of time the possible approaches to conflict management can only increase your effectiveness as a generalist social worker.

Working under Supervisors

Your interpersonal relationship with your agency supervisor will always have special significance in the macro environment. Highlight 2.10 describes the many things you will depend on her for. Because of the importance of your relationship with your supervisor, we will spend time here discussing how you can best put your micro skills to use within this special context.

Social work is a profession that has heavily embraced the value and use of supervision. Barker (1991) defines supervision as "an administrative and educa-

tional process used extensively in social agencies to help social workers further develop and refine their skills and to provide quality assurance for the clients" (p. 230). Shulman (1991) reinforces this by emphasizing that the purpose of supervision is improvement of service to clients. Highlight 2.10 summarizes some general expectations of supervisors.

Obviously, highlight 2.10 primarily addresses workers' expectations of supervisors. However, supervisors also have responsibilities to their agencies and to other administrative personnel. Moreover, many of their roles are complex. The following sections will describe: the administrative and educational functions of supervisors; supervisors' other functions; how to use supervision most effectively; and potential problems that may arise in supervision.

Administrative Functions of Supervisors

In their administrative function, supervisors do such things as assign cases to workers, review case plans,

---

HIGHLIGHT 2.10

WORKERS' GENERAL EXPECTATIONS OF SUPERVISORS

The following are some general expectations workers frequently have of their supervisors (Sheafor, Horejsi, & Horejsi, 1991; Shulman, 1991):

1. *Be readily available for consultation on difficult cases.* Kadushin (1977) defines social work consultation: "Consultation is regarded as an interactional helping process—a series of sequential steps taken to achieve some objective through an interpersonal relationship. One participant in the transaction has greater expertise, greater knowledge, greater skill in the performance of some particular, specialized function, and this person is designated consultant" (p. 25). In other words, a worker expects his supervisor to help him out when he is confronted with a problem or an exceptionally difficult case. Hopefully, the supervisor will use her own well-developed micro skills to assist in the communication process.

2. *Make certain that workers are knowledgeable about agency policy.* Agency policy includes the rules that tell workers which actions among a multitude of actions they may take and which they may not. Additionally, the policy may specify how an agency is structured, the qualifications of supervisors and workers, and the proper procedures agency staff should follow as they go about their daily work routines. Workers depend on immediate supervisors to keep them abreast of changes in agency policy. Workers also depend on supervisors to continue monitoring their work to make sure they remain in compliance with policy.

3. *Provide input to higher levels of administration regarding line workers' needs.* Workers rarely have direct lines of communication with high-level agency decision-makers. Thus, workers must depend on their own supervisors to communicate workers' need upward so that this information reaches people in power who can make changes and meet needs. Chapter 4, "Understanding Organizations," will discuss formal and informal communication channels in much greater depth.

4. *Facilitate cooperation among staff.* Workers expect their supervisors to coordinate their work and the work of others so that together they can accomplish what they're supposed to. In the event that workers disagree with each other or enter into some conflict, supervisors can step in and mediate. Workers depend on supervisors to help attain some resolution on any number of problematic issues.

5. *Nurture workers and give them support when needed.* Workers depend on supervisors to encourage them to perform well. Workers hope that supervisors will praise them when they do their work well. Often, workers look to supervisors when they need to vent feelings or discuss issues.

6. *Evaluate workers' job performance.* Workers expect supervisors to evaluate the strengths and weaknesses they demonstrate while doing their jobs. Workers depend on supervisors to get them back on track when they do something wrong or ineffectively. Workers often need constructive criticism. Frequently, supervisors have direct input in the matter of raises workers receive based on performance.

7. *Facilitate workers' development of new skills.* Supervisors by definition assume positions superior to those of workers. Workers depend on their supervisors to be more knowledgeable than they are. Thus, workers look to supervisors to help them develop new skills and improve their expertise.

and discuss progress on individual cases. Accomplishing these functions helps ensure that the agency's work is being completed in a proper and timely manner. Supervisors thus monitor the agency's direct service provision to clients. Supervisors also help workers stay in touch with changes in the agency. In a sense, supervisors occupy a middle ground between the worker and the agency administration. In this role they serve as a two-way communication link.

We have established that supervisors convey to higher administration how well agency services are being administered. They also provide information from agency administration to workers providing services directly to clients. Sometimes the information conveyed from the administration is positive. For example, it might concern an announcement that the agency received an award for excellence or that the staff's annual vacation time will be increased. Once I worked for a private agency whose administration decided to give all staff an extra day off their respective birthdays. The staff applauded.

Other times, however, the administration will convey information through supervisors that will not be positive. For instance, you might be told that your caseload will be increased significantly. Or you might be instructed that you and your co-workers will have to remain on call and carry a beeper every other Saturday night.

In these latter cases, supervisors can be placed in very precarious positions. They may be given directives to convey information to you that they know you will not like. Yet they may have had little or no input into the content of such directives. It's easy for you as a worker to become angry or disgusted at hearing bad tidings and direct your negative feelings toward your supervisor. The point is that it is helpful to be sensitive to a supervisor and her position. Supervisors won't always be able to quell external demands or help you as much as you need, despite their good intentions. They will have their own job constraints and demands with which to contend.

Supervisors can also assist workers to become more effective in their assigned roles. If a worker is having difficulty, the supervisor should determine the reason (Gambrill & Stein, 1983). For example, is the problem a lack of knowledge or skill? If so, what can the supervisor do to assist the worker in gaining what she needs?

Perhaps, there is no reward system for good job performance. Consider a social worker whose program is repeatedly over budget. Rarely is anything said about this. When the worker finally ends a year within budget, there is no recognition or acknowledgment. The worker ends up asking herself, "Should I work so hard at cutting costs and keeping within my budget when no one cares anyway?" The following year she is once again over budget. A supervisor should know what workers find rewarding and try to build in some type of reward structure.

Consider another issue. Is the worker somehow being punished for doing a good job? This can happen easily with workers who have been staying on top of the workload, getting paper work completed on time, and otherwise performing in an exemplary fashion. A common reaction is to give this person more to do since "she can obviously handle it." Simultaneously, other workers who are less successful at balancing the job's demands are excused from additional assignments. In effect, such behavior serves to punish the good worker and reward the poor one.

Educational Functions of Supervisors

Supervisors have a multifaceted educational role. They can aid workers by helping them improve their knowledge and skills. They can help practitioners establish priorities among work tasks. Additionally, supervisors can help workers develop increased self-awareness and orient workers to both agency policy and social work values.

Supervisors of more experienced workers may play less of an educational role and act more as consultants. Highlight 2.10 established that consultation involves giving expert advice about some specific case or problem. Supervision implies that the supervisor has greater power and assumes responsibility for providing workers with direction.

Barker (1991) compares consultation and supervision: "Unlike supervision, which is relatively continuous and encompasses many areas of concern, consultation occurs more on an ad hoc or temporary basis and has a specific goal and situation focus" (p. 48).

Experienced workers often benefit from a supervisor's consultative approach on difficult cases. Of course, whether a supervisor should assume a consultative role is likely influenced by the worker's level of education and competence. Ideally, the supervisor can switch from one role to another depending upon the supervisee's needs.

Other Functions of Supervisors

Like many middle-management roles, the supervisor's job is not easy. Supervisors are caught between higher level administration and their own supervisees who operate at lower levels in the agency's structure of authority. Yet workers expect a supervisor's assistance in negotiating the very system that pulls supervisors in opposite directions. A case in point involves a field-placement student in a hospital setting who angers a physician. The physician misunderstands the student and is going to have the student reprimanded. The student's field instructor (her supervisor) intercedes to clarify the situation. Thus, the matter is resolved to everyone's satisfaction. The student really needs such supervisory assistance. This illustrates how workers often expect supervisors to help them deal with real everyday problems.

Workers also expect support from a supervisor. Unfortunately, supervisors must play a combined role as teacher-administrator-supporter. Sometimes the roles of supporter and teacher clash with the supervisor's administrative role. For example, supervisors might be called upon to reprimand or discipline supervisees. Likewise, supervisors might be asked to follow a specific course of action that is inconsistent with workers' needs.

For example, the upper-level administration of a social service organization abruptly decides to stop sending letters to clients reminding them of their appointments. The administration decides that this will cut the costs of paper, worker and secretarial time, and postage. However, as a result, less than half of the workers' clients show up when they are supposed to. Workers are mortified. Inadvertently the administration has severely interfered with the workers' ability to do their jobs.

Using Supervision Effectively

Effective use of supervision hinges partly on your own behavior and characteristics as a worker. Communicat-

ing clearly and regularly with your supervisor can get you the help you need for working with exceptionally difficult situations and finding resources you would not otherwise know about. The following are some helpful suggestions for maximizing your use of supervision (Austin, Kopp, and Smith, 1986; Sheafor, Horejsi, & Horejsi, 1991).

Use Your Communication Skills with Your Supervisor

Use the communication skills discussed earlier in the chapter with your supervisor just as you do with clients and other colleagues. Check to be certain that the messages you hear are clear. Ask questions. Rephrase a question if you don't think your supervisor understands what you mean. Paraphrase your supervisor's answer to ensure you understand what was said.

When your supervisor uses a word you don't understand or one that does not make sense, ask what she means. Sometimes people will use letters or acronyms (For example, NASW, CSWE, OSHA, KUMQUAT, or PIGWART). If you don't know what it means, *ask*.

Plan your messages to your supervisor carefully ahead of time, especially the written ones. Keep in mind the following questions:

> What am I trying to get across?
> Who will receive my communication?
> When is the best time to communicate?
> Where is the best place to communicate?
> How should I communicate?
> Why am I communicating?
> (Austin, Kopp, & Smith, 1986, p. 517)

Written communication is important. Decisions that require a supervisor's agreement should often be put in writing. One way you might do this is by sending a memo to your supervisor, summarizing her instructions or your mutual decisions regarding some plan of action. This documents the fact that you have your supervisor's support.

Keep Your Records Up-to-Date

Agencies run on records. A common source of irritation between coworkers and supervisors concerns re-

HIGHLIGHT 2.11

GAMES SUPERVISORS AND SUPERVISEES SOMETIMES PLAY

The supervisory relationship can be a complex one. In any supervisory dyad, both people are unique individuals with distinctly different personalities. Communication is rife with the potential for misunderstandings, conflicts, and manipulation. Power, of course, is also involved. As a result, there are a number of games workers and supervisors can play. Because they are games, they prevent real issues from being addressed out in the open. Games can also corrode relationships.

Kadushin (1968) has cited a number of games about which it is good to be aware:

1. *I'll be Nice to You If You'll Be Nice to Me.* This game involves a supervisory relationship in which both parties are afraid to give any negative or constructive feedback. They avoid real issues by complimenting each other. This is fake interaction. Remarks are rarely genuine. The purposes of supervision are not fulfilled because of the participants' hesitation to assertively confront each other and the issues.

2. *Therapize Me.* This game involves the supervisor delving into the worker's personal life and issues. This is inappropriate. If workers need counseling—as many of us do at various times during our lives—they should receive it outside their agency setting from another professional whom they pay. It is also inappropriate for workers to use their supervisors' time in this manner and for supervisors to pry into their workers' personal lives. The purpose of maintaining a working environment is to get the necessary work done, nothing else.

In the event that a worker is experiencing personal crises or emotional problems, it is appropriate for a supervisor to provide that worker with feedback. The feedback should focus on the worker's job performance and how personal issues might be affecting that performance. It is also appropriate for a supervisor to suggest that the worker get some counseling to help resolve the problems that are affecting his behavior at work.

3. *Good Buddies Don't Evaluate.* This game usually entails a supervisor who feels uncomfortable holding a superior position over workers. In order to avoid having to sit down and evaluate workers' performances, the supervisor becomes friends, and, in effect, personal equals with workers. The problem here, once again, is that this game interferes with the purposes of supervision. Workers and supervisors fail to get constructive feedback from each other. Workers are cut off from having access to the supervisor's expertise and assumption of responsibility over them. A worker needs a supervisor, not a friend, to keep her on track.

4. *Of Course, I Know Much More Than You Do.* This is a game of one-upmanship. Either the supervisor or the worker consistently reveals that he knows much more than the other. Sometimes you might have people like this in your classes. You know, there is someone who sits in the front row and, with an exceptionally condescending tone, corrects the instructor at least twice each class period.

5. *Poor, Helpless, Little Old Me.* In this game the employee dependently leans on the supervisor for almost everything. In essence, the worker "plays dumb." She asks the supervisor to validate almost everything she does. In this way she doesn't have to do much thinking. She manipulates the supervisor into doing all of her thinking for her. She can also avoid responsibility for mistakes. In the event that she makes one, she can blame her supervisor because he "said it was OK" or "told [her] to do it that way."

(continued)

6. *Information is Power.* This game occurs when one or the other in the supervisory relationship withholds information. A worker can withhold information from a supervisor in order to avoid the supervisor's scrutiny. For example, a worker seriously edits the facts about a particular client case. He does so because he feels he should be doing more with the case. Omitting information keeps the supervisor in the dark concerning what the worker is not doing.

Likewise, a supervisor can keep information from an employee in order to maintain greater control over that employee. Consider a supervisor who keeps one worker from knowing that her colleagues have a considerably smaller caseload than she does. In effect, not telling her that she's doing more than her share keeps her doing it and getting things done for the supervisor.

7. *Labeling the Psychological Ploy.* This game requires a supervisor or worker who avoids salient issues by labeling them as some psychological ploy.

For example, a worker says, "I am very concerned about my client's alcohol problem. How do you think I should proceed?"

The supervisor responds, "It sounds as if you don't feel very confident in that area." In this way the supervisor both blames the worker for ignorance and avoids providing any concrete assistance.

8. *Pose Questions to Answer Questions.* As with "Labeling the Psychological Ploy," this game is used to sidetrack real issues. Instead of answering a question, a worker or supervisor responds with another question. This behavior, of course, throws the responsibility for answering a question back to the person who asked it in the first place. For example, a worker might ask a supervisor, "Can I take Friday afternoon off?" The supervisor responds, "What would happen if I let the whole unit off on Fridays? Who would be around to service clients?" This response avoids giving an answer. Instead, it places the responsibility for finding an answer on the worker.

cordkeeping. Keeping up-to-date records is frequently difficult. The pressure of ordinary business makes it hard to take time away from serving clients to maintain case records. However, recordkeeping is essential for accountability. You are accountable to your supervisor, and he or she, in turn, is accountable to higher levels of administration. If you fail to keep up with required recordkeeping, it will reflect badly on your supervisor. Additionally, your successor will have a tough time figuring out your cases if there are not records.

Plan Your Supervisory Agenda Ahead of Time

Most workers have a set time they talk with their supervisor. Use this time to the fullest. Think about the topics and ideas you want to discuss. List the questions you have. Make sure you cover the items on your list before you leave the session. If sufficient time is available, you might even give your supervisor a copy of your agenda beforehand so that he or she can think about the topics

prior to the meeting. However, be sensitive to your supervisor's reactions to this structured approach. Be careful not to be too aggressive or pushy. Coming on too strong is threatening to some supervisors.

Put Yourself in Your Supervisor's Shoes

Use empathy with your supervisor. She is an individual with her own feelings, interests, biases, and opinions. Think about both what she needs to know and what she needs to communicate to you. It is helpful to get to know your supervisor as well as possible. How might you best respond to her own needs and issues?

Display an Openness to Learning and Improving Yourself

Displaying an openness to learning means that you should be willing to accept criticism and to use it to improve your work. It also means you must be able to admit when you don't know something or even when you have made a mistake. This is often hard to do. It is difficult to admit to one's lacks or failings. However, the willingness to seek help is basic to leaning. Your supervisor should be considered a resource that you must be willing to use (that is, of course, if your supervisor is competent).

Demonstrate a Liking for Your Work

Major complainers and whiners are usually very unappealing to both supervisors and others. It is better to emphasize the positive aspects of your work, including those facets you especially like. Generally speaking, if you do not like your work, you should quit and pursue other opportunities. Continuing to hold a position that you find unsatisfying can lead to burnout and a diminished interest in fulfilling your helping role. (Chapter 15 discusses stress-management techniques for avoiding burnout in substantial depth.)

An illustration of this point comes to mind. Several years ago two probation and parole agents came to address an Introduction to Social Work class. Both had been in the corrections field for many years and had talked to other classes several years earlier. During the current talk they referred to their clients in derogatory terms, criticized their agency and agency colleagues, and displayed a high level of dislike for their work responsibilities in general.

By the end of the class, it was evident that both social workers had become burned out about their jobs. They were no longer operating within a social work value system. Following their departure the instructor had to spend some time undoing the negative impressions the speakers had left regarding what social work was all about. Of course, the instructor never again invited them back to the university, although they might have served as good examples for a class on stress and burnout.

Work Cooperatively with Other Staff

Much of social work requires teamwork (chapter 3 discusses teamwork more fully). Your supervisor will expect you to work well with other social workers and with professionals from other disciplines. Be sensitive to how your behavior affects others. Show respect for the competence and talents of your peers and coworkers. Be tolerant of what you see as their shortcomings. Try to see the world from their perspective and understand why they feel and act the way they do.

Give Your Supervisor Feedback

Supervisors can benefit from feedback as much as workers. Tactfully let your supervisor know what you like and dislike. If you have specific needs that your supervisor can appropriately fulfill, share them. Use the suggestions for giving feedback found earlier in the chapter.

Forewarn Your Supervisor about Problematic Situations

Supervisors should be alerted anytime a case becomes especially problematic. When you don't know about the implications of a particular course of action or how it might affect the agency, share this information with your supervisor. Get help. Don't wait until things have developed to crisis proportions before talking to your supervisor.

Learn Your Supervisor's Evaluation System

Ask your supervisor for the basis upon which you will be evaluated. It might be an evaluation form or a description of the evaluation process in the agency's policy manual. You job description can also help orient you to what you're supposed to be doing and accomplishing. Regardless, you should know far in advance what criteria your supervisor and agency will use to evaluate you. Hopefully, there will be no, or few, surprises during an evaluation meeting.

Evaluation systems may be formative, that is, ongoing. Such evaluations provide regular feedback, thereby allowing workers to make corrections as the need arises. Likewise, evaluation can be summative when they occur periodically. These evaluations tend to be more general in that they summarize progress and accomplishments over a longer, designated period of time such as a year or six months. Some agencies and supervisors use both formative and summative approaches in conjunction with each other.

Problems in Supervision

Thus far, we have tried to enhance your understanding of what supervision involves, including the supervisor's perspective. We have also provided some positive suggestions for helping your supervisor help you. In general, perhaps, we have painted a pretty rosy picture. However, it is important to remember that just as there is no perfect world, there is no perfect work environment. Likewise, there are no perfect supervisors. Complaints about supervisors are common. Sometimes they are valid; other times they are not.

There will be times when, despite how hard you try, you will be unable to get formal quality supervision. Highlight 2.11 illustrated a number of unproductive games that can be played in the supervisor/supervisee relationships. Other problems may also occur, including simple misunderstandings; supervisors' taking credit for your work; supervisory incompetence; problems with delegation; laziness; and inability to deal with conflict, among many others. Some of these are illustrated in highlight 2.12.

Simple Misunderstandings Between Supervisor and Supervisee

Because it is a communication-based process, supervision is subject to simple misunderstandings. For example, we've all probably had the experience of saying something to somebody and later that person insists he never heard what we know we said. Hearing without listening is amazingly common. We often use it to block out things we don't want to hear. Many people read the paper and watch television simultaneously. It is likely that they are not paying close attention to what's on television until they hear a word or phrase that triggers their attention. We even have a phrase for this, "tuning out."

Another common communication problem, discussed earlier in the chapter, is that words and phrases do not always mean the same thing to both sender and receiver. This occurs frequently in the supervisory relationship.

Consider a supervisor who summarizes his evaluation of a worker's performance by writing, "Dan does a pretty good job of completing his work on time." The supervisor intends this description to reflect very positively on Dan's performance. Dan, however, feels the term "pretty good" is negative and detracts substantially from a positive evaluation. Clearly, each person interprets the same words in a totally different way.

Many of us hear only what we want to hear. Children, for instance, often hear the parental "maybe" as a more definite "yes." Another child-related example of listening comes to mind: I was showing my father some pictures of a recent exotic vacation to the Costa Rican jungle while my nieces, three and five, and nephew, seven, had their eyes glued to the television screen watching *Return of the Jedi*. The three totally ignored what I had to say until my father asked, "What's that?" I replied, "Oh, that's a horde of army ants devouring a tarantula." Spontaneously, all three children jumped up and dashed over to view a picture of the huge spider's remains. After a quick glance, all three returned to the TV.

Selective listening can also occur during the supervisory process. Supervisors can be equivocal. That is, they can make confusing statements subject to various interpretations. Workers then may interpret these remarks either as encouraging or discouraging, depending upon what the workers want or expect to hear. The only way to eliminate this problem is to listen actively and then verify that your understanding of the message is accurate.

Supervisors Who Take Credit for Your Work

There are times when a supervisor might not give you the credit you think you deserve for your work or may take credit for what *you* have done. At such times, you may choose to use the suggestions for confrontation and assertiveness described earlier in the chapter to work toward a fair conclusion. However, some supervisors in some situations will take the credit for your work regardless of what you do or how tactfully assertive you are. This is unethical, but it can happen. Scenario A in highlight 2.12 presents such a situation.

So what do you do? By the nature of the supervisor/supervisee relationship, your supervisor will probably have more power than you have—that is, unless your mother owns the agency. You might first decide how important it is for you to get the credit that is due you. Was it more important that something was accomplished than that *you* accomplished it? In Scenario A, crucially

---

HIGHLIGHT 2.12

WHAT WOULD YOU DO?

The following scenarios are taken from actual supervisory experiences. Each involves real problems that could theoretically happen to you. In each case, think about how you would use the recommendations we have just discussed to pursue some type of resolution with each respective supervisor.

Scenario A:
Taking Your Credit

You are a social worker at a diagnostic and treatment center, in a large urban setting, for children with multiple developmental and physical disabilities. Your primary role involves helping parents cope with their child's disability, making referrals to appropriate resources, doing some family counseling, and interpreting the physicians' and therapists' findings and recommendations to parents in words the parents can understand.

The city abruptly cuts off funding for transportation to the center. Many of your parents are very poor and don't own vehicles. Most of the children have such extreme physical difficulties that city buses can't accommodate them.

After gathering facts, you call various local political leaders and share with them your serious concerns. Directly because of your efforts, the local city board chairperson sets up a meeting of the council to address and remedy this transportation issue. You are very proud of yourself because you feel you are primarily responsible for mobilizing this change.

You share the news with your supervisor. You indicate enthusiastically that you are planning to attend the meeting on the specified date. She responds by saying, "I don't think you need to attend this meeting. I''ll go instead." You emphasize how hard you've worked on this endeavor and that you would *really* like to attend. You suggest that you could both go.

She responds, "No, I don't think so. I'll go." You are devastated.

What would you do?

Scenario B:
The Communication Gap

You are a newly hired social worker for a unit of boys, ages eleven to thirteen, at a residential treatment center for youth with serious behavioral and emotional problems. Your responsibilities include counseling, group work, case management, some family counseling, and consultation with child care staff concerning your unit's behavioral programming. Two of the dozen boys in the unit have been causing you particular trouble. They are late for your weekly counseling sessions, sometimes skipping them altogether. When you do talk to them, they don't respond to your questions. Rather, they walk around the room, talk about how you don't know what you're doing, use pencils to pick holes in the furniture, and call you vulgar names.

You are at a loss regarding what to do with these two clients. You go into your weekly one-hour supervisory sessions and explain the situation to your supervisor. He makes a number of vague suggestions, such as videotaping some of your sessions, making home visits, and talking about the boys' behavior with them. By the end of your supervisory session, you feel you've gotten nowhere. You couldn't pin down any specific suggestions and still do not understand what you should do. You have difficulty understanding what your supervisor is saying. You can't "read" him. Sometimes when he makes a statement you don't know whether he expects you to laugh in response or take him seriously and say, "Oh, gee, that's too bad."

What would you do?

(*continued*)

HIGHLIGHT 2.12—(Continued)

Scenario C:
The Angry Response

You are a social worker at a health-care center (nursing home) who has a variety of clients diagnosed as "mentally ill." Every six months, a staffing is held at which social workers, nurses, therapists (speech, occupational, physical), physicians, psychologists, and psychiatrists summarize clients' progress and make recommendations. It is your job to run the staffing and write the summary.

You are new at your job and are not familiar with how things are run at this agency. You find that during the staffing, the psychiatrist is very verbal. You would even describe him as "pushy." You feel intimidated and uncomfortable asserting your own opinions, which are somewhat opposed to his. His advanced education, status, and self-confident demeanor make you feel that his points are probably more important and valid than yours.

After the staffing, your supervisor, who was also in attendance, takes you aside. His face is red and his voice has a deadly, steel-like calm in it. He berates you for letting the psychiatrist take over the staffing. He surprises and upsets you so that you do not hear many of the specific things he says. You just know that he is furious with you and that he has implied or stated that you are incompetent. He walks off in a huff.

What would you do?

Scenario D:
Sexual Harassment

You have the strong feeling that your supervisor, who is of the same gender as you, gives opposite gender supervisees preferential treatment. For instance, s/he acts friendlier and more casual with them, directs more comments and questions to them during meetings, and seems to give them preference for their vacation choices. You also have heard

they're getting higher raises when you feel your own work performance is at least as good as theirs, if not better.

What would you do?

Scenario E:
Problems with Delegation

You are a caseworker for a social services agency in a rural county. Your job includes a wide range of social work practice from investigating child abuse charges to working with families of truants to providing supplementary services to the elderly so that they can remain in their own homes. You have a heavy caseload, but feel very useful. In general, you really like your job.

The problem is that your supervisor insists on reading every letter and report you write before it goes out. You think this is a terribly time-consuming waste of effort. In many instances, it also delays your provision of service. Finally, you feel it's condescending and implies a lack of confidence in your professional abilities.

What would you do?

Scenario F: No Action

You are a social worker in a large urban community center serving multiple community needs. Services include counseling for emotional and behavior problems, provision of contraception, reactional activities for adults and youth, day care for children of working parents, meals for elderly citizens, some health care, and a variety of other services. Your job focuses primarily on counseling the center's clients who are referred to you for this purpose. You enjoy your job and are proud of being a professional social worker.

The problem is another social worker who has his office next door. He has a similar job, but is assigned a different caseload and a slightly different range of responsibilities. The bottom line is that you seriously question his professional competence.

You've observed him doing what you'd describe as "comic book therapy" with the children and adolescents on his caseload. In other words, his clients come in and select comic books from his vast collection instead of receiving any real form of counseling. He has boasted on several occasions that he went into social work only because he was offered a scholarship because he has a Spanish surname, he demonstrated the appropriate qualifications, and the program needed to increase its minority enrollment. He, by the way, openly admits his inability to speak Spanish and his lack of Hispanic ethnic identity.

One day you walk up to say hello to one of your clients whom you unexpectedly see reading something in the center's waiting room. You client, a fairly bright, articulate boy of thirteen places his hand over a portion of a picture in the book. You think to yourself how odd that is because his hand is placed over the rear of a horse. He does look surprised to see you. He remarks that the horse's long white mane is pretty. You observe that the mane reaches the

ground and extends along another foot. This also strikes you as peculiar. Finally, you ask him what the book is about. He sheepishly shows it to you. The picture depicts a castrated horse (hence, the elongated mane and tail due to hormonal changes). The book's title is *Washington Death Trips*. Among other items included in the book are pictures of dead babies in caskets, people who have butchered over five hundred chickens by hand for no reason, and various infamous murderers. You learn that your colleague lent your client this book.

You are furious. Not only does this colleague offend your professionalism and your professional ethics, he has also had the gall to interfere with your client. You immediately go to your supervisor, who is also his supervisor, and complain about the incident and your feelings. Your supervisor, a well-liked, easy-going, but knowledgeable and helpful person, hems and haws. You believe that your supervisor is afraid to confront your colleague.

What would you do?

---

needed transportation was restored. How important is it, really, that the worker responsible get the credit (even if the worker is you)?

If you as the worker do feel that receiving credit is very important, what would you do? Would you go to an administrator above your supervisor for help and risk your supervisor's wrath? Would you learn a lesson from the experience and keep the information from your supervisor the next time? Would you try to put it out of your mind and go on with your daily business? Would you start looking for another job? There really is no perfect answer. It would be your responsibility to identify your various options, weigh the pros and cons of each, and decide what to do.

Supervisory Incompetence

Some supervisors are simply incompetent. The Peter Principle, states that there is a tendency for employees to rise in an administrative hierarchy until they reach their level of incompetence. Theoretically and ideally, you should be able to go to your supervisor for help. What if you get a supervisor who does not have the necessary skills to do the job? The old saying that you can't squeeze blood out of a turnip comes to mind. If a supervisor does

not have the expertise, he can't share it with you. Scenario B in highlight 2.12 hints at this problem.

One suggestion for coping in this situation is to find others in the agency who can help you when you need it. This must be done tactfully, however. You should avoid threatening an incompetent supervisor by openly exposing his or her incompetence unless you want to suffer hostile retributions. You can seek support from his other supervisees and begin documenting his incompetence. However, this also places you in jeopardy if he should find out. It can be very difficult to win in such cases as power and usually administration are on your supervisor's side. You might just accept the situation and go on with your own business.

Laziness

Laziness on a supervisor's part is similar to incompetence in that either way you probably will not get the help you need. Laziness can be dealt with as you would deal with incompetence. You can try to talk assertively to your supervisor, seek other sources of help and information, form coalitions with other supervisory victims, ignore the issue, or quit. There may be more potential for improvement if the supervisor has the necessary competence, but just does not want to work hard. Incompetence and laziness can, of course, also exist in the same supervisor. Administrators over the lazy supervisor's head need to know about the situation. Therefore, think carefully before enabling the supervisor by doing his work for him or reminding him of agency deadlines.

Problems with Delegation

A primary administrative task for supervisors is mastering the art of delegation. Delegation means assigning responsibility or authority to others (*Webster's Ninth New Collegiate Dictionary*, 1991, p. 336). Sometimes supervisors have trouble delegating tasks to employees and operate under dynamics opposite to those of the lazy supervisor. Lazy supervisors try to avoid work. Non-delegating supervisors are often workaholics whose problem is that they don't trust anyone, including their own supervisees, to do the work well enough. Scenario E, in highlight 2.12, illustrates a delegation problem, in that the supervisor insists upon reading every single word the worker writes. In this case the worker's options include assertively confronting the supervisor about the problem, emphasizing the unnecessary costs in time and efficiency, learning to live with the situation, or getting another job. This particular scenario actually happened. According to the worker, the supervisor was driving him crazy. He couldn't take it anymore and got another job.

Inability to Deal with Conflict

We have already addressed the issue of conflict and shown how difficult it is for many people to deal with. This can also be true for supervisors. Highlight 2.12, scenario F, describes a situation in which a supervisor feels uncomfortable about confronting a supervisee, so he simply does not do so. If you cannot depend on help from your supervisor, you may have to address the conflict yourself by following the suggestions provided earlier. Another alternative, as always, is to ignore the issue and work on learning to live with it.

Postscript

In summary, life with supervisors will not always be ideal. We have mentioned only a few of the many issues

that can arise in the supervisor/supervisee relationship. When a problem occurs, all you can do is use your communication skills to your best advantage, identify the alternatives available to you, weigh the pros and cons of each, and decide on the course of action you feel will be most advantageous for you.

On the other hand, you may also have supervisors who will serve as primary mentors to you. A mentor is someone who encourages you to do your best, exposes you to new knowledge and ideas, and provides you with exciting opportunities to develop your skills and competence. Just as there are bad supervisors, there are truly excellent ones. This section has emphasized some potential negative experiences because they are so difficult to deal with. Good supervisors are wonderful.

Chapter Summary

This chapter emphasizes the significance of micro skills in the macro environment. Basic micro skills including eye contact, attentive listening, facial expressions, and body positioning are reviewed within macro contexts. A wide range of communication skills including simple encouragement, rephrasing, reflective responding, clarification, interpretation, providing information, emphasizing people's strengths, summarization, eliciting information, and the use of "Why?" are reexamined from a macro perspective.

Appropriate assertiveness in macro scenarios is explained. The assertiveness continuum, including nonassertiveness, assertiveness, and aggressiveness is examined. Advantages of assertiveness are proposed. Assertiveness training is briefly explained. The special relationship between women and assertiveness is identified.

Conflict and its resolution are explored. The pros and cons of conflict are evaluated. Personal styles of conflict are differentiated. Finally, seven steps for conflict resolution are proposed. The importance of communication throughout the conflict resolution process is emphasized.

The importance of working effectively with supervisors is stressed. Administrative, educational, and other functions of supervisors are recognized. Suggestions for using supervision effectively are provided. Potential supervisory problems are discussed.

CHAPTER THREE

Using Mezzo Skills in the Macro Environment

"Sure, I owe you one," said Gray Mfume to Jack Christiansen. Gray had just agreed to attend a community meeting on child abuse in Jack's place. Jack, who had announced his move to a new job in another community, had done many favors for Gray over the years and both were interested in the child welfare field. Jack had helped organize a community meeting to discuss what further steps might be taken to prevent child abuse, a topic of increasing concern in the city of Eagle Bluff following a series of shocking child abuse cases.

Jack had supervised the child welfare intake unit responsible for all initial investigations of child abuse in the county. His sudden departure would leave a void in Eagle Bluff. Additionally, Gray would really miss his friend and colleague.

The community meeting was to be held at the Morgan Neighborhood Center. It would involve representatives of various private and public agencies such as Lutheran Social Services, the local Department of Social Welfare, and interested citizens representing service clubs such as Kiwanis. Gray wasn't particularly worried about his role in the meeting since he was not responsible for organizing it. He would attend as a favor to Jack, but as a staff member at a home health-care agency with no responsibility for child abuse intervention, he felt somewhat removed from the subject.

When the meeting ended, however, Gray had agreed to help establish a Parents Anonymous chapter in Eagle Bluff. (Parents Anonymous is a private organization dedicated to helping child abusers help themselves. It is run by volunteers and uses group work principles to help members learn more effective parenting and coping skills.) At the time, he knew very little about what would be involved in this activity—planning meetings, networking among professionals, managing conflict, and eventually serving as a member of the Parents Anonymous advisory board. (The advisory board would help set policies, raise funds, and support the activities of the Parents Anonymous group.) The process of intervening in the community to establish a new service such as Parents Anonymous would require many skills for dealing with both task and treatment groups. (Task groups include such things as advisory boards, boards of directors, and committees. Treatment groups include support groups, such as Parents Anonymous, and therapy groups.) Addressing such a significant community problem with other interested, motivated community members would test Gray's skills both as a leader and as a facilitator.

Introduction

As Gray was to learn, creating change at the community level requires several mezzo level skills. This is because most of what gets accomplished at the macro level is done by groups or teams. Thus, being successful at changing organizations and communities requires understanding how teams and task groups work. It also requires a number of skills for participating in and leading groups and teams.

In this chapter we will begin by defining networking and describing how the knowledge and skills required for networking can support macro level interventions. We also will use networking as a springboard to talk in general about skills needed for working in and with teams. As mentioned above, much of the change that occurs at the organizational and community level occurs through the efforts of teams of people—professionals and citizens.

Planning and conducting meetings are also essential tasks for achieving large system change, but they are basically mezzo level skills. Anyone who has ever watched a committee or large group meeting may have been struck by the terminology used to get business accomplished. Motions, minutes, second, tabling, and amendments are all concepts drawn from what is called parliamentary procedure. Achieving goals in most groups requires a certain level of systematic organization. It requires procedures that allow tasks to be accomplished in an efficient and effective manner. It also necessitates a system for recording decisions. Because of their significance, skills to help groups make decisions using parliamentary procedure will be thoroughly explained.

Finally, the last portion of the chapter will cover the perennial problem of conflict. Managing conflict, particularly in groups, organizations, and communities is an important skill. Understanding the principles involved enhances your own potential for effective conflict management.

This chapter will:

- Define and discuss the role of networking at both mezzo and macro levels.
- Review the role of teamwork in agencies and identify some useful tips for functioning as an effective team member and leader.
- Describe some effective techniques for planning and conducting meetings.
- Examine the use of parliamentary procedure for transacting business in organizations and groups.
- Address the difficulty of coping with conflict, and provide some recommendations for effective conflict management.

Networking

Barker (1991) defines a network as "a formal or informal linkage of people or organizations that may share resources, skills, contacts, and knowledge with one another" (p. 155). As a social worker you will often hear the term networking and may wonder what it means. It can be confusing because networking really has two related but different meanings. According to Barker (1991) networking occurs when the social worker attempts to "enhance and develop the social linkages that might exist" among clients and others, such as family and friends. In this definition, networking helps connect clients to others who can help them. For example, reconnecting a homeless person with her family may help her begin a new life. Thus, networking can be an important means of helping individual clients.

However, networking "is also used by professionals to indicate the relationships they cultivate with other professionals to expedite action through the social system" (Barker, 1991, p. 155). These linkages may be between different professionals or between professionals and other groups, such as paraprofessionals, citizens, and others (Johnson, 1992). Networks create a synergistic (or multiplying) effect by using the power inherent in multiple agencies or people to help with a social work intervention. In networking the worker helps connect these individuals, groups, or organizations and combine their efforts to achieve ends not possible by any of the organizations or people working alone. For example, the case which started this chapter was an example of networking. Jack helped bring together all those concerned with the issue of child abuse to consider alternative methods for dealing with this problem. The follow-up work by Gray built upon this networking.

Importance of Networking

Why is networking important to social workers? Five basic reasons are described below.

Clients Benefit from Informal Helping Networks

First, research has shown that clients benefit from being part of informal helping networks (Gottlieb, 1983; Gourash, 1978). Few of us as individuals or organizations can exist without working with others. We are interdependent and we network to ensure that our needs can be met (Maguire, 1984). Networks help make individuals feel more confident of their ability to weather a personal storm and help reduce stress. Additionally, networks can usually act/react much more quickly than can formal agencies.

HIGHLIGHT 3.1

NETWORKING IN ACTION

Gray used his networking skills to help implement a Parents Anonymous group in Eagle Bluff. While his own agency was not involved in child-abuse-related services, his contacts in the community were quite extensive. The contacts he made on behalf of the PA group included:

1. Soliciting referrals from the local protective services division of the Department of Social Welfare
2. Persuading a church to provide a meeting location for the group

3. Soliciting donations from private donors and church groups
4. Obtaining television coverage of the existence of Parents Anonymous through a local station
5. Persuading a local private college to provide printing of advertising materials on the PA group

Only through the combined efforts of public agencies, private organizations, and individuals was the success of this project assured. Networking enhances the problem-solving ability of individual workers.

Networks Reach Out to Clients

Second, networks can reach clients who would otherwise not seek out services. Sometimes clients have concerns about being labeled crazy or sick, or being otherwise stigmatized.

Networks can provide help in a culturally sensitive way, essential when working in cross-cultural situations (Biegel, 1987). New immigrants, for example, can often overcome cultural barriers by connecting with others from their homeland who arrived earlier and have already settled in. A Hmong Mutual Assistance Association may provide services to Hmong refugees (immigrants from an area of Laos) without causing them the embarrassment that might be associated with other mainstream agencies. Carefully used, networks can sometimes reach clients who would not normally be served or seek services from formal agencies. Working through tribal organizations is often a more effective way to reach underserved Native American populations.

Gary (1978) notes that it is typical for many African Americans to seek help for personal problems from their informal networks. He says such networks may be composed of people known in "bars, barbershops, peer groups, gangs, and storefront churches" (p. 39). Gordon and Jones (1978) also point out that some social networks may operate in churches, social clubs, neighborhood associations, fraternal associations, and lodges while others are formed on street corners, in parks, and on porch steps. Both Malcolm X (1965) and Claude Brown (1965) describe in their autobiographies how these informal networks helped them cope with oppression and hostility by providing support and encouragement. Devore and Schlesinger (1987) also note that ethnic networks help "buffer stress" attributable to minority status (p. 274). They also help encourage minority clients to use available health-care resources and can augment mental-health services provided by formal agencies.

It is especially important to be aware of the networking roles played by churches since they are more and more frequently offering direct services. Specific services may include support groups for single individuals and adolescents, counseling, and renewal groups for married couples.

Networks are very important for certain classes of clients. People experiencing chronic mental illness often have a very small group of people in their network.

Because of the nature of their illness, most of their friends and family members cease to be ready resources. Some will drift away from the clients while others may be estranged because of the difficulty of interacting with the client. Expanding the size of their network is crucial to help this population manage their lives.

In rural areas fewer formal resources and services are available because of the lack of funding and/or because there are not enough clients with a specific problem to justify services. Networking is critical in these areas and often requires the worker to learn the names and identities of those providing various forms of care. This includes "welfare workers, grocers, barbers, insurance agents, ministers, civic leaders, school teachers, health department nurses, and county officials" to name a few (Hepworth & Larsen, 1993, p. 480). Knowing local resource people is important because there is often no central agency to which clients can be referred. Ideally, it is useful to know what kinds of services or resources are provided, by whom, for how long, what significance this help has for the recipient, and how the recipient perceives the help provided (Tracy, 1990; Whittaker & Garbarino, 1983). You can expand your networking capabilities in rural areas by asking those you already know to introduce you to some of their friends and associates. This is a useful way to build interest and involvement while expanding your own capacity as a networker.

Networks Assist Formal Resources

The third value of networks is that they augment the more formal resources provided by you, your agency, or other social service organizations. Informal networks may offer advice, information, support, feedback, and sometimes concrete resources such as money, clothes, or other tangibles. Of course, not all the people in our networks are helpful. Some people actually create stress in others, some are not available when we need them, and some are helpful only in certain kinds of situations. Think of those people you would want around you in a time of emotional crisis. Are there some individuals who would make matters worse? Perhaps there are others who cannot provide emotional support, but would gladly lend you money or a car if you needed it. Many clients have similar networks of informal helpers and resources whom they can turn to in times of difficulty.

HIGHLIGHT 3.2

NETWORKING FOR LATCHKEY KIDS

Grady Wray is a social worker at the Child Advocacy Council, a private social service dedicated to better serving the needs of poor children in Spring Harbor. She worries about the number of children who have no parental supervision after school and are at risk of becoming involved in drugs. These latchkey children care for themselves after school because their parents are still at work. Grady convenes a meeting of representatives of several organizations in the community, all of whom have a stake in services to children. All of the individuals invited are colleagues whom Grady considers to be within her own network of resources. Agencies represented include the YWCA, the Parent-Teacher Association, the Girl and Boy Scouts, and the Department of Human Services. The participants decide that, while each has some knowledge of the problem from the perspective of his or her own agency, they are not sufficiently clear about the scope of the problem they face. The group decides to undertake a needs assessment with a sample of elementary schools in Spring Harbor. (A needs assessment is a formal effort to identify specific problems and to define services not being provided in a community.) The needs assessment shows that, indeed, a serious problem exists. Literally hundreds of elementary school children are without supervision from the time school gets out until their parents get home from work.

Armed with this data, Grady's original network expands to include school administrators with an interest in addressing this problem. This larger group then begins to discuss options. Because of the cost of beginning a full-scale program and their lack of knowledge about what should be done, the administrators agree to try a time-limited project. Beginning the following fall semester, the school system will provide before- and after-school recreational child

Latchkey children care for themselves after school because their parents are still at work.

care at four strategically located schools. A year later, the success of the program encourages the system to expand the child-care facilities to all Spring Harbor schools. Eventually, over two thousand children participate. The program, offered to parents and children at modest cost, include recreational activities, snack time, and small group discussion sessions.

Other clients may need help in reviewing their own networks of friends.

Networks Help Navigate Through Formal Systems

The fourth major reason that networks are important is that expediting action through a social system is often necessary if clients are to get services to which they are entitled (Barker, 1991). Too often, bureaucracies and red tape prevent clients from getting what they need in a timely fashion. (Bureaucracies and red tape will be discussed much more thoroughly in chapter 4.)

Social workers have multiple opportunities to develop relationships with other social workers and with a myriad of professionals from various disciplines and agencies. The ability to build and maintain those relationships may be the key to helping clients negotiate the system and meet their goals. For example, a phone call to the right person, a recommendation to the appropriate individual, even an instruction to the client to be sure to mention your name to the other professional, may prove to be all that is needed in some situations.

The network-building usually occurs on a personal basis as you meet individual workers and professionals in other agencies. More formal efforts may be made when agency administrators or staff deliberately set about contacting each other to facilitate service delivery. Agency administrators commonly worry about unnecessary duplication of services coupled with gaps in service. Through networking with administrators from different agencies, one agency decided to end its home health-care services while other agencies expanded their efforts in this area. (Home health-care agencies provide a variety of medical and follow-up care for clients, many of whom would otherwise need to be hospitalized or placed in nursing homes.) This decision allowed the agency to refocus on unmet needs and to use scarce resources more wisely. Regular meetings between and among agency representatives also can lead to macro change efforts to close service gaps, change problematic laws and regulations (policies) or lobby for additional funding. An example of the use of networking to fill a service gap appears below.

Besides formal meetings such as the one in highlight 3.2, there are other ways to encourage and facilitate networking among social agencies. *Service fairs* provide opportunities for various agencies to set up tables with brochures and information about the agency's services. For example, all agencies serving the elderly might participate in an Elder Care Fair open to both professionals and the public. Possible participants include the local area agency on aging which is part of a national network of agencies serving the elderly (Barker, 1992), nursing homes, home health-care agencies, hospice agencies, hospitals, and organizations such as the American Association of Retired Persons (AARP) and the Retired Senior Volunteer Program. Yet another method of networking is through periodic meetings of a community welfare council where representatives of all community social agencies meet over lunch. At the meeting, new programs are summarized, new staff introduced, and ideas suggested for dealing with common problems. For example, several agencies dealing with an influx of gang activities in the community might decide that they could be more effective by sharing information. Cooperative endeavors can emerge out of this networking.

Clearly, social workers must understand the importance of networks and networking both for clients and for their own effectiveness as helpers and change agents. The absence of effective networking in a community can be embarrassing, waste resources, and hurt clients. For example, Biegel and Naparstek (1982) found that priests providing counseling services in the same area were not aware of each other's roles as counselors. In addition, mental health clinic administrators located less than one-half mile apart had never met, though they served the same neighborhood. Similarly, lay helpers were often unaware of other such helpers living nearby. Obviously, not knowing who else is providing services to your clients reduces your ability to be of assistance. You simply don't have all the information you need about the resources your clients could use. By getting to know other agencies in your community, you can become a resource for your own agency about other available community services.

Networks Help Workers Cope

A fifth value of networking cited by Sheafor, Horejsi, and Horejsi (1991) stresses the importance of networks in helping workers cope with their own professional stresses and strains. Your network of friends and professional colleagues can share your frustrations and discuss with you the difficult challenges all social workers face.

Thus networks can be used to satisfy client needs and to keep workers functioning better as well. In addition, networks for professionals can help us reality test and recognize problems in our own agencies. Too often we get so used to the way things work in our own agencies that we lose sight of better ways of doing things. Talking with colleagues from outside our agencies can help us recognize a larger reality of possibilities and potentials.

We often develop our own networks when we contact other agencies for clients. The individual workers with whom we collaborate can become a resource for us in our own lives. Of course, networks also allow us to develop referral sources and potential places for referring our own clients. They allow us to learn from others and to adapt their new ideas to our situations and agencies. Joint programs may emerge from such sharing of information.

Networks are not necessarily constant. This is to say that memberships in networks may change as needs dictate. Most important, however, networks are mutual. In other words, aided members must expect to help others in a similar fashion. This is one of the principles behind most self-help groups such as Alcoholics Anonymous. When working with clients in groups, we can help group members learn to rely on one another in times of need. We can also help group members think about how they might expand their own networks outside the group. Members of a group can sometimes meet at each other's homes or call each other periodically, thus serving as resources for one another. For example, members of a Parents Anonymous group offered to help each other out by babysitting during times when one member or another felt particularly stressed and in danger of losing control. Networks survive and thrive when that mutuality is observed. Helping each other out in times of need is an absolute necessity.

Types of Networks

Networks may be classified into categories based upon the *type of relationship* among members, the *degree of intimacy* members share, the *difficulty level* of the help needed, and the *size* of the network. For example, close, intimate relationships among members of a network are likely to provide different sorts of resources than those without such closeness. In these situations, people are so close to us and so important that they offer help with

no expectation of reciprocity. In less intimate networks, there is likely to be the expectation of a quid pro quo (getting something in return).

Sometimes the difficulty level of the help needed or the length of time help will be needed makes a difference. Asking to borrow a friend's car to drive to the store for soda is much less an imposition than asking for that same friend's car to take a five-week trip to Alaska.

Networks may be composed of individuals, small groups of people, self-help groups, or self-help organizations. Barker (1992) defines a self-help group as an organization that provides "mutual assistance for participants who share a common problem with which one or more of the participants have coped successfully." Examples include Alcoholics Anonymous, Parents Anonymous, and Parents Without Partners. Maguire (1984) notes that networking is the basis for self-help organizations because of the reliance on relationships to provide various resources in times of need.

Yet another kind of network springs up only from time to time as need arises. Members of a community may join together to raise funds for a family experiencing a major problem. Examples include loss of a home through fire, major medical expenses, or similar catastrophic events.

Inherently, networks are "based on one-to-one relationships" (Sheafor, Horejsi, & Horejsi, 1991, p. 431). Consequently they are idiosyncratic (unique to the person) and flexible. As mentioned earlier, they change as needed. Also, network members must be willing to play the same role with others if the mutuality is to survive. Interpersonal relationships help keep networks going over rough spots. You can't underestimate the role of personal liking and a good working relationship in helping a network prosper and survive (Maguire, 1984).

For example, Veronica was the program assistant (formerly called a secretary) for the Foreign Adoptions Unit of a large private adoption agency. Ja Dawn and Moustafa also worked in the unit, along with about a dozen other staff. Veronica was part of an informal information network comprised of a number of program assistants in the agency. She also had an exceptionally good relationship with Ja Dawn, whom Veronica brought into this informal network.

Many times Veronica would hear about major changes planned for the agency through her informal

In the aftermath of a recent Midwestern flood, volunteer service people such as this Red Cross worker helped assess damages in this disaster-stricken home. In this example of cooperative efforts, a social worker alerted the Red Cross to this man's plight.

network or fellow program assistants. She often learned this information before it reached her own supervisor through the agency's formal communication system. The informal communication channels which Veronica's network provided were much quicker than the more formal channels. (Formal channels will be discussed more thoroughly in chapter 4.)

The point here concerns the quality and significance of personal relationships in the networking process. Veronica and Ja Dawn had a good relationship. Thus, whenever Veronica heard some news, she would immediately share it with Ja Dawn. Of course, the relationship was reciprocal in that Ja Dawn would also help Veronica whenever possible. This included sharing information and assisting Veronica when things got too hectic in the agency. Other staff, such as Moustafa, never became part of the network because his actions toward Ja Dawn were less helpful and sensitive. His tendency to try to read the mail on Ja Dawn's desk and the fact that he treated her like a lowly servant precluded his ever being invited into the network.

Problems in Using Networks

A common source of difficulty arises when professionals interact with informal networks. Too often, professionals do not value the contributions of informal networks. Rather than encourage their existence, they ignore or otherwise put down these networks. The risk that professionals will downplay the contributions of others is always present. It is a given that informal networks lack the ethical principles, professional training, and community sanction governing the social work role. Their contributions, however, more than match those of the formal systems in duration, intensity, and quantity.

It is much more appropriate for the social worker to view the client's network as an ally in the helping process. It may even make sense to recruit others to become part of the helping effort. The Dial family is a good example. When Mr. Dial died suddenly in a mine cave-in, family members turned to Mr. Dial's son-in-law for help in handling funeral arrangements, dealing with the estate, and providing emotional support. Alicia Hurt, the hospital social worker who initially helped Mrs. Dial, noted that John Dial, the couple's son was never mentioned as a possible source of assistance despite the fact that he lived only a few minutes away from his mother. Alicia encouraged Mrs. Dial to call her son and involve him in making some of the many decisions needed at this most difficult time. By reaching out to broaden Mrs. Dial's network, Alicia gave the client an additional resource and reduced the need to rely on the son-in-law who lived in another city. It also helped rebuild Mrs. Dial's confidence in her own son and strengthened their relationship.

When working with a client's informal network, it is also important to avoid taking such an active leadership role that the client feels incompetent. The social work role should be to help marshal the resources needed by the client, with the client taking the lead whenever possible. This is not an easy task and is especially hard for some new professionals who don't yet have the maturity to allow others to lead or who are threatened by non-professionals.

Potential problems can also occur within formal networks themselves. As we have seen, networks can be strengthened by positive relationships among members. The absence of positive relationships can, conversely, reduce the network's effectiveness. For example, some agencies or workers may see themselves as having higher status than others. In a recent natural disaster, some social workers declined to help because the assistance clients needed, which included locating housing, food, and clothing, was "beneath them." These workers, who saw themselves as therapists, were willing to offer individual and family therapy, but did not feel they should simply help someone find a place to sleep.

Another problem which hinders formal networks is failure to share information with other network members. Mike Clover, a social worker educator, was asked to testify at a legislative hearing on a proposed social work licensing law. The law would require licensing of both BSWs and MSWs and was supported by a large network of social workers in the state. Mike did not inform key members of the network that he did not support licensing BSWs. In the middle of his testimony he responded to a question from a legislator by saying, "Well, if that's a problem, why not just license MSWs?" His failure to share information (namely, his position on licensing BSWs) caught the licensing network members off guard and threatened their progress in getting social workers licensed in the state.

Finally, networks composed of representatives of different agencies can disintegrate when those agencies do not support the network's activities (Johnson, 1992). The State Division of Aging never sent a representative to the meetings of a coalition (another type of network) trying to get additional funding for a foster grandparent program. The foster grandparent program was designed to get the elderly involved as substitute grandparents for children who had no grandparents of their own. The Division of Aging did not consider this program to have a high enough priority and refused to allow their workers to participate in the coalition. Overcoming these obstacles requires consistent effort over time. Johnson (1992) suggest it is important to recognize and acknowledge the mutual interests of different agencies and resources. A good first step, for example, might be to point out that five different agencies in one community are all interested in helping the homeless. This can help them recognize their similar goals and values. In the example above, even though a private agency would have operated the foster grandparent program, the program was designed to help the elderly. Assisting the elderly was also the goal of the Division of Aging. Keeping their mutual goals in mind could have resulted in a more effective effort to get additional funding for the foster grandparent program.

Another way to help networks is to provide various avenues of communication (e.g., face-to-face talks, newsletters, memoranda) to bridge the communication gaps. When cooperative opportunities present themselves, serving as a cheerleader and booster for the activity may help ensure equal commitment from others. Sometimes this is more easily done than at other times. Recent floods in the Midwest and hurricanes in the South have brought people and organizations together to help those most affected by the disaster. Cooperative efforts were encouraged by celebrities and coordinated by existing agencies. They involved thousands of volunteers and staff from many different agencies. On a more local level, efforts to hold fundraisers for victims of medical emergencies, fires, and similar calamities show the capacity for a community to cooperate in seeking specific benefits. The potential synergy (multiplying of effect) available when professionals and informal networks collaborate is enormous.

Worker Roles in Networking

As noted above social workers may be involved with networks from many different angles. We may serve as a "clearinghouse" (Maguire, 1984, p. 203) for self-help organizations. Knowing which organizations provide which services to which groups is essential for making effective referrals or for finding a common ground for working on larger macro issues. Social workers may also help start a network (as did Gray Mfume to combat child abuse, described earlier in this chapter). Maguire's (1984) list of possible roles for a worker in assisting a self-help network appears in highlight 3.3.

Networking is an important mezzo level skill because it both ensures clients receive needed assistance and provides a means to address larger problems in the community. It is a bridge skill in that it is useful in working with individual clients (e.g., by referring them to a self-help group), addressing needs of groups of clients (e.g., helping existing networks flourish and grow), and meeting needs at the community level (e.g., establishing new groups and networks). It is also important in helping us survive as social workers and improve the quality of the services we provide. Also it increases the repertoire of services available to those we serve.

While we have stressed the role of working with

groups so far, it is important to understand that micro level interventions are important to networking. For example, strong interpersonal relationships can help keep networks going over rough spots, just as happens in couples and families. The knowledge gained from tending and maintaining networks also can prove useful at the macro level. When major opportunities to get positive changes appear (or when crises threaten existing programs) it is easiest to assemble those who already have a vested stake in the outcome. By your knowledge of the community and its agencies, you will be in a stronger position to help in this process. Knowing that there are five agencies in the community serving the homeless makes it much easier when you discover that state grants are available to coordinate services to this population. If you were unaware of the existence of these agencies you might miss an excellent opportunity to improve services to the homeless.

Working in and with Teams

As a social worker you will have multiple opportunities to participate as a member of a team. In many settings social workers practice routinely as members of teams. *Interdisciplinary teams* are common in settings in which service to the client requires the expertise of multiple disciplines (for example, psychology, social work, nursing). This is often the case in hospitals and residen-

tial treatment facilities. In other situations the team includes only social workers, each responsible for overseeing some aspect of the client's case plan. A county social service department might assign some social workers to work with children in foster care while others provide service to the children's parents.

In other macro situations you will be invited to serve as a team member grappling with larger issues. For example, you may serve on an agency board of directors or advisory committee. You may be part of a team or task force charged with managing the problems caused when a large employer shuts down its factory in your community. These offer you excellent opportunities to have an impact on the larger environment.

Despite the various factors that can affect teams (membership, size, tasks), certain common elements characterize effectively functioning teams. Teams exist to work on identified problems. The problem may be gang violence, drug dealing in a community, or improving services to the elderly. To be effective in solving those problem, all teams require clear roles and accountability for the work of each member. They also need an effective communication system. Finally, all teams will benefit from an emphasis on fact-based judgments. This means that the team's decisions rest on facts, not on the whims or desires of individual members (Larson & LaFasto, 1989). While these features are important for all teams, the most effective teams exhibit still other characteristics. These include clear goals, structure and membership tied to goals, commitment of all members, a collaborative climate, and standards of excellence. They also require external support and recognition and principled leadership. In this section we will expand on the characteristics of effective teams and try to identify some ways in which you can improve your competence as a team member.

Characteristics of Effective Teams

Larson and LaFasto (1989) have studied effective teams in a variety of settings. Their research suggests that effective teams share at least nine common characteristics. These nine factors appear to operate whether the team functions in a human-service situation or in a business. Clearly, certain factors will be more important in some settings than in others.

Clear Goals

It has been said that if you don't know where you're going, you'll never know if you get there. This is certainly true of effective teams. All members of the group must understand the purpose and goals of the group. Clarity of goals, however, is not sufficient. The goals must be considered worthwhile. Each member must believe that what the team is attempting to do is desirable.

Structure and Membership Tied to Goals

Just as agencies organize in different ways depending upon their goals, so teams must be structured in ways that help goal achievement. If the goal is to help a community solve a massive drug problem in its downtown area, a problem-solving team will probably be required. Problem-solving teams are composed of people who trust one another and can stay focused on the issues of importance.

Another structure is the creative team. Creative teams are to come up with a variety of possible products or ideas and need the autonomy to consider alternatives. Rigid systems may thwart rather than support creativity. These teams function best with a minimum of supervision and rules.

Creative teams also need members who are self-starters and don't have to rely on others for their ideas.

If you can think of a friend who always seems to come up with interesting ideas, you probably know a prospective member of a creative team.

A third structure is the tactical team (Larsen & LaFasto, 1989). Tactical teams are brought in to carry out a plan. For example, a tactical team might be brought in to help a community deal with a natural disaster. The team members might have expertise in areas such as helping trauma victims and developing community programs to cope with future disasters. Disaster teams require clarity with respect to their goals, roles, and tasks. The importance of thinking clearly about team structure should be obvious when we recognize how easy it would be to have the wrong type of team on a job. Consider a team of social workers representing five different agencies. Their charge is to find ways for their agencies to collaborate to provide better service to clients. All members were chosen because of their creativity and wealth of ideas. In their agencies they often recommended changing this or that to make the organization function better. They also tended to be critical and likely to challenge accepted ways of doing things. Each of these characteristics is helpful when the goal is to come up with new and creative ideas for agency-to-agency collaboration.

At the conclusion of their work, the team recommends a new joint system of providing service to multiproblem families. The new system would have a team approach whereby all members of the team would work collaboratively. The agency directors, believing that the new model could be very effective, decide to assign the workers who designed the system to the team responsible for implementing the system.

By now you can see where this is leading. Because creative teams and tactical teams require different structures and people, assigning the same people to both types of team is not likely to work. People who are highly creative and individualistic may not be as effective when the task is to operate a program on a regular basis. They may even find the highly directive nature of their new tasks at odds with their creative orientation. The creative team members simply get bored with the system's implementation and see it as drudgery. Of course, creative teams may also come up with a plan that is difficult to operate because it is not practical. Therefore a team comprised of a combination of creative and tactical members may be most effective.

In short, it is important to think carefully about

team goals and then select the structure that will best accomplish them. It is also important to choose people who have the technical competence and the necessary personal attributes to do the job. Some people work well with others and can submerge their individuality to reach group goals. Others are equally competent from a technical standpoint, but are more difficult to work with. Each has a place, but not necessarily on the same team.

Commitment of All Members

Effective teams are likely to have members who display a team spirit. This means they identify with the group and look forward to participating in team endeavors. Each member commits to the team and expects other members to be similarly committed. Contrast this to a group whose members do not enjoy working with one another, avoid volunteering to do group tasks, and generally act as though they are the only ones on the team with good ideas.

Collaborative Climate

The collaborative climate in well-functioning teams is notable for the high degree of trust felt by individual members. Part of this trust rests upon consistent behavioral expectations. In other words, members usually know how the other members will act or think. This gives them confidence in the others because member behavior becomes predictable.

Members can be honest and open in their discussions with other members and will respect the contributions of other members. Compton and Galaway (1989) stress the importance of accepting and validating the abilities and competence of other members of the team. Collaboration breaks down when social workers begin to believe that they are more effective than other team members. Attitudes such as "He's a nurse. What does he know about case management?" are going to cause problems.

Collaboration is also threatened when members get territorial. Territorial members start by drawing an imaginary line in the sand and saying, "I do this and no else on the team can handle this area except me." As you can imagine, both situations will lead to problems. It is easy to get into win-lose situations and hard to get out of them, so it is best to avoid them entirely. (Win-lose

situations are those in which one party clearly wins while the other clearly loses. It often causes anger and dissatisfaction in the losing party.) Believing that each member can make an important contribution is essential as is mutual respect. It is permissible and even healthy to allow disagreements to surface because it is important to have as many people as possible support the final decision.

On the other hand, *groupthink* is always a risk. (Janis, 1982). In groupthink situations, members do not do an effective job of problem solving or analyzing alternatives. Instead, they simply go along with what they perceive to be the sentiments of the majority. Groupthink occurs when too much emphasis rests on collaboration and conformity and not enough attention is given to thinking critically about alternatives. Members become too concerned with maintaining the "we" feeling and submerge their hesitations and concerns rather than risk disagreeing with their peers. Encouraging critical thinking is important even while striving to maintain a climate of collaboration. Critical thinking involves challenging assumptions, verifying facts, questioning opinions not supported by data, and being willing to consider ideas that others have rejected.

Standards of Excellence

Most effective teams have agreed upon standards of excellence for which they strive. A standard of excellence is a measure of the value or worth of an action. For example, an agency I once worked with always had workers who were outgoing, personable, and friendly. It did not seem to matter who they hired, because all members seemed committed to providing a warm, friendly atmosphere for clients. Not only did they recruit members who had these characteristics, but they believed that reaching this standard was so important that they would exert various pressures to maintain it. The pressure might be exerted by individual members, the team leader, or the team as a whole. It could also include agreed-upon consequences for those who do not meet the standard.

Sometimes the team is subjected to outside pressure to maintain standards. This might occur when an agency administrator raises questions about why the interdisciplinary team is not responding as rapidly to case referrals as was typical in the past. The agency had always prided itself on responding to referrals within twenty-four hours of receiving them. Now the average time has become seventy-two hours. The standard of excellence has not been maintained.

External Support and Recognition

We have seen that members of effective teams see themselves as a "team." In addition, many effective teams are perceived by people outside the team as somehow special. The team may be recognized for its special expertise and may receive external praise and support for its actions. For example, a community appoints a special team to work with employees who have lost their jobs due to plant closings. This team receives high praise from the news media and other groups in the community because it helps employees get other jobs or take college and vocational courses to develop new skills. The team's success in this endeavor is respected in the community. This external reward strengthens group cohesion and reinforces the special nature of the team.

Principled Leadership

Principled leadership gives a consistent message about the role of the team. It gives members the freedom to take risks in pursuit of the standard of excellence. Ideally, leaders can suppress their need to showcase their own personal accomplishments. Instead, the leader focuses on the accomplishment of other members. In your career as a social worker, you will have many opportunities to work with various types of teams. Many will be effective and will share the characteristics Larson and LaFasto (1989) describe. Others will be effective, but share only a portion of the features characterizing effective teams. Some teams will be ineffective because they lack many or most of the characteristics described above. As a member and potential team or group leader, it is important that you know what makes a team effective. Your contributions can help the team reach its goal.

Planning and Conducting Meetings

From the prior discussions of networking and teamwork, it may appear that social workers spend a fair amount of time in meetings. This is often the case. Social workers do spend time in team meetings, groups, staff meetings, and community meetings. Some of this time is wasted because designated leaders run the meetings ineffectively. All of us have been in poorly run meetings that seemed to lack purpose, direction, or a sense of closure. People talked about issues that were of no concern to anyone else there and sometimes monopolized the discussion *ad nauseam*. A handful of people dominated the discussion, or conflict got out of hand and became threateningly personal. These problems often arise in meetings. Despite the potential for problems, there are many ways to make meetings efficient and productive. Some helpful techniques are suggested below.

Plan Ahead

Preparation for meetings is critical. Before planning a meeting you should always clarify its purpose and identify objectives to be achieved in the meeting. Activities in the planning stages include identifying the participants, selecting a time and place for the meeting, providing participants with an agenda, and arranging the physical environment (setting up chairs, locating a microphone and a flip chart or blackboard, if needed). Think ahead about possible follow-up meetings and consider the need for formal reports (including their potential authors) (Sheafor, Horejsi, & Horejsi, 1991).

Clarify Purpose and Establish Objectives

The meeting's purpose should be clear both to you and to those you invite to participate. Is the purpose to plan a new service, carry out a project, or discuss common problems experienced by group members? Meetings can have many ends. They can be used to organize people, share information, or resolve differences. Is this to be a single meeting or merely the first of several meetings that will occur over the next few months? What are the meeting objectives? Do you hope to identify twelve new couples for possible inclusion in the new couples' communication course your agency is offering? Is the group expected to select from a list of candidates the person who will become the supervisor for the court services unit? Will you finish the meeting with a new set of policies and procedures for handling referrals from the intake to the ongoing services unit? Clarify and specify the meeting's desired goals before the meeting begins.

Select Participants

Sometimes you have little control over who attends a given meeting. If it is a meeting requiring agency representation, the agencies themselves will decide who represents them. Other times you will call a meeting and invite people to participate. Always include participants with a mixture of capabilities. Invite individuals who are knowledgeable about the topic under discussion. Ignorance does not produce good outcomes. Likewise, include members committed to the outcome of the meeting and capable of carrying out their responsibilities. A good mix of vocal and reserved members is important in order to balance the two extremes. On the one hand, some members may talk incessantly but not listen. On the other, participants may be so quiet that no discussion is generated.

Depending upon the situation, you may need to consider whether attendees will need transportation, child care arrangements, or other services to assist them in their participation. This may be a consideration concerning who you invite, especially if you are unable to provide these necessary services. Before you can hold a successful meeting, you must have participants who show up.

Select a Time and Place

Always give some thought to the meeting's *date* and *time*. Otherwise, well planned meetings can become flops. Don't hold the meeting on a religious holy day. Also consider participants' personal schedules: Early morning meetings are difficult for anyone responsible for getting children off to school or day care, and for those who have to travel long distances.

Sometimes even your best efforts can go wrong. I once scheduled a meeting at a national professional social work conference, unaware that, at exactly the same time the Pope was speaking across town. Not surprisingly, the Pope won this contest. Hardly anyone attended my meeting.

Whenever possible, preschedule regular meetings by setting your meeting times in advance so people can plan their schedules around them. This increases the likelihood that attendance will be high and lets people know you respect their time. Send a memo or notice to participants as early as possible, even weeks in advance, to assist group members in planning their own schedules.

Don't hold meetings and eat simultaneously. Trying to conduct meetings over meals is often not productive. Most people find it difficult to concentrate on eating, talking, listening, and thinking all at once. Either eat first and get on with business, or schedule the meal to follow your work session. This may serve as a positive reinforcer for completing the work on time, since people will look forward to finishing the task and eating.

Consider meetings location carefully. Hold meetings in meeting rooms—not in your office. The meeting's setting is very important. Will the meeting location offend or put off anyone who might like to come? For example, if you were planning a meeting of two rival street gangs, you would hold it at a neutral site rather than in the territory of either of the gangs.

Hold meetings in locations that simplify accomplishment of group business. Is adequate parking available? Will people be readily able to find the meeting site? Did you include a map if needed? Is the room large enough to accommodate participants? Is ventilation adequate? Are the chairs comfortable and a table available? Do you need a microphone, blackboard, flip chart, and so on?

Additionally, consider the seating arrangements and overall room layout. Should people sit around a table, on chairs in a circle, or in theater style? The purpose of the meeting should determine the arrangements. For example, a round table facilitates discussion by all participants. Likewise, a lecture podium at the front of a room facing rows of chairs facilitates a lecture format in which one individual at a time speaks to the audience.

Prepare an Agenda

An agenda is a list of topics to be addressed at a meeting in some sort of prioritized order. The agenda lists the time and place of the meeting and sometimes those who are invited to participate. Retain extra copies of the agenda for those who do not bring their own copy to the meeting. Highlight 3.4 provides a sample agenda.

HIGHLIGHT 3.4

EXAMPLE OF AN AGENDA

Agenda
Community Welfare Council
January 21, 1996
Red Cross Building, Room 102
6:00 pm

1. Approval of minutes of December 20, 1995, meeting
2. Treasurer's report
3. Announcements
4. Preliminary discussion of social work month celebration (March)
5. Discussion/action on by-law revisions
6. Approval of budget for 1996
7. Old business
8. New business
9. Adjournment

Note that the agenda's list of topics is usually brief and concise. Lengthy explanations concerning how the topics will be addressed are inappropriate. The agenda simply lists general topics to be covered at the prescribed meeting. Other agendas may identify the nature of each topic, that is, whether it is an item for information only or requires action by the group.

Distribute printed matter before the meeting. Don't expect meeting participants to read and understand lengthy written material handed out at the start of a meeting. Send this material in advance with the agenda so attendees know in what order this material will be addressed. The most important topics should appear near the middle of the agenda when people are most attentive and least important items at the end. The first portion of the agenda can be devoted to approval of minutes from the previous meeting and minor items that require little discussion. Sometimes it is possible to estimate the amount of time a discussion item will take in order to determine how many items the agenda should have. Agenda items usually fall into the following categories: announcements (general information of interest to members); decision items (topics requiring

the group to arrive at a decision); and discussion items (items requiring deliberation, but no action). It is often best to handle them in this order for several reasons. First, announcements may be relevant to discussion of items placed later on the agenda. Therefore, the members should hear this information early in the meeting. Decision items require much harder work in most groups and should be placed at the point when members have the most energy. Discussion items can be handled at the end since the group does not need to reach a decisions.)

Start Meetings on Time

Don't wait for stragglers. If you set the time for the meeting at 3:00 P.M., start promptly at 3:00 P.M. Doing this rewards those who are on time and teaches latecomers that your are serious about the schedule. Only the hardcore continue to arrive later after they learn that your meetings start on time. If you are a member of a group instead of its leader, you can still suggest that the leader begin the meeting as scheduled. This can modify their behavior to become more prompt as well. In some groups those who arrive late are noted in the minutes—an embarrassment they usually want to avoid. Sometimes there is merit in allowing a brief get-together time before the meeting, perhaps with coffee and cookies, so people can relax a bit. Either way, the meeting should begin as scheduled.

Introduce participants briefly (perhaps restricting these to name and agency), reexplain the purpose of the meeting, hand out any additional material, initiate the first topic on the agenda for discussion and, if appropriate, encourage action.

State Ending Time at the Start

Right at the beginning of the meeting, let people know when it will end. Stick to that time. Don't allow meetings to go on endlessly. Conversely, don't be afraid to end a meeting early if your work is done. Some of the most productive meetings dwindle off to oblivion and lack of conclusion because no one suggests ending them when the real business is concluded.

Let People Know How Much of Your Time They Can Have

If you are meeting with clients, colleagues, or others, let them know in advance what your schedule is. For example, specify that you have twenty minutes, forty-five minutes, or even an hour and a half. This way they are more likely to stay on task. It also makes it easier when you must conclude the meeting since they know you have somewhere else to go.

Keep the Group on Target

Your role in a group may vary considerably. For the most part, we are assuming here that you play a leadership role. As the leader you must start the discussion and keep it going, clarify and summarize what others have said, and provide suggestions for new ways of thinking about or carrying out ideas.

Part of your task is to keep the group moving and on target—focused on goals and operating within time constraints (Burghardt, 1982). Encourage and allow all

members to speak and ensure that quiet members are drawn out by making such comments as, "Don, we haven't heard your perspective on this. What do you think?" or "Ann, I know this issue has been especially problematic for your agency—any reactions to the suggestions we've heard so far?"

Promotion of harmony is important, but again not at the expense of thinking critically about the options. For example, some group leaders try to maintain harmony by stifling disagreements or differences of opinion. Often, it is better to hear all points of view and then discuss the best one instead of trying to create a false sense of harmony.

You might also make a point of seeking out quiet members and encouraging them to participate. Another task of the leader is to test for agreement whenever apparent compromises appear to be achieved. Don't assume that everyone understands the proposed compromise. You also can't assume that quiet members agree with the compromise simply because they have not expressed opposition. For example, you might say something like, "Bob, I know you have reservations about this plan. Are you comfortable enough with what is being suggested?" This gives Bob an opportunity either to show support for the plan or to voice hesitation and concerns.

Use humor to relax the group or to break the tension. Self-depreciating humor which pokes fun at yourself is often acceptable. Making fun of other members is not.

It is essential to avoid personal attacks and not let others engage in them. It is one thing to criticize or challenge an assumption or proposed solution. This is part of what critical thinking is all about. Making negative comments about other members or questioning their motives, however, only makes the situation worse. It invariably produces additional tension in the group. Generally speaking we wish to keep tension low because we want an environment where people feel safe to participate (Sheafor, Horejsi, & Horejsi, 1991).

Sometimes we may need to interrupt a meeting participant who talks too much. Those who hog the discussion can discourage others from participating. Long-winded speeches may be interrupted by a comment such as, "Mickie, I think we need to see if there are other points of view on this" or, "We need to bring closure on this topic, Minnie, unless you're buying us all supper." We also need to watch for silence, especially when it masks anger or other strong feelings. People who disagree wholeheartedly may be uncomfortable discussing it without the leader making it clear that differences of opinion are sought. At the same time, if an idea seems a bit off target, don't shoot it down immediately or let others do so. Creative ideas sometimes take getting used to. Give them a chance to be aired and considered. Also call on members with higher status last so that their opinions do not intimidate members with lower status who may disagree.

Staying on task and ensuring that all items get covered in sufficient depth is important. Sometimes you can structure this process by suggesting how members might handle certain topics. For example, you can identify items on which there is already unanimity and approve them together. This is sometimes called a *consent agenda*. Complex items such as approval of a lengthy document might be best done *ad seriatim* (item by item) rather than by letting people jump from one section to another. Periodically summarize the areas of agreement and sum up when decisions have been made. Avoid discussing irrelevant topics or rehashing previous decisions. If new topics are brought up, it is often better to place them on future agendas. This practice avoids last minute surprises or maneuvers, and helps the group avoid discussion of a topic for which some members are unprepared. If appropriate, a new business item can be referred to a committee. For example, a suggestion that the group hold a raffle might be referred to the finance committee rather than discussed in the larger group. Keep necessary reports brief. Longer reports should be submitted in written form and distributed to members in advance of the meeting. When oral reports are needed, ask for succinctness and place a time limit on each report. When you have set such a limit, stick to it assiduously.

Sometimes members try to bring premature closure to a meeting to avoid dealing with a sensitive topic. In other situations, members rush to a decision without giving sufficient attention to an important item. In both situations it is better to remind members that the topic needs their full involvement and discussion. It may also be necessary to encourage the group to consider other alternatives. For example, in a recent hiring situation, a search committee was about to recommend that two candidates be invited to come for interviews. Though the group appeared unanimous in selecting these two candidates, the group leader stated his concern that both

the candidates were male and that the positions for which the applicants were applying had previously been held by two women. The group leader reminded the search committee that if both candidates were hired, the unit composition would have changed from 50 percent male and 50 percent female to 75 percent male and 25 percent female. After considering the implications of this decision, the search committee decided to invite additional women candidates who met the position qualifications.

This is a tough job. Tropman, Johnson, and Tropman (1992) summarize the tasks by noting, ''The chairperson must be able to lead and push, set limits, increase participation, and resolve differences. All these tasks must be accomplished in a dignified manner'' so that the leader is always perceived as fair, impartial, and interested in all the members (p.5).

End the Meeting on Time

We noted earlier that meetings should be concluded on time. However, there are times when a leader should suggest ending a meeting. Jay's (1984) suggestions for when a meeting should be ended appear in highlight 3.5 on page 108.

Whenever possible, end a meeting on a high note. Summarize accomplishment, point to the good efforts of the group or of individual members, and discuss what steps will be taken to follow up on the group's decisions. Make sure that any action to occur between meetings is assigned to someone.

Plan for Follow-Up Meetings

You may have already planned for additional meetings. Perhaps you have set a schedule of meetings for the next few weeks or months. If so, the important task now is to get the minutes (official record of actions taken by the group) to the participants. Minutes should show when and where the meeting was held, who was present, and the name of the chairperson. It should list the agenda items discussed, record decisions made, and list those who have tasks to do. The ending of the meeting should be included with advance notice of the next meeting, if known.

The minutes should be approved by the group at the start of the next meeting. The process of planning

---

HIGHLIGHT 3.5

ENDING MEETINGS

Meetings should be ended whenever any of the following is evident:

1. *More facts are required.*
   If a decision cannot be made without certain facts, the meeting should be ended or the group should move on to other agenda items that can be handled.
2. *The group needs the input of people not present.*
   This may occur when it becomes apparent that others not present will have significant roles to play in carrying out the group's plan. Sometimes the person was invited to the group but could not attend. Other times it becomes evident during the meeting that others should be asked to participate in the discussion.
3. *Members need more time to talk to others.*
   Some issues are so controversial that those present don't want to make a decision without consulting others. Agency representatives, for example, may wish to talk the matter over with their administrators or supervisors before making a decision.
4. *Events may change the decision in the immediate future.*
   If a future event (such as a court decision, funding decision, or similar event) will significantly affect the decision the group is trying to reach, it may be best to end the discussion and wait for the event to occur.

5. *There is not enough time to deal with the topic adequately.*
   Occasionally, we simply run out of time to discuss a subject in sufficient depth or to hear all opinions on a topic. It is better to end the meeting than to run overtime or to make a premature decision.
6. *A subgroup can handle this more easily than the entire group can.*
   An example of this is the decision by a board of directors to refer a discussion on the budget back to the budget committee and ask them to take another look at cutting costs. The difficulty of large groups handling certain topics is evident. Perhaps the issue is rewriting the bylaws of the organization. It is often difficult for a large group to write any document. Usually the task is given to a smaller group to work on first. Sometimes the decision requires input from those with greater knowledge about a specific topic (like the budget committee).
7. *A decision has been reached.*
   Clearly, when the group reaches a decision, the meeting should be ended (or another agenda item addressed). Reaching a decision is the most common reason for ending a meeting. Generally groups should not end a meeting to avoid dealing with controversial topics, because the decision is difficult, or because the group's decision might be unpopular.

---

the next meeting then starts over, as described above. Of course, involved participants and meeting location may or may not remain the same. Highlight 3.6 provides a brief sample of minutes of a meeting.

Note that the minutes of this group do not describe who moved and seconded various motions. Most groups would record this information in the minutes.

Parliamentary Procedure

The previous section referred to concepts such as minutes and agendas. These are items commonly used in groups operating under what is usually called *parliamentary procedure*. Parliamentary procedure is a highly structured technique used by groups of various sizes to make decisions and conduct business. It originated in the fourteenth-century as a set of rules for guiding the English parliament. The model of parliamentary procedure described in *Robert's Rules of Order* (Robert, 1970), first published in 1876, is the most commonly used set of procedures. Groups generally agree in advance to use the rules so that there are no last minute disputes about how decisions will be made. Most deliberative bodies (legislatures), large task groups, and many smaller task groups use *Robert's Rules* to facilitate their work. In fact, the bylaws and constitution (the rules by which most formal organizations operate) usually specify that the group's meetings will be conducted using *Robert's Rules*.

HIGHLIGHT 3.6

MINUTES OF A MEETING

Minutes
Community Welfare Council
January 21, 1996

The meeting was convened at 6:00 p.m. by President Michael Torphy. Members in attendance included Janice Piles, Alice Yips, Nathaniel Washes, Sids Rancid, and Edward Leaks. Absent (excused) was Wrentam Magruder who was attending a conspiracy conference in Dallas.

The minutes were approved as distributed. The treasurer's report was accepted. After a brief discussion about social work month, the matter was referred to the special affairs committee. They will report at the next meeting.

The bylaw revisions were approved by the required two-thirds majority. They will become effective after mailing to all members.

The budget was approved with one change. It was moved, seconded, and carried to move $1000 from the contingency fund to the staff travel account.

There was no old business and no new business. The meeting adjourned at 7:30 p.m.

Respectfully submitted,

Alice Yips, Secretary

Advantages and Disadvantages of Parliamentary Procedure

There are several advantages to parliamentary procedure. Perhaps foremost is that it allows minority elements of the group to be heard and their ideas to be considered. All group participants are allowed an opportunity to express their opinions. This helps protect minority factions and allows them to address their concerns before the rest of the group. Parliamentary procedure is also a much faster means of resolving some issues. Attempting to reach consensus (general agreement among all members) may take much more time. Consensus requires convincing everybody present of the wisdom or acceptability of an idea. With parliamentary procedure, decisions can be reached as soon as a majority of those present are in agreement.

However, parliamentary procedure can be manipulated. The nature of parliamentary procedure is that debate is heightened and encouraged which may lead to win-lose or we-they types of confrontations. For exam-

ple, the majority can win a vote on an issue over the objections of a minority. This can end up making the losers angry. Those who don't understand parliamentary procedure often find themselves being silent or unwilling to risk looking foolish.

Basic Parliamentary Concepts

In parliamentary procedure, the business of the group occurs in the form of *motions*. Motions are proposed actions that the group is asked to support. Thus, a member of an agency board of directors may make a motion to approve accepting a donated vehicle from a local car distributor. Another may move to approve the budget for next year. The motion might be stated as follows: "I move we accept donation of the minivan from Larson Automotive and thank Mr. Larson for his most generous gift." A second member who agrees with this motion signals this support by saying, "I second the motion." The motion or proposal is then open for debate or discussion by the members. A motion which is not seconded normally cannot be discussed by the group. This prevents individuals from taking up the group's time by forcing discussions on topics no one else supports. Technically, motions generally fall into four categories: privileged, incidental, subsidiary, and main.

Privileged Motions

Privileged motions deal with the agenda itself but not with any particular business before the group. For example, motions to recess or adjourn are privileged motions because they affect the agenda. In the case of a motion to *recess*, the mover is asking to temporarily suspend deliberations of items on the agenda and to take a short break. A motion to *adjourn*, on the other hand, is appropriate when one wishes to end all deliberations until the next meeting. Because privileged motions can essentially end the group's deliberations entirely, they have the highest priority of the four categories.

Incidental Motions

Procedural in nature, *incidental motions* relate to the business under discussion. Examples include *points of order* and *points of information*. These motions are used when the mover is concerned about some aspect of the way business is being transacted. For example, a member of the group might notice that the discussion no longer relates to the motion on the floor. Perhaps a motion to approve purchase of a computer system has evolved into a discussion about whether the offices for that agency are accessible to the physically challenged. At that point the member might say, "Point of order." That motion, which does not require a second, requires the chairperson (or group leader) to call on the speaker. (Other dimensions of the leader's role will be described later in this chapter.) The speaker might then say, "I believe the motion on the floor is to purchase a computer system. The discussion seems to have strayed off target." This motion is a good one for dealing with such lapses.

Point of information is a motion used when a participant is not clear about something occurring in the meeting. The chair may call for a vote on a motion when some people aren't clear about the intent of the motion. It is common then to say, "Point of information." The

chair will recognize you. Getting the chairperson's attention in such a way is called being *recognized*. Once recognized, you might say, "If we vote in favor of this motion, does that mean that we can't change the budget until next year? The chair would then clarify the intent of the motion and answer your question. Both motions are important but are used somewhat infrequently.

Subsidiary Motions

Subsidiary motions help deal with motions currently on the floor. These include motions to table, postpone, or amend the matter under debate.

Each of these motions in some way handles an item on the group's agenda. For example, a motion to *table* or *postpone* essentially delays action on the proposed motion. A motion to *amend* is used when you wish to change the proposed motion in some way. See highlight 3.7 for a more complete description of these and other motions.

Main Motions

Main motions introduce the primary issue before the group. No other motion can be placed on the floor when a main motion is introduced. Introducing a new proposal for debate asking to reconsider a motion previously voted on, or requesting to remove an item previously tabled are examples of main motions. Ironically, given their title, main motions have the lowest priority since all other motions described above can be use in some way to prevent or end debate on a main motion.

The primary principle established by parliamentary procedure is that each person has a right to be heard without interruption. The person who makes a motion speaks first on the topic. Afterwards, all members must have an opportunity to speak if they so wish. Debate must be related to the motion on the floor and cannot be on superfluous matters not before the group. It is not wise to allow a topic to be debated before an actual motion is on the floor. To do so encourages rambling and confusing discussions lacking in focus. Once each person who wishes has had a chance to speak, the leader (chair) asks if there is any further debate. If there is none, the group then votes on the proposal. Sometimes a member of the group wishes to stop debate and bring

HIGHLIGHT 3.7

COMMON PARLIAMENTARY DEFINITIONS

Ad hoc committee:	A special committee assigned one primary responsibility and then terminated.
Adjourn:	To end a meeting officially.
Agenda:	An official list of business to be discussed or decided at a meeting.
Amend:	To add, delete, or substitute words or portions of a motion. Example: ''I move to amend the motion on the floor by . . .''
Bylaws:	The major rules of an organization, usually more detailed than the constitution.
Call the question:	A motion to stop debate and immediately vote on the matter before a group.
Committee:	Any portion of the total group assigned a specific task. Examples are standing committees that always exist, ad hoc committees created as needed, and committees of the whole in which the entire group acts as one giant committee.
Constitution:	A document that describes the basic laws and governing procedures of an organization.
Debate:	Discussion of topics a group is addressing.
Executive committee:	A subgroup composed of the chief officers of an organization, often including one or more elected members. Responsibilities include transacting business between meetings of the entire group or organization.
Filibuster:	Speaking for the primary purpose of taking up time and not permitting a group to vote on a topic.
Majority vote:	Greater than one-half of the total of persons voting or ballots cast.
Minutes:	The official record of decisions reached by a group.
Motion:	A proposal, requiring action, submitted to a group. Example: ''I move we donate $100 to the Community AIDS Project.''
Nomination:	A formal propsal for some office. Example: ''I nominate Mary for treasurer.''
Plurality:	The receipt of more votes than any other person, but less than a majority. May occur when three persons are running for the same office.
Point of order:	A statement to the presiding officer of a group that a mistake has occurred or a rule should be enforced. Example: ''Point of Order. I believe we already have a motion on the floor that requires a vote before we go on to other business.''
Proxy:	A signed statement giving another person the right to vote in one's place.
Quorum:	The minimum number or proportion of members needed to legally transact business. Usually this appears in the constitution or bylaws.
Recess:	A short break in a meeting.
Refer to committee:	A motion to delegate work on some specific matter to a smaller group.
Second:	An indication of approval of a proposed motion. Example: ''I second the motion.''
Seriatim:	A method of discussing and voting on a document section by section.
Standing committee:	Committee that continually exists and handles certain types of business. Example: Personnel, Finance, Nominations.
Table:	A motion to indefinitely postpone action on a motion already on the floor. Example: ''I move to table approval of the budget.''
Unanimous:	Any vote on which there is no dissent. In other words, all members vote in favor of (or against) a proposition.

HIGHLIGHT 3.8

CLASSES OF MOTIONS

Privileged Motions	Incidental Motions	Subsidiary Motions	Main Motions
Establish time of adjournment	*Point of order*	Table a motion	General main motions*
Call for adjournment	*Point of information*	Call for an immediate vote	Reconsider a motion previously voted on*
Call for recess	*Request for a revote*	Extend or limit debate on a motion	
Question of privilege	Appeal decision of the chair	Postpone a motion temporarily*	Rescind a motion under consideration
	Object to consideration of a motion	Refer a motion to a committee*	Resume consideration of a tabled motion
	Request suspension of the rules	Amend a motion*	
	Request to withdraw a motion previously made	Postpone a motion indefinitely*	

Note: Motions in italic do not need a second. An asterisk denotes motions that are debatable.

---

a matter to a vote. This can be done by saying, "I call the question." This motion is not debatable. Calling the question requires a vote and immediately halts discussion on a matter if it is supported by two-thirds of those voting. It is commonly used when debate becomes circular and nonproductive, positions are not changing, or members are eager to make decisions about the issue and get on to other items.

Ordinarily, all motions need a second. In highlight 3.8, those in italics, however, do not need a second. Certain types of motions are debatable and others are not. In highlight 3.8, those motions with an asterisk are debatable. Under most circumstances a simple majority of members is all that is needed to pass any given motion. A two-thirds majority must pass the following motions:

- Object to consideration of a motion (done when an item is considered inappropriate or when the matter has already been decided at a previous meeting).
- Call to suspend the rules (this allows a group to operate outside *Robert's Rules* for a limited period of time).
- Call for an immediate vote (call the question—discussed previously).

- Limit or extend debate (may set a one hour limit, for example, on discussion of an agenda item).
- Rescind a motion under consideration (does away with a motion currently being discussed).

In point of order motions (discussed earlier), the chair's decision is final unless appealed to the group. A decision can be appealed to the group by saying, "I appeal the decision of the chair." The motion to appeal requires a second but cannot be debated. The chair will then ask, "Shall the decision of the chair be upheld? Those in favor say Aye" (yes). Then the chair calls for "no" votes and announces the decision of the body.

When it is time to vote, the chair will say, "All those in favor of the motion, say aye." It may be best to state the motion to be voted on or to have the secretary read the motion. (The secretary is an elected member of the group, responsible for keeping the official record—minutes—of the organization.) At that point all favoring the motion will respond "aye." then the chair will call for all "no" or "nay" votes. The chair will decide which side prevailed based on this voice vote and announce the results. Sometimes members vote by raising their hands or by using paper ballots. This is especially true when the vote is close. Normally a simple majority must approve a motion. If a tie occurs in the voting, the motion does not pass. Sometimes the chair may vote to break a tie or to create a tie. Whether the chair is allowed to vote is often specified in the bylaws of an organization. A chair may choose not to vote to break a tie even when given that privilege by the bylaws.

As mentioned above, a motion may be amended. This means it may be changed by a member proposing to add or delete something. For example, to amend a motion that authorizes purchase of a computer system, a member might say, ''I move to amend the motion by placing a limit of $2000 on the amount to be spent for each computer.'' This amendment also needs a second and would be voted on before the vote on the main motion. If approved, the amendment would then become a part of the original main motion. After consideration of all amendments, group members would vote on the main motion.

It should be clear in advance who is eligible to vote. Those who cannot vote should be identified. Some groups have classes of membership, some with voting privileges and some without. Sometimes visitors may be present who lack voting rights. If there is any possibility of confusion, calling for a show of hands rather than a voice vote allows you to count those entitled to vote.

There are other rules governing parliamentary procedure. These include specification of a quorum (the minimum number of members who must be present to conduct business and make decisions) and use of an agenda. As mentioned earlier, most groups have a leader or chairperson responsible for helping the group conduct its business. A secretary keeps the minutes (official record of a group's actions). Other officers may be needed depending upon the type and size of the group. Possibilities include a treasurer (who handles the group's dues and money) and perhaps a vice chairperson (who replaces the chair when that person can't be present). Larger groups may create subgroups or committees to which certain business is sent for review. It is common, for example, to have both standing committees (permanent committees such as a finance committee and a personnel committee) and special ad hoc committees (temporary committees established to address some specific issue) set up to handle specific bits or categories of business. Committee members and the chairperson of each committee are usually appointed by the chair of the larger group. In less formal groups, members may volunteer to serve on a committee.

The smaller the committee, the less likely it is to use more formalized parliamentary procedures. Less formal procedures may allow a group to act quickly, especially if there is substantial agreement and no need for actual votes. In general, committees and subcommittees (smaller committees within larger committees) are likely to use less formal procedures. Committees and subcommittees often meet between meetings of the larger group and report their activities at regular meetings of the larger group. Committee membership may be as small as three members or as large as necessary to handle a given task.

Occasionally you will hear the term *steering committee*. A steering committee is sometimes created to help run an organization that does not want to become too formal. For example, a new neighborhood association may select a steering committee to help them get started. Once organized, they may select officers, set up bylaws, and the like. Such groups may reject formal titles such as chairperson or president. At the same time, the members of the steering committee are often the most political individuals in the group. In other words, they are the real movers and shakers.

A social worker skilled in the use of parliamentary procedure can be of enormous assistance to many groups. Knowing how to make motions, amend, and otherwise properly handle the group's business can make work go smoothly. Parliamentary procedure provides an orderly, predictable mechanism for handling a group's issues and decision making fairly. However, while parliamentary procedure provides a set of rules to guide groups in their deliberations it was never meant to serve as an obstacle. Ultimately, the wishes of the group must prevail even if a violation of *Robert's Rules* occurs. For example, while parliamentary procedural rules are clear and designed to help the group, they are not always followed closely. Sometimes the procedures called for in the rules become barriers to accomplishment of group goals. Smaller committees may decide to operate by consensus and dispense with voting on items when the group is in agreement. In addition, in legislative bodies, it is possible for a person to waste the body's time by endlessly speaking on a matter before the group. Often called *filibustering*, this method may stymie a body and prevent it from conducting its normal business. In these situations groups may adopt other less cumbersome methods or decide to temporarily suspend some of the usual rules of parliamentary procedure.

Managing Conflict

Conflict is a fact of life, normal and, often, healthy. Disagreements over goals, methods, ideas, or almost any other topic can lead to conflict. For professionals, sources of conflict can include clients, coworkers, supervisors, or agency administrators. Conflict may occur between providers of service and consumers, between professionals with differing perspectives on service, between units or organizations seeking the same scarce resources, between organizations with sharply divergent goals and missions, or between management and workers, to name a few typical scenarios. Conflict may be based on affective (emotional) factors such as personal animosity or on substantive matters such as how many workers are needed to serve child abuse victims. The latter category is more easily dealt with because these disputes can be resolved through reasoning, acquiring additional data, and engaging in normal debate.

Conflict is common in groups and should not be viewed as problematic (Johnson, 1992). Expecting conflict should be a given—you can't bring people together with different experiences, needs, desires, and goals without having some degree of conflict. Conflict can be positive and lead to new ideas and change. It can even get people excited about a topic (Rubin & Rubin, 1986). Conflict over ideas can help generate alternative solutions.

Conflict, however, can also be negative when it becomes an attack on the individual rather than on the person's ideas, gets enmeshed in a debate over values (instead of alternatives or ideas), or involves personalities. Personality conflicts are quite common and seem to reflect the inability of people to appreciate each other's strengths and good points. Personality conflicts are almost invariably negative for the two parties and, often, for those around them.

Conflict can be scary if, in the past, it has led to outbursts, fightings, and violence. People who associate differences of agreement with violence (perhaps occurring in their families, in other relationships, or in communities) are often very uncomfortable with conflict. Recognizing this is the first step toward meeting our goal—managing conflict.

Unfortunately, conflict is uncomfortable for many of us in human services. We prefer collaborative relationships where we work together pleasantly and get along well. Yet organizations and groups must engage in conflict for a variety of purposes. Overcoming obstacles (such as staff's negative attitudes) to your agency's effort to provide adequate services to gay and lesbian clients is a possible conflict with which you might deal. Conflict sometimes achieves ends not otherwise attainable, such as when people are denied their basic rights and collaborative approaches have not been successful in resolving the issue. In groups, conflict is a normal stage of development and without it the group often cannot move on to the next stage, namely, solving its problems. When you have an opportunity to select the member of a group, it is helpful to choose people who have at least some degree of tolerance for conflict and acceptance of its inevitability. Highlight 3.9 gives an example of how a social work intern handled conflict in a hospital setting.

There are at least four potential forms of conflict that we may routinely encounter. These include interpersonal conflict, conflicts over resources, representational conflicts, and intercessional conflict. *Interpersonal (one-on-one) conflicts* occur when two or more workers disagree over something. It could be an assessment, the best plan for a case, or who got promoted ahead of whom. Their disagreement can rise to the level of conflict if both sides hold strongly to their views and are unwilling to compromise.

Another form of conflict occurs over the use of, or access to, *scarce resources* such as money, time, attention, or power. One unit in an agency may receive a larger share of funds for new positions or may be suffering greater losses when the agency has to cut back on existing positions. Conflicts over resources are nearly inevitable because we never have enough money, people, or other items to meet all the existing demands.

Representational conflicts can also occur when one person represents a group whose interests differ from those of other groups. Worker-management conflicts are of this nature. The person who is engaging in a conflictual approach may simply be representing another group. Efforts to advocate for the interests of one group may be perceived as conflictual by opposing groups.

Sometimes you must intercede between two or more groups (people) in conflict. These are *intercessional conflicts*. An example might be mediating a family dispute that has pitted the parents against a specific child. A variation of this occurs when the entire family is at war with one another and the worker, as counselor, is supposed to intercede. As you can see, conflict is a natural part of our work as social workers.

Once we recognize that conflict is almost inevitable, the goal becomes finding ways to manage or cope

---

HIGHLIGHT 3.9

CONFLICT IN THE HOSPITAL

Allison is in a dilemma. As a BSW student completing her field experience in a hospital, she is aware that the doctors make the primary decisions regarding patients. One hospital physician, Dr. Jones has made it clear that Ms. Ortega will be discharged tomorrow. He will not prescribe a nursing home stay, though many elderly patients with similar injuries recuperate in such environments. Allison, who has talked to Ms. Ortega and her family, knows that the woman cannot take care of herself at home until her broken hip has healed.

Unfortunately, Dr. Jones finds Ms. Ortega a difficult patient. As Ms. Ortega is Hispanic, the language barrier compounds the problem. He is adamant that she be discharged, though she really lacks a place to go. Allison cannot overturn the doctor's decision.

There is little her supervisor could do about the case. Finally, Allison decides that her duty to the patient outweighs her duty to follow Dr. Jones's orders. She telephones Ms. Ortega's regular doctor in Pleasanton, a small town about forty miles from the hospital. Allison explains the situation in detail to Dr. O'Reilly. Dr. O'Reilly then orders a nursing home stay for Ms. Ortega.

Allison realized that only another doctor could overrule Dr. Jones and prescribe temporary nursing home care. Since Dr. O'Reilly is Ms. Ortega's regular doctor, his decisions carry more weight than that of a hospital staff physician. Allison has made certain that Ms. Ortega's needs are met. Dr. Jones never does find out about Allison's intercession.

---

with conflict. Part of our role is to help people recognize conflict when it occurs and deal with it as straightforwardly as possible. Confirming differences of opinion and validating that people have a right to them is part of this process. Conflict should not usually be buried, but handled openly. Attaining positive outcomes in conflictual situations can be quite an achievement. Johnson (1992) recommends discussing and negotiating the differences lying behind the conflict. By carefully listening to the points of view and reasons of both sides in a conflict, we find it easier to search for commonalities that link the conflicting parties. As part of this process you must critically examine the logic behind a person's position, and reexamine assumptions which undergird individual positions. She suggests some general steps (detailed in highlight 3.10) for managing conflict.

Conflict in coalitions (alliances of different factions in a community) is also common. If groups have been at odds with each other in the past, it is not unusual for members to remain suspicious. Groups that have historically been oppressed often enter coalitions doubting the sincerity of other group members. They may doubt whether the other parties share their concerns or are as committed to changing things as they are.

In coalitions where people represent a specific group, it is common for them to be torn between their responsibilities to the coalition and to their original organization. When you are part of a group working on getting a bill through the legislature, you may feel compelled to compromise your group's position in order to forge a working relationship with other coalition members. Compromise is often required to get bills passed. The coalition may push you to agree to a compromise even though it may not be as good for your group as you would have liked. This can be ameliorated somewhat if all parties recognize the greater good that brought them together in the first place. A coalition of professional groups working for licensing of social workers and other human service providers found themselves often in conflict over issues such as the relative power of each group on the proposed licensing board and the wording of specific portions of the law. There were disagreements over what categories of professionals (for example, social workers, professional counselors, and marriage and family counselors) should have positions on the board. Should this Board have equal representation among professionals or be weighted based upon the number of professionals to be licensed? Finally, by staying focused on the ultimate goal of getting all their groups licensed, the coalition learned to successfully manage major conflicts.

Bisno (1988) has helped our understanding of conflict by discussing both the types of conflict that you might encounter and a variety of conflict management strategies. The following section draws heavily upon his insights.

Types of Conflict

Categorizing conflict helps us recognize that there are many types of conflict. As a result our ways of managing conflict may change. Bisno (1988) highlights six different types of conflict: interest/commitment conflict, induced conflict, misattributed conflict, illusionary conflict, displaced conflict, and expressive conflict.

Interest/Commitment Conflicts

Interest/commitment conflicts are characterized by basic genuine clashes of opposing interests of commitments. Recent disagreements over abortion clearly exemplify this. On the one hand, some people are strongly supportive of women's rights to control their bodies and believe that women must have reproductive freedom. On the other hand, some people are just as convinced that abortion is a form of murder and should be totally abolished.

Induced Conflict

Induced conflict is created to reach goals that cannot be attained directly. In essence, you stir up conflict to gain support from one side or another in a disagreement. In a university social work program one faculty member, Jimmy, routinely struggles to induce conflict among the other program faculty. Jimmy approaches faculty members and says critical things about other faculty members. Jimmy might say to Lois, "Clarke has been taking materials you wrote and claiming credit for writing them." Then Jimmy tells Clarke, "You know, Clarke, it look to me like Lois is not pulling her share of the load around here. It seems like you're getting stuck with all the work." By inducing conflict, Jimmy keeps everyone upset at everyone else. This makes it unlikely that any coalitions will form in opposition to his ideas. This increases his power and influence and

seemingly makes him each person's only friend. It should be noted that Jimmy's behavior is not ethical. However, in actual situations, interpersonal behavior, including that of professionals, sometimes *is* unethical. In this situation, Jimmy placed personal gain (power) generated by conflict above the well-being of his colleagues and the department.

Misattributed Conflict

Misattributed conflict involves an honest mistake. It is conflict based upon incorrectly attributing behavior or ideas to people or groups. It can be based on stereotyping or simply mistaken thinking about what someone said or did. It is important to recognize this is a real source of conflict, even though the source has been incorrectly identified. For example, Elwood Drab hung up the phone and turned to his assistant with a look of pure frustration. "That was Jim Boyles, our lobbyist at the capital. He says the bill to provide grant money for new drug abuse programs just got bottled up in the senate's public health committee. Jim thinks the committee got pressure from the public employees' union, who were afraid the bill would lead to more money for private programs and shifting jobs from the state to private agencies. Set up a meeting with union president Tura Lye and let's hit this thing head on. There is no way that this bill threatens state jobs, and we need to convince her of that." With that, Elwood set off on a collision course with the union president. Unbeknownst to Elwood, however, was the fact that the union did not oppose the bill. Rather, the source of the problem was a state senator who had heard that the grant program would teach students about drugs in schools, an idea he vehemently opposed. Elwood was to discover his mistake too late. He had attributed the conflict to the wrong adversary. Moreover, he failed a basic premise of critical thinking, namely, that you base your actions on sound evidence. Since lobbyist Jim Boyles only "thought" the union was a problem, Elwood should have gotten his facts straight first.

Illusionary Conflict

Illusionary conflict is similar to misattributed conflict in that it rests on a mistake. Here, though, we are not dealing with something that actually happened but was blamed on the wrong person or group. In illusionary conflict, the disagreement rests on misperceptions or misunderstandings arising from confusion about, or lack of knowledge of another party. In other words, there is no real conflict at all. An example may help explain this. Juan proposes the creation of a new unit in his agency to deal with perpetrators of domestic violence. The proposal is placed on the agenda of the board of directors for approval. At the last minute, Juan learns that Sally, the assistant director, has asked that the proposal be dropped from the agenda. Juan is furious, thinking that Sally is opposed to serving perpetrators because of her background working with victims of domestic violence. He goes to her office steaming, expecting a conflict over the proposal. When he gets there, Sally explains that she asked to have the proposal dropped because the Board would not have time to consider the idea at this meeting because of other more pressing concerns. She promises Juan that it would be back on the next agenda with her full support.

Displaced Conflict

Displaced conflict is directed at people or concerns other than the real party or source of conflict. This arises when you get upset at work and take it out on others at home, or vice versa. You are really unhappy with a conflict in one area, but allow the conflict to carry over into some other totally unrelated area.

Expressive Conflict

Expressive conflict rests primarily on a wish to express hostility, aggression, or other strong feelings. In other words, conflict exists because someone is blowing off steam. Expressive conflict can occur when people who have not been responding assertively hold their feelings in over a long period of time and then finally explode over some minor issue.

Conflict arouses strong feelings and emotions in most people. Typically, social workers are no more fond of conflict than the rest of the population. We want to help people, to be liked and appreciated. Most important, unlike attorneys, we lack conflict training. Despite these hurdles, however, we can employ a variety of conflict management strategies when we are forced to deal with conflict. Johnson's (1992) suggestions for possible ways of resolving conflict appear in highlight 3.10. These are relatively simple approaches which can be easily employed.

Advanced Conflict Management: Guidelines and Strategies

Johnson's general guidelines for resolving and preventing conflict will not work in every situation. You may not wish to resolve the conflict but to use it to achieve professional goals. In such situations, you require advanced conflict management skills, addressed below.

There are three general guidelines for using advanced conflict management strategies. The first is always to assess both your power and that of your adversary. This is important because some conflict resolution strategies require you to use your available power. Knowing what power the adversary has will help you select the appropriate strategy. Sandra has lobbied hard

---

HIGHLIGHT 3.10

STEPS IN MANAGING CONFLICT

1. Seek clues to conflict—do not ignore it in anticipation that it will go away.
2. Define conflict as a group issue, not an individual one.
3. Listen to all points of view and recognize similarities and differences.
4. Clarify ideas and positions when they are unclear.
5. Avoid win-lose situations.
6. Work for cooperation, not competition.

with members of the city council to get them to approve funding for a new summer program for children. Just one hour before the council is to meet, Henry Waddle, a local doctor, calls Sandra and tells her he is going to attend the meeting and speak in opposition to her proposal. Sandra explains why the program is important and says she welcomes his expression of reservations about the proposal.

After talking with Dr. Waddle, Sandra quickly assesses her situation. Five of the seven council members have told her they will support her proposal. She knows that Dr. Waddle is considered something of a nuisance because he is always speaking against spending money on social programs. Sandra correctly surmises that she has more power (in the form of pledges of support for the program) than does Dr. Waddle. She knows she can even afford to lose one of her supporters and still win by a four to three vote. Thus, she decides that she does not have to exert any more energy or effort to counter Dr. Waddle's influence.

The second guideline is to avoid full disclosure of your power. Never let the adversary know exactly how much power you have. This can be effective in two ways. First, the adversary may assume you have more power than you do. This works to your advantage. Second, since the adversary does not know the amount of power you have available, it makes it doubly difficult for him to respond. Think of it as a chess game. If the opposing player does not know whether you have a powerful queen or only a bishop, s/he will have a hard time knowing what to do.

A third guideline is always to use power sparingly. Use only as much as needed to reach an objective. This avoids the possibility of overkill and still leaves your opponent in the dark about your strength. In the case above, Sandra could call others who might try to dissuade Dr. Waddle from coming to the meeting. Or she could tell Dr. Waddle how many votes she already has, thereby disclosing her own strength. Rather, Sandra plays it cool and never lets her opponent know how much support she has. Nor does she try to influence Dr. Waddle by having others call him. Such a tactic might lead him to think that the program has little support on the council and that his statement can change the outcome.

Other advanced strategies for conflict management are described below. In each we will suggest when the approach might be used and suggest some appropriate strategies and tactics to reach the goal of conflict management.

Forestalling or Sidestepping Conflict

Sometimes it is better to forestall or sidestep conflict. This might be true when conflict is unnecessary because other approaches offer more promise, when the costs are too high, when conflict is inappropriate, or when the issues are not that important. Dinh Trong is in such a situation. Dinh is discussing with a fellow social worker how to handle a situation with her supervisor. The supervisor, Marvin, has just told Dinh that the agency plans to phase out its refugee mentor program when the grant expires next year. Dinh strongly supports the program but is a brand new worker in the agency. Her colleague cautions Dinh that she is still in her probationary period, so she is especially vulnerable to being fired. Engaging in a conflict with Marv right now will probably cause more trouble than it's worth. Since the grant has another nine months to run and Dinh will be off probation in three months, her colleague suggests she avoid a conflict right now. Dinh follows the recommendation.

Of course, these strategies are characterized by avoidance and their use can prevent future problems. For one thing, you can identify potential areas of future conflict. Using this information you can anticipate where problems are likely to occur later. Although Dinh decides not to act now, she certainly knows that Marv is a potential adversary in her efforts to keep the refugee mentor program.

Another way to avoid serious problems with conflict is to ensure that people feel free to criticize or raise questions about policies, procedures, or decisions. Some agencies seem to have an in-house critic who serves as a lightening rod for worker concerns. Instead of avoiding such people, listen to what they are saying. Often, they can provide advance warnings of problems or conflictual situations.

Of course, you also can avoid conflict by denying that any disagreement exists. This ignores the problem in hopes that it will go away. It is characterized as the "head in the sand" approach and is not very fruitful because it does not lead to resolution of the conflict. While Dinh can pretend that she and Marv are in agreement, this will not really be the case.

Another tactic is to leave the agency. This approach, of course, is drastic and should be used only in extreme situations. Dinh can quit over the issue of eliminating the program she supports, but will also lose her ability to influence future events.

Finally, you can simply give in and agree that the opposing side is right. This can be done when you are actually convinced that the other side has a better argument or position. It can also be done because you simply do not have the energy or ability to influence certain events. Again, the tactic used depends on the amount of power at your disposal and the seriousness of the issue.

Generating Conflict

Another approach to managing conflict is to create it. You can use this strategy when other non-conflictual approaches have failed or when you have sufficient power or influence to win on an issue. This approach also assumes that the cost of conflict is acceptable. The strategies include identifying potential conflicts and situations where conflict would be desirable. Then conflict itself is created through a variety of tactics. Had Dinh been an experienced worker with strong support from her colleagues, she might have told Marv that the idea of eliminating the refugee mentor program was dead wrong. She could have insisted on presenting her case to the agency director and brought in other workers who felt the same way. She could also have mobilized community support for the program. Again, this approach works best when you know you have enough power or influence to win the conflict.

Confilct can also be created through strategies such as consciousness-raising, whereby you attempt to get others who have been neutral to see the seriousness of the issues. This tactic has been useful in helping women recognize the many ways in which they are oppressed in a male-dominated society. Women's consciousness can be raised concerning self-esteem, assertiveness, and male-female communication issues.

Another tactic is exposing false consensus—or showing that the emperor lacks clothes. This is based on the old children's story of the emperor who was convinced that he had just put on a beautiful set of clothes when in fact he was naked. He paraded through the city and no one pointed out that he had nothing on. Most of the citizens were pretending that there was no problem.

Finally, a child, not understanding why the adults were behaving this way, shouted that the "emperor has no clothes!" Sometimes it is important to point out that there really is a problem even if no one else wants to mention it. You can also use this when you think others are not happy with the situation and only need someone to help them challenge the status quo.

Encouraging and articulating areas of disagreement (instead of accentuating commonalities) is another useful tactic to generate conflict. This helps to polarize issues and people. Then, if people see that others don't share their views, they can decide whether the issue is important enough to warrant further conflict.

Conflict Management by Covert Means

Conflict can also be managed by *covert means*, which are subtle ways of managing conflict. Because they are hidden, opponents may not recognize the power used against them. This approach can work when the user can't cope with overt conflict, perhaps because his or her situation is too precarious. It might also be used when the costs of open conflict are too high for the conflict generator or when an opponent won't play by the rules in resolving the conflict. Perhaps the opponent is avoiding conflict by denying it exists and refusing to talk about it. Dinh could have quietly passed the word to the refugee community, their supporters, and others interested in the mentor program about Marv's intention to end the program. Without getting drawn into the conflict herself, she could encourage others to mobilize their power to ensure that the program survives. This reduces the risk to Dinh, who is still a probationary worker. The risk of using covert means is that one treads awfully close to the edges of ethical behavior. It should be used only under the most compelling circumstances.

Other strategies of value include passive resistance, concealment, and manipulation. Passive resistance means that you simply drag your feet in ways that create problems for the opponent. This might take the form of turning in important forms late. It also could include operating strictly by the book. An example is a secretary whose job description states she spends approximately 20 percent of her time typing. When she reaches the 20 percent mark each week, she simply refuses to do any more typing that week. Of course, this rankles her supervisor and those who depend upon her typing.

Concealment means exactly what it says. You do not let the other party know what you are doing. You hide your plan and your activity. This strategy works because the other party doesn't know what you're up to.

Manipulation means that you influence others without their being aware of it. This takes great skill and must be done in a way that does not compromise your ethical integrity. Alice leaves little anonymous reminders in her supervisor's mailbox about how rigid the supervisor can get. The reminders include a plaque that looks like a one-way street sign. It reads:

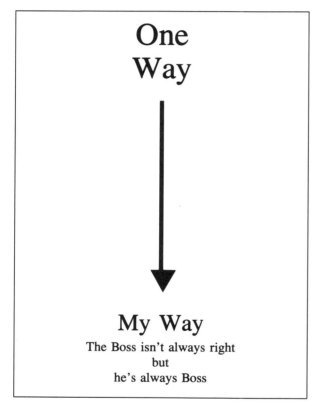

One
Way

My Way
The Boss isn't always right
but
he's always Boss

The boss gradually became more flexible, partly because of the gentle manipulation used by the worker to suggest the need to change.

While the strategies identified above are broad approaches to conflict, one can use other more specific techniques or tactics. The six tactics which accompany these strategies can vary dramatically. They include negativism, noncompliance, stonewalling, deceit, seduction, emotional extortion, and divide-and-conquer.

Negativism and noncompliance with rules. Work-ers in a social service agency decide to deal covertly with a disputed agency policy specifying that they must exit by a certain door in the building instead of the one closest to their parking lot and offices. The agency director is concerned about the security of employees using this door, but the workers have to walk an extra block to reach their cars. They consider this a nuisance since they are always in a hurry. Nearly every worker in the agency deliberately uses the parking lot exit as a show of noncompliance with the policy.

Stonewalling. This simply means refusing to act on a matter. It is a favorite tactic for dealing with policies that you find abhorrent. Operationally, it means that you refuse to enforce the policy, although you may not do this openly. Perhaps the policy requires workers to have their paperwork up-to-date before they can take time off. Supervisors who disagree with the policy might simply look the other way and refuse to enforce the rule.

Deceit or deception. This approach is not completely honest. Deception might be used to make others think you have more power than you really do. A community group convinces the county board to support a new program by arranging for each member of the board to receive multiple letters on the topic. Since few people take the time to write their elected representatives, a dozen letters on a single topic make it seem that there is widespread support for the new program. Actually, the group interested in the program numbered about a dozen. Another related method is *seduction* or the offering of inducements to convince neutral parties to join you or to convert opponents to your side. This method is routinely used in Congress and state legislatures. It works because one senator, for example, from the state of New York, wants the support of other senators to pass his bill providing new money for a subway system in New York City. To get the support of others, he offers to add to his bill a provision in which the state of Kentucky gets increased government subsidies for tobacco farmers. Of course, inducements such as this increase the cost of government.

Emotional extortion. One party with sufficient influence can induce another to change by withholding something valued by the other. The thing of value could be attention. Making others feel guilty about their behavior is another form of emotional extortion. Of course, these strategies are often at odds with ethical considerations.

Divide and conquer. This tactic reduces the influence of the adversary and neutralizes opposing players by approaching opponents individually or by bringing up subjects which produce a split within the opponent's ranks. One key member of a group might be offered a chance to achieve his own personal goals if he switches sides or remains neutral in a conflict. It is also possible to split a group's solidarity by getting it involved in a debate over which there is substantial disagreement. Those opposed to abortion, for example, are often divided about whether abortion is ever warranted. A bill to outlaw *all* abortions might be defeated because many abortion foes recognize its value in cases of rape, incest, or a threat to the life of the mother. Thus, the group's solidarity could be ruptured when it comes to lobbying for this particular bill.

Conflict Management by Emergent Agreement

Managing conflict through *emergent agreement* works when one side convinces the other to change. Perhaps this follows the introduction of new evidence. For example, you might resolve differences by gathering data. Of course, both sides must be willing to look for new answers. Agreements resolved by the introduction of new data usually involve lower stakes and limited costs and risks. On the other hand, conflicts arising from differences in values does not yield easily to new data or information.

Another tactic to produce an agreement is called *coactive disputation.* Essentially this means that both parties are willing to consider joint problem solving, use facts to settle disputes, and remain open to persuasion. Thus, a group trying to pass a licensing law for mental health practitioners might sit down and try to resolve their differences so that they can jointly support a single bill. If they let their differences become a barrier, no one group will get what it wants. By working together to solve their disputes they emerge a stronger force for change.

Conflict Management by Negotiated Agreement

Negotiated agreement occurs when both sides see negotiation as a logical way to end their disagreement. Negotiation is "the process of bringing together those who are opposed on some issues and arranging for them to communicate clearly and fairly, to bargain and compromise, and to arrive at mutually acceptable agreements" (Barker, 1991, p. 154). It works when there are no large disparities in power between the two sides. Labor unions and businesses often reach negotiated agreements because both stand to lose substantially if they remain at an impasse. Employers cannot run their businesses without workers and workers cannot live without their paychecks. Thus, there is pressure on both sides to compromise.

Regular, patient communications and good listening skills can often help you arrive at an agreement. Messages need to be clear to reduce potential confusion. Confused people often say no to ideas they don't understand. Since the primary strategy here is negotiation, the tactics logically follow: define the issues of disagreement, use objective criteria for settling the dispute, and seek mutually beneficial outcomes. An employer and the workers' union, for example, might agree to use a specific index of inflation as the basis for future raises. This is an objective criterion by which to determine how much workers' wages should rise next year.

Conflict Management by Indirect Means or Procedural Measures

This approach is employed under two basic conditions—first, when both sides cannot or will not negotiate; second, when other management approaches are unpalatable. The typical solution is to submit the disagreement to a third party or arbitrator. An arbitrator is a third party who both sides agree can help settle their differences. In some cases arbitration is required by law. Many public school districts and teacher's unions must by law submit their labor disputes to binding arbitration. In binding arbitration the arbitrator's decision is binding on both parties. This way they allow another party to settle things without having to resort to more drastic tactics such as striking.

Conflict Management by Exercise of Authority/Power

Exercising authority or power can simply overcome the opposition. Typically, the more powerful side uses it against the other less powerful faction when other methods either won't work or are unacceptable.

Tactics include enforcing rules rigidly, setting limits, going on strike, ordering the opponent to act a certain way, or firing the conflicting person(s). These more drastic approaches have many drawbacks. The fact that one side is clearly the loser in the conflict is a problem. Other approaches such as negotiating provides solutions from which each side can claim some satisfaction.

As we stated at the beginning of this section, conflict is natural and predictable. Anticipating that it will occur, learning about various types of conflict, and considering ahead of time the possible approaches to conflict management can only increase your effectiveness as a social worker.

In addition, understanding organizations (the subject of chapter 4) and communities (chapter 8) requires that you appreciate the role that conflict plays in both of these areas. The achievement of social work goals in these areas often demands that you use, resolve, or accept conflict.

Chapter Summary

This chapter begins with a discussion of the importance of networking and identifies why this mezzo level skill is so important in bringing about and sustaining macro level change. Various types of networks are discussed, along with the problems which can occur. Workers' roles with networks are also reviewed.

The importance of teamwork is examined. The chapter focuses on characteristics of effective teams and reviews the kinds of teams with which a generalist worker might be involved.

Planning and conducting meetings are other important skills for social workers. The chapter describes the steps needed to ensure an effective meeting. A most important set of skills used in larger groups, parliamentary procedure, is considered in detail.

Finally, the chapter concludes with a review of the role of conflict and the different types of conflict which can emerge. A variety of conflict management approaches are discussed at the end of the chapter.

CHAPTER FOUR

Understanding Organizations

Suppose you are a newly graduated social worker. All those years of grinding out papers and all-nighting it before exams have finally paid off. You have been looking at the Sunday wants ads for "social workers," "counselors," "health care workers," "case managers," and any other titles you think might apply to you. You are finally going to be making money at a job instead of paying money out to get your education.

You're faced with a number of questions. What kind of social work do I want to do most? In what social work field am I most likely to get a job? How much money should I ask for? What might each job be like? What is the agency advertising the position like?

There are many additional questions you might ask yourself as you are about to enter the world of agency life. These include:

Who will do the hiring?
What will my supervisor be like?
How much vacation will I get?
What rules will the agency have?
Will the agency dress standards be formal or informal? What exactly should I wear?
What working hours will be required?
How much freedom will I have in my work?
What will my clients be like?
How will my clients respond to me?
What will the agency staff expect me to know already?
How much training can I expect to get?
What will my coworkers be like?
How will if I fit into a staff already used to working with each other?

Introduction

This chapter will introduce you to work in organizations. We have established that an organization is a type of macro system. When you begin working in an organization, you become part of that larger system. In order to fit in as well as possible, it is important to understand how such large systems work. When the system is not working as well as it could, you may decide to try to change it. Such action requires substantial understanding of how organizations are run.

Frequently, professionals just beginning their social work careers find the direct interaction and work with clients fascinating and exciting. Larger systems such as organizations and communities hold much less allure. However, generalist social workers must have a solid foundation of knowledge and insight into how

these large systems function in order to do their jobs effectively. This chapter aims to provide you with insight into how organizations function as the context which you will practice social work.

This chapter will:

- Explain the meaning of organizations, social service, and social agencies.
- Identify some of the major types of organizational theories including classical scientific management theories, human relations theories, Theory X and Theory Y, and systems theories.
- Explain organizational operations from a systems perspective.
- Explore the nature of organizations including agency settings, organizational goals, the macro context of organizations, and organizational structure.
- Examine what it is like to work within a bureaucracy.
- Describe a total quality approach to management as one example of a management style that significantly contrasts with traditional bureaucracy.
- Appraise the exceptional problems of social service organizations.
- Identify other common problems workers frequently encounter while working within organizations.

Organizations, Social Services, and Social Agencies

Before saying another thing about organizations and your social work practice within them, we need to clearly define the terms involved. These include *organization, agency,* and *social services*. A range of systems concepts used in describing how macro systems operate will also be defined and discussed.

Organizations

Organizations are defined as "social entities that are goal-oriented, deliberately structured activity systems with an identifiable boundary" (Daft, 1983, p. 8). Within this definition there are four essential concepts.

First, organizations are *social entities*. That is, organizations are made up of people with all their strengths and failings. Organizations prescribe how people should behave and what responsibilities employees are to assume in their jobs. Thus, patterns of behavior develop in organizations.

Second, organizations are *goal-directed*. They exist for a specified purpose. Social service organizations are there to provide services and resources to help people in some way. It is important to understand what an organization's goals are. It is also vital to assess whether the organization's goals are really beneficial for clients. Finally, it is crucial to examine whether the organization is, in reality, attaining its goals for clients.

The third key concept in the definition is that organizations are *deliberately structured activity systems*. Daft (1983, p. 8) describes what this means. "Activity system means that organizations have a technology—they use knowledge to perform work activities. Organizational tasks are deliberately subdivided into separate departments and sets of activities. The subdivision is intended to achieve efficiencies in the work process. The deliberate structure is also characterized by a conscious attempt to coordinate and direct the separate activities" (p. 8).

Organizations, then, have structures that include policies for how the organization should be run, hierarchies that direct how personnel are supervised and by whom, and different units working in various ways to help the organization function. For instance, a family services organization might have one staff unit providing marriage and family therapy, another unit providing "family life education," and still another unit working on "community activities to enhance healthy family development" (Barker, 1991, p. 82). Each unit pursues different activities to achieve the agency's general goal of providing family services. Of course, not all organizations provide social services. Other organizations have structures, too. For example, a toilet-seat factory, also an organization, might have one unit responsible for designing seats, one for manufacturing them, and another for marketing them.

The fourth major concept in the definition of organization involves *identifiable boundaries*. That is, it is very clear who is part of the organization and who is not. It should also be evident where resources come from and what services are provided.

The term *organization*, then, is a broad concept. Organizations comprise groups of people, tools, and resources structured to accomplish any of a wide range of objectives (Barker, 1991). For instance, organizations include the Girl Scouts of America, Tenneco, the Pentagon, Enthronement of the Sacred Heart Archdiocesan Center, and the John Birch Society. The following sections will explore more thoroughly the specific types of organizations in which social workers practice.

Social Services

This chapter on organizations that provide social services to clients. *Social services* include the work that social work practitioners and other helping professionals perform for: improving people's health; enhancing their quality of life; "helping people to become more self-sufficient; preventing dependency; strengthening family relationships; and restoring individuals, families, groups, or communities to successful functioning" (Barker, 1991, p. 221). That is quite a mouthful. In essence, social services include the wide range of activities that social workers perform in their efforts to help people solve problems and improve their personal well-being. Social services may be *institutional*, including such services as financial assistance, housing programs, or education provided by public organizations (Barker, 1995). They might also include *personal social services*. These are "social services with a basic purpose to enhance the relationships between people and between people and their environments and to provide opportunities for social fulfillment" (Barker, 1995, p. 279). Such services usually target specific groups or particular problems such as family planning, counseling, or services directed at groups such as children or the elderly (Barker, 1995).

It should be noted that the term *human services* is very similar to social services. Specifically, these are "programs and activities designed to enhance people's development and well-being" (Barker, 1991, p. 105). Often, the two terms are used interchangeably.

Social Agencies

A *social agency* is an organization providing social services that "is usually staffed by human services personnel (including professional social workers, members of other professions, subprofessional specialists); clerical personnel," and sometimes volunteers (Barker, 1991, p. 217). Social agencies generally serve a defined client population who experience a defined need. Services are provided according to a prescribed set of policies regarding how the agency staff should meet this need.

A number of different concepts can characterize social agencies. For example, social agencies can be public, private, or proprietary. *Public* social agencies are run by a designated unit of government and are usually regulated by laws impacting policy. For example, a county board committee oversees a public welfare department and is responsible for establishing its major policies. (Of course, such a committee must function in accordance with state or federal governments that provide at least some of the money for the agency's programs.)

Private social agencies, on the other hand, are privately owned and run by people not employed by government. They are nonprofit social agencies. That is, they are run to accomplish some service provision goal, not to make financial profit for private owners (Barker, 1995). They usually provide some type of personal social services (Barker, 1995). Funding for services can range from tax money to private donations to grants to service fees. A board of directors presides over a private agency, formulating policy and making certain that agency staff run the agency appropriately.

Proprietary or for-profit social agencies provide designated social services, often quite similar to those provided by private social agencies. However, a major purpose of the proprietary social agency is to make a profit for its owners.

It should be noted that the terms ''social services,'' ''human services,'' and sometimes ''social welfare'' are often used interchangeably when referring to organizations, agencies, and agency personnel. From our perspective, the terms social services agency, social services organization, and social agency mean essentially the same thing. Therefore, these three terms will be used interchangeably throughout the book.

Organizational Theories

In order to work within organizations, evaluate them, and sometimes work to change them, it is helpful to understand the major theories regarding how organizations operate. Such a perspective is also useful in determining what kinds of organizational structures are most effective in which client situations.

Many organizational theories have been borrowed from business and management literature. Businesses and social service organizations have many things in common. Both need resources (money) to run. Likewise, both produce products via some kind of process. For example, a business might manufacture lawnmowers. A social services organization might seek the ''product'' of improved family functioning.

There are many theories concerning how organizations really work. Some of them directly contradict others, probably because there is such a vast range of organizational structures, functions, and goals. There are tremendous differences even among social service organizations in terms of structure and function, let alone among other types of businesses.

Sarri proposes (1987) a number of major theoretical perspectives on how organizations are or should be run; these include ''classical scientific management theories,'' ''human relations theories,'' and ''systems theories'' (pp. 30–32). Additionally, we will explore another organizational perspective addressed in the management literature, namely *Theory X* and *Theory Y*, a subset of human relations theories.

Classical Scientific Management Theories

Classical scientific management theories emphasize that specifically designed, formal structure and a consistent, rigid organizational network of employees are most important in having an organization run well and achieve its goals (Holland & Petchers, 1987; Sarri, 1987). Each employee holds a clearly defined job and is told straightforwardly exactly how that job should be done. This school of thought calls for minimal independent functioning on the part of employees. Supervisors closely scrutinize all work. Efficiency is of utmost importance. Performance is quantified (that is, made very explicit as to what is expected), regulated, and measured. How people feel about their jobs is insignificant. Administration avoids allowing employees any input regarding how organizational goals can best be reached. Instead, employees do their jobs as instructed, as quietly and efficiently as possible.

Traditional bureaucracies demonstrate classical scientific management theories. Bureaucracies emphasize: highly specialized units performing clearly specified job tasks; minimal discretion (that is, opportunity to make independent judgments and decisions) on the

Traditional bureaucracies demonstrate classical scientific management theories. A good example of such an organization is the Federal Bureau of Investigation, headquartered in Washington, D.C.

part of employees; and numerous specific rules to maintain control. The Social Security Administration, the Fargo Department of Social Services, and the Federal Bureau of Investigation are examples of large bureaucracies.

Human Relations Theories

Human relations theories emphasize "the role of the informal, psychosocial components of organizational functioning" (Holland & Petchers, 1987, p. 206). The idea is that satisfied, happy employees manifest the most productivity. Important concepts include "employee morale and productivity; . . . satisfaction, motivation, and leadership; and . . . the dynamics of small-group behavior" (Sarri, 1987, p. 31). Organizational leaders strive to enhance their workers' morale. Thus, effective leaders are important.

Likewise, the immediate work group (a mezzo system) is critical in human relations theories. Employees are encouraged to work cooperatively together and participate in group decision making. Employers encourage employee input concerning organizational policies and practices.

Theory X and Theory Y

The management styles of administrators and supervisors in organizations have considerable impact on the productivity and job satisfaction of employees. Douglas McGregor (1960) developed two theories of management styles. He theorized that management thinking and behavior are based on two different sets of assumptions, which he labeled Theory X and Theory Y. These theories are addressed here because in a way they are a subset of human relations theories, with emphasis on treatment of employees. Most management approaches, however, incorporate aspects of more than one theory. Theory X, for instance, reflects aspects of classical scientific management in its focus on hierarchical structure.

Theory-X managers view employees as incapable of much growth. Employees are perceived as having an inherent dislike for work, and presumed to attempt to evade work whenever possible. Therefore, X-type managers believe that they must control, direct, force, or threaten employees to make them work. Employees are also viewed as having relatively little ambition, wishing to avoid responsibilities, and preferring to be directed. X-type managers therefore spell out job responsibilities carefully, set work goals without employee input, use external rewards (such as money) to force employees to work, and punish employees who deviate from established rules. Because Theory-X managers reduce responsibilities to a level where few mistakes can be made, work becomes so structured that it is monotonous and distasteful. The assumptions of Theory X are, of course, inconsistent with what behavioral scientists assert are effective principles for directing, influencing, and motivating people.

In contrast, Theory-Y managers view employees as wanting to grow and develop by exerting physical and mental effort to accomplish work objectives to which they are committed. Y-type managers believe that the promise of internal rewards, such as self-respect and personal improvement, are stronger motivations than external rewards (money) and punishments. A Y-type manager also believes that under proper conditions, employees will not only accept responsibility but seek it. Most employees are assumed to have considerable ingenuity, creativity, and imagination for solving the organization's problems. Therefore, employees are given considerable responsibility to test the limits of their capabilities. Mistakes and errors are viewed as necessary to the learning process, and work is structured so that employees can have a sense of accomplishment and growth.

Employees who work for Y-type managers are generally more creative and productive, experience greater work satisfaction, and are more highly motivated than employees who work for X-type managers. Under both management styles, expectations often become self-fulfilling prophecies.

Systems Theories

A systems approach "construes the oraganization as a social system with interrelated parts, or subsystems, functioning in interaction and equilibrium with one another. It thinks of the organization as an adaptive whole rather than as a structure that is solely rational-legal" (Holland & Petchers, 1987, p. 207).

Systems theories emphasize the interactions of the various subsystems involved. Additionally, the importance of the environment and the impacts of other systems on the organization are stressed. In some ways, systems theories are more flexible than many other theories. Irrational, spontaneous interactions are expected rather than ignored. Systems theories emphasize constant assessment and adjustment.

Which Organizational Theory Is Best?

No one really knows which organizational theory is best. As time passes, these theoretical perspectives rise and fall in popularity. It is beyond the scope of this text to explore organizational theory other than by providing a foundation to help you understand human behavior in the context of macro systems.

Because of its flexibility and the complexities of working with real clients, this text will view organizations primarily from a systems perspective. As we have discussed, various organizational theories emphasize different views of organizations and of what you should consider most significant about them. Regardless of the theory chosen, you can readily use a systems approach to describe the processes involved in organizational life. The *Encyclopedia of Social Work* describes virtually all management approaches

in the context of systems theories (Austin, 1995). Each management theory can be examined using systems theory concepts.

Additionally, accreditation standards for all social work programs emphasize the concept of work with "systems of all sizes" (Council on Social Work Education [CSWE], 1992a, B5.7.6, B6.9; 1992b, M5.7.6, m6.11). Therefore, the following discussion will focus on organizations from a systems perspective. However, we will occasionally allude to other more specific management approaches. For instance, classical scientific management theories offer interesting views of bureaucracy.

Social Agencies as Systems

A theoretical or conceptual perspective provides you with a symbolic representation or picture of the world—in our case, the world of organizations. Systems theories make up a broad category of such symbolic representations. They involve concepts that emphasize interactions among various systems. They stress "the relationships among individuals, groups, organizations, or communities," and "they focus on the interrelationships of elements in nature, encompassing physics, chemistry, biology, and social relationships" (Barker, 1991, p. 233). In other words, systems theories provide a broad approach to understanding the world that can be applied in a multitude of settings.

General systems theory, on the other hand, is a subset of the larger body of systems theories. General systems theory more specifically aims at analyzing "the behavior of people and societies by identifying the interacting components of the system and the controls that keep these components . . . stable"; it then emphasizes living things "from microorganisms to societies." (Barker, 1991, p. 92). This contrasts with the larger category of systems theories which can be applied to virtually anything. This book adopts terms from general systems theory, as we consider organizations' and communities' living human systems.

A number of terms are extremely important in understanding general systems theory and its relationship to social work practice. They include system, boundaries, subsystem, homeostasis, role, relationship, input, output, feedback, interface, differentiation, entropy, negative entropy, and equifinality.

A *system* is a set of orderly and interrelated elements that form a functional whole. A large nation, a public social services department, and a newly married couple are all examples of systems. For our purposes, we will refer primarily to social systems, that is, those systems which are composed of people and affect people.

Boundaries are the repeatedly occurring patterns that characterize the relationships within a system and give that system a particular identity. Boundaries establish how various units in a system relate to each other. An analogy to a boundary is the membrane surrounding and enclosing a living cell (Barker, 1991, p. 26). A boundary may exist, for instance, between parents and their children. Parents maintain family leadership and provide support and nurturance to their children. A boundary may also exist between the protective service workers in a large county social service agency and those who work in financial assistance. Each orderly and interrelated group is set apart by specified boundaries in terms of its designated job responsibilities and the clients it serves. Yet, each group is part of the larger social services agency.

A *subsystem* is a secondary or subordinate system, a smaller system within a larger system. Obvious examples of subsystems are the parental and sibling subsystems within a family. Likewise, a group of protective services workers in a large social services agency system forms one subsystem within the agency, and the financial assistance workers another. These subsystems are set apart by designated boundaries, but they are still part of the larger, total agency system.

Homeostasis is the tendency for a system to maintain a relatively stable, constant state of balance. If something disturbs the homeostatic system, that system will work "to adapt" and "restore the stability previously achieved" (Barker, 1991, p. 103). A homeostatic family system functions in such a way that it can survive and family members can stay together. Likewise, a homeostatic social services agency works to maintain its ongoing existence. However, neither the family nor the agency is necessarily functioning as well or effectively as possible. Homeostasis merely means maintaining the status quo. Sometimes that status quo can be ineffective, inefficient, or seriously problematic.

For example, families with alcohol- or other drug-dependent members often strive to maintain a homeostatic state. That is, such families work to maintain whatever stability they have instead of working

to solve the substance abuse problem. Homeostasis can be uncomfortable, painful, or distressing, but at least it's predictable. Likewise, a community may strive to maintain its homeostasis despite the fact that its political leaders are excessively corrupt. Community members may hesitate to depose their leaders because potential replacements scare residents even more. At least the residents already know about the leaders they have. The unknown is scary even though it might be better. It also might be worse.

A *role* is "a culturally determined pattern of behavior that is prescribed for an individual who occupies a specific status" (Barker, 1991, p. 203). In other words, each individual in a system assumes a role in that system. A person in the role of professional social worker is expected to behave in certain professional ways as defined by the professional Code of Ethics. Each of us probably fulfills numerous roles because we are involved in multiple systems. Social workers may assume the roles of spouse and parent in their family systems in addition to their professional role of BSW or MSW. Likewise, the same practitioner may assume the role of executive director in the National Association of Social Workers' state chapter.

A *relationship* is "the mutual emotional exchange; dynamic interaction; and affective, cognitive, and behavioral connection that exists" between two or more persons or systems (Barker, 1991, p. 199). For example, a social worker may have a professional relationship with her agency supervisor. Ideally, they communicate and interact in order to maximize the worker's effectiveness. Relationships may exist among virtually any size systems. Workers in an agency may have relationships with each other, and one agency may have a relationship with another agency. Such interagency relationships will be discussed later in the context of understanding the nature of organizations.

Input is the energy, information, or communication flow received from other systems. A parent may receive input from his child's grade school principal that the child is flunking physical education. Likewise, a public agency may receive input from the state in the form of funding.

Output, on the other hand, is what happens to input after it's gone through and been processed by some system. For instance, take "the status of a client's problem at the time of case termination" (Chess and Norlin, 1988, p. 27). A client may be referred to an agency with an identified problem, for instance, of heroin addiction.[1] This client received treatment. The agency has taken its input and translated it into a process, namely treatment. When the treatment process or intervention is completed, the client's progress is evaluated. Whatever progress or lack thereof the client has made becomes part of the agency's *output*.

This text will continue to address the importance of evaluating whether a system's output is worth its input. In other words, is the agency using its resources efficiently and effectively? Or can those resources be put to a better use by providing some other type of service?

Consider the client we just talked about with the heroin problem. The client receives six weeks of treatment. He subsequently walks out of the agency and rushes home to stick a needle in his vein for a heroin injection. To what extent do you think the treatment was effective? Virtually any type of treatment is expensive. In this client's case, was the input worth the output? It certainly doesn't seem so. If the agency typically sees little progress at the end of treatment for clients, you'd probably question the agency's usefulness. Should the agency's treatment process be changed to achieve better results (that is, output)? Or should the agency be shut down totally so that resources (or input) could be better invested in some other agency or treatment system?

Feedback is a special form of input. It involves a system receiving information about that system's own performance. As a result of *negative feedback*, the system can choose to correct deviations or mistakes and return to a more homeostatic state. A supervisor may tell a social work supervisee that she is filling out an important agency form incorrectly. This allows the worker to correct her behavior and begin to complete the form appropriately.

Positive feedback is also valuable. It occurs when a system receives information about what it is doing correctly in order to maintain itself and thrive. For example, receiving a significant raise as the result of an excellent job performance review provides feedback to a worker that she is doing a good job. Likewise, receiv-

ing a specific federal grant gives an agency feedback that it has developed a plan worthy of such funding.

An *interface* is "the point of contact or communication between different systems, organizations, or individuals" (Barker, 1991, p. 117). One interface is the written contract between a field instructor in an adoptions agency and a student intern placed under her supervision. At the beginning of the semester, they discuss plans and goals for the semester. What tasks will the student be given, and what levels of performance will be expected? With the help of the student's field liaison (that is, the student's college professor), a written contract is established that clarifies these expectations. Contracts generally involve written, oral, or implied agreements between persons "as to the goals, methods, timetables, and mutual obligations to be fulfilled" during some period in their relationship (Barker, 1991, p. 50).

At his midterm evaluation, the student receives a grade of D. Although he is devastated, he still has half of the semester to improve. Focusing on the interface between the field instructor and the field intern (in this case, the contract they established at the beginning of the semester) provides direction concerning what to do about the problem. By reviewing the terms specified in the contract, the instructor and student, with the university liaison's help, can elaborate on problems and expectations. Where did the student go wrong? Which of the student's expectations did the field instructor fail to fulfill? They then can establish a new contract concerning the student's performance for the remainder of the semester.

It is still up to the student to "make or break" his field experience. However, the contract (or interface) provides a clearly designated means of approaching the problem. Having the field instructor and field liaison vaguely tell the student that he needs "to improve his performance" probably would not do much good. Rather, identifying and using the interface in the form of the student/instructor contract provides a specific means for attacking the problem. For example, the student's expectations might include observing a designated number of staff meetings, reading specified client records, and successfully completing goals established with two assigned clients.

It should be stressed that interfaces are not limited to those between individual systems. Interfaces can characterize interactions among virtually any size systems. For example, there is an interface between the adoptions agency providing the student placement men-

---

1. Heroin is "a strongly physiologically addictive narcotic . . . that is made by acetylation of [morphine] but is more potent than morphine and that is prohibited for medical use in the U.S. but is used illicitly for its euphoric effects" (*Webster's Ninth New Collegiate Dictionary*, 1991, p. 567).

tioned above and the university social work program that places the student intern in that agency. This interface involves the specified agreements concerning the respective responsibilities and expectations of each of these two larger systems.

Differentiation is a system's tendency to move from a more simplified to a more complex existence. In other words, relationships, situations, and interactions tend to get more complex instead of more simplified over time. For example, in the life of any particular family, each day adds new experiences. New information is gathered. New options are explored. The family's life naturally becomes more complex. Likewise, as a social services agency continued over time, it will likely develop more detailed policies and programs.

Entropy is the natural tendency of a system to progress toward disorganization, depletion, and, in essence, death. The idea is that nothing lasts forever. People age and eventually die. Young families get older and children leave to start their own independent lives or their own families. As history moves on, older agencies and systems are eventually replaced by new ones.

Negative entropy is the progress of a system toward growth and development. In effect, it is the opposite of entropy. Individuals develop physically, intellectually, and emotionally as they grow. Social service agencies grow and develop new programs and clientele.

Equifinality means that there are many different means to the same end. It is important not to get locked into only one way of thinking. In any particular situation, alternatives do exist. Some may be better than others, but, nonetheless, there are alternatives. For instance, you as a social worker may solicit needed resources for a family from a variety of sources. These may include financial assistance, housing allowances, food stamps, grants, or private charities. Furthermore, you may have to choose among the alternatives available from a variety of agencies.

Viewing Organizations from a Systems Perspective

As social workers, we want to serve our clients as best we can. Because we will probably be working in social service organizations, we want those organizations to be as effective as they can be. We also want other organi-

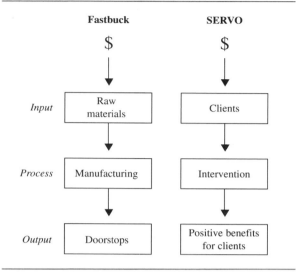

Figure 4.1
Fastbuck and SERVO—Similar Processes

zations with which our clients have transactions to be as effective as possible. The underlying theme is to provide the best resources and services possible to help the people who are our clients. We must maintain constant awareness of how well social service organizations are serving their clients. Therefore, we must continuously assess the effectiveness of organizations. That is, we must ask ourselves to what extent each organization is attaining its designated goals.

Social service organizations can be compared to other organizations such as businesses in a variety of ways. Social service organizations take input (which is, at its most basic level, financial), process this input through service provision, and produce some output (namely, results for clients that, hopefully, are positive). Figure 4.1 illustrates this process and compares it to a business organization. As an example, we will arbitrarily compare social service organizations to a business involved in manufacturing doorstops that we will call Fastbuck. We will arbitrarily call our social services organization Services for Enhancing and Restoring Value to Olive-Growers (SERVO).

Resource Input

Figure 4.1 illustrates how both Fastbuck and SERVO take financial resources and use them to pay for raw material. Fastbuck purchases materials such as metals, chemicals, molds, and plastic to prepare for the production process, getting its funds from sources like investments by stockholders and prior profits from selling Fastbuck doorstops.

SERVO, on the other hand, applies its financial resources to clients, specifically, rural olive-growers approaching or reaching bankruptcy. Social service organizations differ strikingly from manufacturing/business organizations in that their "raw material" is clients (Holland & Petchers, 1987). SERVO secures its resources from public moneys (received from taxes) and a variety of private sources (such as donations, fees, and grants). It then applies these financial resources through some type of helping process. The output is the number of counseling hours with clients and the amount of resources provided.

Process Through Organizational Technology

Both Fastbuck and SERVO then process their "raw material." That is, Fastbuck passes its raw material through a manufacturing production process whereby materials are gradually reshaped, blended, and recombined to produce the desired product, namely Fastbuck doorstops.

SERVO, on the other hand, uses a completely different process on its "raw material." Instead of a manufacturing process, it provides some type of intervention. This intervention can involve counseling, financial assistance, or any other type of social service provision.

Both Fastbuck and SERVO use an *organizational technology* to process and apply their resources. Organizational technology includes all the activities performed to complete the organization's tasks and achieve its goals (Daft, 1992). Fastbuck's organizational technology involves manufacturing and processing materials into doorstops. Likewise, SERVO's organizational technology involves the types of intakes, assessments, interventions, evaluations, and follow-ups the agency undertakes in helping bankrupt or nearly bankrupt clients. One other example or organizational technology is your college classroom. The organizational technology includes the teaching process, the activities and discussions in which you participate, and the information you receive.

Output

Both Fastbuck and SERVO produce output (that is, a finished product) at the end of their processes. Fastbuck produces complete new doorstops ready to be marketed against Chinese and German competition. SERVO, on the other hand, has applied its process (that is, intervention) to produce services that, in turn, have positive effects on and for clients. Such effects may range from improved mental health to improved financial planning and status.

The Nature of Organizations

Meenaghan (1987) eloquently states that the profession has come "to believe that social workers should be trained to see how their agency functioned as a complex organization, what external forces could and would influence and constrain it, and how social workers could act positively, even initiating events in the agency's environment" (p. 83). Social workers must understand how their agencies work in order to do their jobs and help their agencies become more effective. The purpose of this section is not to provide a detailed explanation of organizational behavior. Rather, it is to alert new social workers to factors that can affect their ability to do their jobs.

Organizations are particularly important to you for three basic reasons. First, you will most likely be employed by one. Your organization's policies, goals, and restrictions will directly affect what work you can and cannot do with clients. The second reason for their significance is that often the organization and not the client will be the source of the problem. (We will discuss this later in much greater depth.) You, therefore, will need to evaluate for yourself how well your own organization is functioning in order to do your own work effectively. Third, Hasenfeld (1984) stresses the importance of organizational analysis prior to undertaking any macro level changes. You need to understand a number of dimensions inherent in organizations in order to comprehend and plan the implementation of macro changes.

The ensuing discussion stresses the following concepts: agency settings; organizational goals; the macro context of organizations; and organizational structure.

Agency Settings

Social workers usually work in one of two types of organizational settings: primary or secondary. Each type of setting has implications for effective practice and for the way you will experience your work environment.

Primary Settings

Primary settings are agencies where social work is the main or primary profession employed. Most public social service agencies are primary settings. It is common for the administrators, supervisors, and most of the workers to be social workers and carry social work titles. While there may be other occupations or professions present (for example, homemakers or psychologists), they represent a minority of the staff.

Because most of the staff and administrators are social workers, they tend to share similar professional values and perspectives. Their education and training are typically similar. One benefit of these settings is that workers never have to explain what social workers do. Everyone knows and understand the social work role. This cannot be said of the other category, secondary settings.

Secondary Settings

Secondary settings are characterized by the presence of a variety of professional staff. The main service provided by the agency is not social services. Typical examples are hospitals and schools. In the hospital, medical care of patients is the primary service. Medically trained personnel (e.g., nurses and physicians) comprise the largest segment of the professional staff. Most of the administrative staff and supervisors have medical backgrounds. Social work is just one of several ancillary professions contributing to the overall goal of providing medical care. Other professions include dietitians, pharmacists, and chaplains, to name a few.

The wealth of disciplines and professional perspectives can produce a challenging environment for social work. Typically social workers must learn the language (for instance, medical terminology or relevant abbreviations) used by the other professions. Unlike primary settings, the hospital is likely to operate with a definite pecking order. Physicians are at the top of that hierarchy. Social workers are not. This sometimes means that social work values and perspectives clash with those of the physicians and other medical personnel. The following example illustrates how this can work.

Laura, a hospital social worker, was working with Tom, a sixty-one-year-old patient with Parkinson's disease, and his family. Parkinson's disease is "a chronic progressive nervous disease of later life that is marked by tremor and weakness or resting muscles and by a peculiar gait" (*Webster's Ninth New Collegiate Dictionary*, 1991, p. 856). Tom had been hospitalized for a malfunctioning of his kidneys that had nothing to do with his Parkinson's disease. However, nurses referred Tom to Laura when they observed him falling several times while walking from his bed to the bathroom. These nurses felt that Tom would have difficulty returning home without special equipment such as a walker or a wheelchair. They indicated he might even require special placement instead of returning to his home.

Laura met with Tom. She found it very difficult to understand him, as the Parkinson's disease was seriously affecting his ability to formulate words. However, with some difficulty she was able to discuss his situation with him. He stated vehemently that he wanted to return home. He emphasized that the disease "wasn't that bad" and stressed that he would be all right now that the kidney problem had subsided, if he could just get home!

Laura also spoke alone with Tom's wife, Wendy, age fifty-nine. Wendy felt that Tom was denying the seriousness of his condition. She said that his muscular control and balance had deteriorated significantly in the past four months. Wendy told Laura that Tom had been a professor of engineering at a prestigious private college. She explained that it was very difficult for him to admit to his increasingly serious weakness. Wendy also expressed concern about her ability to care for him adequately at home. Tom was a large hulk of a man, and it was impossible for her to lift him if he fell. She felt that someone needed to be with him at all times. Yet she hesitated to move him out of their home and into a health-care facility. She felt it might break his spirit and his heart.

Laura met with Tom and Wendy individually one more time and, finally, together for their last encounter. She discussed with them a variety of possibilities. These included supportive equipment, widening the doorways in their home and installing ramps for wheelchair accessibility, and referring them to various other support services. The equipment included a beeper Tom could use if he fell. Wendy also began arranging for a visiting nurse to assist Wendy with Tom's care and allow Wendy some respite time to herself.

Laura felt good about her work with Tom and Wendy. She felt she had helped them establish a viable plan for the present. It could maintain Tom in his own home until his increasing disability required more extensive treatment, such as placement in a special facility. Laura had already contacted the recommended services to establish their availability and viability in Tom's case. The next step was to finalize the plans and put them in place before Tom's upcoming discharge.

Laura came to work the next morning and went around as usual checking her patients' charts to see what was happening and to monitor their progress. When she got to Tom's room, it was empty. Initially, Laura assumed that a nurse or volunteer had taken him for a walk.

However, she was shocked as she read his chart. It stated he was being moved that very day to a health-care facility. What about the plans she had made with Tom and Wendy? What about Tom's adamant feelings about remaining at his own home? In disbelief she stared at the signature of Tom's attending physician, Dr. Strangelove. Dr. Strangelove had totally ignored all that she had written in the chart about Tom's discharge planning. How dare Dr. Strangelove do this! How dare he act as if she did not even exist.

Luckily, Laura was so busy that day that she had little time to think about Tom, Wendy, or Dr. Strangelove. By the next morning she had simmered down a bit. After all, Tom and Wendy had the right to choose their own destinies. She was just there to help them if she could.

When she later talked to the head nurse about the matter, Laura was enlightened about what it means to work in a secondary setting. She found out that the physician's word rules in a medical facility. Apparently, Dr. Strangelove was a personal friend of Wendy's son Devin, who was also a physician. Dr. Strangelove and Devin sat down first with Wendy and later with Tom to discuss their feelings about Tom's condition and his and Wendy's future. Both physicians felt strongly that it was ridiculous for Tom to return home and far beyond Wendy's marital responsibility to "sacrifice" herself for Tom. They had apparently urged and eventually persuaded Wendy to place Tom in a residential facility. It was the head nurse's opinion that Tom was too weak to fight three people at once. So, defeated, he complied with their recommendations.

Laura was not convinced that the decision was the correct one for either Tom or Wendy. However, she understood that they had every right to make their own decisions regardless of the dynamics involved in the decision-making process. Laura also learned that she had significantly less status than a physician in this secondary setting.

Organizational Goals

An organizational goal is "a desired state of affairs which the organization attempts to realize (Etzioni, 1964, p. 6). Organizational goals serve at least three major purposes (Etzioni, 1964). First, they provide guidelines for the kinds of functions and activities organizational workers are supposed to pursue. Second, organizational goals "constitute a source of legitimacy which justifies the activities of an organization and, indeed, its very existence" (p. 5). Third, goals can "serve as standards by which members of an organization and outsiders can assess the success of the organization—that is, its effectiveness and efficiency" (p. 5).

How does an organization establish its goals? Holland and Petchers (1987) explain: "Official goals represent a translation of social welfare legislation and policy direction into programmatic action or activities. Official goals also indicate value choices and ideological and theoretical stances about human needs or problems. Goals that the organization sets for itself form criteria by which the organization may be evaluated and held accountable" (p. 207).

Social service organizations and agencies, then, formulate goals in order to address any of a wide range of needs and problems concerning human well-being. Social service organizations are supposed to use their resources to address these needs and remedy problems. The establishment of goals directs this process.

In order to understand an organization's functioning, it is helpful to think in terms of official goals and operative goals (Perrow, 1961, p. 856). *Official goals* "are the general purposes of the organization as put forth in the charter [often called a *mission statement*], annual reports, public statements by key officials and other authoritative pronouncements"; *operative goals*, on the other hand, "designate the ends sought through the actual operating policies of the organization" (p. 856). Official goals entail what the organization publicly says it is *supposed to do*. Operative goals are what the organization *really does* in its day-to-day practice with clients.

Why must we make the distinction between official and operative goals? Because "official goals may predict little about organizational behavior" (Hasenfeld, 1983, p. 87). In other words, official goals may have very little to do with an agency's actual operative goals. Reasons for this will be discussed more thoroughly when we address the concept of goal displacement.

Multiple Goals

Social service organizations are often complex entities that aim to accomplish multiple goals (Hasenfeld, 1983; Holland & Petchers, 1987). There are a number of reasons for this. First, agencies must hold themselves accountable to legislative requirements and constraints. For instance, an organization providing group homes for children with developmental disabilities must conform to a range of state licensing rules that mandate minimum standards for service provision. These include the maximum number of clients in any particular residence, the amount of space required per child, the staff-to-client ratio, and even the requirement that toilet seats be open or split in the front instead of closed.

Multiple goals also are set because many social service agencies serve a range of client groups. For example, one organization may provide daycare services, vocational training, adoption services, and foster care all at the same time. Each segment of the agency pursues more individualized goals in the context of the larger environment with its more encompassing organizational goals.

Additionally, organizations are accountable to various different segments of the public, each with its own demands. Such publics can include "other human service organizations, interest groups, legislative bodies, and professional associations" in addition to clients being served (Hasenfeld, 1983, pp. 90–91). For example,

a child advocacy group may pressure a social services agency specializing in helping survivors of domestic violence to increase its standards for temporary shelter of mothers and their children. Likewise, professional organizations may require the same agency to provide minimum in-service training sessions for staff in various positions. Hence, the agency must pursue both of these goals in addition to many other goals established for numerous other reasons.

Goal Displacement

One major problem encountered by workers in organizations is goal displacement. Goal displacement was originally defined as "substitution of a legitimate goal with another goal which the organization was not developed to address, for which resources were not allocated and which it is not known to serve" (Etzioni, 1964, p. 10). Holland and Petchers (1987) interpret this by stating that "goal displacement often occurs when the means to a goal becomes the goal itself. In recent years, goal displacement has become a serious concern in human service organizations" (p. 208).

In other words, goal displacement occurs when an organization continues to function but no longer achieves the goals it's supposed to. In social service organizations, it often means that the rules and following those rules become more important than providing service to clients.

It should be noted that goal displacement can lead to positive changes in goals. A classic example is the March of Dimes, which began as an organization dedicated to raising money to eradicate polio, historically a major childhood disease. With the discovery of a polio vaccine, the disease ceased to be a major health problem. Instead of going out of business, however, the organization simply shifted its goal to raising money to combat birth defects. The new goal had one advantage over the polio-related goal. Instead of focusing on a single disease, the organization now directed its attention to a broad category of problems. With such a broad scope, the organization will probably never run out of childhood health problems to combat, so it's unlikely that it will ever again face the dilemma of goal displacement.

This is not a criticism of the March of Dimes or any other organization. It is a fact of organizational life that agencies rarely go out of existence. Once a goal is achieved, most organizations do not disappear. Instead,

Goal displacement can lead to positive changes. When this picture of Danny Kaye and Bing Crosby with poster child Delbert "Denny" Dains was taken in 1954, the March of Dimes was exclusively devoted to eradicating polio. With the discovery of a polio vaccine, the organization changed its focus to combating a broad range of birth defects. It is unlikely that the March of Dimes will ever again experience goal displacement.

they shift their attention to new goals. This process becomes a problem only when the means to the goals assume a life of their own. When this happens, agencies place greater emphasis on getting the files up-to-date than on providing effective services to clients.

General Systems Theory, Organizations, and Goal Displacement

We have established that it is helpful to view social service organizations in terms of general systems theory. Many of the concepts involved are similar to those we use to refer to business and industry. In industry, resources or input is processed by the organizational system which turns out a product, or *output*. Figure 4.2 illustrates this sequence as "systems concepts." Essentially, the same thing happens in social service organizations. They take resources (input) and, in response to social forces and institutionalized values, apply a process (procedure for providing services) to product output (actual service provision or other benefits for clients).

Often when goal displacement occurs, however, the emphasis is placed on the process rather than on the product. The organizational system sees the process of providing services as its major function. The process, rather than it's benefit to the client becomes the organization's *product*.

Goal attainment refers to what is supposed to happen through the intervention process. Illustrated in figure 4.2, the input (in the form of resources) is supposed to be used on behalf of clients through the intervention process. Hence, "$" refers to resources with an arrow pointing to "clients" in the top box. The result is supposed to be positive benefits for clients. Thus, an arrow points from the "$ to clients" box to the middle box, "intervention process." The intervention process is whatever treatment or technology the organization uses to help its clients. Finally, an arrow points from the "intervention" box down to the "benefits for clients" box, illustrating an agency's goal attainment process.

Figure 4.2 also illustrates *goal displacement* on the

Figure 4.2
The Process of Goal Displacement

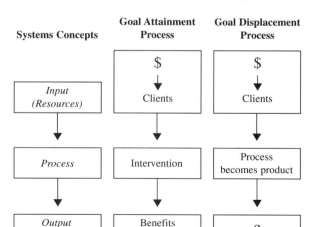

HIGHLIGHT 4.1

AN EXAMPLE OF GOAL DISPLACEMENT— PROCESS SUPERSEDES PROGRESS

A large county department of social services (or public welfare department) is located in the shell of an old department store with high ceilings and myriad small worker cubicles resembling a mammoth beehive. All outside windows have been sealed with bricks because of "heating and ventilation problems." No one really knows what that means. However, everyone inside the building knows that the interior is isolated from the outside world.

When entering the main door of the building, it is extremely difficult to figure out where to find a particular kind of service. This is true even if you're a professional social worker, let alone if you're a client entering the building for the first time. Consider what it would be like if you were a client applying for services from this agency. You probably have to stand in line for fifteen to twenty minutes simply to find out where to go.

When you finally wander into a waiting area for the services you need, you have to stand in line again for another twenty minutes or so to get the forms you must fill out for the services you need. You than take twenty pages of complicated forms, which you must fill out meticulously, and take a seat. The chairs are made of hard plastic. There are large dust bunnies (sometimes referred to as "dinosaur dust bunnies") rolling around your feet. It takes approximately an hour to fill out the forms, assuming you can read English well. You probably do not understand some of the questions so you leave the spaces blank. You then take the forms to the desk, where they are placed in a pile. You wait your turn to see an intake worker (that is, someone who begins the process of providing services). You wait two or three hours.

Finally, your name is called and you are instructed to go to Cubicle 57 to see Ms. Simpson. You enter Cubicle 57 and see Ms. Simpson sitting at her desk, reading your forms. You begin a discus-

sion with her about the additional information she needs to process your application. It seems, she indicates, that a number of critical elements of information are missing. Look at those blanks. She tells you to get the critical information before you continue the application process, but that critical information is somewhere at home. Well, that's all right. Just go home, get it, and start this whole process again tomorrow. At least you know where the waiting room is now.

In this example the organization is supposed to provide services to people in need. However, the complicated process, commonly called red tape, has become more important to the workers than whether clients received needed services or not.

People's access to resources has a major impact on the options available to them and, in effect, on how they behave. Poverty and lack of resources are at the root of many of your client's problems. Therefore, it is crucial to understand how organizations affect resource provision and clients. Such a background can enable you to identify ways to change systems so that your clients really are served better.

Consider the example above. As a worker in that agency, there are several things you might target for change. These include working with other workers and with administration to significantly shorten the tedious forms. You might also explore ways to get information to community residents regarding the documentation and information they must bring when applying for services. Simple things like putting up clearly visible signs instructing people where to go when they first enter the building might be helpful. Suggesting comfortable waiting room chairs might be useful. A variety of ways in which a social worker can foster positive change will be discussed later in this chapter and throughout the text.

far right. Here, input is used to maintain the *process* itself. In essence, the process becomes the *product*. Positive impact on clients are lost and forgotten as agency personnel strive to maintain and complete the process. Figure 4.2 depicts this with arrows leading from the ''$ to clients'' box to the ''process becomes product'' box. The arrow leading from the latter box down to the ''?'' box shows that the actual results for clients have become relatively unimportant and possibly unknown.

The Macro Context of Organizations

The environment context in which a social service organization functions is critically important to the organization's ability to pursue and attain its goals. At least four environmental dimensions have impact on organizations. They include available resources, legitimation, client source, and relationships with other organizations (Holland and Petchers, 1987).

Resources

Hasenfeld (1984) refers to ''resource inputs'' as ''those external units which provide the target agency with its financial basis and those units which provide its personnel'' (p. 24). First, a social services agency must have money to function, to pay staff salaries, rent and/or building maintenance, supplies, telephone, and innumerable other expenses. In order for you to determine whether macro change is possible in an agency, you need to assess whether potential resources are available. How much will your proposed macro level change cost the organization? This is true whether you want to implement a project, develop a whole new program, or amend some agency policy. (These macro interventions will be discussed much more thoroughly in chapters 5 through 7.) What such a macro change will cost is often the bottom line on whether you'll succeed or fail with your macro proposal.

The second critical resource for a social services agency is personnel. What kind of staffing does the agency have? What are their professional credentials? Are staff qualified and plentiful enough to carry out their duties? Are the appropriate staff available for you to implement your proposed macro change?

For example, a debate raged in one state between professional social workers and certain county social service agency administrators. Some of the administrators were social workers and some were not. The battle ensued when professional certification for social workers was initiated in the state. Most professional social workers adamantly maintained that it was critically important for workers calling themselves ''social workers'' to have graduated from accredited social work programs and have the requisite experience.

Some rural county social service agency administrators, on the other hand, staunchly maintained that there were not enough graduates of professional social work programs to fill all the positions available in their rural agencies. They maintained that the only workers they could attract to fill their positions were graduates with other degrees (e.g., in sociology and psychology). They emphasized that most social work graduates are attracted to the state's urban areas.

Much to the dismay of professional social work educators, a faction of sociologists teaching in local universities supported the county administrators' view and lobbied on their behalf. In reality, these sociologists were concerned that graduates with sociology degrees be able to find employment as easily as graduates with social work degrees. This view coincided with the sociologists' own interests, namely, to maintain the number of sociology majors.

Most professional social workers and social work educators were appalled. None of the sociology programs was accredited. Therefore, these programs were not held accountable to standards such as those mandating the teaching of practice skills, the infusion of professional values and ethics throughout the curriculum, a substantial field internship, and a focus on cultural diversity. All social work programs, on the other hand, were required to adhere rigidly to such standards.

Upon further investigation, the state association of social workers established that the major reason the complaining rural county administrators were unable to recruit social work graduates was that these administrators paid minimal salaries. The state social work association determined that hundreds of graduates were being turned out of several state universities within one-hundred miles of these counties. In reality, there were plenty of graduates available to fill positions if the counties would pay salaries appropriate for professional social workers.

This environmental dimension had substantial impact on the county social service agencies' ability to provide professional services. If agencies were not required to hire professional social workers, but could employ any sociology or psychology graduate, regardless of their training in skills and values, quality of service would be seriously curtailed. The agencies' personnel resources would directly affect their ability to provide service to clients.

Legitimation

A second environmental dimension affecting social service agencies is *legitimation*. We have already briefly mentioned the importance of legislative requirements and constraints with respect to an agency's organizational goals. Legitimation is the appropriate status or authorization to perform agency functions and pursue agency goals that is granted by external entities (e.g., local government). An agency must be legally viable. Once established, the agency must continue to abide by the rules upon which its existence is based.

What if an agency does not follow the appropriate rules and regulations? For example, a health-care center for the elderly failed to follow the rules about maintenance of its bedridden patients, especially those with Alzheimer's Disease. Clients' relatives visiting the center reported to the state's licensing agency that they had observed a number of seriously disturbing incidents during her visits. These observations included clients wallowing in their own feces for a day or more, staff slapping clients in the face when the clients refused to cooperate, and employees depriving clients of food as punishment for undesirable behavior. Needless to say, once the health-care center's practices were known and investigated, the agency was closed. It no longer possessed the legitimation and accountability needed to justify its existence.

Client Sources

The third environment dimension affecting agencies is availability of clients. This "array of client sources, which ranges from groups or programs that serve as client referral mechanisms to individuals who directly seek out services for themselves" is critical to an agency's existence and functioning (Holland & Petchers, 1987, p. 208). In other words, an agency cannot last very long without enough clients to sustain it.

One agency provided special therapy services (including social work, occupational, speech, and phys-

ical) to school children in a variety of rural counties. The counties did not initially have enough clients for each to hire its own full-time therapists. Therefore, each county purchased from the agency whatever therapists' time it needed. For example, a social worker or occupational therapist might serve clients in a particular county only one or two days each week, which might be all the service that county needed. Together, the counties provided enough work for the agency to maintain several full-time therapists in each discipline. However, new state requirements for providing adequate service to children were put into place. The counties also began to develop enhanced assessment techniques and procedures. As a result, a number of counties found that they could identify enough of their own clients to hire full-time therapists. Hence, the agency providing special services no longer had enough clients in enough counties. It simply had to shut down.

Relationship with Other Organizations

The fourth environmental dimension affecting organizations is its relationship with other agencies in the macro environment. Analysis of this organizational environment is essential to understanding any particular organization's functioning. How does any social service agency interact with other organizations in its macro environment? Such relationships may fall under the category of *uninvolved, "complementary,"* or *"competitive"* (Holland & Petcher, 1987, pp. 208–9).

1. *Uninvolved relationships among organizations.* Organizational involvement can be placed on a continuum (Emery & Trist, 1961). At one end are agencies that are integrally involved with, and in essence can't function without, each other. Such complementary relationships are discussed below. On the other end of this continuum lie agencies that have virtually nothing to do with each other except for brief, irregular encounters. There is little need to focus much attention on such *uninvolved* relationships. In the middle of this continuum lie organizations that are competitive with each other. This latter type will also be discussed below.

2. *"Complementary" relationships among organizations.* The "availability of complementary services" involves the need of organizations to work together (Holland & Petchers, 1987, p. 208). Agencies are not islands and cannot function in isolation.

They need referral sources for clients. Alternately, they need appropriate resources to which they can refer clients whose needs they cannot meet. Consider a sheltered workshop where adults with developmental disabilities are trained in basic work skills under comprehensive supervision. Such an agency needs other agencies that run group homes and institutional facilities where clients reside when not at work. If clients have nowhere to live, they can't take advantage of the sheltered workshop's activities.

Another example is an organization providing inpatient treatment for alcoholic clients receives virtually all of its referrals from local family-services agencies providing family counseling and local hospitals. Without the cooperation of these referral agencies, the inpatient program would cease to exist. Likewise, the local family services agencies and hospitals would be unable to serve alcoholic clients adequately if the in-patient alcohol treatment program did not exist.

3. *"Competitive" relationships among organizations.* Social service agencies may compete with each other for clients. If the number of clients is relatively limited, the competition can be fierce. We have established that agencies need clients to survive and thrive. For example, one state supported a number of privately run residential treatment centers for boys, ages twelve to seventeen, who had serious behavioral problems. The state purchased services from these agencies because it did not provide such services itself. Purchase-of-service is "a fiscal arrangement between two or more social agencies or between an agency and a government body, usually involving a contract between an agency with funds and another that can provide needed services" (Barker, 1995, p. 307).

For many years the state and counties provided enough clients to maintain all of the centers. No new centers opened because existing agencies adequately served the number of clients. The status quo was maintained. However, when the state decided to build and open its own extremely large treatment complex, the number of clients available to privately run centers significantly decreased. Approximately half of the residential centers were forced to close. They could not solicit enough clients to sustain themselves. The other half of the centers continued to exist because they quickly decided to specialize their services. One center specialized in serving clients with dual diagnoses of both developmental disability and behavioral disorder. Another

center specialized in boys needing treatment because they had been sexually abused.

The new state treatment complex was not large enough to accommodate all of the state's clients who needed treatment. These clients had to go somewhere. The state determined that it was in the state's fiscal interest to continue purchasing services for some clients. The fact that various centers decided to specialize in treating certain problems facilitated the state's decision-making process concerning which clients to treat in its own facility and which to refer elsewhere. Children with special needs and problems were referred to centers that specialized in the treatment of their respective needs and problems.

Organizational Structure

Each agency has its own personality. That is, it is more formal or informal, structured or unstructured, innovative or traditional than other agencies. Especially when you first begin work within an agency, it is important to understand the agency's character. How much freedom will you have in your daily professional activities? What tasks are considered most important (for example, documentation of treatment effectiveness, other record-keeping, administrative conferences, or number of hours spent with clients)? What are the agency's expectations regarding services to clients? Are you as a worker expected to provide services to clients directly or to serve as a case manager for other service providers?

All large agencies (and many smaller ones, as well) have a *formal structure*. Sometimes it is explicated in an organizational chart showing who reports to whom. Such charts depict lines of authority and communication within the agency. Frequently, the agency operates in accordance with this chart, at least with respect to some functions.

Equally often, however, agencies develop *informal structures* and lines of communication. For example, it is typical for an agency to structure its units so that all workers in the unit report to one supervisor. Consider the case of the Brack County Foster Care Unit. Five workers and a supervisor comprise this unit. When workers have questions or problems they are supposed to bring these to the Foster Care Unit supervisor. Often, though, workers in the unit discuss their cases with other workers or with the senior worker in another county agency. This means that the Foster Care Unit supervisor may lack information that might be important to her job.

While this may seem like a bad arrangement, it has some beneficial aspects. Workers who are sometimes uncomfortable talking with their supervisor can get help from other more experienced workers. Sharing ideas and problems helps to produce a camaraderie among the workers. This decreases their stress levels and often leads to better job performance. Human relations theories stress the importance of such interpersonal communication and support in organizations.

The point here is not to praise or criticize informal structures and communication channels. Instead, it is to acknowledge that they do exist and are a reality with which you must deal in your agency. In practice, being aware of both formal and informal avenues within your agency can strengthen your ability to do your job. Once you know all your options and alternatives, you can make more informed choices. This is, after all, a major goal of the problem-solving process.

Three concepts are especially significant when appraising an agency's formal and informal structures. These are *lines of authority, channels of communication,* and *dimensions of power.* The pros and cons of *centralization* versus *decentralization* will also be briefly addressed.

Lines of Authority

All large agencies (and many smaller ones) have a formal structure. An agency's formal structure rests on *lines of authority* (Daft, 1992). For our purposes, authority concerns the specific administrative and supervisory responsibilities of supervisors to their supervisees. Who is designated to supervise whom? Agency policy usually specifies these lines of authority in writing.

An agency's formal structure is often explained in an organizational chart (Lauffer et al., 1977). Positions held by individual staff members are portrayed as squares or circles labeled according to their respective job positions. The hierarchy of authority in an organizational chart is depicted by vertical lines leading from supervisors down to supervisees (Daft, 1992, p. 13). Generally, job positions higher on the chart have greater authority than those placed lower. Lines drawn from higher figures to lower figures identify the supervisors

of staff holding lower job positions with less responsibility and power. In essence, these lines show "who is responsible for whom" (Lauffer et al., 1977, p. 31). The formal organizational structure as demonstrated by an organizational chart, then, indicates how control and supervision are *supposed* to flow.

The chart in figure 4.3 reflects the hierarchy of authority for Multihelp, an agency providing assessment and therapeutic treatment to children with multiple developmental and physical disabilities. Parents bring children with a wide range of physical and behavioral difficulties to the agency to assess the children's abilities in a variety of areas, plan treatment programs, and provide appropriate therapies.

Rectangles in figure 4.3 designate those positions with some administrative responsibility in the agency system. The bolder the rectangle, the more authority and responsibility the position entails.

The executive director has the most authority and is responsible for the overall performance of Multihelp. Below him are five agency directors including the medical director (a physician), and those for accounting, maintenance engineering, food services for clients and staff, and transportation services for clients. Each director (except accounting) is, in turn, responsible for the supervision of other staff further down the hierarchy. The medical director is responsible for overseeing the entire clinical program, including the work of the various departmental supervisors. Departments include occupational therapy, physical therapy, speech therapy, psychology, and social work. Circles at the very bottom of the chart represent line staff who are providing services directly to clients.

If you examine this chart, it is painfully clear how this agency is run, right? If you look at the Social Work Department, there are two direct service workers who report directly to their social work supervisor. It is obvious that these social workers go about their business of providing services to clients, look to their own supervisor for direction, and live happily ever after. The chain of command is so evident that you may be thinking that this entire discussion borders on, or sinks into, monotony.

The catch is that formal organizational charts depict lines of *formal* authority within agencies, showing how communication and power are supposed to flow. Sometimes, an agency's actual chain of command follows the formal chart fairly closely. Equally often, however,

Figure 4.3
Multihelp—An Example of a Formal Organizational Chart

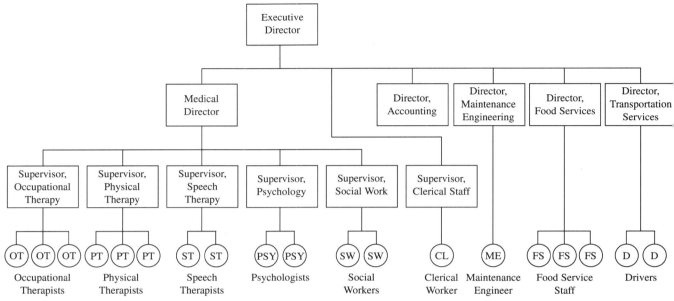

agencies develop *informal* channels of communication and power that are very different from those stated on paper. Let's explore Multihelp's informal channels of communication and dimensions of power.

Channels of Communication

All agencies have "multiple networks of communication by which members relay and receive information" (Resnick & Patti, 1980, p. 51). Communication, of course, is "a process by which information is exchanged between individuals through a common system of symbols, signs, or behavior" (*Webster's Ninth New Collegiate Dictionary*, p. 266). Communication, then, covers the many nuances of how information is conveyed, verbally and nonverbally. It entails subtle inflections, comfort level between communicators, and multitudes of minute gestures.

Formal lines of authority imply that communication is supposed to flow harmoniously and synchronistically along these lines of authority. In other words, supervisees are *supposed* to communicate primarily with their identified supervisors for direction and feedback. Like-

wise, supervisors are supposed to communicate directly with their supervisees and the managers who supervise them. As we will see, in Multihelp this is not the case.

Dimensions of Power

Power involves "the possession of resources that enables an individual to do something independently or to exercise influence and control over others" (Barker, 1991, p. 177). Like channels of communication, dimensions of power are supposed to follow the lines of authority. In the organizational chart, those in supervisory positions are supposed to have actual power (that is, clear-cut influence and control) over their employees. In real-life agency environments, this may or may not be the case.

Informal Structure: Multihelp—An Example

Direct your attention to the Social Work and Psychology Departments illustrated in figure 4.4. We will concentrate on this smaller portion of the organizational chart

Figure 4.4
Contrasting Formal and Informal Structures in Agencies

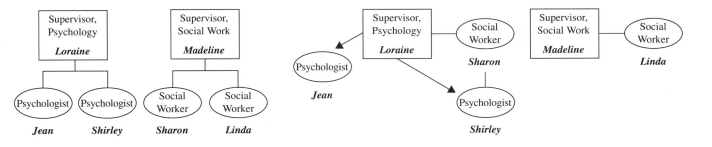

Formal Structure of Authority in Two Agency Departments

Real-Life Informal Channels of Communication

depicting the informal structures of communication and power within the agency. Figure 4.4 contrasts the formal and informal structures of these two agency departments. The *real* channels of communication and dimensions of power among supervisors and direct service staff are very different from those illustrated in the formal organizational chart. The real relationships reflect the personalities and interactions of people who have unique perspectives and identities, strengths and weaknesses, and problems and needs of their own.

The formal structure pictures Loraine, the Psychology Department's supervisor, as responsible for the administration and supervision of both Jean's and Shirley's job performance. Both the latter have master's degrees in psychology. Likewise, the formal structure shows Madeline, the Social Work Department's supervisor, as having direct supervisory authority over both Sharon and Linda, each of whom has a master's degree in social work.

The lower box portrays the real-life informal structure of these departments. Sharon, one of the social workers, has become good friends with Loraine, the Psychology Department's supervisor. Both single, they frequently socialize together and even vacation together. Their positive relationship is reflected by the bold line connecting them in figure 4.4.

Sharon, on the other hand, does not get along with Madeline, her supervisor. It is difficult to define what "having a personality conflict" really means. However, it could describe Sharon and Madeline's relationship. For whatever reason, they do not personally like each other. Additionally, Sharon views Madeline as basically incompetent, lazy, and interested in doing as little work as possible. On the other hand, Madeline perceives Sharon as an overly energetic, impulsive go-getter who acts "just like a bull in a china cabinet." They interact as little as possible with each other. Most communication between them takes place in memo form, with Madeline issuing Sharon direct commands regarding what should and should not be done. Figure 4.4 illustrates Madeline and Sharon's relationship by the arrow that swoops up from Madeline and down again to Sharon. Communication and power consistently flow downward from Madeline to Sharon in a dictatorial, hierarchical fashion.

Madeline, on the other hand, has much in common with Linda, the other social worker. They spend time together and frequently go out to lunch. Madeline views Linda as a calmly competent worker who communicates well and is enjoyable company. In effect, Madeline treats Linda like a friend and equal. Figure 4.4 illustrates this relationship with the linear bond linking Madeline and Linda horizontally.

Now, let's investigate the informal relationships within the Psychology Department. Supervisor Loraine sees Jean, one of her supervisees as a competent professional colleague. Hence, figure 4.4 portrays Jean slightly below Loraine. The connecting arrow flows from Loraine down to Jean because Loraine maintains her supervisory and administrative status with respect to Jean. They essentially like each other on a professional basis. However, neither considers herself a personal friend of the other.

Loraine, on the other hand, perceives Shirley, her other supervisee, in a much different light. Loraine regrets hiring Shirley and has begun to document Shirley's difficulties in performance in preparation for letting her go (dismissing her from the agency). Thus, Shirley is positioned significantly below Loraine, the arrow connecting them running from Loraine down to Shirley. The chain of communication and power clearly positions Loraine in the more powerful, communication-controlling position and Shirley in an inferior, less powerful, communication-receiving status.

However, the plot is even more complicated. Sharon, who is substantially younger than Loraine, is about the same age as Shirley, who is also single. Sharon and Shirley have much in common and have established a firm friendship. They, too, occasionally spend time and socialize with each other. Thus, a vertical line connects them. This indicates that they consider each other equals, friends, and colleagues, despite the fact that Loraine and Shirley's relationship is poor and quickly deteriorating.

Sharon is in an uncomfortable and tenuous position. On the one hand, she values her friendship with Loraine and sees her as a professional ally within the agency who provides her with some leverage against Madeline. On the other hand, Sharon likes Shirley. Sharon understands that Loraine is not perfect (and that she isn't either). Thus, Sharon can listen to Shirley's complaints against Loraine and provide some sympathy. Sharon, however, must be extremely careful not to speak against either Loraine or Shirley to the other person. It is not easy to maintain such a balancing act.

The point here is neither to praise nor to criticize the existence of informal structures of communication and authority. Instead, it is to acknowledge that they exist and are a reality to deal with in any agency, including yours. In practice, being aware of both formal and informal agency structures may strengthen your ability to do your job. Once you know the options and alternatives open to you, you can make better informed, more effective choices.

What eventually happened at Multihelp was that Shirley left for another position in another state. Shirley and Sharon soon lost contact. Six months later, Sharon also left the agency for another social work position that more closely matched her energetic, enthusiastic style. She became a counselor for teens with serious behavioral and family problems. Sharon and Loraine contin-ued to maintain their personal friendship for many years after Sharon left the agency. No one knows what happened to Madeline, Linda, or Jean.

Informal assessment of your agency environment can help you determine how you can best do your job. It can help you to decide how well you fit in and whether you should look for another job.

The Pros and Cons of Centralized and Decentralized Organizations

One other aspect of agency structure merits brief commentary. Organizations can be placed on a continuum regarding their degree of centralization. On one side, there are extremely centralized organizations which resemble those run according to classical scientific management theories. Their lines of authority are clearly established, there is a strict hierarchy, and their units are clearly defined and cleanly separated. Workers have little discretion in making decisions on their own. Responsibilities are defined and implemented from above.

An example of centralization might be a probation and parole department. Clients of any particular officer in any particular unit tend to have very similar characteristics. Procedures and treatment plans are relatively uniform. Clients and officers must abide by clearly defined rules and regulations. Little officer discretion is possible.

On the opposite side of the centralization continuum are extremely decentralized organizations. These organizations offer and encourage great worker discretion. They likely have a wide variety of clients with vastly different problems, issues, and backgrounds. Workers in such organizations, thus, need discretion to make plans for viable solutions. For example, a community crisis intervention organization might be extremely decentralized. Clients coming in for help might have problems ranging from depression to illness to job loss to executive-level stress. Workers need a broad range of discretion to address a wide variety of problems.

Methods of Management

Another way of looking at how organizations function is by comparing management styles that determine how employees are thought of and treated. A number of specific styles have been proposed in recent years. Often, they reflect some combination of the organizational theories described earlier. Therefore, it is difficult to classify them within one organizational theory or another.

We will explore two examples of the many types of styles. They represent two extremes of how staff and clients are viewed and treated. First, we will examine a more traditionally bureaucratic management style. Bureaucracies, of course, emphasize hierarchical power structure with little, if any, input from lower-level staff of clients. Then we will examine an alternative management style, a total quality approach to management. This management approach emphasizes viewing the clients and their input into agency functioning as the most critical factor, the staff who work directly with clients as the next in importance, and so on up the line. Upper levels of administration including the agency director are considered, in some ways, less consequential to the service delivery process.

Working in a Bureaucracy

The concept of bureaucracy was introduced earlier in the chapter under classical management theories. Because it is such a commonly used concept, we will spend some time here addressing practice within bureaucracies. What words come to mind when you hear the term "bureaucracy"? Dullness? Tedium? Boredom? Repetitiveness? Red tape? Sludge?

For whatever reason, most of us have a terrible opinion of bureaucracies. Even one dictionary definition labels bureaucracy "a system of administration marked by officialism (lack of flexibility and initiative combined with excessive adherence to regulations in the behavior of usually government officials), red tape (official routine or procedure marked by excessive complexity which results in delay or inaction), and proliferations (rapid growth by production of new parts, cells, buds, or offspring)" (*Webster's Ninth New Collegiate Dictionary*, 1991, pp. 188, 820, 941, 988). Even this definition is dull.

As we discussed earlier bureaucratic management style emphasizes the importance of a specifically designed, formal structure and a consistent, rigid organizational network of employees in making an organization run well and achieve its goals (Holland & Petchers, 1987; Sarri, 1987). Each employee has a clearly defined

job and is told exactly how that job should be accomplished. This school of thought calls for minimal independent functioning on the part of employees. Supervisors closely scrutinize the latter's work. Efficiency is of utmost importance. How people feel about their jobs is insignificant. Administration avoids allowing employees to have input regarding how organizational goals can best be reached. Rather, employees do their jobs as instructed as quietly and efficiently as possible.

Traditional bureaucracies are made up of numerous highly specialized units assigned to perform specific job tasks. In the formal structure there is little communication among horizontal units, that is, units of approximately equal status that perform different functions. Employees are supposed to "stick to their own business" and get their own specifically defined jobs done within their own units. That's it. Discussion is unnecessary.

Traditional bureaucracies allow very little discretion on the part of workers. Policies and procedures for how to accomplish tasks are clearly specified. In other words, what any particular worker is supposed to do in any particular situation is designated ahead of time. Employees are allowed little, if any, ability or opportunity to think for themselves or make decisions. They are simply supposed to follow instructions.

The policies and procedures are complex and detailed. Regardless of what new situation might come up, workers should be able to consult the "rule book" regarding how they should deal with it.

Value Discrepancies Between Workers and "The System"

Knopf (1979) notes that helping professionals (including social workers) have an erroneous view of the bureaucratic system. He maintains that this view arises from conflicts between personal values and bureaucratic reality. Expecting the values of macro systems to coincide with your own simply sets you up for disappointment.

Helping professionals believe that the primary goal of bureaucracies is to serve clients, while the actual goal of bureaucracies is to survive. Helping professionals believe bureaucracies should change to meet the emerging needs of clients, while bureaucracies resist change and are most efficient when no one is rocking the boat. Helping professionals believe bureaucracies should personal-

---

HIGHLIGHT 4.2

ORIENTATION CONFLICTS BETWEEN HELPING PROFESSIONALS AND BUREAUCRACIES

Orientation of Helping Professionals	Orientation of Bureaucratic Systems
Desire a democratic system for decision-making	Most decisions are made autocratically
Desire that power be distributed equally among employees (horizontal structure)	Power is distributed vertically
Desire that clients have considerable power in the system	Power is held primarily by top executives
Desire a flexible, changing system	System is rigid and stable
Desire that creativity and growth be emphasized	Emphasis is on structure and the status quo
Desire for communication on a personalized level from person to person	Communication is from level to level
Desire shared decision making and a shared responsibility structure	A hierarchical decision-making structure and a hierarchical responsibility structure are characteristic
Desire that decisions be made by those having the most knowledge	Decisions are made according to the decision-making authority assigned each position in the hierarchy
Belief that clients' and employees' feelings should be highly valued by the system	Procedures and processes are highly valued

---

ize services to each client and convey that "you count as a person," while bureaucracies are in fact highly depersonalized systems in which clients (and employees) do not count as persons but are only tiny components of a mammoth system. Highlight 4.2 lists additional conflicting orientations between helping professionals and bureaucratic systems (Knopf, 1979).

Any of these differences in orientation can become an arena of conflict between helping professionals and the bureaucracies in which they work. A number of helping professionals respond to these orientation conflicts by erroneously projecting a personality onto the bureaucracy. The bureaucracy is viewed as being "red tape," "officialism," "uncaring," "cruel," and "the enemy." A negative personality is also sometimes projected onto officials of a bureaucracy, who may be viewed as "paper shufflers," "rigid," "deadwood," "inefficient," and "unproductive." Knopf (1979, p. 25) states:

The HP (helping person) . . . may deal with the impersonal nature of the system by projecting values onto it and thereby give the BS (Bureaucratic System) a "personality." [It is interesting that Knopf refers to a bureaucracy as BS.] In this way, we fool ourselves into thinking that we can deal with it in a personal way. Unfortunately, projection is almost always negative and reflects the dark or negative aspects of ourselves. The BS then becomes a screen onto which we vent our anger, sadness, or fright, and while a lot of energy is generated, very little is accomplished. Since the BS is amoral [that is, the BS can be neither moral nor immoral so the concept of morality does not apply to it], it is unproductive to place a personality on it.

A bureaucratic system is neither good nor bad. It has no personality or value system of its own. It is simply a structure developed to carry out various tasks. However, practitioners may have strong emotional reactions to these orientation conflicts between the helping professions and bureaucracies. Common reactions are anger at the system, self-blame ("It's all my fault"), sadness and depression ("Poor me. Nobody appreciates all I've done"), and fright and paranoia ("They're out to get me. If I mess up, I'm gone").

Behavior Patterns in Bureaucratic Systems

Knopf (1979, pp. 33–36) has identified several types of behavior patterns that helping professionals use in dealing with bureaucracies; they include "the warrior," "the gossip," "the complainer," "the dancer," "the machine," and "the executioner."

The *warrior* leads open campaigns to destroy and malign the system. A warrior discounts the value of the system and enters into win-lose conflicts. Warriors loudly and outspokenly complain about almost everything. They rarely, if ever, get promoted because of an overt "bad attitude." In fact, the warrior generally loses and is dismissed.

The *gossip* is a covert warrior who complains to others inside and outside the agency (including clients, politicians, and the news media) about how terrible the system is. A gossip frequently singles out a few officials as the focus of criticism. Bureaucratic administrators generally hate gossips because they air internal "dirty laundry" outside the agency. Therefore, supervisors and administrators in bureaucracies often make life very difficult for gossips by assigning them distasteful tasks, refusing to promote them, giving them very low salary increases, and perhaps even dismissing them.

The *complainer* resembles a gossip, but confines complaints internally to other helping persons, to in-house staff, and to family members. A complainer wants people to agree in order to find comfort in shared misery. Complainers want to stay with the system, and generally do. Since they primarily keep their complaining secretive and internal, they usually avoid antagonizing the administration and, therefore, maintain their anonymity (and their jobs).

The *dancer* is skillful at ignoring rules and procedures. Dancers are frequently lonely, often reprimanded for incorrectly filling out forms, and have little investment in the system or in helping clients. However, once

inside a bureaucratic system, dancers often manage to "just get by." In essence, they are usually lazy. Dancers generally don't really cause any trouble. They just don't do their jobs very well. It goes against the bureaucratic principle of maintaining the status quo to exert the energy necessary to fire a dancer.

The *machine* is a "typical bureaucrat" who takes on the orientation of the bureaucracy. A machine's intent is to abide by the official bureaucratic rules no matter what. Machines dislike conflict. To them obeying the rules of the letter of the law is much safer. Often a machine has not been involved in providing direct services for years. Machines are frequently named to head study committees and policy groups, and to chair boards. Machines often rise to the level of their incompetence (the Peter Principle), where they may remain until retirement.[2]

The *executioner* is a tremendously enthusiastic and self-motivated individual who has managed to gain power, status, and advancement within the bureaucratic organization. Executioners have no real commitment to the value of orientations of the helping professionals or to the bureaucracy. However, they have learned how to play the game. They manage to hide their anger toward bureaucratic control and red tape. They succeed in disguising their manipulative ploys and fool many of those around them about their true self-centered, hostile motives. Especially when threatened, executioners attack other targeted persons in the organization with energized, impulsive vigor. An executioner abuses power not only by indiscriminately assailing and dismissing employees, but also by slashing services and programs.

This description of bureaucratic systems highlights a number of their negatives, particularly their impersonal qualities. In fairness, it should be noted that an advantage of being part of a large bureaucracy is the potential for changing a powerful system to the advantage of clients. In small or nonbureaucratic systems, a social worker may have lots of freedom, but little opportunity or power to influence large macro systems or mobilize extensive resources on behalf of clients.

---

2. The "Peter Principle" is an observation developed by Laurence J. Peter in 1968 that "in a hierarchy every employee tends to rise to the level of his incompetence" (*Webster's Ninth New Collegiate Dictionary*, 1991, p. 879).

How to Survive in a Bureaucracy

Knopf (1979) gives a number of tips on how a helping professional can best survive in a bureaucracy, including:

1. Whenever your needs, or the needs of your clients, are not met by the bureaucracy, use the following problem-solving approach: (a) Precisely identify your needs (or the client needs) that are in conflict with the bureaucracy, thereby defining the problem. (b) Generate a list of possible solutions. Be creative in generating a wide range of solutions. (c) Evaluate the merits and shortcomings of the possible solutions. (d) Select a solution. (e) Implement the solution. (f) Evaluate the solution. This, of course, essentially follows the problem-solving approach you use in virtually any aspect of generalist practice.

2. Obtain a knowledge of how your bureaucracy is structured and how it functions. Such knowledge will reduce your fear of the unknown, make the system more predictable, and help you identify rational ways to meet your needs and those of your clients. This includes knowledge of your agency's formal and informal structures. Bureaucracies work to eliminate or minimize any informal communication or power structure. Informal relationships interfere with following the rules to the letter.

3. Remember that bureaucrats are people with feelings. Communication gaps are often most effectively reduced if you treat them with the respect and interest you offer clients. Chapter 2 discussed the use of micro skills within macro practice. Many of the same techniques used in micro practice with clients also apply to working with agency colleagues and administrators.

4. If you are at war with the bureaucracy, declare a truce or the system will find a way to dismiss you. With a truce, you can identify and use the strengths of the bureaucracy as an ally, rather than have those strengths used against you. Chapters 5 through 7 discuss how to evaluate your agency environment, regardless of management style, and pursue potential macro interventions.

5. Know your work contract and job expectations. If the expectations are unclear, seek clarity.

6. Continue to develop your knowledge and awareness of specific helping skills. Take advantage of continuing education opportunities (workshops, conferences, college courses). Among other advantages, your continued professional development will help you keep practicing with competence and skill. Continued, regular participation in professional development can maintain mental freshness and stimulation. You can try out new ideas and skills on old tasks and situations.

7. Seek to identify your professional strengths and limitations. Knowing your limitations will increase your ability to avoid undertaking responsibilities beyond your competencies. Chapter 5 more thoroughly discusses how to go about doing this.

8. Be aware that you can't change everything, so stop trying. In a bureaucracy, focus your efforts on those aspects that most need change and that you have a fair chance of changing. Stop thinking and complaining about what you cannot change. It is irrational to complain about things that you cannot change or do not intend to try changing.

9. Learn how to control your emotions in your interactions with the bureaucracy. Counterproductive emotions (such as *most* angry outbursts) particularly need to be controlled. Learning how to respond to stress in your personal life will also prepare you to handle stress better at work.

10. Develop and use a sense of humor. Humor takes the edge off adverse conditions and reduces negative feelings.

11. Learn to accept your mistakes and perhaps even to laugh at some of them. No one is perfect.

12. Take time to enjoy and develop a support system with your colleagues. Use the informal structure of your agency as much as possible. Having others to go to for suggestions, support, and pats on the back is really helpful.

13. Acknowledge your mistakes and give in sometimes on minor matters. You may not always be right. Giving in on one issue may encourage other people to do the same on another one.

14. Keep yourself physically fit and mentally alert. Learn to use approaches that reduce stress and prevent burnout. Chapter 15 discusses stress-management techniques in substantial depth.

15. Leave your work at the office. Do not take all your burdens home with you. If you have urgent unfinished bureaucratic business, either do it before leaving work or don't leave.

16. Occasionally, take your supervisor and other administrators to lunch. Socializing prevents isolation and facilitates your involvement with and understanding of the system. It also helps to enhance your position in the agency's informal structure.

17. Do not seek self-actualization or ego-satisfaction from the bureaucracy. A depersonalized system is incapable of providing this. Only you can satisfy your ego and needs.

18. Make speeches to community groups that accentuate the positives about your agency. Do not hesitate to ask after speeches that a thank-you letter be sent to your supervisor or agency director.

19. If you have a problem involving the bureaucracy, discuss it with other employees and focus on problem solving

rather than on complaining. Groups are much more powerful and productive than an individual working alone.

20. No matter how high you rise in a hierarchy, maintain some direct service contact. Direct contact keeps you abreast of changing client needs, prevents you from getting stale, and keeps you attuned to the concerns of employees in lower levels of the hierarchy.

21. Do not try to change everything in the system at once. Attacking too much will overextend you and lead to burnout. Start small and be selective and specific. Double-check your facts to make certain they accurately prove your position before confronting bureaucratic officials. Once again, this process is explored thoroughly in later chapters.

22. Identify your career goals and determine whether they can be met in this system. If the answer is no, then (a) change your goals, (b) change the bureaucracy, or (c) seek a position elsewhere in which your goals can be met.

A Total Quality Approach to Management[3]

Numerous bureaucracies continue to exist, with all their strengths and weaknesses, but alternative organizational perspectives and management styles are available. For example, management by objectives (MBO) was a popular approach in the past. It focused on goals as the primary driving force of agency life and measured organizational success in terms of how effectively the organization achieved these goals (Netting, Kettner, and McMurtry, 1993). MBO encouraged employees to arrive at an agreement about what objectives or results they wanted, specify what organizational resources each goal required, and establish how long the goal attainment process should take (Barker, 1995).

Here we will explore more thoroughly an example of another management approach, *Total Quality Management (TQM)*, which many social service organizations employ today. Developed by W. Edward Deming (1982, 1986) and others (Crosby, 1980; Feigenbaum, 1983; Juran, 1989), this quality management perspective emphasizes organizational process, attainment of excellent quality service, and empowerment of employees. "Total quality service" (Lutheran Social Services [LSS], 1993) and "service management" (Albrecht, 1988) are related approaches that adopt some of the same primary principles. The remainder of this section on the total quality perspective will stress these common themes.

Defining Total Quality Management

There are a number of definitions of Total Quality Management (TQM). One proposes that TQM is "the application of quantitative methods and human resources to improve the material and services supplied to an organization, and the degree to which the needs of the customer are met, now and in the future" (Mossard, 1991, p. 223). Note that this definition includes emphasis on both *quantitative methods*,[4] reflecting a scientific management approach, and *human resources*, using a human relations outlook. TQM attempts to blend aspects of both theoretical perspectives (Kronenberg & Loeffler, 1991; Martin, 1993).

Barker (1995) defines TQM as "an orientation to management of organizations, including social services agencies, in which quality, as defined by clients and consumers, is the overriding goal, and client satisfaction, employee empowerment, and long-term relationships determine procedures" (pp. 383–84).

Sashkin and Kiser (1993) explain: "TQM means that the organization's culture is defined by and supports the constant attainment of customer satisfaction through an integrated system of tools, techniques, and training. This involves the continuous improvement of organization processes, resulting in high quality products and services" (p. 39). Bedwell (1993) provides a more straightforward description of TQM, stating, "The essence of total quality is simply: Ask your customers what they want; then give it to them!" (p. 29).

It is beyond the scope of this book to describe the

3. The authors wish to thank the administrators of Lutheran Social Services of Wisconsin and Upper Michigan, 4143 S. 13th St., Milwaukee, WI 53221 (especially Robert E. Duca, president and CEO), and Family Counseling Service, 148 Prospect St., Ridgewood, NJ 07450, who readily shared their ideas and materials. The authors also wish to thank Fern E. Behlke, MSSW, Director of Administration for Family Service, 128 East Olin Avenue, Madison, WI 53713, who provided some excellent help and suggestions regarding these materials.

4. Quantitative methods, of course, emphasize clear definitions of organizational expectations, performance levels, and goals, in addition to measurement of results that is as precise as possible.

HIGHLIGHT 4.3

THE GARBAGE CAN MODEL
OF DECISION MAKING

Decision making involves both power and communication. You must have power if any decision you make is to affect anyone else's behavior. You must also be able to communicate your decisions through designated and appropriate channels in order for them to be implemented. We have discussed the formal structure of organizations. Bureaucracies seek to emphasize formal structure and get rid of informal distractions. Therefore, decisions are supposed to be made exactly according to the formal mandates. However, bureaucracies also often have problems in this implementation. Goal displacement is common, as are inefficiencies and overwhelming red tape. Why do such dilemmas develop? What about when the bureaucracy is simply not working right?

There is an interesting alternative model to decision making that might be used to describe processes adapted to bureaucracies. The *garbage can model* of decision making denounces the classical scientific management theories that describe bureaucracies in terms of their hierarchical authority structures and formal lines of communication and decision making (Cohen, March, & Olsen, 1972). This model "deals with the pattern or flow of multiple decisions within organizations," and "helps you think of the whole organization and the frequent decisions being made by managers throughout" (Daft, 1992, p. 363). It is based on the concept of *organized anarchy* (Cohen, March, & Olsen, 1972). Any organization must have some kind of underlying organized formal structure, but the way this formal structure actually operates may be and often is chaotic.

Organized Anarchy

Organized anarchy occurs when three conditions are present (Daft, 1992). First, a high level of ambiguity and uncertainty must characterize the organization.

"Goals, problems, alternatives, and solutions" are poorly or vaguely defined (Daft, 1992, p. 363).

A second prerequisite for organized anarchy is poorly understood technology. Earlier, we defined organizational technology to include all the activities performed to complete the organization's tasks and achieve its goals. In a bureaucracy this entails all ongoing communication, decision making, intakes, assessments, interventions, treatments, evaluations, and follow-ups.

A third prerequisite for organized anarchy is extremely busy staff. They have little time to devote to decision making, and staff turnover may be high.

No Relationship Between
Problems and Solutions

The garbage can model views decision making in organizations as a disorganized, haphazard process. In essence, "decision making is not a sequential series of steps that begins with a problem and leads to a solution" (Daft, 1992, p. 360). Solutions and problems are not necessarily related to each other because decision-making processes are viewed as the potential result of four distinct and separate elements within the organization (Daft, 1992). One might view these elements as ingredients thrown into a garbage-can stew, none of them necessarily having any relationship to the others. A mammoth "waapatuli" party might come to mind (that is, a "bring your own booze" or BYOB party where all attendees bring some type of liquor—usually very cheap—and mix it together in a garbage can or bathtub for all to dip in and share). The four elements involved in the garbage can theory include:

1. *Problems*. Problems arise when solutions are lacking or goals are not achieved. Sometimes effort is ex-

panded to solve the problem and sometimes not. Even when a solution is proposed and adopted, the problem may or may not be solved. Problems have no clear relationship to solutions.

2. *Solutions*. Solutions are a type of output, a produced result of input processed by the system. Solutions may be free-floating ideas that have nothing to do with problems. Or a solution may be generated to solve some problem. In this case, the solution may or may not work. Once again, solutions may or may not be related to any of the other three elements, including problems, inherent in the garbage can theory.

3. *Participants*. Participants are organizational staff who can be fired, promoted, and demoted. Any individual participant's involvement in either a problem or solution is unpredictable. Each concept is unrelated to the others.

4. *Choice opportunities*. Choice opportunities occur when a decision is actually made within the organization. Decisions may be made because the organization is under some type of pressure. For instance, some new law may affect service, or some client may file a suit against the agency, either of which would force the agency to react. Choice opportunities may or may not be related to problems or solutions. Any particular staff may or may not be involved in any particular choice opportunity. It's like one big garbage can filled with problems, solutions, participants, and choice opportunities all stirred up together.

Results of Garbage Can Decision Making

What does the garbage can model of decision making predict will happen? How do organizations continue to survive and function? The garbage can model predicts the following four outcomes (Daft, 1992, pp. 361–62).

1. *Solutions are proposed even when problems do not exist*. Some participant may come up with an idea and frame it as a solution. The solution may or may not work and may or may not be related to any identified problem.

For example, a university administration decided to modernize and adopt a new computer system. A decision was needed regarding what system to adopt. High level administrators appointed a decision-making group of professors and administrators.

The group included no secretary or administrative assistant—the people who would actually use the system on a day-to-day basis. With no practical input from people who would actually operate the system, the decision-making group came up with a recommendation. The group chose a certain type of computer that offered an interdepartmental mail feature. In other words, this particular computer system allowed the various levels of administration to communicate (theoretically) with virtually any department or unit in the university. The proposed system was appealing to administrators because it sounded as if it would be convenient for them.

The idea sounds good, right? In fact, the new system remained almost totally useless for the first year. Its operation was so complicated that the staff using it required excessive, expensive, and timely training to work with it on even a rudimentary basis. Some administrative assistants never did learn and were transferred into other positions where they could avoid the new system. Additionally, the system had almost no memory. In many ways, it was like an old electric typewriter. Few typed items could be saved so most had to be retyped again and again. There were other problems too numerous to describe here.

In summary, this solution (the computer system proposed by the decision-making group) had no relationship to any problem in the agency. Administrative assistants using the new equipment would have preferred either their old equipment or new personal computers which would be more compatible with the equipment used by faculty and other staff. Likewise, the decision-makers really had little or no relationship to the solution, because none of them would actually use the system.

In other words, "if it ain't broke, don't fix it."

2. *Choices are made without solving problems*. This garbage can consequence might also be related to the university computer scenario described above. Not only did no problem exist, but the choice opportunity was not helpful. It was not a useful solution and it was unrelated to any problem.

Another choice opportunity decision that did not solve a problem was made in a large county social services department. State budgets were being cut,

(continued)

taxes were not increased, so the department's budget actually shrunk, especially in terms of inflation rates. The top administrators had to make choices regarding where to spend funds and where to cut. They decided that it was more important to maintain their current staffing levels than to increase funds in other areas, such as staff raises and basic supplies. As a result, large number of staff kept their jobs but only minuscule raises were given. Staff were perplexed as their salaries plummeted in terms of buying power. The supplies situation almost reached critical mass. Supply cabinets were locked to control use. Even pencils and paper had to be requested on appropriate forms. Staff felt they had to monitor each paper clip and staple they used.

In summary, the organization made a choice, namely, to maintain staffing levels and cut elsewhere. However, instead of solving problems, the decision created more.

3. *Problems may persist without being solved.* Because problems, solutions, participants, and choice opportunities have virtually no established relationship with each other, problems may continue.

It can be easier for an organization to ignore some problems than to address them.

For example, a large urban school system employed approximately one-hundred social workers in its Pupil Services Department. Dufus, one of these social workers, prided himself on his ability to fight the system—Pupil Services Department. He loved to ferret out problems, or invent them if he couldn't find any. He loved calling attention to himself and being in the limelight. Dufus's typical approaches included telephoning students' parents and organizing them against the school system on some issue or telephoning local television stations and stringently criticizing the school system.

It should be noted that, as a generalist practitioner, you must work to change a macro system in some way when that system is ineffective or simply wrong. However, Dufus never tried to work internally before going outside for help. He did not consider talking to administrators about policy changes, project implementations, or program development. He preferred to complain to outside systems. This helped neither the school system's

implementation process of a TQM philosophy and program. However, to begin understanding how TQM is implemented in a real agency, we will discuss a number of concepts, including: clients as customers; quality as the primary goal; employee empowerment; the use of teams; TQM leadership; TQM tools; customer feedback; and the learning organization.

Clients as Customers

The central theme of TQM is the importance of the customer. The guiding idea for all service provisions is that the customer is satisfied. Who exactly is the customer?

Customers or consumers "are those who directly received outputs of the organization" (Keys, 1995, p. 2019). *Extreme customers* include clients. By labeling clients as customers, we imply higher status. The agency's primary purpose is to serve its clients as other businesses serve their customers. For social service agencies, the concept of the external customer goes beyond the client. Frequently, other agencies, not clients, purchase services, so these other agencies become external customers (Martin, 1993).

Internal customers include "departments that receive the benefit of an output from another department in their organization" (Keys, 1995, p. 2019). An agency's personnel department provides services to that same agency's direct service staff. Therefore, the direct service staff is considered an internal customer. Similarly, an agency's intake unit usually has initial contact with clients. Thus, the intake unit receives input in the form of initial contact or referral. Depending on the client's problems and needs, the intake unit subsequently refers the client to some other unit in the agency. TQM considers this output to the unit receiving the referral. In other words, the receiving unit is an internal customer of the intake unit.

reputation nor its effectiveness. If anything, it ate away at parental involvement, staff morale, and student attitudes.

At any rate, the pupil services administration was frantic. They seemed to address one of Dufus's crises after another. Unfortunately for them, the urban county had an extremely strong union. Once employees passed their six-month probationary period, it was virtually impossible to get rid of them. Administrators steamed and fumed, but their hands were tied. The problems persisted with no solution in sight. The entire department had to grin and bear it. Dufus was there to stay.

4. *A few problems* are *solved*. A ray of hope! Some light at the end of the tunnel! The garbage can theory, with all of its complexity and confusion, does predict that some problems will eventually get solved. When we consider all the ongoing processes within an organization, we see that sometimes solutions are generated to solve problems and good choice opportunities are offered.

What Is the Answer?

Cohen and March (1974) recommend three ways to cope with organized anarchy and the garbage can stew of elements. First, they recommend that workers take enough time to address any problems they consider important. This reflects our basic advice regarding whether or not to undertake a macro level change (described in chapter 5). Second, workers need to try and try again if at first they don't succeed. In other words, workers shouldn't give up once they decide to address some problem or issue. Third, it is good for workers to maintain a substantial number of projects. It is likely that some will succeed just by virtue of many efforts being made. It is also important to remember that many projects will wither away.

A Final Note on the Garbage Can Model

The garbage can model reflects a somewhat cynical view of organizational behavior. It represents one view of organizations. It is useful in establishing that many issues in large organizational macro systems are beyond anyone's control. Many things occur in organizations that make little sense. Acknowledging that imperfection and illogic exist is a realistic approach, one that is important to keep in mind.

Staff who directly serve client customers are considered very important. Such staff are themselves customers because they receive output (support and resources) from other agency units in order to provide services to clients. Because these staff are considered customers, TQM stresses that they also should have high status and receive good, supportive treatment.

The internal customer concept can be confusing. Therefore, for clarity and simplicity, the remaining discussion will apply the word customer only to clients.

Quality as the Primary Goal

In TQM, quality is the primary goal (Barker, 1995; Martin, 1993). However, quality is a difficult term to define. There is "no universally accepted definition" (Martin, 1993, p. 27). Each organization must determine for itself what quality means in terms of its own service provision. For example, Lutheran Social Services of Wisconsin and Upper Michigan defines six components of quality including "accuracy," "consistency," "responsiveness," "availability," "perceived value," and "service experience" (LSS, 1993, p. 8).

Accuracy measures the extent to which actual service provision matches customers' expectations. To what extent do customers feel they are getting the services they sought and hoped to receive?

Consistency is "service accuracy over time" (LSS, 1993, p. 8). Are customers consistently getting the appropriate services, or is service provision unpredictable?

Responsiveness refers to timeliness of service provision. How long do customers have to wait before they get the attention and services they need?

Availability is the ease with which customers can obtain services. To what extent are services actually delivered to customers who request and need them?

Perceived value concerns the extent to which customers feel satisfied with the service. To what extent are services worth customers' expense, time, and energy plus any possible annoyance or frustration they suffer? To what extent is the service worth its total cost?

The *service experience* sums up the total service event. What is the customer's sum total evaluation of each word spoken with staff? How do customers perceive the agency, taking into account all their encounters with it? This covers each interaction with the agency and each tiny aspect of that interaction. What was the time like that clients spent sitting in a waiting room chair? How clean were those chairs? Were they comfortable? How long were they forced to wait? How were the clients greeted when they finally met with their workers? What is their total summary impression of their total treatment experience?

Each social service agency must specify its own definition of quality in the context of its own mission statement. A mission statement summarizes an agency's mission, that is, its official goals. What is the primary function an individual agency intends to accomplish? This would vary markedly from an organization composed of dozens of group homes for adults with physical disabilities to an organization aimed at curbing and preventing domestic violence. The following is an example of the mission statement presented by a family counseling agency: "Recognizing the family, in all its forms, as the cornerstone of our society, Family Counseling Service of Ridgewood and Vicinity seeks to provide support and counseling to both families and individuals throughout their lives" (Family Counseling Service, 1993).

Employee Empowerment

Empowerment involves providing people with authority or power. A total quality approach espouses "participative management" (LSS, 1993, pp. 20–27). Participative management means placing the major responsibility for effective service on direct service workers. TQM emphasizes the importance not only of customers, but also of employees in the agency units that directly serve the customers. Likewise, other agency units providing input to direct service units are considered important because of their support to the service providers. For example, supervisory input is important primarily because it aids in the service-provision process.

In some ways, you might envision TQM as an upside-down pyramid. In a typical bureaucratic organization, the power structure as reflected in a formal organizational chart, is a triangle or pyramid with the agency director sitting at the pinnacle. Below her might be assistant directors, beneath them managers, below them supervisors, and, finally, at the very bottom, the many workers. The pyramid's shape, of course, reflects the relative number of persons involved at each level. There is only one agency director. There are fewer supervisors than direct service workers. Finally, there are fewer direct service workers than there are clients. In TQM, because the client customers or consumers are given precedence, those providing service directly to them are considered, in a way, the most important. The agency's clients, the customers, thus form the top level of the inverted pyramid because they are considered the most significant. Right below them would be the direct service workers, beneath them the supervisors, and so on in the reverse order of the bureaucratic pyramid. The agency director and perhaps its board of directors would be placed at the very bottom of the inverted pyramid.

TQM emphasizes each employee's importance. Matza (1990) describes such empowerment as "getting employees—especially front line employees—to take care of the customer" (p. 21).

Use of Teams and Teamwork: Melding Mezzo and Macro Practice

A total quality approach espouses not only empowerment of individual employees, but also "team empowerment" (LSS, 1993, pp. 20–27). This involves giving the responsibility for service provision to designated groups that work together. In effect, it means giving power to teams of agency workers. Teams are "task-oriented groups of five to fifteen employees who are responsible for planning and producing an entire product or process. In so doing, they are independent (self-directed) and may manage many activities that were formerly performed only by supervisors or managers" (Keys, 1995, p. 2021). Therefore, teams can identify problems and issues, discuss potential alternatives, make decisions about how to proceed, set goals, and evaluate progress.

Specific teams might consist of groups of staff members who either provide similar services or serve

HIGHLIGHT 4.4

THE SEVEN SINS OF SERVICE

Albrecht (1988) stresses the need to focus consistently on the quality of service provided to customers (or clients). He identifies "seven sins of service" that organizations commonly commit and that work against maintenance and enhancement of service quality. They include "apathy," "brush-off," "coldness," "condescension," "robotism," "rule book," and "runaround" (pp. 14–16).

Of course, according to professional social work ethics, our clients or customers should always be our top priority. In an ideal world this would be so. In the real world, however, staff members are individuals with individual weaknesses and failings. These seven sins of service are often committed. From an organizational perspective, of course, staff include everyone from the agency director to various levels of administration to professional social workers and other helping professionals to clerical staff to maintenance staff. Regardless of job title or responsibilities, each is, in essence, a representative of the agency. Albrecht maintains that it is absolutely essential for all staff to avoid the seven sins described below.

Of course, as professional social workers, we are supposed to be warm, empathic, and genuine. We are always to treat the customer with respect. However, these values are more difficult to maintain when we have twenty-three customers waiting impatiently for service or if we absolutely have to finish, by 4:30 P.M. today, an eight-page report that we haven't started yet or if we have an excruciatingly painful migraine headache. During these times, Albrecht would say that it's especially important to vigilant about the seven sins. Each of the seven organizational sins is explained below.

1. *Apathy.* Albrecht describes the "DILLIGAD" syndrome, or "Do I Look Like I Give a Damn?," á la comic George Carlin (p. 15). In other words, it's easy for staff to focus on getting their jobs over with so that they can go home and live their own lives. Apathy arises from boredom with customer interactions and lack of concern for the *quality*, usefulness, or effectiveness of the service provided.

2. *Brush-off.* This consists of getting rid of the customer if possible by passing the buck and doing as little work as possible. A staff member might tell a customer that he can't answer her questions accurately and send her to another department, probably on a wild goose chase.

3. *Coldness.* This "kind of chilly hostility, curtness, unfriendliness, inconsiderateness, or impatience" is intended to convey to the customer "You're a nuisance; please go away" (p. 15). It is difficult to maintain a warm, interested interpersonal stance every minute of the day. Some customers may be hostile, feisty, or demanding, and you as a worker may be tired, fed up, or disgusted.

4. *Condescension.* Treating customers with a disdainful patronizing attitude implies that you as the worker are more knowledgeable and, essentially, better than the customer. When you condescend, you treat people as if they were not very bright: "Now don't you worry about this. I know best and I'll take care of everything. Trust me."

5. *Robotism.* When you treat each customer identically, without changes in facial or verbal expression, or ask the same questions over and over to different customers, you are not responding to individual differences. Such differences don't concern you. Your main intent is to get the job done as fast and efficiently as possible while using as little brain power as possible.

6. *Rule Book.* If you want to think as little as possible, use the rule book to give the organization's rules and regulations absolute precedence. "Go by the book" totally and completely without any hint of compromise. I once called a weight-control clinic for information on exercising and maintaining my weight. A

(continued)

HIGHLIGHT 4.4—(Continued)

young woman answered the phone, obviously reading a boilerplate blurb about losing weight at the clinic. I asked her if the clinic also helped people *maintain* their current weight, not lose any more. She answered by rereading the identical blurb she just had read to me. I asked her the same question two more times, after which she repeated the same blurb. Finally, exasperated, I said, "Can't you think for yourself or what?" and hung up.

Although this did not occur in a social work context, it does exemplify the sin of "rule book." The

young woman answering the phone was instructed apparently to read her blurb and not say anything else. As a result, trying to get any help from her (in this case, information) was totally useless and frustrating.

7. *Runaround.* Stalling customers is a common "sin." Workers tell a customer to call someone else for the information first, or to go to Window 217 and fill out the appropriate twenty-seven page form. Runaround entails using as little of your own time as possible, while wasting the customer's time.

---

the same category of customers. Teams generally meet on a regularly scheduled basis such as once each week for about one-half hour (LSS, 1993). Team members are expected to work cooperatively on the customers' behalf. Ongoing resolution of any conflicts among team members is emphasized. Negative internal staff conflict does not benefit clients, so it is not tolerated.

Working as a team has several advantages over working as separate individuals (LSS, 1993). First, a team allows the presentation and sharing of many ideas, perspectives, and experiences. Second, team members have a wider repertoire of skills than any one individual. Third, the entire team "owns" its conclusions, recommendations, and results. Fourth, members can teach each other skills in addition to sharing knowledge and information.

The *team* concept should be distinguished from that of a *group*. Groups do not necessarily work cooperatively, individual roles may be unclear, participation of individual members may be hampered or discouraged, and frequently individual group members are seen as "stars" instead of cooperative co-participants (LSS, 1993, p. 18). The team perspective, on the other hand, encourages performance of the team, allowing the entire team to gain recognition and respect in the agency. TQM emphasizes cooperation instead of competition (Martin, 1993; Muckian, 1994b).

A Total Quality Approach to Leadership

Strong support and leadership from top management is critical in implementing TQM (Gummesson, 1991; Martin, 1993). TQM leadership must focus on the process of making all aspects of the organization's functioning excellent (Joiner & Scholtes, 1985). This includes supplying support to all agency units, especially those providing services to customers. Essentially, leaders should "serve as integrators and facilitators, not as watchdogs and interventionists" (Kanter, 1989, p. 89). Leaders often assume the latter role in traditional bureaucracies.

Establishing a Culture of Quality

One task leaders must accomplish is the establishment of a "culture of quality" (Martin, 1993, p. 80). *Organizational culture* is "the set of values, guiding beliefs, understandings, and ways of thinking that is shared by members of an organization and is taught to new members as correct" (Daft, 1992, p. 317). TQM provides a very different organizational culture than the traditional bureaucracy. We have established that a culture reflecting a total quality perspective is "characterized by teamwork, cooperation, open communication, flexibility, autonomy, and empowerment"; the culture is "focused on . . . service to . . . customers (LSS, 1993,

p. 74). As all employees must be involved in the total quality approach, agency leaders must visibly demonstrate their commitment to TQM (Brown, Hitchcock, & Willard, 1994, p. 3). Leaders are responsible for "changing the organizational culture from one that dwells on status quo to one that gets excited about change" (Bedwell, 1993, p. 30).

For example, one agency director whose private nonprofit family services organization had adopted a TQM perspective illustrated her commitment in a very concrete way. Historically, staff would park in the best spots in the parking lot each workday morning because they always got there first. Customers, who regularly got there later, would get the parking spots furthest from the building—if there were any spots left at all. Traditionally, the agency director assumed "ownership" of the best parking spot at the agency's main door. The assistant director took the second-best spot, and so on down the line. The day-time janitor was assigned the worst employee spot.

Reflecting the TQM philosophy, the director demonstrated the importance of serving customers and giving them priority by ordering that customers should be left the best parking spots. Staff were relegated to the worst. The director herself chose the spot in the farthest corner of the lot, next to an appallingly foul-smelling dumpster. She also rallied some of the agency's precious funds to purchase extra parking spaces for customers in a lot adjacent to the agency.

Another example of how agency leaders can demonstrate their commitment to TQM principles involves a family service agency that had held it board of directors meetings at noon each Friday since 1946. The boardroom where their meetings were held was the only large meeting facility in the agency. Therefore, it was used for a variety of agency activities and business, including staff meetings, staffings on individual cases, and educational activities for customers. When the agency adopted the TQM management philosophy, the board solicited and received feedback from customers. One recommendation was a stress-management class would be held at noon on Fridays. Because TQM emphasizes customers' importance, the board changed its meeting time to another day and time, despite some inconveniences for board members.

It should be noted that the board of directors in a traditionally bureaucratic agency would assume the topmost status in an agency. In effect, they function as the agency director's boss. In traditional bureaucracies top leaders usually receive top priority for access to agency resources such as prime meeting space.

A Long-Term Perspective

Note that TQM takes substantial time and resources to implement (Martin, 1993; Muckian, 1994a). It takes massive effort to establish the team concept and the others aspects of TQM. An organization needs to teach its staff new roles and expectations. It is management's responsibility to organize a TQM structure, gain staff support, and educate staff about expected responsibilities and performance. Thus, it is critical for management to clarify for staff the objectives and means of achieving them, to nurture staff's faith in the total quality approach, to engender trust in its success, and to make staff feel that it is "personally worthwhile for them" (Albrecht, 1988, p. 116). Since this is not a management text, we will not address details about how management might go about this process.

TQM Tools

A range of tools for implementing TQM have been established and refined (Keys, 1995). For example, many types of charts are used "to show progress (or lack of progress) in the quality-improvement effort and hence areas that require further decision making" (Keys, 1995, p. 2021). *Benchmarking* is another tool. It involves a formal undertaking of surveys, extra-agency visits, and training "to compare the quality of an organization's processes and activities to the standards of recognized leaders in the field as a target for improvement" (Keys, 1995, p. 2021).

Customer Feedback

Since customer satisfaction is paramount, agencies must solicit information from customers in order to strive for greater effectiveness. This can be done in a variety of ways (Albrecht, 1988; Martin, 1993). For one thing, the agency can administer customer satisfaction surveys or community surveys that solicit information from customers or residents about agency services. Staff can also conduct extensive interviews with individual customers to identify and examine their feelings. Likewise, the agency can focus on customer complaints and undertake extensive investigations. Suggestion boxes for anonymous feedback can be placed in accessible places. Finally, the agency can assemble groups of customers (focus groups) to discuss services and make suggestions for quality improvement.

It should be emphasized that not only is customer feedback regularly solicited, but the agency *uses* this feedback to improve its service provision. There are many ways an agency might incorporate feedback: by prioritizing client and agency needs, planning new goals, and undertaking new projects and procedures.

The Learning Organization

Ongoing evaluation of service effectiveness is an absolute necessity in TQM. The concept of ''the learning organization'' involves continuous striving for improvement (Keys, 1985, p. 2020). The learning organization ''adopts a climate of openness and trust; people are unafraid to share their ideas and speak their minds. Barriers between managers and employees are eliminated and, ideally, everybody works together to support the collective well-being'' (Bennett & O'Brien, p. 44). TQM education for staff is ongoing (Keys, 1995).

Employees in teams are consistently encouraged to assess processes and procedures and make improvements. Thus, change occurs continuously. This contrasts strongly with traditional bureaucracies that usually work to maintain the status quo.

The Exceptional Problems of Social Service Organizations

There are a number of problems plaguing social service organizations that other private businesses don't have. Most are based on the fact that working with people is infinitely complicated.

As worldwide population continues to expand, resources continue to shrink. Shrinking resources make funding and financial support become more and more difficult to get and competition more intense. It makes sense that organizations producing higher quality prod-

ucts (more effectively) at lower costs requiring less input (more efficiently) are more likely to survive than those which are less effective and efficient. Earlier, we compared the business Fastbuck with the social service agency SERVO. Fastbuck will show a profit and thrive if it produces high quality doorstops at competitive prices. Likewise, SERVO will be more likely to survive and thrive if it can prove that is client outcomes are positive and valuable.

Before you as a practitioner can begin to assess the effectiveness of organizations for your clients or suggest changes to improve services, you need to understand some of the problems organizations face. Organizational problems are almost never easy to address and change. You need to recognize the magnitude of the problems and their causes. Organizational problems include uncertainties in the environment, vague processes, and vague goals. Goal displacement, another common problem, has already been discussed.

The Shifting Environment

The environment in which social service organizations strive to exist is constantly in flux. Social forces impact other macro organizations and influence political policies which, in turn, modify the availability of funding. Thus, as Holland and Petchers (1987) explain: ''Financial support from public and private sources must be sought, maintained, and protected while community expectations and priorities shift from one problem or need to another. Legal requirements and policies regulating operations undergo modification. Service technologies evolve in new directions, not always in consonance with consumer or public preferences'' (p. 208).

Funding mechanisms vary widely. Social and economic forces jar social service organizations with unpredictability, suddenness, and severity. Thus, to survive and effectively meet their goals of helping clients, these organizations must be keenly aware of external influences and their effects. Organizations must also be able to react readily to changing needs and demands.

Vagueness of Process

Interventions performed by a variety of individual practitioners and other staff are very difficult to measure

HIGHLIGHT 4.5

HIGHLIGHT 4.5

EMPOWERMENT WITHIN THE ORGANIZATIONAL CONTEXT

Empowerment is "an intentional, ongoing process centered in the local community, involving mutual respect, critical reflection, caring, and group participation, through which people lacking an equal share of valued resources gain greater access to and control over those resources" (Cornell University Empowerment Group, 1989, p. 2). A primary thrust of generalist social work practice is to empower clients as individuals, families, groups, and community residents. We seek to enhance clients' right of choice, participation in decision making concerning their own well-being, and the availability of resources for them. A "goal of effective practice is not coping or adaptation but an increase in the actual power of the client or community so that action can be taken to change and prevent the problems clients are facing" (Gutierrez, GlenMaye, and DeLois, 1995, p. 250). How then can organizations as mightier forces than individual practitioners encourage the empowerment of large groups of clients and citizens?

Gutierrez, GlenMaye, and DeLois (1995) identify a range of factors working for and against an agency's ability to empower large groups of people. They selected six private social service organizations oriented to serving client "populations that have been associated with empowerment-based services" (p. 251). These included two agencies focusing on women's services, two on people of color, one on young people, and one on the elderly. The researchers interviewed both direct service staff and administrators, using taped interviews with an established format to identify environmental variables working for and against client empowerment. They identified four obstacles to, and three positive supports for, empowerment in the organizational context.

The first obstacle to empowerment involves "*expectations of funding sources*" (p. 252). Involving clients in the decision-making and service-provision process on a large scale takes time and energy. More people are involved. More communication is necessary. Therefore, the empowerment process is time-consuming. Funding sources must be sensitive to the significance of empowerment. They must consider it valuable enough to pursue despite increased costs in time and money. In view of these requirements, funding agencies do not necessarily give precedence to encouraging client participation.

The second impediment to empowerment is the "*social environment*," the macro context in which organizations function (p. 252). Other agencies not supportive of the empowerment concept may not encourage referrals to or from empowerment-based agencies. Likewise, competition among agencies works against empowerment in that empowerment is best established when people and agencies work together toward this end. Finally, rivalry for people's participation in the community obstructs the empowerment process. Community residents and practitioners have just so much time and energy. It becomes more difficult to involve people in the empowerment process if they are also integrally involved in other organizations and processes. These might include neighborhood centers, advocacy groups, professional organizations (such as the National Association of Social Workers), or parent/teacher organizations.

"*Intrapersonal issues*" are the third barrier to an organization's ability to seek client empowerment (p. 253). Sometimes, the basic attributes of clients or workers interfere with the empowerment process. For example, to what extent can people with serious mental or physical disabilities participate in the empowerment process? Some practitioners express frustration at the time and energy involved in pursu-

(*continued*)

HIGHLIGHT 4.5—(Continued)

ing empowerment when they see only limited success.

The fourth obstacle to organizational empowerment is "*interpersonal issues*" (p. 253). These involve the interactions and relationships between clients and practitioners. Some workers express serious concerns about how difficult it is to let go of their control and direction of the intervention process. This is especially so when empowered clients choose alternatives that place them at risk. For example, a client who is a survivor of domestic violence might *choose* to return to a destructive, abusive situation. It is difficult for some workers to accept their clients' right to choose when the workers see the choice as inherently bad.

In contrast to the obstacles, three supports are identified for organizational empowerment. The first is "*staff development*" (p. 254). This includes in-service training and other educational activities the agency provides to empower the staff themselves. Agency encouragement to develop new ideas, programs, and skills is another aspect of empowerment. Practitioners are encouraged to put forth extra efforts and to take initiatives in the organizational empowerment process for their clients. Agency sensitivity to staff needs is another facet of staff development. Workers indicate that reinforcement of their efforts through such means as promotions, meritorious financial rewards, and responsiveness to personal needs such as scheduling flexibility rejuvenates them.

A second support to empowerment is an "*enhanced collaborative approach*" (p. 254). This in-

cludes a teamwork perspective on the agency environment. Staff feel empowered when administration and boards of directors listen to their concerns. They are encouraged to pursue organizational empowerment when they feel an aura of safety and camaraderie with peers. Peer review of work is helpful under these circumstances. Workers are more likely to take risks to develop a shared treatment and empowerment organizational philosophy.

The third support to empowerment is "*administrative leadership and support*" (p. 255). When administrators foster this and practitioners realize it, "an atmosphere of empowerment" is established (p. 255).

Examining the aggregate findings of this study, what management approach appears to encourage organizational empowerment? How do the study's result comply with the concepts involved in a total quality approach to management?

Indeed, staff development, collaboration, and leadership all coincide with primary total quality concepts. Perhaps, it would be wise for organizational administrations to consider incorporating such concepts into their own management strategies and approaches. Gutierrez, GlenMaye, and DeLois (1995) conclude that "those organizations that empower workers by creating an employment setting that provides participatory management, the ability to make independent decisions about their work, communication and support from administrators, and opportunities for skill development will be more capable of empowering clients and communities" (p. 256).

---

and monitor. They are not like manufacturing machinery that punches out slabs of metal. The slabs can be measured. Raw materials can be made uniform. Effectiveness can be evaluated in terms of the machine's accuracy and efficiency (that is, how fast and perfectly the machine can punch out slabs). In this context, unlike that of the social services, work routines are predictable, repetitive, and relatively easy to monitor and control.

Professional staff in social service organizations vary widely, and clients probably vary even more widely. Therefore, social service organizations bring multiple, immeasurable, human factors to the intervention process. Because people vary more than inanimate materials like metal slabs do, practitioners who work with people must have more flexibility than metal slab punchers. That is, workers in organizations need discretion in working with their clients. This makes monitoring the intervention process more difficult.

Vagueness of Goals

Accountability, which is of critical importance to social work practitioners today, is "the state of being answerable to the community, to consumers of a product or service, or to supervisory groups; also, a profession's obligation to reveal clearly what its functions and methods are and to provide assurances to clients that its practitioners meet specific standards of competence" (Barker, 1991, p. 2). Individual practitioners and whole agencies are called upon to prove that their performance is productive and valuable by defining specific, measurable goals and monitoring the extent to which these goals are achieved.

Superficially this sounds good, but think about it. How can a practitioner prove that a client has been helped? One way is to define specific behavioral goals, which will be discussed at greater length in another chapter. This takes substantial time, effort, and expertise.

If you're teaching physically abusive parents child management techniques, how do you know when you've been successful? When they can pass a written test on specific techniques? When the parents strike their children only on the hands and rump instead of on the head? When they strike their children only once each day instead of a dozen times as they did in the past? Human behavior is difficult to define and measure.

Evaluating an entire organization, or even a program's, outcomes including goals, effectiveness, and efficiency is infinitely more difficult than evaluating the outcomes of micro or mezzo interventions because of the strikingly increased number of variables involved. In order to evaluate program outcomes, Holland and Petchers (1987) emphasize that, first, "service content must also be made clear, with uniform definitions describing program activities. They continue that "for consequences to be attributed to an activity, it is necessary to state exactly what a client has received from a given treatment or service and to determine whether that content has remained consistent over the course of the intervention" (p. 213). This is not an easy task.

It should be noted, however, that despite such difficulties social service agencies continue to make progress in the area of defining both process and goals. Chapter 6, "IMAGINE How to Implement Macro Intervention," will review setting specific behavior goals and objectives, while chapter 10, "Evaluating Macro Practice," will discuss a range of evaluation methods.

Other Common Problems Encountered in Organizations

Here we will describe some common problems encountered by people who work in any organization, including social service agencies. These include: impersonal behavior, rewards and recognition, agency policy and worker discretion, and traditions and unwritten rules.

Impersonal Behavior

The goals of accountability and efficiency can create difficulties for workers and clients. Sometimes agencies engage in behavior intended to be businesslike but perceived by the workers as impersonal. For example, one agency director, in order to reduce postage costs and cut the time workers spent on clerical tasks, decided to eliminate the appointment letters that workers would type on their computers and send to clients who lacked phones. The letters told the client when the worker was planning a visit and asked the client to let the worker know if this was not satisfactory.

No one quarreled with the wish to save money, but many workers were upset because they would be forced to go to clients' homes without giving the client prior notice. To many workers this seemed inappropriate and unprofessional behavior, even a violation of clients' rights. It could also be more time consuming. The director did not share these opinions and overruled the worker's objections. Finally, tired of arguing social work values against business values, one worker calculated the cost of driving across the county to see a client who wasn't home. The wasted mileage cost exceeded the cost of sending out the appointment letters. After some discussion and debate, the director canceled the policy and allowed the workers to send appointment post cards once again.

Rewards and Recognition

A second characteristic of most agencies is that thay do not distribute rewards and recognition as well as most workers wish. In school, it is common to get periodic feedback on your performance. Papers are returned with comments and a grade. Exams are returned soon after they are given with the grade evidently displayed. After each grading period instructors give grades in each course. Many people prefer this regular system of reinforcement and expect something like it to exist in the agencies where they work.

Unfortunately, much of the good work social workers do will never be recognized. It is simply not noticed in the busy life of the agency. Other good work will be noticed, but for many reasons no one will comment on it. Supervisors may come to take the good work for granted, and not believe it needs regular reinforcement. Clients may appreciate our efforts, but are too involved in their own situations to show their gratitude. Sometimes supervisors like our performance but clients do not. For example, workers who take child abuse cases to court are unlikely to have the offending parent praise their efforts. Consequently, a good guiding principle is to learn to reinforce yourself. This means you must take pride in work you do well, and accept that your work will not always be acknowledged.

Agency Policy and Worker Discretion

Earlier chapters have noted that agencies establish and operate within a system of policies. These policies can guide the behavior of workers and clients, and provide direction in situations that are common in the agency. An agency policy may require workers to sign out when they leave the building. This makes it easier for supervisors, administrators, and clients to know where workers are at any given moment. In effect, it is a form of accountability and makes sense to most workers.

Many new workers feel overwhelmed with all the policies, rules, regulations, and procedures they must learn and abide by. They may think that policies control or constrain their every action. In reality, workers have enormous discretion about how they do their jobs because policies, by their very nature, must be general enough to apply in many different situations. This means that no policy can foresee all the possible events, nu-

ances, and complexities of any given case. Policies set general guidelines, but workers are responsible for using their discretion or judgment with specific cases. Thus, these policies do not present a real barrier to effective social work. Workers must be prepared to apply their professional knowledge and skills and realize that they cannot rely on agency policy to dictate decisions in the field.

For example, suppose you are a practitioner working for a family services agency that specializes in helping parents learn how to control their children's behavior. Agency policy might prescribe eight weeks to work with parents and demonstrate improvement in their children's behavior. However, you and the parents have relatively wide discretion in determining what specific behaviors to work on. Should you focus on the children's tantrums, their refusal to eat anything but pizza and Hostess Twinkies for supper, or their almost constant nagging for attention? The decision is a matter of discretion.

Traditions and Unwritten Rules

Another characteristic of agencies is that, like other systems, they have both written and unwritten rules. The written rules frequently appear in a regulation manual or personnel handbook. The unwritten rules are related to the organization's informal structure, reflecting who has power and who communicates with whom. As in families, the traditions and unwritten rules are often learned only through verbal exchanges with more experienced group members. Sometimes they are learned only when the novice worker inadvertently violates a rule of tradition.

A case in point arose when a new MSW graduate, Gary Hughes, took his first job at a huge state mental hospital. Each Wednesday afternoon at 2:00 P.M., all the social workers at the hospital gathered around a large conference table. The purpose of the meeting was to improve communication among the social work staff. The hospital's social services director and its formal policy encouraged social workers to feel free at these meeting to raise issues causing them problems or making their jobs more difficult. Gary was confused. The social services director, Harvey Steinenfrank, who supervised four social work units, had offered Gary a job right out of graduate school. Gary had done his first field placement at the hospital and the director liked the quality of his work.

Gary's direct social work supervisor, Jannell Fesselfuff, seemed distant and acted as though she resented Gary's presence. Although she was always polite and professional, Gary felt Jannell did not really want him around. Finally, Gary decided to use the Wednesday afternoon meeting to discuss his feelings. All social work staff, supervisors, and Harvey attended these meetings.

At the meeting Gary shared his feelings with the assembled group. Jannell tactfully acknowledged that she felt as though Harvey, the social services director, had "dumped" Gary in her unit without talking to her about Gary's status beforehand. Jannell apologized for taking out her anger at Harvey on Gary. Harvey apologized to Jannell for not consulting her before assigning Gary to her unit. The air appeared to clear and Gary felt much better.

After the meeting, Jannell took Gary aside and told him she was upset because he brought the topic up at the meeting. She stressed, "We never discuss anything important at these meetings. We just meet because Harvey likes us to get together. If you have a concern, please talk it over with me first and we'll work it out." Later, Gary learned from talking to other workers that Jannell was right. The group had an informal rule that they never discussed anything important at these meetings. To do so was to violate the workers' informal policy and expectations.

The importance of this example is that informal rules and traditions can affect our work. We learn best by observing others and asking privately about things that appear to be rules. Learning about informal rules by breaking them can be painful.

Chapter Summary

This chapter defines organizations, social services, and social service agencies. A variety of organizational theories are presented including classical scientific management theories, human relations theories, Theory X and Theory Y, and systems theories. General systems theory concepts are defined and organizations as systems are explored. The nature of organizations is investigated, including primary and secondary agency settings, organizational goals, goal displacement, the macro context of organizations, and organizational structure. The latter includes lines of authority, channels of communication, and dimensions of power.

Two methods of management are examined. The traditional bureaucratic approach is explained. Orientation conflicts between professionals and the bureaucracy are identified. Suggestions for surviving within a bureaucracy are provided. A garbage can theory of decision making is discussed and related to bureaucratic management. A Total Quality Management (TQM) approach is discussed. Major concepts include: defining TQM; clients as customers; quality as the primary goal; employee empowerment; use of teams; TQM leadership; establishing a culture of quality; a long-term perspective; TQM tools; customer feedback; and the learning organization.

Finally, the exceptional problems of social service organizations are identified. These include the shifting environment, vagueness of process, and vagueness of goals. Other common problems encountered in organizations are discussed, including: impersonal behavior, rewards and recognition, agency policy and worker discretion, and traditions and unwritten rules.

CHAPTER FIVE

PREPARE—Decision Making for Organizational Change

As the social worker at an elementary school, you notice an increasing number of children coming from turbulent homes. With each passing year the truancy rates rise. Children's grades deteriorate and their illicit drug use soars. They need something, some kind of help. But what? Your job is to intervene individually with those children who are suffering the most severe crises. You do some individual counseling, make some family visits, run a few support and treatment groups, and attend numerous assessment and planning meetings.

In a new social work journal, you read about a new type of alternative programming for children who are at risk of developing the kinds of problems you're seeing. One idea in particular catches your eye. A school in Illinois has developed a "Friendship Program" for children-at-risk. Volunteers are solicited form social work students at a nearby university. The volunteers attend a dozen training sessions to learn how to work with these children. Each volunteer is then paired with an individual child and subsequently becomes the child's "special friend." The required commitment period is one year. Volunteers' responsibilities include spending time with their assigned child at least once a week, being available to talk when the child needs to, and providing a positive role model for the child.

In a way it reminds you of Big Brothers/Big Sisters programs where volunteers "work under professional supervision, usually by social workers, providing individual guidance and companionship to boys and girls deprived of a parent" (Barker, 1991, p. 23). However, in this Friendship Program, the child may or may not be from a single-parent home. The Friendship Program's prerequisite for participating children is that school staff designate them as being at-risk of problems including truancy, deteriorating school performance, and drug use. School staff have substantial latitude regarding the criteria to use for identifying a child as "at risk." However, typical criteria include a recent divorce in the family, extreme shyness and withdrawal, academic problems, and other social difficulties.

You think, "Wouldn't it be great if my school system had a program like that in operation? How would you go about establishing such a program? It is not included in your job description. It is possible for you to start something like that? Would it be worth your effort? Whom would you talk to about it? How might the school administration feel about starting up a program? What would it cost?

The above situation illustrates a major thrust of this chapter. Chapter 4, "Understanding Organizations," discussed various dimensions or organizations to help you understand the agency environment in which you will work. This chapter has one primary intent, to propose and explain a seven-step decision-making process to use when deciding whether or not to pursue macro intervention within your agency environment.

Introduction

Historically in social work, the term "community organization" referred to an intervention approach in which social workers and other professionals worked with groups of people to collectively bring about some social change. Traditionally, social workers were trained primarily in skills oriented toward community organization instead of in skills working directly with individual clients, groups, and families. Students trained in community organizing were expected to get jobs in agencies whose primary goal was community organizing. However, the social and political climate is very different today. Resources are scarce, and agencies engaged primarily in community organization are much less common.

Today's generalist approach intends to supply beginning social workers with a wide range of micro, mezzo, and macro skills for helping individuals, groups, families, organizations, and communities in a wide variety of situations. This necessitates maximum flexibility. Most beginning social workers get jobs that concentrate on helping individuals (micro systems) or families and other groups (mezzo systems) (Yessian & Broskowski, 1983; Hull, Ray, Rogers & Smith, 1993). Consequently, if macro change efforts are going to be undertaken, they will most likely be generated by social workers employed in agencies providing primarily micro and mezzo services. This is the perspective of this text. Because macro practice as such is rarely a goal of today's social service agencies, the worker must be able to move the wheels of change from a job not intended for that purpose. This requires a sound understanding of what goes on in agencies and how they work. The preceding chapter addressed many issues inherent in agency work.

This chapter emphasizes macro practice changes. The changes we are talking about here are very different from those that agencies formally engage in. Usually, agency administrators implement changes as part of their administrative responsibility, or agency authority figures solicit help and advice from outside consultants (Holloway, 1987). In both instances, formal authority figures (such as an agency director or board of directors) initiate and control the change process.

You might assume that agency administrators have, theoretically, greater qualifications and experience than direct service practitioners who have less responsibility for overall agency functioning. Likewise, you might assume that agency administrators automatically make good decisions. In an ideal agency that would be the case. However, in the real world, administrators make decisions for a multitude of reasons including: regulations governing them outside of the agency; monetary restrictions on agency functioning; insufficient information about what is going on at the direct service level (often due to the administrative layers of bureaucracy that act to buffer, summarize, edit, and censor information before it can get from the bottom up to administrators); or even interest on the part of administrators in some personal gain.

In our context, organizational change involves the actions of practitioners with little or no administrative power (that is, those who usually work directly with clients or have lower-level supervisory status). Our position is that such practitioners can seek to actualize changes in agency policies, programs, or procedures so that the agency will serve clients more effectively (Holloway, 1987). For whatever reason, agency administrators may not do what you think is right, necessary, or ethically responsible. In these instances, it becomes your responsibility as a direct service practitioner or lower-level supervisor to identify problems and instigate change. Such organizational change has also been called "change from within" (Resnick & Patti, 1980), "internal advocacy," (Patti, 1983), and "change from below" (Brager and Holloway, 1978).

Four factors usually define the context of organizational change (Holloway, 1987). First, such change begins with staff who have lower levels of power and authority within the agency. These staff seek to influence administrators with significantly greater levels of power. Ideally, of course, agency administrators encourage constructive suggestions from staff. However, in real life this is often not the case. Administrators may even discourage such communication for reasons such as the protection of their own egos or their concern for what they consider more global and important than staff input.

A second factor in organizational change is that lower-level or line staff express concerns about some problem or issue within the organization that transcends their own job descriptions and domains of responsibil-

ity. A third factor is that staff approaches go beyond those the organization has formally established. For example, the worker initiating the change might have to participate in special meetings out of his or her usual job experience. Indeed, the worker might have to confront superiors about issues involved. Confronting supervisors is not normally part of a worker's job description. Finally, the fourth factor in organizational change is that the whole process is undertaken for the benefit of the organization's clients.

Initially, we will look at the types of organizational changes usually involved when you initiate change from within. Later, we will describe the decision-making process involved in pursuing organizational change.

This chapter will:

- Introduce macro practice organizational changes involving projects, program development, and agency policy.
- Introduce and explain a seven-step process entitled PREPARE for assessing organizational change potential.
- Illustrate various steps in the decision-making process, including identifying problems, evaluating macro factors working for and against change, establishing primary goals, identifying relevant people of influence, assessing potential financial costs and potential benefits to clients and agency, evaluating professional and personal risk levels, and evaluating the potential success of a macro change process.
- Demonstrate the application of the PREPARE process through an extended case example.

Change in Organizations

As a social work practitioner, you will likely encounter times when your agency is accomplishing tasks ineffectively, is not doing something it should do, or is simply doing the wrong thing. Holloway (1987) points out that some problems facing human services organizations are "profound," while others are very "subtle" (p. 731). Specific problems might include the following:

"The agency does not reach out to potential clients, the agency is insensitive to clients' definitions of problems, it serves those for whom public sympathy is high and refuses to serve others, it makes referrals for its own rather than the client's convenience, or it offers one kind of service to meet all needs" (Holloway, 1987, p. 731).

When such organizational problems exist, it is your

responsibility to try to help your agency improve its service provision to clients. The National Association of Social Workers Code of Ethics (1993) states that it is your professional responsibility to put clients' interests above anything else, including those of the agency.

Macro changes within an agency are of two types (Netting, Kettner, & McMurtry, 1993): changes made to improve the resources provided to clients and changes made to enhance the agency's working environment so that personnel can perform more efficiently and effectively, thus improving service provision to clients. Such changes can involve undertaking projects, initiating and developing programs, and changing formal agency policies (Kettner, Daley, & Nichols, 1985).

A Word about Innovations

One way to look at organizational change is to frame it as an *innovation*. Rothman, Erlich, and Teresa (1981) introduce and define innovation as "any program, technique, or activity perceived as new by a population group or organization" (pp. 21–22). Thinking about macro change in organizations as innovations provides a bright, optimistic context for organizational change. Innovations imply freshness, creativity, and gusto. They can involve tried-and-true methods that are known well elsewhere but are totally exotic in your own agency. Or innovations can be brilliant ideas you creatively think up yourself for how to improve the functioning of your agency.

Once again, note that agency administrations may not recognize such brilliant innovations and ideas, let alone support them. Therefore, much of this and the next two chapters will address how to maximize your potential for initiating and implementing some macro change when resistance is likely.

Undertaking Specific Projects

The first type of potential macro change you are likely to encounter in your agency environment is the undertaking of some special *project*. The term project "refers to the development of specific sets of short-term, result-oriented activities providing support or direct services in response to unique conditions, problems, needs, or issues, in community or organizational context"

(Kettner, Daley, & Nichols, 1985, p. 39). Projects then are time-limited, short-term, and specific. Projects generally are undertaken only for some designated period of time, usually no more than a year. Unlike program development or policy changes, projects are temporary.

Other definitions and uses of the term project involve ongoing, permanent, or semi-permanent organized, goal-oriented activities. Consider, for example, the Milwaukee AIDS Project that has provided services to persons living with AIDS and their families for many years and will most likely continue to do so. By our definition, however, such a project is really a "program." (Programs will be discussed in a subsequent section in this chapter and again in chapter 7, "IMAGINE Project Implementation and Program Development.") We will, therefore, continue to define a project as a time-limited endeavor.

Projects are usually specific regarding the client population they serve and the final objectives they will pursue. Projects also likely cost less than new programs and have fewer repercussions than major agency policy changes, a fact that makes them more appealing to administrators.

Kettner, Daley, and Nichols (1985, pp. 161–63) cite two broad categories of projects. First, *service projects* address needs or issues requiring some new, innovative, or untried approach. Consider a worker at a residential treatment center for behaviorally disordered boys. This practitioner may initiate a project to determine the effectiveness of involving siblings along with parents in the family counseling that staff provide. If the project is found effective, the worker might urge the agency to incorporate such treatment into its policies or develop an ongoing new program to continue this practice. The research project would be evaluated and then terminated because projects are temporary. However, the worker and agency may then begin a new macro process of policy revision or program development.

Service projects do not necessarily involve time-limited research orientations. They can be undertaken to complete other short-term tasks. Once the designated task is completed, the project is over. For example, workers may undertake the task of rewriting their old job descriptions to more accurately reflect what they are currently doing.

The second type of project, the *support project*, involves short-term endeavors aimed at specific ends that support some other agency activity. Workers might organize a fundraising campaign for resources to build a new addition to their agency or take on a project to develop an in-service training curriculum to develop the skills they feel they need.

Initiating and Developing Programs

The second type of macro change that might face you as a practitioner is the need to develop a new *program*. Rapp and Poertner (1992) describe a program as "an aggregate of actions directed toward accomplishing a single goal"; they continue that "social programs attempt to find workers satisfying and fulfilling work" (pp. 29–30). Social programs then provide the means by which workers can offer clients services and resources. Programs are "relatively permanent structures designed to meet ongoing client needs"; they "carry out policies that are intended to meet community or organizational goals" (Kettner, Daley & Nichols, 1985, p. 33).

Each social agency or organization can have any number of programs. For example Lutheran Social Services, a national organization with agencies throughout the United States, hosts a number of programs; these include adoption services, mental health services, services for people with developmental disabilities, services for elderly people, and a variety of others (Barker, 1991).

Program development is not an aspect of most direct service jobs. Why, then, might you as a practitioner, consider trying to set up a whole new program? Because you see a major gap in the service delivery system that needs to be filled. You recognize clients' needs that are not being met.

For example, you might be a state probation officer. You notice a significant increase in your caseload (that is, those client cases assigned to you and for which you're responsible) of men committing acts over and over again that in your state are considered misdemeanors. A misdemeanor is a minor crime, less serious than a felony, that generally results in incarceration for less than six months (Barker, 1991, p. 146). Your clients are doing things such as speeding while driving under the influence and petty shoplifting of CDs. As their probation officer, you see them doing thoughtless, "dumb" things that simply get them several-hundred-dollar fines and several-month jail sentences over and over again.

You think this is senseless. There must be a better way to deal with this problem and help these men become responsible for their behavior.

At a conference you hear about a deferred prosecution program being run in an adjoining state. This program provides men arrested for such misdemeanors with alternatives to fines and jail terms. They can opt to participate in a twelve-week group run by two social workers. Group sessions focus on enhancing self-esteem, raising self-awareness, improving decision-making skills, developing better communication skills, and encouraging analysis of responsible versus irresponsible behavior. It might be noted that the program was initially funded by a grant (often referred to as "soft money," meaning temporary and limited funding). However, it was so successful that the state decided to implement and pay for it in several designated counties by using "hard money." "Hard money" means relatively permanent funding that becomes part of an organization's regular annual budget.

At any rate, men who participated in the program were found to have a significantly reduced recidivism rate. Recidivism rates refer to the proportion of men who repeat misdemeanors. A recidivism rate of 25 percent would mean that of one-hundred men, twenty-five would commit another misdemeanor and seventy-five would not.

You think, "What a wonderful idea!" You begin to consider how to initiate such a program in your agency. This can be the beginning of program development.

Or suppose you are a counselor at a large rural residential facility for adults with developmental disabilities who are considered unable to live in the community by themselves. Your job involves teaching basic daily living skills such as how to dress oneself and make one's own bed. Additionally, you run socialization groups and activities for clients to teach them to relate to and get along with each other. Finally, you work with your clients' families to help them make visitation arrangements and address any other problems that may come up. Sometimes, for instance, parents have difficulty controlling their adult child's behavior during the child's home visits.

The problem is that you are especially concerned about six of your clients. You feel they are not being stimulated enough to develop their full potential. You think that with some special training and help, they

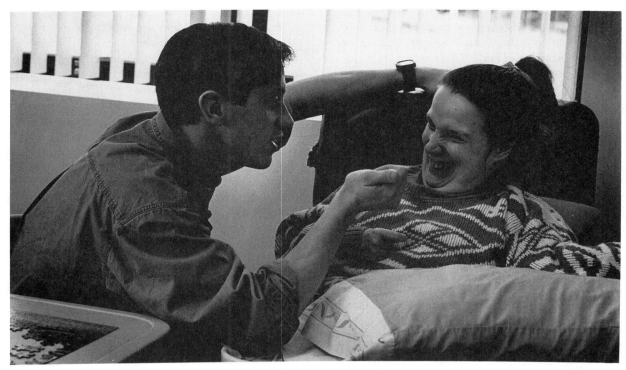

How does one begin the process of program development? At this day treatment center, a social worker helps an adult who has developmental disabilities. The worker feels that the center needs a new program with respect to patient care. He'll need to "learn the ropes" concerning how to get a new program off the ground.

would be capable of living either in a group home or in individual apartments with some supplementary support. This support might include teaching them how to cook, do laundry, pay bills, and possibly obtain employment. You feel they would be able to grow in such a setting, enhance their self-esteem, and become more productive members of society.

However, no such program exists in your area. There are neither group homes nor social workers assigned to provide supportive services to enhance the independence of clients like yours. Now what? How might you begin exploring the possible initiation of program development?

Changing Agency Policies

Agency or organizational policies are the guidelines that govern how an agency operates. Policy dictates what should and should not be done in the agency setting.

Policies may be formal or informal. *Formal policies* are written down and clearly specified, often in a policy manual. *Informal policies*, on the other hand, are not overtly stated, yet still guide and influence agency staff's behavior.

The policy manual, by the way, may be the most important document in your agency. It compiles the rules and regulations that govern your responsibilities, rights, restrictions, and benefits. A policy manual is usually excruciatingly dull. It is not written to stimulate the reader's interest. Rather, policy manuals usually consist of complex, legalistic language that is very difficult to understand clearly. Such manuals do, however, provide you with a statement of the agency's formal goals, procedures for working with clients, instructions for requesting vacation time, and grievance procedures to follow if you think you have been mistreated. Therefore, it is vitally important that you receive your own copy of the manual when you enter the agency or have ready access to someone else's, such as your supervisor's. Policy manuals are very dull when they don't apply to you, but tremendously interesting when you need them to answer your questions and find out about your rights.

Formal and informal policies formulate the core plan for what the agency does and how it does it. Policies involve both internal operation (process) and provision of services to clients (output). Internal operation includes administrative arrangements and specific procedures for how the agency is run. For example, formal policies involving internal operation can address the lines of authority within the agency (who supervises whom). Such policies can also specify how many sick days and vacation days employees have available and how such time is accumulated (a specific agency procedure). Often, sick time and vacation days are accumulated on the basis of time worked in the agency. You might accrue one sick day for every month of completed work and two weeks vacation for every year.

Formal and informal agency policies also concern how services are provided to clients. They can specify the proper procedures for completing a family assessment, the forms to fill out as progress notes, what kinds of services will be provided to clients, and many other aspects of worker-client interaction.

Formal and informal agency policies usually represent long-established ways of doing things in the agency. As such, agency policies affect virtually all agency personnel and clients.

It is easy for practitioners entering the field to assume that agency administrators and supervisors are responsible for ensuring that the agency has "good" policies. Agency policies should be effective and efficient so that clients receive the services they need. They assume that is what administrators get paid for. Administrators are supposed to keep the agency running well so that workers providing direct services to clients can do their jobs. However, often this is not the case. For example, a type of goal displacement may occur where the original goal of serving clients is gradually replaced with a new goal of maintaining the service process. Process becomes more important then results. Often tasks such as keeping records up to date become more important than the quality of services provided to clients.

Sometimes agency policy reinforces problems such as goal displacement. A formal policy might read that crisis intervention workers in an agency must attend weekly staff meetings at regularly scheduled time despite the fact that their clients may be experiencing ex-treme crises at these meeting times. Thus, agency policy requires crisis workers to attend meetings rather than address their clients' crises.

Another example of a problematic formal policy is one that requires clients to fill out a twenty-seven-page admissions form before they can receive services. Perhaps a large percentage of the agency's clients are Hispanic people who speak very little English. If the admissions form requires that potential clients be highly articulate in English, the agency essentially prohibits Hispanic clients from receiving service. Because of the language difference, the agency blocks clients from getting what they need.

Still another example of a problematic policy involves an informal requirement that all members of a family must be present for the initial intake interview. If individual family members refuse to attend such interviews for any of a variety of reasons (such as employment during meeting times, lack of interest, or resentment about social service involvement), such families would be denied access to treatment.

Our final example of a problematic agency policy concerns workload. Assume that agency policy requires you to make one home visit to each of the one hundred families on your caseload every forty-hour work-week. Including traveling time, it takes you approximately two hours to do each home visit. Therefore, in order to fulfill agency policy, you must make two hundred hours worth of home visits in your forty-hour work-week. Obviously, even if you omit eating lunch and using the restroom, this is impossible. Agency policies frequently create such dilemmas. Perhaps when the agency policy was instituted, caseloads averaged twelve families instead of one-hundred. Established policies are often appropriate at their conception, but can become outdated. Over time, with increasingly stringent budgets, caseload numbers gradually creep up. For practical reasons, this agency policy needs to be changed. Caseloads could be cut drastically, the requirement that each family be visited weekly be deleted, or some other fairly drastic policy change be made in order to make the policy congruent with what is possible.

There will be times when you feel that formal or informal agency policies interfere with, restrict, or even totally prevent you from doing the best possible job with clients. You as a practitioner working directly with clients on a daily basis may be more in tune with "what's going on out there." It makes sense for you to identify

A problematic policy is one that requires that all members of a family be present for the intake interview. Here, a mother and her children who receive public assistance are being interviewed. How might the worker improve current policy to make service provision more effective and efficient?

the impediments and difficulties confronting you every day. Therefore, even if it's not your designated job to change policy, it may be in your and your clients' best interests to do so.

Informal versus Formal Agency Policies

Informal agency policies can be confusing. As we have indicated, they are implicit, unwritten rules about how the agency should operate. Often they are elusive and difficult to pin down. Many staff simply assume that "everybody knows about *that.*" Unless an agency newcomer is psychic, he may behave totally inappropriately simply by being ignorant of the unwritten rules. Sometimes these informal policies entail simple expectations for superficial actions. Other times they prescribe important rules of conduct, the violation of which is not to be taken lightly.

Suppose you're a new worker at a Veteran's Administration Hospital. You work in the vocational rehabilitation unit with clients who have mental or physical disabilities. Your main tasks are to assess your clients' abilities, refer them to the appropriate training facilities, and eventually help clients find jobs in the community. You have been on the job exactly six work days. You walk into your first multidisciplinary staffing. You are one of a number of staff from various disciplines who are there to provide information and make decisions regarding treatment planning for a series of clients.

You feel you have done your homework and read through the ponderous section of the agency's policy manual that described multidisciplinary staffing procedures. You are energetic, enthusiastic, and eager to make a good impression on your new supervisor and colleagues. You have worked with similar clients before and have taken special related courses in college. You feel confident and appropriately assertive.

During the meeting you make six well-thought-out statements regarding your beliefs about the treatment of two clients. At the end of the meeting, you pat yourself on the back, thinking, "Wow, that was good. I must've made a good impression. Knowledgeable. Not too pushy. What more could they ask?"

After the meeting several staff walk quickly past you without making eye contact. You think, "That's odd. What's up with them?"

A physical therapist sheepishly approaches you as you walk out the door. You have spoken to her several times informally and feel that you really hit it off. She says, "I don't mean to be rude, but perhaps someone should have told you some things about our staffings. The case manager [not you on this occasion] usually comes in with the treatment recommendations in pretty good shape. We all have an understanding that whoever is managing the case (including following up on recommendations, monitoring progress, and writing up reports) talks to those of us who are involved ahead of time for our input. If we started from scratch with every single case, we'd never get anything done."

How would you feel? In this case two informal policies or implicit rules were unknown to you. First, staffings here provided opportunities to finalize already established plans, not to discuss or initiate loads of new ideas. Participants keep talking to a minimum in order to get through the process. The physical therapist did not refer to the second rule, which is that new staff are not supposed to talk much at meetings until they are at the agency at least three months. By this time, other staff have had time to get to know them and will give more credibility to their ideas.

How could one prevent such an "oops" experience? The fact that many policies are informal means that they probably will need to be learned informally. That is, talking to other staff about informal expectations, rules, and policies is probably a good plan. In this situation, prior to the staffing you might have talked to colleagues about how staffings are run, especially about how they differ from the description in the policy manual.

Three types of informal agency policies are discussed briefly below. They include policies involving practice procedures, agency goals, and personnel (Netting, et al., 1993). Remember, however, that we will focus on them in the context of informal policies. Practice procedures, agency goals, and personnel may also involve clearly established formal policies.

Informal Policies on Practice Procedures

Practice procedures refer "to the way organizations or individuals within them go about doing their business"

(Netting, Kettner, & McMurtry, 1993, p. 235). Some practice procedures are formalized policies. For example, an agency might specify that goal attainment scaling, a specific method of evaluation, is used to monitor clients' progress.[1] Chapter 10, "Evaluating Macro Practice," discusses goal attainment scaling in greater detail.

Knowledge and understanding of informal policies on practice procedures is infinitely important from the macro perspective. The way tasks are *actually* carried out in agencies (as opposed to how they are theoretically *supposed* to be carried out) directly impacts clients' well-being. Consider an agency where formal policy requires that cases be discussed and plans developed during periodic formal case staffings. Because of heavy caseloads and limited time, in reality most workers informally discuss clients' cases whenever they can snatch a few seconds of time. Sometimes they do so in hallways, other times while having a drink after work. These informal practices downgrade and sometimes even eliminate regular, responsible discussion of cases during staffings to make certain that case plans are effectively on track. Assuming a macro perspective in this instance, you might want to initiate and implement a change in the informal procedure so that case plans are once again discussed on a predictable basis. This might involve addressing the issue with other staff and administrators. Likewise, it might require initiating renewed formal case staffing procedures that are more efficient and doable.

Practice procedures within agencies vary widely and endlessly. Examples include counseling techniques, record-keeping methods, and admissions processes. For example, you might want to propose that progress notes be written using an established agency form instead of just scribbled in the form of a note citing the date the client was seen and your impressions. You might suggest a procedure for decreasing each client's intake pro-

---

1. Goal attainment scaling provides an individualized means of monitoring a client's treatment progress in interpersonal communication skills, parent effectiveness skills, and the like. Sheafor, Horejsi, and Horejsi (1988) describe three steps for establishing an individualized scale: "1. Identify major areas of functioning in which intervention is expected to have an impact . . . 2. Assign a number to each goal area to indicate its importance in comparison with other goal areas toward which the client is preparing to work. . . . 3. Specify five levels of possible outcome in relation to each goal area" (p. 398). The status of individualized goals can then be measured before, during, and after intervention to measure progress toward goal attainment.

cess from three steps (that is, initial phone contact, individual interview, and family interview) to two steps (namely, initial phone contact, when individual information is collected, and family interview).

Another example of an informal policy concerning agency procedures is causing problems for Ms. Winfrey, a newly promoted supervisor of the large Supportive Services Unit (for the elderly) in an urban social services agency with two-thousand employees. Unit staff provide supportive services to elderly residents in their own homes to help them remain as independent as possible. For example, unit staff help clients access services, pay bills, get food and medicine, and connect with required resources.

Ms. Winfrey's new job requires her to supervise five direct service workers. The first day of work after returning from her two-week Rocky Mountain National Park summer vacation, Ms. Winfrey's administrative assistant, panicking, storms into her office. The assistant gives Ms. Winfrey a handwritten note from the agency's Executive Director, Mr. Sawyer. Ms. Winfrey is awestruck. She has seen the Executive Director only a few times, and has never before received a handwritten note from him. This means serious business. What could possibly be wrong? She's only had her new job for a month. What could she have done? The note reads:

8/29/95
Ms. Winfrey,
    Please submit the absence reports for your staff immediately. They are due the fifth of each month.
    T. Sawyer

No one told Ms. Winfrey that absence-reports forms existed, let alone that they were due to someone on the fifth of each month. The policy was not contained in any document she knew of. Apparently, several administrative assistants in Mr. Sawyer's office tried to contact her. Due to her illness, her vacation, and a malfunctioning telephone answering machine, the messages never got through. Finally, as a last resort, Mr. Sawyer took his very expensive time to address this extremely petty issue. Apparently, the agency loses major funding if timely absence reports are not religiously submitted to the powers-that-be.

Ms. Winfrey is flabbergasted. Apparently, the agency personnel expect new administrative staff to learn such procedures by osmosis or ESP. She had no idea how important this procedure was.

Eventually, Ms. Winfrey chalks the incident up as a mistake that was not really her fault. However, she *never* again forgets to submit the absence report when it is due.

INFORMAL AGENCY GOALS. The last chapter discussed organizational and agency goals and their importance. Rothman, Erlich, & Teresa, (1981) reflect on their significance: "The collective welfare of practitioners' clients and constituents is profoundly affected by the organizational structures and goals of social agencies. Changing an organization's goals thus becomes a key task for many practitioners, and failure to accomplish this objective is frequently a great hindrance to effective practice" (p. 51).

Sometimes formal goals reflect an agency's real goals and sometimes they do not. Informal agency goals often replace formally stated goals. In these instances, the informal goals become the real goals the agency strives to reach. Goal displacement is a good example. Commonly, in goal displacement the *process* of getting things done replaces the importance of actually getting things done (Etzioni, 1964). This is the case even though the formal goals still stress the importance of the output or services provided.

INFORMAL PERSONNEL PRACTICES. Agency treatment of personnel is integrally involved with formal and informal communication channels discussed in the previous chapter. Many potential sources of conflict can result in macro practice intervention. For example, staff might cooperatively organize to try to overthrow an administrator they intensely dislike (Netting et al., 1993). There are no formal policies for doing that.

An administrator's significantly preferential treatment of staff in her unit, giving opportunities to a privileged few, may infuriate the unprivileged many. A supervisor might use his power and discretion to give privileged staff better cases, choice of limited vacation time, and more flexibility of hours. The unprivileged may then mobilize to develop and institute new formal policies to curb such unfair practices. Policies could structure the procedure so that it had to be fair.

Be wary, however, about trying to put new policies in place to constrain the actions of one or two individuals. When those individuals leave their positions or the agency, you will be stuck with the policy. One group of practitioners resented how their supervisor divided cases. His personal friend, a woman with whom he had an intimate relationship, received the most interesting and least chaotic (therefore, least difficult and time-consuming) cases. The remaining unit practitioners worked to develop, and urged administration to adopt, a policy that forced supervisors to divide cases equally and randomly. Passed through higher levels of administration, the supervisor lost most of his discretion regarding the assignment of cases.

Abruptly, both supervisor and friend left the agency for other positions. The remaining staff and the new supervisor were then burdened with the old policy. The new supervisor was much fairer and more democratic. The old problem of unfair treatment was gone. Without that problem, staff would have preferred holding staff meetings where clients could be assigned on the basis of each staff's expertise. They all preferred to have input into case assignments. However, this was not possible due to the rigid, newly adopted policy. Staff and new supervisor were then faced with two choices. They could live with the new system that severely restricted discretion and flexibility or they could start a new macro change process, expending time and energy to recover a more flexible policy. Staff's other concern was their credibility with administration. They feared they would look as if they could not make up their minds and would simply be ignored. In effect, they were stuck.

Beginning the Change Process

Macro interventions are often complex. Practitioners usually must think about the problem and potential solutions in a general way before beginning any change process. There are a number of dimensions to consider. Resnick (1980b) emphasizes that macro change requires four critical elements including ''the change catalyst [we will use the term *change agent*], the action system, the innovation proposal, and the action plan'' (p. 188). The *change agent* is the person who feels some change within the agency is needed. In our context, you. You as the change agent begin to think about a perceived problem you feel requires change, and then you initiate the change process. The *action system* is the people and resources you will organize and employ to help you work toward the needed change. It includes you and the people who work with you to achieve the change. If you undertake the change yourself, you will be both the change agent and the action system. The *innovation proposal* is the basic idea you want to implement. Fi-

nally, the *action plan*, like any other plan in generalist social work practice, is a detailed blueprint for how to go about achieving the desired change.

As a change agent—the practitioner who sees something wrong and is willing to expend effort to change it—you can either choose to initiate the process yourself or unite with other social workers in your agency who have similar feelings about the problem (Resnick, 1980c). The latter approach is usually superior because it gives you more power and influence. Either you alone or your coalition becomes the action system.

At this point there are two major tasks to consider (Resnick, 1980c). First, you need to identify the action system's potential goal. What do you want to accomplish? Do you want to incorporate flexible hours into the agency's policy so that clients may be seen on evenings or weekends? Does your agency need to establish a crisis intervention line to respond to clients' needs more quickly? Do your adolescent clients need somewhere to congregate and participate in wholesome recreational activities as an alternative to gang membership? What is your final goal?

The second task involves thinking about the potential opposition you anticipate in trying to reach your goal. Will agency administrators balk at greater costs or at changing established procedures? To what extent will co-workers and workers in other agency units either impede or support your ideas?

The Process of Organizational Change

We have established that the problem-solving process follows seven basic steps. These include: engagement; assessment (including defining issues and collecting and assessing data); planning (including contracting); implementation (selecting and implementing appropriate courses of action); evaluation (including using appropriate research to monitor and evaluate outcomes, and applying appropriate research-based knowledge and technological advances); termination; and follow-up.

We have also established that the generalist perspective proposed here is oriented toward solving problems at multiple levels of intervention. That is, such problems may involve individuals, families, groups, organizations, and/or communities. In effect, this generalist approach means that virtually any problem may be analyzed and addressed from a wide range of perspectives that could potentially involve any size system.

At the point you decide to access the possibility of macro change, you switch into a new, more complicated mode. First, you must determine whether a macro change is a viable alternative. You might learn that no macro change is feasible and drop the whole idea. Second, you must choose the most desirable type of macro change. You can pursue changes in an organization, a community, or a social policy (The latter two will be discussed much more thoroughly in later chapters. This chapter focuses on organizational change.) Finally, you must select and follow your strategies for whatever type of change process you choose.

Macro level change is more intricate because so many more micro, mezzo, and macro systems are involved. It is also more extensive because it pursues goals outside your everyday job description. In addition, you assume greater risks. We will discuss these risks later in the chapter.

This chapter proposes a seven-step process to evaluate whether your goal is potentially worth a macro change effort within an organizational setting. Brager and Holloway (1978) term this phase "initial assessment." You acknowledge a problem exists and judge whether you have the potential resources to pursue change. Figure 5.1 summarizes this process. Note that you do not necessarily have to follow PREPARE's steps in the exact order in which they are presented. The important thing is to remember all of the variables involved when considering undertaking a macro level change. We use PREPARE as an aid to help you remember each of these dimensions.

Step 1: *PREPARE*—Identify *Problems* to Address

The first step in the process for organizational change is identifying the *problems* you feel are most significant. This often takes some time for you to clarify in your own mind specifically what needs to be addressed. In any macro environment, including an organization, there are bound to be a multitude of imperfections and problems that vary drastically in degree of severity. What problem or problems are most severe and in need of attention? About which problems are you most seri-

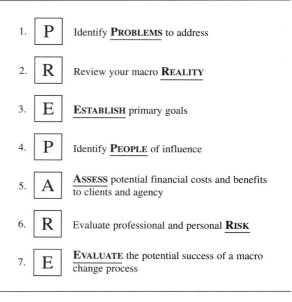

Figure 5.1
PREPARE: An Assessment of Organizational
or Community Change Potential

1. P   Identify **PROBLEMS** to address

2. R   Review your macro **REALITY**

3. E   **ESTABLISH** primary goals

4. P   Identify **PEOPLE** of influence

5. A   **ASSESS** potential financial costs and benefits
       to clients and agency

6. R   Evaluate professional and personal **RISK**

7. E   **EVALUATE** the potential success of a macro
       change process

ously concerned? Can you ethically live with the problems despite inconveniences, or do you feel you must address them directly at the macro level? Finally, how can you most concisely identify the problem requiring macro level intervention?

This first step in the PREPARE process involves five facets of substeps that are listed below.

Substep 1: Decide to seriously evaluate the potential for macro level intervention.
Substep 2: Define and prioritize problems.
Substep 3: Translate problems into needs.
Substep 4: Determine which need(s) you will address.

The following sections discuss each substep in greater depth. Then, each will be applied to our case example involving Spiro, Farica, and the other protective services unit staff.

Substep 1: Decide to Seriously Evaluate the Potential for Macro Level Intervention

The first step entails thoughtfully considering the intervention's potential success. It requires exercising criti-

DECIDING TO GO MACRO—
A CASE EXAMPLE

Social work students are usually eager to get into the field and work with clients of their own. It is often difficult for them to understand the significance of working in an organizational environment when they have not yet had the experience. They may also have difficulty comprehending the complex decision-making process necessary before initiating macro change. Agencies are full of individuals with distinct personalities. Each individual has strengths and weaknesses, personal opinions and quirks. A macro change process involves many unique variables. Our intent is to make the decision-making process for pursuit of macro change more vivid and relevant to you. Therefore, we will follow a case example through each of the seven proposed decision-making steps.

The Scenario

The setting is a Protective Services Unit in the Yalobusha County Department of Social Services in Plattesburgh, Wisconsin. The unit is composed of six workers and a supervisor. Farica, the unit's supervisor, is very worried about the significant increase in the workers' caseloads over the past year. It is becoming nearly impossible to handle even the crises on the workers' caseloads, let alone give adequate attention to each and every case assigned. State law requires that each reported case be investigated within twenty-four hours after intake. In reality, a worker is lucky if he or she gets to it within four days. Farica's staff is being forced to violate the law.

The Personalities

Farica, a raven-haired, heavyset, intense person, is a motivated individual who works extremely hard to do a good job. She is very concerned about her clients' welfare. If anything, she takes her work too seriously.

Farica hates being the unit supervisor, a job she accepted four months ago. She doesn't like her colleagues very much and abhors taking responsibility for their mistakes. She has a tendency to fly off the handle when angered. She accepted the supervisory position under duress when the prior supervisor left. At that time, one of the unit staff had to take the job because a budget freeze prohibited any new hires. The problem with other staff taking the position was that either they didn't want it (and all the headaches that came with it), or they were not interested in attending to administrative detail (an absolute requirement). Farica has been with the agency about ten years.

Spiro, short, blonde, and ordinary-looking in appearance, has been in the unit twenty-five years. He considers the unit a kind of home for him. He feels it is somehow *his* unit and is dedicated to its welfare. Spiro thinks of himself as a "great guy" and by far the most qualified and best worker in the unit. Spiro has anything but low self-esteem and thinks he is always right.

Spiro didn't want the supervisory position because he is much too busy earning a substantial income through his booming private practice. Spiro is highly motivated to achieve and is very responsible in his work. He typically likes to complete things two weeks before others even know they are due. He gets really annoyed when obstacles get in his way when he is performing his job.

Tina, an attractive, petite woman, is very articulate and concerned with her own performance. She wants to do a good job and get positive feedback from colleagues and supervisor but is not certain she really wants to be in social work. She has been with the agency five years. She is a bit paranoid about others

(*continued*)

<hr>

HIGHLIGHT 5.1—(Continued)

criticizing her and her work. She takes offense relatively easily. She hesitates to become involved in any projects that are not directly related to her own job.

Archie, a tall, thin, relatively handsome individual, has been in the unit almost as long as Spiro. He essentially feels he is tenured and is sitting back doing what he has to until he can retire in three years. He has a blustery manner and tends to be abrasive. People who don't know him are easily intimidated by his height and manner, which accounts for the fact that he frequently gets his way. He is very concerned about the welfare of his clients, however, and will expend substantial effort for those he thinks are "worth it." Archie is terrible with detail and spelling. He is not highly creative.

Dylan, a 320-pound giant of a man, who considers himself quite intellectual, is more adept at thinking of global ideas than at completing day-to-day, mundane tasks such as paperwork. He's been with the unit approximately seven years. He has a laid-back approach to work and life. If things don't get done today, they will tomorrow or the next day. Or somebody else will eventually take care of them. He does the minimum required, however, to accomplish his job. He is also seriously concerned with children's welfare so is willing to expend effort on their behalf.

Barney, of average height and weight, bald with a bushy dark brown mustache, is another laid-back individual who is not in a hurry to get anything done. It is very important to him that people consider him a nice guy. He also strongly believes that everyone must be treated equally so he virtually never takes sides for or against his colleagues. He is very concerned about his clients and does most of his work.

However, he has a very difficult time making decisions and often seeks direction from colleagues, usually Spiro and Dylan. Barney spends a lot of time worrying about what he might have forgotten. He's been with the agency four years. Barney and Dylan are good friends, as they feel they have a lot in common. They can sit and talk together about global issues for two full hours and when they're finished, they can't summarize a thing they've said.

Ann, a relatively quiet yet assertive person, is very concerned about her clients and doing a good job. She is generally well-liked by colleagues because she is cooperative and easy to work with. She participates in group projects to some extent and generally carries her share of the work burden. However, she is very busy working part-time on her master's degree, which is distracting her. She has only been with the agency a year and a half. She likes her job and strives to have colleagues accept her.

Attending to the Problem

Spiro and Farica are the most acutely concerned about the enlarged caseload. Spiro is disturbed because he is the most committed to the unit and worries about failing to obey the law by meeting the time requirements. Farica is perturbed, too. She is worried about clients' welfare in addition to her own ability to fulfill her supervisory responsibilities, namely, seeing that her staff serve clients effectively. Other staff are concerned about the problem, but not that much.

What should be done? Should a macro change be attempted? Or should they all just sit tight and see what happens?

<hr>

cal thinking skills to make decisions regarding how to pursue your professional practice. During this first step, address the following questions:

a. How heavily is the problem impacting clients' well-being?
b. Is the problem serious enough to merit macro change?

c. Are you willing to think through and appraise the actual potential for you to make a difference?
d. Are you certain that your clients would support such a macro change and that it is in their best interest?

If you sincerely feel and rationally determine that the pursuit of macro change is the *right* thing to do, then you should proceed to Substep 2.

HIGHLIGHT 5.2

CASE EXAMPLE, PREPARE: IDENTIFY PROBLEMS TO ADDRESS—SUBSTEP 1

Substep 1: Decide to evaluate seriously the potential for macro level intervention.

Spiro is our identified change agent because he feels most strongly about the caseload problem. He thinks seriously about the questions posed in substep 1 above. Yes, the problem *is* impacting clients'

well-being. It *is* serious enough to merit the efforts that must be expended to cause a macro change. He himself is willing to pursue it. He feels certain that it *is* in his clients' best interest. Certainly society and the families involved would like to arrest and halt child maltreatment.

Substep 2: Define and Prioritize Problems

This substep in the problem identification process involves deciding which problems to address. Specifically, identify problems, prioritize them in order of their severity, and choose those that you will work on. Rothman (1984) emphasizes that at least three aspects of each problem merit attention. *First, exactly what client*

population will be affected? What are the demographic characteristics of the client population? Exactly who will benefit from the macro change?

Second, *what type of problem is it? Whom does the problem affect? Exactly how severe is it?*

Third, *what is the root of the problem?* How did the problem start? What variables serve to perpetuate it? How is the problem sustained by other systems in the environment? Such appraisal helps you think about

---

HIGHLIGHT 5.3

CASE EXAMPLE, PREPARE: IDENTIFY PROBLEMS TO ADDRESS—SUBSTEP 2

Substep 2: Define and prioritize problems

1. *What is the client population?* The clients are families whose children are being maltreated. Specifically, clients include all such cases referred to the agency.

2. *What type of problem is it? Who is affected by it? How severe is it?* The problem involves all the clients who are not being served. It also involves families that are receiving less attention than they

need. Spiro estimates that possibly fifty families are currently affected. He determines that, yes, the problem *is* severe.

3. *What is the root of the problem?* The foundation of the problem is that abusive families need attention and help to strengthen coping skills and minimize risk. Lack of staff time and attention prevents clients from receiving the help they need. There is really one designated problem, so prioritizing does not apply in this case.

Figure 5.2
Identify *Problems* to Address—Substep 2

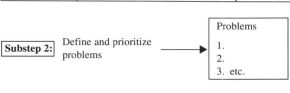

the problem in various ways and understand it more fully.

Frequently, problem identification is more an emotional evolution than a rational statement of facts. Resnick (1980c) maintains that "the process is more like an emotional pulling together of a group of people who desire to right some wrong in the organization" (p. 203). You can begin focusing on some organizational facet that either directly or indirectly interferes with effective service provision. The more you think about it, the more ideas you can generate about how to solve the problem. Later, you can talk to colleagues about the issues involved. You can test the waters to see what others think and who might be on your side. As you continue discussion, you can think about the problem in new and creative ways. Frequently, the problem's solution evolves over time as new ideas are integrated (Resnick, 1980c).

After evaluating problems prioritize them, starting with the one that's most severe and requires the most immediate attention. Sometimes there is only one primary problem. Other times, there may be several. Decide which one or ones to target. See figure 5.2, substep 2, in the problem identification process.

Substep 3: Translate Problems into Needs

Problems, of course, are any sources of perplexity or distress. Many times they arise from lack of resources. Clients come to agencies because they have problems to solve. It is your and your agency's job to help them accomplish that.

Needs, on the other hand, are "physical, psychological, economic, cultural, and social requirements for survival, well-being, and fulfillment" (Barker, 1991, p. 153). The way to prepare for figuring out what an agency can do to better serve its clients is to translate

agency and client problems into needs. See figure 5.3, substep 3, identifying problems to address.

Hansenfeld (1987) suggest five phases for clarifying and substantiating an unmet need in order to prepare for program development within your agency (pp. 454–55).

First, get background data and information to clarify exactly what the need is. You can use substantiating data to prove that the need is significant enough to merit intervention. You can obtain facts from statistical reports kept by public agencies. Census data are often helpful. What are the characteristics of community residents? Public and private agencies often keep information on requests for service that cannot be met. Research studies sometimes document needs. Be creative. Think about what kinds of facts would help to prove the need. Who else might be interested in the problem and the need? Where might other interested parties make documentation available?

You might be a school social worker who identifies the *problem* that many of your clients are heavily involved in drug use. You determine that these clients *need* a drug education and treatment program in the school setting. Although drug involvement might be considered a community problem, you feel that the school system is the appropriate organization to address this need. Where can you find facts and statistics to establish the need in order to convince the school to address it?

One source might to police statistics. How many drug-related arrests have been made? Can the lack of treatment programs and referral sources be documented from police records? Another source might be specific local schools. What records are available regarding drug problems and seizures? Are research reports addressing similar adolescent populations available to support the need for drug rehabilitation programs in general?

A second phase in clarifying and substantiating an unmet need is to recognize and specify other agencies or programs in the community that already address the identified need. If the need is being met elsewhere, why start a new program? Return to the example of the adoles-

Figure 5.3
Identify *Problems* to Address—Substep 3

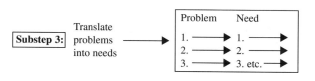

HIGHLIGHT 5.4

CASE EXAMPLE, PREPARE: IDENTIFY PROBLEMS TO ADDRESS—SUBSTEP 3

Substep 3: Translate problems into needs.

After identifying the problem clearly in his mind, Spiro goes through the steps to translate problems into needs.

1. *Getting background data.* Spiro goes to Farica who keeps summary records of all cases referred to their unit. Together, they determine from the data that there is a current backlog of twelve cases needing immediate assessment attention and forty-two cases requiring more extensive treatment. Analyzing the data, together they determine how many hours the typical case requires.

2. *Assessing services provided by other agencies.* Spiro already knows that his unit is the only agency providing this service in the area. His unit is the centralized resource receiving all referrals.

3. *Getting ideas.* Spiro talks with his colleagues to get their thoughts about the problem. He doesn't bother talking with Archie because he doesn't think Archie has any ideas. This is interesting because Archie no long speaks much to Spiro. One day Archie abruptly told Spiro that Spiro always steals his ideas. Spiro responded that he didn't think Archie had any ideas to steal, and around it went. They no longer spoke to each other. With other staff members, Spiro considers various ways of looking at needs. On the one hand, workers need more time to spend with clients. One way of getting this would be to decrease the number of clients. This alternative, of course, is not possible because all clients must be served.

The other workers come to a consensus that more staff are needed. The workers cannot do an adequate job of treatment without spending sufficient time with each family. However, they'll need more funding to add more positions. Neither Spiro (as a direct service worker) nor Farica (as unit supervisor) has access to information about funding. They do know, however, that several months ago, when the prior supervisor left the agency, there was no funding to replace her.

4. *Involving clients.* One phase of treatment for families who are agency clients involves a support group for abusive parents. Tina is responsible for running the group and usually does not like any interference. Spiro asks her if he can speak to the group members at their next meeting. Tina feels somewhat threatened, but she reluctantly concedes. Spiro then attends the beginning of the next group meeting, explains the problem to clients, and solicits input from them regarding their feelings. The fact that these clients continue to be involved in a support group implies that they value the agency's services. Otherwise, they would not expend the effort to attend. As expected, they support Spiro's idea about the unit's needs.

5. *Considering a needs assessment.* Spiro determines that a formal needs assessment is not necessary. Not only does he review records with Farica, but they also prepare and administer a limited-term functional job analysis procedure. That is, over a two-week period, Farica monitors each unit staff person's time. Staff are provided forms that divide their typical work activities into categories and are required to record the type of activity in which they are involved for each fifteen-minute period of work time. Categories of activities include face-to-face interviewing with clients, travel time, and time for keeping records. Farica and Spiro determine that staff are, indeed, working as efficiently as possible. Staff simply do not have enough time in a day to perform their jobs adequately. Spiro and Farica decide that further investigation using a formal needs assessment would be a waste of time.

cent drug problem. If a local hospital is already offering a treatment and rehabilitation program, further program development may be unnecessary. Rather, your intervention approach must then be to educate teens and parents about the problem and the hospital program. You could also facilitate their access to the existing program. On the other hand, establishing that *no* relevant programs exist strengthens your position that a program is needed.

You can find out about other services in a variety of ways. First, consult a resource directory if there is one for your area. Second, consult supervisors and colleagues regarding their knowledge of other services. Third, consult the telephone yellow pages to find out if there are any resources you are not aware of. You can talk to anyone you think might have ideas. You can also consult your own records if you think they might be helpful.

The third phase in clarifying and sustaining an unmet need is talking to other professionals serving similar clients. Find out how they perceive the problem and the need. They might enhance your understanding of what's involved and give you ideas about how to proceed.

The fourth phase emphasizes client involvement. As a school social worker, you might talk to students and find out how they perceive the problem and the need. You might also talk to community residents to test their feelings and potential support. For example, parent-teacher associations, church groups, and community businesspeople and professionals might provide further insight into and support for your plans.

The final phase in substantiating an unmet need is considering the value of a more formal needs assessment. Needs assessments are formal evaluations of client needs within the organizational context and of resident needs within the community context. "Problems, existing resources, and potential solutions" are methodically taken into account in order to "document needs and establish priorities for service" (Barker, 1991, p. 153). Such studies can establish very specific needs in a convincing manner.

Substep 4: Determine Which Need or Needs You Will Address

Macro systems are complicated environments. Thinking in general systems theory terms, there is a constant flow of input, process, and output. Agencies are dynamic interdependent webs of resources, clients, services, workers, policy, programs, and administration. At any particular time in your work career, you will likely have many things on your mind. Even when you notice a problem in agency policies or programs, you should carefully assess what needs are most critical to address. You cannot do everything. You have only so much time, energy, and general resources.

Step 2: PREPARE—Review Your Macro and Personal *Reality*

One major factor in deciding whether to pursue a macro level intervention is a serious appraisal of your *reality*.

HIGHLIGHT 5.5

CASE EXAMPLE, PREPARE: IDENTIFY PROBLEMS TO ADDRESS—SUBSTEP 4

Substep 4: Determine which need or needs you will address.

Spiro decides that clients need more of the workers' time. He thinks the best way to address the defined need is to seek additional staff from the administration. Trying to get funding for more staff on his own is too awesome of a task. He has no access to any information about funding and no power to solicit resources himself. He and Farica have fortified their argument by analyzing the staff's workload and establishing that there is too much work for staff to complete effectively.

That means the actual conditions, in your working environment and in your personal characteristics, that may affect the macro change process. We define *macro reality* as the macro environment in which you work. It includes the numerous systems, subsystems, and other elements of your agency's internal operation and the agency's own macro environment. When considering macro intervention, ask yourself what your macro reality involves. What variables might work for or against you, either from within or from outside the organization, in your pursuit of macro intervention? How *realistic* is your chance of success in implementing this macro change?

Reality also refers to your own *personal reality*, the personal strengths and weaknesses that might affect your ability to effect a macro intervention in the macro environment. Therefore, step two of the PREPARE process has two substeps:

Substep 1: Evaluate organizational and other macro variables potentially working for or against you in the macro change process.

Substep 2: Assess your personal reality—the strengths and weaknesses that might act for or against successful change efforts.

Substep 1: Evaluate Macro Variables Working For or Against You in the Macro Change Process

Numerous variables in the agency and the external macro environment can work for or against you in the macro change process. Analyzing "data about the various forces that may affect a change agent" is often referred to as a *force field analysis* (Sheafor et al., 1981, p. 493). In other words, it is critically important to identify, analyze, and scrutinize the variables within the macro environment that might work for or against the change process. Such variables affect at least five arenas. They include (1) resources and funding, (2) constraining regulations or laws, (3) the political climate of the agency, (4) the external political climate, and (5) other factors (Holloway, 1987).

Resources

First, how do you perceive the resources and funding available in your agency? Did the agency just receive a major grant or donation? Is the agency looking for ways to use these resources? Or is internal funding so tight that staff are being laid off right and left? What types of resources do you think you'll need? Will the change be a minor project requiring only a few weeks of staff time? (Staff time is expensive.) If staff are spending time on a macro project, how will their regular work get done? Who will take over or pay for the extra work? Will the necessary change require development of a whole new program costing half a million dollars or more?

For each of the four variables involved in the evaluation of your macro reality, write a brief description of how you perceive the respective situations. Then evaluate the extent to which each variable works for or against your goals. Rate each from extremely positive to extremely negative. See figure 5.4, substep 1, in the assessment of your macro reality.

You may notice that there is no central neutral category in the rating scheme, so you are forced to decide whether the variable is positive or negative. Otherwise, it's too easy to take a neutral, wishy-washy position that fails to help in your decision making.

Constraining Regulations

Second, are there any regulations or laws against your goals? For example, suppose your idea is to expand twenty agency group homes for adults with developmental disabilities from six male clients to twelve male and female clients. Your rationale is to provide greater opportunities for socialization and relationship-building. However, state licensing regulations mandate that such group homes may not have more than eight clients maximum.[2] In this scenario, your idea for macro change would be doomed to failure because it did not follow the designated rules.

Internal Political Climate

Third, what is the political climate in your agency? Does your administration urge employees to develop and try out new ideas. Or does your administration watch em-

---

2. State licensing of facilities like group homes involve "granting a formal governmental authorization to do something that cannot be done legally without authorization" (Barker, 1991, p. 132).

Figure 5.4
Assess Your Macro and Personal *Reality*—Substep 1

Substep 1:

Evaluate organizational and other macro variables potentially working for or against you in the macro change process. These include:

Variable	Brief description	Extremely positive	Mildly positive	Mildly negative	Extremely nega-
Resources (Funding)					
Constraining regulations or laws					
Agency political climate					
External political climate					
Other factors					

ployees like private investigators and try to limit the time employees spend in the restroom? We discussed different types of leadership and their consequences in the last chapter. A large bureaucratic organization with a strict hierarchy of authority would probably be much less likely support an innovative idea than a small, growing agency that actively responds to new concepts and quickly implements changes.

FACTORS AGAINST CHANGE. Three factors act against change in the agency environment (Resnick, 1980c). Therefore, you need to address them when considering a macro change. First, an organization that has undergone a number of major external alterations and upheavals in recent months will probably be more resistant to change. Organizations as systems tend to seek homeostasis. Change generates anxiety and effort to address the unknown. It is logical that an organization would seek some peace and quiet in order to regain its equilibrium.

A second potential factor acting against organizational change exists if the agency is wedded to a specific philosophy or treatment modality. For example, a mental health agency espousing psychoanalysis would probably bristle at the idea of converting to a behavior modification approach.

The third variable working against agency change is the age of the agency and longevity of its staff. Consider an agency initially established fifty years ago. Its administration and staff, who have been around forever, are more likely to resist change than the administration and staff of a new agency that is readily responsive to new approaches and ideas.

BUREAUCRATIC SUCCESSION. One positive opportunity for change occurs in the first three months of a new administrator's tenure after the previous one leaves. This is referred to as bureaucratic succession (Pawlak, 1983). It is common for an organization to enter a "lame duck" period for the last few months an administrator is in power. Staff generally don't bother to think of anything new or make any changes because the new administrator might turn them upside-down anyway. Why bother to expend extra energy when you don't know how a new administrator will feel about your ideas? On the other hand, the new administrator is "both vulnerable and receptive to influence" (Pawlak, 1983, p. 206). A new administrator doesn't yet know the ropes. She needs to explore and identify the agency's formal and informal policies and communication channels.

Pawlak (1983) proposes six ways a practitioner can use bureaucratic succession to advantage in effecting positive macro change. First, you can offer suggestions to those responsible for hiring the new administrator, suggesting what qualifications they should specify for the new position.

HIGHLIGHT 5.6

CASE EXAMPLE, PREPARE: ASSESS YOUR MACRO AND PERSONAL **REALITY**—SUBSTEP 1

Substep 1: Evaluate organizational and other macro variables potentially working for or against you in the macro change process.

Spiro follows the evaluation suggestions for this substep as illustrated in figure 5.4. Suggestions include evaluating the following variables:

1. Resources and funding.

Brief description: Resources are unknown. There have been rumors about funding crunches. However, other units have gotten minor staffing increases in the past three months.

Evaluation: Mildly negative. (Spiro thinks there might be funds available if administration is convinced more staff is really necessary. Spiro knows that administrators have some funds available to distribute at their discretion. After all, other units have gotten the staff they needed. Spiro feels that bringing his case to the administration's attention and making it strong enough will result in some positive action, namely, a staffing increase in his unit.)

2. Constraining regulations and laws.

Brief description: Laws require that staff respond within time limitations. Staff can't possibly do so. Therefore, the staff is forced to break the law.

Evaluation: Extremely positive. (Spiro thinks that the agency is not in compliance with laws and regulations regarding what its staff is supposed to do. He believes this is a persuasive factor for administrators. They want to comply with legal requirements in order to look good in the public's eye. When an agency does not look good, there's always a chance it will lose public funding.)

3. Political climate within the agency.

Brief description: Spiro characterizes the agency's internal political climate as "business as usual." Administration generally supports its units and their respective staffs as they do their jobs.

Evaluation: Mildly positive. (Spiro determines that the agency has not undergone any major upheavals recently. The agency's general philosophy is to attend to the public's basic needs. There has been no recent bureaucratic succession. Actually, the agency's administration is pretty set in its ways. However, since Spiro can think of no clearly negative factors in the agency's climate, he decides it is mildly positive.)

4. External political climate.

Brief description: The general public is basically supportive of providing services to combat child maltreatment (including physical, sexual, and emotional abuse in addition to neglect). However, funding appears to be tight.

Evaluation: Mildly positive. (Spiro decides that the external environment's potential influence is positive because of strong feelings about abuse. This positive influence is bolstered by the law requiring responsive attention to referrals. However, he determines this is only mildly positive because of the overall general lack of resources for programs. In other words, he feels his unit and its work could compete fairly well with others for any funding that might be attainable. However, he does not know what kind of funding is available.)

Second, you can pursue becoming a member of the agency's search committee. Frequently, agencies assign task groups to conduct job searches, especially when the position is one of substantial authority within the agency.

The third way to use bureaucratic succession is to write a position paper outlining your ideas and your proposed macro change. A fresh administrator is generally eager for information. She would, thus, be more open to what you have to say.

Fourth, you can suggest that the agency's adminis-

HIGHLIGHT 5.7

CASE EXAMPLE, PREPARE: ASSESS YOUR MACRO AND PERSONAL REALITY—SUBSTEP 2

Substep 2: Assess your personal reality—strengths and weaknesses that might act for or against successful change efforts.

Strengths: Spiro sees himself as extremely competent and hardworking. He feels he has an excellent reputation within the agency. He is very willing to expend the necessary energy to undertake macro change and is fairly confident of success.

Weaknesses: Unfortunately, Spiro is not very adept at evaluating his own weaknesses. He really sees himself as having none. In reality, his major weakness is his need to succeed and get his own way. The implication is that if he would acknowledge this weakness, he might better perceive how people above him could resent his pushing them too hard.

---

trative power structure be amended to increase staff participation in decision making. You can seek to increase the worker discretion allowed in various job roles. Or you can urge the agency to use advisory committees to increase input.

Fifth, you can collaborate with fellow practitioners and present the proposed macro change to the new administrator as a group. More supporters tend to enhance an idea's influence.

The sixth way to use bureaucratic transition is to encourage the agency to establish a task force to ease the new administrator's adjustment to this new organizational environment. To have greatest influence, you could also become part of that task force.

External Political Climate

The fourth question to ask when evaluating organizational and other macro variables involves the agency's external environment. What is the political climate outside your agency like? Would the community and governmental structure be likely to support or obstruct your idea for macro change? For example, what if implementation of your idea would require a lot of money? What chances would you have if community residents were irately protesting the tax increases they already had?

Other Factors

Other factors affecting potential macro change can include virtually anything not included in the four categories above. It could be a catastrophic natural disaster like a flood or hurricane, causing most attention and resources to focus on providing food and shelter to victims. Likewise, it could be an economic upheaval such as a major industry leaving or arriving in town. Finally, a factor with potential impact could be an event like a sexual harassment, racial discrimination, or fraud charge within the agency. Take into consideration anything that would distract administrators' and public attention from your macro change effort.

Substep 2: Assess Your Personal Reality— Strengths and Weaknesses That May Act For or Against Successful Change Efforts

The second substep in the assessment of your macro environment's reality targets your own personal qualities. These include the strengths and weaknesses that may act for or against a successful change effort. As in micro and mezzo practice, it is vitally important to assess your own personal traits before proceeding with a macro change proposal. Personal assets include such variables as your personal relationships with colleagues and administrators in the agency. Deficiencies or weaknesses include such aspects as lack of sufficient knowledge about the problem and needs you want to address.

Rothman et al. (1981) cite a number of specific personal factors that act either to facilitate or hinder your ability to work toward macro change within your agency. You should evaluate each asset and weakness on a scale from very good to very bad, as figure 5.6 suggests. Assets involve: positive interpersonal relationships with other staff members, immediate supervisor, and various levels of administration; personal loyalty and dedication to the agency; your reputation within the agency; your understanding of client problems and needs; your ability to initiate macro change within the limitations of your own job role; and your own level of "self-confidence" (p. 43). Limitations include: lack of understanding of the community and how the agency fits into the community's total service delivery system; personal stress currently being experienced, such as a death in the family or a personal illness; debilitating exhaustion and fatigue; overinvolvement

with your own job; and insufficient time. Rate each limitation from serious problem to no problem.

Step 3: PREPARE—*Establish Primary Goals*

How can you fulfill your identified needs? What is your ultimate goal—that is, what will fulfill the need and solve the problem? What goals do you think you might be able to accomplish within the reality of your own macro environment? It is too early to establish detailed, specific objectives. However, you should be able to set your sights on some distant target. *Establishing* a primary goal can provide you with general direction as you evaluate macro intervention potential and establish plans.

Goals generally have two characteristics (Resnick, 1980c). First, we have established a process whereby goals are derived from some identified *problem*. Second, the problem can be translated into some *specific need*, which suggests ideas about what the change should involve. Resnick (1980c) describes goals:

HIGHLIGHT 5.8

CASE EXAMPLE, PREPARE: **ESTABLISH** PRIMARY GOALS

Spiro has already defined the problem: clients need more service time from workers. Translating this problem into a *specific need*, Spiro decides that his goal is to increase the time workers within his unit can devote to service provision. He does not have enough details yet to decide exactly how he might go about this. His main idea is to increase the number of staff, which will allow each worker more time to serve clients.

When considering the concepts related to goal selection, Spiro foresees his goal as being relatively permanent—"relatively" permanent because fund-

ing cuts and changing regulations can often alter the fabric of agency life. Abrupt changes such as dismissal of staff can result. Thus, Spiro considers his proposed goal to be as permanent as possible.

The second concept relevant to goal selection is deciding which goals have the greatest impact. Spiro's primary concern is for his own unit. Therefore, whether his goals have more widespread impact does not concern him.

The third concept relevant to goal selection is simplicity. Spiro feels his goal is as simple as he can propose, namely, adding more staff.

Figure 5.5

Evaluating Personal Characteristics for Macro Practice: Macro Practice Builds on Macro Practice Skills

It is just as important to evaluate your own personal characteristics, strengths, and weaknesses in macro practice as it is in micro or mezzo practice. We have established that skill development in generalist practice evolves. First, you must know how to engage and interact with other individuals (micro practice skills). Next, you must expand your skills to working with groups of individuals (mezzo practice skills). Finally, you must acquire skills to work with and within agencies and communities (macro practice skills). Each level of skills builds and expands upon the earlier level(s).

It is important to assess your personal strengths and weaknesses that may act for or against a successful change effort. This is very similar to the process of self-awareness you underwent when developing your engagement and interviewing skills. You will use the same interpersonal skills working with people in macro practice as you do in other levels of practice. Your own behaviors, mannerisms, and characteristics will work for or against you in macro practice just as they do in micro or mezzo practice.

Picture yourself working with staff, administrators, and clients in the context of an agency. Answer the questions and follow the instructions below:

1. Complete the following four *who are you* statements. They can be adjectives, nouns, or longer statements. If you had to summarize who you are, what would you say?

   I am _____ .

   I am _____ .

   I am _____ .

   I am _____ .

2. What adjectives would you use to describe yourself? Circle all that apply. They are in no particular order or priority. They are just meant to stimulate your thinking about yourself.

HAPPY	SAD	HONEST	DISHONEST	SENSITIVE	INSENSITIVE	TRUSTWORTHY	UNTRUSTWORTHY	CARING
UNCARING	OUTGOING	SHY	WITHDRAWN	FRIENDLY	UNFRIENDLY	RELIGIOUS	NOT-VERY-RELIGIOUS	
NERVOUS	CALM	FORMAL	INFORMAL	AGGRESSIVE	ASSERTIVE	TIMID	CONFIDENT	
NOT-VERY-CONFIDENT	CAREFUL	CARELESS	CAPABLE	INCAPABLE	INDEPENDENT	DEPENDENT		
AFFECTIONATE	COOL	WARY	BOLD	CHEERFUL	WITTY	UNASSUMING	THOROUGH	EASY-GOING
DETERMINED	CLEVER	RESPONSIVE	STRONG-MINDED	WEAK-WILLED (SOMETIMES)	LEISURELY			
INDUSTRIOUS	CONTROLLED	SPONTANEOUS	SERIOUS	FUNNY	TOUGH	PLEASANT		
DARING	EAGER	EFFICIENT	NOT-SO-EFFICIENT	ARTISTIC	TACTFUL	INTOLERANT		
VULNERABLE	LIKABLE	SMART	UNDERSTANDING	IMPATIENT	PATIENT	IMAGINATIVE	WORDY	
CONCISE	OPEN-MINDED	FUNNY	ORGANIZED	SOMEWHAT-DISORGANIZED	CONSCIENTIOUS	LATE		
EMOTIONAL	UNEMOTIONAL	CONTROLLED	OPEN	CREATIVE	CURIOUS	SENSITIVE	SINCERE	PRECISE
A-LITTLE-HAPHAZARD	COOPERATIVE	PLEASANT	ETHICAL	BRAVE	MATURE	EAGER	SPUNKY	

3. How would you rate yourself on the following traits?

	Very good	Mildly good	Mildly bad	Very bad
Relationships with other staff	_____	_____	_____	_____
Relationship with supervisor	_____	_____	_____	_____
Relationship with administration	_____	_____	_____	_____
Dedication to agency	_____	_____	_____	_____
Your reputation within the agency	_____	_____	_____	_____
Your understanding of clients	_____	_____	_____	_____
Your ability for pursuing macro change within job role	_____	_____	_____	_____
Your self-confidence	_____	_____	_____	_____

Figure 5.5 (*continued*)

4. How would you rate yourself on the following traits:

	Very serious	Moderately serious	Mildly serious	Not at all serious
Lack of understanding of community service system	___	___	___	___
Personal stress	___	___	___	___
Exhaustion and fatigue	___	___	___	___
Overinvolvement with job	___	___	___	___
Insufficient time	___	___	___	___

5. Cite your four greatest strengths. They can be anything from personal qualities to talents to accomplishments. They don't have to be in any particular order or priority.

Strength A _____

Strength B _____

Strength C _____

Strength D _____

6. Cite your four greatest weaknesses. These don't have to be in any order of priority either.

Weakness A _____

Weakness B _____

Weakness C _____

Weakness D _____

7. How do you think your personal strengths will help you work with other staff, administrators, and clients in macro practice situations?

_____

_____

8. What weaknesses, if any, do you think you need to work on to improve your ability to work with staff, administrators, and clients in macro practice situations?

_____

_____

Examples of goals may range from the establishment of regular meeting times for physicians, social workers, and nurses in a hospital to discuss cases, to the shifting of the program focus on a social work unit from individual services to a group or community service. A goal may be as minute as designing a new face sheet on a case record or as major as establishing a workshop to improve administration-staff relationships (p. 212).

Three concepts relevant to goal selection are potential for permanence, greater influence, and acceptance (Resnick, 1980c). First, give precedence to a goal that the agency is likely to integrate permanently. Don't waste effort on temporary remedies to permanent problems. Second, choose a goal that is likely to influence more agency units over a goal with more limited effects. The agency is more likely to maintain goals that will affect a greater number of units and personnel. Third, select goals that are simpler to manage over those that are more complex and require a lot of administrative effort. Administrators are usually busy and preoccupied with a wide range of concerns. They are thus more

Figure 5.6
PREPARE—Identify Relevant *People* of Influence

Potential Action Systems	Name	Potential Support			
		Very good	*Mildly good*	*Mildly bad*	*Very bad*
Individuals in the organization					
Groups in the organization					
Individuals in the community					
Groups in the community					
Others					

likely to accept and support goals requiring less of their energy.

Step 4: PREPARE: Identify Relevant *People* of Influence

Whom do you know who might be available to help you make the changes you want to pursue? Potential action systems might include specific *people* or groups within either the organization or the surrounding community. Probably people with access to influence or power within the agency are most significant. Are there any others you could go to for help? Do you have a former supervisor or professor who could help you develop a strategy?

It's too early in the process to make detailed plans and establish specific objectives for how to accomplish your goals. However, you can start thinking about potential plans and objectives. Identify individuals and groups within your agency and community who could potentially *help* or *hurt* your cause. Subjectively rank the support you anticipate from each on a scale from

very good to very bad. You will be able to use this information later when you begin to work on expanding your base of influence and support. See figure 5.6, which illustrates how you might identify relevant people of influence.

Leadership Styles of Decision-Makers

Administrators have individual personalities, qualities, and flaws just like anyone else. It is important to take these differences into consideration when thinking about which leaders can be most helpful to you in the change process.

Personalities and priorities are related to leadership styles. Lauffer, Nybell, and Overberger (1977) identify five basic types of leadership styles, including "climber," "conserver," "zealot," "advocate," and "states[person]" (pp. 13–15). These styles offer interesting food for thought. Keep in mind, however, that many people demonstrate a mixture of these distinctive styles.

The *climber* "tends to closely control subordinates

HIGHLIGHT 5.9

CASE EXAMPLE, PREPARE: IDENTIFY RELEVANT **PEOPLE** OF INFLUENCE

Spiro first thinks about the agency administrators with the power to make financial and program-related decisions. Three administrators in the organizational chart have direct responsibility for the protective services unit. Bob, the agency director is a reasonable, caring person who likes Spiro. In the past Spiro has volunteered for a number of projects Bob proposed. Spiro did a pretty nice job and Bob appreciated his efforts. However, Bob has much more to think about as head of the entire agency than one relatively small unit. Spiro sees Bob as a statesperson type of leader with some tendencies to be an advocate.

Harold, a stiff, unemotional person who is hard to read, is assistant director and second in command. Spiro sees him as a conserver. He is authoritarian in his approach to people below him. However, he is more involved in internal budgetary decisions than Bob and wields substantial influence over how funds are spent. Spiro and Harold don't get along very well. Spiro gets along best with people who do what Spiro tells them to do. Spiro resents his lack of influence over Harold. One positive note, however, is Harold's concern for obeying the rules (such as the law regarding abuse cases). Spiro feels Harold may listen to an argument emphasizing the legal rationale.

Theresa, the general supervisor (directly above Farica as unit supervisor and below the assistant director) is unpredictable in her treatment of the protective services unit. She makes haphazard decisions and often attends to details the unit staff feel are irrelevant rather than focusing on what staff consider important. For example, she is very concerned about the exact mileage reported on mileage reimbursement sheets, but is totally disinterested in treatment plans or goals. Spiro views Theresa as a climber. She appears to have a very close relationship with Harold. In their interaction, Harold seems to listen

to her suggestions, and in return she does whatever he tells her to do. Spiro does not get along at all well with Theresa. She has criticized his suggestions several times. Once again, Spiro does not get along well with anyone who doesn't consistently let him have his own way.

Farica, as unit supervisor, has the most direct link with administration. She seems to get along fairly well with Theresa. However, Theresa is inconsistent in her treatment of Farica. Sometimes, Theresa is supportive and sometimes not. Farica's relationship with Harold and Bob appear adequate. She, too, has volunteered for some of Bob's projects. He appears to respect her, although their relationship is not as close as Bobs' and Spiro's. Spiro feels his own relationship with Farica is relatively good. She generally cooperates with his suggestions. He feels to some extent he can manipulate her to support him.

Spiro also feels that his immediate colleagues will support him. He envisions addressing the issue at an upcoming unit staff meeting. Barney, not a powerhouse of ideas himself, usually goes along with Spiro's suggestions. Dylan is easygoing enough to agree. He usually just wants to maintain collegial relationships with unit staff. Ann wants to avoid conflict at all costs so will probably go along with Spiro. Archie and Tina usually keep quiet and go along with the majority opinion. Despite Spiro's anticipated support of unit staff, they have little real power to help. Spiro does want their support, however. Just in case the plan fails and anything negative results (for example, hostile reactions from administrators), he does not want to be the only one to blame. If he gets the entire unit to support him, any blame or bad feelings will be diffused.

Spiro decides that these agency administrators are the most relevant people of influence. There is also a Community Advisory Committee made up of

(continued)

influential people in the community and of people who were clients in the past. The committee's purpose is to provide feedback and suggestions directly to Bob and Harold. The committee's strength and influence generally depend on the energy and commitment of its current membership.

About fifteen years ago, the Protective Services unit was in a similar predicament regarding desperate understaffing. At that time Spiro went to the Community Advisory Committee, explained the situation, and asked for help. At the time he was unit supervisor. Spiro also went to the local newspapers and alerted them to the situation. Under this public pressure, the agency director (the one before Bob) added two staff positions to the unit.

Finally, Spiro considers seeking funds outside the agency. The county supplies most of the funds. He could ask the county board to increase funding, but why would they listen to him? He is too low in the agency power hierarchy to matter. He knows that specified channels exist for making budget and funding requests.[a] The board would wonder why he didn't go through his agency channels. Seeking funds through grant writing or donations is also too uncertain. It takes too much time and effort to pursue these options with little hope of successful return.

In summary, Spiro feels that the potential of support from Bob is mildly good, from Harold mildly bad, from Theresa very bad, and from Farica very good. Spiro also thinks the potential for using both the agency's Community Advisory Committee and the press are very good.

Note

a. It should be noted that funding channels for public agencies responsible to various legislative bodies are very different than funding channels for private agencies whose funding sources often vary widely.

to ensure nobody else is seen as a rising star'' (Lauffer et al., 1977, p. 13). These supervisors and administrators are very concerned about themselves and their own career moves. They tend to interpret any bright ideas on their subordinates' part as threatening to their own status. Therefore, they probably will not support a subordinate's proposal for macro change. They might even confiscate the idea and take it as their own. You can target a climber as a person to influence if you think he or she might latch on to the plan and exert pressure to have it adopted. However, don't expect to get any credit for the idea.

The *conserver* toils to preserve the homeostatic status quo. Like climbers, conservers are very concerned with and interested in themselves and their own work. Conservers are sometimes called typical bureaucrats. They revel in filling out forms on a routine and timely basis. They tend to be strong proponents of goal displacement. Quality of service is not of much concern to them unless it involves their higher priority of following the rules. They generally abhor fresh and innovative ideas that might disrupt the steady flow of paperwork. Obviously, you would not get much support for macro change from a conserver.

The *zealot* is a go-getter who exudes energy and loves creative innovation. However, zealots are also very preoccupied with themselves. Zealots think they know best regardless of others' opinions. They expect subordinates to be their faithful devotees. They may or may not listen to a macro change proposal, depending on how it fits into their view of the universe. You might approach a zealot with your innovation whether you think he'll agree with it or not. However, don't expect him to spend much time listening to your ideas. Zealots and climbers are more likely than conservers to support an innovation. A zealot is a little less likely than a climber to steal your idea.

The *advocate* is ''a person who has exceptionally high commitment to the goals of the organization or unit of which she or he is a member, or to a client population serviced by the agency'' (Lauffer et al., 1977, p. 14). Advocates are skilled administrators. They can protect their corner of the agency from such external threats as funding cuts and can mediate disputes among their own staff. Advocates are generally straightforward, primarily concerned about the well-being of both clients and agency. Advocates are probably the best administrators to approach with good, innovative ideas. They are the most likely to work toward the benefit of the agency and its clients. They are least likely to put their egos first or to steal your ideas. Because they tend to be assertive, they can be powerful allies.

HIGHLIGHT 5.10

CASE EXAMPLE, PREPARE: **ASSESS** POTENTIAL COSTS AND BENEFITS TO CLIENTS AND AGENCY

What are the potential costs?

Spiro does not have access to specific budgetary information. However, he does know that staff are occasionally added to other units in the agency. He thus supposes that resources are available if you can develop a good enough argument for them.

Will the results be worth the effort?

Spiro strongly believes in the unit's work and goals, and he feels strongly that the potential results are worth the effort.

Might alternative solutions produce more benefits at less cost?

Spiro can't think of any viable alternative to pressing administration for additional staff. He and Farica have established that their unit is using its time as efficiently as possible.

Who gets the benefits and who pays the costs?

Spiro feels that clients will directly benefit and that the agency is responsible for paying the costs.

The final leadership category is that of *statesperson*. These people are "more concerned with the welfare of society as a whole than with the agency or a particular client population" (Lauffer et al., 1977, p. 14). A statesperson can be extremely helpful as a proponent of a new idea. One of his/her strengths lies in establishing excellent public relations with others. These are usually good people to target for potential positive influence. However, they are not good at attending to detail and carrying through on long-term proposals. They lose interest relatively quickly. Therefore, a statesperson might be very helpful at the beginning of the macro change process, but useless once the proposal has been adopted.

Rationales for Internal Advocacy

Patti (1983) speaks of internal advocacy as championing or defending the rights of clients from the practitioner's perspective when such advocacy is not part of the job description. It is our professional and ethical responsibility as social workers to make certain that clients receive their due rights and services. There are four rationales or arguments for legitimacy that you can make to agency administrators on behalf of your quest for posi-

tive organizational change (Patti, 1983). They include:

1. You know a lot about the problems and issues involved. In essence, because of your special knowledge, involvement, and skill, you can "assist the organization in coming to a more rational and effective solution than has heretofore been available to deal with the issue in question" (p. 220).
2. You are on the agency's side. You are simply trying to help the agency comply with its stated goals of providing effective services to clients.
3. Your advocacy is necessary to supplement the agency's formal communication network. It is not always possible to communicate information and ideas clearly through a number of administrative levels or individual administrators. As a result, administrators may be deprived "of the data they need to assess accurately the effects of the agency's programs and procedures" (p. 220).
4. It is your right to express your feelings and ideas to improve both service delivery and your ability to do your job. This last argument is best used when supported by a group of staff.

The decision to advocate for organizational change is a tough one. The above arguments may help you. You need to clearly establish your legitimacy as a change agent within the organization before beginning to imple-

Figure 5.7
PREPARE—Evaluate Professional and Personal *Risk*

To what extent are you in danger of:	No danger	Some danger	Moderate danger	Serious danger
1. Losing your job?				
2. Decreasing your potential for upward mobility?				
3. Seriously straining work relationships?				

ment the change. Even then, however, administrators can always just say no. You are then stuck with employing other tactics or halting your change attempt completely.

Step 5: PREPARE—*Assess* Potential Costs and Benefits to Clients and Agency

Any macro change requires some new input. Such input can be in the form of actual money spent, but also in how you might miss out on other good opportunities where your time would be better spent (Rubin & Rubin, 1992). This is often referred to as *opportunity cost*, an important consideration in your *assessment* of potential costs and benefits. You could also lose political and social influence with those who disagree with your proposed change (Rubin & Rubin, 1992). For example, if you are constantly asking for extra funds for some project, administrators may get sick of you and ignore your requests. Then you would lose some of your potential power or influence. Colleagues might resent you for pushing your own agenda, and your social interaction with them might be affected.

It is very difficult to estimate potential costs in terms of actual money needed, but you do need to think about costs in a general way. Does your macro change require half a million dollars for new staff and office space when you really don't know that any funds are available? Might your macro proposal require a few hours a week of several staff members' time plus supplies and minor financing for publicity to advertise a new service?

Rubin and Rubin (1992, p. 391) suggest asking three questions before pursuing a new project. First, will the results be "worth the effort?" Second, might "alternative solutions produce more benefits at less cost?" Third, "who gets the benefits and who pays the costs?"

Step 6: PREPARE—Evaluate Professional and Personal *Risk*

Ask yourself three questions before seriously undertaking macro change in an organization (Resnick & Patti, 1980), and evaluate the potential *risk* of each. First, to what extent are you in danger of losing your job? Do you perceive no, some, moderate, or serious danger? Second, to what extent will such macro change efforts decrease your potential for upward mobility within the agency? Might you make enemies who could stand in the way of future promotions? Third, to what extent would your efforts for macro change seriously strain your interpersonal relationships at work? See figure 5.7, step 6 in the PREPARE process.

Lose My Job

At this point, you might be thinking, "What do you mean, lose my job?!!! Why would I do anything to endanger my job?" often the problem with trying to change an agency's policies or practice is that you will have to "fight against the flow" of your agency's energies and established practices. Losing a job has a number of obvious consequences including "inconvenience,

---

HIGHLIGHT 5.11

CASE EXAMPLE, PREPARE: EVALUATE YOUR PROFESSIONAL AND PERSONAL RISK

To what extent is Spiro in danger of losing his job?

The agency has a strong union. It's almost impossible to fire staff once they receive a positive two-year review. Therefore, Spiro feels that he is in no danger.

To what extent is Spiro in danger of decreasing his potential for upward mobility?

Spiro is quite satisfied staying in direct service and maintaining his clients in private counseling. If he were interested in becoming an agency administrator, he would probably evaluate himself as in serious

danger. Administrators don't promote "troublemakers." However, since he has no intentions of going into administration, he decides the situation presents no danger to him.

To what extent is Spiro in danger of seriously straining work relationships?

Spiro is most concerned about relationships with colleagues he sees on a daily basis. He sees no danger in straining his relationship with Farica. He does see moderate danger, however, in straining relationships with higher level administration, especially Theresa and Harold.

---

possible embarrassment with friends and family, income loss, forced geographical mobility, and the burden of explaining negative job references" in addition to "loss of professional identify" (Patti, 1983, pp. 214–15).

Change requires energy and effort, not only on your part, but on the part of everybody who is the least bit affected by the proposed change. Macro changes, by definition, involve large numbers of people. These include both clients and practitioners providing clients with services.

However, as we've discussed, sometimes agency policy and/or practice is wrong or ineffective. At such times you will need to evaluate your own personal and professional risk if you engage in macro change and weigh the severity of risk against the need and potential for positive macro change.

Patti (1983) cites at least two ways to deal with the threat of job loss. First, you can treat such a threat as a distraction from the real issue, namely, that some facet of the organization needs to be changed. Second, you can assume the perspective that job loss may be the price you have to pay in order to ethically fulfill your professional responsibility.

Hinder Upward Mobility

Most newly graduated practitioners, especially those with little experience, are overjoyed to land their first job. They are fascinated with new tasks and new clients. However, within the larger scheme of things, you probably envision a longer-term career path for yourself. This perspective stretches far beyond a single job, let alone your first professional one. A career may involve different fields of practice and different client populations. It may also involve upward mobility, that is, gaining job positions of greater responsibility and authority within the agency's personnel structure. After working in an agency for a while, you may begin to target the positions you would ideally like to have. Perhaps you begin seeing yourself in your own supervisor's position. Or you might think even further than that and see another position higher in the formal hierarchy that appeals to you. You might like to have a job with more responsibility and a higher salary. You might even plan your progress through a series of jobs within the hierarchy. Where might you see yourself ending up in five, ten, or even twenty years? Might you aspire to the Executive Director's spot, or would your own supervisor's job be more appealing to you? Would you rather stay in direct contact with clients, as many practitioners choose to do?

At any rate, you need to undertake macro change very carefully and tactfully. If supervisors and administrators higher in the structure begin to see you as a troublemaker, your risk increases. They may not want to promote someone whom they see as difficult to work with or dissatisfied with agency authority and practice. Looking at macro situations from administrators' perspectives is helpful and interesting. Even in flexible, innovative agencies, the task of the administrators is to keep the agency running, and indeed, running smoothly. Therefore, when considering macro change, it is important to consider who in the agency might bristle at your suggestions and who might pat you on the back. All agency administration should be considered and handled very carefully.

Strain Interpersonal Relationships at Work

The third risk to consider when pondering macro change is how your actions could affect your *relationships* with coworkers, supervisors, and other administrators. Interpersonal relationships with supervisors and other administrators are tied directly to the potential consequences discussed above, namely, those concerning keeping your job and pursuing upward mobility.

You should also consider how your actions will affect your relationships with your colleagues. Will some of them see you as a Dudley DoRight kind of character, looking to make yourself more visible to administration and thus more important? Will they be threatened by your suggestions because these suggestions may affect how they do their own jobs? Maybe they don't want to change. Remember, any change takes some degree of effort. People often resist expending extra effort.

You should carefully consider the extent to which you see others—including co-workers, supervisors, and administrators—supporting your macro change ideas. Getting together with an informal group of colleagues to discuss issues and muster support is a strongly recommended means of decreasing your own risk while increasing support for change.

Consider "Covert Operations"

Covert operations might bring to mind military spies operating an intricate web of undercover activities in some foreign nation. Here such covert operations or activities refer to communication and actions designed to hide their true purpose. They involve interactions intended to manipulate the reactions of others without straightforwardly and honestly explaining your intent.

Covert activities may include at least four scenarios. First, you act covertly if you omit presenting some of the facts. Second, emphasizing only those aspects of an argument that are in your favor is a form of covert activity. Third, manipulation of others by selecting what information to tell them and what to conceal is covert. Finally, anything else with generally sneaky undertones is probably a form of covert activity.

Sometimes a situation may be so severe or intolerable that you feel you must resort to covert activity because you can see no other way. However, covert activity in the field is generally considered to "violate the professional norm of openness" (Holloway, 1987, p. 735). Practitioners should carefully consider covert options before undertaking them. Brager and Holloway (1978) indicate that covert activities should be used only when three conditions exist. First, agency administrators are putting their own personal gains and interests before those of both clients and agency. Second, practitioners are provided no official, agency-sanctioned means of input into what goes on in the agency. Hence, covert activities would provide the only means of having such input. Thirdly, you have already attempted to initiate macro change openly and were put down for it, or you know you would be put down for such change if you tried it.

The Other Side of the Coin

Evaluating your risk potential when deciding whether or not to pursue a macro level change is very important. However, note that sometimes involvement in macro activity will enhance your standing in an agency. It can demonstrate initiative and a sense of responsibility that others might highly respect. To a great extent, it depends on who is evaluating you and your change effort.

HIGHLIGHT 5.12

CASE EXAMPLE, PREPAR**E: EVALUATE** THE
POTENTIAL SUCCESS OF A MACRO CHANGE
PROCESS—SUBSTEP 1

Substep 1: Review the prior PREPARE *process, and weigh the pros and cons of proceeding with the macro change process.*

Spiro determines that client need, the organizational and external macro environment, his own strengths, potential support, and the potential benefits far outweigh negative macro variables, personal weaknesses, potential resistance, financial costs, and his own risks. Therefore, he decides to proceed.

It is difficult to establish financial benefits in this case. What is the value of children being nurtured and taken care of rather than abused and neglected? Financial benefits are often difficult to establish when addressing issues involving service provision to needy people. When you can think of financial benefits, however, you will have a powerful argument when approaching decision-makers.

Step 7: PREPAR*E—Evalute* the Potential Success of a Macro Change Process

This final step in the PREPARE process involves your *evaluation* and determination of whether to continue your change efforts or stop right here. It consists, essentially, of the following two substeps.

Substep 1: Review the prior PREPARE process, and weigh the pros and cons of proceeding with the macro change process.

Substep 2: Identify possible macro approaches to use, roughly estimate their potential effectiveness, and select the most appropriate one.

Substep 1: Review the PREPARE Process and Weigh Pros and Cons of Proceeding with the Macro Change Process

In coming to a decision about whether to pursue your prescribed macro change, it is important to review the thoughts, facts, and perceptions identified in PREPARE's preceding six steps. Specifically, appraise cli-

ent need (as established in step 1 of the PREPARE process), positive organizational variables in your macro reality and your personal assets (step 2), potential support from people of influence (step 4), potential benefits (step 5). Then weigh these variables against negative organizational variables in our macro reality and your personal deficiencies (step 2), potential resistance to change efforts from relevant people of influence (step 4), potential costs (step 5), and your own potential risk (step 6). Figure 5.8, step 7 in the PREPARE process, illustrates how you might evaluate the potential success of your proposed macro change effort.

As you evaluate the overall potential for a successful organizational change effort, you might ask yourself a number of questions regarding the pros of pursuing macro intervention. Are the problems and needs great enough to require the effort it would take to make the required changes? What macro variables inside and outside the organization would support such efforts? What personal and professional strengths do you yourself bring to the change effort? Whom could you count on for potential support? Would any financial benefits result from the proposed change?

After evaluating your potential pros, weigh them against potential cons. What variables would probably work against your change efforts? What negative macro

---

HIGHLIGHT 5.13

CASE EXAMPLE, PREPARE: **EVALUATE** THE POTENTIAL SUCCESS OF A MACRO CHANGE PROCESS—SUBSTEP 2

Substep 2: Identify possible macro approaches to use, roughly estimate their potential effectiveness, and select the most appropriate one.

Spiro considers a variety of possible macro approaches. One is to go through administrative channels level by level, from Farica to Theresa to Harold to Bob. He know, however, that Farica has consulted Theresa informally in the past about needing staff. Theresa's response was vague and negative. Considering this and his own poor relationship with Theresa, he does not think talking to her is a viable approach.

We have already mentioned other options as going to the county board to requesting funding, writing grants, or asking for donations. The former idea is inappropriate because Spiro would be usurping agency administrators' roles and could look ridiculous. The latter two ideas are vague and time-consuming, and are only temporary remedies anyway.

The macro method Spiro has been developing and clarifying in his mind involves the same approach he successfully used fifteen years ago under another administration. Namely, he can use the agency's Community Advisory Committee to plead his cause, in addition to taking his pleas to the press. The current advisory committee is exceptionally active. Its chairperson, Danielle, is extremely bright, dynamic, and committed to positive change.

In summary, Spiro chooses a strategy involving a personnel change. This falls within our category of changing agency policy. This type of change has both formal and informal dimensions. On the one hand, Spiro is essentially requesting a formal redistribution of funds to his agency unit. On the other hand, such a decision concerning expenditures involves the informal judgments of formally designated decision-makers.

---

variables inside and outside the organizational environment would work against your change efforts? What personal and professional weaknesses of yours would interfere with your change efforts? Who would resist change? How serious would such resistance be? How much would the change, if implemented, cost? Is the cost feasible? How serious are these deficiencies? Finally, what risks would you confront in pursuing the change effort? How might your actions affect keeping your job, retaining upward mobility, or preserving relationships with colleagues and others?

At the end of this decision-making process, you must conclude one of three things. First, you might make a definite commitment to continue the change process. Second, you might determine that the time is not right. You could postpone the change process to another time. Third, you might decide that the potential for ef-

fective organizational change is too poor to continue your efforts. In this case, you would terminate the process, essentially forget about the idea, and go on with your ordinary work activities and responsibilities. In any case, at this point you must make a definite decision about what to do.

Substep 2: Identify Possible Macro Approaches to Use, Estimate their Effectiveness, and Select the Most Appropriate One

Substep 2 of the final phase in the PREPARE process is the transitional stage between *deciding* to pursue a macro change effort and actually *doing* it. At this point,

Figure 5.8
PREPARE—*Evaluate* the Potential Success
of a Macro Change Process

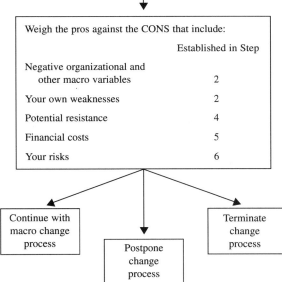

Evaluate the PROS that include:	
	Established in Step
Client need	1
Positive organizational and other macro variables	2
Your own strengths	2
Potential support	4
Financial benefits	5

Weigh the pros against the CONS that include:	
	Established in Step
Negative organizational and other macro variables	2
Your own weaknesses	2
Potential resistance	4
Financial costs	5
Your risks	6

Continue with macro change process

Postpone change process

Terminate change process

point, you have committed yourself to pursuing some type of macro change. You have a pretty good idea about what type of macro approach you want to pursue. Approaches include those directed at changing agency policy, developing new programs, or undertaking some more limited project. Chapter 6, "IMAGINE How to Implement Macro Intervention—Changing Agency Policy," will continue where this chapter leaves off in the macro change process. We will follow the choices and activities of Spiro, Farica, and the others involved in Spiro's macro intervention. Additionally, a number of other macro practice applications (for example, the establishment of a sexual harassment awareness program in a large public agency) will be studied.

Chapter Summary

This chapter introduces a range of organizational changes including the undertaking of projects, program development, and changing agency policies. Agency policies can be formal or informal.

A seven-step decision-making model—PREPARE—for the assessment of organizational change potential is explained. Steps include: identifying problems to address; assessing your macro reality; establishing primary goals; identifying relevant people of influence; assessing potential costs and benefits to clients and agency; evaluating professional and personal risk; and evaluating the potential success of a macro change process. Each step is explained and is shown to have a number of substeps. Each step is discussed in the context of a continuing case example concerning a large public agency's Protective Services Unit.

CHAPTER SIX

IMAGINE How to Implement Macro Intervention: Changing Agency Policy

Recall the case discussed in chapter 5, "PREPARE: Decision Making for Organizational Change." The setting is the Protective Service Unit of the Yalobusha County Department of Social Services located in Plattsburg, Wisconsin. The unit is composed of six workers and a supervisor. Farica, the unit's supervisor, is very worried about the significant increase in the workers' caseload over the past year. It is becoming nearly impossible to handle even the crises on the workers' caseloads, let alone give adequate attention to every case assigned. State law requires that each reported case must be investigated within twenty-four hours after intake. In reality, a worker is lucky to get to it four days later. Farica's staff is being forced to violate the law. It is physically impossible to do the job that the law requires them to do.

Spiro, you recall, in one of Farica's supervisees. Arrogant and self-satisfied on the one hand, he is deeply committed to the agency and its service provision on the other. Hence, he becomes the change agent. He draws in Farica, his colleagues in his protective services unit, and the Community Advisory Committee to become the action system. He has proceeded through the steps to determine whether to pursue macro intervention and decided that, indeed, it is necessary. Now what?

Introduction

This chapter builds on the material covered in chapter 5, the decision-making process focused on whether or not to pursue some type of macro intervention. At this point, we assume this decision is positive. Macro intervention is the route of choice. This chapter, then, addresses how to proceed. We will continue with the example used in chapter 5, following Spiro and Farica in their effort to increase their unit staff. How do you go about implementing a macro change concerning agency policy? What steps should Spiro, Farica, and other action system members pursue in order to achieve their desired goals? This chapter will address these and other questions concerning macro change.

This chapter will:

- Explain the IMAGINE process for proceeding with a macro intervention.
- Discuss concepts involved in conceptualizing the macro environment for change, including the client, change agent, target, and action systems.
- Describe the application of mezzo concepts to macro practice in the context of forming an action system.
- Explain the importance of establishing clear goals and objectives.

- Evaluate the use of collaborative and adversarial strategies when neutralizing opposition to the proposed plan.
- Describe formal and informal agency policies.
- Discuss changing policies on agency goals, personnel practices, and practice procedures.
- Apply IMAGINE to Spiro and Farica's macro intervention scenario.
- Define the concept of cultural competence and show how it might be enhanced in an agency setting.

The Problem-Solving Process and Organizational Change

We have established that the macro change perspective we assume here is that of a direct service generalist practitioner with little or no administrative power. In your own specified job role, you are expected to participate in certain types of work with clients. For example, if part of your job is to counsel jobless people and assist in their job search, that is exactly what you do. You do not have to ask permission to try to influence decision-makers to get the job done. In macro generalist practice, however, you must virtually always extend yourself beyond your specified job role. You always target a change that affects more than just your own work. Therefore, there are some differences between macro generalist practice, on the one hand, and micro and mezzo generalist practice on the other.

Macro generalist practice does follow the basic problem-solving process of engagement, assessment, planning, implementation, evaluation, termination, and follow-up. However, two factors differentiate macro generalist practice from micro and mezzo. First, the change process involves many more people and systems than problem solving with individual clients or groups of clients. Second, a major part of macro generalist practice involves mustering support from colleagues and influencing decision-makers to affect change at the macro level. Therefore, the macro problem-solving process is more complicated than that at the micro and mezzo levels.

Chapter 5, "PREPARE—Decision Making for Organizational Change," introduced the three major arenas in which you are most likely to target agency change. They include changing an agency policy, implementing some kind of project, and developing a program. The first phase is to follow the procedure for assessing orga-

Figure 6.1
IMAGINE—A Process for Initiating
and Implementing Macro Change

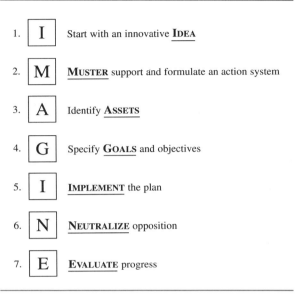

1. **I**   Start with an innovative **IDEA**

2. **M**   **MUSTER** support and formulate an action system

3. **A**   Identify **ASSETS**

4. **G**   Specify **GOALS** and objectives

5. **I**   **IMPLEMENT** the plan

6. **N**   **NEUTRALIZE** opposition

7. **E**   **EVALUATE** progress

nizational change potential, also introduced in chapter 5. The subsequent phase is to pursue the actual organizational change process. The remainder of this chapter will explore and discuss this change process.

IMAGINE: A Process for Organizational Change

We proposed a paradigm (model) termed *IMAGINE* as a guide for initiating and pursuing macro change within organizations. The meaning of each letter in the acronym IMAGINE is illustrated in figure 6.1. The IMAGINE change process can be applied to virtually any type of organizational change.

We will elaborate on each of IMAGINE's seven steps, then apply each to Spiro and Farica's organizational situation as described in chapter 5. As you may recall, their particular situation relates to an agency policy change concerning agency personnel.

IMAGINE: Start with an Innovative Idea

The first step in the IMAGINE process is to identify and start with an innovative *idea*. At this point in the process, we assume that you have already expended some time and effort thinking about the potential macro change. More specifically, you have progressed through the assessment steps to decide whether or not to proceed with a macro intervention. You have weighed strengths and weaknesses, risks and benefits. You have also determined whether you would like to pursue a more limited project, more extensive development of some program, or a change in agency policy. This step is applied to Spiro and Farica's case illustration in highlight 6.1.

IMAGINE: Muster *Support and Formulate an Action System*

The second step in the IMAGINE macro change process involves *mustering* support from others. We assume that you will have no agency-designated power in your own job role to initiate macro change all by yourself. Therefore, regardless of the type of macro change, you need help. You would already have identified some relevant people of influence as you undertook the decision-making process for pursuing macro change. When selecting your designated change strategy (that is, an agency policy change, project implementation, or program development), you need to determine specifically whom you want to influence and how to do it most effectively.

Conceptualizing the Macro Practice Environment

To better understand the macro change process, it is helpful to conceptualize a number of systems interacting within an environment. As we have discussed earlier, general systems theory implies dynamic, connected interactions among any number of systems and subsystems. These systems are of various sizes. To help you picture the whole interactive process in your mind's eye, we will elaborate upon a number of relevant systems concepts. Our intent is to give you a clear picture of what the general macro change process involves. Specifically, we will discuss four types of systems critical to the change process. They include the client, target, change agent, and action systems (Pincus & Minahan, 1973; Resnick, 1980b; Resnick, 1980c).

THE MACRO CLIENT SYSTEM. The *macro client system* includes those people who will ultimately

Spiro, one of Farica's staff, is concerned about the personnel issue for a variety of reasons. (Spiro's and Farica's situation is reviewed at the very beginning of this chapter.) We have identified Spiro as our change agent. He has considered a range of variables including organizational resources and constraints, relevant people of influence, personal strengths, and risks involved. Spiro recalls that about fifteen years ago, the protective service unit was in a similar predicament, desperately understaffed. At that time

Spiro went to the agency's Community Advisory Committee, explained his situation, and asked for help. He also went to local newspapers and alerted them to his unit's personnel shortage and the subsequent impact on clients. The result was the successful addition of two staff members. After deliberating over these past experiences, Spiro determines that the best way to solve the problem now at hand is to seek additional staff from administration.

---

benefit from the change process. It usually involves some particular client population, having similar characteristics and receiving similar agency services. The macro client system is made up of any number of individual client systems. For instance, the macro client system might include all the clients with developmental disabilities at a sheltered workshop, in addition to these clients' families.[1]

Figure 6.2 depicts the macro client system. Two large circles are illustrated, one representing the agency system and one the macro client system. The scenario portrays you as the worker. You are represented by a small circle inside a slightly larger circle that illustrates your agency unit or division. Other small circles within the agency environment represent administration and other agency units. The agency system circle depicts only four of the latter smaller circles. These circles are intended to represent any number of units. The number depends on how many units are encompassed by whatever agency you work in.

The second large circle to the right of the agency system circle represents the *macro client system*, those clients receiving services and resources from your agency. Smaller circles within the macro client system circle illustrate that, in macro practice, many *individual client systems* make up the larger macro client system.

The arrow leading from the agency system circle to the client system circle represents *service provision*. The agency system provides the macro client system (made up of all the agency's individual client systems) with services and resources.

Finally, note the arrow leading from the circle entitled "you the worker" to the agency service system's provision arrow. Your potential macro practice role allows you to effect macro changes that can impact many clients instead of only one or two. Ultimately, we view macro change as a means of enhancing services and resources provided to larger numbers of clients. You can choose to play a direct role in this process.

The Change Agent

In a macro practice perspective, the *change agent system* is the individual who initiates the macro change process. In our context you, at least initially, are the change agent. Later on as you gain support and join coalitions with others who also believe in the proposed macro

---

1. A sheltered workshop or sheltered employment involves job-training vocational rehabilitation services for people with various disabilities or needs for rehabilitation (in this case, developmental disability); additionally, these workshops provide testing services and social skills training (Barker, 1991).

Figure 6.2
The Macro Client System in Macro Practice

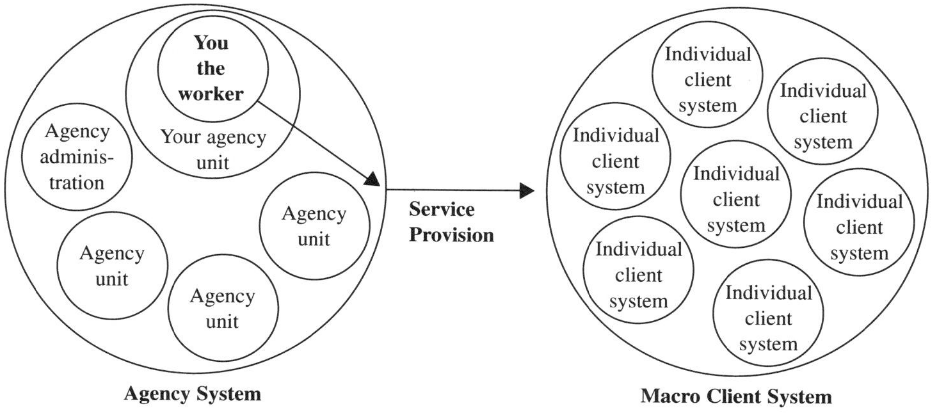

Agency System

Macro Client System

change, you as an individual change agent would become part of a larger action system dedicated to changing the status quo.

A Note about the Agency as a Change Agent System

Frequently in social work, the term *change agent system* refers to an agency involved in the implementation of some macro change. This book assumes the perspective that the vast majority of your opportunities to pursue macro intervention will be outside the context of your designated job with its formal job description. In reality, you will most often act as a catalyst to modify policies, implement projects, or develop programs within your own agency. It follows, then, that your agency or various units within it may not support or even agree with your proposed macro change. Your agency then becomes the target of your change efforts rather than a helper in the change process. This is true, at least initially, in the change process. Therefore, we will generally refer to the agency as the *agency system* instead of the change agent system.

The Target System

The target system is "the individual, group, or community to be changed or influenced to achieve the social

work goals" (Barker, 1991, p. 234). We have already indicated that frequently our own agency or some subsystem within our agency becomes the target system, that is, the target of our change efforts.

As the macro change process continues, the target system may change. At first, it may be a specific group of decision-makers somewhere in the agency that you target to influence. Later, this group of decision-makers may join you in your quest. They may become part of the action system, working together with you to implement the proposed macro change. The target system may then become another influential unit within the agency system. Or you may even decide to target the top administrator.

Figure 6.3 illustrates the target system concept. The large circle represents the total agency system. The *action system* is illustrated as a circle within the large agency system circle. You as the *change agent* are part of the action system. Arrows run from you to three other circles inside the action system circle. Each of these is labeled "action system member." These arrows illustrate that you as the change agent initiated the action system and developed its membership. Three circles are depicted. However, the action system can consist of any number of members, depending on the change agent's plan.

Another arrow runs from the action system to another circle that is designated the *target system*. This target system is made up of some decision-makers or people with power that you feel you must influence in

Figure 6.3
The Target System

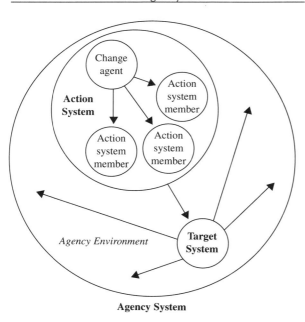

Agency System

order to effect the proposed macro change. Several arrows run from the target system into the general *agency environment*. These arrows reflect that the target system could have an impact on other portions of the agency environment so that the agency is able to adopt the change.

In summary, figure 6.3 depicts a three-stage process. First, you as the change agent initiate the macro change by formulating the action system. Second, the action system as a unit attempts to influence the target system to accept the validity of the proposed macro change. Third, the target system (hopefully) implements the proposed change within the agency environment so that the entire agency goes along with it.

The Action System

The action system includes those people who agree and are committed to work together to attain the proposed macro change. As a change agent, you need to select supporters for your action system very carefully. It is best to muster support from staff who are well respected and competent (Resnick, 1980c). The administration is

then more likely to have positive feelings about individual action system members and potentially to react positively to members' proposals and plans. Believable action system members lend credibility to the suggested change. (See highlight 6.2 for the application of these concepts to our case illustration.)

Formulate an Action System: The Application of Mezzo Concepts to Macro Practice

We have defined the action system as the people and resources you will organize and employ to help you work toward the needed change. It includes the change agent (presumably you) and those people who work with you to achieve the change.

Building an action system involves the use of mezzo skills. It is critical to attend to three major mezzo factors when formulating an action system; these include "composition, understanding of and commitment to purpose, and group leadership and participation skills" (Resnick, 1980c, p. 211).

Composition of the Action System

Resnick (1980c) suggests that two aspects of composition are particularly relevant. The first concerns how many members the group should have. If the group is too large, the process becomes complicated. It is then easy to get bogged down in interpersonal disagreements or multiple agendas. On the other hand, if the group is too small, it may be limited to creativity, information, and personpower to complete the plan. Resnick (1980c) suggests that a five-person action system is ideal in terms of limiting complexity and enhancing communication. As the implementation process proceeds, more members can be added when new tasks arise.

The second aspect of action system composition concerns the characteristics of individual group members. There are at lest four suggestions for selecting and approaching potential action system members (Resnick, 1980c). First, consider interpersonal variables. Select people who generally get along and communicate well with each other. Archenemies would probably carry old vendettas into the new macro proposal arena. Second, do not include people having vast differences in power within the organization. People with lower status may feel intimidated by more powerful others. On the other

CASE EXAMPLE: CONCEPTUALIZING RELEVANT SYSTEMS IN THE MACRO ENVIRONMENT

As Spiro conceptualizes what he is trying to do, he defines the various systems he needs to work with. The macro client system is the clients his unit serves. He is initiating the macro change to benefit them and to fulfill the legal obligations designed to protect and help them (namely, for workers to abide by the twenty-four-hour assessment requirement). The target system is upper level administration, specifically, Bob, the agency director, and Harold, the assistant director. They are the agency decision-makers ultimately responsible for acquisition and assignment of agency staff. Spiro himself is the change agent as he is initiating the change. Finally, the action system includes Spiro, his supervisor and colleagues in the unit, and the agency's Community Advisory Committee.

hand, people with higher status may assume more control when working with group members of lower status. Third, do not automatically exclude potential members who can make only limited commitments. The effort they can afford to expend may be very useful. You cannot expect everyone else to have the same level of commitment and motivation regarding the proposal that you do. Finally, try to keep communication straightforward and aboveboard. Keeping secrets and criticizing other group members behind their backs only serves to erode morale and detract from the group's task, namely to initiate and undertake the macro change.

UNDERSTANDING OF AND COMMITMENT TO PURPOSE. When forming an action system, make sure you clearly explain the major goals of the innovative idea. Also, describe how you perceive action system members' roles and how much time and effort you anticipate requiring of them. You need to make certain that members are committed to the purpose and goals of the macro change in order to avoid problems and misunderstandings later on.

GROUP LEADERSHIP AND PARTICIPATION SKILLS. Any newly composed group needs time to establish interactional and decision-making patterns. This is a significant process in itself, apart from trying to achieve the macro goals the group was established to accomplish. It is important, then, to pay attention to communication patterns. Before the group even begins, can you foresee a personality conflict between any members? For example, does one potential member perceive herself as a free-spirited, but devotedly committed nouveau "hippie" (á la the 1960s) and another as a staunchly regimented professional in a three-piece-gray-suit-world where changes should be made only after methodically, even tediously, thorough planning?

Or can you predict that two or more individuals will vie for power in the group? Who would be the most effective leader? You may or may not be the best choice as leader. Sometimes, this is a difficult thing for one's ego to accept. The important thing is to achieve the proposed macro change. (See highlight 6.3 for the application to our case situation.)

IMAGINE: Identify Assets

Regardless of the type of macro level change, you will need to determine what *assets* are available to implement the change. This is the third step in the IMAGINE process. Assets involve resources and advantages in your favor that will help you to undertake and complete your proposed change process. Assets can include readily available funding, personnel who are able and willing to devote their time to implementing the change, and

---

HIGHLIGHT 6.3

CASE EXAMPLE: **MUSTER**
SUPPORT AND FORMULATE AN
ACTION SYSTEM

Spiro has already thought about the potential people both inside and outside his agency whom he might call upon for support. They include his unit supervisor and colleagues, the agency's Community Advisory Committee, and the local newspapers.

Spiro presents his idea formally at the next unit staff meeting. To his surprise, Farica, whom he expected to endorse the idea enthusiastically, is hesitant. She states that she knows the unit needs more staff, but she worries that such tactics may alienate the administration, especially Theresa, Farica's direct supervisor. This concerns Farica in particular because Theresa, as supervisor, is responsible for Farica's actions. Farica feels it is very important to maintain a good working relationship with her.

However, the other staff (including Tina, Archie, Dylan, Barney, and Ann) are more supportive and appear to be happy someone has opted to take the lead. Surprisingly, Archie, who usually stays out of these matters, voices spirited support. He is the only staff in addition to Spiro who was around the last time the unit used this tactic fifteen years ago. Eventually, the unit staff come to a consensus that they have no choice but to pursue Spiro's idea.

The unit approves a motion asking Farica to send a memo to Theresa with copies to Bob and Harold to alert them to the unit's needs. The memo is addressed to Theresa because it must go through the appropriate chain of command from bottom to top. Otherwise, higher levels in the agency's power hierarchy will most likely tell Farica to go through the proper channels, (namely, Theresa) anyway. This would uselessly delay the process. It is common practice to send copies of memos to people higher up in the chain of command. This alerts them to issues without requiring a response. A memo requires a response only from the person to whom it is addressed. Farica is aware that sending copies of the memo to Bob and Harold places pressure on Theresa to respond appropriately. Since they are her direct supervisors, Theresa would probably want to please them.

In the unit meeting, Spiro suggests that the memo include the fact that the client support group encourages the unit's plea for help. Spiro wants the identification of need to be as strong as possible. Because the unit is sending a formal request, the administration cannot plead ignorance and say they were unaware of the unit's needs.

Spiro also meets with the agency's Community Advisory Committee. He explains the situation and pleads for their help. Danielle, the chairperson, is taken with Spiro's self-confidence and charisma. She urges the other members' support. The advisory committee passes a motion in favor of Spiro's plan. They will await suggestions from Spiro concerning what specific strategies to pursue.

---

office space where the change activities can occur (see highlight 6.4).

IMAGINE: Specify Goals and Objectives

IMAGINE's fourth step concerns specifying *goals* and objectives. At this stage in the process you have already identified your primary goals during your assessment of macro change potential. Chapter 5 elaborated on this process. Goals provide you with direction regarding how to proceed with your macro intervention. What do you really want to accomplish? How can your clients' major needs be met through macro change? What are your primary and necessary end results?

Primary goals are usually so broadly stated that

HIGHLIGHT 6.4

CASE EXAMPLE: IDENTIFY **ASSETS**

In his assessment of macro change potential, Spiro has already identified a variety of strengths. These include: the constraining laws that unit staff are unable to follow; the agency's motivation to comply with regulatory laws; the public's concerns about the treatment of child abuse; Spiro's own competence and his reputation in the agency; Spiro's positive relationship with Bob, the agency director; client support (as received from Tina's client support group); and the backing of the agency's Community Advisory Committee. It is important to keep these in mind throughout the macro change process and integrate them as thoroughly as possible into the intervention plan.

HIGHLIGHT 6.5

CASE EXAMPLE: SPECIFY **GOALS** AND OBJECTIVES

Spiro's general goal is to increase unit staff's time to address clients' needs. He has further refined this goal to increasing the number of unit staff. In order to do that, he establishes an initial plan in the form of the following objectives:

1. Farica *(who)* will write the memo to Theresa including recommendations made at the staff meeting *(what)* by this Friday, Nov. 12 *(when)*.
2. Spiro *(who)* will meet with the agency's Community Advisory Committee to suggest to them that they draft a statement supporting the staffing increase *(what)* at their next meeting, 7:00 P.M. Tuesday, Nov. 16 *(when)*.
3. Spiro *(who)* will ask the advisory committee to have the statement completed and submitted to Agency Director Bob *(what)* by the following Friday, Nov. 19 *(when)*.
4. Spiro *(who)* will check to make certain that objectives 1 and 3 are completed *(what)* by Monday, Nov. 22 *(when)* and then contact the two local newspapers *(what)*.
5. Spiro *(who)* will urge the two newspapers to print the stories as soon as possible *(what)*, hopefully by Monday, Nov. 29 *(when)*.

---

it is virtually impossible to identify how they will be achieved. For example, you might want to improve conditions in the family planning center where you work. Or you might want to change the agency policy that requires clients to come to the agency only during business day hours.

In order to reach such broad goals, you must specify exactly how to achieve them. This breaks primary goals down into a series of objectives. An objective is "something toward which effort is directed, an aim . . . or end of action" (*Webster's New Collegiate Dictionary*, 1991, p. 815). You might think of objectives as sub-

A goal in the IMAGINE process might be eliminating graffiti. An objective would be having teenagers paint murals on the defaced walls.

goals. Sub-goals are smaller, more easily met goals that lead to the accomplishment of a primary goal. Additionally, objectives are behaviorally specific regarding what is to be done and how success will be measured. In the following discussion, objectives and sub-goals will be considered identical.

You can consider these goals along with their objectives as the strategies by which to implement the plan in this step of the IMAGINE process. For example, what might one mean by a goal of "improving conditions in a unit at a residential treatment center"? Objectives might include painting the walls, improving the disciplinary system, or developing recreational groups. However, these objectives require additional specific steps of their own for completion. Who will paint the walls? When will the job be done? Who will pay for the work?

Objectives may also have action steps. In other words, an objective might itself have some prerequisites in order for it to be accomplished. Thus, action steps might be specified for a particular objective. For example, prior to painting the walls, someone must be designated to select the color and order the paint. In essence, action steps help to clarify tasks and responsibilities. They can also help to prevent you from wasting time and energy.

Writing Clear Objectives

Establishing objectives involves specifying "the steps that must be taken and the time needed to reach those objectives" (Barker, 1987, p. 64). Two necessary ingredients in objective-setting, then, are *steps* involved in the intervention process and the *time limitations* for each step. The basic formula for delegating responsibility is to specify *who* will do *what* by *when*. "Who" is the individual specified for accomplishing a task. "What" involves the tasks the individual has to complete in order to achieve the goal. Finally, "by when" sets a time limit so that the task is not lost in some unforeseeable future.

The following are examples of objectives:

Harry Carey *(who)* will notify all unit colleagues about the upcoming inservice *(what)* by noon on March 15 *(when)*.

I *(who)* will write a five page paper describing the new treatment approach *(what)* by 9:00 A.M. on Friday, October 13 *(when)*.

Ms. Fidgety *(who)* will contact the designated community leaders for information about housing needs *(what)* by next Tuesday *(when)*.

You might now be asking yourself, "Why is it important to be so precise?" The answer is that if you aren't explicit regarding who has the responsibility for accomplishing the task, it's likely that the task won't get done.

For example, you as a student are probably very busy. You are likely not to have much time to do anything but your required coursework. It would be nice to do a lot of in-depth reading on topics that interest you. However, you probably assign this a relatively low priority. You do what you have to do first. It's the same

---

HIGHLIGHT 6.6

CASE EXAMPLE: **IMPLEMENT** THE PLAN

The advisory committee drafts and sends the memo to Bob, as directed. Farica writes the memo and Spiro carries out his objectives as planned. The newspapers both print the story, one on Saturday, November 27, and the other on Sunday, November 28. Spiro waits impatiently for the administration's response.

---

with generalist practitioners in the field. As a social worker you will probably have an abundance of clients and will constantly strive to prioritize what needs to get done first. If it's not your specifically identified responsibility to complete a task by a certain deadline, it's easy to put it off . . . and off . . . and off. Such tasks rarely if ever get done.

It's interesting to note the phrase, "get done." It is as if the task will magically do itself without any human intervention. In other words, this phrase is one to carefully scrutinize and, probably, to avoid.

In addition to being specific, objectives should be measurable. That is, it is important to specify exactly when and how an objective will be met. For example, if your objective is to contact five designated community leaders, you have not met your objective if you were able to contact only three of them. You would not meet your objective until you had contacted all five.

IMAGINE: Implement *the Plan*

IMAGINE's fifth step involves implementing the established plan. All macro changes need a plan to give them direction. Which decision-makers need to be contacted as part of the target system? In what order should they be contacted? What should they be told? What recommendations should such decision-makers be given? Implementation is the actual doing of the plan. The plan's goal or end result is to establish the macro change.

Macro changes usually require regular communication and negotiation. Because some number of people are involved, the formula for change completion is usually both complex and fluctuating. Therefore, you will probably need to monitor the plan carefully to keep the change process on course as you continue working toward your goal. (See highlight 6.6.)

IMAGINE: Neutralize *Opposition*

IMAGINE's sixth step is neutralizing (overcoming) any opposition to your macro plan. The macro change process does not usually involve a direct linear thrust whereby all objectives proceed perfectly as planned. Rather, the process usually follows a twisting path full of surprises. Goals, objectives, and plans often need modification in view of vacillations in the macro environment. People change their minds. New elements such as funding cuts enter the scene, seemingly out of nowhere. You may be assigned to a new supervisor. The larger the target of change and the agency environment, the more likely that new factors will develop to influence the change process.

As you encounter new issues and impediments, continuous influence of decision-makers remains important. Significant facets of such influence involve elements to consider before talking to administrators, anticipation of their logical reactions, the phases of resistance to expect, and the use of collaborative and adversarial strategies.

Communicating with Decision-Makers

A critical point in the macro change process is reached when you present your plan to your target system. It is important to consider three things prior to your meeting with target system members; these include role determination, articulation of formulated plan, and practice before the meeting (Resnick, 1980c).

Role determination means deciding in advance who will attend the meeting and who will say what. It is wise to choose action system members who you think will have the strongest positive impact on the target system (for example, decision-making administrators). You want to maximize your potential to influence decision-makers on your behalf.

Next, you should determine who introduce the subject, who will present the rationale, who will respond to what types of questions and so on. In essence, establish who will have the role of leader and who will assume the role of expert in the event specific facts are requested or of mediator if conflict arises between action and target systems.

The second task before holding your formal meeting with the decision-making target system is to perfect the way you will describe and present the issue, your concern, and your recommendations for change. This should be crystal clear in your mind. The action system should also spend time identifying as many potential arguments as possible against the proposed plans. Your group can then think about and prepare responses to any queries or objections decision-makers may raise. For example, administrators might say that the proposal's costs are too high or there are not enough staff to complete the necessary tasks. In this event, how would you respond to defend and explain your proposal?

The third assignment before addressing the target system is to practice by role-playing the meeting. Action system members who will actually meet with decision-makers can play themselves. Other volunteers can play the decision-makers and voice the decision-makers' presumed concerns. This is a good way to further explore the issue and the plan. The better prepared you are to address concerns voiced by target system member, the more convincing your proposal will be.

Logical Administrative Reactions

It is of ongoing importance to examine and understand the concept of change from an administrative point of view. Often, "external constituencies, which are frequently in a position to affect the flow of inputs (for example, money, legitimacy, and influence) upon which the agency relies for maintenance and survival, can and often do contain the decision-making discretion that can be exercised by an administrator" (Patti, 1983, p. 217). The top administrator must view the agency and its needs as only one system within the mammoth external environment. Administrators may have constraints such as licensing regulations or funding requirements of which you as a practitioner are unaware. This is not to relieve administrators of their responsibility for providing effective services to clients. However, it is helpful for you to know as much as you can about the agency and its interrelationships with other systems in the macro environment before implementing the macro change process. The more information you have, the better prepared you will be to utilize assets and anticipate problems.

Keep one other thing in mind concerning macro change in organizations. The size of the organization is probably inversely related to the ease with which macro change can be accomplished (Patti, 1983). It is often tremendously difficult to make significant changes in massive agencies such as state departments of social services. Such organizations have multiple levels of administration. A dedicated red ant trying to move a huge mountain of brownish-gray sludge comes to mind. Each bureaucratic level provides new opportunities for information and ideas to become distorted, diluted, and forgotten. It is likely much easier to know and target influential decision-makers in smaller agencies. Such agencies have smaller staffs. Thus, there are usually greater opportunities to know and understand individual personalities and these people's responsibilities and attitudes.

Phases of Resistance

Resnick (1980c) suggests that you might as well anticipate four stages of resistance as you try to muster support for your macro plan. The first stage delivers a monumental dose of negativism. You might hear any of a wide range of negative responses. "That proposal simply can't work!" "How did you come up with such an irrational idea?" "My Uncle Olaf always used to say, 'if it ain't broke, don't fix it.'" Critics are usually outspoken, and potential supporters lie hidden in the woodwork. This is often a very frustrating stage.

However, if you persevere and do not give up, you

are likely to enter stage two of the resistance process. By this time people have already mulled over the issues and thought about possibilities. Critics tend to die down a bit and supporters slowly start to emerge. This phase may allow you to increase the strength of your action system as you identify potential supporters for your macro change proposal.

Stage three of the resistance process is characterized by conflict. Decision-makers must decide whether to go with the proposal or not. Once again, with good planning and perseverance, you have a chance of achieving your goal.

Finally, stage four of the resistance process occurs after you have initiated the proposal and it is already being implemented. Resistance may still be skulking in your internal agency environment. Overt conflict has probably gone undercover. Do not be deceived that all is perfectly well. People who do not believe in or like your proposed macro plan may persist and work covertly against you. Beware of potential obstructions. You must continue to nurture and monitor your macro process in order for it to survive and thrive.

Collaborative and Adversarial Strategies

We have established that there is a wide range of strategies to pursue when initiating a macro change. One way of looking at this broad range is by placing these strategies on a continuum. The continuum reflects your perceptions of how much the target system is likely to go along with your proposed plan.

Patti and Resnick (1980) define and explain "collaborative" and "adversarial" strategies (pp. 224-25). Collaborative strategies are those used when you don't anticipate dogged or profound resistance on the part of decision-makers. Such strategies assume that it is better to work *with* than *against* the existing organizational system. Collaborative strategies also assume "that the target system is rational, open to new ideas, and acting in good faith" (Patti & Resnick, 1980, p. 224).

Adversarial strategies, on the other hand, are those used when you expect decision-makers to express mildly significant to extremely vehement resistance to change. You may choose to use these strategies when you feel there is no potential for collaborative strategies or when collaborative approaches have failed. Therefore, adversarial strategies, those basically setting the action

system *against* the organizational structure, are preferable when those are the only approaches that might have a chance to work.

Another way of looking at the continuum is in terms of "persuading" versus "pressuring" (Austin, Kopp, & Smith, 1986, pp. 123–28). When using collaborative strategies, your intent is to persuade decision-makers to agree with your point of view by presenting a logical and convincing argument. There are four basic steps in persuading (Austin, Kopp, & Smith, 1986). First, you articulate the problem clearly and succinctly. Second, you allow time to discuss, mull over, and answer decision-makers' questions. Third, you state your macro change proposal (in essence, the solution to the problem) clearly and straightforwardly. Fourth, you summarize any progress you have made with the decision-makers and any agreement regarding how to proceed.

COLLABORATION AND PERSUASION. Three methods of initiating persuasion include (1) establishing something in common and starting from there, (2) straightforwardly sharing your honest feelings, and (3) "the blunt assault" (Austin, Kopp, & Smith, 1986, p. 126). Establishing something in common can involved stating some aspect of the problem or proposed solution with which you know both action and target systems will agree. For example, you might say, "I know that we all are seeking effective service delivery for our clients."

Sharing honest feelings may entail getting right to the point, even if the target system receives the point negatively. For instance, you might state, "I understand that you are opposed to a major change. However, I feel it is necessary to share my serious concerns with you."

The blunt assault takes sharing honest feelings much further. It should be used rarely since it falls much closer to pressuring on the continuum than the other two approaches. For example, you might say, "I have to be honest. I totally disagree with your position. I will be forced to fight you on this one. Let me explain to you why I feel this strongly. . . ."

Austin, Kopp, and Smith (1986) cite eight additional strategies for using persuasion:

1. Educate the decision-makers. Provide detailed, specific information. Help decision-makers understand the problem and see it more clearly from your point of view.

2. Discuss options. What potential solutions are there to your described problem? You can subsequently review with decision-makers the potential advantages and disadvantages of your proposed plan.

3. Ask if a trial or partial policy, project, or program change is possible. Perhaps, some partial proof can begin to establish your idea's validity.

4. Suggest that a committee be formed to discuss and consider the proposed plan. The committee could be composed of a range of staff including representatives of both the decision-making target system and the action system.

5. Creatively identify how target and action system members could spend more time together to develop communication channels and become familiar with the issues from both sides. This might mean planning a special meeting for this purpose. Likewise, it might require an in-service training session to present information to the target system about the problem you are addressing.

6. Appeal to the decision-makers' sense of fairness, ethics, and right and wrong. What is the most ethical approach to service provision for clients? What goals are most important for the agency to pursue?

7. Develop a rational argument to support your proposed plan. Choose information that strongly supports your macro proposal. You might even write a summary for decision-makers to review during the meeting and keep for later reference.

8. Specify to decision-makers what the negative consequences of the identified problem might be. How will ignoring the problem or maintaining the status quo result in costs to them? Describe the seriousness of the costs. The greater the costs of stagnation, the greater the perceived benefits of change.

BEING AN ADVERSARY AND PRESSURING. Pressuring is a much "pushier" approach than persuading. Pressuring involves using forces and even coercion to achieve your goals. It involves much higher potential risks than persuading. Decision-makers are much more likely to react to this approach with bristling resistance and hostility.

Use pressuring only when three conditions are present (Austin et al., 1986). First, you have tried everything else, including persuading, and nothing has worked. Second, you feel very strongly that you must pursue the macro change. You can't just let it go. Third, you think you have a substantial chance of attaining your goals. If you think there is little or no chance, why bother wasting your energy and exposing yourself to risk?

One example of pressuring is the use of a formal grievance procedure. A grievance is "a formal complaint about some procedure or regulation that is not being followed, and that has resulted in some harm to the complainant" (Barker, 1991, p. 96). Many agencies have specific policies that identify a formal process to undertake if you think you have a valid grievance. The procedure usually designates a formal group whose task is to review your grievance and determine whether you were treated fairly or not.

Austin et al. (1986) cite the following nine strategies you can pursue when pressuring for change:

1. Circulate a petition to gain collective support and submit it to administration for consideration. A petition is a formal written request signed by any number of persons stating their support of the request.

2. Stage open confrontations regarding issues with decision-makers during regular staff meetings. You might also initiate public forums and invite interested parties to come and hear both sides of the issue.

3. Involve sanctioning agencies in the external environment. For example, you could cite agency regulatory violations to regulatory agencies. You could tell funding sources about problems that might lead these sources to withdraw resources. Please note, however, that administrations generally abhor this type of strategy. Administrators responsible for and committed to maintaining the agency's functioning and good standing understandably feel betrayed when "traitors" air the agency's dirty laundry for all the world to see.

4. Go to the newspapers, television, and radio with information that will bring agency problems to public attention. As in point 3 above, however, be warned that agency administrations usually hate this type of tactic.

5. Encourage staff or clients to interfere deliberately with service provision. This strategy halts the regular flow of agency activity and often interferes with funding and service. Staff might refuse to complete any paperwork until some specified problem is solved.

6. Initiate a strike. Strikes can obviously stop or seriously impede service provision. However, being on strike additionally means getting no paychecks. It may also mean getting fired.

7. You can organize concerned personnel and others, including clients, to picket the agency. Once again, administrations are usually very annoyed with tactics that cause the public to view their agencies negatively.

8. You can take the issue to the courts. Administrators also hate this strategy. It not only brings problems to public attention, but also costs a lot of money, both for the agency and probably for you.

9. You can undertake formal bargaining. This would probably take place when employees are members of a union and have elected representatives to settle issues for them.

Remember that when choosing to pressure people in power, you increase your own risk. Risks may range from causing powerful people to hold negative opinions of you and label you a "troublemaker," to causing your supervisors to fire you. (See highlight 6.7 for the application of the concepts involved in neutralizing opposition to our case situation.)

IMAGINE: Evaluate *Progress*

The final step in the IMAGINE macro change process involves *evaluating* the intervention's progress and effectiveness. In all such processes there is an ongoing need to evaluate progress made toward your goal. Are you progressing as planned? Or, are you "stopped dead in the water?" In the latter case, what can you do to get back on track?

There are two major purposes of evaluating progress. First, evaluation can monitor the ongoing operation and activities involved in achieving a macro level change. Second, evaluation can target the end results of your macro intervention. The monitoring and evaluation functions are complementary (Kettner, Daley, & Nichols, 1985). On the one hand, monitoring looks at the macro level change throughout the IMAGINE process. On the other, evaluating end results addresses the effectiveness of the process after it has been completed. How well have you achieved the goals you set out to achieve? Evaluation will be discussed more extensively in later chapters. (See highlight 6.8.)

Application of IMAGINE to Macro Intervention

The case example explored above, involving Farica and Spiro, provides an example of how you can target agency policy for macro change. The particular policy we addressed was a personnel issue. We have established that personnel issues are included under the agency policy umbrella (instead of other types of organizational change, such as project implementation or program development).

The remainder of this chapter will elaborate on changing agency policy. The IMAGINE process will be applied to this dimension of macro change in some depth.

Changing Agency Policy

We have already established that policy in its simplest form can be thought of as rules. More specifically, policy is "the explicit or implicit standing plan that an organization or government uses as a guide for action" (Barker, 1991, p. 175). Policies thus provide rules or directions for functioning and activities adopted by any macro system. Policy's purpose is to provide rational, predictable guidelines for a system's operation, especially with respect to how resources are distributed (Kettner, Daley, & Nichols, 1985). Policy dictates what should and should not be done within the agency setting.

As this chapter addresses organizations instead of communities, our attention will focus on agency policy and how to change it. Agency or organizational policies are the guidelines that govern how agencies operate. Policy as it applies to communities will be addressed in later chapters.

Kettner, Daley, and Nichols (1985) discuss the differences between policy on the one hand, and both program development and project implementation on the other: "Designing policy is different from designing and structuring programs and projects in several significant ways. Policy establishes principles and guidelines for change, while programs and projects define the details of implementation" (pp. 143–44). In other words, policies usually stress *general guidelines* for total agency functioning. Programs and projects, on the other hand, provide much more *specific detail* for what activities are performed within an agency.

Chapter 5 established that agency policies formulate the core plan for what the agency does and how it does it. Policies involve both internal operation and provision of services to clients. Internal operation includes administrative arrangements and specific procedures for running the agency. These include lines of authority within the agency and types of benefits (for example, sick leave, vacation time, or health care) that employees receive. Formal and informal agency policies also concern how services are provided to clients. What specific services are available? Under what conditions do workers meet with clients? Are meetings held in

HIGHLIGHT 6.7

CASE EXAMPLE: NEUTRALIZE OPPOSITION

Theresa calls Farica at 7:45 A.M. on Monday, November 29, the first workday following the news articles' printing. Theresa never calls anyone first thing on Monday morning unless it is urgent. Farica's secretary Julie tapes a message to Farica's office doorknob to make sure Farica sees it first thing. Farica dreads seeing a note on her doorknob. It always means that, as Farica's mother would say, "Theresa's got a bug on her liver."

Theresa typically calls Farica when she is livid and probably loaded for bear. Farica thinks Theresa must be furious about the strategies for getting more staff. She has been worried about that ever since Spiro initiated the plan. On the one hand, Spiro's suggestions are best for the unit. She has supported Spiro, but not too visibly. On the other hand, Farica has anticipated going outside of the agency for help would infuriate the powers that be. She has desperately tried to remain on the fence and out of the line of fire. Now she feels as if she is looking down the barrel of an elephant gun.

Farica decides the time has come to face the music. As unit supervisor, she is supposed to manage and control her supervisees. She returns Theresa's call immediately. Theresa answers in a scathingly sharp tone of voice. She pointedly scolds Farica for allowing Spiro to speak with the Community Advisory Committee and asks if it was he who called the newspapers. Farica humbly responds that, yes, it was he. In reply, Theresa raises her voice and vehemently states that Farica and Spiro are *never, never, never* to go outside the agency with agency business again. Furthermore, Theresa wants to meet with them both immediately. She abruptly hangs up.

Farica is disgusted. She feels as if Spiro has manipulated her into being the target of the administration's rage. This is why she hates being the super-

visor. As such, she becomes ultimately responsible for everyone else's "mistakes."

Farica walks down the hall to Spiro's office. With his typical charming smile, Spiro says hello and asks her how it's "goin'." She responds that it's "goin'" terribly and tells him about her conversation with Theresa moments earlier. She also tells him that Theresa wants to meet with them "immediately!"

As the two walk to Theresa's office, they hypothesize that Bob and Harold must also be furious. That must be why Theresa called Farica first thing in the morning. Higher administration probably put pressure on Theresa, as Farica's direct supervisor, to handle the situation pronto.

Farica and Spiro subsequently have a very unpleasant hour with Theresa chastising them for their major blunder, namely airing the agency's dirty laundry in public. Finally, Theresa instructs them to write a formal request to her for needed staff and include adequate documentation. Theresa emphasizes that she will decide what to do about any possible staffing needs. She also tells Farica and Spiro that she will send them a memo to be placed in their permanent personnel files regarding their poor judgment and behavior. She commands that this never happen again!

Farica and Spiro return to Farica's office. Spiro whines about how insensitive administration is and about Theresa's horrible personality. Together, they write a ten-page memo requesting more staff. Farica submits it to Theresa that same day. The other unit staff walk softly around the unit throughout the day, thankful they were not the targets of administrative wrath.

Both Spiro and Farica made some errors and misjudgments. Mistakes are common when instituting macro change. Such change is usually a difficult and complicated process. Spiro and Farica failed to understand the fiscal strain that Bob and Harold were experiencing from the agency's funding sources. Making problems public hurt rather than helped the agency's chances for receiving more resources. Psychologically, if people controlling funding sources thought the agency was not doing a good job and was suffering serious problems, these people would only put pressure on Bob. They would indicate that he had better solve the problems now and prove to them that he had done so. Bob, in turn, would put pressure on Harold. Harold, subsequently, would pressure Theresa, and Theresa would lean on both Farica and Spiro. Funding sources might also withhold resources until they were convinced that the agency was running smoothly and doing its job as it was supposed to.

Spiro and Farica had misjudged the situation. Farica, as unit supervisor, had not submitted a formal request for more staff to Theresa. Yes, Farica had approached Theresa informally on a number of occasions. However, one of the typical rules of agency life is that if a request isn't written down, it doesn't exist. Hence, Spiro and Farica perceived that they had already pursued the collaborative strategy when they had not pursued it to its fullest. The first rule of using pressure in an adversarial situation is to make certain that you have already tried everything else, including every possible means of persuasion.

As it turns out, Farica must proceed to educate agency decision-makers about the unit's staffing problems. Spiro and Farica have run into the typical first phase of administrative resistance, namely, a massive *"No, it is not possible under any circumstances!"*

A week after the confrontation, Theresa writes Farica a memo stating that due to funding constraints it is not possible to add new staff at this time. Farica and Spiro then decide that they need to get more information and suggest more specific, viable options. Farica sees Spiro as a strength in the further pursuit of their primary goal. He is motivated, knowledgeable, and hard-working, albeit rather aggressive and egotistical. She feels Spiro can provide her with much-needed assistance in the quest for additional staff.

Farica and Spiro proceed to talk with other agency units that have acquired additional staff. They learn about some other arguments that appear to be persuasive in the administration's eyes. For example, documenting that staff are already expending more effort than is required is important. Farica documents that staff already work about nine and one-half hours instead of the required eight hours per workday. She can thus diffuse the possible misconception that unit staff are lazy and don't really need the requested help.

Another supervisor tells Farica about two retirements in units not nearly as pressed as Farica's. Perhaps, Farica can suggest to administration that these positions, or portions of them (in the form of part-time instead of full-time staff) could be reallocated to her own unit. Of course, Farica will present such suggestions in a very helpful and humble manner.

In subsequent communication involving both verbal and written contacts, Farica and Spiro emphasize that children are literally being hurt by the agency's lack of attention to their problems. In this way they try to respond to the decision-makers' sense of fairness and ethics.

Farica calls other Protective Services units in surrounding counties. She asks them about their caseloads and establishes that her staff to client ratio is indeed excessive in comparison. Her workers have significantly more clients than other similar units. This provides yet another persuasive argument to administration on the behalf of getting additional staff.

Two months pass. Farica finally sends Theresa a memo. In it Farica asks about and establishes an argument for the addition of two more staff. In reality, Farica thinks that such a proportionately large increase in a relatively small unit is unrealistic. Adding two more to a staff of seven represents almost a 30 percent increase. However, Theresa does allocate to Farica four quarter-time positions.

(continued)

HIGHLIGHT 6.7—(*Continued*)

You might ask, "Why four part-time positions instead of one whole person? Doesn't adding a bunch of part-timers only make things more confusing?"

The answer is that part-time staff usually cost the agency less. Such staff are paid less and don't receive the same benefits that full-time staff receive (for example, paid vacation and full health insurance.)[a] They are also not as well protected by union rules. Remember how once an agency staff person receives "tenure" in Farica's and Spiro's agency, she essentially has a permanent job position. Within this particular agency, administration can pretty much hire and fire part-time staff at will. This allows administrators significantly more flexibility in how they allocate their resources.

You might ask another question about how ethical it is for administration to offer only part-time

positions with poorer benefits to new staff. That is a good question. It poses an ethical dilemma. An ethical dilemma is a situation in which it is impossible to comply with two or more ethical principles at the same time. For example, in this agency's case, the administration has a difficult choice. It must either offer less money and benefits to new staff or fail to serve clients in serious need. The administration, therefore, decides it's more important to provide benefits to clients than to staff.

Note

a. It should be noted that, although part-time staff may appear to cost less on paper in terms of salary and benefits, such staff generally cost the agency more in terms of administrative "workload" (i.e., supervisory time, staff meeting time, in-service training, etc.).

---

workers' offices or in clients' homes? How long should such meetings take? What types of information must workers gather from clients? Agency policies concern these and any number of other questions about worker-client interaction and intervention.

Formal and Informal Agency Policies

Chapter 5 explains that agency policies may be formal and informal. *Formal policies* are written down and clearly specified, often in a policy manual. *Informal policies* are not overtly stated, yet still function to guide agency staff's behavior.

The policies addressed in Farica and Spiro's example involved both formal and informal dimensions. Acquisition and distribution of personnel is formal, in that such actions require formal funding prerequisites and formal integration of staff into the agency's hierarchy of employees. Informal policies, concern the everyday decision-making processes of people in power. Decision-makers in Farica and Spiro's situation included Bob, Harold, and Theresa. Such decision-makers have substantial informal discretion regarding how they will

allocate agency staff. This offers only one example of the types of policy changes you may decide to target in your own agency.

At any point in your role as an agency worker, you may decide that some agency policy, either formal or informal, is unfair, outdated, or inappropriate. First, you should review the decision-making steps illustrated in chapter 5 to decide whether or not to pursue macro change. Next, you can follow the IMAGINE process to implement a policy change.

Types of Changes in Agency Policy

There are three major types of agency policy changes. These include policies on agency goals, on practice procedures, and on personnel practices. Each of these may involve both formal and informal agency policies.

Whenever a worker decides to pursue an agency policy change, she should first answer two questions (Netting, Kettner, & McMurtry, 1993). Will the change result in improved service delivery and resources to clients? And will the change result in improved working conditions for staff so that they will be better able to

---

HIGHLIGHT 6.8

CASE EXAMPLE:
EVALUATE PROGRESS

Toward the end of the change process, Spiro and Farica form the primary action systems since other action system members are no longer actively involved. In their pursuit of the designated macro change, namely, increasing staff, they are forced to seriously evaluate their change efforts. Because of total lack of administrative support and receipt of administrative chastisement, they determine that their original plan was ineffective. They need to develop some totally new strategies.

At the completion of the macro change process,

Farica and Spiro can also evaluate their overall effectiveness. What exactly have they been able to accomplish? They have gained the equivalent of an additional staff member for the unit, at least in terms of the time someone will be available to work in the unit. In effect, Farica and Spiro decide that their efforts have been successful. Now or at some point in the future Spiro or Farica may decide to undertake a new macro change effort. They can target either a similar or a very different need to enhance the unit's level of service provision and effectiveness.

---

serve their clients in a more effective or efficient way? The bottom line is that, regardless of type of policy change, the ultimate beneficiaries of that change should be your clients.

Changing Agency Goals

Chapter 4 discussed organizational and agency goals and their importance. In essence, an organizational goal is "a desired state of affairs which the organization attempts to realize" (Etzioni, 1964, p. 6). Goals propose what an agency wants to accomplish. Rothman, Erlich, and Teresa (1981) reflect on the significance of goals: "The collective welfare of practitioners' clients and constituents is profoundly affected by the organizational structures and goals of social agencies. Changing an organization's goals thus becomes a key task for many practitioners, and failure to accomplish this objective is frequently a great hindrance to effective practice" (p. 51).

Sometimes formal goals reflect an agency's real goals and sometimes they do not. Informal agency goals often replace formally stated goals. In these instances, the informal goals become the real goals the agency strives to reach. Goal displacement is a good example. The *process* of getting things done replaces actually getting things done as the agency's priority. This is the

case even though the formal goals still stress the importance of the output or services provided.

Chapter 4, "Understanding Organizations," discussed goal displacement and other potential problems with organizational goals. In your role as agency worker, you may see that goals have become outdated. Over time, goals may become either too high or too low for the agency to accomplish effectively and efficiently. Agency goals may also become too complex or too numerous to accomplish realistically.

Changing agency goals can be significantly more difficult than changing other agency policies. Agency goals are broad and affect a wide range of agency personnel. Therefore, changing goals requires careful consideration, a broad support base, and the help of administrative decision-makers. Targeting agency goals for change requires following the same basic assessment and IMAGINE processes you would use for other changes. However, you would proceed on the understanding that the accomplishment of change would probably be more difficult.

Changing Policies on Personnel Practices

Spiro and Farica's example above portrayed one type of policy change, that of increasing or reallocating personnel. There are any number of other personnel policy changes that will merit attention at some point in your agency life. Other types of formal or informal policies concerning personnel include job position responsibilities, staff benefits (such as salary, health insurance, and vacation), methods of evaluating staff performance, and physical working conditions. At any point that you feel some agency condition affects staff's ability to function optimally on behalf of their clients, you may target and pursue a policy change.

Changing Policies on Practice Procedures

Practice procedures refer ''to the way organizations or individuals within them go about doing their business'' (Kettner et al., 1993, p. 235). We have established that these policies may be formal (clearly written down in an agency policy manual) or informal (implicit expectations that all staff are expected to know and follow even though they are unwritten).

Both formal and informal practice procedures vary endlessly from one agency to another. Examples of agency policies on practice procedures include rules governing intervention approaches, record-keeping methods, and staff evaluation criteria. Any aspect of worker-client intervention and interaction that you feel should be improved can be targeted for policy change.

Using IMAGINE to Change Agency Practice Procedures

To illustrate the application of IMAGINE to changing a policy on practice procedures, we will use a new example. You are a social worker in a small rural hospital. Your duties include: assessments; provision of information; clarification of medical conditions; individual and family counseling; referral to necessary resources, discharge planning; and follow-up. You are concerned about the efficiency and effectiveness of a policy requiring the head nurse of each unit to sign each of your progress notes at the end of each day. The original intent was to double-check all written documents for accuracy. However, it turns out the head nurses don't have time to read the reports anyway. They typically initial each of a large stack of progress notes at the end of each day without reading a word of them. You feel that you and the two other hospital social workers are experienced

and competent enough to complete progress notes without having them checked by unit head nurses. You already have a social work supervisor, and you resent the current policy, which gives the head nurses supervisory responsibility for your work.

IMAGINE: START WITH AN INNOVATIVE **IDEA**. You begin with the innovative idea of changing the required reporting system in order to decrease wasted effort on the part of you and other hospital staff. You go through the suggested steps for evaluating whether to pursue a macro change, in this case a change in agency policy about practice procedures. You determine that the overall potential for positive change is good. You develop the following innovative idea. The hospital should abolish the practice of asking head nurses to review social workers' progress notes on a daily basis. Instead, the social work supervisor should spot check the workers' notes periodically to maintain control of their quality.

IMAGINE: **MUSTER** SUPPORT AND FORMULATE AN ACTION SYSTEM. You consider the agency's power structure and the potential for achieving a policy change. Your supervisor is a personable, competent woman, generally well-liked among hospital staff. She gets along fairly well with the unit head nurses and with the hospital director. You feel your supervisor would provide substantial support for your ideas. She feels strongly that social workers should assume responsibility for completing their work in a professional, ethical, and conscientious way. Thus, she probably is not crazy about the head nurses' supervising social work productivity. Additionally, your supervisor spot checks her supervisees' work anyway. Periodic review of daily progress reports would add little to her workload. This could be important because she probably doesn't want to make her job any more difficult or time-consuming than it already is.

You also feel your two social work colleagues would support your idea. They feel as you do about having the unit head nurses check their work. They also find it inordinately cumbersome to collect their notes each day from patient records, run around to find the unit head nurses, and get these nurses to stand still long enough to initial the records.

Your proposed action system, then, will consist of you, both your colleagues, and your supervisor. This,

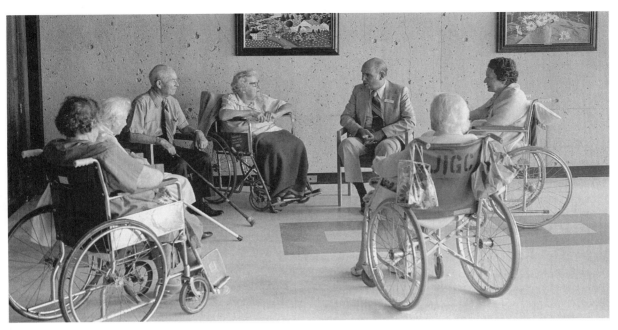

By formulating an action plan, the social worker in this hospital setting uses IMAGINE to change the policy requiring that the head nurse review his notes on a daily basis.

of course, assumes that all three will agree to participate in the macro change process.

IMAGINE: IDENTIFY ASSETS. You own assets include your good work record, the fact that you consistently complete your written work in a timely fashion, your excellent relationships with your two social work colleagues, your fairly good relationship with your supervisor, and your fairly good relationships with most hospital staff, including all but one of the unit head nurses. You do tend to butt heads with one head nurse who has an exceptionally condescending attitude toward you and other non-nurses and non-doctors. You swear that Ms. Hardhat eats nails for breakfast.

Another asset is your supervisor's good relationship with the hospital director and with most other hospital staff—except for Ms. Hardhat. Still another asset is the fact that your intent is to increase efficiency without relinquishing quality of work. Your immediate supervisor will still monitor your work. Your guess is that the unit head nurses (except for Ms. Hardhat) will welcome discontinuing a bothersome, time-consuming, and, in effect, useless task.

IMAGINE: SPECIFY GOALS AND OBJECTIVES. Your basic goal is to amend the policy stated above, which requires unit head nurses to check over and initial your daily patient progress reports. Replacing this practice policy, you recommend that the social worker supervisor periodically spot check workers' daily progress notes. This is to ensure their completion and quality.

Specific objectives leading to this goal include the following:

1. You will talk to each of your two social work colleagues by a week from Friday to solicit their support.
2. You will talk to your social work supervisor by two weeks from Friday to solicit her support.
3. You will determine with your supervisor the potentially most effective strategy for implementing the policy change. For example, should she approach the unit head nurses or the hospital director about the proposed change? Should recommendations be made via a memo or in person? Should the entire social work department or just the supervisor meet with decision-makers?
4. You will specify further objectives for meeting your goal after discussing them with your supervisor (e.g., meeting

---

HIGHLIGHT 6.9

ESTABLISHING A CULTURALLY COMPETENT ORGANIZATION

One dimension of agency policy that may merit your attention in assessing possible macro change is *cultural competency*. Cultural competence in the organizational context is "a set of congruent behaviors, attitudes, policies, and structures which come together in a system, agency or among professionals and enables that system, agency or those professionals to work effectively in the context of cultural differences" (Benjamin, 1994, p. 17; Cross, Bazron, Dennis, and Isaacs, 1989, p. 13). So cultural competence is a multi-focused, unifying thread connecting staff behaviors and attitudes, agency policies, and formal structure. This intertwining theme should emphasize that every aspect of an agency's performance should be sensitive and responsive to the cultural diversity of its clientele. How can the agency make clients from diverse cultural backgrounds feel as comfortable as possible in accessing agency services? How can practitioners best communicate with clients from diverse cultures? How can staff be taught to maximize their own cultural competence? What agency policies, practices, and goals work for or against cultural competence?

You will be employed by some social services agency. Will that agency be culturally competent? You might assume, "Well, of course. It's the only ethical way to be," or "All social workers are trained to be sensitive to cultural diversity." In fact, agencies may be neither culturally competent nor particularly sensitive. Perhaps most agencies can improve on or expand their cultural competence. Agencies might need to provide continuing education for employees or expand the range of cultural competence to specific cultural groups. Some agencies may need to take a long, hard look at the entire concept of cultural competence and make major revisions in their mission statements and overall goals.

Cultural Incompetence: A Case Example

Isaacs-Shockley (1994) critiques the current juvenile justice system with respect to its lack of cultural competence. She suggests that a six-point scale exists upon which agencies can be rated from extremely culturally incompetent to extremely culturally competent. She maintains that the juvenile justice system as it operates today is located between "cultural destructiveness" and "cultural incapacity," the two least culturally competent points on the scale (Isaacs-Shockley, 1994, p. 19).

Culturally destructive agencies "exhibit attitudes, policies and practices that are destructive to cultures and consequently to members within the culture." She continues that in such organizations, "bigotry, coupled with vast power differentials, allows the dominant group to disenfranchise, control, exploit, or systematically destroy the minority group and its culture" (Isaacs-Shockley, 1994, p. 19). In such agencies some designated culture is considered superior to other cultures that should be subjugated, controlled, and perhaps exterminated. South Africa's prior apartheid policy comes to mind.[a]

Agencies falling into the cultural incapacity category, the second worst point on the cultural competency scale, "do not intentionally or consciously seek to be culturally destructive; rather, they lack the capacity to help persons or communities of color. The organization remains extremely biased, believes in the racial superiority of the dominant group, and assumes a paternal posture towards 'lesser' races and cultures" (Isaacs-Shockley, 1994, p. 19). Such agencies may overtly or covertly provide fewer resources to those whose culture is considered inferior, maintain racist policies, or reinforce negative stereotypes.

Isaacs-Shockley identified at least seven ways in which the juvenile justice system lies between the culturally destructive and culturally incapacitated points of the continuum (p. 20). First, clients are likely to be "African American, male and poor" (p. 20). Second, after entering the system, people are much less likely to reach higher educational levels or obtain better jobs than are others who are not involved in the system. Third, despite the fact that people entering the system are more likely to have "emotional disabilities, substance abuse, child abuse and learning disabilities," they will most probably neither be assessed nor receive help for these problems (p. 20). Fourth, many attitudes "the discretionary decision-makers within the juvenile justice system hold about people of color (i.e., police officers, probation officers, prosecutors, etc.) are often based upon strong and deeply embedded racial biases and stereotypes" (p. 20). Fifth, families and communities of those youth involved in the system are allowed little input and participation. Sixth, there is a significant power imbalance in the system in terms of staff and administration, as most employees are from the dominant culture. Seventh, the system's focus is on punishment instead of treatment.

Assessing Cultural Competence

What, then, can be done to improve the juvenile justice or any other system for the enhancement of its cultural competence? First, you as a practitioner should apply the PREPARE process to determine the viability of a macro change effort. Consider the extent of the change you are suggesting. On the one hand, you might consider making major changes in a larger organization's mission statement (which directs all of the organization's efforts). This would require significantly greater effort and resources than making a more minor but constructive change in agency in-service training policy (for example, requiring the incorporation of training sessions focusing on cultural competence).

After undertaking the PREPARE process, you might decide to pursue a macro level change. Then you would follow the IMAGINE procedure to make and implement your plans.

The following discussions regarding potential questions to raise and possible alternatives to pursue are not intended to conflict with PREPARE and IMAGINE. Rather, they are intended to enhance your ability to think about and examine the specific issue of cultural competence in your agency.

Mason (1994) suggests examining questions similar to the five presented below, which are aimed at assessing an organization's cultural competence:

1. *How responsible is the organization in responding effectively and efficiently to the needs of the culturally diverse people it serves?* Does the agency have a good grasp of the cultural diversity of its clientele? Must further research be performed to identify target client groups? To what extent are staff culturally competent in their individual interactions with clientele? What types of training and education would improve employees' cultural competence?

2. *In what ways can a culturally competent staff, regardless of an individual worker's cultural background, assist the agency in actualizing its mission of cultural competence?* How can staff best work together to serve clientele from culturally diverse backgrounds? How can staff help each other obtain relevant knowledge and skills?

3. *In what ways could services be administered different in response to the needs of the agency's culturally diverse client population?* Are services being provided where they are readily accessible to culturally diverse client groups? If not, how might the agency make such services more accessible? Is the communication between agency staff and clients as effective as it could be? Should workers offer services in different languages so clients from diverse cultural groups can better understand? Can agency personnel solicit information from significant community leaders or from clients to identify and pursue better service provision in terms of cultural competence?

(continued)

HIGHLIGHT 6.9—(Continued)

4. *What is "the vision of services" to the culturally diverse community (p. 5)?* How might you best "envision the system as it should be and . . . identify ways of funding such a system" (p. 5)? How could you maximize the involvement of people representing the diverse cultures your agency serves? How might you empower community residents? Can you and others helping you identify new potential resources for the community and the agency? Such resources might include "assisting with staff and board recruitment, encouraging . . . donations, identifying advocacy resources, and promoting parent or community education and support groups" (p. 5).

5. *How might you determine that the goal of cultural competence has been achieved?* What specific goals and objectives might you identify to provide clear proof that your mission has been actualized? (This chapter stresses the specification of goals and objectives in an earlier section). What task groups might you and the agency establish to review progress, refine recommendations, and keep efforts on task?

Recommendations for Attaining Cultural Competence

After exploring the extent of your agency's cultural competence by answering questions such as those raised above, what can you do to improve the situation? Mason (1994) summarizes a number of suggestions regarding planning. One involves the identification of the client system. What aspects of cultural diversity are reflected by the client population? How would you most clearly define these client groups? Are you talking about one group or several?

Another planning suggestion entails an assessment of your agency's staff training needs concerning enhancement of cultural competence. What knowledge and skills do practitioners have? What do they really need to improve upon? What are their strengths and what are their deficits?

Figure out what obstacles stand in the way of your serving culturally diverse clients. Do they involve language differences, lack of administrative support, inadequate resources, or meager staff motivation? What problems should be your targets of change?

A further planning proposition concerns the development and achievement of goals. PREPARE focuses on the establishment of primary goals while IMAGINE addresses goal-setting in a much more detailed and specific manner. The final planning suggestion entails establishing measurements to verify that goals have indeed been attained. How can you prove that the agency has enhanced or attained its cultural competence?

Responding to the Juvenile Justice System Critique

A loose end remains in this discussion of cultural competence. What about the juvenile justice system? It is easy to complain about any system. Fixing it is more difficult. As with most problems in providing social services, financial resources are the bottom line. The trick is to figure out how to implement changes that will result in maximum benefits and minimal costs. What aspects of the huge problematic dilemmas reflected in the juvenile system would you attack first? Trying to resolve all of the issues at once would be a mammoth task. However, here we will attempt to break down some of the issues into smaller pieces, raise a few questions, and review some ideas and possibilities.

Several themes run through the criticisms of the systems presented earlier. One theme is punishment instead of treatment. People entering the juvenile justice system are more likely to have problems (such as substance abuse) and decreased chances for success in traditional society (that is, less chance for a good education and job). What ideas might you have to turn this around? Ideally, how would you try to increase the juvenile justice system's cultural competence?

Establishing policies that provide for treatment of problems such as substance abuse and emotional disability might empower clients. Such support might help them get to a point where further education and training, in addition to good jobs, are at least realistic possibilities. Being a crackhead does not allow for much learning and concentration nor provide a very good impression when applying for a job. How might one get funding for such a treatment program? Might you write a grant application (addressed more thoroughly in chapter 14, "Developing and Managing Agency Resources")? Could you convince politicians by proving that the total cost to society would be substantially less if young people leaving the system were healthy and capable?

What about emphasizing education and training within the system? This too costs money. However, what if you could establish policies that provided rewards for academic achievement? What if you could develop policies to emphasize development of self-esteem and to aid in decision making concerning a future career path? Are there ways in which you could try to prove that these tactics would be cheaper for society in the long run, and would also humanely encourage people to lead productive, satisfying lives?

Another theme of the criminal justice system critique presented earlier focuses on unequal power. The argument is that decision-makers in the system are biased against certain cultural groups, that most decision-makers are not of these diverse cultures, and that the families of young people in the system have no input into what goes on in that system. Additionally, the point is made that impoverished African-American young men are significantly more likely to become involved in the juvenile justice system than are other groups.

What about biased decision-makers? What types of policies could be developed to encourage or require training focused on cultural competence? Could citizens who support public politicians be educated regarding the importance of such a policy? Could they, in turn, put political pressure on these politicians to make far-reaching changes in how things are done in the juvenile justice system? What about recruiting more culturally diverse staff? How might that be done? Could potential applicant populations be identified and targeted? What are the reasons that such recruitment is not successfully occurring already? Could communities and families of clients contribute ideas about how such policies might be changed?

The questions are endless. The problems are awesome. However, the point here is that there may be ways in which you can start to make changes on the behalf of enhancing cultural competence, regardless of your agency work setting. Even tiny changes can begin the process of positive shifts in agency policy. Little by little, you might begin to work toward the goal of increased cultural competence for yourself and your agency.

Note

a. Apartheid is "a policy of segregation and political and economic discrimination against non-European groups [formerly] in the Republic of South Africa" (*Webster's Ninth New Collegiate Dictionary*, 1991, p. 94).

with your target system of decision-makers to describe your proposed change).

IMAGINE: **IMPLEMENT** THE PLAN. Implementing the plan, of course, simply means carrying out your objectives. Throughout this process you can monitor your effectiveness. As it happens, things go fairly smoothly, except for some bristling on the part of Nurse Hardhat.

IMAGINE: **NEUTRALIZE** OPPOSITION. Nurse Hardhat presents the primary opposition to your action system (the social work department). Your social work supervisor initiates a meeting with the daytime unit head nurses. At that time, Ms. Hardhat's expressed hesitations about the proposed changes are quickly dismissed. Other unit head nurses commend the change for allowing greater efficiency and creating less paperwork for them. They don't get along that well with Ms. Hardhat either, and they refuse to support her.

IMAGINE: **EVALUATE** PROGRESS. Two months after initiating the practice policy change and formulating the action system, you evaluate your progress. Your measurement of success is the fact that the new policy has been formalized, is included in the hospital's policy manual, and has become part of normal daily hospital operation. Further, there have been no problems experienced with the new system.

Chapter Summary

This chapter proposes IMAGINE, a process for undertaking macro change. Steps in IMAGINE include the following: (1) start with an innovative *idea*; (2) *muster* support and formulate an action system; (3) identify *assets*; (4) specify *goals* and objectives; (5) *implement* the plan; (6) *neutralize* opposition; and (7) *evaluate* progress. IMAGINE can be applied to changing agency policy, implementing a project, and developing a program.

The macro practice environment is conceptualized, including the macro client, change agent, target, and action systems. Mezzo concepts are applied to macro practice in the context of formulating action systems.

IMAGINE is applied in detail to a case scenario directed at changing agent policy. Collaborative and adversarial strategies are described with respect to neutralizing opposition to the proposed macro plan. Formal and informal agency policies are explained. Changing policies on agency goals, personnel practices, and practice procedures are discussed. Attaining cultural competence within the organizational context is addressed.

CHAPTER SEVEN

IMAGINE Project Implementation and Program Development

The following are some positive reflections on macro practice:

How might you be able to make your job more interesting?

If you could do anything you wanted to improve service provision conditions for your clients, what would you do?

What kind of innovative program could your clients really use?

What kind of project in your agency would you really like to sink your teeth into?

The above stand in stark contrast to the following negative, rather depressing attitudes:

It's hopeless. There's nothing a plain old direct service worker like me can do to change the system.

The system's too big and impersonal. Why should I waste my time trying to fix it?

I'm just an old cog in the wheel. I don't really matter in the big picture.

Introduction

Macro practice can be an exciting, rewarding part of your professional life. Targeting large systems for change can result in momentous benefits to large number of clients. In the last chapter we introduced the IMAGINE process for macro change. We applied this process to changing an agency policy. This chapter will apply the IMAGINE process to two other types of macro level interventions, project implementation and program development.

This chapter will:

- Suggest types of projects within agencies you might choose to pursue and programs you may choose to develop.
- Apply the IMAGINE process to project implementation and program development.
- Discuss in depth the special implications of IMAGINE when implementing a project of developing a program.
- Examine and evaluate the usefulness of Program Evaluation and Review Technique (PERT).

- Apply PERT charts to planning an inservice project and developing a sexual harassment awareness program.

Initiating and Implementing a Project

In addition to agency policy change, the second type of macro change that you are likely to come across in your agency setting is implementation of a project. Projects are directed at completing some time-limited and specific goal. This contrasts, of course, with developing a program (usually established as a permanent part of an agency's structure and service). Projects can involve testing some new treatment approach or technique, raising funds, completing a report about some aspect of agency functioning, or developing a curriculum outline for an in-service training program (Kettner et al., 1985).

As a direct service practitioner or lower level supervisor, you will probably have more and easier opportunities to plan and implement projects than to develop full-scale programs. It may also be easier to initiate a project than to change an agency policy. Workers undertaking projects usually have greater control over the tasks at hand because a project has a more limited scope. Sometimes only the change catalyst's own work and time is affected if she is the only one working on the project. Resources, of course, are a major concern. If resources are available along with permission and support from decision-makers, then the potential for carrying out a project is probably pretty good.

One assumption here is that you, as the worker initiating a project, will remain integrally involved throughout its implementation. Changing agency policy usually has much broader effects on numerous other staff. Many staff may be required to implement a policy change. Likewise, program development often requires a larger action system than does a project. Such action systems may be composed of a number of people, even a very large number of people. Therefore, you may remain significantly less integrally involved in program development.

The IMAGINE process to initiate and implement a project for your agency is described below. Some aspects of planning and implementing an agency inservice training program within the IMAGINE framework will also be discussed.

IMAGINE: Develop an Innovative Idea

We will assume that you have already completed the assessment of macro change potential as described in chapter 5. You have defined and prioritized problems and translated them into needs. You have decided which needs to address and have identified your primary goals. You have also begun to assess variables working for and against your primary goals, influential people, your own risk level, and the client need. Finally, you have decided that undertaking this project is the way to go at this point. Your idea is becoming more and more clearly formulated in your head. Highlight 7.1 proposes various types of projects you might propose in an agency setting.

IMAGINE: Muster Support

Determining who you will need to muster support for your project, attend to two variables. First, determine who else in the agency might be interested in helping you undertake the project. Who else feels strongly about the issue or would benefit from the project's success? Second, whom do you need to obtain permission from in order to undertake the project? Certainly, at least your immediate supervisor. Remember that a macro project is not within your own job description. Therefore, you need administrative support, at least from your supervisor and, perhaps, even from higher authorities, in order to proceed.

IMAGINE: Identify Assets

There are four basic types of assets to consider when initiating a project (Kettner et al., 1985; Matthies & Waalkes, 1974). The first involves *time*. Significant aspects of time include the anticipated duration of the project and the amount of staff time necessary to complete it. What *skills* are needed, and who has them? Are special therapeutic or accounting skills needed to pursue the project? Are the special skills of a consultant necessary? Third, what type of *staffing* is necessary to complete the project? How many staff need to be involved? How much secretarial help is needed? Fourth, what *costs* will accrue with implementation of the project? For exam-

ple, will the project require paper, postage, long-distance phone calls, or mileage reimbursement? Must you hire a consultant to help with a research design or an expert to present a certain specialized type of in-service training?

IMAGINE: Specify Goals and Objectives

At this point in the IMAGINE process, you have already identified your primary goals during your assessment of macro change potential. Chapter 5 explained this process. We have established that goals provide direction regarding how to proceed.

Goals can probably never be too specific. They should be clearly stated so that it is as easy as possible to determine that they've been attained or that they have not. However, many times goals are very basic and broad. Consider the goals "develop an in-service training program" or "evaluate new vocational techniques." These primary goal statements and other goal statements like them don't give you a clue about how to achieve them. Where do you go to meet that need? How would you begin your planning process?

As in other types of generalist intervention, goals for implementing projects can usually be broken down into smaller action steps called *objectives*. Objectives delineate how you might go about achieving your ultimate goal. They must be both behaviorally specific and measurable.

Suppose that you want to raise some money for a group of needy clients. In order to achieve such a broad primary goal, you need to begin specifying exactly how to achieve it. This produces a series of action steps of objectives. Who will publicize a fundraiser? Who will participate in raising the money? Who are possible contributors? How will money be funneled to people in need? These and many more specific questions need to be addressed.

IMAGINE: Implement the Plan

Setting goals and objectives is an integral part of establishing a "project design" (Kettner, Daley, & Nichols, 1985, p. 164). A project design or plan is like a map of the entire project from beginning to end. One useful

HIGHLIGHT 7.1

EXAMPLES OF PROJECTS IN MACRO PRACTICE

Projects, by definition, are relatively short-term, limited endeavors with specific measurable goals and objectives. There are no limits on the type of project you might dream up for your agency. Below are some examples of potential projects. It is up to you as you work within your own agency setting to establish what the agency's and clients' needs are. Then only your own imagination will limit what type of project you would like to undertake. Of course, you must follow the IMAGINE process to determine the project's feasibility. Nonetheless, personal creativity is key in project development. Examples of projects follow.

Meeting Clients' Special Needs

You might decide that your clients need clothing. A one-time clothing drive among community citizens would help. Or you might suggest a drive for Christmas gifts. In either case you establish a client need and plan how to meet it by initiating and implementing a project.

Fundraising Projects

Fundraising can be used for anything from research on a specific physical disability to building a new office building. It often comes under the auspices of a project because of its limited, short-term, goal-oriented nature. Chapter 14 describes fund-raising in greater depth.

Evaluation of Effects Due to Agency or Community Changes

Sometimes, changes implemented in the agency or surrounding community will affect your ability to serve clients. In such cases, you may determine that a project will be useful to evaluate the effects of the change. You might also decide that a project could assist the agency or its clients to adjust to the change.

Suppose your agency administration decides to change the crisis intervention services it provides to community residents. Administration determines that clients can receive a maximum of one month of crisis intervention services, instead of the current three-month maximum.

You are horrified. You feel this change will seriously impede your agency's ability to provide adequate services to clients. You realize that it is essentially an administrative cost-saving measure. However, you think the administration will listen to you if you can prove that such a change will have serious negative consequences for clients. You plan a research project to evaluate the effectiveness of such short-term intervention procedures.

Changes in the surrounding community can also affect an agency's ability to serve clients. Community decision-makers may decide to build a superhighway through the middle of the community where most of your clients live. Your clients are outraged, but they feel helpless and trapped. You have already tried to take an advocacy approach. You tried persuading decision-makers to reroute the highway to another industrial area with less population. However, for various reasons your attempts failed.

Now you consider ways to ease the transition of clients from one neighborhood to another. You begin planning a relocation project involving local realtors and landlords. You begin to think about establishing a centralized system aimed at pairing displaced homeowners and renters with new housing locations. An idea for a project is born.

Evaluation of New Intervention Approaches

You may become aware of new, more effective intervention approaches for clients. A new approach might be a specific new technique that would be relatively easy to incorporate into agency practice, such as adopting a token system for child-behavior management in a day-care center. A token system or token economy involves ''the therapeutic procedure, used in behavior modification . . . and various institutional settings, in which the clients are given tokens, slips of paper, or coupons whenever they fulfill specified tasks or behave according to some specified standard'' (Barker, 1991, p. 237). Clients may then exchange the tokens they've earned for good behavior in return for items or privileges they desire.

On the other hand, new intervention approaches may involve a radical change in theoretical orientation for agency practitioners. For example, after considering current research, you might determine that a shift from a psychodynamic to a behavioral treatment approach would enhance service provision and effectiveness. In either of these cases, you might consider implementing a project to evaluate the effectiveness of the proposed intervention approach. Testing the approach or technique on a smaller scale can help determine whether a major agency adoption of the approach is worth the effort.

Suppose that you work in a state probation and parole department and watch scores of people age sixteen or under pass through the revolving doors of ''the system'' again and again. You think about how senseless this is. You also note how expensive it is for the system. You come up with an idea for providing extra, intensive attention to first offenders to help them keep from returning in the future. You understand this has the potential to be a full-fledged program. However, at this point you know administrators would not buy such a radical idea without proof. How about a demonstration project, letting you implement a short-term intervention approach and then evaluating the results? If the results are positive, that is, effective and efficient, there might be a chance to develop an entire new program.

You might be a protective services worker with an increasingly large caseload of families accused of some form of child maltreatment. Sometimes you feel that your periodic visits are like trying to plug a widening hole in a dike with your little finger. You have an idea about providing group parenting classes for some of your clients. Maybe this would be a way of offering more service to more clients in the time frame you have available. You also think about incorporating a self-help group for abusers under the umbrella of the project. Such a limited-term project might prove very effective.

Implementing Internal Agency Changes

You feel that your agency job description, written a decade ago, no longer really applies to what you do every day. You think it might be more helpful to you and your colleagues if you had a more accurate description to guide you in your day-to-day activities. You propose to your supervisor the short-term project of revising your job description.

Perhaps you work in a large hospital social services department. Your supervisor is responsible for overseeing dozens of staff. As a result, you rarely have time to consult her about what to do with some of your most difficult cases. You come up with the idea that it would be helpful if you had access to a hospital staff psychologist for consultation purposes. The psychologist has not nearly the weighty responsibilities in this particular setting that your supervisor does. You talk to your colleagues and supervisor about your idea at the next group supervision meeting. You suggest undertaking a project in which a group of interested workers would examine the possibility of implementing this idea.

Providing Internal Services to Your Agency Staff

Some projects involve the development and provision of services to agency staff. For example, you begin to see a huge number of cocaine-addicted clients

(continued)

HIGHLIGHT 7.1—(Continued)

added to your caseload. You talk to some of your colleagues and find that they're experiencing the same problem. You think about a series of in-service programs aimed at helping practitioners address this problem. You initiate the idea of establishing a short-term project consisting of six in-service training sessions for you and your colleagues.

Another example involves a group of adults who have developmental disabilities. Many of them work at a sheltered workshop run by another agency, you find that you often have difficulty understanding ex-

actly what your clients do at the workshop. You think your colleagues working in similar group homes run by your agency feel the same way. You propose a field trip to the sheltered workshop. You feel this would provide you and your colleagues the opportunity to talk to workshop staff and find out exactly what is going on in this major aspect of your clients' lives.

Source: Many of these projects are examples suggested by Kettner, Daley, and Nichols in *Initiating Change in Organizations and Communities* (Monterey, CA: Brooks/Cole, 1985).

means of formulating and illustrating a plan is through the use of a PERT (Program Evaluation and Review Technique) chart (Federal Electric Corporation, 1963). PERT charts are flow charts or time charts "that show what steps need to be taken in what order . . . . Such charts can help [action] group members anticipate and reduce problems while providing a sense of direction for projects" (Rubin & Rubin, 1992, p. 402).

PERT charts illustrate a series of tasks or activities in the order that such tasks should be done. The original PERT charts developed for industry were quite complicated and intricate. Today's use includes a variety of simpler formats adapted to individual and small group use. Therefore, we refer to the PERT formats illustrated in figure 7.1 as being "amended" or revised.

You can depict PERT chart tasks horizontally or vertically. Necessary activities might be pictured in boxes connected by horizontal or vertical lines. Thus, there are usually a number of horizontal and vertical rows consisting of activity boxes connected by lines above or below the time line. Each horizontal or vertical sequence of activity boxes connected by lines reflects the plan for how each goal should be achieved. Figure 7.1 illustrates three types of amended PERT chart formats.

PERT charts assume a number of forms. In addition to having either a horizontal or vertical format, they illustrate individual tasks in various ways. For example, you can use sequentially connected circles of simple statements instead of specifying tasks in boxes. Like-

wise, in a complicated chart you can use a series of codes, such as numbers or letters, to indicate tasks or time frames instead of writing them out. You would then provide a key to explain the meaning of each number or letter.

It should be noted that for the purposes of simplicity and clarity, the PERT chart illustrated in figure 7.1 displays only *one* task accomplished by one person. In reality, multiple project tasks must often be accompanied simultaneously by different members of the action system. One or more of your tasks might depend upon others completing their tasks first. For example, another member of the action system may develop a list of resource people for the in-service program and your report depends upon having this data available. Thus, PERT charts can become more complex as tasks and participants increase in number.

PERT Charts Illustrate Goals

PERT charts provide pictures of how the five elements involved in planning relate (Barker, 1991). The first element in planning entails the plan's goals and the objectives, here referred to as tasks, necessary to complete the goal. A PERT chart readily identifies the project's goals. Figure 7.1 illustrates a variety of amended PERT formats. Each portrays the goal of presenting informational findings at a designated agency meeting. This is a pretty straightforward and simple goal.

Figure 7.1
Examples of Amended PERT Chart Formats

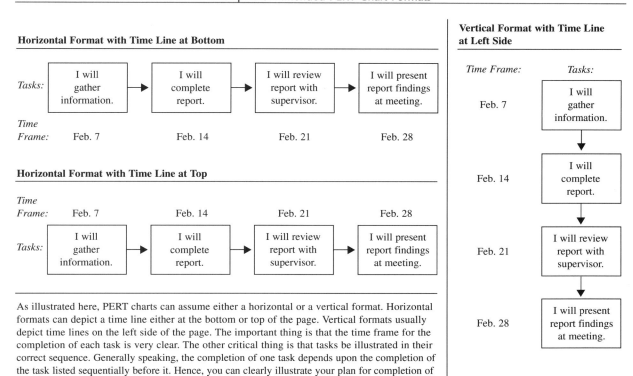

As illustrated here, PERT charts can assume either a horizontal or a vertical format. Horizontal formats can depict a time line either at the bottom or top of the page. Vertical formats usually depict time lines on the left side of the page. The important thing is that the time frame for the completion of each task is very clear. The other critical thing is that tasks be illustrated in their correct sequence. Generally speaking, the completion of one task depends upon the completion of the task listed sequentially before it. Hence, you can clearly illustrate your plan for completion of some designated goal in a step-by-step sequence.

PERT Charts Portray Specific Tasks

The second element in planning concerns the specific tasks and activities necessary for achieving each goal. Such tasks are the equivalent of the objectives or action steps you need to accomplish in order to attain your ultimate goal. Before presenting an informational report, you need to get the information. You probably also want to check it over with your supervisor for approval before sharing it with other agency staff at an agency meeting. You need to have something in hand to show to your supervisor. Therefore, you need to write the report first.

PERT Charts Depict Task Sequence

The third important element in planning is specifying the necessary order in which activities should take place.

Figure 7.1 shows three different ways to illustrate the same series of tasks.

Rubin and Rubin (1992) make three suggestions about such charts. First, make sure that the sequence of tasks makes sense. For example, you would complete a report before submitting it to administration for approval. Second, make sure you note to yourself what objectives and activities should be given top priority. What activities are absolutely necessary to achieve the most important goals? You can use this to guide you when you are rushed and must make fast decisions about what you can and cannot do. Finally, think about the potential barriers and problems you might face when implementing the activities on the chart. Anticipating problems before they occur can give you ideas about how to prevent or solve them. This process, often called a *force-field analysis* is described more thoroughly in chapter 5's discussion of the **PREPARE** process.

The PERT charts depicted in figure 7.1 have the goal of presenting an informational report at a designated agency meeting. The end result or final activity in the sequence, then, is your presentation of the report at the actual meeting. However, before being able to accomplish that, you must gather the information you need. Second, you must pull the information into a form that makes sense. You must do this in preparation for presenting it for your supervisor's approval and eventually to other agency staff. Finally, you must sit down and review the completed report with your supervisor. All this must occur in the designated sequence so that you can present the report at the meeting, your ultimate goal.

PERT Charts and Necessary Resources

The fourth element in planning involves the resources needed to complete the plan. The charts illustrated in figure 7.1 make a number of assumptions about resource availability, even though they do not mention specific resources as such. For one thing, they assume that whatever information you need for the report is available to you. The report might involve anything from an assessment of clients' needs to exploration of parking availability in your agency's lot. If the information you need to complete the report is not available, you will probably have to include additional steps in your PERT chart. For example, before the first illustrated step identified as "I will gather the information," you might start with "I will identify information sources."

Another assumption in figure 7.1's PERT chart is that you will have ready access to your supervisor to review findings with her. And it is also assumed that you will have the basic supplies with which to write the report.

PERT Charts Establish a Time Frame

The fifth element in planning is the time line for the plan's completion. How long will it take to complete each task and activity necessary for achieving goals and objectives? How much time should you allow yourself to complete various aspects of the plan? How long should the entire plan take?

The horizontal formats have time lines on the bottom or top of the charts. The vertical chart has the time line located on its left-hand side. The time lines in these particular charts illustrate weekly deadlines for achieving each of the four objectives. The intent is to complete each objective and, eventually, reach the goal by the indicated target date. Each PERT format in figure 7.1 depicts completion of the following tasks in the following order: (1) gathering information by February 7; (2) completing the report by February 14; (3) reviewing the report with your supervisor by February 21; and (4) presenting the report findings at a designated meeting by February 28.

Time lines on PERT charts can reflect virtually any units of time. Figure 7.1 depicts weekly units. However, time lines can reflect days, months, or years, depending on the specified goals.

How do you establish the activity sequence and the time frame for each objective? Young (1978) suggests asking three useful questions to determine the sequential activities for a PERT chart. First, what are the primary activities needed to complete each primary goal? Dissect each goal or objective into a series of independent "action steps" (Rubin & Rubin, 1992, p. 405). Make certain that all the steps are necessary to actualize the goal.

The second question is, who will be responsible for accomplishing the activity? If more than one person is involved in implementing the project, the individual responsible for completing each task should be noted on the chart.

The third question concerns how long you think it will reasonably take to complete each activity. This should be clearly noted on the chart. Each activity should be completed by the time indicated.

Advantage of PERT Charts

Advantages of PERT charts are numerous (Kettner, Daley, & Nichols, 1985). They provide a general outlook on the entire project planning process. This allows you to coordinate a number of activity sequences at the same time in addition to foreseeing potential snares. Likewise, PERT charts establish time frames and deadlines for evaluating progress.

Case Example: A PERT for Developing an In-Service Training Program

Figure 7.2 illustrates a PERT chart for initiating an agency in-service training program. Suppose you are working in an agency and you develop the bright idea. You think you and your colleagues could really use

Figure 7.2
An Example of a PERT Chart for Developing an In-Service Training Program

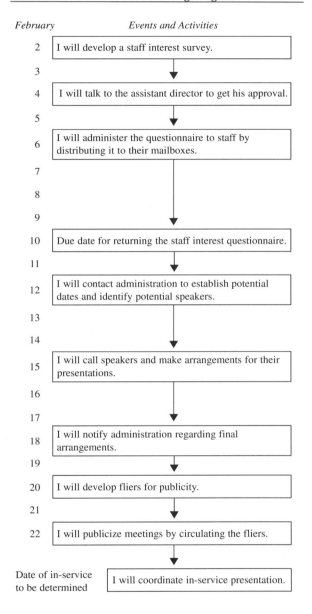

February	Events and Activities
2	I will develop a staff interest survey.
3	
4	I will talk to the assistant director to get his approval.
5	
6	I will administer the questionnaire to staff by distributing it to their mailboxes.
7	
8	
9	
10	Due date for returning the staff interest questionnaire.
11	
12	I will contact administration to establish potential dates and identify potential speakers.
13	
14	
15	I will call speakers and make arrangements for their presentations.
16	
17	
18	I will notify administration regarding final arrangements.
19	
20	I will develop fliers for publicity.
21	
22	I will publicize meetings by circulating the fliers.
Date of in-service to be determined	I will coordinate in-service presentation.

some input and training on a certain aspect of practice—resolving ethical dilemmas, dealing with hostile clients, or testifying in court. Whatever, you determine that an in-service is a good idea. You also decide that it is worth your effort to initiate the idea and try to implement it.

The following section applies PERT to developing such an agency in-service training program.

In figure 7.2, the time line is illustrated on the PERT chart's left-hand side. Your intent is to complete the planning process for the in-service training program during the month of February. Therefore, dates indicated include February 2 through 22. As the lower left-hand side of figure 7.2 indicates, dates for the actual in-service programming are to be determined. This is because you cannot finalize these dates until you check with both administrators and speakers to establish convenient dates.

It should be noted that, as you pursue any macro goal, your micro- and mezzo-level generalist practice skills come into play again and again. You use these skills as you communicate with, attempt to persuade, and possibly confront each individual or group of individuals within the macro system you are trying to persuade or change. Thus, we will discuss this example of a PERT chart in the context of a specific agency with specific personnel. All such staff have individual personalities (it's tempting to use the word ''peculiar'' instead of ''individual'').

By February 2, you will develop a staff interest survey that polls staff regarding their interest in an in-service training session. Since you already have an idea about what you think is needed, you might ask them questions such as, ''On a scale from 1 to 10, how interested are you in the proposed topic?'' or ''On a scale from 1 to 10, how likely are you to attend such an in-service?'' You might also ask staff for ideas regarding what they feel are the most essential in-service topics. This last question may determine whether your proposed topic is indeed the one that staff would support most heartily. It might also help gather ideas for future in-services.

You know that you need agency approval for expending staff time. You might also need some monetary support to pay the person presenting the training sessions. Such payment, of course, depends on what speaker you get.

The first step in getting agency approval is checking out your idea with your direct supervisor. Your supervisor is a bright, straightforward person who loves the outdoors and has a gruff manner. You've often thought that he was probably a lumberjack in another life. Although he is forceful, he also has a very democratic style. You know that he typically encourages staff to pursue innovative ideas with little interference. As you anticipate, your direct supervisor gives you a clear "go ahead."

The next person from whom you need permission in order to proceed is the agency's assistant director. Your plan is to make an appointment with her by February 4 to show her the questionnaire and discuss your in-service idea. You anticipate more resistance from this administrator than from your supervisor.

The assistant director is an intense person who seems to need excessive control over what goes on in the agency. She is hesitant to "rock the bureaucratic boat." She wants no uncontrolled changes to disrupt any of the agency's daily routines. She typically scrutinizes every tiny detail before providing support for any new project or proposal.

However, you feel that you can persuade her by emphasizing the need for continuing education units (CEUs). These are given for training provided to professionals after they receive their formal degrees and are working in the field. Some state licensing boards for social workers require practitioners to complete a designated number of CEUs annually or biannually in order to continue in the profession. This is the case in your state. The fact that CEUs are required fortifies your argument to the assistant director that in-service training is necessary. You can also argue that providing such training in your own agency saves substantial staff time. Staff who attend do not have to spend lengthy travel time to get to the training. You continue that this will be training that staff clearly want and need. You emphasize the importance of the questionnaire in terms of verifying interest and need. Finally, you stress that you have some speakers in mind who would require little if any funding. (For local speakers, the minimum support usually required is reimbursement for mileage to and from the presentation and provision of any meals needed during the period they allocate to your agency. An honorarium may also be given in appreciation of their time and effort. This may be of any amount.) In your conversation with the assistant director, you ask if any funding is available for expenses and honorariums for local speakers or to pay consultants or experts brought in from further afield.

Predictably, the assistant director emphasizes that local speakers would be better. You think she really means that local speakers would be cheaper. However, you do have some good local people in mind, so you are willing to go along with her wishes.

With the assistant director's okay, you copy the questionnaire and distribute it to staff. You complete this process as planned by February 6. You state the due date for returning the interest questionnaire as February 10. You realize that some staff will probably not return their questionnaire on time. As a matter of fact, since you have worked in the agency for quite a while, you can pretty much predict who will return their questionnaires as requested and who will drag their feet.

For example, consider Reid, whose desk and office are stuffed with stacks and stacks of papers gradually tipping over like crumbling skyscrapers and spilling onto the floor. Reid is renowned for losing anything one gives him. However, you have come to expect this and never give him original papers, only copies. When he inevitably loses them, you believe he must take responsibility for his actions so you usually proceed without his input if he doesn't get it to you within a reasonable period of time in this case, you decide, February 10.

To compensate for staff who fail to return questionnaires on time, you plan to talk briefly with some of the tardy types on February 10 and administer the brief questionnaire verbally. If enough staff express their interest by promptly returning questionnaires, those who do not respond will not matter that much.

By February 12 you contact the assistant director again to share the questionnaire results. During a phone conversation with her, you are able to report adequate support from staff, identify potential dates when administration would allow staff to attend, and pinpoint potential speakers. You clarify with the assistant director that staff will be encouraged to attend the in-service training during regular work hours, but will not be required to attend. You and the assistant director feel that getting some time off of their regular workload to participate in this activity will provide an adequate incentive.

It should be noted that when you first establish your project plan via a PERT chart, you assume that both administration and other staff will ultimately support your project. If at any point they don't, you can either halt the planning process and forget the whole idea or build in the necessary steps to overcome their resistance.

You anticipate a busy time between February 12 and 15. You must summarize the information gathered on the questionnaires and contact potential speakers. You have already established a series of possible in-service dates with the assistant director. You allow yourself an additional three days, from February 15 to 18, for potential speakers to check their schedules and get back to you. On February 18 you notify both your direct supervisor and the agency's assistant director of your finalized plans. The agency will sponsor the in-service on March 22. It is critically important not to do anything in developing such a project without notifying the administration regularly about where you are in the planning process. Although in this case you have already solicited administrative support, you still need to maintain it.

By February 20 you have made up simple fliers to alert staff to the in-service's speakers and dates. You choose hot pink paper for the fliers in order to get staff's attention. Finally, you circulate fliers to staff mailboxes by February 22. You breathe a sigh of relief until March 22 approaches. At that time your responsibilities will resume as you oversee the in-service itself, introduce the speakers, and generally trouble-shoot for any potential problems.

IMAGINE: Neutralize *Oppositions*

After implementation, the sixth step in the IMAGINE process is neutralizing any opposition. Here it means addressing any impediments that obstruct your project's progress. In the case of the in-service training program, opposition might assume the form of another agency supervisor complaining about the in-service as a waste of his staff's time. Or something unexpected might come up to interfere with the project. For example, your speaker might call you at 6:30 A.M. on the day of the in-service to tell you that she's got a horrible case of the flu and so can't make it. Whatever potential problems develop, it will be your creative job to figure out solutions.

Murphy's Law states that "anything that can go wrong, will go wrong" (*Webster's Ninth New Collegiate Dictionary*, 1991, p. 781). Corollaries to Murphy's Law include the following:

1. Nothing is as easy as it looks.
2. Everything takes longer than you think.
3. If there is a possibility of several things going wrong, the one that will cause the most damage will be the one to go wrong.
4. If you perceive that there are four possible ways in which a procedure can go wrong, and circumvent these, then a fifth way will promptly develop.
5. Left to themselves, things tend to go from bad to worse.
6. Whenever you set out to do something, something else must be done first.
7. Every solution breeds new problems.
8. It is impossible to make anything foolproof because fools are so ingenious.
9. Nature always sides with the hidden flaw. (Bloch, 1977, p. 11)

One more corollary might be added to this list: Murphy was an optimist.

The point here is not to become totally depressed, throw in the towel, and forget the whole idea, but rather acknowledge that situations, and the variables in any particular situation, change constantly. If this is the case in micro systems, it is certainly the case in large, complex macro systems. It's important to remember that specific plans like PERT charts are wonderful. However, you must also be wary of unexpected changes curtailing the best planned activities and causing projects to run amuck. Therefore, it's important to remember always to be vigilant and flexible. Plans can and often should be changed. You need to navigate your project through the entire implementation process, responding to new issues, needs, and problems as they arise.

Essentially, two major responsibilities characterize the neutralizing opposition step in the project implementation process. First, ongoing *coordination* is necessary to keep all participants involved in the implementation process working together and on schedules. The second responsibility involves regular *checking* that each designated activity sequence is completed in a timely and effective manner. Each completed step reflects progress toward the designated goal.

IMAGINE: Evaluate *Progress*

You should state project goals and objectives so clearly that it is readily apparent when each objective is met. When proposing objectives, keep in mind how they will be evaluated. Littlestone (1973) reflects, "If, from the outset, evaluation is considered concurrently with other planning steps, a rigor is introduced that will aid in testing the feasibility of each step in the planning process" (p. 13). In other words, establishing specific, easily measurable goals at the very beginning of the planning process will make measuring their attainment easier.

Program Development

The second macro intervention approach this chapter addresses is program development. Along with initiating agency policy changes and implementing projects, you may well have the opportunity to set a whole new program in motion in your agency.

We have established that a program is "an aggregate of actions directed toward accomplishing a single goal" (Rapp and Poertner, 1992). Social programs provide the means for generalist practitioners to offer help and services to clients. Program development is important when necessary social programs don't exist or when they are inadequate to meet clients' needs. Then you may determine that you need to pursue program development. Highlight 7.2 presents a series of examples illustrating why generalist practitioners need program development skills.

We propose a number of steps to follow in the program development process. We have arbitrarily designated their order. Sometimes in real practice you will not follow these steps in order. Your plan and process will depend on a wide range of variables from agency environments to administrative personalities to designated job descriptions. However, these eighteen steps reflect the issues and activities you should consider when trying to develop a program. The steps are grouped according to the IMAGINE paradigm.

A case example follows the explanation of the program development process. The example addresses the development of a sexual harassment awareness program in a large social service agency. This particular example of program development depicts only one of the many types of programs you might initiate within your own agency.

Application of the IMAGINE Process

*I*MAGINE: Develop an *Idea*

The first step in the IMAGINE paradigm for macro practice intervention involves developing an *idea*. You become aware of some deficit in available resources or some malfunction in service delivery. Two suggestions address this phase of the program development process. They include making certain you work with your client and clearly articulate your program goals.

WORK WITH YOUR CLIENT SYSTEM. Working with the client system means that you must work closely with those people who will be receiving the services provided by the new program. In macro practice it entails working with other professionals, organizations, and agencies that can help you initiate and implement the new program. Other individuals and systems can help provide you with information about clients' needs. They can also assist you in the program development process. Working with the client system means that you remain open to feedback and strive to be responsive to the needs of others involved in the process.

Suppose your intent is to develop a program for homeless people in an urban community. It is absolutely essential to involve homeless clients integrally in the program development process. What good would it be to enthusiastically expend a great deal of energy developing a plan you think would be good for them if it is not something they want or feel they need? Perhaps converting an old department store into a series of apartments would be an utter turn-off to potential clients. They might be more interested in refurbishing deserted homes owned by the city because of their prior owners' failure to pay taxes. In this case, the homeless people who would benefit by the program would need a way to purchase the homes and the resource assistance necessary for fixing them up if they do all the work. Some cities support urban homestead programs in which deserted homes are sold to people for $1 and materials for home refurbishment (paint, wood, and pipes) are provided. People purchasing the homes agree to fix them up to abide by city codes (concerning electric wiring, heating, and water standards), live in the homes for some specified period of time (at least two or three years), and eventually pay back the city for the repair materials the city provided.

ARTICULATE THE PROPOSED PROGRAM'S PURPOSE. The purpose (or primary goal) of the proposed program must be very clear in your own mind. You must be able to articulate it clearly and straightfor-

WHY PROGRAM DEVELOPMENT IS RELEVANT TO YOU

Below are three vignettes illustrating how direct service workers can run into dilemmas that block them from providing needed services. What would you do if you, as a professional generalist practitioner, ran into similar glitches? Each dilemma could be solved through undertaking program development.

Dilemma A

You are a social worker in a Veteran's Administration (VA) Hospital in East Los Angeles. The VA, a federal organization established in 1920, provides people who have served in the military with a wide range of services to enhance their overall health and welfare; services include those directed at physical and mental illness, vocational training, financial assistance, and a host of others (Barker, 1991, p. 247). Specifically, you work in a unit that provides short-term housing and alcohol- and other drug-abuse (AODA) treatment for homeless veterans. You're finding that more and more of your clients come to you and tell you they simply can't find any full-time jobs, even for minimum wage. You find yourself thinking more and more frequently, "Even a full-time minimum wage job is pretty much a bummer in terms of taking care of yourself."

The issue, you believe, boils down to adequate job training. Why can't the VA provide educational and vocational training, or finance its purchase through some other agency? You have looked for resources to help your clients get back on their feet. They need work that is relatively permanent, provides an adequate standard of living, and enhances their self-esteem. What you and your clients really need is a job training program with a strong educational component. But there isn't one. Now what?

Dilemma B

You are an intake worker for the Sheboygan County Department of Social Services. The county is primarily rural with a smattering of small towns. You job is primarily to receive calls from people requesting services, gather initial information about them and their problems, provide them with some information about your county services, and make appropriate referrals to the agencies they need.

You are alarmed at the growing number of calls about elderly people having difficulty maintaining themselves in their own homes. Most calls come from neighbors or relatives, and some from elderly people themselves. Examples of concerns include: worries about falling and remaining stranded for days; forgetfulness such as leaving the stove's gas burner on; lack of transportation to get to important—for example, doctors'—appointments; difficulties in understanding complicated health insurance and Medicare reimbursements; and depression due to loneliness and isolation.

You typically refer such callers to the department's Protective Services for the Elderly unit. However, you know that all that unit can do is make an assessment home visit and either refer to a local nursing home or terminate the case. That's depressing. Many of those people only need company and supportive help to maintain their independent living conditions.

You have heard of programs providing such support elsewhere in the state. It would be great to have a program whose staff could visit similar clients, help them with daily tasks, transport them to recreational activities, and generally provide friendly support. Such programs would help these elderly people and

(continued)

HIGHLIGHT 7.2—(Continued)

---

allow them to remain in their own homes. There is no such program in your county. Is there anything you can do to initiate one?

Dilemma C

You are a school social worker in large, urban Warshawski High School. The pregnancy rate is soaring. Twenty-one percent of all female students become pregnant by the time they graduate (or would have graduated, since many drop out because of pregnancy). A Planned Parenthood agency two miles away provides counseling about reproductive choices, contraception, and related health services such as pregnancy tests and physical examinations in preparation for using contraception. However, not many students are using its services.

The school requires all students to participate in a Family Life Education program (except for those students whose parents withhold permission). This program includes some content on human sexuality, including basic "plumbing" information (who has what sexual parts and what those sexual parts are called). This involves details about fallopian tubes and epididymises. There is also content on sexually transmitted diseases that espe-

cially emphasizes HIV (human immunodeficiency virus) transmission and the prevention of AIDS (Acquired Immune Deficiency Syndrome). Other content stresses abstinence, focusing on the "Just Say NO!" approach to avoiding pregnancy. Both the school board and the school administration strongly forbid the discussion of contraception. They have openly stated that such content only encourages promiscuity by giving students permission for sexual experimentation.

You feel strongly that students need additional accurate information on sexual issues, such as contraception and emotional relationships. They also require ready access both to contraceptives and to counseling on contraceptive use. Students are not getting this and, thus, suffer the consequences. You are aware of the research establishing that such programs have significantly decreased pregnancy rates and the transmission of sexually related diseases in other high schools in similar settings. What can you do?

Each dilemma represents the type of predicament that may well face you in practice. You may find yourself in a social work position with a fairly clear *job description*. Job descriptions are just that. They describe the specific tasks and responsibilities

---

wardly to others in order to solicit support (Hasenfeld, 1987). A program's mission has three facets. First, clearly define and document the unmet client needs.

For example, you might be a social worker for a county department of social services. You job involves helping clients who receive financial assistance under the Aid to Families with Dependent Children (AFDC) program.[2] You provide counseling and assist these women in their job searches. You discover that most

of your clients, primarily single mothers with one to four children, have tremendous difficulty finding reasonably priced and satisfactory day-care facilities to care for children while mothers work. In order to develop either a day-care program or a referral program for day-care facilities, you would need to document clearly the need for such a program by performing a needs assessment. Needs assessments are "systematic appraisals made by social workers and other professionals in evaluating their clients' problems, existing resources, potential solutions, and obstacles to problem solving" (Barker, 1995, p. 251). You might develop a questionnaire for public assistance recipients examining their day-care needs. Or you might consult the state licensing agency that licenses day-care facilities to find out how many

---

2. AFDC is a public assistance program established by the Social Security Act of 1935. Specifically, federal and state funding "provide financial aid for needy children who are deprived of parental support because of death, incapacity, or absence" (Barker, 1991, p. 8). Eligibility is based on the individual family's need for resources.

you will be held accountable for while performing your job. Some job descriptions also include educational and certification requirements or types of experience required in order to get the job to begin with and continue to hold it. Generally, job descriptions summarize the tasks you get paid for doing. However, in the dilemmas, the workers found that what their clients sorely needed was not available. There were gaps in the service delivery system. That is, significant numbers of people had needs that, to the worker's knowledge, no agency or program was addressing.

It was not really in any of the workers' job descriptions to do anything about these problematic client situations. However, each worker was forced to face each problem with increasing frequency. These problems, through no fault of the workers, were seriously impeding their ability to serve clients effectively.

We have established that one of the many reasons that macro practice is important for generalist practitioners is that many times "The System," whichever one it may be, is not doing the right thing. Usually, either the system is not serving clients the way it is supposed to (consider our earlier discussion of goal displacement), or, as in the above dilemmas, the services clients need simply do not exist. Hence, we address the concept of *program development*. A program needs to be developed in order to meet clients' needs.

There will be times in a worker's career when resources desperately needed by clients will not exist. At these times, workers must determine whether it is possible, practical, and worth their effort to pursue the development of some new program. Often, workers will not be alone. There will be others—clients, administrators, colleagues, and persons in other agencies—who also support the establishment of badly needed services. Most frequently, workers' job descriptions, established by others working in "The System," will not include anything about changing the system. This includes the development of new, needed services.

It is essential to remember that you as a worker derive your sanction for macro action within agencies and communities from your professional obligations to clients. This is a basic requirement of the social work profession as espoused in the Code of Ethics. In essence, you as a social worker have a professional obligation that transcends your job description. Professional social workers are not plumbers doing a technician's job. The Code emphasizes that your primary responsibility is to your clients. That places upon you the obligation to pursue changes even if the agency doesn't initially sanction them. You may give up eventually because the barriers are too great. However, you cannot ignore your professional responsibility. What information do you need? What variables must you consider? What skills do you require? Finally, how do you start the process?

facilities and what kind are available in your area. You could call each facility and get information about costs, hours, and whether they care for infants or not.[3] If you can establish on paper with real facts and statistics that the demand for day care significantly outweighs that which is available, then you have strengthened your argument for program development. Your argument would be further enhanced if you could establish that providing day care would save money. In essence, enabling mothers to work by providing access to day care might ultimately be cheaper than the prior level of public

assistance. This might be true even if the county supplemented the mothers' day-care costs.

The second aspect of a program's mission that requires articulation involves the clientele who will receive services. Exactly whom will the program serve? In the day-care program example, clients would include women receiving public assistance and their children. Essentially, anyone who applied and was accepted to receive assistance could potentially apply for a job and, ultimately, use the day-care services. Such participants would be included in the designated client population.

A third aspect of any potential program that needs articulation concerns the services the program would provide. In other words, clearly state the purpose of the program so that everyone involved understands what the

---

3. Many daycare facilities do not accept infants and children who are not toilet-trained because of the additional care and attention such children demand.

The first step in the IMAGINE process is to develop an idea. The social worker might see the need for a community shelter so that persons such as this homeless man do not need to sleep in the street.

proposed program would do. Continuing with the day-care example, such a program might include provision of day-care services by qualified providers. The plan might require potential day-care providers to undergo some type of screening process before being hired. Daily day-care services might be located at a centralized location in the community and be open from 6:00 A.M. to 6:00 P.M. every day except Sunday. The agency might accept children of any age, including infants.

IMAGINE: *Muster* Support

Phase two of IMAGINE is mustering support from others to help you through the program development process. It is difficult, if not impossible, to initiate and establish a new program or service completely by yourself. You need support from a variety of other sources (Hasenfeld, 1987). As the change catalyst you can solicit a steady source of support by establishing your action system. Such a group "then gathers resources and influence, actively representing the new program's objec-

tives, and fights for its support in the community" (Hasenfeld, 1987, p. 455). Additionally, a group forming an action system can help you: identify and articulate the primary goals for the proposed program; specify the client systems that will receive services; target potential financial resources for the programs; and share information about the program and its goals with other groups, agencies, and organizations within the community such as city council, county government, mental health board, United Fund (Hasenfeld, 1987, p. 456).

Choose action group members very carefully. Chapter 3 on using mezzo skills in the macro environment examined task groups and their membership. You want motivated individuals who are seriously interested in the proposed program. You might also solicit support by including influential community professionals, religious leaders, and businesspeople. They can provide the credibility you will need to succeed. Community members likely consider such prestigious people important and will listen to their views. Therefore, influential community leaders' support lends the program greater credibility.

HIGHLIGHT 7.3

ETHICAL QUESTIONS ABOUT DAY CARE AND THE OPPRESSION OF WOMEN: FOOD FOR THOUGHT

The example chosen here to illustrate the need to articulate a program's purpose when initiating program development is that of providing day care for children of women receiving public assistance. Superficially, this may appear to be a straightforward, basically simple idea. However, when considering any kind of program development, a worker must think about the many possible implications the program could have for clients. A number of questions surround the provision of day care in the situation described including the following:

1. *To what extent would provision of day care as described force women to work outside the home when they feel their rightful place is at home with their children?*
2. *How ethical is it to strongly encourage or force single mothers to work outside the home when they can earn only a meager, inadequate income*

anyway? Single mothers may have little or no technical or professional training. Therefore, any work they get will likely pay very low wages. Taking all women into account, women today earn about 70 percent of what men earn (Renzetti & Curran, 1992). This income disparity is partly due to the fact that women are clustered in relatively low paying occupations such as secretary and office support staff, compared to men who are more likely to assume higher paying jobs such as those in skilled trades (carpenters or electricians) (Renzetti & Curran, 1992).

3. *To what extent is it fair to make single mothers work outside the home in addition to assuming all responsibilities for both household and care of their children? Is it fair to force women to do both jobs when the same pressures do not generally apply to men?*

Finally, you might select action group members for their specific areas of expertise. For example, a certified alcohol- and drug-abuse counselor could provide valuable input as to how a drug rehabilitation program should be structured. Likewise, a lawyer whose practice targets juveniles or a police officer knowledgeable about youth could contribute relevant information regarding the legal aspects of working with juvenile drug abusers.

From members of this action group you might establish a more formalized "board of directors, . . . advisory council, or . . . an internal task force within an existing agency" (Hasenfeld, 1987, p. 457). A board of directors is "a group of people empowered to establish an organization's objectives and policies and to oversee the activities of the personnel responsible for day-to-day implementation of those polices. Social agency boards of directors are often made up of volunteers who are influential in the community and reflect

the views prevalent in the community" (Barker, 1987, p. 17). Such a formalized group can lend support, credibility, and community influences.

ALLOCATE RESPONSIBILITES TO A DESIGNATED TASK GROUP OR ADVISORY COUNCIL. Much earlier in the macro change process, as you were deciding whether to pursue such change or not, you identified relevant people of influence. Such people may be very useful in helping you achieve your macro change goals. It is helpful to allocate responsibilities to a designated task group or advisory council (Hasenfeld, 1987). You can solicit such a group's help by asking them to discuss issues, make plans, and prepare objectives. Chapter 3 discusses task groups in detail.

Avisory councils or advisory boards are committees that provide "needed information, expert opinion, and recommendations about how to acheive an organiza-

These children are attending a Head Start program in Chicago's Robert Taylor homes. Operation Head Start was once an idea. Today it is a nationally recognized preschool program.

tion's goals'' (Barker, 1991, p. 7). Such an advisory group functions much like a task group.

IMAGINE: Identify *Assets*

IMAGINE's third step is identifying your assets. What variables will aid you in the program development process? Consider three issues: preparing the agency for change, conducting a feasibility study, and soliciting necessary financial resources.

PREPARE THE AGENCY FOR CHANGE. Before actively pursuing program development, you must prepare the agency for the change process; Brager and Holloway (1983, p. 200) call this preparation *preinitiation*. Preinitiation includes three major tasks, all of which increase some change component in your favor.

First, you must enhance the *assets* in favor of the change. Earlier in this chapter we discussed formulating your action system. Now identify who in the agency would be most useful in helping you make the change. Who is in your target system? Explore the informal communication network. Whom do you trust and respect in the agency, regardless of formal position? With whom do these people associate? Can you expand your support network indirectly through them? Whom does the executive director or top administrator trust? Might there be ways to influence the people at the top through others lower in the hierarchy whom the top people trust?

The second variable in preinitiation is enhancing your own *''legitimacy''* (Brager & Holloway, 1983, p. 202). What personal and professional power can you muster? Often you can increase your expertise regarding the proposed program. Ask yourself what would augment your position with administrators. What facts about the program and how it meets client needs might influence the target system in your favor?

The third variable in preinitiation is increasing the *stress level* related to need for program development. Brager and Holloway (1983) explain that another task at this point is influencing ''prochange and restraining forces so as to induce or magnify stress relating to the particular problem area'' (p. 203). They continue, ''Unfortunately for change efforts, human service workers tend to perceive their function to be stress reduction. But change is unlikely to occur unless discomforting tension accompanies an attempt to change the status quo.''

One useful method of escalating stress is by pointing out to others in the agency how the discrepancy between what the agency is doing (current policy or practice) and what it should be doing (proposed program) is significant and intolerable. This reinforces the argument in favor of the proposed program.

Note, however, that increasing stress levels puts you at risk of being associated with that stress. Some of the stress's negativity may rub off on you. You are best off when you can position yourself as a concerned advocate for the agency instead of as an irritating complainer. Here, again, it is probably helpful to seek support and corroboration from other individuals and groups in the agency. When you are grouped with others on an issue, it is more difficult for opponents to single you out and point the finger of blame in your direction. Any blame or negativity becomes more dispersed and diffuse.

CONSIDER IMPLEMENTING A FEASIBILITY STUDY. To help identify your assets, consider implementing a feasibility study (Hasenfeld, 1987). A feasibility study is a systematic evaluation of the resources necessary to achieve your program development goals (Barker, 1987). In other words, you can explore how realistic your hopes of success are in developing this new program. How much will staffing and facilities cost? What kinds of backing can you expect from the community housing the program and from other community agencies?

What other types of resources might be available? Hasenfeld suggests five potential sources: grants, assistance from local government, private donations by individuals and agencies, services and goods donated by other agencies, and volunteers.

One especially beneficial resource for many agencies is the United Way. This agency is "the national federation of local organizations established to systematize and coordinate voluntary fundraising efforts. The money raised through the United Way is used to fund social agencies, nonprofit human services organizations, and some health, education, and recreation programs in local communities" (Barker, 1987, p. 169).

The main point is that you need to determine whether you have enough resources to continue with your program development plan. If you can't possibly afford to implement the program, you might as well halt the process right here.

SOLICIT THE FINANCIAL RESOURCES YOU NEED TO INITIATE THE PROGRAM. You should already have identified possible funding sources. Now you need to transform the *potential* funding sources into *actual* funding sources (Hasenfeld, 1987). Where will your financial support actually come from? Who will make definite commitments to give you needed resources? In this process you must convince people controlling targeted resources that your proposed program merits their attention, support, and whatever money you need. You may also want to instigate a fundraising crusade, a macro technique discussed more extensively in chapter 14.

IMAGINE: Specify *Goals* and Objectives

The fourth step in the IMAGINE process is formulating clear action steps or objectives leading to your priori-

tized goals. You identified specific problems during the initial phase of the macro intervention process. At this point you are proceeding to develop a program. A significant number of your agency's clients are homeless or are not getting access to the health care they need. Your intent is to designate the order in which you'll address your specified problems. Your proposed program will begin to take shape according to the problems you determine are most important to solve.

We have consistently emphasized that goals and objectives must be very clear. This applies to agency policy change, project implementation, and program development. It also applies to macro, mezzo, or micro levels of intervention. Goals in macro practice should be just as clear and measurable as in any other type of intervention. Specifying the performance expected, the conditions under which that performance is to occur, and the standards by which success is measured is just as necessary in macro practice as in micro practice.

Consider a possible objective in developing a program for adolescent drug abusers—to provide an inpatient, six-week treatment program (performance) for all identified drug-abusing teens in a specified geographic area (conditions) aimed at having at least 90 percent of clients remain drug-free for six months after leaving the program (standards). Inpatient programs, by the way, are those that require clients in treatment to live in the facility day and night.

Such a goal would also require its own action steps or objectives for successful completion. What steps would need to be followed to develop this program? *Who* would need to do *what* by *when*? Macro practice, of course, involves more individuals and groups—in addition to agencies, policies, and organizations—than does micro practice. Therefore, you might anticipate needing more action steps than you would, for example, when working with a single individual. Action steps for achieving macro change can require the cooperation of any number of individuals and groups before primary goals can be accomplished.

CONSIDER DEVELOPING A PERT CHART. As we discussed earlier, a PERT (Program Evaluation Review Technique) is a tool for plotting your intervention plan in a linear manner. PERT charts designate what participants are responsible for completing what tasks. They also specify time frames. In undertaking a project, a PERT chart allows you to view the entire program development process from beginning to end. It also allows you to see how various phases of the process fit together. Remember that in a macro situation a PERT chart may include a number of simultaneous activities, each with its own PERT timeline. The line development is coordinated with common reference points. In other words, the chart illustrates multiple activities and the time frames for each. (Such a chart is illustrated in figure 7.4 at the end of this chapter.)

DESCRIBE HOW THE PROGRAM WILL PROVIDE SERVICES. Before implementing the program, you must describe clearly how the program will actually provide services (Hasenfeld, 1987). How will the program work in its day-to-day functioning? Suppose you initiate a drug rehabilitation program. What types of treatment techniques will the drug rehabilitation counselors be expected to use? What kind of training do they require? Will there be an outpatient program in addition to the inpatient one? An outpatient treatment program offers clients "treatment at a health care facility without being admitted for overnight stays or assigned a bed for continuous care" (Barker, 1987, p. 113). How will the inpatient units be run? What type of treatment will clients have (group counseling, individual counseling, or job-seeking assistance)?

It is important to specify details that describe how the program will be run. What specific kinds of services will the program deliver to clients? Exactly how will the program achieve its specified objectives?

IMAG*INE: Implement* the Plan

IMAGINE's fifth step is the actual implementation of the plan. You present the macro change goal to the agency, a process called *initiation* (Brager & Holloway, 1983). At this point it is best to have as much influence as possible, which includes any assets favoring change such as your own professional legitimacy and the existence of increased stress levels that convince decision-makers to pursue new solutions. You must carefully consider the identified target system's receptiveness to your idea. It is helpful to play out possible scenarios in your mind. Try to anticipate how the target system will react to your proposal. How might the proposal best be introduced to maximize its potential acceptance?

Ask yourself three questions about how to influence

others who can provide support (Brager & Holloway, 1983). First, who should hear the initial proposal? What individual or group within the agency would be the most supportive and influential? It might be the top administrator, but it might not. It might be an individual or group of individuals lower in the administrative hierarchy. Perhaps you can target persons who are potentially more supportive of your idea than the top administrator. You then can find out how much influence these others have with the top administrator (or other ultimate decision-maker).

The more support you can muster for your idea, the greater your potential for success. Support from a broad and varied base (such as a number of disciplines or supervisory units) carries more weight than a narrow, homogeneous base (only one social worker or one small social service unit).

The second question is, who should present the proposal? We have discussed the importance of professional credibility. If at all possible, this individual should have strong influence with those hearing the proposal. Sometimes it is best to introduce the proposal as a member of a group. Other times, an especially credible, well-respected individual can be designated to present the idea. When appropriate, this may be you.

The third question is, how can you best present facts, issues, and goals to the target system? How can information about the proposed program be presented most positively to decision-makers? Try to frame the proposed program to reflect or conform to various aspects of the decision-makers' value system. For example, if you talk to a decision-maker who feels agency accountability is a top priority, it is in your best interest to emphasize that your proposed program enhances accountability.

GET THE PROGRAM GOING. After initiation, getting the program off the ground involves an *implementation* phase, the period between the agency's acceptance of the program development plan and the plan's actual operation (Brager, & Holloway, 1983). During the implementation period or in the early days of running the program, you may need to focus on nurturing participating staff's support, considering a trial run, starting out small, and formalizing necessary contracts.

NURTURE PARTICIPATING STAFF'S SUPPORT. The first matter to consider during implementation is the participating staff's support. You must encourage, gain, and maintain support from the employees who actually carry out the intervention (Brager & Holloway, 1983). You might anticipate some hesitation and resistance on their part. All involved in implementation must understand why the proposed program is important. Strive to answer their questions, continue to seek their support, and thank them for their efforts. Continuously monitor any changes to make certain workers remain on track.

Sometimes the agency must hire new staff who have the necessary credentials. These staff also need to fully understand how the program is structured and operated. Explain all procedures as clearly as possible. Using a PERT chart can help, but make sure all involved staff understand it.

HOW ABOUT A TRIAL RUN? One possibility to consider when developing and beginning a new program is a trial run (Hasenfeld, 1987). Instead of plunging full speed ahead, try out the program with a few clients for a brief period of time to identify any flaws. Such flaws can be addressed and remedied more easily when programs start up. At this point, you have not established any precedents. It is very important that the new program be responsive to needed changes and improvements.

CONSIDER STARTING OUT SMALL. Rothman, Erlich, and Teresa (1981) emphasize that "the likelihood that an innovation will be adopted by a larger population is increased if the innovation is first utilized by a small group of opinion leaders. This small initiating group may be characterized as style setters, information disseminators, key communicators, spark plugs, or gatekeepers, among other descriptions" (p. 22). They suggest that your chances of having a program implemented significantly increase if you first try out one part of the proposed program or use a limited number of clients to create a test case. This way you can showcase your innovation at lower cost and with much less risk. You also have an opportunity to demonstrate your idea's effectiveness before its total application as a program plan.

FORMALIZE ANY CONTRACTS THAT MIGHT BE NEEDED. Contracts can be useful in program development on a variety of levels. Contracts can be used to solidify the agreements made in action groups or on a board of directors.

Purchase of service contracts described earlier might be established with other agencies to provide services your program cannot offer. For instance, your agency might contract with another agency to provide vocational rehabilitation counseling, instead of trying to provide it. Your program might employ contracts with food suppliers and professional laundry facilities to take care of inpatient clients' daily needs.

IMAGINE: *Neutralize* Opposition

We have established that you must be wary of potential opposition throughout your change process. Two suggestions can assist this phase of the program development process: anticipation of a "honeymoon period" and the maintenance of ongoing administrative support.

ANTICIPATE A "HONEYMOON PERIOD." A "honeymoon period" often occurs when a new program starts out (Brager & Holloway, 1983, p. 206). This period is often marked by high levels of enthusiasm and interest on the part of involved staff. Theoretically, as on a real honeymoon, life appears full of roses. Problems seem nonexistent.

However, after some time has passed, unanticipated problems may occur. This makes sense. You must begin implementing a new idea before you can possibly discover all the potential snags. Only after clear identification can you begin to work out the inevitable real-life problems. At any rate, staff interest and enthusiasm may wane as working on the new program becomes more humdrum. You can revitalize the program development process by giving it your continued attention and emphasizing the gains staff have made.

MAINTAIN ADMINISTRATIVE SUPPORT. Another relevant element in getting a new program going is maintaining the continued interest of the crucial decision-makers (Brager & Holloway, 1983). Sometimes these people are part of the original target system. Other times the target system changes over time as the action system implements its plan. Regardless, it is important for you to monitor whoever has responsibility for the program's ongoing existence and success. Once the initial excitement wears off, it is easy to be distracted by other new ideas, problems, or pressing agency needs. Providing decision-makers with regular progress reports regarding accomplishments made and goals attained can solicit and maintain their interest and support.

IMAGINE: *Evaluate* Progress and Effectiveness

As with any other type of generalist intervention, evaluation of your progress is critical. For program development this means monitoring daily progress, assessing the overall program's effectiveness, and establishing ongoing program services.

MONITOR DAILY ACTIVITIES AND EVALUATE PROGRAM IMPACT. A bottom line for any program is that it has to work. Services provided must be effective and efficient if the program is to become a viable part of agency service provision. Two concepts are particularly important concerning evaluation programs; *monitoring* is the day-to-day observance of the agency's performance and *impact analysis* is the evaluation of the program's effectiveness (Rubin & Rubin, 1992, p. 411).

MONITORING YOUR PROGRAM. Monitoring daily program functioning involves appraising how efficiently services are provided and learning how effectively clients are being served. *How* services are delivered to clients is just as important as *what* services are delivered. Clients should be able to depend on a service being provided in a timely, predictable fashion. Scheduling appointments and meetings should be done according to clearly defined procedures. Many questions need addressing. Is the target client population actually benefiting from the services? Do clients have ready access to what they need? Are the services provided the ones that clients want and need?

Monitoring also concerns checking the staff's work. Are personnel able to fulfill their job responsibilities adequately? Are they prioritizing and completing the most critical tasks before attending to minor details? Staff should have straightforward, accurate job descriptions. They should all know exactly what tasks they are responsible for. Finally, billing (if needed) should be organized and predictable.

Monitoring also involves evaluating the program's costs and benefits (Rubin & Rubin, 1992). Are the benefits sufficient to justify the costs?

Rubin & Rubin (1992) make one other important point concerning program monitoring. The evaluator should distinguish between *effort* (that "measure the energy or money spent by the organization to accomplish its goals") and *outcomes* (that "measures the changes brought about by the program") (p. 412). Earlier we talked about goal displacement, that is, when maintaining procedures becomes more important than helping clients. Often in large bureaucracies, keeping records and obeying rules become paramount. A lot of effort can be expended to maintain procedures. However, the actual outcomes in terms of getting clients what they need can take a back seat. Intervention effectiveness can even be totally disregarded. Rubin and Rubin (1992) stress that it is important to measure both effort and outcomes in order to get a clear picture of agency functioning.

IMPACT ANALYSIS. *Impact analysis* evaluates a program's outcomes. There are at least two types of measures in impact analysis (Rubin & Rubin, 1992). First, some outcomes are factual and can be readily observed. For example, you can count the number of homeless people placed in temporary shelter care. You can also count the monetary benefits indigent clients receive. The second kind of outcome is reflected in "reports of personal satisfaction" on the part of clients (p. 412). You can develop and administer a questionnaire to clients to solicit their feelings and opinions about the program's effectiveness.

ESTABLISH HOW SERVICES WILL BE PROVIDED ON AN ONGOING BASIS. The final step in IMAGINE's implementation phase establishes how services will be provided on an ongoing basis (Hasenfeld, 1987). *Institutionalization* (or stabilization of change) is the cementing of the change into the structure of the system, a process that involves two major tasks (Brager & Holloway, 1983, p. 207). First, clearly specify and record standardized procedure for continued implementation of the change. Ideally, these should become part of the ongoing agency policies and procedures manual. Second, link the new program as much as possible with other units and aspects of the organization. This is important so that the unit does not become an isolated entity. Isolated programs are easily hacked off. They have fewer supporters when decisions are being made about agency priorities. Having more agency units support and rely on the services broadens the base of the service's support. Likewise, any decision-makers trying to delete the services will run into stronger resistance.

Program Development: A Case Example

Programs can involve almost any type of service or event. Examples include programs to help crack abusers, survivors of sexual abuse, single parents, HIV positive children, homeless people, or elderly people residing in their own homes. It is impossible to give you a formula for developing a specific program for a designated agency setting. There are just too many variables, and the possibilities are literally infinite. Therefore, this chapter intends to present general guidelines you can follow and modify as needed in your program development. To illustrate program development, we will examine the development of a sexual harassment awareness program in a large public agency with special emphasis on the application of a PERT chart to facilitate the program development process.

IMAGINE: Develop an Innovative Idea

Sexual harassment has become an increasingly significant national issue. Lawsuits and publicity have raised public consciousness and escalated administrators' fears of legal liability, because administrators can be held legally responsible for inappropriate treatment of staff in their own agencies.

We will examine the development of a sexual harassment awareness program in the Ogalala County Department of Social Services. The change catalyst in our example is Cindy Cepsowicz, the supervisor of the agency's foster care unit. She has always been a strong proponent of women's right and is increasingly conscious of the sexual remarks and gestures she sees being made around the agency. She feels that there is a strong need to educate personnel regarding sexual harassment and to provide a means to help staff who are victims. She formulates the goal of establishing a sexual harassment awareness program.

In this particular example, the potential client system includes the agency staff instead of the agency's clients. This is an internal agency issue which needs to

be addressed so that staff can function more effectively on the behalf of their clients. Staff also need to develop their sensitivity to sexual harassment so they will treat each other and their clients appropriately.

IMAGINE: Muster *Support*

As the change catalyst, Cindy talks to other colleagues who she thinks have similar concerns and verifies that indeed they do. The colleagues she identifies for the initial action system include two of her supervisees, two other unit supervisors, a direct service worker from another unit, and the agency's personnel director. Each person in the action system is committed to the idea that sexual harassment is a serious problem that needs to be addressed within the agency environment. Each action system member is also willing to work on developing a plan of action and to address the issue with administration. The action system forms a task group.

IMAGINE: Identify Assets

Cindy, with her assertive leadership ability, organizational skills, and attention to detail, becomes the natural leader of the action system. Their first step is the development of a clearly defined rationale for developing a sexual harassment awareness program.

Cindy has already identified other staff members as strong proponents of her idea. Support from staff is a major asset in the implementation of her plan. By integrating supportive people into an action system, she has enhanced her own legitimacy. This strengthens her position it is important for the agency to address the issue.

Another means of increasing Cindy's legitimacy is by strengthening her program development proposal with facts and specific suggestions. Cindy first educates herself about sexual harassment and the types of behavior it commonly involves. She researches recent court decisions in sexual harassment cases to clarify the issues facing her agency. She constructs a strong rationale to convince administrators to implement a program.

Developing a strong argument for Cindy's case can escalate administrative stress levels. Administrators must understand their responsibilities in the maintenance of a sexual-harassment-free working environment. Worrying about legal problems they may face if they do not establish a program can cause administrators stress. This demonstrates that escalating stress can motivate decision-makers to do something (in this case, develop a program) to alleviate the stress.

Cindy decides that no feasibility study is necessary. She feels her support and rationale for program development are strong enough to merit administrative attention. Her proposal for program development calls for some staff time, office space, and supplies. She feels the agency is large enough that these resources can be assigned to her proposed program with relatively minor shifting of internal funds. Cindy's specific plans are explained more thoroughly in the following section on goal development.

IMAGINE: Specify Goals and Objectives

The action group decides that the best plan is for Cindy and the personnel director to meet with the agency director. The agency director, who is ultimately responsible for all agency business, becomes the target system. She is the decision-maker whose support is necessary to get the program off the ground. She also happens to be a personal friend of the personnel director. This personal influence can only help Cindy's cause.

The three meet. The agency director is impressed with Cindy's organization and preparation. She gives the okay to establish a part time position and initiate the program. The primary program goals are twofold. First, the program's coordinator will provide education to staff concerning sexual harassment issues. Second, the coordinator will advocate for victims. She will be available to address problems informally, thereby defusing potentially explosive situations.

Cindy and her action system develop an extensive plan for the program's development. They recruit within the agency for the part-time coordinator and establish a PERT chart to direct and monitor program development.

It might be noted that Cindy herself chooses not to apply to be the program's coordinator. Although she firmly believes in the cause and the program, she feels her own job keeps her more than busy enough. She is happy with her role of getting the program off the ground and letting the new coordinator take over from there.

Establishing a Sexual Harassment Awareness Program for Employees (SHAPE)

We have established that PERT charts are useful goal-setting and monitoring tools for anything from planning a surprise birthday party to setting up an in-service training program (described earlier in this chapter) to developing a whole new program. Shown here is a PERT chart for establishing a Sexual Harassment Awareness Program for Employees (SHAPE) within Cindy's large bureaucracy.

The primary emphasis is on the establishment of a PERT chart to assist in the program's implementation. However, in order to understand the importance of various program goals, you need to understand the issues involved. Therefore, prior to describing the goals themselves, the definition of sexual harassment, its frequency, and its legal foundation are discussed in highlight 7.4. The program itself is discussed in detail. A similar program could be implemented in any of a variety of other organizational settings.

Description of SHAPE

SHAPE aims to educate staff about sexual harassment issues and to provide informal mediation when complaints arise. In order to understand the intricacies delineated on the PERT chart, we will explore the proposed program and its goals in some depth. This will also provide you with a potential model for initiating and developing a similar program in your own agency.

SHAPE provides a viable alternative to confronting sexual harassment in a large organizational setting. By supplementing the existing formal complaint procedure (a vehicle to address any kind of complaint, including those involving sexual harassment), SHAPE offers an informal means of both preventing sexual harassment and of stopping it in a nonpunitive manner. Specific educational strategies targeting various units of the organization and the outside communities are utilized. Specific alternatives for victim advocacy and informal mediation are defined and actively pursued.

Federal legislation supports SHAPE and its goals. For the purposes of this scenario, we assume that state law provides strong support. We have already established that the agency's director supports development of SHAPE. Within this context SHAPE prescribes a

HIGHLIGHT 7.4

WHAT IS SEXUAL HARASSMENT?

Consider the following vignettes:

A young social worker just started in her first professional position. She feels this is an ideal job for her. She's working with a client population she enjoys and she's located in a choice geographical area. Her new male supervisor is constantly putting his arm around her and touching her. It might be his way of showing his supportiveness, but the other day during a supervisory session, he places his hand on her knee. On the one hand, she does not like him very much personally, and abhors his behavior. On the other hand, she feels she has no choice but to grin and bear it. This job means a lot to her.

A male social worker needs his supervisor's support for case consultation, salary increments, and fair delegation of job responsibilities. His female supervisor has made several sexual advances to him and has invited him over to her home several times. She has implied that if he doesn't start responding to her, he will not be happy in his job for very long. In passing, she mentioned the possibility of placing him on emergency call every weekend.

A male administrator holds monthly organizational meetings requiring all staff to attend. He often makes comments about how the ''girls,'' meaning his female practitioners, will probably have difficulty being assertive enough with their more aggressive clients. Several times he has initiated the monthly meeting by asking some of the younger, more attractive female workers to sit in the front so he can ''appreciate the view.'' He is noticeably more likely to address questions and issues raised by his male workers than those raised by his female workers.

The preceding vignettes illustrate incidents of sexual harassment, a serious form of sex discrimina-tion that has gained considerable public attention. Not limited to business and industry, it also affects social service organizations and bureaucracies. One recent study surveyed half the members of the National Association of Social Workers' Iowa chapter and found that over one quarter of the respondents had experienced sexual harassment at work (Maypole, 1986).

Sexual harassment is illegal. Title VII of the Civil Rights Act of 1964 covers discrimination on the basis of sex along with discrimination on the basis of race. Legal precedents have been established to include sexual harassment as a form of sex discrimination (Maypole, 1986). Title IX of the Higher Education Amendments of 1972 prohibit sex discrimination from taking place specifically on university campuses. Individual state laws also prohibit sexual harassment and provide legal recourse to victims.[a] Finally, agency policies may prohibit sexual harassment and provide procedures for victims to file complaints or grievances.[b] The major publicity and public fascination that accompanied the Clarence Thomas and Anita Hill ordeal in the early 1990s emphasized the issue's significance.

Sexual harassment includes unwelcome sexual advances, requests for sexual favors, and other verbal or physical conduct of a sexual nature under the following conditions: submission to such conduct is required as a condition of employment or education; submission to such conduct is used as a basis for decisions that affect an individual's employment or academic achievement; such conduct creates a hostile, intimidating, or anxiety-producing work or educational environment.[c]

In sexual harassment, there is always an element of unequal power and coercion. Sometimes a victim is promised a reward for sexual cooperation. For instance, sexual harassment occurs when a female direct services worker, seeking promotion to supervisor, is

(continued)

HIGHLIGHT 7.4—(Continued)

pressured to endure physical touching and kissing by her male agency director to maintain a good relationship and receive a positive promotion decision. Other times punishment may be threatened. A female worker may be pressured to submit sexually to her male supervisor in response to threats that resistance could result in her dismissal as part of a cost reduction plan. At other times, sexual harassment consists in the perpetrator becoming overly and inappropriately personal with the victim, either by sharing intimacies or by prying into the victim's personal life. A supervisor can overstep the boundaries of his role by questioning a supervisee about his or her love life.

Sexual harassment can victimize both males and females. In this respect it is a human rights issue. A member of either gender can be the victim of arassment, offensive behavior of a sexual nature. A female supervisor in a position of power could pressure a male supervisee for sexual favors.

Sexual harassment also occurs when verbal re-marks make the work atmosphere offensive or stifling. Sexual remarks not related to the work at hand can interfere with productivity and performance. For example, female staff might be forced to endure condescending derogatory remarks from male coworkers who comment on the women's anatomy or sneer at their inferior ability.

Notes

a. For example, the state of Wisconsin's Fair Employment Acts as amended in 1978 prohibits sexual harassment.
b. For example, the University of Wisconsin System Board of Regents have stated in their Resolution #2384 of May 8, 1981 that sexual harassment ''is unacceptable and impermissible conduct which will not be tolerated.''
c. The definition of sexual harassment is taken from Resolution #2384 of the Board of Regents of the University of Wisconsin System dated May 8, 1981. The Equal employment Opportunity Commission has published a similar definition of sexual harassment in ''Guidelines on Discrimination because of Sex, Title VII, Sec. 703,'' *Federal Register*, 45 (April 11, 1980).

---

part-time coordinator who oversees program development and provides services. The coordinator will devote ten hours of her forty-hour work week to running the program. The portion of a position allotted to the coordinator's tasks is modifiable according to agency size. Larger organizations demand more time and attention than smaller agencies. The important thing is to adopt a well-defined policy on sexual harassment to support the program coordinator's position. Responsibilities must be clearly stated in the coordinator's job description.

SHAPE is an informal means of combating sexual harassment. SHAPE supplements the potentially punitive formal complaint procedure. SHAPE emphasizes prevention of sexual harassment and halting any harassment that might be occurring.

Cindy's action group determines that the coordinator's role consists of five basic duties. Primary among them are educational programming and informal mediation. The coordinator will offer educational presentations about sexual harassments to as many agency personnel as possible. The coordinator will also serve as the official contact person and informal mediator on any informal sexual harassment complaints. Furthermore, counseling the offended individual regarding available alternatives and preferred courses of action may be involved. The coordinator's approach will emphasize solving the immediate problem and establishing a positive, supportive work environment, to whatever extent that is possible.

The coordinator's other duties will include monitoring existing formal procedures to ascertain their relevance and their responsiveness to sexual harassment complaints. Finally, the coordinator will submit formal reports directly to the agency's director concerning progress, problems, and necessary program changes.

Cindy's action system selects a potential coordinator. It then solicits the agency director's concurrence and permission. Subsequently, the action system and new coordinator create a PERT chart to direct program development and activity. The program goals they establish are explained below.

Educational Programming

Educational programming is one of SHAPE's foremost goals. Agency personnel need education about what sexual harassment is and what can be done about it. First, the agency's personnel structure must be analyzed and arbitrarily divided into units. Programming initially targets top level administration such as the agency director, assistant director, and unit division supervisors. The coordinator then arranges educational sessions for units from administrative structure down to individual departments. The coordinator typically asks each unit to sponsor a presentation on sexual harassment issues during its regular unit meeting times.

The coordinator offers specific suggestions for stopping or averting sexual harassment to each unit she addresses. She tailors content to each unit's particular circumstances, using examples that unit staff can understand and identify with. She encourages staff to avoid using sexist terminology and references to anatomical gender differences when speaking to each other or to clients.

Educational presentations examine various forms of sexual harassment, the personal rights of victims, and how victims can take advantage of SHAPE. The coordinator suggests ways to discourage and stop sexual harassment. Recommendations include telling the offender calmly and straightforwardly that the behavior is offensive and inappropriate, seeking emotional support from peers, looking for witnesses to corroborate complaints, and documenting informally and briefly specific details of the harassment. The coordinator strongly encourages staff to contact SHAPE about any sexual harassment problems they encounter.

The coordinator can also target the agency's regular in-service training program. Half-day conferences with "brown-bag" lunches provide periodic educational opportunities. Using such opportunities for education about sexual harassment flows well with the agency's normal operation. It neither disrupts staff schedules nor takes away from staff's work time.

Informal Mediation and Advocacy

In addition to providing education, the coordinator offers informal mediation and advocacy. In the event that a staff member makes a sexual harassment com-

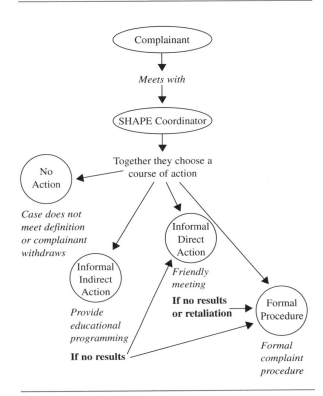

Figure 7.3
Procedural Flow Chart for SHAPE

plaint to SHAPE, four specific courses of action are available to the coordinator in her counseling role (see figure 7.3). First, a *no action approach* is possible when the complaint does not meet the definition of sexual harassment or the offended party withdraws. Second, the coordinator may choose the *informal indirect approach*, offering education on sexual harassment to the alleged offender or to the group of which he/she is a part. No accusations are made. Direct confrontation is thus avoided. Third, an *informal direct alternative* is available wherein the coordinator stages a friendly meeting with the alleged offender. This may occur with or without the complainant present. Finally, the coordinator may refer the complainant to the *formal complaint procedures*. Here the coordinator can continue to function as advisor to and advocate for the complainant. With each course of action, the coordinator maintains confidentiality to the greatest extent possible.

No Action

Some complaints may be received that do not involve actual sexual harassment. In that event the SHAPE coordinator might choose to pursue *no action*. She must evaluate each situation carefully to determine whether it falls within the definition of sexual harassment described above. Complaints inappropriate for SHAPE intervention may include: sexual harassment of agency personnel in the external community, which have nothing to do with the agency; disputes between supervisor/administrative personnel and their supervisees that have no sexual overtones; and affirmative action issues not related to gender.

For instance, a male employee leaves the agency for another position and then calls the SHAPE coordinator to complain that his female supervisor had been sexually harassing him. He says his former supervisor gave him tasks he considered inappropriate and criticized his work performance unfairly. On further discussion, the coordinator finds neither sexual discrimination nor sexual overtones. Rather, the problems seem to lie in the supervisory relationship and in differences of opinion over the appropriateness of various job tasks.

Occasionally, the coordinator takes a ''no action'' approach when an individual opts to withdraw a complaint. The complainant may decide that he or she misinterpreted the behavior in question. In other cases the coordinator may conclude that the complaint is so vague or illogical that pursuit of any further action is unwarranted.

Informal Indirect Action

The coordinator may take informal indirect action when she determines that it is best to avoid a direct confrontation. However, she still must do something to address the sexual harassment. Informal indirect action usually involves an educational presentation to, and discussion with, the offender's unit or department. The coordinator avoids making specific allegations. Rather, she provides examples to illustrate variations of sexual harassment that resemble, but are not identical to, those the complainant has reported.

The coordinator uses various criteria to determine whether informal indirect action is the appropriate course to take. First, she carefully examines the seriousness of the sexual harassment. In a situation in which

serious sexual advances are being made, more severe and immediate action might have to be taken. Other variables include: the unit's prior exposure to educational programming, its perceived receptivity to such programming, and the programming's potential usefulness in remedying the specific problem.

Three circumstances characterize situations that call for informal indirect action. First, the complainant may choose to remain anonymous. Frequently, a direct confrontation with the offender, detailing the specific circumstances under which the harassment occurred, would make it obvious to the offender who the complainant was. This possibility can be very intimidating to the victim.

Second, it may be questionable whether sexual harassment has actually occurred. This following example illustrates how a combination of these circumstances can lead to informal indirect action.

Two male employees, colleagues of a woman in their supervisory unit, initiate a complaint to SHAPE on her behalf. The SHAPE coordinator contacts the woman, and she describes the problem. She states that her male supervisor is giving her undue attention both inside and outside the agency. The supervisor has called her at home several times and has sought her out at work for no professional reason, questioning her about progress on a variety of work assignments.

Without consulting the SHAPE coordinator, the young woman formally transfers to another agency unit the following week. Discussion during a later interview reveals several new aspects of the situation. The young woman apparently had been doing a very marginal job in her initial agency assignment. On the one hand, the young woman feels that the supervisor's attentions were excessive. However, on the other hand, she appreciates his efforts to help her with her work. Her male colleagues were more concerned about the situation than she was. She indicates that her decision to transfer to another unit was primarily based on her own poor performance in her first position, not on the supervisor's attentions. The young woman states that the issue does not merit further attention. Therefore, the SHAPE coordinator drops the complaint.

However, the coordinator still makes an educational presentation to the agency unit of the supervisor in question. She discusses the issues involved in sexual harassment and explains SHAPE. The coordinator purposely uses examples of a male supervisor telephoning female employees at home and giving them undue attention to illustrate this supervisor's inappropriate behavior. She hopes that the targeted supervisor will integrate the information and apply it to his own future behavior. In the event that further complaints are made about this same supervisor, more definite action may be necessary.

The third set of circumstances calling for informal indirect action involves inappropriate, offensive comments, jokes, or materials. A group of male staff members might congregate in the cafeteria and make sexual comments about passing female staff such as, "Look at the big bazooms on that one." Other examples include the open display of offensive photos depicting nude women or cartoons illustrating sexist jokes.

One other means of informal indirect action is useful, information and suggestions not to the victims themselves, but to staff in whom victims have confided and who have contacted SHAPE about the problem. Sometimes victims do not know about SHAPE and their rights or are uncomfortable approaching a stranger (the SHAPE coordinator) about a personal sexual harassment issue. Dissemination of information and suggestions via the contact person can be just as effective as communicating directly with the victim.

For example, a staff person consults SHAPE about a gay male worker in his unit. The staff member is concerned because this worker is the object of substantial ridicule and hazing by fellow workers. Because of its sexual nature, the SHAPE coordinator considers this behavior sexual harassment. The coordinator supplies the staff person complaining about the incidents with several suggestions regarding how both he and the victim might discourage and curb such harassment. The coordinator also discusses the alternative procedure of filing a formal complaint with the agency. Finally, the coordinator urges the staff person to encourage the victim to contact SHAPE for help. Shortly thereafter, the hazing subsides. Both further contacts and the formal complaint process become unnecessary.

Informal Direct Action

In the event that informal indirect action is inappropriate or ineffective, the next more severe alternative is informal direct action, an informal meeting between the SHAPE coordinator and the offending party. This alternative consists of several steps.

First, the complainant and the SHAPE coordinator agree that action needs to be taken. The intent of informal direct action is to make the harassment stop, not to bring punitive action against the offender. Second, the SHAPE coordinator and a designated top level administrator (for example, the agency's director or assistant director) meet and discuss the situation. The coordinator describes specific plans for dealing with the situation. Third, the coordinator and the offending party meet. The offending party has the right to have a third person present if he so desires. The purposes of this meeting are to present the problem as the complainant perceives it, discuss the offender's perspective, gather additional information if necessary, seek resolution if possible, and educate the offender regarding sexual harassment. The fourth step is a later meeting with the complainant to determine whether the harassment has stopped. The final step is providing the agency's director with a summary of the situation's current status.

The following example illustrates how this procedure might be followed. Two young female staff separately complain to SHAPE that a male supervisor has made sexual advances to them while each was alone in his office discussing a case. Specifically, both women complain of him touching them on the arms and knees and placing his arm around them. One woman states the supervisor attempted to kiss her. The SHAPE coordinator notifies the agency director of the situation and describes plans for meeting with the alleged offender. Both complainants prefer to remain anonymous. The SHAPE coordinator calls the offender and makes arrangements to meet in the SHAPE office, which is located in an inconspicuous place within the agency.

Upon arrival, the accused offender is irate that the SHAPE coordinator has contacted him. The coordinator initiates the meeting with the alleged perpetrator by stating that complaints have been made. She offers specific details of the complaints. Discussion focuses on the fact that employees have complained, not on whether the behavior actually occurred. The coordinator emphasizes the well-being of staff members in their work environment. She clearly defines individuals' rights and options when confronted by sexual harassment. Confidentiality is stressed. Her intent is to educate the alleged offender regarding the types of behavior that will not be tolerated. The meeting ends on a relatively cordial note. The day following the meeting, the coordinator contacts the two complainants and describes what happened. Both complainants report that they are satisfied that the coordinator has handled the situation and will not seek further action unless the harassment reoccurs. Finally, the SHAPE coordinator updates the agency director regarding the situation's progress.

Formal Procedure

At any point during the procedure, it is the complainants' prerogative to initiate the formal complaint process. A formal action for sexual harassment is pursued in the same way as any other complaint. Most frequently, complainants elect to take such action when other less severe alternatives have failed, when the SHAPE coordinator determines that the case is of such a serious nature that this is necessary, or when the complainant desires punitive action.

In the event that the formal procedure is followed, the coordinator may provide support and guidance during the ensuing hearings. Victims frequently need assurance of their rights and information about each step in the formal complaint process.

A major strength of SHAPE is that the coordinator is never placed in the position of determining guilt. That responsibility is relegated to other formal bodies. This frees the coordinator to function as support and advocate for the complainant.

Planning the Program: Development of a PERT Chart

At this point, you should understand the proposed sexual harassment awareness program in substantial detail. We will now show how a PERT chart can be used to implement the actual program. For the purposes of our discussion, we will assume that you have been chosen as the coordinator. The program's goals and activities have already been established, so you as the coordinator will follow the PERT chart described below. Of course, this is only a sample PERT chart. Specific steps in the process and objectives pursued to complete goals will vary according to the program plan, the organization's structure, and the staff involved.

For our purposes, SHAPE has four major areas in which goals are set. These include initial planning, education, referral sources, counseling, and evaluation.

The first thing to consider is initial planning. How do you get such a program off the ground? Figure 7.4 is set up vertically, that is, from top to bottom, in order to fit a textbook page format. In real life, the format would as likely be horizontal, that is, leading from left to right. The time frame illustrated runs from February 1998 to March 1999. Establishing a new program often takes substantial amounts of time, in this case, over a year. Many details merit serious attention. Many wrinkles need ironing out.

INITIAL PLANNING. In developing a program like SHAPE, first visualize how the program will fit into the agency's structure and functioning. For example, where will the office be located? Who will serve as the support secretarial staff? Who will answer the phone to receive complaints about sexual harassment? How will the program be publicized to agency personnel?

As we begin to explore figure 7.4's PERT chart, remember that we are operating under a number of assumptions in this example. For one thing, the coordinator, theoretically you, has already been selected. For another thing, the program has already been designed. Its goals have been identified. The agency has a firm grievance policy in place that supports your role as educator and informal advocate. A grievance is "a formal complaint about some procedure or regulation that is not being followed, and that has resulted in some harm to the complainant" (Barker, 1991, p. 96). Agencies typically are required to explain established grievance procedures in their policy manuals. You, of course, would need to be well aware of your role in helping complainants about sexual harassment pursue the designated grievance process.

Finally, we will assume that the budget has already been developed. In addition to involving one-fourth of your own salary and benefits, the budget would probably include specific amounts for items such as supplies, copying, postage, educational resources, educational videos, secretarial help, travel and conferences, and publicity needs such as brochures. Figure 7.5 illustrates a simplified budget. As program coordinator you would begin developing your PERT chart with all of the above assumptions in mind.

The five major categories illustrated in figure 7.4's PERT chart include initial planning, education, public relations, counseling, and evaluation. The first task needing attention, of course, is initial planning. This entails brainstorming with administration and other col-

Figure 7.4
A PERT Chart for the Sexual Harassment Awareness Program for Employees (SHAPE)

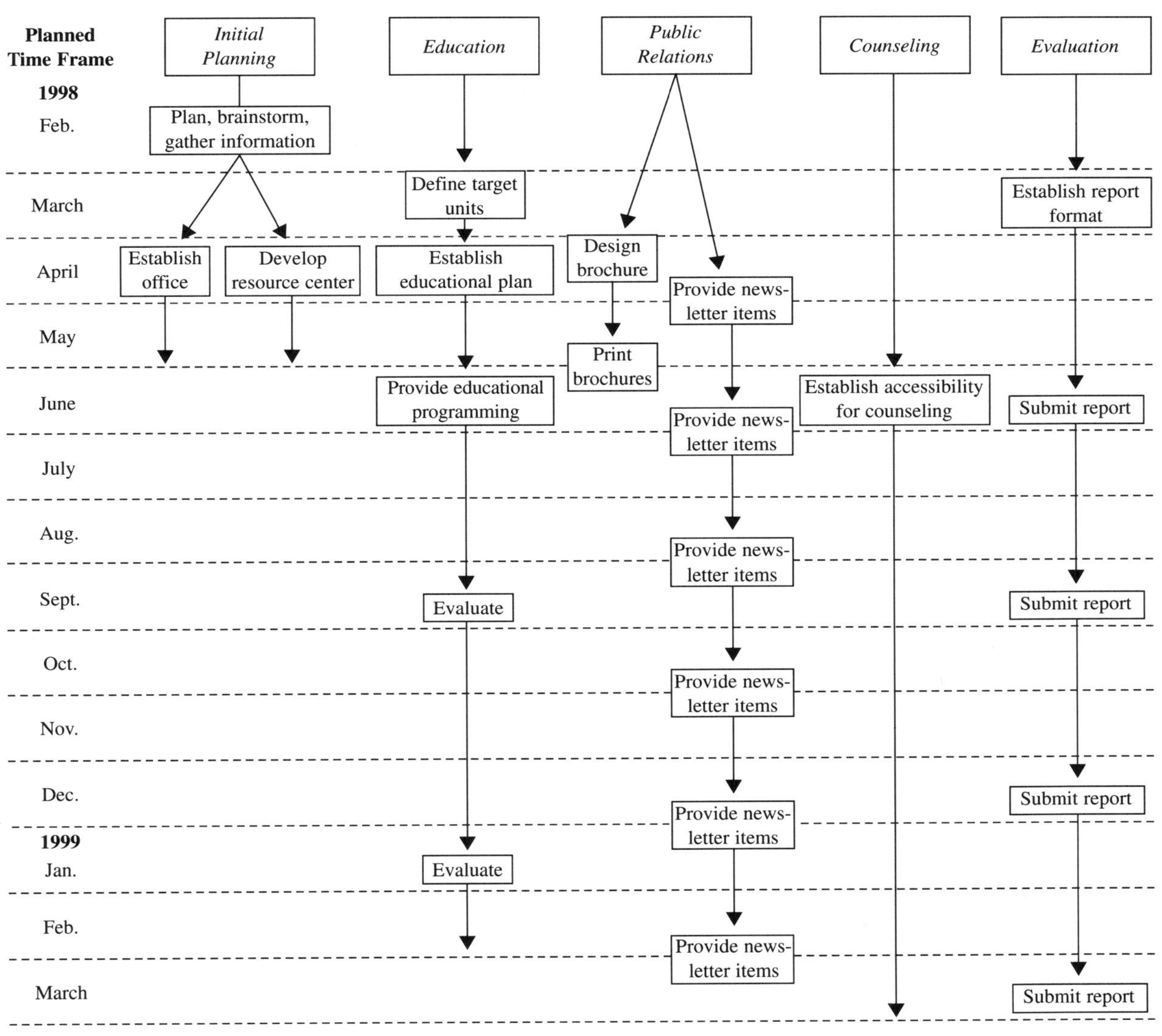

leagues concerning the extent of the sexual harassment problem and their feelings about it. You would also seek to educate yourself more thoroughly about sexual harassment issues, especially with respect to their legal aspects and the counseling of victims. The PERT chart indicates that you would begin this in early February, (specifically, February 1 when your part-time position

begins). You would continue through early April (specifically, April 7). Due to space limitations, it was not possible to specify monthly dates in the PERT chart. Therefore, we will specify the due dates here as we discuss the chart itself.

You would aim to set up SHAPE's office from April 8 through May 31. This objective would include

Figure 7.5
A Budget Summary for SHAPE

Projected Needs	Cost
1. Supplies	$ 600
2. Copying	300
3. Postage	150
4. Library Resources	600
5. Travel and Conferences	1,000
6. Telephone	800
7. Brochures	800
8. Miscellaneous	500
Total:	$4,750

locating office space and getting administration approval. You would need a place where employees could come to you confidentially. They would need to feel comfortable talking with you about such an intimately disturbing problem as sexual harassment. A preferred location would thus be out of the mainstream of agency traffic (not, therefore, an office right next to the reception area), yet one that could be easily found (not an office hidden in a corner of the agency's basement that could only be found after winding along a maze of heating ducts).

You would need to find a secretarial assistant. Since this is only a part-time position, perhaps you could use a secretary assigned to another agency unit. She might also answer the SHAPE phone and take messages when you are out of the SHAPE office performing your other job duties. It is important, however, not to coerce a secretary or administrative assistant to add to her own workload and do SHAPE's work. This tactic would only cause her to resent SHAPE and you, and resist doing the job. Perhaps you could check with administration to add to her salary in view of these additional responsibilities. Or you might negotiate a decrease in some of her other workload. Otherwise, you might discover that every important document you give to her winds up hopelessly lost.

A second aspect of gathering information is the development of a resource center. The PERT chart indicates that you will pursue this goal concurrently with establishing the SHAPE office. You aim to complete the resource center by May 31. Since one of your intents is to educate staff concerning sexual harassment, you need material. To this end, you could perform a library search or call other professionals involved in similar

endeavors, such as the Affirmative Action offices of public agencies or the state office of Equal Employment Opportunity. One of your goals is to start developing a reference library for your own professional education and for other staff in need of this information.

A related question is where the resource materials would be located. Is there enough room in the SHAPE office to accommodate them? Might administration give you another room for such a purpose? Does the agency already have a resource area to which your materials could be added?

EDUCATION. As the agency's designated educator concerning sexual harassment issues, you would need a systematic plan for educating virtually all agency employees, from the agency's executive director to the nighttime custodial staff. You will have to determine how best to reach them. You could try personal educational presentations or send relevant brochures and reading material to staff.

You decide that ideally it would be best for you to talk individually to each of the agency's units. How might you go about doing this? First, examine an agency administrative chart that includes all staff, from top to bottom in the agency's power structure, and shows how supervisory responsibility is structured. You could probably identify some obvious target units. For example, a Protective Services unit for the elderly includes a supervisor and eight workers who meet for weekly group supervisory sessions. Perhaps you could speak to them on sexual harassment during a portion of one of their regular meetings. Thus, you could develop a systematic plan for speaking to each agency unit. You could do it in any way that you chose, from alphabetical order to making random presentations according to how individual unit meetings fit into your own work schedule. You determine that you will define your target units by April 7 and finish such an educational plan by May 31 (both of which are illustrated on the PERT chart in figure 7.4).

In summary, first you designate your target units. Second, you establish an educational presentation schedule. Finally, you follow your own proposed schedule and begin your educational programming.

PUBLIC RELATIONS. The third dimension of tasks illustrated in figure 7.4's PERT chart involves the goal of establishing positive public relations. In order to come to you for help, people need to know that you exist. You might develop a descriptive program brochure. Information could include the definition of sexual harassment, a variety of brief examples, its illegal status, your own agency's policy, and maybe a clever cartoon to catch people's attention. You could distribute these during your educational sessions and give them to complainants coming to you for help. At some point you might even place them in the mailboxes of all agency personnel. However, you are a little skeptical about this approach because you know how staff love to process paper without reading it. However, you will work on designing the brochure during the month of April, targeting May 15 for its completion date. You will have two-hundred copies printed by June 1, in time for your first series of presentations.

The second major way of notifying agency staff that you exist is through writing articles for the agency's bimonthly newsletter. You could start with some basic definitions of sexual harassment and progress to providing vignettes of sexual harassment that explore and highlight the problems involved. Additionally, you could discuss the legal basis for action against sexual harassment. Legal updates are another possibility. Figure 7.4's PERT chart indicates that you will submit your first item to the newsletter by May 1. You will then continue to submit items by the first of every other month (that is, July 1, September 1, November 1, January 1, and March 1). By then you will have gathered enough resources to have plenty of information to submit for newsletter publication.

COUNSELING. SHAPE's fourth dimension of tasks involves the provision of counseling when needed. As indicated in the PERT chart, you anticipate making this service available by June 1. At that point you will also start your educational presentations. Staff should begin to know who you are and where the office is. Set regular office hours that are clearly posted on the door. They can also be publicized in the agency newsletter. Your phone number should also be publicized and available, with a secretary assigned to answer the phone during most office hours.

EVALUATION OF SHAPE FUNCTIONING. The final dimension of tasks aims for the goals of successfully evaluating SHAPE's effectiveness. Any program needs some form of evaluation to determine

whether it is worthwhile or not. You as coordinator are directly responsible to the agency's director. Therefore, you need a means of being accountable to her. You decide to provide her with a record of your accomplishments. You will summarize for her the number of educational programs given, the names of staff members who participated, the number of complaints you handled, and your budgetary reports. You will submit these summaries to the director every three months. The PERT chart indicated that such reports are due on June 30, September 30, December 31, and March 31, respectively.

IMAGINE: Implement *the Plan*

The fifth step in the IMAGINE process for macro intervention involves Implementing the plan. During this phase you actually initiate the program and get it off the ground. You would follow objectives described in your PERT chart and monitor your progress. Such monitoring can entail the evaluation of whether you are achieving your objectives in a timely manner as planned or not.

The suggestion of nurturing participating staff applies primarily to your secretary as you are the primary staff person involved in the program. We have emphasized that maintaining good relationships with support staff such as secretaries or administrative assistants is extremely important in any program.

You determine that a trial run is unnecessary in that the program is relatively small. It involves only one-quarter of your job position time in addition to secretarial time. In essence, you are starting out small. You do not foresee any future need for expansion at this point. Because you will be providing the services, no formal contracts are needed concerning agreements with other agencies or consultants.

IMAGINE: Neutralize *Opposition*

IMAGINE's sixth step involves maintaining an ongoing wariness about potential opposition. We have established that often when a program is first initiated there is a honeymoon period. This time interval is typically characterized by good (almost too good to be true) relationships with program participants and agency staff.

As time passes, the honeymoon period passes, and any potential problems surface. Neutralizing opposition involves becoming aware of problems as they appear and dealing with them to the best of your ability.

IMAGINE: Evaluate *Progress*

Periodic evaluation is already built into SHAPE's goals. You are to provide summaries of accomplishments to the agency's director every three months. This report make you accountable for your activities. Summaries document the extent to which you prevent sexual harassment problems through educational programming, address any problems that do occur as they surface, and validate your usefulness by preventing major legal incidents. Additionally, the program structure is such that you can consult with the agency's director at any time to seek guidance and help.

Chapter Summary

This chapter applies the IMAGINE process of macro intervention to project implementation and program development, specific suggestions for relating the IMAGINE process to each of these two types of macro intervention are explored.

Program Evaluation and Review Technique (PERT) charts are examined and PERT charts proposed to implement an in-service training project and to develop a Sexual Harassment Awareness Program for Employees (SHAPE). With respect to the latter, issues concerning sexual harassment are addressed. Suggestions for curbing and halting sexual harassment are provided.

CHAPTER EIGHT

Understanding Neighborhoods and Communities

Residents on South Sunrise Street were very angry. Their quiet residential neighborhood provided ample sidewalks for children to ride bikes and play. A nearby shallow creek paralleling their dead end street even provided a place for kids to wade in the warm summers. Several years ago, the city informed residents that eventually the street would be widened. At that time, the city planned to add two more lanes of traffic to South Sunrise but these would be built on the other side of the creek, away from their homes. Residents were unconcerned because this plan did not affect their quiet working-class neighborhood.

Abruptly, the city changed its plans. One balmy late spring morning residents received letters from the city announcing a new plan. Rebuilding of South Sunrise Street would commence next month, and not on the other side of the stream as previously promised. As they read, residents saw visions of mammoth bulldozers and steam shovels appearing out of nowhere. They envisioned barricades set up at the street's entrance, complete with threatening ''KEEP OUT—RESIDENTS ONLY'' signs. Residents were shocked and horrified. This plan would greatly widen the street, gobbling up front yards, sidewalks, and trees. The city's plans would shorten already steep driveways to angles difficult for mountain goats to master, and forbid residents and their guests from parking in front of their homes. The increased danger to children from this plan, the lack of involvement of street residents in the planning process, and the fear that this change would seriously diminish their quality of life spurred residents into action.

Residents pulled together quickly and formed the South Sunshine Community Improvement Committee. Electing a president, they also sought assistance from a social worker who lived on the street. Members met with city officials (including the neighborhood's city council representative and the director of public works, both of whom wielded significant power over city street planning). They informed legislators of their plight and seriously lobbied to halt what they considered a neighborhood disaster.

Finally, after strenuous effort, decision-makers began to understand the plight of South Sunrise residents. After careful deliberation and consideration of alternative strategies, plans were changed. Instead of widening South Sunrise, the city chose a street two blocks over, which proved to be a better target of change. The latter ran through a large plot of land occupied by several huge warehouses. As no one lived there, widening that street would have no similar injurious effects on community residents.

As a result of their efforts South Sunrise residents were able to maintain what they considered a good quality of life in their neighborhood. In addition, they opened a new channel of communication with city planners through their newly established Community Improvement Committee. Planners not only listened to residents on the street widening issue, but also indicated a willingness to hear what residents had to say about other neighborhood concerns.

Members of the Morningside Neighborhood Association worried about the possible closing of Franklin School, the only school serving this working-class neighborhood. The school board had closed down other city schools, so a precedent had already been set. Without the school, neighborhood children would have to take long, tedious city bus rides to another school miles away. Their friendships, after-school activities, and study time would be seriously disrupted. Having no readily accessible school would discourage new young families from moving into the neighborhood, a goal the neighborhood was striving to accomplish.

Residents feared that closing the school would mean the end of their neighborhood as they knew it. They were already threatened with overcrowding from several student-rental properties and with parking problems caused by a nearby university.

Two years ago, the neighborhood association mustered its energies and prevented Burp's Brewery, a large beer production plant, from moving into the area. The brewery had caused multiple problems in another location, which was why it had to move in the first place.

Association members had become increasingly successful in getting the city to tailor regulations to benefit their neighborhood. Their efforts had resulted in greater emphasis both on maintaining single-family homes and on setting clear limitations on the types of businesses, public institutions, agencies that could move into the area. Now, working together, association members set out to convince the elected school board not to close the neighborhood school. The neighborhood association entered into lengthy negotiations with public decision-makers. By exerting constant pressure on both the school administration and school board, the association finally got its way. The board decided to keep Franklin School open. Morningside Neighborhood Association members were ecstatic. It had taken massive effort, but they had won.

Introduction

Upon graduation, generalist social workers find themselves working in a wide range of social service agencies providing direct services to individuals, families, and groups. As workers provide services, they encounter problems of varying degrees of seriousness and intensity. Take, for example, the case of Serge Menendez, an eighteen-year-old male high school graduate, who is desperately yet unsuccessfully seeking work. Or consider Mike Gleason who dropped out of high school and has even less potential for finding an adequately paying job. Finally, think about Debra Whitetail, fourteen, who just had a baby. She wants to finish high school but has no one to help her care for her daughter. Debra's own mother died when she was four. Debra now lives with her grandmother who works full-time and can't afford to quit to babysit for Debra's daughter.

When dealing with individual clients, it is easy to lose sight of the broader social issues and problems that affect them. In reality, the problems extend far beyond the individual cases mentioned above. Each of these problems involves huge issues.

For instance, Serge is not alone. In poor school districts, as many as 50 percent of the students with high school diplomas lack reading and writing skills needed for employment. Likewise, Mike is just one student in a school district where dropout rates of 30 percent to 50 percent are not uncommon (Committee for Economic Development, 1987). Finally, Debra's lack of adequate child care is also part of a larger problem. While as many as one million licensed child-care slots are available, the actual need approaches six million (Emig, 1986). Debra's experience is shared by many other girls. She is just one of a million teenagers who become pregnant each year. Eighty percent of these pregnancies are unintended (Children's Defense Fund, 1987). Clearly, the welfare of individual social-service clients is inextricably linked to policies and programs established by people in authority above you.

It is also true that social workers must view individual clients' problems in the context of the complex macro environments in which these clients live. When a child drops out of school, it may be the result of individual lack of motivation, lack of supervision by alcoholic parents, or any of a number of other factors unique to the child's particular family. However, when 30 percent of a school's enrollment fails to graduate, the explanation cannot rest solely on the individual dropouts or their families. Generalist practitioners must constantly keep this in mind.

The community and neighborhood exert significant influence upon individuals in most areas of the world, including the United States. Poor communities are often unable to provide high quality schools and recreational facilities. Run-down neighborhoods may expose children to drug dealers, drive-by shootings, and gang violence.

The problems cited earlier—youth unemployment, school drop-outs, and teen pregnancy—affect young people. Of course, a myriad other problems affect people of all ages and from all walks of life. Lisa Swanson, age two months, remains on life-support equipment. She was born to a cocaine-addicted mother almost three months early. Her chances of survival are still not considered very good. Vladimir Nurotuscki, who is living with AIDS, has great difficulty finding access to necessary health care. Norma Ray, sixty-one, is homeless and suffers from increasingly serious Alzheimer's Disease. She has no money and nowhere to go. Each of these individuals exemplifies a large group of people suffering from similar problems. The generalist perspective requires us to confront macro problems and issues affecting many people as we address our individuals clients' needs.

The importance of understanding the community cannot be overstated. Most people access resources at the community level regardless of whether the program funding originates at the local, state, or national level. It is at the community level that government is potentially most responsive to individual citizens. Quality of life issues are most profoundly confronted at the local level. Being forced to live in substandard housing, being victimized by drug dealers and drive-by shootings, or having to choose between paying the rent and eating this week seriously diminish the quality of one's life. The absence of a day-care program for Debra, homeless people sleeping in the doorways of closed downtown businesses, and the fact that almost a third of Mike's peers will drop out of school and into a lifetime of poverty are cases in point. The examples cited at the beginning of this chapter suggest that some of the larger problems confronting society can be addressed, at least in part, at the local level. Also, the responsiveness of local elected leaders makes it easier to address shared concerns and problems.

This chapter stresses the importance of understanding the communities and neighborhoods in which we live and work. The ability to understand these entities, comprehend clients' situations as existing within a context, and identify critical areas of need is essential. It is important not to lose sight of the forest when we are dealing with individual trees (our clients). Simultaneously, our responsibility as generalists is to intervene, when appropriate, to ensure that clients receive needed services, equitable treatment, and adequate resources. Remember that the generalist provides services to individuals, families, and groups in addition to *organizations* and *communities*.

This chapter will:

- Discuss the role of social workers in neighborhoods and communities.
- Define communities and neighborhoods in terms of their functions and types.
- Review the systems perspective and the community as an ecological and social system.
- Describe social stratification in the community.
- Consider community economic and political systems.
- Examine power in the community context.
- Describe the functions and types of neighborhoods and the ways in which neighborhoods act as helping networks.
- Address the process of assessing communities and neighborhoods.

The Role of Social Workers in Neighborhoods and Communities

As a social worker in a public or private human service agency, you may not initially see a role for yourself in either the neighborhoods or the larger community. After all, you were hired primarily to investigate child abuse and neglect cases, or to provide case management for chronically mentally ill clients, or to perform perhaps a hundred other professional chores your agency expects. Immersed in case responsibilities, it is easy to forget one of the things that makes social workers different from other professionals. Namely, social workers are concerned about the *social environment*. Generalist practitioners have a professional obligation which is drawn directly from the Code of Ethics of our profession. According to the National Association of Social Workers (NASW) Code of Ethics (NASW 1990), each social worker has a responsibility to:

- Prevent and eliminate discrimination against any person or group on the basis of several factors including race, sex, and age.
- Ensure that all persons have access to the resources, services, and opportunities they require.
- Expand choice and opportunity for all persons, with special regard for disadvantaged or oppressed groups and persons.
- Promote conditions that encourage respect for human diversity.

- Advocate changes in policy and legislation to improve social conditions and to promote social justice.
- Encourage informed participation by the public in shaping social policies and institutions.

In addition to NASW, the Council on Social Work Education (CSWE) (1984) further describes social work's purposes. Social workers are concerned about relationships between individuals and society's institutions (such as schools, government agencies, courts, and employers). Social work commits itself to "the promotion, restoration, maintenance, or enhancement of the functioning of individuals, families, households, social groups, organizations, and communities by helping them to prevent distress and utilize resources" (CSWE, 1984, p. 106). Further, the profession expects social workers to engage in legislative advocacy, lobbying, participation in local and national coalitions, and running for public office. This is an incredible array of expectations for our field.

What this means is that a responsible social worker has a much broader mandate than do other human service practitioners, such as psychologists or marriage and family therapists. This is particularly so at the macro level. Sometimes you will become involved in a neighborhood or community because of a specific case (individual, family, or group) with which you are working. At other times you will become involved because several agencies' representatives join together to address a problem extending beyond their individual walls, and, they will invite you to participate. At still other times, you volunteer to become involved because the need is there and you have the interest, knowledge, and skill to positively impact the outcome.

Social workers engage in a broad and colorful spectrum of activities when they intervene in neighborhoods and communities. Quality of life issues such as those mentioned earlier are critical to neighborhood and community residents. They are so significant and widespread that social workers have to choose what to target for action and what to ignore. Zoning and housing codes directly affect the quality of life of homeowners and renters alike. (Zoning and housing codes are a combination of city, state, and federal laws and regulations that cover everything from the safety of your plumbing, water, and electrical systems to the number of unrelated people who can live in a home or apartment. Housing codes usually require, for example, hot and cold running water, bathrooms, and heat in a house or rental unit.) Imagine what it would be like if there were no rules governing what a landlord could do to a tenant. Your client could be thrown out of an apartment with no notice at all if it were not for these kinds of codes and regulations. Without these codes, landlords could turn off the heat and water supply simply because they disliked their tenants. Social workers sometimes involve themselves directly in getting such codes adopted or, enforcing codes already in place.

A social worker might lobby a city government to have abandoned, deserted, deteriorating homes in an urban ghetto sold for $1 each to community applicants. The applicants would agree to repair and upgrade these homes themselves in return for ownership. Likewise, social workers might pressure a neighborhood developer to set land aside for parks and recreational purposes. Or a social worker might find herself struggling in a neighborhood to overcome residents' opposition to a proposed group home for the developmentally disabled. Resident are terrified by, and obsessed with, the many myths characterizing disabled people.

Generalist practitioners employ a vast array of skills to effect changes for clients. Vayda and Bogo (1991, p. 273) identify some additional typical activities requiring these skills:

1. *Assessing needs through use of interagency committees.* You may recall the interagency needs assessment in chapter 3 which focused on the needs of latchkey children in a community.
2. *Identifying service gaps, and recommending new programs.* You constantly confront the fact that young people have no social activities after school unless they are involved in sports. You suggest developing an after-school drop-in center with activities of interest to adolescents.
3. *Advocating for policy changes in response to needs identified by grassroots community organizations.* You learn that children living in a homeless shelter with their families are not enrolled in school because school policies require children to have a permanent residence. Consequently, these children fall desperately far behind in school. The Community Homeless Coalition asks you, as a school social worker, to help them change the school policy.
4. *Participating in professional association action groups.* You become involved with the local NASW chapter in lobbying for a new state law to prevent employers from firing gay and lesbian workers solely because of their sexual orientation.

Wyers (1991) believes that social workers can be particularly effective in the macro areas because they are more likely to recognize and define social problems. Additionally, they can help design appropriate programs to combat problems. Finally, they can argue for new policies and programs to address these problems. Wyers' point is that, as an agency worker, you are most likely to be acutely aware of how agency policies or state and federal regulations affect your clients. As you know, your involvement in these activities may arise either as part of your job or in addition to it.

Likewise, a neighborhood association may ask a social worker to represent it in efforts to dissuade the city from widening a street and cutting down all the mature growth trees. As a social worker in the local neighborhood center, you are the logical person to turn to for assistance. In a recent case a single dogged individual lobbied endlessly to convince the highway department to move a street design three feet off its proposed center to save sixty mature oak and maple trees. The highway department grudgingly agreed. The result was the loss of only a handful of minor scrawny saplings. Neighborhood property owners, all of whom were low- or fixed-income elderly residents, rejoiced.

Of course, social workers are also residents of their neighborhoods and citizens of their communities. In either capacity, you may end up in a leadership role as you help your fellow citizens address some issue. Social workers' ability to solve problems, to work with people in groups, and to understand systems help them in their roles as citizens.

Obviously, here we are most concerned about your role as a generalist practitioner, so we will focus most of our attention on this role. As a social worker, your primary function is delivering existing services (such as case management or linking clients to services), helping to develop new resources (by lobbying for more funds or new programs in your agency), and modifying old services to benefit clients (such as identifying more effective ways of intervening with victims of sexual abuse). You are concerned about the individual, but always within the social environment. You will simultaneously view the community as the context of your practice as well as a potential target of change if clients are not getting resources or services they need. You will ultimately need skills in advocacy, research, assessment, evaluation of policies and programs, conscious use of self, the ability to link theory and practice, a commitment to change hurtful policies (Wyers, 1991, p. 247). Obviously, everyday agency demands for competence will require many of these skills. The social work profession requires still other skills for meeting professional expectations extending beyond the narrow window of agency practice.

Using these skills requires a great deal more knowledge about communities and neighborhoods. Just as you can't hope to work with people without understanding human growth and behavior, you cannot practice competently in the community without a similar knowledge of its growth and dynamics. The remainder of this chapter will help you understand communities and neighborhoods, the contexts of your macro practice.

Defining Community and Neighborhood

For decades social scientists have debated the meaning of community. Though definitions vary, most have similar components. The first is that a community occupies a *shared physical space*. In other words, it has defined boundaries. Thus, a community's boundaries might include all the area west of Peculiar Street, east of Banshee Avenue, south of the Sharptooth River, and north of Pineapple Boulevard. We can mark these boundaries on a map. They clearly separate one community from another.

A second component of the definition is *social interaction*. That is, community members interact with each other in a way different from their interactions with people outside the community. Social interaction in communities can revolve around employment, recreation, church, or a myriad other purposes. Typically the interactions occur frequently and face-to-face.

A community's third component is a *shared sense of identity*. Community members often form a strong affiliation and identify with their community. They will say with pride that they live in Chicago, Los Angeles, Tokyo, Oosberg, or Memphis.

Of course, for some residents the sense of identity is stronger than for others. Newcomers often do not feel the same degree of identification with a community as those who have lived there all their lives. Nor might the community readily accept newcomers. When running for city council (the city's elected governing board), the author remembers once being referred to as a "newcomer" in a newspaper article. That he had been a resident for eight years was irrelevant when others had lived in the community for decades. Being labeled a newcomer was almost equivalent to being called an ax murderer.

Combining the elements listed above, we conclude that a community occupies shared physical space where residents engage in social interaction and maintain a shared sense of identity. These definitions are helpful because they allow us to understand much of what goes on in a community. The intense attachment and sense of belonging and identity that long-time residents share helps explain, for example, why newcomers sometimes feel left out. It also explains why a smaller community might fight attempts by a larger adjoining city to annex (legally incorporate) its space.

Neighborhoods share some of the same features as communities. According to Barker (1991, p. 154), a neighborhood is "a region or locality whose inhabitants share certain characteristics, values, mutual interests, and styles of living. Typically, a community is composed of many neighborhoods. In each, the degree of neighborhood identity is often even greater than the sense of identity found in the larger community. If you think about your home community, you may recall many recognizable neighborhoods. The standard of living is likely to be similar in a given neighborhood while the community may have a wide variation in living standards. Housing prices or rental rates are similar within individual neighborhoods, further providing a sense of commonality. We will discuss neighborhoods in more detail later.

Functions of Communities

What does a community do for people? Why do people cluster in neighborhoods and communities? Warren (1978) has identified five functions all communities serve. The first is *socialization*, the transmission of values, culture, beliefs, and norms to new community members. *Values* are those principles a group considers important. Honesty is a value. *Culture* includes customs and ways of doing things. Shaking hands when greeting strangers is a custom. *Beliefs* are ideas that members assume are true, but may not be verifiable, such as, a belief in a supreme being. *Norms* are a community's expectations for how its members should act. For example, attending school is an expected behavior (norm) for most children.

Socialization occurs through both formal and informal mechanisms. Formal mechanisms include laws, rules, and procedures adopted by a community's legal bodies. Informal mechanisms entail any informal transmission of such information. Informal norms may be transmitted to new community members through other community members' comments or reactions. A neighbor might casually note, ''Yeah, look how much rain we've been having, and look how long your grass has grown.'' This neighbor really wants to convey that the lawn is in desperate need of mowing. Or a neighbor might say, ''You got any offers for that '72 Chevy pick-up truck parked in the frontyard yet? This neighbor is suggesting that the pick-up truck makes the frontyard look like a junkyard (and perhaps that's where the truck really belongs).

A second function of communities is the *production, distribution, and consumption of goods and services*. All communities provide a variety of services and products consumed by residents. This includes housing, food, and perhaps banking and street maintenance. Communities encourage and regulate construction of homes, apartments, and commercial buildings. Some communities have a greater variety of goods and services available than others. While specific individuals carry out these functions and provide the goods and services used by individuals and families, the community is the context in which this exchange occurs.

Social control is another community function. This involves setting limits on behavior by creating and enforcing laws via police and other official bodies. In practice, social control is the enforcement of community norms and values, Such control ranges from enacting twenty-five-miles-per-hour speed limits on city streets (when children are not present) to setting maintenance codes and requirements for individual homes. The city may restrict the number of people allowed in any one dwelling unit and set standards for how large the yard must be for a new home. It may also restrict what you can do with your home. (City regulations might forbid using your apartment as a massage parlor, for example.)

Mutual support is yet another community function. This function means that community members take care of one another. It ranges from informal action, such as giving directions to strangers, to formal actions, such

as providing social services for identified groups of citizens. Examples of social services include child protective services for abused or neglected children, probation and parole services for criminals, and shelter for survivors of domestic violence, to name a few. Self-help groups and networks as described in chapter 3, also provide avenues of mutual support.

Finally, each community provides for, the *participation* of its residents. This means that residents have the opportunity to interact with others through recreation, talking, church-going, and other forms of socializing. Obviously, some members of a community participate more than others in these interactions. Shut-ins and institutionalized patients have much less opportunity to interact with others in the larger community. This social dimension of a community is often what people speak of when they praise a community's qualities. They may refer to a community as very open or friendly, or cold and ''tight knit.'' This reflects the commentator's sense of the community's quality and quantity of participation.

While the definitions and functions described above apply primarily to communities, they apply almost equally well to neighborhoods. As we have seen, a neighborhood is ''a region or locality whose inhabitants share certain characteristics, values, mutual interests, and styles of living (Barker, 1991, p. 154). However, neighborhoods cannot offer the same breadth of services to residents (such as police forces supplying social control). Neighborhoods do carry out the other functions, however. Highlight 8.1 contrasts two communities of approximately equal size and their capacity to carry out common functions.

Types of Communities

Communities can be classified according to several dimensions, using size, economic health, or ethnic diversity as variables. We can also look at several very special types of communities which serve unique needs of inhabitants. These include reservation, bedroom, and institutional communities.

Perhaps, the most common classification system is size. The largest type of community is the metropolis. *Metropolitan communities* are large cities that serve as the surrounding area's business and economic center. They may actually be composed of multiple cities located in close proximity to one another. Such multiple

HIGHLIGHT 8.1

EXAMPLES OF
TWO COMMUNITIES

Hyerville is a community with a rich history. Founded by merchants hoping to serve farmers in the surrounding area, it quickly became a center for manufacturing of items the rural community needed. Early in its history, the community produced farm machinery, wagons, dairy equipment, and tools. The town prospered quickly, growing in population and reputation. Townspeople helped found a local university, built many churches, and took a great deal of pride in their community.

Within fifty years of its founding, however, Hyerville was in trouble. Manufacturing companies shut down due to economic hard times and consumers' changing interests. Wagons were no longer needed when automobiles became available. The university, once a positive feature of the community, has become a focus of its discontent. The school's enormous growth has brought too many students crowding into

the old mansions along Main Street, parking their cars all over the residential areas near campus, and engaging in vandalism after weekend drinking bouts. While there are several small manufacturing companies in town, the university is now the town's dominant employer, offering jobs mainly to well-educated outsiders. Local residents resent the institution "on the hill."

Despite this resentment, residents of Hyerville are generally very neighborly. Although it takes a while for them to accept newcomers, they find ways to welcome them. Block parties and invitations to join churches and social clubs are regularly offered. Residents generally know their neighbors' names, not to mention where they work, what kind of car they drive, and where they shop. Hyerville is a "neighborly" community in which to live.

Compare Hyerville to Spikeville, a city of ap-

cities might include a large central city surrounded by suburban and satellite cities. (Suburban cities are small cities which adjoin another larger city, while satellite cities are located near, but not adjacent to, the central city.) For example, the metropolitan community of Madison, Wisconsin, comprises the city of Madison and adjacent cities of Middleton, Sun Prairie, Verona, and many smaller towns that serve as bedroom communities for Madison. These metropolitan communities may be thought of as a system with multiple subsystems of various sizes. They are a unified system in the sense that together they perform all the functions described earlier (Warren, 1978). Metropolitan communities vary in size from about fifty-thousand to several million residents.

There are also a variety of *nonmetropolitan communities*. Nonmetropolitan communities differ from metropolitan communities, again, mainly in terms of size. Johnson (1992) discusses six different types of such communities. These include:

1. *Small cities (15,000–50,000 population)*. Small cities are legally organized entities, usually with their own police department and several other city departments.
2. *Small towns (8,000–20,000 population)*. Small towns are usually not legally organized, or "chartered." The town may offer few, if any, services, relying on the county or parish to provide such basic services as police protection.
3. *Rural communities (under 10,000 population)*. Rural communities often consist of a very small town surrounded by townships. The community provides no services and, thus, usually relies on the county or parish.
4. *Reservation communities*. Reservation communities are located on American Indian reservations recognized by the federal government. They vary in size depending on the number of residents in the particular reservation.
5. *Bedroom communities*. Bedroom communities are predominantly residential in nature, with little if any industry or business. Their residents work in nearby communities. That is, residents sleep and find recreation in their home communities but work in nearby cities with more business and industrial opportunities.

proximately the same size. Unlike Hyerville, which has a downtown business district and a couple of discount stores, Spikeville has nothing. Built as a residential community to house railroad workers, it quickly followed the economic misfortunes of the railroad. Without businesses of its own, Spikeville has been forced to increase residential property taxes to pay for its school system.

To raise additional money, Spikeville encourages new home building by offering home sites at greatly reduced prices. Inexpensive housing has gone up quickly. However, there is no sense of attachment to the community as there is in Hyerville. People do not know the names of their next-door neighbors, let alone what they do for a living. Without local business and industry, virtually everyone in Spikeville works outside the city. As a result, the city becomes largely a "bedroom community" to which people return after working somewhere else. This further reduces the sense of community identity.

Let's look briefly at how these two communities differ in terms of the functions they provide. Both communities provide socialization through their respective school systems. Other socialization mechanisms, such as participation in community activities, is much greater in Hyerville where residents largely spend their entire day in the community. As for the production of goods and services, Spikeville performs this function less well than Hyerville. Without a business sector, residents are forced to acquire goods and services outside the community. Hyerville, on the other hand, has an abundance of small shops, stores, and discount stores, as well as several other businesses and professional services.

Both communities provide social control through laws and local police departments. Both also have housing and health regulations and inspectors, but Spikeville seems less willing than Hyerville to enforce its rules. In addition, both communities provide certain kinds of support. However, Spikeville does so to a lesser extent. It has few social service agencies and makes few formal attempts to assist those in need. Finally, participation exists to a much higher degree in Hyerville. The availability of opportunities for people to spend time together is greater there because people both work and reside in the community.

It is clear that even cities of comparable size can be more or less effective in fulfilling their functions, depending on a variety of factors. Of the two cities, which one would you find more attractive as a place to live?

6. *Institutional communities.* Institutional communities have one major employer which may overshadow the whole surrounding area. Therefore, sometimes they are called "company towns." The company or institution may own all or a large portion of the available housing stock, renting it to their employees. By virtue of this ownership and of their control of employment, these institutions often have enormous influence on community events. Residents have much less freedom when the employing organization literally controls the community through ownership of most property. Once a person leaves the employ of the company, the company maintains control of the property. A variation of the company town is the community dominated by a single large employer. Examples include college towns, and communities with other large government facilities, such as prisons and mental hospitals. While not as overwhelming in their impact as industrial company towns, these employers may still exert an enormous influence on life in the community.

As you can see, the first three communities differ from one another primarily by their size, whether they are legally chartered, and whether they provide services to residents. The reservation community is characterized not by size but by the composition of its population (Native Americans) and the unique relationship of the community to the federal and state governments. Reservations are geographical areas set aside by the federal government to serve as communities for identified populations of Native Americans. Tribal governments have jurisdiction over some functions on the reservation, including law enforcement, while the federal government has a role in assisting the reservation communities by providing financial and medical services.

Bedroom and institutional communities differ from one another primarily in terms of the functions which they perform for their residents.

Of course, any system of categorization of communities leaves gaps and involves overlaps. For instance, some small towns of 10,000 people could also be referred to as rural areas because of the overlapping size definition. Thus, it is important to understand that one can define and describe communities by specific size rather than relying solely on such simple labels as "small town" or "rural community." In addition, some communities which rely largely on the recreational industry for their livelihood may have an official population as small as 10,000 but swell to many times that size during the "season." Examples are Branson, Missouri, Wisconsin Dells, Wisconsin, Gatlinburg, Tennessee, and Estes Park, Colorado.

Communities may also be classified on the basis of ethnic composition or degree of homogeneity/heterogeneity. For example, a community may have a mixture of people of many nationalities or socioeconomic classes or be dominated by a particular group. In some cases, while a diversity of ethnic groups is present, one group predominates. Miami, for example, has a very large population of Cubans. This has important implications for life in the community. Stores cater to specific population groups, and residents are often politically active to ensure that needs of their group are considered.

Other communities are predominantly affluent and others are primarily working-class. Still other communities may be more diverse but have ethnic enclaves such as Chinatown, Little Saigon, or Polish Hill. These factors are important in understanding what goes on in a community. For example, ethnic enclaves may offer special services to members of that minority group. Support groups and networks for Hmong (who migrated to the United States from Southeast Asia after the Vietnam War), for example, may be found in a particular area of the city. Language differences can complicate such community problem as education and human services. Similarly, a community's economic strength and resources may allow new social services to be developed or may severely limit what is possible.

Clear community boundaries are not always easy to establish. While the boundaries of cities are easily identified, community boundaries may be more diffuse. An ethnic community might be located primarily in one city but spill over into adjoining areas. The diversity of communities is compounded when one realizes there are almost 20,000 municipalities (cities) in the United States, about 17,000 townships (legally recognized geographical areas which may or may not have elected leaders), and over 3,000 counties (Rubin & Rubin, 1986,

Some communities have ethnic enclaves, such as Boston's Chinatown.

p. 118). The concept of community is further confused when we use the term to refer to non-place entities such as the "gay community" or the "legal community" (Fellin, 1987). These communities share a common sense of identity but are not geographical entities like cities or towns.

What is most important, however, is that neighborhoods and communities serve a variety of purposes for residents. They also come in different sizes and compositions. The effective worker, trying to understand a particular community's dynamics, would be wise to consider which of the functions described earlier are being carried out and which are not. It would also be helpful to know which type of community is under scrutiny. For example, is this a rural community or a metropolitan one? Is it an ethnic community or a reservation community? This knowledge is helpful in assessing a community, but is not in itself sufficient to direct your efforts as a change agent. In the next sections we will consider the community as an ecological and social system, and explain ways of understanding and assessing the community in a practice context.

Using the Systems Perspective

Generalist social workers use general systems theory to understand the relationships among various components of our society. Systems theory posits that these elements relate to one another in an orderly, functional manner. For example, the human body is a system, in that all of the various internal systems (e.g., circulatory, nervous, respiratory) relate to one another in a specific and predictable manner. Likewise, a human being can be seen as one element in a system that includes his family, employer, friendship group, and larger units such as school, church and community. Compton and Galaway (1989) view social systems as a series of boxes nested one inside the other. Figure 8.1 illustrates this view.

Thus, if you think of yourself as the person in the center, you recognize that you are part of a much larger set of systems. First, you are part of a family system composed of your family's other members. Next, your family is a system within the community. Likewise,

your community is a system within the state where you reside. You can carry this analysis further in both directions, considering either larger or smaller systems. For example, your state (e.g., Missouri, Wisconsin) is part of a larger system called the United States. Similarly, as the person in the center, you are composed of smaller units or internal systems (subsystems) such as circulatory or nervous.

As we grow up, we tend to see the community through our parents' and other family members' eyes. Of course, members of the community may view us as members of a particular family instead of as individuals. They might say, ''He's a Johnson kid. What did you expect?'' Or ''Like father, like son.''

In one sense, this diagrammatic model is helpful because it may be seen as circumscribing (or limiting) one's behavior. If the environment (including the family or community) is unacceptably restricting the person's behavior, she or he may seek to change the environment somehow. For example, a family that places unrealistic expectations on a child may need help in recognizing and changing their demands. Helping the family change is an appropriate social work role.

Similarly, if we want to understand individuals and families, we have to consider the influence of the community on both of these systems. Social workers must become more aware of the relationship between the individual and the environmental forces that have impact on that individual. Unemployment affecting several families may have nothing to do with the personal inadequacies of the family members. It might have much to do with what is happening to jobs in the community. Social workers must look beyond the individual and focus on the larger social system to accurately assess client problems. In short, human behavior is a function of the interactions among the cultural, social, biological, and psychological aspects of our environment. This perspective and the recognition that we must identify and build upon client strengths is the essence of generalist practice.

Kettner, Daley, and Nichols (1985) have also provided a systems model for viewing social work practice. They refer to five primary systems: *initiator, client, target, change agent*, and *action system*. The individual or group that brings a problem to the forefront is the initiator system. This may be an individual client, a group of clients, another professional, or an interested third party. The person initiates the process by identi-

Figure 8.1
A Social Systems Model

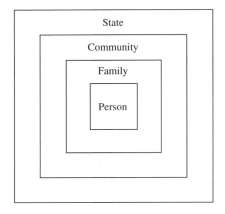

fying a problem or perhaps by suggesting a more effective way of doing something. For example, the social worker mentioned in chapter 3 who raised concerns about the needs of latchkey children was an initiator. She brought various groups together to discuss the problem. John Rogers, a social worker who helped form a neighborhood association, pursued that course because it was a more effective way to address neighborhood problems than having individual residents try to handle things themselves.

The "problem" may be reported to a worker or an agency that we refer to as the *change agent* system. This term is used because social workers are charged with responsibility for helping improve (change) circumstances and situations for their clients. The agency of which we are a part is thus a change agent system since the entire agency's goal is to facilitate improvement for clients. You may have heard social workers called change agents. The concept comes from this model.

The target system includes those individuals, organizations, or community elements that need changing. We might, for example, want a member of the city council to change her vote on a housing project for the homeless. Perhaps we want the building inspector to enforce existing building codes so that poor clients do not have to put up with leaky plumbing and unsanitary conditions. Or maybe police officers tend to stop and question minority individuals on the street more often than nonminorities, and we want to ensure equal treatment. In each of these cases, the person or organization that we want to change is a target system.

The client system consists of those who will benefit directly or indirectly from the change. The client system is also the initiator system when the client initiates the change by bringing it to your attention. A client infected with AIDS who asks your help in getting health-care when the local nursing home has refused him admission is an initiator. He is also the intended beneficiary or client system.

Action systems are those individuals, groups, or other entities that will carry out the effort to cause change. Sometimes this effort will be conducted by the social worker, sometimes by others. If we are trying to get the police department to treat oppressed groups more fairly, it might be best to have the city manager or city council manage the change. (The city manager is the chief administrative officer in some cities and the council is the chief legislative body. Managers supervise all city staff and the council supervises the city manager.) After all, they may be in the best position to put pressure on the police department and administration. Here the city manager or council would be the action system.

As we have seen above, one individual or group may play multiple roles. Thus, under the right set of circumstances, the social worker may be initiator, action system, and change agent system all in one. In other situations the worker may play only a single role. Taking the idea illustrated in figure 8.1 a bit further, we can focus on the worker in the center box within his/her agency (the next larger box). Being a part of a larger system also means that agency rules, expectations, and traditions constrain the worker. Understanding these ideas should help the worker maintain perspective. For example, the worker must recognize that she is influenced by systems that include her employer and, as mentioned earlier, the social work profession itself.

The Community as an Ecological and Social System

You need to understand several theoretical perspectives in order to understand and change systems (Vayda & Bogo, 1991). These perspectives include ecological, social systems, social structural, organizational, and human behavior theories.

Ecosystems or *ecological theory* (Germain & Gitterman, 1980) emphasizes the importance of the transactions between systems within an environment. For example, take the experience that many people of color have in their interactions (transactions) with police departments. The tendency of law-enforcement personnel to stop an African American driving through a predominantly white community definitely affects how the person of color views the police department. Thus, you can understand how various groups in a community might have very different perspectives on such social institutions as law enforcement, schools, and employers. These transactions are the primary focus of ecological theory. When you try to understand human behavior within the social environment, it is important to remember that the community is part of that environment. How people experience their social environment has a major influence on their expectations about the future and their trust level in social institutions (including social workers). Intervening at the macro level requires a solid recognition of the community as an ecological system. Social workers must often focus on how two or more systems interact. Characteristics of the community—such as size, racial composition, age of residents, population density, and the extant (existing) social structure (e.g., who has power, resources, and influence)—are important aspects of every community. They will be particularly helpful as we figure out when and where to intervene.

In addition, every community can be viewed as a *social system* with all the associated characteristics, including boundaries, homeostasis, stressors, task and maintenance functions, and subsystems. Communities have *boundaries* (borders or dividing lines) that separate them from their environment. These may be political, physical, or psychological boundaries. Political boundaries are city or county limits or wards or precinct divisions. Physical boundaries might include rivers, roads, or other geological features. Psychological boundaries are psychic separations from others. Gay and lesbian communities have a sense of identity that creates a boundary between them and non-gay-and-lesbian groups.

At the same time, all communities respond to change like any other system. That is, they tend to seek *homeostasis* or *equilibrium* (relative balance) and attempt to maintain the status quo when threatened by outside *stressors*. Stressors are forces that disrupt the homeostasis of a system. Examples in people's everyday lives include getting married, losing a job, moving to a new community, divorce, illness, and various catastrophes. In the lives of communities, stressors might include loss of a major employer, bankruptcy (this has affected several cities and, recently, Orange County, California), rapid growth or decline in population, scandals involving city government or officials, tragedies such as the bombing in Oklahoma City, and even pressure to change conditions in a community (such as attempts to pass legislation protecting the rights of gay and lesbian residents).

Communities perform both *task and maintenance functions* as they seek to maintain a range of services, attend to the needs of multiple audiences, and respond to special interest groups. Task functions include such mundane activities as snowplowing, street maintenance, and police and fire protection. Maintenance functions, more social in nature, are activities that help make peo-

Stressors of many kinds affect communities. In recent times, the bombing of the Alfred P. Murrah Building in Oklahoma City stands out as one of the most severe stressors in modern American history.

ple feel positive about living in a community. Examples are the Fourth of July fireworks, Christmas and holiday street lighting, and recreational facilities like swimming pools and beaches.

While the community is often seen as providing assistance to its residents, the relationship between citizens and their community is hardly one-sided. Many *primary groups* (e.g., families) help the community function. Individuals, families, and groups *use* community services, thus helping to justify the existence of those services. In addition, many groups contribute their own services to augment those provided by the community itself. Self-help groups offer services not normally available from traditional agencies. Service clubs and similar organizations extend city services by contributing money, time, or personpower to projects that benefit the community. Thus, a Kiwanis club may donate money and materials to build a park shelter. The Junior League may donate time to improve the appearance of a shelter for domestic violence survivors. College organizations and local businesses may volunteer to clean up city streets or highways as a way of helping communities.

In addition, each community may be viewed as a collection of subsystems (defined earlier) including economic, political, health, education, social welfare, etc. that often interact with and affect each other and other systems inside and outside the community (Fellin, 1987). *Social structural theory* focuses on understanding how these various subsystems affect the individual and group. Attention is directed to how some social structures (systems) empower clients and others oppress them. For example, a city hospital may treat poor patients so badly that they quit going there despite their need for medical care. Another city job program may actually involve clients in the development of policies and procedures affecting them. The hospital oppresses clients while the job program empowers clients. The latter gives clients a sense of importance and control over their lives while the former does not. Understanding how all these social structures (systems) interact with each other and with community residents and groups can tell you a great deal about the health and desirability of a community.

Organizational theory is important in understanding how bureaucracies function, especially in relation to provision of services. Chapter 5 discussed organizations and organizational theory more thoroughly. Here we will simply review such concepts as *authority, lines of communication, hierarchies,* and *job descriptions*.

Authority refers to the people in any organization who control the means of effecting change. Every position has a certain amount of authority and each organization member has some ability to use that authority at his or her own discretion. *Hierarchy* is the term for the layers of organization wherein people are situated in terms of power, responsibility, pay, and other variables. All members of an organization report to someone else above them in the hierarchy or chain of command.

Lines of communication are means by which information is transmitted in an organization. We might expect information to follow the hierarchy or chain of command up and down an organization (for example, from agency director step-by-step down to line staff or vice versa). Yet, in many situations the lines of communication don't follow the formal change. Some organizations have informal connections between members that facilitate the sharing of information. Other organizations seem to pass information only one way (such as top to bottom) and show little interest in hearing what people lower in the hierarchy are thinking.

Finally, *job descriptions* are written policies governing what a particular person in the organization is supposed to do. Earlier we mentioned the secretary whose job description called for typing 20 percent of the time and who refused to type more than that. Job descriptions can be very narrowly written or very broadly constructed. When you try to understand why a community governmental unit—such as a police department, a human services agency, or a parks and recreation department—is unresponsive to citizen needs, it is sometimes helpful to find out how the organizational factors of authority, lines of communication, hierarchies, and job descriptions contribute to the problem.

The final tool we use is *human behavior theory* (or theories, since there are several commonly employed). These theories are more useful for understanding the behavior of individuals and families and less useful for larger systems. However, the role of adaptation and stress (common to many human behavior theories) is useful in understanding how and why individuals behave in a certain manner when dealing with larger systems such as organizations and communities. Some groups, denied social or economic justice, lose any confidence in the willingness of larger systems (education, police, or social services) to help them. They adapt to injustices by becoming apathetic, angry, or both.

Similarly, behavioral theory, which suggests that much of our current behavior is the consequence of past learning, may also help us understand why individuals in an organization or community act the way they do. Being victimized by drive-by shootings can cause an entire neighborhood to lock its doors, refusing to help neighbors, and keeping its children constantly indoors. When this happens, the quality of life in the neighborhood is clearly affected.

Rational theories, which posit that actions and feelings arise from our thinking process, are also important. Suppose we wish to change the minds of members of a target system. If a decision maker believes that you have little community support for your ideas, she is not likely to give you what you seek. If she becomes convinced that you have great community support (whether you do or not, what she *thinks* is significant), she is more likely to accede to your request.

Through the use of multiple theories you can become more effective in dealing with larger systems in the environment. If you understand why things are the way they are you are in a much stronger position to change them. You have more insight into how systems work and, therefore, how to change them. These theories can guide your practice because they provide clues about what approaches to take to bring about change.

Additional Perspectives on the Community

Ideally, the most effective communities respond to the needs of all population segments. Often, however, certain portions of the community (such as the homeless) seem to be ignored either because they lack power or because they are invisible, or both. Needs come to the attention of a community as a function of many factors. For example, when asked what constitutes a "good" community, residents will often identify both positives and the absence of negatives. The community's aspects may include: it's a safe place to raise kids; the cost of living is reasonable; parks and recreation services are excellent; and schools are good. Negative factors might include a high crime rate, air pollution, traffic problems, and inadequate school funding. Clearly, the list of qualities is highly individual. So how does a community focus on meeting a particular type of need? A need is often brought to community attention by people with a specific agenda. For example, wealthy and influential citizens concerned about public safety and crime convince the police force to crack down on drug dealers. In the process, the police department begins to stop every person of color they see on the streets on the ground that they might be drug dealers. The needs of one group in this community have created problems for another group. In another city the community responds to a vocal minority by undertaking efforts to preserve historic buildings, beautify city streets, and improve traffic flow on Main Street. Elsewhere, primary efforts focus on economic development, bringing in new businesses and jobs, and combatting job losses occasioned by local plant closings. In each case, the city is responding to needs expressed by only a portion of its residents.

It is important to recognize, then, that a community may choose to focus on some aspect of problem solving or resource utilization merely because of a strong interest group's lobbying. On the other hand, a community may expend resources and efforts based on a planned needs assessment or a comprehensive review of community problems. A needs assessment is a systematic effort to identify problems, needs, or demand for service. These are often, but not always, undertaken before launching new programs.

Again, ideally, given the enormous resources (financial, organizational, and human) available in a community, most citizen needs should be met. However, this is often not the case. The nature of the community as a system means that it is subject to numerous influences. These include its subsystems (local groups, organizations, and residents) and its own larger environment (other communities, state and federal governments, and large economic entities). The combination of pressures from its larger environment and its subunits can be seen in many ways. To better understand how this works, Fellin (1987) suggests looking at one of the primary factors impacting any given community and its ability to meet community needs—competition.

The first fact of life about communities is that they are often battlegrounds for groups and organizations competing for resources. Competition is the struggle within a community by various groups, all seeking to put their interests and needs ahead of any others. The competition may be waged over the best use of certain land or the most important items in a city budget. Various segments of communities compete for resources and attention. People who want better streets compete with those who want more police protection. Advocates for new schools compete with those who seek property tax reduction and limits on spending for education. The director of a city's parks and recreation program competes with the city streets department director for limited city funds. Will it be a new tennis court or new asphalt for Main Street? Should we spend money on bike trails or new sidewalks?

Competition is essentially a political activity in which many valid needs vie with other equally valid needs. Consequently, when you advocate for a particular program or need you are always competing with others. It does not mean that the other needs are illegitimate nor that your objectives are less worthy if they do not receive funding. All it means is that you are more (or less) successful in convincing those who control the resources that your own case has merit. The reality of competition is sometimes a surprise to new social workers who assume that a need properly documented and presented will usually, or even always, be met.

Fellin (1987) discusses other characteristics useful

for understanding communities: centralization, concentration, invasion, and succession. *Centralization* is the practice of clustering business services and institutions in one area of the community. For example, most communities have a central business district, though this may no longer be the principal retail sector of the community because of the prevalence of shopping malls. Often the downtown shopping district has been replaced by another form of centralization—the urban mall. In another example of centralization, auto dealerships often locate adjacent to each other. Communities, through zoning and other land use restrictions, frequently attempt to centralize certain businesses in specific areas. Perhaps it is an industrial park where all new commercial or manufacturing plants are encouraged to locate. Other communities have zoned districts so that adult book stores are centralized in a particular location. Zoning laws are a major means of ensuring that homeowners do not find an industrial corporation building suddenly popping up next door. It is also why subdivisions of expensive homes are approved and rules established excluding less expensive homes.

Another characteristic of communities, *concentration*, is the tendency of certain groups to cluster in a particular section or neighborhood. There are several reasons for this. Housing in this area may cost less, residents may seek to locate closer to family and friends, or discrimination in housing may force people to concentrate in certain areas. Recently a local newspaper undertook a study of landlords' reactions when Hmong refugees sought housing. When Hmong individuals called about apartments listed in the newspaper, landlords, recognizing the callers' accents, said the apartment was already rented. When a non-Hmong person called immediately afterward, landlords told them the apartment was available. Such blatant oppression and discrimination often results in housing segregation. New in-migrants concentrate in the only community area where they do not experience such treatment, in neighborhoods populated with others of their nationality/ethnicity. Of course, the concentration of large, poor families in certain neighborhoods can cause other problems, such as overcrowding of available units.

Another community characteristic, *invasion*, is the tendency of each new group of in-migrants to force existing groups out. Invasion primarily affects housing. Thus, African Americans living in a neighborhood may begin to leave as Asian Americans move in. They, in turn, will leave when some other group begins to move into (invade) the neighborhood. Eventually this can lead to older neighborhoods becoming more rundown, even though at one time they were very nice areas in which to live. A corollary of invasion is the process known as *gentrification*, the tendency of upper-middle-class families to move back into downtown and near-downtown residential areas. Paradoxically, as these families turn second floors of businesses into lofts and rehabilitate large older homes, they also are invading an established neighborhood. These restored homes and buildings rise in value, and poorer residents are forced to move out. When this occurs, those forced to move often end up in another undesirable neighborhood, putting pressure on existing residents to relocate (see highlight 8.2).

Another form of invasion occurs when certain types of land use begins to change. The conversion of large single-family homes into apartments may force the remaining single-family home-owners to sell rather than be surrounded by multifamily housing. When they do so, their homes will likely face the same fate, namely conversion to multifamily homes. Of course, the converted multifamily housing provides shelter for a greater number of persons than did single family homes. However, those forced out are often lower- or fixed-income elderly.

In a similar fashion, a predominantly retail downtown business district may lose its businesses as vacant storefronts are invaded. As these storefronts become insurance offices, counseling centers, and law offices, they produce less foot traffic than businesses such as department stores. Consequently, an office center may eventually replace the old business district.

Invasion is usually followed by *succession*, the gradual replacement of the original occupants of a community or neighborhood by new groups. It is common to see a neighborhood that first housed Irish immigrants, then African Americans, now housing Hispanics. Succession, of course, can continue indefinitely in some areas of a community because it usually creates less expensive housing which is attractive to low-income families and individuals.

Centralization, concentration, invasion, and succession typically occur in most communities. Understanding each of them helps social workers better predict what will happen in their communities. Concentration helps us understand why large numbers of Hispanic cli-

---

HIGHLIGHT 8.2

KEY CONCEPTS FOR UNDERSTANDING COMMUNITIES

Competition: The struggle within a community by various groups, all seeking to have their interests and needs considered more important than other needs.

Centralization: The practice of clustering business services and institutions in one area of a city.

Concentration: The tendency of certain groups (particularly ethnic groups) to cluster in a particular section or neighborhood of a community.

Gentrification: A pattern whereby upper-middle-class families move back into downtown and near-downtown residential areas, turning second floors of businesses into lofts and rehabilitating large older homes.

Invasion: A tendency of each new group of in-migrants to force out or replace existing groups previously living in a neighborhood.

Succession: The gradual replacement of the original occupants or residents of a community or neighborhood by new groups.

---

ents are living in substandard housing yet refuse to move. Similarly, gentrification becomes real when African American clients are forced out of their near-downtown neighborhoods to make way for wealthy professionals bent on rehabilitating these buildings. Being about to pinpoint the factor responsible for the problem can help identify the best avenue for intervention. Gentrification of a former multifamily housing unit usually requires rezoning or permission to change the use of the property. Gentrification can be prevented by communities that refuse to permit this change of use or re-zoning.

Community Resource Systems

All communities have a variety of resource systems available to help residents. Three primary types include informal, formal, and societal. *Informal* (sometimes called natural) resource systems include family members, coworkers, friends, neighbors, and others who provide emotional, social, or more tangible types of support.

A second type of resource system is the *formal* or membership organization. These systems include social or fraternal organizations (e.g., Elks, Kiwanis, Rotary, League of Women Voters, etc.) in which people hold memberships. Other examples include labor unions, professional associations such as NASW, scouting organizations and churches. Churches may provide members spiritual support or more tangible benefits, such as emergency financial assistance. Too often, social workers neglect to explore the role of clients' religious and spiritual values and church affiliations. Workers thereby exclude an important resource for many clients.

Societal resource systems are institutionalized organizations or services such as private and public social service agencies, family service agencies, and libraries. These resource systems are established to provide specific kinds of assistance to community residents. Social workers employed in public and private agencies tend to think of these systems first when clients experience problems. Familiarity with these formal resource systems makes it easy to overlook other, more informal systems.

An important lesson in understanding your community is that learning is a continuous process. Even experienced social workers may not be aware of the myriad resource systems available to help with any given problem. Consequently, we often operate with less than complete knowledge of our own communities.

Knowledge of a community's various resource systems is essential if you are to help individual clients or groups of clients with similar problems. If you know that the Church of Our Lady of Perpetual Misery provides low-cost meals to its shut-in members, your client (a member of the church) can receive help at little cost from people whom she already knows. This may be preferable to connecting her with some other societal resource system she knows nothing about and with which she is not comfortable. Knowledge of resources is also important because you may wish to consult specific resource systems to learn more about community needs. For example, asking the local National Association for the Advancement of Colored People (NAACP) for assistance in pinpointing needs of that ethnic group may be more efficient and effective than talking to a multitude of individual African Americans.

Learning about a community often requires more than simply reading a community resource directory, however. Most communities have local gathering places where certain groups meet. In one case in the author's experience, a local restaurant served this function. Many influential formal and informal leaders in the community (e.g., business owners and city officials) gathered there for breakfast and discussed major community issues. Most mornings you would see community residents greeting friends, moving from table to table to talk, and sharing opinions on various topics. Subjects discussed could include everything from the proposed new landfill to rumors about the city manager's car accident. (Was he drinking?) More could be learned about the community by listening and observing there than by reading an entire resource directory.

Figure 8.2 shows the vast variety of resource systems and organizations that exist in a single city. Those listed here are only a very modest sample of the entire system. As you look at the figure, you can recognize two of the three types of resource systems, formal and societal. Governmental units, educational organizations, and social service agencies are examples of societal resource systems. Civic, spiritual/religious, consumer, business/trade, and professional groups are considered formal resource systems. Each of these groups, organizations, or services might benefit at least some of your clients at some point in their lives. Not

knowing about these community resource systems reduces your ability to link individual clients and groups with needed services.

The existence of the array of resource systems illustrated in figure 8.2 does not necessarily mean that most needy members of a community have access to them. In some communities, informal resource systems such as relationships among neighbors may be more significant for clients. Clients may rely on neighbors for help in times of need. In other communities there may be greater reliance on formal structures and societal institutions. New resources may need development when existing systems are either unresponsive to client needs or are simply not available. For example, the absence of a community shelter for battered women means that these individuals have nowhere to turn when they are in danger.

One major advantage of the systems and ecological perspectives is they permit us to step back and see a problem through a wider lens. We can view problems in the context of the larger systems in which those problems exist. We might realize, as we consider the problem and the array of community resources available, that the problem is simply bigger than the community. For example, community problems such as plant closings may have more to do with federal tax laws and foreign ownership of a local company than with the quality of the local work force. Tax laws that encourage closing down a company and deducting the loss from one's corporate taxes can subtly encourage such shutdowns. This has virtually nothing to do with people living in the community. Similarly, new economic needs in the macro environment may cause changes in family structure. Changing economic factors may require both parents to work in order for the family to survive. Such factors permeate society and are not limited to just one community.

A community may lack the means, autonomy, or authority to do anything about a particular problem, such as changes in family structure. In addition, federal or state laws may limit the right of a community to raise money through taxation or to clean up a polluted industrial landfill. Often, these problems, if they are to be solved, require the resources and involvement of multiple levels of government.

Occasionally, community apathy or lack of citizen involvement amplifies community problems. In some communities residents believe no one can do anything

Figure 8.2
Community Resource Systems

formal & societal

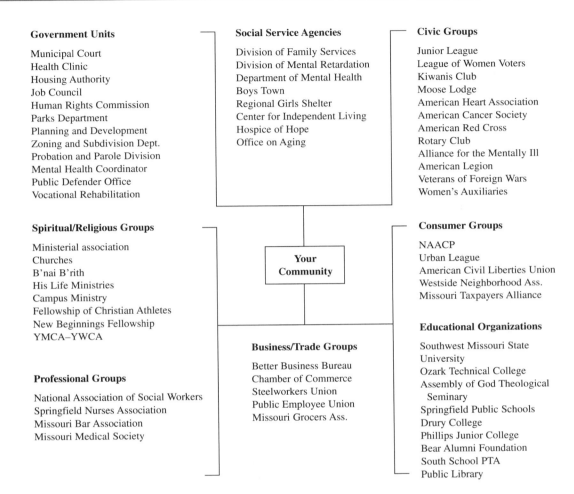

Government Units

Municipal Court
Health Clinic
Housing Authority
Job Council
Human Rights Commission
Parks Department
Planning and Development
Zoning and Subdivision Dept.
Probation and Parole Division
Mental Health Coordinator
Public Defender Office
Vocational Rehabilitation

Spiritual/Religious Groups

Ministerial association
Churches
B'nai B'rith
His Life Ministries
Campus Ministry
Fellowship of Christian Athletes
New Beginnings Fellowship
YMCA–YWCA

Professional Groups

National Association of Social Workers
Springfield Nurses Association
Missouri Bar Association
Missouri Medical Society

Social Service Agencies

Division of Family Services
Division of Mental Retardation
Department of Mental Health
Boys Town
Regional Girls Shelter
Center for Independent Living
Hospice of Hope
Office on Aging

Your Community

Business/Trade Groups

Better Business Bureau
Chamber of Commerce
Steelworkers Union
Public Employee Union
Missouri Grocers Ass.

Civic Groups

Junior League
League of Women Voters
Kiwanis Club
Moose Lodge
American Heart Association
American Cancer Society
American Red Cross
Rotary Club
Alliance for the Mentally Ill
American Legion
Veterans of Foreign Wars
Women's Auxiliaries

Consumer Groups

NAACP
Urban League
American Civil Liberties Union
Westside Neighborhood Ass.
Missouri Taxpayers Alliance

Educational Organizations

Southwest Missouri State
University
Ozark Technical College
Assembly of God Theological
Seminary
Springfield Public Schools
Drury College
Phillips Junior College
Bear Alumni Foundation
South School PTA
Public Library

---

about the problem, so why try. In other cases a lack of shared values prevents the community from taking concerted action. Residents in several communities battled over the need for additional schools and public facilities such as libraries. Such struggles may pit elderly citizens on fixed incomes (who value low taxes) with little investment in the schools or libraries against parents and school officials (who value good schools). Unable to agree, they cannot join forces to address the community's education needs.

You cannot understand communities completely without looking at demographic development, the role of social stratification, and the impact of economic and political systems on a community's health. In the next three sections we focus on each respectively.

Demographic Development of Communities

It is helpful to understand more about the economic, ethnic, social, and educational characteristics of a community. You may want to know how many people in your community fall below the poverty line (a subsistence level of income). Such information is called demographic data. Specifically, demographic data describe a community in terms of such factors as race, gender, education level, and economic class. Thus, you could describe a given community as 40 percent African American, 30 percent Hispanic, and 30 percent white. Normally, the best source of information on demographic data is the U.S. Bureau of the Census. The Census Bureau divides each community in the United States into what are called census tracts, based solely on numbers of people living in a given area. They serve as a handy way of dividing a community for study and analysis. Traditionally, population size has been used to distinguish between communities. We use terms such as city, town, village, and metropolitan area to designate communities of differing sizes. The definition of *urban*, for example, usually applies to a community with a population of over 2,500 people that is incorporated (that is, legally chartered) with the state. Incorporated communities are permitted to do such things as levy taxes and can qualify for certain kinds of state financial aid. Being chartered or incorporated bestows the state's formal recognition upon a community. *Metropolitan areas*, similarly defined by size, are cities with a population of at least 50,000. The term *suburb* refers to incorporated areas adjacent to a larger central city. As mentioned earlier in the chapter, metropolitan areas may include other smaller cities. We tend to use the term *rural* for everything that does not fit one of the above designations.

Urbanization and Suburbanization

Two primary trends, urbanization and suburbanization, have strong effects upon communities. *Urbanization* is the trend in which multitudes of people move to large metropolitan areas and away from rural, outlying areas. Urbanization has historically been a major factor in the growth of most large U.S. cities. The rate of urbanization is affected by transportation systems, communication systems, and employment opportunities. For example, the development of automobiles and trains made it possible for people to get into the city. In the early 1900s, the availability of factory jobs attracted millions of rural residents to the larger central cities such as Chicago and New York. In the process, many social

problems developed, including child labor, residential segregation, poor sanitation, and other offshoots of the rapid growth of central cities. A modern equivalent of this trend is the large numbers of legal and illegal immigrants flocking to cities while better educated professionals move away. The result is another example of succession, discussed earlier.

A second trend with major influence on American communities is *suburbanization*. While movement in the early part of this century was toward metropolitan areas (urbanization), the trend since 1940 has been toward suburbanization. In suburbanization, residents deserted large cities and moved to smaller communities nearby. This movement was encouraged by the development of the interstate highway system, mass transit systems, and tax advantages for home ownership. (By deducting interest on home mortgages, federal and state governments help support home ownership.) The desire for larger homes and more yard, changes in job location, lower property taxes, and fewer city problems combine to encourage suburbanization. Companies opening branch offices outside the central city also encourage employees to live away from the city. Of course, those who benefit most from this trend are the most upwardly mobile members of our society, composed disproportionately of white, middle-class Americans. As a result, the phenomenon sometimes is called *white flight*. Increasingly, the large urban city has become the home of minorities of color, citizens with lower incomes, and others not able to take advantage of the trend.

Gentrification

Although much recent movement has been away from the central cities, there is a notable exception—*gentrification*, the movement of upper-middle-class professionals and families back to the central city. Their purchase and renovation of older buildings result in increased value of buildings surrounding their properties (many of them currently rented to lower-income families). As these properties become more valuable they are sold to other newcomers. Property values increase, and so do rents. This forces lower-income individuals and families to seek housing in less expensive areas. For social workers, this can produce an ethical dilemma. On the one hand, rehabilitation of rundown buildings improves the quality of life in a community and prevents further deterioration. On the other hand, the process eventually hurts low-income families and individuals who may have few other housing choices. Do we encourage housing rehabilitation or focus on maintaining affordable housing for the poor? Are the choices mutually exclusive? These are difficult questions to answer. Innovative solutions are needed. For example, federal support for rebuilding dilapidated areas of cities (urban renewal) resulted in some communities redeveloping blighted business and residential neighborhoods. It also forced large numbers of the poor from their homes and resulted in further overcrowding of other parts of the city. Achieving the goals of rebuilding a community without hurting those displaced by the effort takes new and creative ideas.

Rural Communities

We have not said much about rural communities. While many stereotype such communities as lacking sophistication and services, there has also been a growing trend to relocate in rural areas, particularly in the West. Migration from California places pressure on more rural states nearby, such as Nevada and Oregon, as newcomers seek a more relaxed, less expensive style of life.

There is a substantial body of literature on rural communities and on social work practice in rural areas. Brill (1990), for example, makes some excellent observations about rural communities. She notes that rural communities often have many of the same problems that urban areas have, but fewer of the services needed to cope. The strong value systems in rural areas and the pressure to conform to longstanding traditions may make it more difficult for newcomers to fit in. At the same time, rural residents are often more willing to help each other in times of need. Informal resource systems may be stronger, though societal resource systems may be less numerous than in metropolitan areas.

The worker new to a rural area may find herself with relatively fewer colleagues, less supervision, and less personal privacy than she would have in an urban area. Value conflicts with rural residents may also arise. For example, pressure on individual residents to conform to community norms may conflict with the social worker's belief in client self-determination. Similarly, a community belief in self-reliance may result in opposition to development of new societal resources. Residents

may believe that people should be able to help themselves instead of relying on publicly supported programs.

Where Is the Best Place to Live?

Over the years there have been periodic analyses of the relative advantages of living in the city versus the suburbs versus rural areas. These comparisons, published in newspapers and popular magazines, do not always recognize that each location has its own advantages and disadvantages. Rather than relying on stereotypes of various communities, you should use the same nonjudgmental attitudes appropriate to working with diverse clients. In each community you will need to learn the strengths and weaknesses of resource systems, the important values and norms of residents, and how to use those factors in improving the quality of life for clients.

Social Stratification

Social stratification, or the division of a society into categories (e.g., income, social class) is both a conceptual tool and a fact of life. On the one hand, it is often useful to consider larger groups as composed of various subgroups. Depending upon your interests, you can stratify a community by race, gender, or age, all useful dimensions. For example, we may want to know about the types of jobs held by residents. Thus, we are likely to use a stratification system for types of employment (e.g., working class, blue collar, white color, and so on). If we look at a community and discover, for example, that a disproportionate percentage of the population are women over age sixty-five, this information may suggest the need for more social services, health care, or housing for this age and gender population. Similarly, stratifying the population by level of education may reveal a sizeable population with little formal education. Armed with this information, we might delve further into this group's educational and training needs. A needs assessment focused on this group might show that they need vocational training to prepare for jobs in local industries. Needs assessments are systematic efforts to identify needs in a community. This information can help us develop priorities. A needs assessment may be accomplished through surveying community residents, studying official government data such as census information, and reviewing agency files or other similar records. Needs may also be identified by inviting members of a target population to a meeting to discuss their needs or by asking relevant community officials (such as ministers, the mayor, or agency directors) to provide their views.

On the other hand, social stratification is a tool used to discriminate against groups who differ by gender, race, or sexual orientation. Anytime we behave differently toward those with an identifiable characteristic such as skin color, the negative side of social stratification is evident because we have used some characteristic as an excuse to deny group members' individuality.

In the United States we frequently find social class stratification. This system divides people into categories based on socioeconomic factors such as income and education. The primary purpose of this information is to better understand our society and the vast disparities within it. Only when you understand the facts can you begin to target pieces of the system for change.

The number of actual categories in any stratification scheme is arbitrary. Thus, you may see references to lower class, middle class, and upper class, or perhaps lower middle, middle, and upper middle class. A more recent addition to the nomenclature is *underclass*, a term that refers to the poorest of the poor. This group is considered almost permanently trapped by social and economic factors such as discrimination, lack of education and marketable job skills, and personal factors such as chronic mental illness. It is composed disproportionately of minority groups. Members of the underclass are among the most oppressed groups in our society and perhaps the most difficult to help. Despite the drawbacks of categorization, information on social stratification helps us recognize and understand the unique problems of such population segments. In other words, if you don't thoroughly understand the problem, you can't begin to solve it.

Community Economic Systems

Economic systems, whether at the national, state, or local level, are concerned with the "production, distribution, and consumption of goods and services" (Fellin, 1987, p. 119). This process of production, distribution, and consumption is one of the community's primary functions. The community is connected closely to our economic system. Everything from Stevens' Supermarket to General Motors is involved in fulfilling this community function. Economic systems also include professionals such as doctors, attorneys, and social workers, in addition to service companies such as restaurants, laundries, and other service-giving businesses.

There is also an "underground" economic system (Fellin, 1987) consisting of off-the-books businesses, such as child and lawn care, bartering, and even gambling. All of these exist without maintaining records, paying taxes, or otherwise participating in the aboveground, or legitimate, economy. Lower-income clients may well benefit from these underground activities at one level or another. For example, clients who provide babysitting for middle-class families may be paid in cash. No income taxes are deducted nor Social Security taxes paid. Because no records are kept, providers of service may not report this income to the Internal Revenue System. Not abiding by the rules can save money, but is illegal. While clients may benefit by having more money in their pockets, they risk getting caught. Equally important, people who don't have Social Security deducted do not get credit for this work when they retire nor have Social Security disability/survivor's benefits.

Underground bartering also exists. A dentist fixes the teeth of his plumber who agrees to put in a new bathroom for the dentist. No money changes hands and no records are kept. The size of the underground economy is unknown but believed to be sizable. By understanding that it exists side by side with the money economy and why people participate in it, you will better grasp how your community's economic system operates.

We have established that the economic condition of a community is crucial to its health. For example, out-migration of businesses, closing of major employers, and other negative happenings can cause unemployment and personal stress for community residents. Such out-migration causes the community to lose tax revenues, thereby hampering its ability to maintain schools, pay social workers, or pave streets. A person who loses her job because of a deteriorating economic situation suffers personally by losing income, suffering decreased self-esteem, and perhaps even encountering forced relocation. Work provides not only income and benefits to residents, but also a sense of belonging and satisfaction with one's life. This satisfaction and sense of participation can enhance or detract from people's connection to the residential community where they live. Unemployed workers may be less likely to contribute to or participate in their communities. They are more likely to be concerned about their own situation. Communities need jobs and taxes to help fund basic services. Likewise, residents need employment to feel positive about themselves, provide an adequate life-style, and feel a part of their communities.

Feeling alienated from one's community and hopeless about the future are common characteristics of some inner city residents. We have referred to people experiencing these feelings as the underclass. Fellin (1987) has captured the ideal when he says what we really want in our communities is a "low level of unemployment, a minimal level of discrimination in hiring . . . , a program of affirmative action for employment of special populations, an adequate health and welfare system and educational system, adequate protection (fire, police, safety), adequate public services and recreational facilities and programs, and opportunity to earn adequate income above the poverty level" (p. 121).

Like most other aspects of our lives, economic systems are affected by decisions made at all three levels of government, federal, state, and local. Federal and state taxing, local land use, and federal transportation policies may all have an impact on a company's decision to relocate in a community, expand operations, or move away. Ready access to highways, airlines, or railroads may make it easier for a company to ship its goods across the country or around the world. Local gifts of land or reduced taxes also help corporations decide to locate in a community. Lower state taxes may help some companies select a given state for expanding their operations. Other companies will consider such factors as quality schools and access to a strong labor pool as critical incentives.

The enormous emphasis communities place on recruiting new businesses is testimony to the importance of the economic system on the local level. Communities and states offer millions of dollars in tax breaks, loan forgiveness, and outright grants to attract and retain major employers. One community was so anxious to get a major employer in its new industrial park that leaders evicted a small cement company because the prospective new tenant considered it too messy.

The crucial fact is that a healthy economic system supports the vast majority of the social programs and services in which social workers practice. In other words, taxes paid by corporations and wage earners pay directly or indirectly for most social services. Thus, you cannot overestimate the importance of the economic system. Also, failures of the economic system often directly impact clients and services. Thus, while we may take pride in what the American economic system can produce, we must also recognize its limitations. Unemployment, plant closings, layoffs, and low-wage jobs are all part and parcel of our economic system. Understanding the community requires that we understand the role of the economic system in that community and the importance of human and social services to meet the needs of those affected by that system.

Community Political Systems

The term "political" has a negative ring for many people. It conjures up images of smoke-filled rooms and shady deals, decisions made for wrong and selfish reasons, and sometimes questionable actions by government officials. For our purposes, however, the political arena is where most decisions affecting social work practice are made. Funding for the programs that serve our clients, pay our salaries, and support our agencies comes largely from the federal, state, and local governments. Government may support the development of programs benefiting the community, but this same government may undercut and diminish those programs. This occurs when a governmental unit (federal, state, or local) decides to fund social service programs, refuses to fund them, or funds them insufficiently. These decisions are so important to us and our clients that we cannot afford to avoid involvement.

Formal Organizations and Informal Political Processes

At the community level, the political system includes formal organizations like city government (where funding decisions are made) and "informal political processes and activities" (Fellin, 1987, p. 127) . Informal political processes are evident when certain people in the community exert significant power over decisions made by government officials. The processes are infor-

---

HIGHLIGHT 8.3

GOVERNMENTAL ACTIVITIES IN THE COMMUNITY

Designing community programs:	Programs such as Neighborhood Watch that involve neighborhood residents in crime prevention activities is one example.
Allocating funds:	Monies for homeless shelters, general assistance, and playgrounds are simple examples.
Providing services for citizens:	Basic services like police and fire protection are in this category.
Building projects:	This might include jails, county care centers for the elderly, and community centers.
Awarding and supervising contracts:	Counties and cities often contract with private agencies to provide needed social services.
Determining and enforcing laws:	This function is carried out by both the legislative branch (e.g., city council) and the administrative branch (e.g., police department).
Making and enforcing regulations:	Logical examples are housing, health, and sanitation ordinances.
Negotiating agreement:	Decisions involving location of streets or highways are in this category.
Mediating disputes:	This may be done when city agencies are at odds with each other or with segments of the community. Some communities have contracted with agencies to provide mediation services to residents covering everything from child custody to landlord-tenant disputes.
Planning for the community:	Cities are usually solely responsible for planning local parks, streets, and sewer/water service.

---

mal because such people are not elected by citizens nor accountable to community residents. For example, a local banker may actually control or affect many of the decisions made by elected officials.

The political system can encourage or discourage participation of community residents, especially minorities. Some communities, for example, have made it difficult to register voters by discouraging voter registration drives. Actions by federal and state political systems affect local matters in many areas such as housing, roads, and health. Highlight 8.3 provides a good summary of activities that characterize government involvement in the community (Rubin & Rubin, 1986 p. 111).

As mentioned earlier, there are three levels of government which affect decisions within the community.

The federal government has multiple responsibilities. It funds many social programs, maintains the U.S. monetary system, oversees interstate commerce, and provides for the national defense. Finally, it protects the civil rights of U.S. citizens. Sometimes, the federal government acts in partnership with state government. An example is the recent federal welfare reform law. This law establishes general rules allowing states to qualify for certain federal welfare funding. However, once those rules are met, states may develop their own policies with respect to specific programs.

State governments fund most health and mental health services that social workers and others provide. They also play a role in education, providing financial support for local school districts and enforcing rules regarding how this financial support is spent.

Local governments (county or city) often provide health and social services. They also provide fire and police services. Clearly, there is much overlap among levels of government. Sometimes there is tension and conflict. This is especially so when federal or state rules are unpopular at the local level. For example, states may set rules restricting the ability of a community to spend money on its school system. Often, however, there is effective cooperation.

Political decision making at the local level is different from that at the state or federal level. While debates at the upper levels often revolve around party lines (e.g., Democrats versus Republicans), local politics are more concerned with issues that cut across party lines. Snow removal, street maintenance, sidewalks, and good schools are issues that rarely involve political parties. A city council, for example, may consist of people from across the political spectrum (Democrat, Independent, Republican) who vote the same way on most major issues. To put it succinctly, there are no Republican sewer systems and no Democratic streets. Consequently, it is sometimes easier for local elected officials to reach compromises and agreements despite the fact that they may significantly disagree on national political issues.

The formal structure of the community political system has several components. These include the official governance structure consisting of elected officials (e.g., mayor, city council), the city bureaucracy, the staff who carry out the city functions described in highlight 8.3, and appointed committees (such as the city planning commission or police and fire commissions) which advise the elected officials in their respective areas. The formal political structure also includes citizen participation. Formal citizen involvement can occur through organizations such as the Chamber of Commerce (an association of business owners). Informal involvement takes place both through the personal power and influence of individual community members and through the power structure. The power structure, usually outside the formal government structure, consists of business leaders and others with major influence over what goes on in a community. Power in a community has an impact on all aspects of community life. The influence of powerful people may determine whether or not a homeless shelter is built or a group home for the emotionally troubled adolescents is allowed to locate in a given neighborhood. The next section will continue discussion of the community's power structure.

Power in the Community

The political system determines who makes decisions in a community (Fellin, 1987). This is really a power issue. Therefore, it is critical to understand how power operates within communities. This section will present a definition of power, consider types and sources of power, and explore the relationship between power and conflict.

Defining Power

Power may be defined as "the ability to move somebody or some group or organization to do something they may not want to do" (Meenaghan, Washington, & Ryan, 1982, p. 117) . Highlight 8.4 on page 286 provides an example of the influence of power.

From another perspective, power may also be seen as the ability to prevent someone from doing something they want to do. Such negative power is more difficult to detect. Let's reconsider the situation described in highlight 8.4. If Peter had wanted to adopt a pro-family policy for the shelter but had learned that the city manager wanted as many people served as possible, he might have dropped the idea altogether before ever proposing it. An exercise of power has occurred in both cases, but is not as evident in the second example because there is no visible power struggle and others never know the influence the city manager exerted.

Types of Power

We also distinguish between potential and actual power. *Potential power* is power that has not yet been exercised. Potential power exists when we can influence others but have not done so. *Actual power* is the *use* of power to influence others. Sometimes potential power is not used because it would not be appropriate or because the payoff for using the power is questionable. A person might not exercise because others might construe it as bullying or throwing one's weight around. Such overt use of power can make the more powerful person look bad. Sometimes people elect not to use power because they don't see how they will benefit from forcing a decision one way or another. People tend to use power only when it is in their interest to do so. When there is nothing

---

HIGHLIGHT 8.4

POWER AT WORK

Peter Kracker was an intense administrator with excellent skills for managing new organizations. As director of the new community shelter for the homeless, he was anxious to show he could run an efficient program. One of his first policies, borrowed from another similar shelter he had operated, was to institute a same-sex policy. This policy meant that the shelter would serve only clients of the same gender. The policy allowed Peter to house more homeless people because he could create barracks-style physical arrangements with rows of beds for homeless men. Peter was quite proud of his accomplishment. His facility, originally designed to house forty people per night, now held sixty-five each night.

At his third meeting with city officials (who were providing 75 percent of the shelter's funding, the city manager raised some concerns about the new policy. He had read that policies such as this were common in homeless shelters. However, they fueled the breakup of families by forcing family members to live apart. Often, they resulted in women and children being denied shelter entirely.

Peter defended his position and argued that he could serve more clients using his system. The discussion became quite heated until the city manager made it clear that he would not place the shelter in the budget next year unless Peter adopted a more pro-family policy.

Peter said that under the circumstances he would revise the policy so that families could be housed at the shelter. If that action was needed to satisfy the funding source, he could hardly afford to act differently. Peter had just encountered an exercise of power. The city manager had the power to make or break Peter's program. If Peter wanted the program to survive, he had to comply with the city manager's desires.

---

important at stake, there may be no motivation to use power.

Sources of Power

Sources of power vary (Meenaghan, Washington, & Ryan, 1982). A financial asset such as money is commonly recognized as a source of power. Other sources include business ownership, community status, possession of information, or linkages to other individuals, groups, or organizations with power. One person may have multiple sources of power or only a single source. A wealthy business owner has money, business ownership, and community status as sources of power.

Power tends to be concentrated in a relatively small number of people. Because of this, it is important to know how to detect who has this power. One primary method, the *reputational* approach, involves simply asking others about who has power. Truly powerful people are likely to be mentioned most frequently. The *issues* approach is another means of detecting power. It assumes that there are always important community issues under consideration and that those who are influential in addressing these issues are powerful people. Identify the most important issues and then observe which persons are most influential. Those people most involved in making decisions are likely to be the most powerful.

A third method of detecting power is the *positional* approach. The positional approach assumes, reasonably enough, that those who hold various important positions in a community also have power. Thus, one would assume that the city manager, mayor, and president of the city council hold power. The same would be said of persons holding titles such as chairman of the board or executive director.

It is entirely possible, however, that those with official positions have relatively little power. In some situations others with no official positions may actually be making decisions. The richest person in town may be directly involved in decisions affecting the local college, the county board, and the school board despite holding no official position in any of these bodies. His ideas are listened to because he has money, prestige, or other sources of power. Therefore, it is better to use the positional approach in tandem with another method to avoid overemphasizing the importance of official positions.

Note also that some people are accorded power in one area but not in another (Johnson, 1992). Thus, one may look to a person for leadership in business but not in civic or political matters. There is also evidence that power is not always static. That is, power may be fluid and shifting in some situations while remaining constant and concentrated in others. This means that holding power depends upon the situation: an individual has power in one situation but not in others, but some people consistently wield power in all decisions.

Other factors may affect power. Those who own local businesses are more likely to have power than those who manage businesses that are part of a chain. Chain store managers move around every few years and put down few roots in a community. Transitory community residents are less likely to hold power, so they usually have limited community influence. Communities that have many businesses (especially locally owned) are also likely to have more people with power than are communities with only one or two major businesses. This occurs because there are more people with experience in leadership and more people with the resources to exert power.

Power and Conflict

Power becomes more visible in times of community conflict. Powerful people may be involved in a number of community issues, including disputes over road locations or sidewalk placement, labor strikes, locations of group homes, and similar matters. These situations upset the community's equilibrium and challenge the status quo. The issues may be significant, such as deciding whether to grant millions of dollars in tax breaks to lure an employer into town. They may also be relatively insignificant such as determining the proper action to take when high school students are caught having sex in the school hallway. Note that what is considered significant or insignificant varies widely from one issue to another. The latter issue could split the community even more than such significant issues as the gain or loss of a major employer. During conflicts like this, you are most likely to observe those with power influencing the outcome.

For the most part, our attention has been focused on communities, and we addressed neighborhoods only in passing. The following section will explain the functions of neighborhoods, their types, their role as social networks, and the importance of neighborhood organizations.

Neighborhoods in America

Neighborhoods exist throughout the United States and the world. All of us grow up in neighborhoods. Most of us have memories of our old neighborhoods. Neighborhoods are the contexts for primary and secondary groups (families and friends). They are also the place where our earliest interactions with others outside our family occur. The neighborhood's influence on residents can be considerable. When you hear the term neighborhood you might think of a place with dwellings and other buildings such as schools. We also think of neighborhoods in terms of their physical characteristics—a "new neighborhood" or a "rundown neighborhood."

The term neighborhood does not have a single accepted definition. Neighborhood may refer to a geographical area such as the third ward, Beacon Hill, or Marlborough Estates. It may also describe the social relationships or activities that occur among people in an area ("a friendly neighborhood"). For our purposes, we will define a neighborhood as a geographical area where significant social relationships occur among residents. This is perhaps the most important factor in what people consider their "neighborhood." One's sense of belonging is part of this subjective social factor. Of course, we often try to foster this sense of belonging through zoning ordinances and covenants designed to maintain a certain sense and feel to a neighborhood. Zoning ordinances, you may recall, are local laws designed to ensure that all the properties in a neighborhood are compatible. Covenants are similar standards that can even govern what residents may or may not do on their own property. For example, your neighborhood covenant may state that you are not allowed to put up a clothesline or install a swimming pool.

Earlier we described all systems as having boundaries. Neighborhoods are no exceptions. All neighborhoods have some sort of boundaries that separate them from the larger system (or other subsystems and neighborhoods). Residents usually define and are clearly aware of such boundaries. Sometimes the boundaries are more psychological than physical. Often there are natural boundaries, however, such as major streets, rivers, railroad tracks, or other geographical features. Even ethnicity may divide one neighborhood from others.

Frequently, outsiders define the neighborhoods. School boards may decide where to establish the boundaries between one school and another. They require a certain neighborhood's children to attend a certain school. These decisions often provoke reactions from neighborhood residents who think of a particular school as theirs and don't want their children to go to another school.

Functions of Neighborhoods

Neighborhoods have many functions. The most typical include: political, social, economic, and institutional. *Social functions* include providing friendships, status, socialization, mutual assistance, and informal helping networks. Residents may select a neighborhood because it provides status, comfort, or an opportunity to interact with neighbors. While significant, the relationships one has with neighbors are often not the most important ones in a person's life. Rather, they represent resources in times of need. Neighborhoods are important to social workers for this same reason—they represent untapped resources for helping clients.

Neighborhoods may also contribute to one's sense of well-being or help at-risk populations such as the elderly feel they have someone to turn to. Often, they offer the kind of assistance that could not be acquired elsewhere. Neighbors may babysit for each other's children, borrow one another's vehicles, ask for help with projects, borrow tools and equipment, serve as sounding boards for unhappiness about community issues, and provide emergency assistance. Most important, relying on one's neighbors does not carry the stigma of reliance on formal systems. You can ask for assistance from neighbors without being seen as bad or weak. Of course, not all neighbors are resources. Some inner city neighborhoods are threatened by drug dealers, crack houses, and random violence. Although their usefulness as a

resource may be much less, residents still consider the area "their" neighborhood.

Neighborhoods may also carry out *institutional functions*. These include providing employment, connecting new residents to older residents, providing access to specific services, and otherwise helping neighborhood members integrate. Institutional functions are performed by neighborhood schools, local offices of larger community agencies, churches, and the like. Organizations that help this process include Parent-Teacher Associations, fraternal organizations (e.g., the Elks), ethnic organizations, block clubs, and neighborhood centers.

Neighborhoods also serve a *political function*, allowing members to become involved in the political process to influence elected and appointed decision-makers. One of the ways neighborhoods create a balance of power in the larger community is through the use of neighborhood organizations. Neighborhood organizations are groups formed to help the neighborhood achieve specific goals such as renovation of older buildings. We will discuss neighborhood associations later in this chapter. Other types of political functions include activities such as encouraging people to vote, pushing the city to provide better police protection from drug dealers, or fining landlords who allow their buildings to deteriorate. Becoming involved in this sort of self-advocacy activity often increases residents' political sophistication. Such participation enhances residents' confidence and allows them to become further involved in the political process, an example of empowerment. Residents may campaign for specific candidates, seek political action on issues they are concerned about, and otherwise lobby for their agenda.

Economic functions of neighborhoods include provision of housing and places to shop. These are the functions most threatened by technology, changing demographics, and changes in the nature of businesses. For example, neighborhood shopping centers and markets are becoming much less common as large malls and supermarkets proliferate. Illegal practices such as redlining further reduce the value of the housing in a neighborhood. Redlining is "the practice by certain financial institutions of designating an area of a city as being too risky and unprofitable to lend money to those who want to rebuild or refurbish buildings there. The term came from the red line that various institutions drew on maps around ghetto areas to identify those locales that would not be funded'' (Barker, 1991, p. 197).

As mentioned earlier, communities (and neighborhoods as well) are often devastated by economic shifts caused by mergers, acquisitions, downsizing of companies, and other economic factors. While these are perhaps beneficial for the corporation, the impact on families and neighborhoods is usually not. Some states have now passed laws requiring corporations to notify their communities when planning to leave the community. A portion of those thrown out of work may never find equivalent employment. Many are out of work for significant periods. Many, if not most, end up with a lower standard of living even after they find suitable employment. Some are forced to sell their homes and seek less expensive housing in other parts of the community, thus disrupting their neighborhood ties.

In some communities, plant-closing task forces have been established to help residents cope with these catastrophes. Such task forces typically include representatives of social and human services, educational and vocational training institutions, and employment agencies. Some states have put in place efforts to help those affected—through retraining and education funds, and job seeking assistance.

In contrast, a rapid influx of new companies, jobs, or residents may also prove disruptive to a neighborhood or community. A small bedroom community finds itself with more students in school. However, it lacks the economic tax base to provide adequate education to them all. This occurs because the corporations employing the children's parents are located in other taxing jurisdictions.

Types of Neighborhoods

Neighborhoods are of several types. There are neighborhoods composed of highly mobile residents who will be there for only a short time. Despite this, a neighborhood may maintain a degree of solidarity and integration (organizing block parties, or neighborhood-watch programs). Another type consists of residents who have lived there all or most of their lives. Other neighborhoods are characterized by the lack of integrating mechanisms. They are almost disorganized in a social sense. People feel little sense of commonality with their neighbors and there are no neighborhood activities to help build this sense of community. Thus, we can define neighborhood type by looking at degree of transiency and cohesion among residents. Transient neighborhoods with little cohesion are less likely to function as informal resource systems.

We also categorize certain neighborhoods by giving them different names. The term *ghetto*, for example, is a ''bounded residential area in which a defined racial or ethnic group is forced to live'' (Choldin, 1985, p. 236). Other neighborhoods are called *slums*, indicating they are run down, deteriorating, or otherwise blighted.

We also refer to ethnic neighborhoods when ethnic similarity among the residents is great. Most sizable cities and many smaller ones have defined ethnic neighborhoods: Frenchtown (Tallahassee), Chinatown (San Francisco), Clark Park (Detroit). The degree of residential segregation that occurs in these neighborhoods challenges the image of the melting pot. The melting pot, as you may recall, was an idea that everyone in America, regardless of country of origin, would somehow blend into the mix and become ''an American.'' Sometimes, entire communities move toward ethnic similarity. Over twenty-five major cities with populations over 100,000 have minority groups as their single largest group (Hallman, 1985). A more apt description of the mix of peoples found in America would be a salad bowl.

The development of ethnic neighborhoods can be traced to a variety of factors. Like the rest of the population, the most oppressed and poorest members of society seek housing they can afford. The somewhat lower costs of housing in certain areas act as a magnet to attract lower income residents. Housing discrimination in other parts of a community may encourage this process. Minorities of color may find it difficult to get bank loans for purchasing a home or impossible to rent existing properties in more desirable neighborhoods. In addition, the ethnic neighborhood provides at least one advantage, the opportunity to live with others who share cultural similarities. This combination of factors helps explain why ethnic neighborhoods have residents from a range of economic classes living together, a pattern not common in other residential neighborhoods.

Neighborhoods as Helping Networks

Neighbors can be part of an informal network of helpers; they can provide everything from day care to crime prevention (Halley, Kopp & Austin, 1992). It is important to learn who are the natural helpers in the community. In one neighborhood several neighbors relied on one person for help fixing anything and everything. When the water heater broke in the middle of the night that neighbor was called first. When another neighbor needed help putting up a new mailbox or assembling a bunkbed for his kids, the same neighbor helped out. When a nearby sorority house furnace went out one winter night, members of the sorority sought this person's help again. This person had become one of the natural helpers in the neighborhood.

Devore and Schlesinger (1987) summarize the importance of neighbors as a source of friendship and support in many ethnic neighborhoods as well. Neighbors can be a "source of caring and healing" (p. 274) for both physical and emotional problems. Neighbors can provide temporary or regular child care for each other, join in a neighborhood-watch program, or simply listen to the concerns of their neighbors.

Neighborhood Organizations

America has been called a nation of "joiners" because of our tendency to join organizations. We join churches as well as organizations for business, social, political, self-help, and service purposes. Young neighborhood residents may join gangs for some of the same reasons—social or economic benefits. Neighborhood Associations are organizations formed by the residents of an identified neighborhood to address common needs and concerns. These concerns might arise when properties in the area are neglected or crime frightens residents into action. By organizing, residents can exert greater pressure on city officials to take action. Depending on the problem, goals might include more frequent police patrols or demolition of dangerous buildings. Perhaps residents would like more people to buy older homes in the neighborhood and repair them. Another goal might be to prevent vacant homes from being used as crack houses.

Associations have many positive benefits for the community and neighborhood. They encourage cooperative efforts to address common difficulties faced by all residents. The efforts of individual residents also affect others. When one person becomes involved in an effort to improve the neighborhood, others may begin to feel that something can actually be accomplished, and they too may pitch in.

Associations may be formal organizations with bylaws, dues, and several membership categories or informal networks that meet in a resident's living room. Programs and goals can be as simple as getting a bad railroad crossing repaired or as complex as developing a grant program to help low-income residents buy their homes with little or no down payment. A social worker might play a number of roles in these types of associations. You might be involved in starting a neighborhood association when concerned residents bring a problem to your attention. You may also work with other associations as they grapple with the same problems you face: low-income clients living in inadequate, poorly maintained housing or gang violence running rampant in the neighborhood.

It is estimated that there are over 100,000 neighborhood organizations in this country (Biegel, 1987) . The vast variety of organizations and the benefits they seek are staggering. They run the gamut from those interested in better police protection in their neighborhoods to those actually providing social services and advocacy for community interests. Neighborhood organizations may exist for single purposes or for multiple reasons. They may seek to improve housing conditions, enforce existing city laws, or prevent deleterious activities such as drug dealing from occurring in the neighborhood. Many associations begin in response to a crisis such as burglaries in the neighborhood or the threat to South Sunrise Street mentioned at the start of the chapter. They usually become sufficiently broad to continue their operation after the threat has been overcome (another example of goal displacement). The Neighborhood Watch program in cooperation with local law enforcement is one such effort. Most important, neighborhood associations help connect people to their neighborhoods and communities. They allow residents to get involved, to exert influence on the political process, to get help, and to help others. They also provide a resource that we as social workers can use.

Often community residents band together to achieve ends that could not be accomplished by individuals. For example, one community worried about the lack of locally available health care. It subsequently created an inexpensive health-care system to serve the entire area. The community located an abandoned potato warehouse and converted it into a health center, offering

HIGHLIGHT 8.5

TWO EFFECTIVE NEIGHBORHOOD ASSOCIATIONS

Brentwood was once an affluent neighborhood. Large Victorian homes lined the street for three blocks, though many had been converted into apartments over the years. The transition from single-family to multi-family housing had been difficult, but the mixed use neighborhood was beginning to pull together. Now a new problem appeared on the horizon. The old Bailey estate (the house had burned to the ground two years ago) was for sale. A local auto repair shop had shown interest in buying the property and using it to store cars awaiting repair. Residents had visions of their children being crushed under wrecked cars, trapped in trunks, and generally having to live next to a junkyard.

The Neighborhood Association held raffles and bake sales, and solicited donations to raise enough money to buy the property from the owner and convert it into a park. Using funds donated by a local civic club, they purchased playground equipment and turned ownership of the property over to the city.

The Altoona Betterment Association had already made a name for itself by aggressively asking owners to maintain their rundown properties. Writing to individual owners, the association pointed out what needed to be done (mainly, clean-up of debris and repair of rental properties.) They also pressured the city to provide sufficient police protection so that drug dealers were forced out of the neighborhood.

A low-income housing project for senior citizens had been built in the area because of the efforts of the association. Now they were about to take a more important step, namely attracting a physician to their neighborhood. The physician, new to the area, was planning to open a family-care office and build his practice. After repeated encouragement from the association and pledges of cooperation in fixing up and maintaining an old Victorian house, the doctor agreed to open his practice in the neighborhood.

---

free services to low income residents. Community residents talked local doctors into donating time each week to work in the health center. In addition, residents began an emergency health-care fund for indigent residents who needed more serious medical care. Using fourth-year students from a nearby medical school, the community developed a health advocacy plan. Highlight 8.5 gives examples of two positive community organizations whose efforts resulted in significant positive community change.

Highlight 8.6 illustrates a list of neighborhood organizations in a small city of about 150,000 population. The number and variety of organizations is fairly typical of many other communities. Each organization undertakes a variety of activities on behalf of residents of the neighborhood. Some focus on crime prevention, others on property maintenance. Some are concerned about ensuring an adequate supply of low-income housing

while others worry more about parking problems caused by students at the local high school and college.

Local newspapers may carry news of neighborhood organizations. New residents may be welcomed, meetings announced, and accomplishments of residents' children praised. Newspapers can help neighborhood associations in other ways. One newspaper prints weekly pictures of neighborhood properties that are eyesores. Besides spotlighting and potentially embarrassing the property owner (almost all of whom are absentee landlords), the newspaper interviews city officials responsible for enforcing ordinances requiring maintenance of buildings. This puts pressure on officials as well. The publicity helps force landlords to improve their properties and provide better living conditions for their low-income tenants.

Neighborhood associations are an excellent source of information for new residents. The large number of

---

HIGHLIGHT 8.6

NEIGHBORHOOD ORGANIZATIONS

The following examples show the wide variety of neighborhood associations possible.

Rountree Neighborhood Watch Group
Rountree Urban Conservation District
Wellington Hills Homeowners Association
Cinnamon Square Property Owners Association
Citizens Association for the Betterment of Western Springs
Mid-Town Neighborhood Association
North Central Neighborhood

North Sutter Betterment Association
Phelps Neighborhood Association
Ravenwood Homeowners Association
Rountree Area Advisory Committee
Sherman Avenue Project Area Committee, Inc.
United Neighborhoods Organization, East
Walnut Street Historical Neighborhood Association
Westside Community Betterment Association
Woodland Heights Neighborhood Improvement Association

---

city offices that provide neighborhood services may be unknown to the resident or the newcomer may find the long list overwhelming. Social workers new to a community might also find neighborhood organizations useful as they try to determine what to do about existing problems encountered by their clients. A list of potential neighborhood resources appears in highlight 8.7.

As you can see from this list, cities often try to address a number of community and neighborhood problems. In addition, they engage in other endeavors not normally known to residents. For example, cities actively seek new businesses and workers. Attracting workers and their families to a community is important in keeping a city progressive and alive. Recreation departments provide the usual park programs, golf courses, and swimming pools for neighborhoods, but are also active in creating tot-lots (programs for very small children), gang diversion activities, employment programs for teenagers, and drug-abuse prevention programs. Social workers involve themselves in many of these by providing services, helping to implement programs, or simply advising officials.

Fire departments provide fire prevention and fire safety programs while health departments wrestle with immunizations, AIDS, family violence, and infant mortality. Planning and Zoning departments are instrumental in locating day- and child-care facilities in a community, and police departments often work with other agencies to address family violence, gang activities, and

community policing (a program of having police walk their neighborhood beats, meeting residents in their homes and at neighborhood gatherings, and planning joint crime-prevention efforts). Libraries may serve as meeting places for support groups of various types. They also offer information and referral services.

Putting It All Together: Assessing Communities and Neighborhoods

Once you begin to understand the dynamics affecting communities and neighborhoods as systems, it becomes easier to assess a particular neighborhood or community. It is important to understand the purposes of such an assessment. You could undertake an assessment to prepare for moving a new agency into a community. An assessment might help you respond to an identified community problem. Community assessment could help you orient yourself to a new environment as you begin a new social work position. Remember that your ethical obligation and role as a social worker is to go beyond the responsibilities of your official job description and work to improve conditions affecting society. To do this you will need to learn a great deal as you begin your first job.

In assessing a community, you can turn to many sources of information. These may include census re-

HIGHLIGHT 8.7

NEIGHBORHOOD RESOURCES

Finding out where to turn for assistance for problems in one's neighborhood can often be frustrating. Many different city offices have multiple purposes. Titles of offices don't always help. The list below is from a medium size city. As a social worker, you might wish to develop a database like this for your own use as you help clients confront problems they encounter in their neighborhoods.

Abandoned or unsafe buildings: Building Regulation Dept.

Overcrowded housing (more than 3 unrelated people): Building Regulation Dept.

Housing rehabilitation loans: Planning and Development Dept.

Illegal use of property (zoning code violations): Building Regulation Dept.

Zoning information: Planning and Development Dept.
Inoperable vehicles parked in yard: Health Dept.
Abandoned vehicles on street: Police Dept.
Tall weeds (over 12 inches): Health Dept.
Trash, appliances, auto parts left in yard: Health Dept.
Parking in front yard: Police Dept.
Noise disturbance: Police Dept.
Dangerous or stray animals: Health Dept.
Neighborhood planning: Planning and Development Dept.
Neighborhood Watch Program: Police Dept.
Operation I.D. engraver: Police Dept.
Street lights: City Utilities Dept.
Carpool information: Community Development Dept.
Bus Routes: City Utilities Dept.

---

cords, planning agency documents, and business development plans. These are often available from city agencies such as the planning department, regional planning agencies, chamber of commerce, or industrial park boards. Newspapers are often a good source of information on current issues, such as finding out how a particular problem developed. Many papers report on the background of a current community problem, trying to highlight (not always accurately, however) important dates and names. Other sources of data include libraries and books about the community's history. Especially if you work in a particular neighborhood—in a neighborhood center, homeless shelter, or similar facility—you might also wish to secure a map of the community or neighborhood. If you are focusing your efforts on a neighborhood, consider enlarging your map to provide greater detail. You also may wish to locate a city directory which lists all residents by street rather than alphabetically. This will tell you who lives on the streets in your neighborhood.

As you learn about a community, you can create and maintain a database of important officials and individuals simply by jotting down on note cards (or in a computer data base if you have access to one) the names and titles of these people as their names emerge in the news. This way you will always know who the critical people are in your community and who could be a resource for a particular problem.

Depending upon need, it may be useful to focus on a certain segment of the total picture. You might augment information gained from reviewing official documents, such as census records, with data gathered by talking directly to decision-makers and other key informants. Key informants are knowledgeable persons in the community with special expertise in your area of interest. The latchkey programs the text described earlier used key informants to determine the extent of need for such programs. Typical key informants might include school principals, ministers, neighborhood association officers, ethnic group leaders, city officials, and business leaders. In this manner you can learn about interrelationships and connections of which you were not previously aware. A local minister may serve as administrator of a nursing home, be a senior member of a major civic organization, and sit on the board of directors of the local bank. Lobbying this individual in one context, can

---

HIGHLIGHT 8.8

A MODEL FOR COMMUNITY ASSESSMENT

Name of neighborhood or community

Location: including physical setting, location, boundaries, and relationships to other communities, etc.

Population characteristics: including size, age and gender distribution, nationality, ethnicity, religion, etc.

Income: by subgroups (women, minorities, etc.), poverty rate

Community attractiveness: characteristics that attract and hold residents, such as climate, cost of living, amenities

Housing: types, conditions, (e.g., unoccupied homes could be a sign of poor housing or something as innocent as cottages used only part of the year)

History: Why did people settle here? Where did early residents come from? What changes have occurred over time in population attitudes, beliefs and values, important events?

Geography: What characteristics have helped or hurt the community (e.g., location on a major river often means business develops in a strip along the river, may also mean periodic flooding, cheap electricity, affects street patterns and transportation, etc.)

Other factors: e.g., mobility of residents, etc.

Education: educational characteristics of population for men and women, school dropouts rates, differences among subgroups (e.g., minorities), financing, buildings, student-teacher ratios, programs for special needs children, extracurricular programs

Social/cultural systems: parks, cultural resources, recreational activities, social clubs, and organizations

Commerce and Industry: major employers and industries, unemployment rates, local or absentee control of business, role of unions, future prospects, stability of industries, etc.

Religion and churches: role and influence of

Governmental type: e.g., city manager, mayor, council

Political factors: role of political parties, voting patterns (who, what percentage), major issues, tax structure, elected versus appointed officials, financial stability, law enforcement, and other city services

Social and health systems: number and type of hospitals and clinics, primary social service agencies, problems and limitations of each, responsiveness of services, informal helping systems, planning bodies

Sources of information: radio, tv, newspapers, prominent individuals who speak for population segments

Quality of education: programs of note, condition of facilities, special problems such as court ordered integration, higher education availability

Power distribution: use reputational, positional, or issues methods to assess

Miscellaneous: major community difficulties, steps being taken in response, gaps in services and facilities, important issues include identifying concerns of the community (who is concerned and why?), learning what has been done in the past to deal with problem, discovering the antecedent conditions that led to this situation, assessing the strengths and limitations of the community for dealing with the problem

---

HIGHLIGHT 8.9

KIDSPLACE

The assessment that led to the development of KidsPlace began with a community survey of 6,700 children to find out their needs, interests, perspectives, and hopes. From their survey city officials discovered a wide variety of needs, from steps at the aquarium so that younger children could see the exhibits to information about shelters for runaway children.

Several hundred volunteers (including social workers) helped draft a series of goals. They then carried them out with the combined support of private and public social service agencies and resources. These included creating bike routes for kids, expanding playground facilities, reducing bus fare so kids could ride at less cost, developing an annual Kids-Day when admission to various recreational and cultural events is free. Stores posted window signs indicating that children could safely seek help there. Such help could mean having a place to go to the bathroom or to call their parents. City budget development processes now weighed children's needs. More basic changes included zoning law changes making family day care an allowable use for buildings. This was an important change because city zoning laws can cause difficulty for anyone trying to open a day-care center. The KidsPlace model of planning and services has proven successful enough to be replicated in several cities (Cheyne, 1987).

---

also influence him in his other roles. The confluence (merging) of interests make this individual very important in the local community and give him significant actual and potential power. No single source of information could have disclosed this series of connections.

There are many models for assessing communities (Sheafor, Horejsi, & Horejsi, 1991; Meenaghan, Washington, & Ryan, 1982; Netting, Kettner & McMurty, 1993). Most share similar components or suggest gathering information on specific topics. A typical assessment model appears in highlight 8.8. It might be used for major projects such as development of a new agency, expansion of social services, or comprehensive planning to improve a community's human services.

Understanding the community and its problems is essential to be effective in improving our clients' quality of life. Only then can we combat community-wide problems. In social work we select interventions based upon our assessment of the problem. While highlight 8.8 presents a comprehensive model for assessing a community, other methods are available for more limited goals. A good example of this is evident in highlight 8.9. It depicts a community grappling with its children's needs.

The community described in highlight 8.9 used a survey of community children to focus on specific needs. They then used that data to plan and carry out a set of interventions.

Chapter Summary

This chapter addresses a range of roles that social workers might play in neighborhoods and communities. Neighborhoods and communities are defined. Ecological and systems perspectives help us understand the complexity of communities. Various demographic factors in the development of communities are considered, including urbanization, suburbanization, and gentrification. The impact of social stratification on the community and on neighborhoods is discussed. The community as an economic and political system is highlighted. Neighborhoods in America are carefully reviewed in terms of functions and types. The role of neighborhood organizations is explained. Finally, putting all this information together as a community assessment leads the way to community planning and intervention.

CHAPTER NINE

Macro Practice
in Communities

"Officer needs assistance!" With his last breath, police officer John Bennett radioed for help and then collapsed. As he lay dying in the parking lot of the temporary domestic violence shelter on Byron Street, his assailant escaped into the dingy rundown neighborhood. Although the location of the shelter was supposed to be a secret, the man had located his estranged wife and threatened to kill her. Officer Bennett, responding to a call from the shelter, was shot and killed. The man was later arrested, tried, and sentenced to prison. Ironically, the death of Officer Bennett helped spur efforts to protect victims of domestic violence and led to one of the most effective community organization efforts in the history of Richland City.

Just about everyone in the tiny community of Ozaukee showed up. The mayor and sheriff attended. So did the police chief, school officials, and church leaders. Also present were representatives of all the service clubs (Kiwanis, Rotary, etc.). the community meeting was a response to the death of Frank Vanet, a seventeen-year-old killed by a fellow student. Though his assailant had told many people before the killing that he was going to shoot Frank and had even showed them his gun, this did not change the tragic outcome. "How could this happen in our community? This isn't New York where people don't care about one another," said the president of the Parent-Teacher Association. The apparently gang-related incident galvanized the people present. As a first step, they agreed to organize a huge town seminar focused on gangs and gang violence. Later steps would come out of that town meeting.

Central Springbok was close to becoming one of those neighborhoods where nobody will live. People were leery about the older homes needing repair. They preferred to settle in newer neighborhoods. Steve Odom was tired of hearing that nothing could be done to convince people to live there. As a member of the Board of Directors of Commercial Bank, his opinions were important in the community. At his last Rotary Club meeting he heard Annie Wentmeyer, a social worker from the Springbok Community Action Agency, describe how central Springbok was an example of a neighborhood on the edge. As he talked with her afterward, Steve learned that other communities had successfully revitalized similar neighborhoods by making the purchase of homes there more attractive through offering low interest loans and homesteading arrangements. In the latter, cities that had foreclosed on properties because the owner didn't pay the taxes offered the homes to families who agreed to fix them up and live there.

At the next meeting of the bank board, Steve presented his idea for encouraging low-income families to move into central Springbok. He suggested offering low interest loans, with 3-percent down payments, and no closing costs. Following some discussion of its feasibility, the bank board directed its president to begin the program as soon as possible.

Introduction

Sometimes it takes a tragedy to spur community action on a problem. The first two case examples above illustrate that traumatic events can sometimes make a community face a problem head-on. Other times, a good idea produced at a propitious time can have similar impact and benefit. The last case example shows how sharing ideas can sometimes spur others to action. Each community described above attended to a problem and initiated concrete steps to change things.

Social workers are often more aware of community problems than other professionals. After all, they work in the community, often in contact with the most oppressed populations. They make home visits to the poorest neighborhoods and daily confront myriad social problems. Social workers often witness the impact of unemployment, crime, drug use, health problems, gang violence, and educational troubles. Along with police officers, social workers are perhaps more likely than any other professionals to confront these social ills.

Sometimes, social workers are employed to deal directly with community problems. In one state, for example, the state division of Alcohol and Drug Abuse employs community organizers to investigate neighborhood needs and implement programs to meet those needs. One neighborhood's need might be the creation of a neighborhood phone directory identifying resource persons such as baby sitters and lawn caretakers. Another might involve holding a neighborhood block party or potluck dinner to bring residents together. The ultimate goal is always reduction of chemical-dependency risk factors such as community disorganization and lack of attachment to one's neighborhood.

Unfortunately, except for the few social workers employed by community organizations (like Annie Wentmeyer, mentioned above), most of us are not hired to deal directly with these larger issues. As employees of various agencies, we provide direct service to those who experience these social problems. We often deal with the aftermath of community problems. In other words, we may deal with family problems (stress, child

HIGHLIGHT 9.1

COMMUNITY CHANGE ACTIVITIES

The community change activities described in this chapter are certainly not an exhaustive list of what is possible. Indeed, community change activities can involve grand as well as minor goals. They include programs to rehabilitate neighborhood housing, maintain pressure on slum landlords, and develop low-cost food cooperatives to help members reduce their food bills. Other programs focus on developing and maintaining small neighborhood parks, establishing a credit union for a low income neighborhood,

and patrolling neighborhoods to counter criminal behavior. Still other efforts aim at developing a community newspaper to cover local activities, creating self-help groups for widows, and providing medical care to the Chinese population to reduce the need for nursing-home placement. The programs addressed in this book are merely a subset of what is possible when we begin to address community needs.

Source: Rubin & Rubin (1986).

abuse, poverty, etc.) partly attributable to widespread unemployment resulting from the closing of a major shipyard. Does this mean we can avoid responsibility for trying to solve the larger societal and community problem? Can we stand by and let our clients and other citizens suffer injustice and lack of resources? The answer, of course, is no. Our professional obligations supersede our allegiance to our individual agencies. Our responsibilities to our profession and society dictate that we try to do something whenever possible.

This chapter will:

- Look at some ways direct service social workers can become involved in changing their communities.
- Apply the PREPARE and IMAGINE models (introduced in chapters 5 and 6) to community problems.
- Give examples of how social workers can have an impact on their respective communities.
- Consider different types of community change.
- Review the steps in the problem-solving process supported by the PREPARE and IMAGINE models.

Change in Communities

Wanting to make your community and society a better place to live is a natural desire. Social workers have a unique opportunity to influence their communities be-

cause social work is the only profession that mandates working with both individuals and their environments. Consequently, social workers are often active in the community level. That involvement may take the form of signing petitions to support or protest some proposed action. It may also include involvement in political processes by voting, working for candidates, contributing time and money to political campaigns, and working with others to improve living conditions. Additionally, social workers can demonstrate on behalf of causes such as developing services for the elderly or improving the quality of drinking water. Likewise, they can act against problematic practices such as destruction of neighborhoods through banks' refusing home loans. They can also target culturally insensitive planning such as scheduling community-wide activities during periods in which certain groups celebrate their religious holidays. Highlight 9.2 describes an example of how social workers can work with others to improve the quality of life in a community.

To be an effective community change agent, you must master several techniques of, and approaches to, implementing change at the macro level. One of our biggest strengths as social workers is our ability to work with others and make changes affecting large numbers of people. People working together can usually make greater changes than individuals working alone. The

HIGHLIGHT 9.2

SOCIAL WORKERS IN THE COMMUNITY

Entwistle (1992) describes the collaborative activities of several social workers and others who formed a group to help a community solve some of its drug- and alcohol-related problems. Participants included representatives of the police department, members of Urban League (a community service agency), a social worker specializing in dealing with gangs, a substance-abuse consultant, and the director of a Hispanic social action agency. They divided into several action groups, one of which dealt with treatment and rehabilitation of chemically dependent persons.

Because low-income persons could not take advantage of costly inpatient treatment programs, the action group gathered leaders of local treatment programs and explained that free beds for the indigent were needed. As a result, agency directors agreed to provide fourteen free beds for low-income clients. Another group agreed to coordinate allocation of the beds.

A third action group focused on influencing the criminal justice system. Members met with judges to ask for more stringent jail terms for drug dealers. Another action group centered its efforts on holding absentee landlords responsible for drug dealing in their buildings. Yet another group lobbied the city council to ensure that no new liquor licenses were granted to facilities located near schools or existing liquor stores. All of these efforts made group members realize they could influence the system.

As an outgrowth of their attention to the community problems, the members discovered another critical need: lack of adequate health care and health insurance for low-income elementary school students. The action group then organized a group of pediatricians, general practitioners, and specialists to provide free emergency care to children who were hurt or became ill at school. Volunteers transported students to physicians' offices or clinics.

The program was eventually expanded to include mental health providers, dentists, pharmacists, and laboratory services. Churches, social clubs, and local industry donated money for x-rays, medications, and other medical items. Over two-hundred children received care in the first year, and volunteers handled such routine tasks as office work, transportation, and locating follow-up services. Eventually, the program expanded to almost all schools in the community. A five-year evaluation project accompanied the program to measure its impact and ensure that it continued to meet community needs.

micro (individual) and mezzo (group) skills you have learned will be equally useful at the macro level. Chapters 2 and 3 provide a useful review of these skills. Here, we will describe other macro approaches that should add to your repertoire of social work skills. Social workers use change strategies ranging from letter writing to legislative advocacy to concerted social action. Social action is "coordinated effort to achieve institutional change to meet a need, solve a social problem, correct an injustice, or enhance the quality of human life" (Barker, 1991, p. 217). Connaway and Gentry (1988) distinguish social action from advocacy, noting that social action is dedicated to creating *new* programs while advocacy is designed to ensure that *existing* rights are honored and *current* programs are accessible.

A Philosophical Perspective on Macro Practice

Burghardt (1982) emphasizes that social workers should acknowledge the basic philosophical underpinnings needed for community change efforts. Such underpinnings are the basis of the values guiding social workers' practice. These include "trust that people, given genuine alternatives, will act with decency, humanity, and skill" (p. 12). In community work you are working *with* people instead of *for* them. To do otherwise is to risk becoming a manipulator who uses others (Freire, 1972). People must accept ownership of their problems and work to help themselves. Our planning occurs with people and our strategies "must be based on some sound objective that corresponds to the actual conditions and perceptions of people's lives" (Burghardt, 1982, p. 12). In other words, what we try to do must relate directly to what the *beneficiaries* of our efforts think is important, not what we think is important. This is consistent with the social work rule: Start where the client is.

Burghardt also recognizes that social workers must work and live within the boundaries of professional values. This requires that we avoid the trap of thinking the end justifies the means. *How* we achieve our goals is very important. Earlier, more radical approaches to community change often did not recognize this limitation (Alinsky, 1972). There are still groups in society that believe the ends justify the means. Some abortion protestors burn medical clinics, assault medical personnel, harass patients, and physically bar people trying to receive medical services. Their perspective is that the end justifies almost any means, a value orientation with potentially catastrophic consequences if adopted by the whole of society. It is essential not to leave our ethical standards behind when we work in the community. We should remember that as social workers we work in a political environment. Our actions directly affect how others perceive, respect, and treat us.

Perspectives on the Community

Fellin (1987) and Kramer and Specht (1975, p. 17) point out that we can view the community from three different perspectives. First, the community is the *context* in which we practice. Whether we are direct service workers, supervisors, planners, or community change agents, we all practice in a community of some sort. The community, as the place where we work, significantly influences what services we provide and what problems we address (or ignore). It also affects the types of change

efforts that are feasible. Economically poor communities, for example, often lack the resources to meet human needs as readily as wealthier areas.

From the second perspective the community is the target of our change efforts. In other words, the community *is* the thing we are seeking to change. If a community remains unresponsive to the needs of a significant segment of its population, then that community must change. Macro change is required when communities or institutions constrain individuals by limiting their opportunities (social or personal) (Fellin, 1987, p. 3).

When we target the community for change, our efforts are directed at causing that change. We may accomplish this through creating new services, improving the delivery of existing services, or replacing the political leadership. Consider the problem of gang violence that plagues many cities. Many communities respond to gang violence by hiring more police, but others approach the problem more creatively. A Streetworkers program in one large city targets actual and potential gang members. This program is designed to end the gang violence destroying the quality of inner city life. Streetworkers act as mediators between police and gang members to reduce the reoccurrence of violent incidents. Mediators seek compromise and suggest alternatives to settling problems by resorting to violence. Preventing a problem is a more positive approach than simply increasing the number of police who are available to pick up the pieces after the damage is done.

Finally, from the third perspective, the community is the *mechanism* for change. That is, the community can actually solve its own problems by drawing upon the talents and mutual interests of community members. Consider Ozaukee, mentioned at the start of this chapter. That community is undertaking to prevent gang-related values and violence from undercutting residents' concern for fellow citizens. A broad cross-section of the community is working to ensure that others do not suffer the fate of Frank Vanet, the murdered teenager.

Approaches to Community Change

There are at least three separate orientations from which we can tackle community problems (Fisher, 1984). One orientation emphasizes working with the power structure in a consensual, gradual way that focuses on service delivery. Social workers have historically been involved in organizations sponsored by the traditional establishment. These include social settlement houses, neighborhood and community centers, and the United Way. The United Way is a "national federation of local organizations established to systematize and coordinate voluntary fund raising efforts. The money raised . . . is used to fund social agencies; nonprofit human services organizations, and some health, education, and recreation programs in local communities" (Barker, 1991, p. 243).

A second orientation focuses on conflict, mediation, and challenges to the power structure. The goal is to obtain or maintain power and develop alternate institutions to meet existing needs. Examples include tenant organizations and community reform movements. This approach finds the current system of services inadequate, unresponsive, and unwilling or unable to change. We will talk about this more when we look at conflict tactics.

Neighborhood maintenance is the third orientation. This approach combines a consensual, peer pressure system with legal action and political lobbying to improve property values, maintain neighborhoods, and deliver services. Neighborhood associations (described in chapter 7), civic clubs, and property owner organizations are typical mechanisms used in this approach. They all serve to improve and maintain neighborhoods. Smaller scale examples of specific activities are organizing bike-safety programs for local children and holding self-defense classes for neighborhood women.

As social workers, you may operate from any or all these orientations during your career, depending on several variables. These variables include the nature of your job, the amount and type of sanction from your agency, your personal time, and the type of community problems you encounter. This chapter will offer examples illustrating each of these approaches.

Beginning the Change Process

We have discussed the problem-solving process in previous chapters. However, it is helpful to remember that this process works at all levels of intervention, from micro to mezzo to macro. As you know, steps in the problem-solving process include assessment, planning, intervention, evaluation, termination, and follow-up. We will follow these steps in this chapter as we consider a variety of community problems.

Figure 9.1
PREPARE—An Assessment of
Community Change Potential

1.	P	Identify **PROBLEMS** to address
2.	R	Review your macro **REALITY**
3.	E	**ESTABLISH** primary goals
4.	P	Identify **PEOPLE** of influence
5.	A	**ASSESS** potential financial costs and benefits to clients and agency
6.	R	Evaluate professional and personal **RISK**
7.	E	**EVALUATE** the potential success of a macro change process

PREPARE: Assessing Potential for Community Change

Because the PREPARE and IMAGINE models provide a detailed breakdown of the problem-solving process, we will use these models in this chapter (see figure 9.1).

Step 1: PREPARE—Identify *Problems* to Address

Identifying problems in the community is not usually difficult. Problems have a way of making themselves known without much effort on our part. In the case that began this chapter, three communities learned of problems in various ways. Regardless of how a problem comes to light, several substeps are needed to identify the problem you are going to address. These were discussed in chapter 5 and will be reviewed here. First, you must seriously evaluate the potential for macro level intervention. Second, you must define and prioritize the problems. Third, you must translate the problem into needs. The final step is to determine what needs you will address (since it may not be feasible to tackle all that you have identified).

The next section describes some of the more common ways that problems come to our attention using case examples for illustration.

IDENTIFICATION BY NEWS MEDIA REPORTS. Sometimes, the news media reports a sensational event that underscores the existence of a community problem. One community learned of a gang infiltration problem when the news media reported police attempts to apprehend those responsible for gang "art work." This case is explained in highlight 9.3.

IDENTIFICATION BY SOCIAL SERVICE PROVIDERS. Still other problems are identified by those who provide social services. In one state, leaders of four social welfare departments (Mental Health, Elementary and Secondary Education, Social Services, and Health) met over breakfast to discuss their collective unhappiness with problems their individual agencies couldn't seem to handle. Although their combined budgets equaled several billion dollars, the money did not seem to help. Their primary concerns included keeping children in school as long as possible, helping them remain safely in their homes, and keeping them out of prison.

The group formed what they called "The Sustaining Program," designed to find ways to deal with neighborhoods and school districts beset with frequent homicides, drug dealing, armed children, high incidence of child-abuse, and rising high-school dropout rates. Settling on a trial program, they identified a series of schools in various cities to serve as pilot sites. These sites became test, or pilot, locations to try out new ideas and approaches. One facet of the program provided individual counseling to students in these schools. Another initiated latchkey programs for children lacking adult supervision after school. The latter programs also helped the children with their homework. Program counselors made home visits and encouraged parents' participation in school affairs, further helping to connect parents with the school system. Favorable evaluation of the program led to its expansion in other city locations. Subsequently, still other cities adopted the model for application in their schools.

HIGHLIGHT 9.3

GANG GRAFFITI

The city of Thistle is a booming community of 150,000 residents. Lately gangs and gang "wannabees" have begun to appear in the community. This initially becomes evident through the graffiti gangs used to mark their territories and provoke other gangs. The local newspaper reports a series of violent incidents apparently related to territorial issues.

In response, a citizen's committee composed of representatives of several civic and social service organizations is formed. The committee evaluates the situation and decides that an intervention is needed. By doing so, they carry out substep 1 in the problem-identification process. In substep 2, they prepare to deal with the media-defined problem of gang graffiti and identify as their first priority the removal of the markings. This will destroy the gangs' territorial markers, remove the provocation for other gangs, and eliminate an eyesore.

By translating the problem into a need—graffiti removal—the committee completes steps 3 and 4 (translating problems into needs and determining which needs to address). Operation Paint Out is launched to beat the gangs at their own game. Volunteers are recruited to paint over gang graffiti. Soon, almost every display of graffiti has been painted over by members of the volunteer Paint Out Corp. A defaced wall is repainted in fifteen minutes by a group of teenagers, at least one of whom had once considered joining a gang. The experience helps convince him and other youngsters that gangs are destructive to their community. The gang concept is not so romantic, after all. This paint-out effort is only one of several steps the community pursues to take back the city from the gangs.

IDENTIFICATION BY VICTIMS. Occasionally, those most directly affected by a problem bring it to our attention. For example, a neighborhood association became concerned when absentee landlords began to violate city laws about numbers of unrelated persons living in the same residence. The overcrowding in some homes and apartments contributed to maintenance problems and health and sanitation difficulties, and generally increased neighborhood deterioration. The association approached the city council to strengthen relevant laws and to urge that landlords be fined or jailed for law violations.

Sometimes, a single agency identifies a problem and undertakes a solution. For example, a local organization dedicated to improving the supply of low-income housing pointed out that nearly 6,000 people in the community were living in cars, shacks, or other substandard housing. They organized a community meeting featuring local entertainers to raise money for their next project. The organization, which builds homes for low-income families, requires these families to pay 1 percent of the cost of the building, maintain payments on a no-interest loan, take living skills classes, and donate time to help build homes for others. To involve the community in the process, the organization asked residents to sign up to buy nails, lumber, paint, and other materials. Because supply costs varied, almost anyone could help. One person could purchase a box of nails for $2 and another a front porch for $300.

DESCRIBE PROBLEMS CLEARLY. Of course, it is not sufficient merely to identify a problem. You must describe problems with sufficient clarity that others can understand what needs to be done. The case example involving the police officer (which started this chapter) may clarify how to identify a problem.

Geri was the newly appointed director of an agency operating a domestic violence shelter. As a BSW, she was a committed social worker who cared deeply about her community's residents and her clients. She knew the police officer's death and the community's concern were good starting points for a discussion of domestic violence and the needs of its survivors. At least people were now aware of the "battered wife" problem and of the violence inflicted on women and others. Yet the problem needed further definition. Geri subsequently clarified the problem as follows:

Survivors of domestic violence had no safe place to stay for periods of thirty days or more. The lack of a permanent, secure shelter for battered women and their children was the primary problem. In the long run, such a facility would eliminate the periodic need to find a new home for the shelter, which had been the pattern for several years. In previous years, Geri's organization simply found a person or a group to lend them a house for a short period of time. When the owner wanted the house back, the board had to locate a new shelter. Because the houses belonged to other organizations, it was impossible to provide enough security to prevent entry by angry husbands.

National rates of domestic violence and local police reports made it possible for Geri to estimate the number of women and children physically victimized in Richland City each day, week, and month. This information, publicized in various media and reported to the shelter's board of directors, helped convey the seriousness of the problem. Largely because of increased media attention following the officer's death, the time was right for change.

Recognize that only the most pressing problems are likely to get media attention when so many things are happening simultaneously in a community (Netting, Kettner, & McMurty, 1993). This increases the importance of gathering adequate data about a community problem. For example, a problem affecting a thousand people is easier to address for change than one that concerns only a hundred.

RESEARCH THE PROBLEM CAREFULLY. No matter how the problem comes to your attention, research it very carefully to ensure that you have all the needed data. How serious is the problem? How many people are affected? Describe the problem as carefully as possible. Is this an unrecognized problem not yet acknowledged by others? Is it necessary to spend time educating people about the seriousness of the problem? Is there just one problem, or is there a series that must be prioritized? Is this a long-standing problem that has been ignored, or one for which previous solutions have failed? What factors cause or contribute to the problem? Keep in mind that what appears to be a cause might actually be a coincidence. For example, an increase in gang activity in a community may coincide with an increase in arrests for selling drugs. The two events may or may not be related. Both may reflect major problems in the community caused by lack of legitimate employment and recreational opportunities, absence of appropriate community services, or a decision by the police to target gangs and drug sales. But that doesn't mean one has caused the other.

Causes might be seen differently by different groups. Cultural experiences and values can dramatically affect how people view the same set of events (Netting, Kettner, & McMurty, 1993). Consider seven family members living in a two-bedroom house. Some people might consider this evidence that residents just don't know how to live "normally." Still others may blame greedy landlords for trying to stuff as many people as possible into any available living space. Yet others may believe that such crowding results from lack of available housing for large low-income families. Others think crowding is caused by lending institutions that refuse loans to low-income families, thereby forcing them to live in inadequate housing.

We cited sources of data earlier in this text. Such sources include census records, prior needs assessments, agency reports of services delivered, or media accounts of problems. Any of these may be of value in assessing the extent of community need. Local or regional planning agencies, university or college research centers, or other bodies may have gathered useful information.

Sometimes the absence of local data is a problem. However, it may be possible to extrapolate from national, state, or county data and relate it to your community. You could use state data to estimate the number of births to unmarried teenagers occurring in a community. Such information would be useful if you were trying to highlight the need for family planning services for this age group. This extrapolation would be appropriate if there were few demographic differences between the state and the community. However, an urban community in a predominantly rural state may not find state figures very useful. The circumstances in urban and rural communities may be radically different.

Sometimes data are available to show changes in a community over time. One study surveyed the sexual experiences of teenagers at ten-year intervals. It found that, despite fears to the contrary, teens were not much more sexually active than their parents had been twenty years earlier. This information helped lower anxiety about widespread teenage sexual behavior.

At other times you might want to compare your situation to some sort of average. One community dis-

covered that, compared to other cities of similar size, they had significantly fewer school social workers serving children. Sometimes it is possible to compare your situation to a national standard. You might discover that you have only one third the number of police officers you need when compared to a national standard. This standard might recommend 1.5 police officers for each 1,000 city residents, and you only have 1. Your community's citizens, thus, are less protected. It follows that they may be at significantly greater risk of theft, property damage, and assault.

Completion of the problem-definition stage should enable you to determine, with some degree of assurance, who is affected by the problem, to what extent, and what sort of remedy might be appropriate. You should also have at least an elementary grasp of what will happen if you intervene, and of who the participants in the change process should be. This includes clients affected by the problem, change agents, action systems, and target systems. Recall that the change agent system includes the organizations or agencies that sanction the worker. The action system is "the people and resources in the community with whom the social worker deals in order to achieve desired change" (Barker, 1987, p. 163). The target system represents those you will seek to influence in order to achieve your goals.

Step 2: PREPARE—Assess Your Macro and Personal *Reality*

Assessing your macro and personal reality is the next step to follow in considering prospects for change. Your macro reality includes those organizational and other variables that can work for or against you in the macro change process. Your personal reality, you will recall, is comprised of your own strengths and weaknesses and their potential impact on the change effort. What variables work for and against efforts to respond to the identified community problem? Are people invested in the status quo? Who benefits from the current situation? You will need some sense of how likely the system is to change. How might individuals and leaders in that system respond? Also, knowledge of the available resources would be helpful. Of course, costs must be figured two ways. What are the costs of acting, and what are the costs of not acting? Can you anticipate help from others? How about opposition? Who might be on each side of the fence? Who might straddle the fence and try not to take a position? What you are undertaking is a *force field analysis*, a review of the barriers accomplishing your goal and the factors likely to help you achieve it. Typical barriers include lack of resources (money, people, laws, rules, and so on). They also include individuals or groups who benefit from the status quo. A company that hires only part-time workers at minimum wage avoids paying fringe benefits such as health insurance or retirement. This company benefits from the status quo. Those who work for the company, disproportionately women, might be considered an oppressed population. Their belief that nothing can be done is a barrier to changing the situation.

Positive factors include the availability of money, people, and other resources; motivated individuals, groups, and organizations; the skills of participants; the influence of individuals; the size of your group; and any other force that supports change (Netting, Kettner, & McMurty, 1993; Burghardt, 1982). A large group of influential community citizens is in a very powerful position to bring about change.

Assessing Target Systems

You must also be concerned about the target system to be influenced. If you are trying to get local banks to stop discriminating against people of color when making home loans, you must assess the banking system. Among the factors to consider is the *power* of the target group. Do members of the target group have money, information, media and political influence, or other assets that need to be addressed? For example, bankers are often influential in a community.

To what extent does the target system share your aspirations, values, and goals? The more you have in common with the target system, the more you can employ collaborative tactics rather than conflictual approaches. A human service agency dedicated to providing service to the poor is likely to share your values and goals. This is another positive factor when you are trying to achieve a change in that agency's policy. A company which exploits workers in order to make money for its owners is less likely to share your values. Consequently, the lack of shared values or goals is an impediment.

What are the "consequences of change" for the target system (Connaway & Gentry, 1988, p. 99)? Are the consequences welcome or unwelcome? The more unwelcome the consequences, the greater the likelihood that conflictual approaches will be necessary. Giving workers a raise may make the company's widgets too expensive and cause loss of jobs. This is a very negative consequence. A change in policy which can be explained and achieved so as to bring public praise to the agency or company has positive consequences.

Finally, what are the *general characteristics of the target?* Is it a public organization responsive to public opinion or voters? Is it a private company influenced by its board of directors or stockholders? Is it well organized or poorly run? Knowledge of these characteristics may help you decide how difficult it will be to change the target system and what tactics you should employ to cause that change. Organizations not responsive to public opinion or voters are more difficult to change. A poorly run or badly coordinated organization can be criticized on these accounts and is therefore more vulnerable than an efficient organization. The sum of this information about your target is your force field analysis.

For Geri, the force field analysis was easy. No one in the community would automatically oppose a permanent shelter for battered women. The transient nature of the facility made it hard for police and other agencies to remember where the shelter was located from month to month. In addition, security was always a problem. Because the agency did not own the building, it could not make physical changes to the property to protect its residents. Geri knew that police officers would appreciate a stable place to refer the abused women they encountered. Other social service agencies would also benefit, and ultimately so would clients. Geri's job as program director was to meet the needs of her clients, so her board of directors was likely to support her.

Though relatively new to the community, Geri was full of enthusiasm for the project with a "can do" attitude, a real asset in a social worker. Yet she knew that the effort to find a permanent home would involve many people and require strong community support. Geri summarized the opposing forces as including lack of money, her own and the board's inexperience in tackling major projects, and the fact that she had almost no staff. On the positive side, Geri recognized that the community had often donated money to the shelter (partly in

HIGHLIGHT 9.4

GERI'S FORCE FIELD ANALYSIS

Opposing Forces

1. Lack of money
2. Geri's inexperience
3. Board's inexperience at major projects
4. Shortage of staff

Supporting Forces

1. Past community support and interest
2. Board support
3. Demonstrated need for shelter
4. State grant money for domestic violence
5. Geri's enthusiasm and attitude
6. Relatively inexpensive goal
7. Increased public interest in domestic violence.

response to media attention), and now the need for the shelter was greater. It was often necessary to turn people away because of lack of space. Besides, Geri's review of state and national statistics on domestic violence suggested that the actual incidence of this problem was increasing. The increase had prompted the state to provide grant money to help communities cope with domestic violence. Geri also knew that the cost of purchasing a building would be modest compared to many local fundraising campaigns which sought to raise hundreds of thousands of dollars. Highlight 9.4 illustrates the results of her force field analysis.

Geri did not view the opposing forces as extremely negative. The supporting forces ranged from mildly to extremely positive with items 2, 3, and 5 being most positive. Geri knew she could not accomplish this project by herself and would need to involve others from her board. At the same time, she was new to the organization and this was an opportune time to bring about change. This change in the leadership of the agency (referred to as bureaucratic succession in chapter 4) provided an ideal chance to move in a different direction. The board and Geri were in something of a honeymoon period. In the initial stages of new leadership, there is a tendency for the leader to be given more latitude to try to new ideas. Geri and the board were getting comfortable with each other and each felt very positive about the other. This meant the board was willing to try things

it might later find too threatening. Geri assesses the situation as an excellent opportunity to meet a community need. She decided she could not waste her chance to implement such a macro change.

Step 3: PREPARE—*Establish* Primary Goals

Establishing a primary goal flows from a problem you have already clearly defined. In this case Geri found it easy to establish a primary goal. Since it was no longer feasible to keep using temporary locations and loaned buildings, the community needed a permanent shelter for battered women. She would subsequently direct all her efforts toward this primary goal. In other situations, you could have several goals, so you would have to decide which one was of greatest importance. Geri knew that the potential for permanence of this goal was high, and that achieving it would definitely influence the ability of her organization to meet the future needs of domestic violence survivors.

A goal should generate interest in a given problem so that board members and other influential citizens are motivated to help solve it. Unless you can frame a goal so that it is easily understood and clearly responds to a significant problem, important people are not likely to get involved. This is very important in the next step, identifying influential people.

He beat her 150 times. She only got flowers once.

Every 15 seconds, a woman is beaten in this country.
For as many as four million women, this battering is so severe, they require medical or police attention.
But for nearly 4,000 women each year, the abuse ends. They die.
Help us end domestic violence. Your donation can make a difference.
CALL 1 900-STOP ABUSE
(1 900-786-7228)
$10.00 PER CALL
National Coalition Against Domestic Violence, P.O. Box 18749, Denver, CO 80218-0749, (303) 839-1852

Establishing a permanent shelter for battered women was not difficult once the social worker determined that doing so was a primary goal.

Step 4: PREPARE—Identify Relevant *People* of Influence

Identifying relevant people of influence is sometimes a challenge. As discussed earlier in chapter 5, they are individuals and groups within your agency and community who could potentially help or hurt your cause. Who are the people of influence in your own community? Are there groups whose assistance you might count on? Are there any persons in your organization whom you can ask for help? You want people who bring certain characteristics to the activity. Highlight 9.5 discusses such characteristics.

Geri, you may recall, had a very limited circle of influential contacts and friends. New to the community, she did not know many people. However, her board of directors included persons from many different agencies and organizations. In addition, many board members were members of other groups. Doctors, for example, often serve on boards of other organizations (such as local medical associations). Lawyers serve on many boards and often belong to local civic clubs. If Geri could persuade board members to tap their own circles of resources and influential friends, the possibilities of success expanded dramatically.

Sitting down with the board, Geri helped them identify individuals and organizations they could contact for support of their goal. These included the news media, service organizations, and local philanthropic foundations. Geri also knew about grants that could be applied for and had learned who controlled these funds. As director of the agency, she was frequently asked to address local groups. In fact, both the Junior League and Kiwanis had asked how they might help the shelter. Geri counted those groups as possible sources of support. After talking further with the board, Geri concluded that they had a reasonable-sized network of influential people whom they could approach for help in securing a permanent site for the shelter. This network included a local TV reporter, a newspaper editor, three local service clubs, the local bar association president, and seventeen other community and business leaders.

Step 5: PREPARE—*Assess* Potential Financial Costs and Benefits

Assessing potential costs and benefits to clients and the community is often easy. For Geri, the benefits of a permanent home for the shelter would be enormous. She believed the community would be better served by having the shelter in one place and not having to move periodically to some new location. Permanency would enhance board members sense of identification with the facility, staff, and other agency personnel. Geri's agency could allocate money to make the shelter more secure, thereby providing greater safety for residents. This was especially important because privacy and security are critical for domestic violence shelters. The agency could make its physical environment more attractive to clients and staff. Money spent fixing up the building would produce longer-term benefits because the building would belong to the agency. Physical improvements to the building would increase the value of the property.

Benefits to the clients are usually clear when we formulate a goal. We begin a change process in response to problems affecting clients and our goals reflect our desire to help. However, it is possible to overlook some

---

HIGHLIGHT 9.5

IDENTIFYING PEOPLE OF INFLUENCE

Homan (1994) has suggested getting people who meet the following criteria:

1. *People who get things done.* This includes those with a reputation of providing leadership and accomplishing goals. Past leaders of major fundraising drives might be in this category.
2. *People to whom others look for guidance.* Among these are leaders others turn to for advice and help. They are often established and may be senior members of the community.
3. *People who will become leaders in your organization.* Included here are younger staff members whose enthusiasm and drive are recognized by others.

4. *People who can motivate their peers.* This group includes not only those who are obvious leaders, but also those colleagues who work behind the scenes to get others involved in projects.
5. *People who have connections with other important people or resources.* Among this group would be those who have friendships and business relationships with influential people.
6. *People who have particular skills.* Examples might include those with public speaking ability, writing skills, and mediation skills.

---

aspects of this benefit-to-cost consideration. Efforts to achieve a goal often subtracts from efforts expended for other goals or services. Opportunity costs (referred to in chapter 5) apply in most situations. Geri and her board's effort to secure a permanent shelter could easily take time from their work in meeting current clients' needs. Money spent for a building could also have been spent hiring a social worker to help residents of the temporary shelter or giving raises to the small staff already providing service.

Burghardt (1982) suggests we weigh the costs of using specific tactics to achieve a designated goal. Be aware of how the tactics you are considering affect the political climate you are facing. If the political mood in a community is strongly against new taxes, a campaign to build a new school is likely to fail. Can you move quickly and decisively or must you progress more slowly with less grand objectives? If you ideas are too unrealistic in a given political climate, you may fail, and failure can be costly. It discourages supporters and makes it harder to get their involvement in future projects.

Some costs are more difficult to calculate. Any time you undertake a macro level change effort you risk making someone unhappy. How is this possible? Change is often resisted because it opens people up to the un-

known. What will the future be like if you succeed in your macro change effort? Even if you agree that a new shelter is a good idea, how will it affect the neighborhood surrounding the shelter? Will you have to contend with neighbors who object to a group facility in their neighborhood? This often happens when establishment of group homes or low-income housing units is proposed. Residents may fear this will make their neighborhood less attractive and their property of less value. How much time and energy will it take to overcome this potential barrier? It is safe to say that everything has a cost. You always need to think about such expenses before launching any community project.

Step 6: PREPARE—Evaluate Professional and Personal *Risk*

Chapter 5 identified three types of risks you can incur as a change agent—losing your job, reducing your potential for upward mobility, and straining work relationships. These risks increase when you undertake community-level change. This occurs for several reasons. First, trying to change an element of a community often requires tackling large-scale problems that are resistant

HIGHLIGHT 9.6

GATHERING PEOPLE OF INFLUENCE

Cherrytown had a serious problem that affected its elderly population. Many frail senior citizens could not receive routine medical care because they had no way of getting to the doctor or hospital. While emergency service was available through the local ambulance company, there was no such arrangement possible for routine office visits. The result was that many elderly residents simply gave up going to the doctor. The problem was especially acute for residents with physical disabilities who needed specially equipped vans to get from their homes to medical services. Transportation for routine medical needs was not covered by Medicaid or Medicare, the two primary governmental health-care programs for the elderly.

A recent community needs assessment identified this problem, although it had existed for over ten years. Francine Bodes-Well, social worker for the Council of Churches Elder Service program, thought the time was right to try to do something.

She listed all the influential people in town who had an interest in ensuring that the frail elderly received medical care. In all, she listed twenty-two agency representatives, including the Visiting Nurses Association, the Council of Churches, the Medic-Transport Service, the City of Cherrytown,

and the Mental Health Association. Calling them together to discuss the problem and possible solutions led to the creation of the Eldercare Coalition. A coalition is "an alliance of various factions or . . . groups in a society brought together to achieve a goal" (Barker, 1991, p. 39). Creation of the coalition allowed its members to contribute to solving the problem. A cooperative arrangement allowed the coalition to borrow a bus from the adult day-care center. The coalition then formed an Eldercare Transit Service. Each bus would be assigned a driver and a certified nurse's aide. The service would provide nonemergency medical transportation with fees determined on a sliding scale. Service would not be denied for lack of money, however. Funding for the service came from fees paid to users, contributions from several agencies, and a small start-up grant.

A four-month evaluation of the service found that ridership had risen so dramatically that a second bus would be needed months earlier than projected. Elderly people used the van at a rate that doubled every couple of months, rising from eighteen in the first month to eighty-four at the end of the fourth month. The general level of satisfaction was high, as evidenced by client satisfaction surveys and a survey of agencies whose clients used the service.

---

to change. The resistance you encounter may require more drastic action on your part. Remember that someone always benefits from the status quo and selling change to those who are happy with the ways things are is tough. Those who hold power seldom relinquish it readily. Your efforts to change the situation may cause you to be seen as a troublemaker. Sometimes changing the status quo can be seen as too daunting. Undertaking schemes that seem too grandiose can lead others to believe that nothing can be done.

A third problem is that adopting conflictual strategies can brand you as "unprofessional." After all, you

are supposed to be a social worker helping people, not a rabble-rouser trying to run the community. Fourth, attacking problems that your agency does not view as within your job purview may leave you unsupported. Perhaps neither your colleagues nor your supervisors will accept your new role.

All these examples can be scary to the individual social worker. Even with the sanction of your profession and its values, you always assume some risk. Realistically, however, few social workers lose their jobs for trying to make the communities better places to live. Many, however, lose the support from colleagues who do not feel the same level of intensity about the problem or simply do not consider the goal that important.

Generally, though, the benefits of large scale change efforts are easily identified, and your colleagues can understand why you have undertaken the effort. In addition, they might become part of the group that is helping you bring change. In one community, a social worker concerned about the lack of low income housing helped convince the city and a private company to relocate houses rather than tear them down. Previous plans called for the two entities to raze the properties to make way for other projects. After moving the homes to a new location (relatively inexpensive compared to building new houses), the city and the company could donate them or sell them inexpensively to low-income families who would fix them up. In addition, the company would likey receive a tax benefit for donating the homes. The creative nature of this endeavor attracted the admiration of other social workers who wished they had thought of such a novel idea.

In the case of the new home for the shelter, Geri really ran few risks. She would certainly not lose her job, because her board of directors supported her efforts. As agency director, she was expected to lead and be involved in community activities. It is doubtful the board of directors had this in mind when they hired her; nevertheless, Geri felt there was little chance she would be seen as acting outside her mandate or without sanction. Her one big risk was failure. If she undertook the project and could not make it work, she might lose credibility with her board which might then hesitate or even refuse to support her future ideas. Also, if she did succeed and the permanent home became an expensive problem for the agency, she might incur the anger of her employer—the board. How would the board react if the house got termites, of if the furnace and water heater broke in the first year of operation? These were all risks she was willing to take.

Step 7: PREPAR*E—Evaluate* the Potential Success of a Macro Change Process

After considering the pros and cons of undertaking a community change effort, you ultimately decide whether or not to go ahead. This involves evaluating the potential benefits and success of the change effort coupled with an assessment of the most effective tactics to achieve your goal. Some tactics carry higher risk than others. Conflict or contest tactics are perhaps the most

risky because some people perceive such tactics as unprofessional. Other may be afraid that the tactics themselves will cause problems. Yet conflict tactics may be the only way to achieve your goal. Conflict tactics include bargaining, negotiating, demonstrating, civil disobedience, and lawsuits. Bargaining and negotiating are the least offensive conflict tactics because they are based on the premise that both sides can discuss the problem and arrive at an acceptable solution. Demonstrations, including picketing and public displays of disagreement, are more problematic. They may engender public ridicule from those who don't support your ideas, and they may embarrass the targets so much that they refuse to change their position. Civil disobedience, including refusing to obey the law or other rules, often brings condemnation from "law abiding" citizens and allows others to criticize your tactics as too radical. Finally, lawsuits are an expensive and risky proposition because you may not prevail in court. Court decisions against your side can end up costing you financially. Moreover, judges and juries may decide cases based on very narrow grounds, and you can lose on a technicality even though your position is ethically and morally sound.

Collaborative approaches carry much less risk, but they may not be as effective in getting you where you want to go. Remember, the tactics you adopt must be consistent with your value system. Ends don't justify the means, and your chosen strategy must mesh with the NASW Code of Ethics.

At this point in the PREPARE process, you will be faced with the same three alternatives described in chapter 5. You may elect to: (1) pursue the community change effort, (2) postpone it indefinitely, or (3) terminate the process. In Geri's case, she had already decided that the potential benefits were many and the risks few. Highlight 9.7 presents a review of Geri's evaluation. Geri reasoned that the proposed tactics were unlikely to produce either conflict or bad feelings. On the other hand, had Geri decided not to go forward, others probably would not have thought badly of her nor would a decision to postpone have earned disapproval. In this situation, Geri was as close to a win-win situation as possible. No matter what she did, she was likely to be praised for her decision. However, the benefits of obtaining a permanent community shelter for battered women made the choice clear—she had to go for it.

Once you make the decision to seek some improvement in your community or its service delivery system, you are still not at the half-way point. Though the plan-

---

HIGHLIGHT 9.7

EVALUATING POTENTIAL SUCCESS

Pros

Factor	*Evaluation*
Client need	High client need
Organizational variables	Neutral to positive
Own strengths	Good to excellent
Potential support	Good to excellent
Financial benefits	Unclear

Cons

Factor	*Evaluation*
Organizational variables	No perceived negatives
Own weaknesses	Minor (mostly inexperience)
Potential resistance	Minor, perhaps none
Financial costs	Cost estimates unclear
Geri's risks	Relatively minor

---

ning process is critical, actual achievement of a goal is often the toughest task because there are always unforeseen obstacles to impede your progress. There may be financial costs you could not anticipate or opposition you did not expect. In addition, the planning process in the PREPARE paradigm is largely cognitive or "on paper." Achievement of your own goals requires that you actually do something. This brings us to the IMAGINE model of implementation, which incorporates the intervention, evaluation, termination, and follow-up steps in the problem-solving process.

IMAGINE: A Process for Community Change

Chapter 6 introduced the IMAGINE model for guiding you through the implementation of a macro system change effort. The seven steps of IMAGINE are applicable to most, if not all, community change situations. To illustrate this process, we will continue with our example of Geri and the shelter for battered women (see figure 9.2).

*I*MAGINE: Start with an Innovative *Idea*

The innovative idea you will begin with is the plan you identified for effecting change. By now, you have carefully considered your options and made a decision about the approach most likely to succeed. This approach represents your best assessment, your innovative idea about how to handle the problematic situation confronting you. In Geri's case, her plan was to find a permanent building to house the shelter for battered women. Highlight 9.8 describes yet another innovative idea.

I*M*AGINE: *Muster* Support and Formulate an Action System

Mustering support and forming an action system are essential steps in the process because rarely can we ac-

Figure 9.2
IMAGINE —A Process for Initiating
and Implementing Macro Change

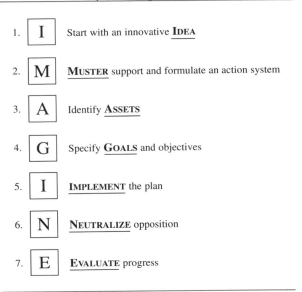

1. **I** — Start with an innovative **IDEA**

2. **M** — **MUSTER** support and formulate an action system

3. **A** — Identify **ASSETS**

4. **G** — Specify **GOALS** and objectives

5. **I** — **IMPLEMENT** the plan

6. **N** — **NEUTRALIZE** opposition

7. **E** — **EVALUATE** progress

complish a major project without enlisting the help of others. Recall that the action system includes people and resources you begin to organize and employ to help you work toward the needed change (see chapter 6). Even Geri, as an agency director, could not achieve her goal without assistance. As a starting point, you have identified relevant people of influence who might be helpful. Geri, for example, identified members of her board of directors and local citizens who could help her in her project. Homan (1994) suggests a useful technique for recognizing the relevant people to whom your action system has access. He recommends asking each person in the action system to list three community leaders he or she would be willing to ask for a favor connected with your project. This is also a sound way of assessing whether your action system is well-connected. If the action system comes up with a sizable number of names, you have a potentially powerful group. If the names are few in number or appear to be relatively unimportant in the community, you have a big problem.

Geri could start with her board of directors, several of whom were very influential members of the community. At a special meeting of the board, she outlined the goal of getting a permanent home for the shelter. Geri had already spoken privately to several board members,

including the chairperson, about her idea. She had also notified the board that she would bring the idea before them for their approval after she did some more groundwork. Geri then outlined some suggestions about how they might proceed and described the steps she and the board members might take to ensure the success of their mission. She suggested the news media could be asked to highlight the idea. She also identified several possible sources of help, from local service clubs with whom she had prior contact and raised the possibility of seeking a state grant to help defray some of the costs of the project. She answered questions and anticipated some concerns board members might have. Reviewing the possible advantages and disadvantages of the proposal, Geri proved that she had thought carefully about this plan. Board members were impressed. "Yes, we made the right decision when we hired her!" one member thought to himself as he heard her discuss the plan. One by one, most board members agreed the goal was attainable. Even doubters recognized that the goal was desirable, though they retained their reservations about whether the plan would work.

As an action system, the board was responsible for helping implement the plan. Through their contacts the board members could probably influence a large segment of the population. Because board members were influential, others in the community would be more likely to take a positive view of the goal than if Geri had undertaken the change by herself. Although the action system contained ten people and was larger than the five-person size recommended by Resnick (1980c), its size was not an impediment.

In this situation, the board was a "naturally occurring" group. (That is, it was not formed for the specific purpose of carrying out this plan.) In other circumstances, you would need to follow the recommendations described in chapter 6 to create your action system. However, the board of directors was an experienced action system. Like any action system, it consisted of people with varying degrees of commitment to the goal. Ultimately, how much time and energy each would contribute varied from member to member. Some members, committed activists who had helped begin the first services to battered women, were behind the project 150 percent. They would devote as much time to this as possible, given their own responsibilities as employees and family members. Other board members were community professionals (lawyers, social workers,

---

HIGHLIGHT 9.8

GETTING FOOD TO
WHERE IT IS NEEDED

April Showers, director of the Mountain City Food Harvest, knew there had to be a better way. While thirty agencies in Mountain City served over five-thousand meals per day to the needy, tons of food were thrown away by area restaurants, bakers, and other food establishments. What if there were a way to get the two together—those who need food and those who have it and must get rid of it? What if, say, leftover chicken from Kentucky Fried Chicken could be given to the Mountain City Kitchen, an agency serving the homeless?

April hit upon an idea. She could contact each eating establishment and ask to bring in pans for the vast quantities of leftover food they have each day. These pans could be picked up in refrigerated vans for transportation to local group homes, shelters for the homeless, and kitchens serving low-income clients. In a matter of less than two years, April's vans plied the city streets thirty-five hours each week, reaching over three dozen businesses. The result was a yearly delivery of eighteen tons of food. To help encourage restaurants to cooperate, April provides receipts for the amount of food donated, which is tax-deductible for the contributing businesses. The result is a win-win situation in which all participants benefit in some way.

---

physicians, pharmacists) who were somewhat less committed to an all-out push to achieve the goal. However, despite their other commitments, these individuals had a wide array of contacts in the community. Their influential help would compensate for their own lack of time to expend on the project.

Geri also knew that board members sometimes have short memories. She checked carefully with the board secretary to ensure that decisions to support this project were described clearly in the official minutes of the meeting. She also verified that the actual steps each member would take were clearly recorded. This record of *who* was going to do *what* by *when* was important for keeping the process on track. (Had Geri known about doing PERT charts, described in chapter 5, she could have devised a written plan to guide the board/action system as it went about its business.)

IMAGINE: Identify *Assets*

Remember that assets are any resources or advantages that aid you in undertaking and completing your change process. Assets include money, people, time, energy, and facilities/office space, etc. Geri had many assets.

First, she had an influential action system with a variety of community contacts. For the most part, the action system was solidly behind the project. Geri's office in the temporary shelter gave her a place to operate as she carried out her tasks. As always, money was scarce, but the potential for getting some grant money and other types of contributions was great.

Although new in the community, Geri was an effective problem-solver, as a BSW social worker she was prepared to tackle a variety of tasks. She knew the goal of attaining a permanent home for the shelter would excite some people. She felt that hardly anyone would be against the idea. Thus, her assets included herself, the contacts and enthusiasm of her action system, and the attractiveness of the goal to other community members.

IMAGINE: Specify *Goals* and Objectives

Normally, the primary goal would already be identified in general terms in the PREPARE process. At this point you need to be even more specific about what you actually want to accomplish and how you will get there. We refer to these subgoals as *objectives*. We call the actual activities needed to achieve your objectives *action steps*.

HIGHLIGHT 9.9

GOALS, OBJECTIVES, AND ACTION STEPS

Primary Goal:	Reduce Gang and Drug Activity in Third Ward
Objective 1:	Develop Neighborhood Watch Program in Third Ward
Action Step 1:	Mrs. Watermolen and social worker Framo Phlegm will call meeting of Third Ward residents at St. John's Church for April 15th.
Action Step 2:	Mr. Newt and Ms. Wart will prepare flyers to be distributed to neighbors and at local grocery by March 25th.
Action Step 3:	Mrs. Watermolen and Framo Phlegm will develop agenda for meeting and Mrs. Watermolen will lead meeting (April 15th).
Action Step 4:	Mr. Newt and Ms. Wart will distribute flyers and Pastor Danish will arrange refreshments for meeting (April 10th–15th).
Action Step 5:	Representatives selected at meeting will contact Police Department to help neighborhood set up watch program (April 25th).
Objective 2:	Increase Police Department patrols of Third Ward
Objective 3:	Eliminate vacant house at end of block as haven for gang

For example, one of the steps in establishing a permanent shelter for Geri's agency might be to designate either herself or some board members to investigate various properties. Before the agency can relocate, the action system must know *where* it can go.

While the terms may get confusing, all major projects benefit from being broken down into manageable pieces with clear indications of what needs to be done, when, and by whom. Using the terms introduced in chapter 6, we identify three possible levels of specificity in goals and objectives. These appear in highlight 9.9.

In highlight 9.9 it is easy to see that any objective might consist of a series of action steps. You might even break each action step down further. Action step 5, for example, could be further specified as Joe Smith and Mary McDonald will speak to Captain Frisbie on April 20 to request help in establishing a neighborhood watch program. Keep in mind that there are often many tasks to accomplish, and someone has to do each of them. Unassigned tasks will not be completed. Tasks without deadlines will probably not be done when they should be. (See highlight 9.10.)

Let's return to our social worker, Geri. Geri had a clear goal, getting a permanent home for the shelter. To get there, however, would take many steps. An outline of some of her objectives and action steps appears in highlight 9.11.

As it turned out, Geri and the board chairperson discovered a variety of buildings they could bring to the board for approval and action. One building's owner would finance the sale with a small down payment from the agency. The other building would require bank financing, but the price was very reasonable. In addition, at least one local service group was willing to co-sign a loan for the building if the agency needed this assistance.

Once the board selected what they felt was the best option, Geri and the board would carry out their plan. This is the beginning of the implementation phase of the IMAGINE process.

IMAG*I*NE: *Implement* the Plan

Burghardt (1982) suggests some general guidelines useful at the implementation stage. He reminds us that it

---

HIGHLIGHT 9.10

GETTING THINGS DONE

Burghardt (1982) provides excellent guidelines for some of the tasks with which you may become involved when undertaking a community change effort.

Holding Meetings

1. Arrange for the location—try to make it accessible for everyone.
2. Advertise the meeting as widely as possible.
3. Set up the chairs, tables, and microphone where you want them before the meeting.
4. Arrange for refreshments.
5. Prepare an agenda of topics to be covered.
6. Arrange for child care, if possible.
7. Be ready to accept donations.

Mass Mailings

Mass mailings are letters, brochures, or other material sent to large numbers of people informing them of events or soliciting their support.

1. Schedule work sessions for mailings (when can volunteers get together to stuff envelopes?) at least three weeks before mailings.
2. Make the experience enjoyable by providing food or music.
3. Have sponge available to moisten envelope flaps and stamps.

4. Try to get a bulk mailing permit allowing mail to be sent for a fraction of the normal cost. Churches and non-profit organizations often have bulk mailing permits already and may let you use theirs. Permits can be purchased at the Post Office.

Leafleting

Leaflets are brochures or other handouts. They might describe your organization's views on a topic or announce meetings and other events.

1. Hand out leaflets where they will do the most good. Consider a person handing out information on a constitutional amendment to roll back taxes and cut government spending. He sets up his table in front of a state office building housing the Department of Health and Human Services. For the most part, the people using the building are clients who benefit from the services and government employees whose jobs are based on those services—hardly persons interested in cutting off their own resources.
2. Use two-person teams to hand out leaflets. This ensures that one is available to talk to those who wish to learn more while the other continues to distribute information. They also keep each other company when things are slow.
3. Be ready to write down the name, address, and telephone number of anyone supporting your cause.

---

is important to recognize the strengths of everyone involved in the implementation process. Some members are good public speakers and others are well organized. You must know your own strong points and those of the people helping you carry out the plan. Some people are more process oriented and others are more task oriented. This means that some members of the action system may move at different speeds. Task-oriented people prefer to get right to the point, complete a task, and move on. Process-oriented helpers want to spend

more time talking about how things can best be done, considering every possibility. Recognize that different tasks depend on different skills. Try to match needs with skills. If some people are better at letter writing, use them for that. Others can work on grants or participate on a subcommittee. Break your activities into smaller tasks so that each action system member has a role.

Holding meetings is one of the most frequent activities in the implementation phase. You will be running

---

HIGHLIGHT 9.11

GOALS AND OBJECTIVES FOR A PERMANENT SHELTER

Goal:	Obtain permanent home for shelter for battered women
Objective 1:	Locate building that will adequately house the shelter and its program (by June 1).
Action Step 1:	Geri will look at real estate ad in newspapers and contact local realtors (by May 1).
Action Step 2:	Banker Smith will learn whether his bank or any other bank in town has foreclosed on (taken back ownership of) a suitable building (by May 1).
Action Step 3:	Board will review available buildings at the May 3 meeting, narrowing list to five possibilities.
Action Step 4:	Geri and board chairperson will visit each building and discuss possible financing of property with seller (by May 15).
Action Step 5:	Geri will explore available grant sources to purchase or remodel building(s) for shelter (by May 15).
Action Step 6:	Geri and board chairperson will report to board about options and give their recommendation (by May 22).
Action Step 7:	Board will act on recommendation and begin process of acquiring building(s) (by May 22).

---

meetings and using the mezzo skills discussed in chapter 3. Little get done without the combined efforts of many people and meetings are often helpful in bringing that combination of people together. As a group leader, you will use skills such as familiarity with Robert's Rules of Order to move business along.

Burghardt also suggests that you involve people as quickly as possible in *doing* things. This keeps them feeling part of the group and give them a sense of accomplishment. He urges staying on task and doing the follow-up work, making phone calls and arranging meetings. A general guideline for your practice is: Do not procrastinate—do it *now*.

Let's turn again to Geri and the shelter for battered women. Carrying out the plan to get the shelter typifies the challenges you face when trying to carry out your plan. There are always twists and turns that you do not expect, complicating your choices and actions. As Geri and the board chairperson pursued their objectives through the series of action steps, it became clear that this was just the start of the process. The decision to purchase a building would lead to even more objectives

and action steps. In that sense, you often carry out a plan and revise it simultaneously. Highlight 9.12 further describes some activities that characterize the implementation phase of this process.

As you can see, several objectives and appropriate action steps are incorporated in the above example. The objective of purchasing a building required action steps related to arranging funding (bank loan). Rehabilitating the property (another objective) required action steps to identify needed remodeling, estimate costs of such remodeling, and write a grant application to cover the costs. This pattern is repeated in almost all macro implementation activities.

IMAGINE: *Neutralize* Opposition

Neutralizing opposition may be either a large task or a small one depending upon how controversial your change effort is. Trying to get the city to drop its plan to run a highway through a low-income neighborhood is likely to encounter major opposition. City officials,

---

HIGHLIGHT 9.12

IMPLEMENTING THE PLAN

Geri and her board of directors agreed to purchase a dilapidated two-story home near a college campus. Once a fine old home, the building was for sale for about 80 percent of its actual value because the owner wanted to sell it quickly. To Geri, however, this meant that there was already 20 percent equity built into the property. (This meant that whoever bought the property already had 20 percent of the home's value invested in it.) Using this information, Geri persuaded the board to seek a bank loan to buy the property, using the 20 percent equity in lieu of a down payment. Board members were excited about the possibility of having a permanent home but were also more than a little skeptical. "It will happen," Geri kept telling them.

Geri learned that a state fund had been established to help support community responses to domestic violence. She wrote a grant application and received a $40,000 grant to rehabilitate the property. Now real progress was possible.

With the grant in hand, board members began to tap other community resources. Geri contacted local church and civic groups and asked for their help. Some "adopted" a room, buying furnishing and paying for needed repairs. The Lions Club agreed to hold a raffle to support the new refuge house, which was named for Officer Bennett, the police officer whose death in a domestic violence incident initiated this chapter. While the amount of money the Lions Club raised was not large, the involvement of this respected service organization encouraged other organizations and individuals to help.

Donations of kitchen cabinets were received. Geri traded an unused garage door opener (the garage was converted to a group therapy room) for a toilet. Influential board members used their business contacts to gain additional help. A lawyer on the board asked his law firm to contribute funds to fix up a staff office. Another law firm did all the paperwork gratis (free of charge). The criminal justice system also found a way to help. Juveniles and adults sentenced to perform restitution (community service) for their criminal conduct were given the opportunity to work off their obligation at the shelter.

Geri contacted a youth conservation organization (sponsored by the state) that worked on several public construction projects in the community. They agreed to build a fence around the shelter and to turn the basement into office space. The social work department of the nearby university provided students as both volunteers and field interns, allowing further expansion of services.

The board of directors of the Bennett Refuge House decided to become more diversified in membership. Members were added representing many different new perspectives: the probation department; the university social work department; news media; civic groups; additional local businesses; and active volunteers. All new members brought with them a variety of contacts and membership in other groups.

---

road planners, business interests, and other groups may stand to benefit from this road. Because of their potential gain they are likely to fight on their own behalf. Overcoming their opposition or changing their minds could be quite difficult.

On the other hand, a plan that initially had no obvious opposition may incur some along the way. In Geri's case a board member might change her mind about the value of a permanent shelter during the discussions about purchasing a building. This board member might conclude that the project was too expensive. Neighbors could have raised concerns about the location of the shelter in their neighborhood. Had the latter happened, efforts would be required to deal with such opposition. Opposition can be handled through collaborative strategies or through adversarial approaches. Collaboration in Geri's case might involve persuasion, communicating ideas to others, educating opponents, listening to opponents' concerns and responding accordingly, and rational argument, to name a few. Had only a few vocal neighbors caused a problem, Geri and her action system could have asked other residents to sign a petition in support of the shelter. The action system could have sent letters to the news media emphasizing the desirability of the shelter and the weakness of opposing arguments.

USING SOCIAL ACTION, CONFRONTATION, AND CONFLICT APPROACHES. Social action involves efforts by groups of individuals to create change in an organization or community. Social action activities need not necessarily involve confrontation and conflict. However, the effort required to cause significant changes in the status quo within large systems often requires different approaches. We have said previously that it is best to start with nonconflictual approaches

whenever possible. They can save energy used up in conflict and avoid resultant bad feelings. Conflictual tactics will likely have repercussions. Moreover, you should not use confrontational approaches on behalf of any client group without first obtaining the group's agreement. Be sure to fully inform clients about possible risks associated with such approaches. Realistically, however, more confrontational and adversarial social action approaches are sometimes needed. Burghardt (1982) provides some helpful suggestions for their use. Social action may take the form of a group lobbying its legislators, lobbying a decision-maker, or writing letters to newspapers or elected officials. (Chapter 10 addresses these skills more thoroughly.) More drastic examples of social action and conflict approaches include such things as strikes, rallies, boycotts, marches, demonstrations, informational picketing, and court action. This type of social action has a rich history, from women's marches for the right to vote in the early 1900s to

---

HIGHLIGHT 9.13

CONFRONTING A BAD IDEA

Golden Lake park is the spiritual home of much of Grand Rapids' African-American community. Every fall for the past quarter century the park has played host to over four thousand people of color with ties to the city of Grand Rapids. This group wants to maintain the park as it has been for the past twenty-five years. When the city park board announced that they were going to build a million-dollar community center in the park, the battle lines were drawn.

Opponents of the idea formed the Community Coalition and enlisted the help of diverse elements of the community. African-American residents felt the move would destroy the park's heritage. The Community Coalition collected more than three-hundred signatures on petitions from homeowners living near the park. Next, they arranged for crowds of people to attend meetings of the city council and speak against the move. More than fifty people turned out to oppose the idea at one meeting, and seventy showed up in opposition at another public meeting.

The coalition also put pressure on the state Department of Natural Resources, which had previously given a grant to help develop Golden Lake Park. The terms of that grant permanently restricted the use of the park to public outdoor recreation, which was not compatible with the building of a community center there. At the coalition's initiation, the state agency told the city that it would be violating the terms of its agreement with the Department of Natural Resources. If the city wanted to go ahead with its plan, the state agency ruled that the city council would have to buy park land equal in value to that which they were using to build a multipurpose community center. Caught between confrontation with the African-American community and the cost of trying to find new park land, the city gave up. A new site for the community center would be sought. The African-American community had successfully overcome or neutralized opposition to its desire to keep Golden Lake Park unchanged.

Social action has a rich tradition in American communities. Here, people join in a gay rights demonstration, thus calling attention to their concerns about homophobia and community safety.

current marches protesting violence against lesbian and gay people. Likewise, the civil rights and antiwar movements used marches and demonstrations to call attention to their concerns.

Similarly, boycotts of products have been used to oppose mistreatment of farm workers, thereby forcing lettuce and wine growers to negotiate with their workers. Workers commonly employ labor strikes to force employers to bargain with them.

More intrusive and controversial approaches to social action include sit-ins, civil disobedience (for example, lying in front of a bulldozer to prevent it from entering a neighborhood), and fasts or hunger strikes (Connaway & Gentry, 1988). The intensive nature of these tactics can lead to burnout. They must be used carefully.

Specht (1969) has categorized more extreme approaches into three overall groups, each increasing respectively in severity.

CLASHES OF POSITION. The first, he calls clashes of position. Clashes of position include actions such as "debate, legal disputes, written statements of intent, or public speeches" (p. 10). To this list we would add bargaining. Because bargaining and negotiating are

such commonly used approaches to social change, highlight 9.14 describes some guidelines for their use.

VIOLATIONS OF NORMATIVE BEHAVIOR. Violations of normative behavior comprise the second category of more extreme approaches to social action in macro practice. They are generally more severe than clashes of position. Specht (1969) defines violations of normative behavior as activities such as "marches, demonstrations, boycotts, protests, vigils (extended demonstrations), rent strikes, dropping out (of an organization), haunting (following one's opponent for long periods), renouncing honors, . . . fasts, and interjection (having large masses of people congregate in an area" (p. 10). That is, they are not illegal activities but are considered outside the norm. They carry greater risk than clashes of position. In fact, today, haunting might be considered stalking and could violate state or local laws.

Burghardt (1982) points out that, while marches and demonstrations can be effective in gaining attention for your cause, they can also take on a life of their own. They can attract vocal opponents and can result in escalating problems. Planning becomes more complex in such instances. For example, marches require

HIGHLIGHT 9.14

BARGAINING AND NEGOTIATING

Bargaining/negotiating (considered identical for practical purposes) is a process whereby two or more parties reach a mutually acceptable decision. It is a common approach to use when engaging in community interventions. Bargaining works best when the decision-maker's image is consistent with your goal. Assume you are working with a group of neighborhood parents who seek more supervised recreational opportunities for their children. City officials who believe they have an interest in helping inner city children are more likely to bargain if their image (their reputation for concern) and your goal (providing recreational opportunities for children) are consistent. Pointing out to city officials that closing a city park at 5:00 P.M. means these children have no place to play and will probably remain unsupervised on the street is going to be persuasive. After all, both of you want a better community and opportunities for these children.

Contrast this with Taxpayers for No Property Tax, a group whose sole concern is cutting city taxes. The willingness of city officials to bargain with them is reduced because the group's values and image are narrowly focused on tax reduction. They can't bargain as effectively because their goal—reduction of property tax—clashes with city officials' obligation to meet the needs of citizens with multiple city services.

A disadvantage of bargaining is that it takes time to arrive at an agreement. Those who can afford the time, can tolerate the stress of prolonged discussion, and have the stamina for bargaining have the advantage. Those who have both a capacity for and an interest in protracted negotiations are likely to have more success. As a result, it is typical for negotiators to act as though they don't mind waiting or to pretend that they are willing to fight against your proposal. In essence, they are bluffing, so it is probably in your best interest to act as if you too have plenty of time, even if you don't. Your adversary probably has time constraints too.

Simultaneously, recognize that threatening to take an action if the other side does not agree carries some risks. If the threat is credible—that is, if the other side believes you can carry out the threat—your position is stronger. At the same time, it is important that the threatened action be proportionate to the goal. A threat to boycott all city services if the park hours are not extended is out of proportion to the solution you seek. Generally, if the threatened action does not seem credible or is out of proportion to the goal, your effectiveness is lessened. Realize that all these tactics exist for the purpose of convincing the other side that you will expend as much energy as necessary to achieve your goal.

Bargainers often put forward positions or requests that neither side thinks are reasonable. This is a time-worn tactic in labor negotiations but not necessary in all bargaining situations. In some situations the tactic of making absurd demands may backfire, making the other side see you as totally unreasonable. If you sense that you and the other party are not that far apart on key issues, try adopting a more reasonable goal instead of ''asking for the moon.''

---

preparation for water supply, medical care, leadership, and signs. You have to coordinate contacts with and request support from other groups who will participate. These could include labor unions, religious groups, community organizations, neighborhood associations, student organizations, and social clubs.

March organizers must develop lists of definitely committed participants to make certain they have enough people for an effective march. Six people walking down the street makes little impact. Organizers want to ensure that participants arrive on time and have backup plans if anyone on their list decides not to come. Timing for marches and demonstrations is also important. Noon and quitting time during the week are considered very effective because of the likelihood that a large number of people will witness the event. Avoid holding demonstrations on holidays or at the end of the week before holidays. Potential participants are probably busy with other personal activities and distractions during such times. Thus, they probably will not show up. Your audience is also likely to be much smaller. If you are marching to raise awareness of a problem, pick specific start and stop points in advance. A length of about one-and-a-half miles is typical (Burghardt, 1982).

Maintaining security during a march or demonstration is also important. March security includes keeping people in line, leading chanting, identifying leaders, and deciding who will carry the medical equipment in case of emergency.

Before the demonstration or march it is important to coordinate placing of signs, distributing flyers, and preparing press releases. Distribute the press releases about a week before the gathering and follow up with an invitation to the media personnel you hope will attend. Press releases should be brief, containing specifics of the march (what, when, where, why, who). Provide the name and number of a contact person. Limit the entire message to a single double-spaced page. Remember that the media like new information, new angles, and/or important people. Often it is wise to schedule a press conference together with a rally (Burghardt, 1982). A rally is simply a gathering of people, usually with several speakers exhorting the audience to support a specific goal. Combining a rally with a march gets both the public and the media involved and is a capstone for your group.

Rallies should begin or end the march. In either case, arrange rally speakers and sound systems in advance. Each speaker should emphasize something different. One might discuss why the march is taking place. Another might describe the problem, while a third might suggest solutions. The event should end with encouragement for future action and identify specific steps that will be taken on behalf of the goal (Burghardt, 1982). Rallies help energize people and recruit others interested in the goal.

VIOLATIONS OF LEGAL NORMS. The approaches with the highest risk, violations of legal norms, include "civil disobedience and noncooperation, tax refusal, sit-ins, . . . and other violations of law" (p. 11). We emphasize that such methods are potentially harmful to the members of your action system and to yourself. Because they are outside legal limits, possible consequences can include arrest, conviction for a crime, and loss of support from colleagues who feel you have gone too far. The recent abortion protest controversy is a good example of this. For many professionals, getting convicted of a crime means loss of a license to practice. It can also result in lose of one's job. At the same time, these methods have historically been used effectively to change community and institutional behavior, laws, and government policies.

It is important to reemphasize that none of these approaches are ends in themselves. You should not undertake them simply for the sake of doing them. Your goals must be very clear. You must view clashes of position, violations of normative behavior, and violations of legal norms all as action steps to obtain goals and objectives. They are not the goals and objectives themselves. Rather, they are used to generate publicity, boost morale, or help locate similarly minded people and groups. To be most effective, social actions need "a clear assessment of its real and potential resources, a focused target, and a program designed to attract as large a group as possible" (Burghardt, 1982, p. 73).

CHOOSE GOALS WISELY. Resources needed for social action include the people expected to help carry out the various activities envisioned. Getting too grandiose in your goals can disappoint people and reduce their future involvement. Predicting that five-hundred people will show up for a protest rally at city hall and having only fifty come is a real letdown. We recommend selection of manageable goals and targets. If you need to change direction after you discover that more is possible—great! It's better to expand your horizons than to have to cut back drastically because your initial planning was unrealistic. The latter makes it look as if you are not a strong group and reduces your credibility. One of the goals of social action is to choose an issue that is likely to get others excited and involved and that will ultimately succeed. This is more effective because it gives participants a sense of purpose and accomplishment.

IMAGINE: *Evaluate* Progress

Evaluating progress is much easier when you have clearly specified your goals and objectives in measurable terms. Writing down the objectives and action steps allows you to see whether all pieces of the puzzle are in place. You thus can tell if each step in the process has been followed as planned. Suppose, for example, that you were supposed to contact your state senator by September 14 to ask his support of a bill licensing BSWs in your state. It is now September 21 and you have not gotten around to doing this. Having a written list of objectives and action steps is a reminder that you have unfinished business. The process of verifying that the steps are being carried out is called *monitoring the ongoing operation*. More important, however, you will be concerned about the results of your process. We will discuss evaluation in more detail in chapter 10. Because we have taken you so far through the case of the shelter for battered women, we'll let you see how it turned out. A brief evaluation appears in highlight 9.15.

The purpose of the evaluation phase is primarily to learn whether the identified goals were achieved. A secondary purpose includes deciding what additional effort, if any, is needed to stabilize the change. For example, without a plan for paying the mortgage on the property, the future of the permanent shelter would be precarious at best. The multiple sources of funds available to the shelter help ensure that is will continue to exist for some time. It will be fairly permanent. In addition, broadening membership of the board of directors provides a wider base of support than previously existed. In macro terminology, we often refer to this as *stabilizing change* because it allows our accomplishments to continue indefinitely.

In this stage you might also look for any negative consequences of the implementation (Kettner, Daley, & Nichols, 1985). Sometimes unexpected (iatrogenic) and problematic results appear. Perhaps the original old house that became the permanent shelter was built over a sinkhole or has a leaking underground fuel storage tank that no one knew about. Perhaps the heavy traffic in and out of the shelter cause parking problems in the neighborhood. Negative consequences may be overcome or adjusted to, or may force you to abandon the project. While you always hope there will be no negative outcomes, expect that some will appear.

TERMINATION AND FOLLOW-UP. Terminate a change effort when it has proven successful, is unsuccessful and can't be fixed, or is too costly to continue. For example, you may have underestimated the obsta-

---

HIGHLIGHT 9.15

EVALUATING PROGRESS AND A FOLLOW-UP

The board of directors purchased the home. Geri and many others helped it become a major player in the human service community. The Junior League continued to support the house by decorating and refurnishing several rooms. The local medical association contributed money for remodeling projects. Church groups and private individuals donated clothes so that residents of the shelter, who often left their homes with few belongings, would have clean, serviceable wearing apparel. While the progress was sometimes slow, neither Geri nor the board lost sight of the purpose of the agency, to protect women and children suffering from domestic violence.

Seven years after Officer Bennett's death, the community finally had a full-fledged shelter for battered women offering individual and group counseling, children's groups, and job training. The shelter also owned and operated a transition house where women and their children could live once they were ready to leave the shelter. Later, the shelter acquired a community meeting building where the board and other community could hold regular meetings. Funding for projects and operations came from donations, grants, fees for service, contracts with various social service organizations, and United Way contributions. Officer Bennett would have been proud.

cles and forces against the project arising from community indifference. Maybe conditions have changed and the goal is no longer as important to your client group. You may terminate the project if unintended consequences are sufficiently negative. If you have to give up on a worthy goal, find out what, if anything, can be salvaged from the effort. Sometimes the failure of one project leads a group to take on another goal that is more attainable.

Do follow-up when you need to ensure that agreed upon tasks and action steps were actually carried out. Perhaps the city agreed to build a new community center but then dragged its feet about allocating the money. This requires follow-up to see that promises are kept. Follow-up is important because too often people and organizations revert to their old ways when "the heat" is off them. Keeping the pressure and heat on them won't produce a diamond, but it will help ensure that they keep their promises.

Chapter Summary

This chapter begins with a discussion of change in the community and a philosophical perspective on macro practice. It includes a discussion of both the ends and the means of change. Perspectives on the community are addressed, along with a brief review of the problem-solving process used throughout generalist social work.

Next, the PREPARE model, designed to help assess and plan for a community intervention, is presented. We also discussed each step in the model, from identifying problems to evaluating the potential success of a change effort. Specific examples are given for each step.

Next, the IMAGINE model for implementing and evaluating a macro change effort is applied to a variety of community problems. A discussion about social action, confrontation, and conflict approaches is also included. Finally, we present a brief overview of the termination and follow-up phases of the change process.

CHAPTER TEN

Evaluating Macro Practice

Angie Amed, usually an enthusiastic effervescent individual, felt overwhelmed and defeated. The youth services program she nurtured and supervised for her agency had operated smoothly for the past six years. Until now, no one had ever challenged her on the program's success. Suddenly, the local United Way office was requesting definitive proof that her program had been successful in meeting its goals. Angie quickly gathered her staff of social workers and activity specialists to discuss the problem. The youth services program had originally been set up as one of many programs operated by her agency. Angie, hired just two years ago, supervised seven staff members. The program offered after school recreational activities and educational programs to a number of adolescents. Her agency's basement was outfitted with pool tables, foosball tables, and even Nintendo. Every day there were as many as ten to fifteen kids there playing and having a wonderful time. Of course, her program was successful—who could doubt it looking at the many kids who took advantage of and enjoyed the program?

As Angie and her group talked, however, some serious problems began to surface. First, the agency kept very few records on the youth who used the services. Worse, there were no specific records on the actual number of adolescents who had participated in the recreational program over the past few years. Moreover, Angie discovered that staff were in disagreement over the program's purpose. Some felt the goal was to divert kids from delinquent activities. Others felt the program was primarily designed to help adolescents develop social skills with their peers. Still others argued that the goal was to keep the kids in school and help reduce the dropout rate.

Unfortunately, when it came right down to it, there were no adequate records to document that any of these goals had been achieved. The United Way's request could not be met. The agency received no funding that year to help pay for staff. When Angie left a month later to take another job, the agency decided it could no longer afford the youth services program and simply eliminated it.

Rosalee Mercado was director of the First Offenders Diversion Project in a city of about 50,000 people. The project, supported by the county government, offered first time offenders an opportunity to avoid getting a criminal record by participating in an eight-week group-based program. Individuals arrested for the first time for such crimes as shoplifting, domestic violence, and similar offenses, after being screened for appropriateness, were referred to the diversion program.

It was time again for Rosalee to make her annual budget request to the county board (an elected board responsible for governing the county). The board had requested that each program provide information on its effectiveness in terms of reaching its intended goals. Rosalee had anticipated this need

several years earlier and had been carefully gathering data. In a few short hours, she pulled together proof that individuals who completed the entire eight-week program were rarely arrested for further criminal activity. First offenders in the county who chose not to participate when offered the opportunity were three times as likely to be re-arrested within the following year. The county's average cost for bringing these offenders to trial and paying for their care in the city jail was five times as high as the cost of paying for the diversion program. Of course, this calculation did not include the effects on the offender's victims, for whom the loss of property or personal injury was much more costly. Rosalee appeared before the county board with detailed data displaying her program's success. Happily, she again received funding for the next year. Board members could brag to their constituents about how well this program was doing and stress that county tax monies were extremely well spend supporting this program.

Introduction

The differences between the two cases cited above show one of the principle reasons for evaluation in macro practice. A program must prove a certain degree of success to receive continued support, whether the money comes from private or public sources. While advocates may support some programs for a short while on faith alone, eventually they will ask for hard data and facts to prove that the programs are working. Records must be maintained to show evaluators what is actually happening, thereby justifying the program's continued existence. Rosalee understood this principle, but Angie did not. Rosalee and her staff clearly realized the sole purpose of her program was to help divert first time offenders from the criminal justice system and thereby reduce their chances of rearrest. Angie and her staff, on the other hand, were not certain about their program's goals, nor had they collected sufficient data to verify its success. Hence, the program folded. In summary, program evaluation is necessary to ensure continued services to our clients and employment for ourselves.

This chapter will:

- Establish a context and overview for evaluation.
- Provide definitions of evaluation.
- Describe the purposes of evaluations.
- Identify barriers to and problems in doing evaluations.
- Discuss various kinds of evaluations.

- Outline the steps in an evaluation.
- Discuss the ethical use of evaluation.

Overview of Evaluation

"Evaluation is a social process of making judgments about the merit, worth, or value of a change. Evaluations make judgments about those change episodes' inputs, throughputs, outputs, and outcomes that have been monitored" (Kettner, Daley, & Nichols, 1985). This means that evaluation measures a number of aspects of a program. These include money; time (input); actual efforts, such as hours expended providing service (throughput); and numbers of clients served (output). It also measures changes in the quality of life for those served (outcomes). Evaluation requires information on how a program is being run and what it has achieved (Rubin & Rubin, 1986). The essential question to ask about all our interventions (micro through macro) is, "Do they work, and how do we know?".

Evaluation research has a rich history at the macro level. Cox et al. (1984) note that in the early 1900s people undertook to measure whether literacy rates were improving for—and employment skills being acquired by—participants in many community programs. Program evaluation research continued during the 1920s and 1930s, focusing on ways to improve the productivity of employees. The New Deal era of the 1930s and 1940s saw repeated attempts to determine whether changing the living conditions of people subsequently changed their behavior. Efforts to measure the success of delinquency prevention programs, treatment of mental disorders, and community change outcomes (such as crime and gang activity reductions) are more recent. While evaluation is fraught with potential barriers and problems, it is important both for professional reasons and for financial accountability to make the attempt. Our ethical responsibility to our clients and to the organizations we serve requires us to ensure that our efforts not only do not hurt clients, but also achieve our intended ends. Moreover, if we don't expend the effort to measure success, others assuredly will, and they might cut off program funding. If we can't prove our effectiveness, we are at the mercy of others. Another intent of evaluation is to accurately measure what we are doing. We often work with professionals from other fields who are well ahead of social work in assessing effectiveness.

Evaluation of effectiveness helps us maintain credibility as competent practitioners in a legitimate profession.

The right time for evaluation varies from situation to situation. Sometimes we evaluate while our change effort is going on. Let's say we are trying to determine whether a public education program aimed at alerting people to the problems of child abuse and neglect is effective. To do this, we might monitor the number of complaints turned in to the protective services unit each month to find out whether the number is increasing. Evaluation may also be done after we conclude an intervention, as in the case of the diversion program that opened this chapter.

Clearly, we can produce different kinds of information depending upon what is most important to know. If we are interested in simply describing what exists, we might use one design. If we want to know whether two or more things are related to one another (correlation)—whether reports of child abuse go up during periods of parental unemployment—we will use another evaluation design. Interest in finding possible cause and effect (such as a public information campaign's effectiveness in recruiting additional foster parents) would likely lead to use of yet another design (Kettner, Daley & Nichols, 1985).

Definition of Evaluation

We have said that evaluation is a process of assessing the worth of an undertaking. We always want to know the degree of success of our efforts, whether what we accomplish is significant, and whether the cost of the effort is worthwhile. Also of concern is how well we perform our roles as social workers, whether the goals we established are appropriate, and whether it is likely that we can achieve these goals in the first place (Cox et al., 1984).

We may also be interested in learning whether the program is serving the numbers of clients we originally envisioned. A successful program that reaches only a very small percentage of the intended population may not be worth its cost. In evaluations we can't operate on the principle that, "If it saves just one child, it's worth it."

Evaluation can also focus on explaining how the outcome we achieved actually came about. This type of evaluation is concerned more with the process than with the outcome.

Evaluation can be defined many ways but always comes down to making judgments about what we are doing. The judgments may concern effectiveness, cost, relationships between events, or numerous other factors.

Purposes of Program Evaluation

Program evaluations have at least five purposes. First, they help us save time and money or avoid wasting precious resources on approaches that either don't work or don't work very well. Second, they allow us to change our programs to make them more effective, identifying areas of strength and weakness. Third, studies showing that a program is effective often help build support for continuing a program. Fourth, we can establish whether a program has really implemented positive changes. Finally, we gain a great deal of personal satisfaction from knowing that our programs are sound and effective (Solomon, 1984). Because evaluation can be done for multiple purposes, we must think carefully about what it is we want to know before we begin an evaluation. Failing to consider the purpose may cause us to select an evaluation design that does not give us the results we seek.

Key Concepts in Evaluation

Of course, like any other specialized endeavor, evaluation has its own terminology and concepts that we have to master to be effective as evaluators. The following section describes and defines the concepts and terms that will be of greatest utility in doing evaluations. These include control group, experimental group, dependent variable, independent variable, sampling and random sample, experimental design, quasi-experimental design, and baseline. Also covered are mean, median, mode, descriptive statistics, inferential statistics, outcome, reliability, validity, standard deviation, chi-square test, and statistical significance.

Control Group

Ideally, one way to know whether your work is effective is to compare your program's success with clients to the success of a similar group of clients not involved

in your program. For example, the diversion program referred to earlier compared the rearrest rate of group members to the rate of those who had committed similar crimes but not participated in the group. The group used for comparison purposes, that is not receiving the intervention, is called a *control group*. While we probably could say that our group did very well because fewer than 20 percent were ever rearrested, it would be less significant if only 10 percent of the untreated control group was rearrested. In the history of social work and community interventions, this has actually happened. Well intentioned interventions do not always work as planned.

Experimental Group

The group that receives no treatment is called the control group, and the one that receives an intervention is called the *experimental group*, because an intervention is essentially an experiment. In an experiment we test a hypothesis (belief) that a certain intervention will produce a certain desired outcome.

Dependent Variable

A dependent variable is "the phenomenon or reaction to be tested or measured when a new stimulus, condition, or treatment is introduced" (Barker, 1991, p. 60). In other words, what are you trying to measure or achieve during a program's intervention process? What variables are you trying to study and evaluate? The variable we are studying is called a dependent variable. If you try to reduce a neighborhood school's dropout rate by implementing a peer counseling program, the school's dropout rate is the dependent variable. We use the variable to measure whether our intervention is working.

Independent Variable

An independent variable involves "the factors that are thought to influence or cause a certain behavior or phenomenon or reaction" (Barker, 1991, p. 112). An independent variable explains changes in the dependent variable. In a group program aimed at reducing delinquency among adolescent males, the program itself is the independent variable. It is the "treatment" variable being evaluated.

Sampling

In many large programs, it is nearly impossible to interview or follow-up on every participant who participated in the experimental group or control group. In addition, it can become prohibitively expensive to do so. As a consequence, we often use a sample or subset of the total group rather than the entire group. There are many ways to select a subset of a population, and this text cannot cover all the methods currently in use. However, one of the most important kinds of sample is called a *random sample*.

Random Sample

A random sample is one in which every element in a population has an equal chance of being selected for inclusion in the sample. If you simply survey people you run into at the supermarket, it will not be a random sample. Only those community members who happen to be in the store at a particular time would have a chance of being selected. You would miss all the people who could not be in the store at that time (all school children, for instance). As a result, your sample would be *biased*. It would not accurately reflect the total population. Random sampling is especially important when we want to show that our sample represents the population. We can't say this as easily when the sample is not random. Under ideal conditions you might assign people randomly to experimental and control groups. This makes it less likely that factors other than the intervention caused any differences in outcome between the groups. Random selection of a sample brings a higher degree of rigor to our attempts to assess a program's effectiveness. It also allows us to use more sophisticated evaluation techniques.

Experimental Design

You might want to know whether your community's anti-drug program is effective. Perhaps the most elabo-

rate method for evaluating a program's efficacy is to use an experimental design. Experimental designs generally involve attempts to manipulate the intervention to determine whether change occurs in a target group. Thus, an experimental design might add to, discontinue, or modify a community anti-drug intervention to determine whether it affected the use of drugs in the area. These designs often use control groups, experimental groups, and random assignment of subjects to the two groups.

Unfortunately, experimental designs cannot be followed in practice because we are not able to randomly assign clients to groups. As a consequence, we must use less rigorous research designs. Among those frequently used is the quasi-experimental design.

Quasi-Experimental Designs

Quasi-experimental designs use some, but not all, elements found of the typical experimental design. Thus, a quasi-experimental design might use a control group and an experimental group but not random assignment of clients to the two groups. Because they meet at least some of the standards for experimental designs, we call these designs quasi-experimental. Social workers must often employ this type of design because we cannot randomly select who participates in our programs.

Baseline

Deciding whether something has changed over time (such as the frequency of domestic violence) requires that we know the original amount or frequency of occurrence of that phenomena. Measuring the amount or frequency of domestic violence in a community produces a baseline. A baseline tells us how often a problem or behavior occurred either at a specific point in time or during a specified period. A child welfare agency has received an average of fifteen reports of child abuse per week for the past two years. The agency implemented a campaign to educate local citizens about child abuse and the importance of child-abuse reporting. Then the agency might use the original average of fifteen reports per week as a baseline to determine whether child abuse reporting has increased or decreased. An increase might indicate the educational program's success.

Sometimes we simply don't have data about something in the past because no records were kept. This leaves us with two possibilities. First, we can create a *retrospective baseline* composed of data collected after the fact from people's memories. Neighborhood residents might not have kept written records of how often in the past they were victims of various crimes, such as theft or vandalism. However, if asked, they can probably recall how often they were victimized in the past year (Nurius & Hudson, 1993).

A second way of gathering data for a baseline when no records have been kept is future-oriented. We gather data between the point of initial contact and the beginning of the intervention. For example, we might begin gathering data when the client initially requests our help in dealing with the neighborhood crime problem. Thus, we are seeking data while simultaneously helping the neighborhood develop a neighborhood watch program. This model of data gathering simultaneous with our intervention is called a *concurrent baseline* (Nurius & Hudson 1993).

While baselines are often helpful in assessing whether change has occurred, they are not always available or necessary to evaluate the effectiveness of an intervention. Let's take a new program which provides Meals-on-Wheels. Since no such program existed previously, the effectiveness of the program during its first year might be evaluated by using the actual number of meals delivered to the elderly. Of course, in subsequent years, we would have the number of meals served in the first year as a baseline.

Mean

The mean is an arithmetical average derived from adding all the entries and dividing by the number of entries. To find out the mean age of neighborhood residents, we add up all their ages and divide by the total number of people in the neighborhood. Let's figure the mean for the five members of a family. Currently, family members are 51, 47, 27, 25, and 48. The sum of those five numbers is 198. Dividing 198 by 5 gives us a figure of 39.6 years. In other words, the mean age of family members is almost 40 years. Calculating the mean age for a neighborhood might reveal that most of the people in the neighborhood are quite elderly. Such a finding has implications for what they can do to take care of themselves.

Since Meals-on-Wheels is a program that has been in existence for some time and can be found in many communities, it should not be difficult to find baseline data for this program in a given neighborhood.

Sometimes we compare the mean of the experimental group with that of the control group to learn whether there is a difference between the two. The diversion project mentioned at the start of this chapter documented that the mean number of postintervention arrests for its "graduates" was lower than the rate for those who did not participate in the program.

Sometimes the mean or arithmetical average is not useful because it provides skewed data. For example, consider the family above when its 104-year-old grandmother was still alive. When her age was added to the 198 years the total was 302, giving the family a mean age of just over 50 years. This suggests a somewhat unrealistic picture of this family. Thus, the problem with using a mean is that it can mislead you when extremes distort the collected data. To eliminate this problem and prove a more useful figure we often use the median.

Median

The median is the centermost figure in a distribution of figures listed from highest to lowest or vice versa. For certain kinds of data, medians provide a more useful basis for comparison. We often compare median incomes of groups or community residents. We do this by taking the annual income figures for each individual, arranging them from lowest to highest, and selecting the figure which appears in the middle of the distribution. The median can be calculated for any set of numbers. Consider the family we described above. Their ages were 51, 47, 27, 25, and 48. To calculate the median age we must reorder them as follows: 25, 27, 47, 48, and 51. Since 47 falls exactly halfway in the middle of this distribution, that is the median.

Mode

The mode is the most frequently observed score in a group of scores. Thus, we might find that the modal number of credits carried by full-time college students is fifteen per semester. This means that of the various numbers of credits which students could carry (typically from twelve to eighteen) most students are carrying fifteen. Fifteen is the mode.

Standard Deviation

A standard deviation measures the amount of variability of observations around a mean. Standard deviations are easily calculated using a computer or programmable calculator. Suppose you examine a community's distribution of wealth. You discover (from looking at income figures) that the mean annual family income is $25,000 with a standard deviation of only $2,000. This suggests that most people in the community have incomes somewhere around $25,000. If the standard deviation was $10,000 it would suggest a wider variation among family incomes (that is, more families with incomes well above or well below $25,000).

Reliability

Reliability is the likelihood that a measurement will yield the same results at subsequent times. If you are trying to find out whether your assertiveness groups are helping to make domestic violence survivors more assertive, you might look for an instrument to measure assertiveness levels. That instrument should also be reli-
able. That is, a person who receives a low assertiveness score should receive about the same score no matter when the instrument is given. The score should change only if the person receives assertiveness training between the first and second measurements. Evaluators usually measure and report reliability so as to reveal whether it is high or low. Thus, an instrument may be about 90 percent reliable (indicating high reliability) or only 50 percent reliable (reflecting relatively low reliability).

Validity

Validity is the ability of an instrument to measure what it is supposed to measure. Thus, valid instruments measure what they purport to measure. A written test used to judge whether a person can ride a bicycle would not be a valid test of bicycle riding ability. Similarly, a test measuring self-esteem should deal directly with matters of self-esteem. Several different kinds of validity are possible. They involve different ways of determining the validity of a given instrument. *Face validity* means that a common sense view of the instrument suggests that it measures what it's supposed to. A test composed of questions regarding historical events from 1945 to the present has face validity as a measure of post-World-War-II historical knowledge. It really does measure acquisition of historical knowledge about that time period. Thus, the test measures what it is supposed to. *Predictive validity*, on the other hand, is a measure of validity based upon the ability of an instrument to predict future performance. If social work exams could accurately tell us which test-takers will become good social workers following graduation, such tests would have predictive validity. That is, they could predict future behavior (in this case, competent social work practice). Whenever possible, use measurements that have high validity and different kinds of validity (such as face, predictive, and so on). They have more value and their results are much more respected.

Descriptive Statistics

Statistics that describe a phenomenon are called descriptive statistics. A mean (referred to earlier) might be used to describe the average age of a population. We might learn that a community has only a 2 percent minority population. This statistic might be helpful in understanding why community residents fear an influx of low-income housing. Their lack of contact with different cultures may be causing their anxieties.

Inferential Statistics

Any set of statistics used to make an inference (or draw a conclusion) about a population based upon a sample of that population is called inferential statistics. Not knowing the average income in a community, we might survey a sample of residents. Based upon the information on income they provide, we would infer the income level of the entire community from that sample.

Outcome

An outcome is a quality-of-life change resulting from social work interventions. A program that reduces the incidence of burglary or drug-selling in a neighborhood produces a definite change in the neighborhood residents' quality of life. Another program that helps domestic violence survivors avoid further injury and encourages them to develop new friendships and resources enhances their quality of life. These changes are outcomes. Of course, we can have outcomes we do not anticipate. Unanticipated consequences or outcomes are common so we must always be aware that they may occur. For example, graduates of an assertiveness training group may test out their newfound skills with an employer who promptly fires them for insubordination. Being fired for being assertive is an example of an unintended consequence.

Statistical Significance

Statistical significance is a measure of the risk that exists in generalizing from a sample to the population. Generally speaking, you want to be able to say that your sample and the population from which it was drawn are identical. Practically, however, it is likely that any sample deviates slightly from the original population. This deviation can be calculated and reported. If you surveyed a sample of people from a community to learn their views on their most pressing problems, you would hope to get results from the sample that you could apply to the entire community. We usually try to limit the risk of error in this process to small percentages such as 5 percent out of 100 percent. To say this differently, we want to be wrong about our belief only five times out of 100. Often statistical significance will be shown in the form of a figure such as $p = .05$ or $p = .01$. This means that there is a 95 percent or 99 percent probability (p), respectively, that the sample accurately represents the population.

Chi-Square Test

The chi-square test is a statistical procedure to compare the expected frequencies in a study to observed frequencies. Expected frequencies are the outcomes which are expected to occur. Sometimes this expected frequency is based on the probability that something will occur. When flipping a coin, you would expect to get a head one time and a tail the next. Thus, for every ten flips of the coin, you would expect to get five heads. On the other hand, if you were looking at a population with 10 percent people of color, you would expect your sample to have the same percentage, namely 10 percent. Observed frequencies are the actual results you get from your coin toss, say, eight heads and two tails, or the real percentage of people of color in your sample (perhaps 25 percent).

The importance of the chi-square test and similar procedures is that they can tell you whether your outcome could have occurred by chance. If you are comparing high school dropout rates and find that the average dropout rate for a school is 7 percent, that is the expected frequency. If you find that the dropout rate for people of color in that school is 34 percent, this is well above the expected frequency. The chi-square test can help you determine whether this is a fluke or indicates that people of color are more likely to drop out.

A chi-square test is also useful in evaluative studies to determine whether the sample being evaluated resembles the total population. If you wanted to know whether your sample differed from the population you could compare, for example, the age, ethnic, or gender breakdown in the sample (observed frequency) with the expected frequencies based upon what exists in the population. A population consisting of 24 percent Native Americans and 60 percent women would lead one to expect similar frequencies in the sample. If the sample did not differ from the population on these dimensions, it could be said with greater assurance that the sample was representative of the population.

Problems and Barriers in Program Evaluation

Trying to evaluate a social work program or project can be quite complicated. There are multiple problems and barriers that can interfere with undertaking the evaluation, interpreting results, and using the results to improve programs. This section identifies six common problems and barriers discussed by Weiss (1984) and others. They include failure to plan for evaluation, lack of program stability, relationships between evaluators and practitioners, unclear evaluation results, evaluation results which are not accepted, and evaluations which are not worth the effort.

Failure to Plan for Evaluation

Too often, the decision to evaluate a program comes well after the program has been in operation. Without a built-in plan for evaluation, including decisions on what information to gather and for what purposes, evaluators are at a loss for ways to proceed. In the case involving Angie Amed and the youth services program that opened the chapter, the program originators never really considered the need to evaluate what they did. When they were eventually asked to prove the effectiveness of their program, they lacked the data and even the means for gathering data. When an agency considers an evaluation plan at the start of the program's operation, it is much easier to gather baseline information, establish management information systems (including forms, computer databases, and the like), and create a time line for evaluation. If the agency waits until the program has already begun, or worse, waits for several years, critical data may not have been recorded or records kept.

Lack of Program Stability

A common evaluation problem is that no program is static. That is, programs typically change over the course of their operation. Staff may learn to do some things better. Clients or the community may change. More or less money may become available. The composition of the staff itself may drastically change. Philosophies and support for the program may wax and wane. Finally, staff turnover may result in commitments to different goals from those pursued by the staff who originally launched the program. Thus, it is likely that the program you started out to evaluate is not quite the same program now. The longer the evaluation process proceeds, the more changes are likely to occur.

This leaves evaluators in a bind because they may not know what has changed. It may not be possible to modify the evaluation design in midstream to accommodate the changes. Or there may be no appropriate way to measure the new "thing" which has emerged. Of course, in reality you can't keep anything in a steady state for long. One option is to test only small parts or components of a program to see if they work, without trying to tackle too large a project at a time. Rather than try to evaluate an entire program, you might decide to focus only on the intake operation. It may be best to test programs over short periods to avoid problems associated with longer time frames. You might decide, for example, to evaluate for only the first year of operation or only the fourth year.

Other options include using periodic measures rather than waiting to the end to assess progress. Likewise, holding changes to a minimum for short periods of time may reduce the possible factors that could confound or confuse the evaluation.

Relationships Between Evaluators and Practitioners

Relationships between those who carry out a program and those who evaluate it can be problematic. Personality differences, which can always arise, are exacerbated by role-related problems. Practitioners are usually concerned primarily with *delivering a service*. Evaluators, on the other hand, are interested in *measuring the effectiveness of that service*. These two roles need not be conflictual, but they can be. When you evaluate a worker's effectiveness, it is easy for that worker to feel threatened. Practitioners may feel like their worth is under examination, a potentially painful situation. At any rate, an evaluation is likely to uncover things that need improvement. Such change is frequently threatening or at the very least uncomfortable.

Evaluators' standards may be more rigorous than those of practitioners. Evaluators are likely to be more interested in the specifics of data collection and encourage random assignment of clients to control and experimental groups. Practitioners, on the other hand, are more concerned with providing service, preferring to do the paperwork later when they have time. Evaluators usually feel that completing required paperwork and keeping records is extremely important. Practitioners sometimes think such paperwork is a waste of time compared to actually doing their jobs with clients. Practitioners are appalled to think that a client would be denied service because that client had been randomly assigned to some control group. Evaluators might want to know precisely how many incidents of gang-related activity occurred after a street-worker program was initiated. Involved practitioners, on the other hand, may see no need to keep precise records of each specific event because they know from discussions with neighbors that things are "getting better."

It is possible to manage this problem if administrators support the evaluation effort, involve practitioners in designing the evaluation, use measures that don't place undue record-keeping burdens on staff, and reduce disruptions in service. If evaluators take these steps, practitioners will feel that they have a bigger stake in the evaluating effort. They will also be less weighed down with paperwork and better able to do their normal work with clients.

Sometimes it is possible to present an evaluation as focused on the theory underlying a particular intervention instead of on the intervention itself. This can make the evaluation process seem less threatening. If an evaluation focuses on the theory behind a particular type of delinquency prevention program (such as after-school recreation), it will appear less challenging to the workers. After all, if the theory behind an intervention is flawed, the workers cannot be blamed for unsatisfactory outcomes.

Finally, it is important to give practitioners feedback during the process so that they see the importance of the evaluation to their practice. This feedback helps practitioners improve services and feel that they are more a part of the evaluation process.

When Evaluation Results Are Unclear

Sometimes even a well-planned evaluation produces equivocal or unclear results. Perhaps we can't really establish that our new neighborhood watch program reduced crime in the neighborhood. Maybe only a modest drop in burglaries occurred. Further, perhaps, the police added another officer to the neighborhood patrol at the same time that we began our program. Maybe *this* was responsible for the small reduction in the crime rate. We can't tell for sure whether the watch program or the added patrol caused the reduction. Often it is difficult to say with any degree of certainty that the goal was achieved because of our efforts. Perhaps the most logical solution to this predicament is to conduct multiple evaluations so that no one explanation can rule out all your findings. It may also be possible to use various statistical techniques to rule out the effects of unexpected changes. These techniques, however, are beyond the scope of this text.

When Evaluation Results Are Not Accepted

Sometimes evaluations demonstrate things that the people involved do not or cannot accept. For example, a program may prove successful but not be continued because it is not politically popular. An evaluation might threaten a favored program or cast doubts on its efficacy. Yet the program is continued and the evaluation ignored.

Recent discussions around the Drug Abuse Resistance Education (DARE) program are a good example. Extremely popular with police and school officials, the program sends police officers into schools to provide an anti–drug-abuse course. Anecdotal reports from police participants are very positive. They make comments such as, "The kids tell you a lot of their problems," or "The children are now much more friendly toward the police." Other comments suggest that "kids are friendly toward one another and feel good about themselves." Yet studies designed to assess whether participation in DARE stops adolescents from using marijuana and other drugs and drinking alcohol found that no significant differences exist between participants and nonparticipants in their use of these drugs. Other studies, summarizing research involving thousands of children,

The DARE program, in which police officers go into schools to provide anti–drug-abuse courses, is considered successful by some and ineffective by others. However, DARE is politically popular wherever it operates.

raise similar questions. Despite these questions the DARE program continues to be praised as effective because it is politically popular.

When Evaluation Is Not Worth the Effort

Some evaluation efforts are simply not worth pursuing. A special event that occurs only once does not necessarily merit evaluation (Rubin & Rubin, 1986). The women's club that donates labor and materials to refurbish the domestic violence shelter is an example of a one-shot project. The neighborhood association that contributes its expertise to repair the roof of one of its elderly members does not merit an evaluation effort. Rubin and Rubin (1986) suggest that you undertake an evaluation effort under only three conditions. First, perform an evaluation only when you are certain that the information gained will actually be used. Second, evaluate only when the cost is low compared to the potential value of knowing whether the program is successful. Third, consider an evaluation only when the result is likely to improve social work practice.

As you can see, many potential problems can affect evaluation efforts. Sometimes you can overcome these

barriers with careful planning, sensitivity to the concerns of those involved in the process, and a willingness to be flexible. The next sections will look at some evaluation designs you might consider using to assess effectiveness of your macro practice interventions.

Kinds of Evaluations

Generally speaking, evaluations can be categorized into two broad categories. These include *formative* or *monitoring evaluations* and *summative* (or *impact*) *evaluations*. Evaluations may also be categorized by whether they are designed to measure the *effectiveness* of an intervention or its *efficiency*.

Formative or Monitoring Evaluations

Formative evaluations focus more on the *process* than on the outcome of an intervention. Formative evaluations occur during the implementation stage and are designed to improve the change effort (Kettner, Daley, & Nichols, 1985). They may gather information on the provision of a service (such as the number of hours of counseling, number of phone calls to the crisis line, or the number of people served per month). They may also focus on more subjective measures, such as clients' or workers' judgment of change efforts. Thus, a formative or monitoring evaluation will reveal whether the program is serving as many clients as initially expected. It will also tell us whether, in the social workers' and clients' opinions, the program achieves its goals.

Formative evaluations do not address whether the effort is worthwhile, or even whether it is more worthwhile than other programs. They focus on describing what the program does and what is happening during the service delivery process. To help in this process, formative evaluations can compare what actually happens in a program to a set of model standards that represent an ideal to which the program can be compared (Royce, 1992) . Various national organizations such as NASW or the Child Welfare League of America produce sets of standards covering a wide range of areas. These include standards for staff qualifications and case management services, among others.

Sometimes consultants are invited to review a program and provide input as to whether the program is operating by accepted practices. Research on effective past programs can also provide helpful guidelines to use in monitoring a program.

Monitoring can be used to assess whether the program is actually serving its intended population. Basic data collected for monitoring purposes might include such things as demographic data on each client (name, age, sex), the problems for which they sought help (emergency shelter, food), the service actually provided by the agency (voucher for food, transportation), and the outcomes achieved (job obtained, no future police contact). It is very important in the beginning planning stages to carefully consider what kinds of information might be helpful to monitoring, because once a program is launched it is unpleasant to discover that needed information has not been collected. If no records are kept on actual services provided, an agency cannot document what it did to help clients. If no follow-up is done, it can mean that we are unable to prove that our services helped clients in the long run.

Summative Evaluations

Summative evaluations (sometimes called impact evaluations) measure the consequences of services provided. They are normally conducted following an intervention and focus on changes occurring in the target population. Is a program actually doing what it says it intends to do? It is achieving its goals? Summative evaluation might focus on whether a neighborhood watch program reduced the number of area burglaries, increased residents' sense of security and peace of mind, or contributed to a greater sense of community among residents. Most program evaluations are summative. Funding sources such as county boards, boards of directors, and legislatures are concerned about whether the program's intended outcomes are achieved. Consider a program aimed at reducing drug-related crimes in an inner city area. Has this happened? Was the incidence of such crimes actually reduced? Were first-time offenders in the diversion program diverted from future criminal behavior (or at least future arrests)? Did the program successfully rehabilitate twenty-five rundown homes in its first year of operation, as predicted in the grant application? These types of issues are most important in summative evaluations. Ultimately, they are also the issues most likely to determine whether a program is continued or abandoned.

Effectiveness and Efficiency Evaluations

Evaluations are also distinguished by whether they concern effectiveness or efficiency. To be effective, an intervention should produce a desirable end product. This might be lowered delinquency rates for a group of teenagers, better school attendance for at-risk children, or fewer incidents of gang violence in a target neighborhood. Most of our evaluations are, in fact, designed to assess whether the intended product was achieved. These are effectiveness evaluations.

Efficiency evaluations, on the other hand, are concerned with whether a program achieves outcomes in the correct manner. For instance, an extraordinarily expensive drug treatment program would be considered less efficient than one that achieved the same goals at lower cost. Similarly, a program that achieved its goals in inappropriate ways (such as through unethical treatment of clients) would not be considered efficient even if its goals were accomplished.

Both types of evaluations (effectiveness and efficiency) are important and useful, depending upon our needs. We are always concerned about determining whether we are effective. We should also concern ourselves about whether our programs are efficiently run.

Evaluation Designs

Planning evaluations for judging the effectiveness or efficiency of a program, whether formative or summative in nature, requires familiarity with some of the most useful designs. There are many evaluation designs to use, depending upon needs and circumstances. The following sections address several of these designs. They include qualitative designs, quantitative designs, one-group posttest designs, pretest/posttest designs, client satisfaction surveys, goal attainment scaling, target problem scaling, case studies, group comparisons, and quality assurance reviews.

Quantitative Designs

Quantitative designs use objective (numerical) criteria (such as scores on a test, number of arrests, or frequency of temper tantrums) to learn whether change has taken place following an intervention. Using baselines, these designs compare change over time in designated target behaviors. Quantitative designs require specificity in identifying the problem, selecting observable indicators of the problems, deciding how measurement will take place (including who will do it), gathering data, and analyzing it.

One advantage of quantitative designs is that you can sometimes aggregate data from many studies in a technique called *meta-analysis*, the combining of the results of several smaller studies (for example, single-subject designs), and statistically analyzing the overall findings. This synthesis and analysis yield more useful results than would be possible with only a handful of cases. Meta-analyses might calculate the average change between clients' scores on baseline data and their scores on the same dimension following intervention. This change is called *effect size* (Gingerich, 1984) because it shows the effect of our interventions. The use of meta-analysis is becoming more common in social work literature. It is described in more detail in Corcoran (1985).

Qualitative Designs

Qualitative designs rely on "nonnumerical examination of phenomena" (Marlow, 1993, p. 66). Qualitative research methods examine a program without using quantitative measures described above. They typically involve in-depth review of a small number of cases, and their goal is to describe or explore the experiences of clients or others involved in the process (Marlow, 1993). Qualitative designs aim at understanding what made a program work for specific clients or what participants would do differently if they could do it over again. Qualitative methods include interviews, review of logs or journals, and similar approaches. Marlow (1993), who has provided a detailed look at qualitative designs, suggests that they are very useful for monitoring purposes. She notes that when combined with quantitative designs, they can provide exceptional detail on program effectiveness.

One-Group Posttest Designs

One-group posttest designs are, as indicated by the title, evaluations that look at a single target group, focusing only on changes that have occurred following interven-

tion (posttest). These designs are used when we lack baseline data that would allow us to compare the change from time A (before an intervention) to time B (after an intervention). The ability to compare pre- and posttest results (sometimes called A-B designs) is more useful to the evaluator. However, often the evaluator is unable to gather baseline data to allow such a comparison. An agency might launch a program to keep kids from becoming involved in delinquent behavior without knowing how much delinquent activity the kids are already involved in. All agency staff can do is look at the youngsters who complete the program and say that 75 percent of them have had no contact with the juvenile justice system. They cannot prove, however, that their program was the reason for the 75 percent non-delinquency rate. Seventy-five percent of participants might not have been involved in delinquent activity before the program even started. Without a baseline, no one can prove that the program is responsible for deterring delinquent behavior.

Pretest/Posttest Designs

Sometimes we have an opportunity to compare a situation after intervention with the situation before intervention. These designs (sometimes called A-B) are more useful than posttest only designs because they allow us to show changes over time. Compare arrests for drug dealing in a neighborhood before and after an intensive neighborhood association effort to report all suspicious persons to the police. While arrests might increase briefly when the program begins, they decline quickly as dealers recognize that the neighborhood is inhospitable. These designs require the existence or creation of a baseline against which comparisons can be made following the intervention. A subsequent section of this chapter will describe these designs and others more thoroughly.

Client Satisfaction Surveys

Client satisfaction inventories or surveys measure general satisfaction with a service or with achievement of specific goals. They can be used to keep a record of complaints received or problems encountered in providing a service. They can also be used to tally positive comments from clients or service users. Ideally, client satisfaction surveys include questions that cover such variables as staff behavior, accessibility of service, fairness of agency policies, and other factors. Client satisfaction data, besides being fairly easy to obtain, is a valid source of certain kinds of information. For example, such data may help explain why clients drop out of a particular program at an unusually high rate or determine which agency services are most well-received. However, client satisfaction surveys are not useful in other situations. A delinquency prevention program should not be considered a success simply because the participants (at-risk adolescents) enjoy the program or recommend it to their friends. The critical variable there is whether the delinquency rate drops following group members' participation in the program.

Goal Attainment Scaling

Goal Attainment Scaling (GAS) is a design used to monitor the progress of individual clients and then to aggregate the data on a weekly, monthly, or yearly basis. At the first step in the process, workers and clients jointly set goals that both believe are reasonable, desirable, and attainable. Using goal attainment scaling can improve the morale of staff and increase their motivation (Stelmachers, Lund, & Meade, 1972). The ability to see actual progress in a case can be very reinforcing. When you try to evaluate whether your agency is effective, it is helpful to have individual case records showing the types and percentages of goals achieved. You are then able to summarize the results of individual worker-client interactions and apply the results to the entire agency.

Goal attainment scaling is a qualitative design and is very flexible. It generally has good face validity and usually does not interfere with the intervention. Its reliability is considered good. GAS can be combined with other measures, such as client satisfaction surveys. For example, evaluation of an after-school latchkey children's program could include a survey of parent and child satisfaction.

Target Problem Scaling

Target problem scaling is a method of monitoring changes in a client's behavior. It is primarily a qualita-

tive design used in simple evaluations. The basic premise is that one identifies a problem, carries out an intervention, and repeatedly measures whether the problem has been reduced, modified, or eliminated. These measures are considered generally reliable though the degree of validity is unknown (Alter & Evens, 1990, p. 64). That is, since the client or worker monitoring the behavior may tend to interpret the changes in behavior in the same way over the length of the intervention, it is likely to be reliable. On the other hand, since the changes are measured by individual interpretation and judgment, validity may be open to question. Asking clients whether they feel less suicidal this week than they did last week (as might be done in a program aimed at helping at-risk teens) will not necessarily yield a valid response. Another example of a measurement chart which one might use to deal with target problems in a neighborhood is shown in figure 10.1.

This form illustrates two concerns expressed by neighborhood residents, fear of walking in their own neighborhood and lack of a place for their children to play. These problems are rated as equally severe (extremely severe, or ES) at the start. As a result of the neighborhood intervention, both problems diminish in severity. People are no longer afraid to walk in their neighborhoods, and the issue of a place for kids to play is not longer so severe. The degree of change in each problem area is also assessed at termination and a year later. Improvement has been substantial with respect to both problems (ratings of 4 and 5). A global or average rating helps give a composite picture of all the problems being addressed. The advantage of such a scale is twofold. First, you can use it to assess changes in a macro-level problem in a single area or neighborhood. You could also combine it with ratings from other neighborhoods to provide a more comprehensive view of residents' opinions. In the latter case, a survey might yield findings about the success of a particular type of intervention (program, policy, or project).

Case Studies

Case studies are qualitative measurement designs allowing the use of a single case or a small group of cases. They allow us to study a problem in some depth to identify the factors that led to a certain outcome. Interviews with neighborhood members can reveal

Figure 10.1
Target Problem Change Scale

Target Problem Name of Rater:_____Alice_____	Target Problem Rating— Severity Scale[a]			Target Problem Rating— Degree of Change[b]		Global Improvement Rating
	Start	Time 1	Time 2	Termination	Follow-Up	
Afraid to walk in neighborhood	ES	S	NP	4	4	
Children have no place to play	ES	ES	NVS	3	5	4

a. Degree of Severity Scale: NP (no problem), NVS (not very severe), S (severe), VS (very severe), ES (extremely severe)
b. Improvement Scale: 1 (Worse), 2 (No change), 3 (A little better), 4 (Somewhat better), 5 (A lot better)

Instructions: This form is to be completed by both the client and the social worker. It may be used at repeated intervals throughout and following the intervention. It can be used for formative and summative evaluations. Each problem should be listed. Global improvement is the mean of the change ratings for all problems.

which factors were most responsible for their increased sense of safety over the past six months. Once we have identified what factors produced which results, we are in a better position to form a hypothesis about our interventions. Ideally, however, results of case studies should be replicated several times before we attempt to generalize about an intervention's success and apply our findings to other programs.

Case studies allow us to use unstructured interviews and ask whatever questions seem helpful in understanding a situation. For example, you might wish to ask neighborhood residents what issues they consider most important. Since each resident may select different issues, it is not always possible to anticipate what they will say. Follow-up questions may be needed to elicit further information. As you can see, this creates a very unstructured interview, but it can yield excellent information that might be missed if you simply asked residents to choose from a list of the five issues you think most important.

Group Comparisons

Group comparisons, as the name suggests, compare outcomes between two or more groups—one of which is the treatment group and the other the control group. The control group may receive no treatment, or it may be exposed to some type of intervention (but not the same type as used with the treatment group). Because we can't usually do random assignment to control and experimental groups as required in true experimental designs, we often use quasi-experimental designs.

Quasi-experimental designs use comparison rather than control groups. In comparison groups we try to match the two groups on important variables such as gender, age, ethnicity, income or social class, and any other variable that might affect the outcome. We might compare two neighborhoods whose residents are of similar ages, gender breakdown, and income. While we cannot randomly assign people to live in a particular neighborhood, we can try to find a neighborhood similar to the one in which we are working. The variables, of course, depend on what you are trying to find out in the study. Typical group comparisons are pretest/posttest designs or posttest only designs. Much of what we attempt to measure in group comparisons can be considered status change. Changes in a client's status include such things as employment, attending school, or taking any specific actions (such as getting a job, moving to an independent living situation, or completing a GED.) Such concrete outcomes make it much easier to compare across groups.

Of course, we can also compare the groups on other dimensions, such as behavioral checklists (used by clients or significant others to monitor changes in behavior) or tests of knowledge (such as knowledge about sex and birth control). The limitation of quasi-experimental designs such as group comparisons is that other factors—such as maturation, preexisting skills, and so on—might have caused the change. Each factor is a potential threat to validity. We cannot be sure (since we did not randomly assign people to guarantee close similarity between the intervention and nonintervention groups) that the changes might have been the result of other factors. For example, we might be quite pleased to find that 90 percent of the at-risk teens in the target group finished high school compared to only 50 percent of the teens in the comparison group. However, it is possible that the target group teens had higher intelligence to begin with or had parents who were more motivated to help their children complete high school. Only random assignment of cases can rule out alternative explanations of outcomes.

Quality Assurance Reviews

A quality assurance review is an evaluation which identifies "patterns of problems with the outcomes of service delivery and then corrects the problem" (Love, 1991, p. 107). It may be an ongoing effort or be conducted primarily when there are perceived problems in an agency's service delivery. Quality assurance reviews can be done by reviewing case files, records of complaints, and letters from clients and/or others receiving service. Quality assurance focuses on finding defects in service and enhancing uniform quality of service. To conduct a quality assurance review requires that an agency have some accepted standard of performance. Perhaps all workers are required to prepare monthly written file summaries of their work with clients. Or maybe every client must have an agreed upon treatment plan in the file. A quality assurance review might focus on whether these standards of performance have been achieved. To do this, you might review every file in the agency or just a subset of files. You might also review agency records to decide whether client-identified problems were resolved and whether adequate records were kept that would allow other types of evaluations. Similarly, if we knew that agency policy requires all reports of suspected child abuse to be investigated within forty-eight hours, we can review records to see whether this level of service was attained. The purpose

of quality assurance reviews is to ensure that the agency or program is meeting its own standards of quality.

Summary of Evaluation Designs

Each design mentioned above can be used to gather information useful for monitoring or evaluating interventions. Some are clearly more useful than others, depending upon the questions we want answered. Those that are focused on process will tell us little about the outcome of the intervention. Other outcome-focused designs won't tell us how we got the results we observed. To do effective evaluation we must consider our purpose before selecting a design. In the following section we will discuss the stages in evaluation and provide examples of useful instruments and tests.

Stages in Evaluation

The steps in an evaluation of a macro intervention are important. Without a blueprint to follow and careful advance planning, it is easy to discover that no assessment of progress can be made. If you do not consider in advance what sort of records and data to collect, you may discover that you don't have the information needed to prove program effectiveness. The following sections will describe the steps to be followed in evaluating a macro intervention. These include: (1) conceptualization and goal setting, (2) measurement, (3) sampling, (4) design, (5) data gathering, (6) data analysis, and (7) data presentation.

Stage 1: Conceptualization and Goal Setting

The conceptualization stage begins with agreement upon the goals to be achieved and the indicators of goal achievement to be employed (Rubin & Rubin, 1986). A goal is a "statement of observable effects that are expected from a set of actions" (Love, 1991, p. 87). If the goal is to deliver a minimum of thirty-five meals per week to elderly shut-ins living in Center City, the goal could be made more specific by indicating that it must be reached by the end of the first year of operation. Normally, we prefer to start with a clear description of where we are and where we want to go. The "where we want to be" is the goal sought through our intervention. Measuring goal achievement is a process of comparing actual accomplishment to intended goals. Those goals may be quantitative, (that is, measurable by some specific amount), such as providing shelter to one hundred homeless persons in the first year, or qualitative (that is, without a set numerical target), such as increasing client satisfaction with services provided by the discharge planning unit. Goals may be set for individuals, units, or entire agencies. Likewise, goals may extend over any time period.

Establishing goals is not always easy. Sometimes the goal seems, initially, too hard to quantify or measure. A goal of increasing such elusive things as happiness or reducing stress is too general. These situations require us to think more clearly about what we hope to accomplish. One common problem involves goals that are so poorly defined they cannot be measured. An agency's goal could be to improve the quality of life of community residents, but "quality of life" is undefined and can involve many different aspects. It is easy to see how evaluators might throw up their hands in disgust. Sometimes goals are unrelated to the actual service being delivered. Some youth agencies operate personal challenge programs, such as rock climbing, rappelling, and wilderness camping. These programs are typically provided to emotionally disturbed adolescents and delinquent youth. The goal in the latter case is to deter the youth from further delinquency, yet the service provided does not necessarily relate to this goal. Sometimes goals are never explicitly stated, only implied. A program might be based on implicit belief that providing after-school recreational activities for adolescents can keep them from using drugs. Yet this goal is never actually articulated. Because measuring achievement of implied goals is very difficult, it is best to err on the side of explicitness. That is, try your best to state your goals clearly and unambiguously.

Feedback Systems

A feedback system is any method employed to help us know whether goals were achieved. We should be able to assess how we are doing in relation to either the starting point or the desired end point. The starting point might be established by using a baseline. The desired end point might be our stated goal. We need to establish a system for periodically gathering data to assess progress toward goals. Weekly or monthly reports on clients seen, problems encountered, services given, and outcomes achieved are typical feedback mechanisms. Evaluations often use benchmarks (short-term indicators of progress) that show how things are going. Feedback systems allow you to monitor your progress and avoid waiting until the last minute to decide whether or not you are moving in the right direction. You might expect that by the end of the first quarter of the year, you would have served about 25 percent of the total number of clients you hoped to serve during the entire year. Comparing quarterly reports to this benchmark helps you know how you are doing and perhaps make needed changes.

All these considerations lead to some general rules for planning an evaluation. These appear in highlight 10.1.

Stage 2: Measurement

In the measurement stage you refine the measures you will use to learn whether the stated goals have been accomplished. If you decide to evaluate a program to help people out of poverty, the poverty rate is one logical indicator. However, you will still need to determine which poverty rate to use and how the rate will be computed. If the goal is neighborhood improvement, you might use such measures as numbers of trees planted or neighborhood residents' perceptions about how the community looks. A crime reduction program might use a measure such as the Uniform Crime Reports disseminated by the FBI. Or perhaps the program's measure would be victimization surveys, asking residents whether they have been victims of specific crimes.

The amount of time and effort staff expend to implement a program is probably more difficult to measure than the number of trees planted in a neighborhood or the number of crimes people reported in the last year. Staff time and effort, by the way, is one significant dimension of agency life and productivity. Would you measure effort as the number of hours practitioners work with clients? Or would effort be defined as the number of clients practitioners see? The amount of input and output must balance satisfactorily or the agency will not survive. Too much input (staff time and effort) and

---

HIGHLIGHT 10.1

GUIDELINES FOR PLANNING AN EVALUATION

Rule 1: Build in the plan for evaluation when developing the program.

Rule 2: State program objectives clearly—avoid remarks like ''to meet the needs of teenagers in Hooten'' or ''to improve the well-being of elderly residents.'' What does meeting the needs of teenagers mean? Which needs? How will you meet them? When will you be able to say you achieved your goal and met the need? Likewise, how can you improve the well-being of elderly residents? What does well-being mean? Which elderly residents? How will you know when you have met your goal. A better example is ''to reduce by 50 percent the number of truancies per month for children in the program.'' Fifty percent is a clearly established percentage. Similarly, you should be able to identify those teens involved in the program. You will have accomplished your goal when you achieve a 50 percent reduction in truancies, not 49 percent nor even 49.9 percent. Your stated goal here is very clear.

Still another example of a well-written goal is ''to increase by 33 percent the number of applications received from prospective foster parents.'' Once again your numbers and expectations are very clear. You can very easily measure progress toward your goal.

Rule 3: Select the indicators you will use to determine whether the objectives have been met. School attendance records would be good indicators for a truancy reduction program.

Rule 4: Choose and use the correct tools and procedures—that is, focus on actual outcomes and people's perceptions rather than on other factors that won't tell you whether things have changed. Rely on official court records rather than on vague recollections of teachers or parents.

Rule 5: Interpret the findings. First, list the facts in a logical order. Second, list the questions that remain unanswered. Third, list your interpretations of the data. Fourth, provide recommendations with options showing the strength and limitations of each option. Your findings should then point you in the right direction to continue improving your program.

---

too little output (achievement of the agency's goals are) probably herald the agency's demise. Regardless, *objective* measures are best. By definition, objective measures are clear and easily interpreted. The more objective the measures, the higher the agreement rate about what they mean.

Of course, if the chosen indicators show no change over time, the intervention may have been unsuccessful—or we may have selected the wrong indicator. Using results of a client satisfaction survey to measure the effectiveness of a crime prevention program would be meaningless. The author once asked employers to evaluate graduates of a particular social work program, only

to find out that the employers rated all the graduates in the upper 25 percent of social workers known to the employers. In fact, employers rated most graduates in the upper 10 percent. In this case, the indicator used was not sophisticated or sensitive enough to gauge accurately what we were trying to measure.

While quantitative evaluations offer certain kinds of information, you might consider using qualitative measures to gather other information. For example, your collection of data from police records indicates that 75 percent of the residents who completed their stay in a halfway house for convicted felons were not rearrested. This would be useful quantitative data. However, if you wanted to learn why people dropped out of the program or what factors led some people to remain to the end, you would likely use a qualitative design. Such designs might involve interviewing each dropout or all participants to identify themes or factors characteristic of those who stayed and of those who dropped out.

Sometimes it is important to know whether the changes we observe are temporary or permanent. Because many programs produce temporary changes in behavior but no permanent modification (somewhat like our driving speed after we spot a police car behind us), they are considered less effective. We may also be concerned about unexpected consequences of our programs. Were people hurt by participating, or were problems exacerbated? Unanticipated consequences have been well documented in the research and can have a very negative impact on clients (Gibbs, 1991).

Stage 3: Sampling

Sampling is the stage at which we decide whether we will gather data from all participants (recall that we refer to this group as the population) or sample part of the population. Often, the costs of gathering data for an entire population are prohibitive. Frequently, it is unnecessary to gather data from everyone, because a well-selected sample can achieve the same results as gathering data from the entire population. Sampling should utilize rules and procedures that meet certain criteria. For example, the size of sample you will need is generally a function of population size, diversity of the population, and desired error level (small samples increase the possibility of error in the results). Experts sometimes disagree on the optimum sample size, but there are formulas to use. Though some of the formulas are complicated, Austin, Cox, Gottlieb, Hawkins, Kruzich, and Rauch (1982) say a sample size of one-tenth of the population is sufficient to eliminate most sampling errors. Yet other authors argue that a sample size of 50 percent is required to rule out error. Mailed surveys (used frequently to gather opinions and data) often get return rates well below this level.

A particular type of sampling, random sampling, was discussed earlier in this chapter and is commonly used in evaluation. In addition to simple random sampling, there are two other types worthy of mention, systematic and stratified.

Systematic Random Sampling

This method simply divides the population by the desired sample size. For a population of five-hundred families served by your agency, you decide on a sample of one hundred to survey. Five hundred divided by one hundred, of course, is five. You than select every fifth person from the population for inclusion in the sample. Some bias could creep in if there were something characteristic about every fifth person that was not true of the rest of the population. That risk, however, is relatively small, and you would still retain some of the advantages of a random sample.

Stratified Random Sampling

Stratified random sampling is used in special situations. For example, you might want to explore the worker-client experiences of clients your agency serves. However, your agency serves only a very small percentage of minority clients, and you are especially interested in their views. A simple random sample might leave you with no minority clients because they compose such a small percentage of the total client population. To avoid this, you might want to ensure that minority clients are proportionately represented in your sample. To do this you can assign numbers to both minority and nonminority clients and, using a table of random numbers (located in most statistics texts), select a proportionate number of minority clients. (A table of random numbers is a list of numbers produced by a computer and is used for selection of random sample members.) If your agency serves one-thousand clients and only one hundred (10 percent) are minorities, then 10 percent of your sample should also be minority. This will help ensure that the sample is representative of the entire population.

As mentioned earlier, random samples allow us to say within a given range of accuracy whether the results we observed in the sample are typical for the entire population. As Marlow (1993) points out, systematic random and stratified random sampling are just two of the random sampling approaches available.

Stage 4: Design

As we have seen, many different designs are available to help us evaluate the effectiveness of our programs.

Experimental and quasi-experimental designs were described earlier in this chapter. Each design has strengths and limitations. Some are easier to use than others, while the others produce more valid and reliable results. The design stage is concerned with selecting an appropriate design and eliminating other possible explanations for the observed outcomes (Rubin & Rubin, 1986). You need to rule out certain other explanations for changes which occur. A drug treatment program that selects only the most promising candidates is likely to be "creaming," selecting the "cream of the crop." When this happens, its results may reflect the characteristics of this group of people rather than substantiating the success of the program. As a result, one cannot say with assurance that the program will work on other populations. Similarly, "maturation" may explain certain outcomes. Maturation is an internal process in which time itself affects the client. A group of adolescents who become less "delinquent" as they grow older may simply be maturing. Delinquent behavior may decrease just because they're aging. Their behavioral changes have little to do with the program in which they are participating and much more to do with their developmental stage. A variety of factors besides creaming and maturation affect outcomes, although these are perhaps the two most common factors (Rubin & Rubin, 1986).

You can sometimes rule out these extraneous factors more easily by using control groups or comparison groups. Likewise, you can select randomly those who are involved in your interventions. Frequently however, you must accept the possibility that other factors may account for the changes observed.

Several designs help control for alternative explanations while others do not. We identified some of these designs earlier. The list in highlight 10.2 provides additional information on these and other common designs, discussing their respective strengths and limitations.

Stage 5: Data Gathering

Data gathered for evaluating, whether goals are achieved or not, can come from several sources (Austin, Kopp, & Smith, 1986). Data gathering may include direct observation by the worker, written surveys sent to clients, interviews with clients or others, and reviews of existing data sources (such as census figures). Some data focus on the program's individual participants,

while some involve more global types of information (such as official government records). At the individual level a worker can review case notes or other official records to learn whether expected outcomes were achieved. If a program was designed to help unemployed workers find adequately paying jobs, agency records may show whether most clients reached this goal. Reviewing each case record, one by one, may be an adequate source of data for this evaluation.

Other data sources are furnished by family, friends, and others with the necessary knowledge about the clients. You may ask their opinions, ratings, or observations of clients. For example, consider an agency program focused on anger control for teens. Parents may be the best source of data regarding whether the program is successfully changing their children's behavior or not.

Workers can also detect changes themselves by observing clients in their natural settings. Observations of school children on the playground or in the classroom may help a school social worker learn whether group activities are resulting in improved peer interactions. Finally, the actual measurement of identified variables is a source of data. Exam scores, changes shown on instruments or scales, and similar measures allow the identification of changes taking place over a given time period.

Data sources are largely aimed at determining whether changes have taken place in individual program participants. There are, of course, other useful sources of data for gauging broader changes. Such sources are described in figure 10.2.

Figure 10.2
Sources of Data

Type of Data	Types of Agency
Census data	U.S. Department of Commerce
Housing data	U.S. Department of Housing and Urban Development
Local employment situations and community needs and plans	Regional planning council
Disease incidence prevalence	State/local health departments
Local needs assessments and community goals	The United Way
Archives and public records	Public libraries

> # HIGHLIGHT 10.2
>
> ## COMMON EVALUATION DESIGNS

1. One-Group Posttest Only Design

By definition, a one-group posttest design involves a single group in which progress is measured only at the end of the intervention. You could use such a design to evaluate the effects of a community drug-abuse-prevention program (Royce, 1992). Program participants are adolescents considered at-risk because of their home situations. Asking "graduates" of the program to complete an anonymous survey describing their drug use following participation in the program could be the posttest. If reported drug use was low or nonexistent (and participants were honest), we might conclude that the program was effective.

The lack of control group and of long-term follow-up are potential problems, however. Other factors may be responsible for the absence of drug use. Since no baseline of prior drug use existed, participants may never have been into drugs. Moreover, the lack of drug use might turn out to be very temporary.

With some posttest only designs, we don't really know whether the clients changed because we have no information on them prior to the intervention. A test of knowledge about illegal drugs given to a group of adolescents following a training program does not prove that their knowledge improved since group leaders don't know what the adolescents knew before participating in the training program.

2. Posttest Only Design with Nonequivalent Groups

This design employs a comparison group that we hope will be similar to our experimental group. Of course, the two groups may not be similar on the variables that matter. Consider a treatment group for adolescent delinquents. You might include in the comparison group others of the same age, gender, life experiences (such as a history of delinquent behavior). The second group allows you to compare results in the experimental group (which received an intervention) with those in the comparison group (which did not). If the experimental group improves (such as by engaging in fewer incidents of school truancy or gang-related behavior), you might claim the intervention program was responsible for the changes.

3. One-Group Pretest/ Posttest Design

This model assesses change over time using the same test, or a variation of the same test, at two points. It works best when you can measure something such as knowledge, attitudes, etc. with a specific instrument. Again, it is difficult to know what caused the change over time. Unlike the posttest only, however, we have greater reason to believe the intervention produced the change.

4. Quasi-Experimental Designs

Several types of quasi-experimental designs may be employed in evaluating outcomes. These include nonequivalent control group designs, time series designs, and multiple time series designs.

a. *Nonequivalent control group designs* use two groups, both of which are given pretests and posttests. The groups are similar on important variables (such as gender and age), but there is no random assignment. This method allows us to rule out some alternative explanations for outcomes because we have tried to control for such things as creaming, maturation, and so on.

(continued)

---

b. *Time series designs* use a series of observations before and after an intervention to gather longitudinal data to help spot patterns occurring over time. This model works when real control groups cannot be used or are not available.

c. *Multiple time series designs* are essentially the time series design with an added control group. They are best for ruling out alternative explanations for observed changes because differences between the untreated control group and the experimental group are more likely the result of the intervention received by the latter.

5. Experimental Designs

An ideal model, experimental designs are most difficult to use in actual practice. Such designs require both random assignment of subjects and a control group which receives no (or different) treatment to compare with the treatment group.

Source: Royce (1992).

Data from all of the sources listed above may allow us to decide whether broad changes are occuring in a community or larger area. You might want to find out whether a community-wide program to immunize children against a specific disease is working. You could compare incidents of the disease before and after the immunization program was carried out. Another example involves efforts to thwart criminals targeting the urban elderly. You can assess such efforts by reviewing law enforcement records of crimes reported to the police before and after the anticrime program was initiated.

Instruments, Tests, and Scales

Evaluating a program's effectiveness is often facilitated when the agency already uses standardized instruments for the quantitative analysis of clients' progress. These instruments can measure specific variables. There are instruments that measure critical thinking and such intangibles as knowledge, attitudes, and behavior. These focus mostly on changes in individuals. A community program aimed at preventing or reducing suicidal behavior by teenagers might utilize an instrument to measure changes in suicidal thoughts or depression. Environmental change measures, such as the Oregon Quality of Life Scale (Bigelow, Brodesky, Steward, & Olson, 1982), assess whether living conditions and other quality of life issues for the client have improved. Such environmental change measures are focused not on the individual's thoughts and feelings, but on tangible changes in such things as quality of housing and access to resources.

Locating measurement instruments can be easy or difficult, depending upon what you are trying to measure. Sometimes a professional journal article will mention an instrument and direct you to where you can find information about it. Other times you might need to consult some of the excellent resources available referred to in figure 10.3 that describe and explain many appropriate instruments.

We will not begin to describe the host of difficulties involved in constructing your own instruments and questionnaires. It is a much more efficient use of your time (and increases the validity and reliability of the instrument) to use existing instruments whenever possible. Factors important in instrument selection are: validity, reliability, the sensitivity to the instrument to any changes caused by the intervention, length, difficulty level for the client, and ease of use. We have already discussed the importance of reliability and validity with respect to research. It is equally important that the instrument actually reflect changes which took place following your intervention. An instrument not sensitive enough to assess changes in assertiveness following an assertiveness training program would not help us evaluate that program. Logically, you would seek an instrument which was not too long (people refuse to fill out

Figure 10.3
Sources of Measurement Instruments and Tests

Brodsky, S. L., & Smitherman, H. O. (1983). *Handbook of scales for research in crime and delinquency.* New York: Plenum.

Conoley, J. C., & Kramer, J. J. (Eds.). (1989). *The tenth mental measurements yearbook.* Lincoln: University of Nebraska Press.

Corcoran, K., & Fisher, J. (1987). *Measures for clinical practice: A sourcebook.* New York: Free Press.

Hamill, D. D. (1989). *A consumer's guide to tests in print.* Austin, TX: Pro-Ed.

Hudson, W. (1982). *The clinical measurement package: A field manual.* Homewood, IL: Dorsey.

Royse, D. (1992). *Program evaluation.* Chicago: Nelson-Hall.

very long instruments) or too difficult. If an instrument uses language and grammar appropriate for college graduates, it might be inappropriate for those without this education. Ease of use is important because complicated or difficult instruments are less likely to be completed by the respondent.

Finally, instruments should not themselves cause changes by leading a client to respond in a certain way (Royce, 1992, p. 133). Most good instruments ask questions in a neutral manner and give no clues as to the ''right'' answers. Most scales and instruments are copyrighted and have some restrictions on their use. Consequently, you must seek permission to use them. Figures 10.4 and 10.5 show two scales that are not copyrighted.

The CES-D Scale was developed to help measure depression and its symptoms. The instrument asks respondents to react to twenty statements concerning behavior related to depression. Respondents are asked to indicate one of the following: ''rarely or none of the time''; ''some or a little of the time''; ''occasionally or a moderate amount of time''; or ''most or all of the time.'' Past evaluations of the instrument have found acceptable levels of validity and reliability (Radloff, 1977).

As you might expect, responses to this instrument have different weights. A zero is given for any response of ''rarely or none of the time.'' Three points are given for a ''most of the time'' response. The statements numbered 4, 8, 12, and 16 are given reverse scores (in other words, 0 points for most of the time and 3 for rarely.

These statements are positive-sounding items unlike the others, and scoring must be reversed to maintain consistency with the negative items in the instrument. Total scores on the instrument may range from a low of zero to a high of sixty. Obviously the higher the score the more likely the person is to have symptoms of depression. If you were evaluating a program that provided intervention to clients experiencing symptoms associated with depression, an instrument like this might serve as a pretest and posttest to determine changes following the intervention.

Another noncopyrighted scale is the Rosenberg Self-Esteem Scale illustrated in figure 10.5. This is a normed instrument that allows comparisons of those who complete it with a broader population. Normed instruments have been given to normal or typical populations and give us a measure of how the average person responds. This instrument asks respondents to indicate strong agreement, agreement, disagreement, or strong disagreement in reaction to ten statements involving self-esteem. Scores on this instrument range from 1 to 4. The statements 1, 3, 4, 7, and 10 are scored in reverse by giving a response of 4 for strongly agree and 1 for strongly disagree. Scores range from 10 to 40 points, with higher scores reflecting greater self-esteem. This instrument has good validity and reliability scores.

Stage 6: Data Analysis

Data analysis is the actual process of assessing the nature and significance of the results obtained. Some types of analysis are relatively simple and straightforward. You may only be interested in explaining single variables (*univariate analysis*) and descriptive statistics (mean, median). Thus, your analysis may concern the mean number of homeless people a program serves per day and the median age of shelter residents. This level of data analysis requires relatively little skill and no sophisticated computers. You can simply count the people the program serves and calculate the median of shelter residents' ages. You might not even need your calculator.

A higher level of analysis is *bivariate analysis*, which determines the degree of association between two variables. You might explore the potential relationship between the number of times a social worker sees a client and the success the client has in finding a job. Here we are looking at two variables (number of hours

Figure 10.4
CES-D Scale

Circle the number for each statement that best describes how often you felt or behaved this way during the past week.

	Rarely or None of the Time (Less than 1 Day)	Some or a Little of the Time (1–2 Days)	Occasionally or a Moderate Amount of Time (3–4 Days)	Most or All of the Time (5–7 Days)
During the Past Week:				
1. I was bothered by things that usually don't bother me.				
2. I did not feel like eating; my appetite was poor.				
3. I felt that I could not shake off the blues even with help from my family or friends.				
4. I felt that I was just as good as other people.				
5. I had trouble keeping my mind on what I was doing.				
6. I felt depressed.				
7. I felt that everything that I did was an effort.				
8. I felt hopeful about the future.				
9. I thought my life had been a failure.				
10. I felt fearful.				
11. My sleep was restless.				
12. I was happy.				
13. I talked less than usual.				
14. I felt lonely.				
15. People were unfriendly.				
16. I enjoyed life.				
17. I had crying spells.				
18. I felt sad.				
19. I felt that people disliked me.				
20. I could not get "going".				

of service to the client and client success in job seeking). We might discover that there is a close positive relationship between these two variables. The more frequently workers see individual clients, the more likely these clients are to successfully find employment. You could also find that there was no relationship between number of meetings and job-finding outcome. You might even find a negative relationship between the two variables—the more contact clients have with workers, the less successful they are in finding jobs. This relationship

Figure 10.5
Rosenberg Self-Esteem Scale

Instructions: Below is a list of statements dealing with your general feelings about yourself. If you agree with the statement, circle A. If you strongly agree, circle SA. If you disagree, circle D. If you strongly disagree, circle SD.

	Agree	Strongly Agree	Disagree	Strongly Disagree
1. On the whole, I am satisfied with myself.	A	SA	D	SD
2. At times I think I am no good at all.	A	SA	D	SD
3. I feel that I have a number of good qualities.	A	SA	D	SD
4. I am able to do things as well as most other people.	A	SA	D	SD
5. I feel I do not have much to be proud of.	A	SA	D	SD
6. I certainly feel useless at times.	A	SA	D	SD
7. I feel that I'm a person of worth, at least on an equal plane with others.	A	SA	D	SD
8. I wish I could have more respect for myself.	A	SA	D	SD
9. All in all, I am inclined to think that I am a failure.	A	SA	D	SD
10. I take a positive attitude toward myself.	A	SA	D	SD

would not appear in a univariate analysis, described above, because univariate analysis explores only one variable. You can use bivariate analysis without the aid of computers but the availability of software packages makes computations much easier.

A third level, *multivariate analysis*, examines three or more variables in relation to one another. A common multivariate technique is *regression analysis*. This is a statistical procedure to determine how much of a change is due to the event under our control (independent variables) and how much to other factors. If the income of people in the job training program increases 10 percent following six months of training, it appears that the program is successful. Assume, however, that the income level of people in the comparison group also went up, but this change is simply due to inflation. Regression analysis would help us determine the actual amount of the increase attributable to the job training program and the amount attributable to inflation. Multivariate analysis generally requires use of a computer and statistical software designed specifically for this level of analysis.

Stage 7: Presentation of Data

The presentation of data must communicate clearly to your intended audience the evaluation's results. Written reports should contain a brief single-page (if possible) "Executive Summary" that highlights the evaluation's most significant findings. Conclusions should flow from the findings. Be prepared for reactions from those who

are unhappy with the findings. There is often a tendency to be defensive about our programs, especially when they are viewed unfavorably by others. The final evaluation report will likely contain six sections (Royce, 1992). Briefly described in the following sections, they include: (1) introduction, (2) literature review, (3) methodology, (4) result, (5) discussion, and (6) references and appendices.

Part 1: Introduction Section

The introductory section reviews the situation that prompted the evaluation in the first place. Here you describe the research questions you want answered. "Did the community education program on child abuse increase the number of reports of suspected abuse and neglect filed with the Department of Human Services in the two months following introduction of the program?" Or "Does an eight-week, self-esteem group for at-risk thirteen-year-olds reduce the number of times these adolescents are referred to the school social worker for disruptive classroom behavior?" Or "Did the implementation of a neighborhood watch program in the Jabberwocky School area reduce the number of burglaries and thefts reported in this neighborhood?"

Part 2: Literature Review Section

The literature review describes any existing research on topics that you discovered as you selected the best

Figure 10.6
Pie Charts

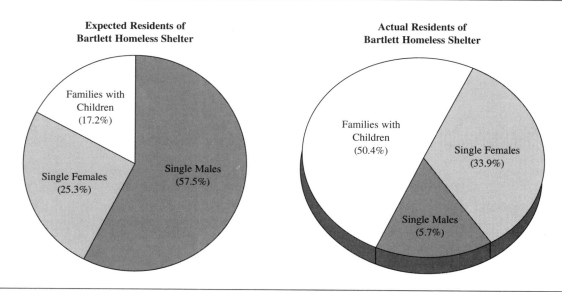

intervention to produce desired changes. To answer the last question cited above, you would want to discuss research on neighborhood watch programs that has examined the success of such programs. The literature review should also show that no research is available on a topic (if that's the case) and describe why this evaluation is taking place.

Part 3: Methodology Section

The methodology section describes the evaluation design and the data collection methods used. If a pre- and posttest without a control group was used, this should be stated. If you gathered data using a self-report form completed by program participants, report this. Likewise, if you used agency records as your primary data source, indicate that. Also state whether you sampled the population or used the entire population for data collection. Explain what sampling system you used. Identify any instruments, scales, or surveys you used and describe to the readers the study's subjects. Finally, discuss the data analysis system selected (univariate, bivariate, multivariate).

Part 4: Results Section

The results component describes your findings with appropriate graphics (charts, graphs) and reports on the findings' importance. Data may be displayed using line graphs, bar charts, three dimensional bar charts, and pie charts. Figure 10.6 depicts a pair of pie charts comparing the expected to actual breakdowns of homeless shelter residents. The shelter expected the resident population to consist of 58 percent single males, 25 percent single females, and 17 percent families with children. The actual population consisted of 50 percent families with children, 34 percent single females, and 16 percent single males. Imagine the implications for the program of these findings. How would a client population of primarily women and children require different attention and services than one made up primarily of single men?

Figure 10.7 shows a line graph, bar chart, and a three-dimensional bar chart, each depicting the same information. Charts and graphs can be varied to clearly show the results achieved. A bar chart can be used to visually compare changes in the shelter's population across two or more years. A line graph can easily show

Figure 10.7
Line Graph, Bar Chart and a Three-Dimensional Bar Chart

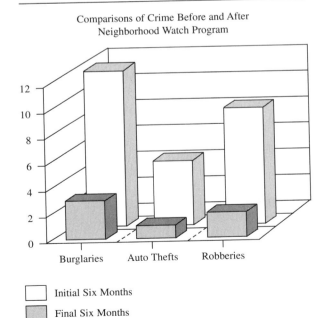

Line Graph

Comparisons of Crime Before and After
Neighborhood Watch Program

—————— Initial Six Months
- - - - - - Final Six Months

Bar Chart

Comparisons of Crime Before and After
Neighborhood Watch Program

Initial Six Months
Final Six Months

Three-Dimensional Bar Chart

Comparisons of Crime Before and After
Neighborhood Watch Program

Initial Six Months
Final Six Months

trends. Generally speaking, you will choose the type of chart that most clearly communicates your data to the reader. The goal is always clarity.

Part 5: Discussion Section

The discussion section briefly summarizes your findings, describes any unexpected findings, and describes any practice implications. Your findings might suggest that the program you are evaluating is not serving the originally intended population. Unexpected findings might include such things as the fact that agency policies are actually making the situation worse and forcing clients to seek help elsewhere. Practice implications might include information such as which intervention worked best with a certain group of clients.

Finally, describe any limitations of the research. One limitation might be that, because subjects were not selected randomly, the results cannot be generalized to any other group. Another limitation might be that the size of the sample was too small.

Part 6: References and Appendices

References include any sources (books, journal articles, and similar items) you consulted in preparing and conducting your evaluation. Perhaps you consulted a statistics book to look up an explanation or definition for a particular method or test. References also include all the literature sources cited at the beginning of the study.

Appendices might include any documents too large to fit into the study itself. For example, a copy of a questionnaire might appear in the appendix. Related reports might also be included in an appendix. So also might letters sent to accompany surveys or to inform clients about a program, and any details too involved for inclusion in the basic report.

Summary of Data Presentation

Always present data as clearly as possible. Think carefully about what to say and how to say it. Use your common sense. If the report is to be read by people with little background in the field (perhaps members of the board of directors), consider how to make the information as easily understood as possible. Trying to impress the readers may end up confusing them. Most people will ignore unclear results. Any tables used in the report should be numbered and titled. Columns of data need headings to tell readers what is presented below. Similarly, rows in a chart should have headings providing helpful information. Again, recognize that different audiences may require different presentations. For example, decision-makers may want a brief summary rather than 457 pages of reports. Public presentation of data requires more use of graphics than might be required for a written report. For example, you might wish to use overhead slides or handouts summarizing data, because reading data from a report can be excruciatingly boring—to you and to your audience.

Ethics and Values in Evaluation

Royce (1992) provides some excellent guidelines for maintaining ethical standards while doing evaluations. He stresses that whenever you contemplate using subjects as part of the evaluation (such as when interviewing or testing), those subjects must be volunteers. Any person volunteering should know the risks (if any) associated with participation. Of course, no one should be harmed because of participating in the evaluation. The privacy of participants should be zealously protected. There have been many examples in the popular press and in various governmental reports of well-meaning practitioners failing to inform clients adequately of the risks to which they were being exposed. In some cases evaluators have deliberately concealed information from participants. Our ethical obligation to clients must guide our interventions and our evaluations.

Sometimes our values can become a barrier to effective action following an evaluation. This can happen, for example, when we refuse to recognize that cost factors do enter into the decision-making process (Rubin & Rubin, 1986). If it costs too much to help individual clients deal with their problems, we need to ask whether we should abandon the program and spend the money on a program which has a payoff. While sentiments such as, "If it helps one person, I'm satisfied," may show your heart is in the right place, this is not an acceptable response when it comes time to measure results. Few funding agencies will continue supporting programs of dubious effectiveness or efficiency when more promising approaches are available.

Chapter Summary

This chapter opens with an overview of evaluation and some of the key concepts it involves. These include experimental design, control group, experimental group, independent and dependent variables, baseline, outcome, reliability, validity, mean, standard deviation, median, mode, sampling, random sample, inferential and descriptive statistics, chi-square test, and statistical significance.

The purposes of program evaluation are outlined along with some common problems and barriers to effective evaluations. Various kinds of evaluation—formative or monitoring, summative or impact, effectiveness and efficiency—were identified and described. A variety of evaluation designs were discussed. These included qualitative and quantitative designs, one group posttest, pretest/posttest, client satisfaction surveys, goal attainment scaling, target problem scaling, case studies, group comparison, and quality assurance reviews.

Stages of evaluation one normally expects to complete during the evaluation process are identified, including conceptualization and goal setting, measurement and sampling, design and data gathering. Also reviewed are data analysis and presentation of the data. Finally, the ethics of evaluation is briefly mentioned.

CHAPTER ELEVEN

Advocacy and Social Action
with Populations-at-Risk

Andrea Munoz was beside herself. After working for years providing shelter and food to the homeless at the downtown complex called The Pantry, she had gotten used to handling problems. She had built The Pantry into the main supplier of shelter and food to the homeless in Orange Harbor using a variety of techniques. Indeed, The Pantry was a remarkable social agency with a wonderful history of working with businesses in the neighborhood, and with other social service agencies. Her success at raising funds and acquiring other resources for the shelter was legendary.

Now the very success of The Pantry was causing a problem. Many of the homeless people who learned of The Pantry arrived in old vehicles that they parked on the street and in the nearby municipal lot. Some slept in their vehicles when there was no room in the old hotel Andrea used for sheltering the homeless. Herein lay the problem.

The neighborhood in which The Pantry was located was a mixture of small businesses and older homes. Locals called the area Parkside because it was adjacent to a large city park. The Parkside Integrity Group (PIG) was a neighborhood association begun several years earlier to deal with a variety of local problems. As PIG became more effective, it successfully produced many changes in the neighborhood. These included better street lighting, more police patrols, and a decrease in drug use and dealing in the area. Now PIG decided that its next project was to reduce the number of homeless people sleeping in their cars in the neighborhood. Well-organized and vocal, the association approached the city council with a request for an ordinance prohibiting overnight parking without a permit. They claimed that sleeping in cars overnight was a common occurrence among homeless people congregating near the central city's two largest shelters and food kitchens. By discouraging this, the neighborhood association hoped to improve the quality of life in its low-income neighborhood. At the same time, The Pantry wanted to give the homeless the same rights due all the community's citizens, namely, worth and dignity. Unfortunately, PIG, an organization that had helped the neighborhood address such problems as reducing crime, drug abuse, and residential deterioration, ended up targeting the homeless population. The homeless clearly became an oppressed group in the community of Orange Harbor. In essence, PIG was trying to evict them from the community.

The city council weighed the needs of two competing groups and voted to ban overnight parking without a permit. This effectively prevented the homeless from using perhaps their last resource, their vehicles. Andrea had lost this battle to the NIMBY Syndrome—Not in My Back Yard. NIMBY is the strange malady in which people support group homes and similar facilities in principle as long as they are not located in their own neighborhoods. The Pantry clients' and other homeless people's lack of political power made the city council's ruling a foregone conclusion. In a struggle between taxpayers, home owners, and the homeless, the latter almost always lose. In other words, those with the power are almost always able to oppress or subjugate those without power. The homeless have no power.

Introduction

Longres (1990) has argued that social workers cannot afford to blame either victims for their situation or the environment or society. A more rational approach is to assess the interaction between the environment and the individual to determine where the problems lie. This process is at the heart of generalist social work practice.

At the same time, you must recognize that certain population groups are at greater risk of being disadvantaged or harmed by actions of other individuals, groups, organizations, or the communities. The homeless described in this case are a typical example. Such groups call for a variety of different macro approaches for social workers including advocacy, social action, and empowerment.

This chapter will:

- Define key concepts involved with macro practice.
- Examine the macro practice issues of advocacy, social action, and empowerment activities with populations-at-risk.
- Discuss what places a population at risk.
- Provide several examples of populations-at-risk.
- Describe the role of the social worker in working with this population.
- Discuss advocacy in detail, with a special focus on concerns about its use, the value and limitations of advocacy, opportunities for macro-level advocacy, and principles guiding macro-level advocacy.
- Review social action, including Alinsky's model, concerns about social action, and legal action.
- Examine some of the most controversial forms of macro practice in the current debate about what is appropriate for generalist social workers to know and do.
- Discuss empowerment.
- Explore legislative advocacy.
- Discuss the role of social workers in legislative advocacy and political activity.

Defining Advocacy, Social Action, Empowerment, and Populations-at-Risk

In order to discuss the role of social workers in advocacy, we must consider social action, empowerment,

---

HIGHLIGHT 11.1

KEY CONCEPTS

Advocacy is representing, championing, or defending the rights of others.

Case advocacy is work on behalf of individuals and families.

Cause advocacy is work on behalf of groups of people.

Discrimination is negative treatment of individuals, often based upon their membership in some group (such as women) or upon some characteristic they share with others (such as a disability).

Empowerment is ensuring that others have the right to power, ability, and authority to achieve self-determination.

Oppressed populations refers to groups that experience serious limitations because others in power exploit them.

Populations-at-risk are those groups in society most likely to suffer the consequences of, or be at-risk for, discrimination, economic hardship, and oppression.

Social Action is a coordinated effort to achieve institutional change to meet a need, solve a social problem, correct an injustice, or enhance the quality of human life.

Social and economic justice exists when every individual has equal opportunities, rights, and responsibilities with all other members of a society. This includes the opportunity to obtain gainful employment, adequate housing, food, and medical care without experiencing discrimination or other forms of oppression.

---

and populations-at-risk. Each concept is briefly defined and discussed in the following sections. A more detailed description of the concept is presented later in this chapter.

Defining Advocacy

As we noted earlier, in its most basic definition, advocacy is representing, championing, or defending the rights of others. All generalist social workers engage in advocacy at some level as part of their responsibility to clients. Macro practice, in particular, often involves cause advocacy. *Cause advocacy* is work on behalf of groups of people who lack the ability (resources, talent, or skill) to advocate for themselves. Cause advocacy should be distinguished from *case advocacy*, in which the worker advocates for individual cases or clients. You are likely to pursue case advocacy in micro practice with individuals and families. At the same time, however, cause advocacy may well grow out of case advocacy. This occurs when multiple individuals or groups experience essentially the same problems.

It is not unusual for a generalist social worker to discern a pattern when working with multiple clients. Perhaps it becomes clear that many clients are experiencing similar problems with a particular agency whose policies discourage them from seeking help. In other circumstances you might learn that certain resources such as day-care centers for low-income working parents are not available in your community. The result is that many parents leave their children in less-than-adequate situations with very poor supervision. Awareness of this situation may well set the stage for cause advocacy. Highlight 11.2 provides such an example.

Social workers have had a rich history of cause advocacy. This includes helping to work for civil rights legislation and fighting for the rights of persons with physical and emotional disabilities and for other populations-at-risk. Advocacy can take the form of merely persuading others to accept your definition of the problem and your suggested solutions, or it can assume a more conflictual approach. As Taylor (1987) observes, "cause advocacy arises from case situations (or community knowledge) and goes on to document the problem

---

HIGHLIGHT 11.2

ADVOCACY PRODUCES SYSTEM CHANGE

Mrs. Ackerman and her two daughters Nadia and Fadia arrived at the Division of Family Services (DFS) office at 9:00 A.M. to turn in their welfare application. They spent four hours in the agency waiting room before getting any help. When Mrs. Ackerman later mentioned this to her social worker at Catholic Charities, Genevieve Moran, she was appalled. "I don't know why they can't do a better job of serving their clients," Genevieve said "I just think this is unacceptable."

With that, she picked up the phone and called DFS. "This is Ms. Moran at Catholic Charities. Is Bob Evans available?" With that call Genevieve took the first of a series of steps. First, she met with Bob to discuss what she perceived to be a common problem, very slow service to clients at DFS. Bob set up a meeting with the secretary/receptionist, financial aid supervisor, and financial aid worker. They decided to adopt a pro-client policy that would provide the following:

1. Each client would receive a set appointment time.
2. Any delays over five minutes would be communicated to the client and no clients would be left to wonder why they were not being waited on.
3. A client satisfaction survey would be used two weeks after the client had been seen to assess clients' attitudes toward the service they had received.
4. Staff training would emphasize the importance of responding to clients in a timely fashion, showing courtesy to clients, and demonstrating respect for the client's time.

Client satisfaction survey results indicated general contentment with the new efforts to treat clients better. Although a single client brought the situation to Genevieve's attention, her advocacy ultimately benefited all clients served by DFS.

---

in many other situations. Cause advocacy serves many people with the same problem by taking a stand for what is theirs by rights from the system. Cause advocacy will go beyond consensus planning to confrontation for change, if necessary. . . . It can empower inadequately served people to work on their problem as a united group to obtain what they need from the system. Cause advocacy can also join people who are hurting with influential citizens and professionals to work toward the same goal" (p. 22).

Defining Social Action

As we said in chapter 9, social action is "a coordinated effort to achieve institutional change to meet a need, solve a social problem, correct an injustice, or enhance the quality of human life" (Barker, 1991, p. 217). Of course, social workers are not the only ones who pursue social action. It may be undertaken by other professionals, agencies, and organizations, churches, cities, and anyone affected by a particular problem. It is important to coordinate social action efforts because rarely is there only one group concerned about the issue or problem. Often there are many, although they may be unaware of each other's interest. Coordinated efforts can also bring more influence to bear than can single individuals or groups. Highlight 11.3 gives an example of the benefits of coordinated efforts.

The example in highlight 11.3 demonstrates a relatively "gentle" form of social action, persuasion through lobbying. Often, however, social action implies a more confrontational approach to problem solving, since more consensual approaches have not proven successful. (Chapter 9 addresses this issue.) This chapter will discuss the debate over whether the social action skills used by social workers in the past are still relevant today.

HIGHLIGHT 11.3

COORDINATED SOCIAL ACTION EFFORTS

Mount Holland is a small community housing a medium-sized state university. Most students at the university are people of color and many are from relatively poor families. Local landlords in the community have turned many older homes into student housing units, crowding more residents into each apartment than the law allows. In addition, these apartments are poorly maintained. A piece of linoleum nailed to the walls of a small closet is presented to students as a "shower stall." Vermin and unsanitary conditions are commonplace.

While students do not like the situation, as a group they are relatively powerless. Complaints to the landlord are largely ignored and efforts to

strengthen housing maintenance regulations have been stymied by the apartment owners. Progress occurs only when the University Student Housing Association and Citizens for a Better Mount Holland (both organizations focused on the needs of their members) combine efforts. The student group is committed to ensuring students decent living conditions. The citizens group is concerned with making the community a safer, more attractive place to live. By lobbying the city council and the Mount Holland Plan Commission and mounting a letter writing campaign, they succeed in achieving enactment of a property maintenance code for the City of Mount Holland.

Defining Empowerment

Empowerment suggests that people have "the right to power, ability, and authority to achieve self-determination." (Hartman, 1993, p. 365). Empowerment is a frequent description of social work's goal with people of color and other commonly oppressed groups. This reflects our recognition that oppressed populations benefit most when our efforts (1) give them the power to help themselves, (2) reduce the negative influences of social and agency policies, and (3) build new helping models which acknowledge the very real problems these groups experience.

Defining Populations-at-Risk

Populations-at-risk are those groups in society most likely to suffer the consequences of or be at risk of discrimination, economic hardship, and oppression. Historically, among the groups most frequently experiencing these societal influences are women, lesbian and gay

people, and persons of color. Persons of color are African Americans, Hispanics, Native Americans, Asians, and Pacific Islanders, to name a few. Examples of what places these groups at risk will be covered later in the chapter. Other groups are also at risk, including the elderly persons with physical, emotional, or developmental disabilities; and those holding religious views significantly different from those of the rest of society. This is not an exhaustive list of populations that may be at risk. Any group that other groups in our society believe to be "different" can be victimized. Those differences can be based on skin color, intellectual ability, belief systems, gender, age, sexual orientation, culture, or class.

Populations-at-Risk

This section will consider three major aspects of populations-at-risk. They are: (1) factors that can contribute to putting a population at risk, (2) some examples of populations-at-risk; and (3) the role of social workers in helping these groups.

HIGHLIGHT 11.4

CAVEATS IN EMPOWERMENT

Empowering client groups requires that we understand their situations and life experiences, especially when these differ significantly from our own. This is particularly true when working with people of color. Lacking personal experience with these groups, we tend to rely on the literature in social work and related disciplines to understand their situation. This can produce disastrous results. Marla Moodie is a new social worker, working with refugees from Southeast Asia. She is very interested in understanding their culture and providing the help they need. She is aware that immigrants often have little power and less access to resources, and are more likely to experience social and economic oppression.

To better understand this important group of clients, Marla seeks articles and books on Asian culture. Although she ultimately reads several well-documented articles about Asians, she is still unwit-

tingly operating on a database of limited value. As Fong and Mokuau (1994) point out, social work literature tends to lump Asian groups together without appropriate differentiation. The result is that the literature generally ignores huge variations between and within groups which significantly limits understanding of specific groups. Empowerment can't take place when we apply inaccurate stereotypes, make assumptions based on limited samples, and try to make a single model fit all members of a diverse group. This is true whether the group we are working with consists of women, people of color, the homeless, or gay and lesbian people.

Marla's efforts result in a fine understanding of Asian life-styles and values as a whole. Unfortunately, she still knows little about the experiences, values, and aspirations of Southeast Asian refugees, the group with which she is working.

Factors Contributing to Populations Being at Risk

Several primary factors can help place a population-at-risk. These include physical differences (such as skin color) and values and beliefs (including religious beliefs) that differ from those of the dominant or more powerful segment of a society. It can also result from preconceptions about the ability or competence of members of a group (such as women). Finally, populations may be at risk as a result of our economic system. Each of these factors will be discussed below.

Being different from other, more powerful groups in society often places a group at risk. Some may consider it human nature to be uncomfortable around those who are different from us. Because we lack experience with those whose characteristics are different from ours, we often avoid them. However, experience has shown that this discomfort can be ameliorated over time as we learn more about the group. We can also discover that

we may share more with those individuals than we thought we did. Our commonality is enormous and our differences become minuscule. Initially, however, our lack of familiarity and discomfort with a population may place them at risk. We may avoid them, hurt them through ignorance, or deliberately engage in actions that will penalize them. A business owner may refuse to hire a person of color because he wears his hair in dreadlocks and has an earring. Cab drivers may refuse to pick up young black males at night for fear of being robbed or assaulted.

Of course, our discomfort with others may be derived from values and beliefs they hold that are widely divergent from our own. Some religious values define homosexuality as sinful, thereby subjecting gay and lesbian people to discrimination. The logic goes something like this: "What these people are doing is bad, so they deserve mistreatment."

The long-standing practice in the military of denying women the opportunity to receive combat assignments is

Before women got the vote, they suffered discrimination, economic hardship, and oppression. These New York City women marched in support of women's suffrage in 1917. Though they have had the vote for many years, women still suffer serious economic hardship.

a similar case in point. Keeping women out of combat, it is argued, is consistent with our need to "protect" them. It is also argued that women cannot perform the same physical activities as men. Allowing them to serve in combat would place them (and their fellow soldiers) at greater risk. However, in the military, opportunity for advancement is usually improved by experience in combat. As a consequence, these policies mean most women do not have the same opportunities as men. Earning promotion is simply easier for a male soldier who has been in combat than for a woman soldier who has not.

Sometimes a group is at risk because others in society define it as economically or socially insignificant. Consider our own government's sad treatment of various peoples of color. Native Americans were herded off their land, shot, and systematically exterminated partly for economic reasons (whites wanted their land) but also because they were defined as barbarians. African Americans were first enslaved for economic reasons and later considered so insignificant that they were not allowed to vote. Women, too, were denied the vote until

1920. Asians were prevented from owning land by the state of California, and the federal government attempted to prevent further immigration of Asians. Most people of color have experienced deliberate governmental efforts to exterminate or subjugate them, or limit them in fulfilling their rights to "life, liberty and the pursuit of happiness." This malevolent behavior was condoned by belief systems which reduced minorities of color to subhuman status or defined them as economically insignificant. The current argument advanced by some segments of the population about the supposed intellectual inferiority of African Americans is a typical effort to reduce the value of these groups.

We have briefly suggested the role economics may play in placing a population at risk. Economic justice has often been denied certain groups in society. Sometimes the argument is made that this treatment is inherent in our economic structure. The nature of a capitalist economic system is to deliver a product at the lowest cost possible which may mean keeping salaries and benefits as low as possible. Companies' common practice of hiring part-time workers (particularly women) to avoid paying benefits (e.g., health insurance and retirement) normally given to full-time employees is one example of a cost-cutting practice. The economic injustice which arises from such practices is justified by views such as, "women don't need these benefits because their husbands have full-time jobs," or "If they were really unhappy with the situation, they wouldn't come to work." The fact that this practice unfairly affects certain groups (women, for example) is ignored. Employers believe it is an effective way to make a bigger profit.

Another example of economic injustice which places groups at risk is evident when businesses decide to move from communities where wages are considered "too high." Two groups are affected by these decisions. Company employees and the community now housing the business are often victimized by what is considered a purely economic decision. Workers lose their livelihoods, homes, and sense of identity. Communities suffer loss of taxes, which may mean they cannot afford to provide city service or repair the streets. An entire community can become a population-at-risk when it is heavily dependent on a major employer who relocates.

Of course, the community which attracts the business is also a population-at-risk. The company will pay workers significantly less than their former employees were getting, a practice which exploits the new hires. Again, this series of decisions is considered good business, as it is designed to maximize profit and minimize cost of producing a product or service. It is a guiding principle behind our economic system.

Examples of Populations-at-Risk

As we have seen above, many factors contribute to a population being at risk in our society. Some groups are inherently at higher risk than others for certain negative outcomes. Several such groups are described in the following sections.

African Americans

We have already described some of the historic discrimination and oppression experienced by African Americans. However, this group continues to be a population at great risk on several fronts (Ginsberg, 1992). Infant mortality rates for African Americans are almost 80 percent higher than for whites. Black women are almost twice as likely to use abortion services as are whites. Black males are over seven times more likely to die as homicides than are white males. The rate difference is about ten times as high for black males between twenty-five and thirty-four years of age. Similarly, African Americans are less likely to survive physical illnesses such as cancer and more likely to suffer from hypertension and strokes. Blacks, who constitute less than 13 percent of the total population, comprise over 30 percent of those arrested in the United States. And they constitute almost one half of those imprisoned in state correctional facilities. These factors help explain why African Americans are considered a major population-at-risk.

Hispanics

Another ethnic group at risk are Hispanics. Hispanics represented 26.5 percent of all federal prisoners in 1990. Moreover the percentage of Hispanic juveniles incarcerated is increasing faster than other groups. Hispanics are also less likely to have completed four or more years of college than either blacks or white. In the trend toward one-parent families, Hispanics experienced a rate increase almost twice that of the rest of the U.S. population in the period 1980–1991. Current debates in the United States focus on reducing the ability of Hispanic and other immigrant groups to benefit from social, health, and economic services routinely available to whites.

Native Americans and Alaskan Natives

Native Americans and Alaskan Natives "have some of the most serious health and social problems of all the groups in the nation" (Ginsberg, 1992, p. 91). In all categories of cause of death from cancer to accidents, Native Americans have a rate higher than that of the rest of the U.S. population. For some causes of death (for example, alcoholism and tuberculosis), the rate is five to seven times higher. Attempts by tribal groups to improve their economic situation through the institution of casino gambling on tribal lands are often met with opposition from whites and from groups opposed to gambling on religious grounds. The continuation of traditional Native American activities such as spear fish-ing (even when guaranteed by treaties) is also met by antagonism and resistance from non-native people.

Asians and Pacific Islanders

Asians and Pacific Islanders, particularly refugees from Southeast Asia who emigrated to the United States after the Vietnam War, experience a host of problems that place them at risk. Without a grasp of the English language and coming from a basically agrarian and rural background, many have great difficulty making the transition to an urban life-style. Traditional customs and norms often clash with those of whites in America. Reliance on family and clan for support often places them outside the usual formal networks of social service providers available to nonimmigrants. In addition, the enormous diversity within these groups is often ignored by white Americans who assume that all Asians have similar experiences, values, and behaviors.

Women

Women have constituted a population-at-risk for some time. From an unwillingness to grant women the vote to more recent manifestations such as lower pay for the same jobs, women remain an at risk group. They are more likely to be subjected to sexual harassment in the workplace, and maltreatment after surviving a sexual assault. Denial of women's right to control her own body also arises during the debate on abortion. The willingness of some men to subjugate women in the workplace and in the home increase the risk to this population.

Lesbian and Gay Persons

One of the population groups most at risk in the United States is comprised of lesbians and gay persons. Lacking the traditional civil rights protection accorded women and people of color, this group often experiences discrimination. This includes the refusal to hire gay or lesbian persons for teaching or other jobs involving children. Based upon a homophobic and irrational fear that members of this group are more likely to cause harm to children, this discrimination is supported by current laws.

Partners of gays or lesbians are often denied the rights accorded other next of kin such as child custody and access to the partner's health insurance. Even the U.S. military, one of the first employers to end racial discrimination, carries on discrimination against gay and lesbian people by discharging anyone who openly discusses being homosexual or who engages in any homosexual act. Needless to say, these restrictions are not placed on heterosexuals in the military. Like the controversy over abortion which attempts to limit the rights of women to control their destiny, denial of rights to gay and lesbian persons places one group in the position of forcing its religious views on the rest of the population.

Other At-Risk Populations

Other groups in our society can be at risk in numerous ways. The homeless risk not benefiting from a community's school system. The transient nature of the homeless population often means that school systems will not accept homeless children because they lack a permanent residence. Trying to reach this population-at-risk takes extra effort. Some communities are using tutors to work with homeless children and adolescents. Tutors also help adults get their high school equivalency degrees, give advice about finding jobs, and teach parenting skills. Programs of this type reach a segment of a population-at-risk normally excluded from social and educational programming. It often takes an advocate for the homeless to supply the special programs they need.

Another population-at-risk are teenagers who have no plans for college. They remain at risk of a marginal economic existence without further training, or some other employment-enhancing education. Vocational opportunities are essential, although some schools systems are oriented primarily to students planning to attend college.

Another group of teens-at-risk are those who have unplanned or unwanted pregnancies. Besides the physical health risk to the mother, both parents have a high risk of poverty, dependence on welfare, and involvement in various other social problems. Advocacy efforts for this group may include increased funding for family planning, opposition to efforts to cut funds for this purpose, and programs which advocate abstinence, birth control, and parenting education. Both conservatives and liberals can agree on such goals that promise long-term benefits for the individuals and for society (Zill & Nord, 1994).

The Role of Social Workers with Populations-at-Risk

Social workers are in an excellent position to help prevent populations from being placed at risk. The profession is often keenly aware of the needs of certain segments of the population who bear the brunt of economic decisions affecting a community. Social workers see the long-term poverty which comes from child-rearing burdens placed prematurely on teenaged girls. We are also trained to recognize the negative impact of discrimination on people of color and other groups, such as lesbian and gay people.

Social workers must also be vigilant regarding how their agencies and other societal institutions interact with high risk populations. We need to review agency policies to see if they work to the disadvantage of any groups. Do we, for example, serve minority populations with the same frequency as other agencies? Or do our practices (lack of minority workers, daytime office hours, or other factors) discourage some populations from using our services? Do our hiring practices discourage minority applicants from applying for positions in the agency?

Likewise, social workers must alert themselves to the community's treatment of populations-at-risk. Do the community's decisions reflect an interest in all segments of the population? Does the city seem to ignore the problems in Hispanic neighborhoods while rushing to provide police services to upscale areas? Are the parks in African-American neighborhoods maintained with the same care as other parks in the city? Are the public hospitals in the community providing a comparable level of treatment for poor patients as for their well-to-do clientele?

Do all the positions of influence in the community seem to go to men, with women rarely offered status or important roles? Does the city allow landlords to discriminate against gay and lesbian people who apply for housing? Does the community really enforce laws protecting the rights and needs of schoolchildren with physical and mental disabilities?

In each of the above situations, social workers can try to prevent groups from becoming at risk. Be alert to what goes on in your community and take an active part in its operation. You can also decide to try to change policies, practices, and procedures which negatively affect at-risk populations. Finally, you can work for systems designed to alleviate the problems experienced by populations-at-risk. One of the most effective methods for achieving these goals, advocacy, is discussed next.

Advocacy

Advocacy is an approach which has been used by social workers for a very long time. This section describes the value and limitations of advocacy, discusses agency commitment to advocacy, and considers opportunities for advocacy. It will suggest some typical concerns about advocacy. Finally, it will provide guidelines for macro-level advocacy, and review some advocacy tactics.

Concerns about the Use of Advocacy

Advocacy is a longstanding social work tradition. However, Taylor (1987) notes that practitioners sometimes have fears about engaging in advocacy. Workers may be afraid of controversy, which is a natural consequence of advocating for an oppressed group or population-at-risk. Some view advocacy as too confrontational and worry about how others may perceive their efforts. For example, an agency director may be averse to having her workers engage in advocacy since board members or other funding groups may be offended by what they perceive as challenges to the status quo.

Being unable to determine the outcomes of advocacy is another potential problem. Some potential advocates fear being considered a troublemaker who is placing the agency at risk. Still other workers honestly believe they cannot produce any change in the system, no matter what they do. This lack of a sense of efficacy is a real barrier for new social workers who lack confidence in their own power. Finally, change produced by advocacy and other means is threatening. Social workers may fear what will happen if they advocate for a change and the change actually occurs. Change and the unknown are often scary.

The Value and Limitations of Advocacy

According to Taylor (1987) the basis for advocacy is our heritage of respect for the worth and dignity of every person and the rights (both moral and legal) which are ours as a part of this society. Advocacy is consistent with the values of the social work profession. We have seen that the groups for which advocacy works change over time—from civil rights for people of color in the 1960s to legislation for the handicapped in the 1990s. In each case, these macro-level efforts profoundly changed the quality of life and opportunities of both groups.

A major benefit of macro-level advocacy is that it can attack core problems rather than merely treating crisis situations. It can help workers feel a sense of participation when they are actively involved in solving a problem rather than merely putting bandaids on it. It can also empower clients to tackle their own issue, thereby leading to development of personal skills and a sense of efficacy.

One factor limiting the effectiveness of advocacy is that by nature human and societal problems often do not lend themselves to massive change. Sometimes all we can do is tackle one piece at a time or take the first steps in the process. Look at the advocacy efforts undertaken to ensure that women (and, fifty years earlier, African Americans) had the right to vote in this country. Although this right was ensured by constitutional amendment it did not guarantee that people would vote. The next step was encouraging people to exercise the right. Getting people to register to vote is still necessary today, and getting them out to vote is yet another step, when less than half vote in presidential elections. These are incremental steps in the process of getting people to participate in the electoral system.

At the same time, some tasks cannot be accomplished now because the climate and conditions for change just aren't there. For example, it is difficult to successfully advocate for bold, new programs when the entire political process is focused on cutting taxes and reducing government spending.

One significant limitation to advocacy is our own lack of courage and of knowledge about how to tackle the problem. Apathy is perhaps the most dangerous threat to progress in combating oppression and pursuing social and economic justice. Some of this apathy stems from lack of faith that one can have much impact on major societal or community problems. In other cases,

doubt over how to begin contributes to a sense of incompetence. Fortunately, advocacy utilizes the same process of problem solving described earlier in this book. While the problem may be much larger than we are used to dealing with, the process for tackling major macro type problems is essentially the same for all generalist interventions.

Agency Commitment to Advocacy

The degree of interest in advocacy on behalf of populations-at-risk varies from agency to agency. Some agencies have a strong advocacy mission inherent in their service giving (Taylor, 1987). Most shelters for survivors of domestic violence are committed to the enactment and enforcement of strong laws against spousal abuse and development of new programs that help women become self-supporting. Other agencies actively pursue outreach efforts to ensure that their services are available to populations-at-risk and groups underserved by existing agencies. Still other agencies such as the American Civil Liberties Union and the Children's Defense Fund are devoted almost solely to advocacy (Clifton & Dahms, 1993).

Unfortunately, some agencies do not see advocacy as an important part of their mission. The degree to which one's agency is committed to advocacy tends to affect the worker's sense of commitment to pursuing large system change. If your agency does not believe that advocacy is important for social workers, it is less likely that you will pursue it. Only your commitment to the profession and your professional obligation to clients are available to motivate and sanction your efforts.

Opportunities for Macro-Level Advocacy

We have identified by example some of the types of advocacy in which generalist social workers may engage. However, we have touched on only a few of the opportunities available to us. Recall that advocacy can help people take control of their own lives and problems, so it can be considered a form of self-help or empowerment (Segal, Silverman, & Temkin, 1993). Advocacy activities might include forming groups of people with similar interests or problems who can work in concert

---

HIGHLIGHT 11.5

ADVOCACY FOR CHANGE—
THINKING BIG ABOUT CHILD CARE

Advocating for change can also be done in ways most social workers might not think about. A few cases illustrate that stepping back and thinking on a larger scale can produce benefits no amount of individual effort can create. For example, San Francisco identified a lack of adequate low cost day care as a community-wide problem. To help remedy the problem, the city imposed requirements on developers of new office projects. Any building project over a specified size was required either to set aside free space for child care or to contribute to a fund providing affordable child care to low- and moderate-income families (Young, 1987). Other cities have adopted similar proposals and social workers have been and can be involved in such efforts through advocacy.

Likewise, to meet the child care needs of students and school staff, some school systems have added in-school child care and after-school care. For those without sufficient income to pay the full cost of child care, other communities establish a sliding scale fee, ensuring that no one is denied care because of income level. In still other communities, the city provides funds to help low-income parents pay for child care in reputable facilities. Facilities not meeting city standards may apply for grants to bring them up to appropriate service levels.

While these examples of advocacy have oc-curred at the city level, it is possible to achieve many of the same goals on a more local basis, such as the neighborhood. A neighborhood center could be an ideal site for a child-care center. Or perhaps a church with unused space could be converted to meet the need for low-income child care.

The important lesson is that social workers must be prepared to intervene at many levels in order to achieve social work goals. It also means we must be concerned about decisions made at every level—local, county, state, and national—because each has the capacity to influence our clients, our programs, and our goals as social workers.

We also need to maintain a broad perspective about who benefits from our advocacy efforts. We should recognize that child care is not a concern only for people with children. Lack of affordable and dependable child care affects others including co-workers, employers, and those who depend upon the worker. Thus, it is an issue which transcends family status. Low-income parents with inadequate child care are at risk of entering the welfare system or leaving their children in situations which do not guarantee their safety and health. Thinking big is a useful habit to develop in macro-level practice.

Source: Young (1987).

---

to achieve goals they could not achieve as individuals. We can also give clients a role in running agencies by placing them on the board of directors or hiring them for certain staff roles.

Advocacy might include efforts to change policies and laws at the institutional, community, or other level. It can also involve planning for new services or modifying the way agencies allocate resources for specific programs.

Another set of advocacy activities can be under-taken with gay and lesbian clients who constitute a population-at-risk. Homophobia (irrational fear and loathing of homosexuals), even among social workers, can result in our failure to address the topic of sexuality with gay and lesbian adolescents. Often this group faces a range of problems and discrimination: they lack support from their families; are at higher risk of substance abuse, suicide, and violence; and suffer from negative stereotypes about sexual orientation held by their peers (Morrow, 1993). Sometimes these stereotypes grow out of deeply held religious beliefs. Other times they result from irrational fears that simply talking about gay and lesbian lifestyles will make people become lesbian or gay, though this is contrary to all evidence (Morrow, 1993; Bell & Hamersmith, 1981). An advocacy role for social workers might include providing information to parents and supporting them as they struggle to accept their own children.

We might also advocate for special programs to meet the needs of this group of adolescents. Developing socialization activities focusing on dating, AIDS, and talking to one's parents might be appropriate (Morrow, 1993). We can also advocate for support groups and school programs aimed at teachers.

Advocacy may involve efforts to change laws that actively discriminate against gay and lesbian individuals. Laws, policies, and practices that prohibit gays in the military, prevent gay parents from gaining custody of their children, or fail to recognize the emotional and economic importance of same-sex unions are appropriate for advocacy. In most states the partner of a dying homosexual has no rights to make medical decisions about the ill person, as legally married spouses are permitted to do. Advocating for changes in the law to recognize the emotional and legal relationships between homosexual partners is an appropriate activity for social workers.

We also know that gay and lesbian individuals experience a higher degree of violence because of their sexual orientation (Hunter & Schaecher, 1987; Hetrick & Martin, 1987). Similarly, recent studies have found gay and lesbian youth at higher risk of suicide than their peers (Proctor & Groze, 1994). This discrimination, the lack of understanding and support, and the acceptance problems experienced by homosexual adolescents contribute to this higher suicide rate. However, once we recognize that groups are at risk, social workers can more effectively advocate for appropriate programs to help reduce or eliminate the risk. Many schools provide literature on lesbian and gay life-styles that do not portray them in a negative or derogatory way. In some communities programs exist aimed at giving homosexual adolescents a place to gather and socialize, a function that the "gay bar" serves for many adults.

At the same time, schools and communities that demonstrate a sensitivity to the needs of lesbian and gay persons are under attack by conservative groups who oppose any positive references to homosexuality. Advocacy can take the form of opposing efforts by these groups to determine what is "normal" and fighting their attempts to impose their religious values on others. It can also involve supporting and voting for political candidates who truly believe in the worth and dignity of all persons, not just those whose sexual orientation matches theirs.

Principles of Macro-Level Advocacy

As should be clear by now, advocacy may be directed toward individuals, groups or organizations, elected or appointed officials, public and private human service agencies, legislative bodies, court systems, and/or governmental entities (such as the Housing Authority). We include this wide array of possibilities because any of them can prevent groups from gaining access to service or can treat them inhumanely. Undertaking advocacy efforts, however, requires that we consider several principles which should inform our efforts.

First, *we should work to increase accessibility of social services* to clients. It is not sufficient simply to offer a service without learning whether the groups we seek to serve are actually being helped. Clients for whom English is a second language will have difficulty completing lengthy forms written in English. If they can't complete the forms, they may not receive the services. We must advocate for our agencies to find ways to serve all those who need help, not just those for whom our service is convenient.

Sometimes the services themselves are satisfactory, but other problems prevent clients from using them. For example, services may be available only during the day when clients are at work. Or there may be long waiting periods before services can be received. Another problem entails service locations which are inaccessible to clients, such as when a building is not accessible to the disabled or when services are offered at sites far from clients' homes.

A second principle for social work advocates is that *we must promote service delivery that does not detract from the dignity of the groups we serve.* In other words, clients should not be put in humiliating or embarrassing situations in order to receive services. Consider a situation which requires clients wait in a filthy, crowded waiting room for hours in order to receive public assistance. It is appropriate to advocate for a change in such conditions because they are an affront to the clients' dignity.

Sometimes services are provided in a fashion that is demeaning to clients. One large county social services agency located workers' desks in a giant facility resembling a remodeled warehouse. There were no walls or partitions between the desks, so anyone within sight or hearing of the workers would know what the client and the worker were talking about. Privacy was almost nonexistent for many clients served by that agency.

A third principle is that *advocates should work to assure equal access to all who are eligible.* Services might be more accessible to white clients than to African-American or Hispanic clients because of the location of the agency or organization, lack of public transportation, or cost of services provided. This kind of service delivery is unacceptable and needs to be changed if we are to provide equal access.

Highlight 11.6 gives examples of when advocacy may be appropriate.

Guidelines for Macro-Level Advocacy

While the above suggestions for action are reasonable, they do not provide sufficient guidance for many advocacy situations. The section below offers general guidelines for advocacy.

Be Reasonable in What You Undertake

When you advocate to change an organization, you are really struggling to change the values, beliefs, and assumptions of the people who make up the organization. Advocacy may be the only reasonable alternative when

---

HIGHLIGHT 11.6

WHEN TO ADVOCATE

Advocacy is appropriate if:

1. *Client groups are refused benefits or services to which they are entitled.* This might happen when an agency staff member unilaterally decides not to provide service to a specific group or when an agency discourages all clients from asking for certain benefits.
2. *Client groups receive services that do not respect their worth and dignity as individuals.* Being talked down to or ignored when seeking assistance is one example of this.
3. *Populations-at-risk are discriminated against because of factors such as ethnic origin, beliefs, or race, and are denied social justice available to others.* Police may routinely stop and interrogate African Americans traveling through a white community simply because of their skin color.
4. *Client groups are provided services that do not come close to meeting their needs.* This can occur when a service is inadequately funded and additional money is needed to ensure that the client groups' actual needs can be met.

5. *Vulnerable groups receive services or treatment which actually cause or compound their problems.* Nursing home residents may be so heavily medicated that they become disoriented and difficult to deal with. The staff then decides further medication is needed to control their troublesome behavior.
6. *Client groups are seriously disadvantaged by the policies of the very agencies that are supposed to help them.* A state institution for the developmentally disabled might actively discourage residents from learning independent living skills because that could eventually result in the closing of the facility.
7. *Clients are prevented from exercising rights available to all citizens.* Sometimes agency foster parents are discouraged from presenting their need for higher payments to elected officials because they "might rock the boat."
8. *Client groups are negatively impacted by agency methods or facilities.* Facilities which are not handicapped-accessible prevent disabled clients from receiving services they need.

Source: Hepworth & Larsen (1990), p. 460.

an organization performs its functions poorly or actually hurts its clientele. Nevertheless, it is difficult to bring about change in some organizations and agencies, especially when there appear to be many changes needed. Obviously, it makes sense to tackle only those things that are reasonably achievable and not try to change everything at once. Remember that people have investments in the status quo. It is easier to get them to change a few things than to undertake wholesale change which threatens their survival. A social worker who wants his agency to hire some bilingual workers to help Spanish-speaking clients is more likely to be successful than a colleague who advocates that supervisors and administrators all take pay cuts to finance an expansion of services to clients. One goal is manageable and requires only that future hiring be directed toward recruitment of Spanish-speaking social workers. The other goal is an affront to administrative staff and would affect the agency in a major way.

Teamwork Often Produces Better Outcomes

While a person working alone can often achieve great ends, teams make it much easier to achieve major outcomes. Macro-level advocacy works best when many people are giving the same message. Joining with others increases your power and influence. Several workers in a county human service agency found that they were unable to help clients needing certain services because there was no resource manual available for the county. (Resource manuals contain lists of agencies that offer various services in a geographical area. They are often organized alphabetically and by the kinds of service provided.) By working with a nearby college they were able to put together a county-wide resource manual. Individually and collectively they lobbied the agency director until she agreed to pay for the printing costs and the expense of mailing the manual to all agencies in the county. While an individual worker might have been able to accomplish this goal, the combined teamwork of the social workers make it much easier to achieve.

Being an Advocate Sometimes Requires That We Not Be Nice

Keep in mind that you can't always be the nice person. Consistently being nice means sometimes ignoring very real grievances and injustices. Trying to change things will cause you to make some enemies from time to time. Remember that today's enemies are tomorrow's allies. The agency director who is upset with you today because you pointed out that he was not providing services to women clients despite his pledge to do so will welcome your support next year when he requests additional funding to expand these services.

Flexibility Is a Strength, Not a Weakness

Be flexible—sometimes an approach may call for being bullheaded and difficult to deal with. Other times you need to be more flexible, warm, and friendly. You must be able to select the appropriate behavior depending upon the need. Mary Andrews is a case in point. She is one of the most gentle, warm, and easygoing workers in the Frunk County Department of Human Services. Everyone likes her. However, when her agency began to propose budget cuts that would significantly reduce services to unmarried teenage mothers, she became the strongest possible advocate. She confronted the agency's administrative council (consisting of supervisors and administrators) with the needs of this group and the potential consequences of ending services to them, and pointed out that proposed cutbacks were contrary to the agency's mission of helping the most vulnerable groups in society. She spoke with passion, marshaled facts, and challenged her superiors to do the right thing. Some of the supervisors were upset at her actions, but her arguments won over the majority. Mary had taken the risk of upsetting people because unmarried teenage mothers had no other advocate in the system.

Sometimes We Win—Sometimes We Lose

Sometimes your advocacy efforts will not achieve your goals, but you may be able to block your opponents from achieving theirs. Or at least you may force your opponents to take your ideas into account. You may not be successful getting the city to create a new homeless shelter, but you may be able to stop them from closing an existing shelter. You might also force them to relocate a proposed highway which threatens an intact, but poor, neighborhood and would create additional homelessness.

Be Prepared to Use a Variety of Strategies

We are not suggesting that advocacy must be a confrontational or win-lose experience. In fact, we have stressed that collaborative strategies should probably be tried first. Taking a matter to court, for example, is a confrontational act which can lead to appeals no matter who wins. Any situation that continually results in a win-lose outcome is likely to frustrate everyone involved. Win-win approaches are more likely to work. Disputes may be resolved through negotiation, arbitration, or mediation.

Advocacy Tactics

A variety of tactics can be employed to advocate for client groups. Most of them are part of the educational preparation of the generalist social worker. These include persuasion, fair hearings, legal action, embarrassment of the target, political pressure and petitioning. We will address each of these in the following sections.

Persuasion

Persuasion can take the form of providing the target system (the one we wish to change) with additional information that may allow them to make a different decision. Hoffman and Sallee (1994) have identified three useful ways to persuade others. One method, Inductive Questioning, simply means asking the target system a series of questions designed to make them think about their original conclusion. If you believe that someone has made a decision based upon faulty information, you can ask them whether that information is available in public records. A follow-up question might be whether anyone has double-checked to see whether the information provided verbally is consistent with the published information. If you are trying to develop a juvenile detention facility in the community (because juveniles who are now detained end up in the city jail with adult felons) the mayor might state that she sees no need for a juvenile detention facility in the community. You can challenge her with a question such as, ''Can you indicate the number of juveniles who were incarcerated in the city jail last year because there was no detention facility? How does that number compare to the average for a city our size?''

A second approach to persuasion is to provide arguments on both sides of an issue. This involves stating not only your opinions and facts, but also acknowledging the opinions, concerns, and facts of the other side. The advantage of this is that it lets the other side know you understand their arguments but still think your position makes the most sense. It also surprises people used to hearing only one side of the argument. Perhaps you are trying to get a program started to provide needles and bleach (for sterilizing needles) for drug users to help prevent the spread of AIDS. You know the research shows that this is an effective method for slowing the AIDS epidemic. At the same time, you must be able to articulate all of the arguments against your idea and have responses for each.

Persistence as a persuader is a strong suit. Most people give up when they meet resistance. The target system may expect you to give in too. A social worker who perseveres, determined but not abrasive, will win points. Suppose you are a part of a group trying to develop a recreation center for barrio children. You have found an abandoned building, and a civic group has promised to provide funds to renovate it. The city manager has promised to check into having the city take ownership of the building, because the taxes on it have not been paid in years. Unless the city owns the building, the project can't go forward.

Despite the promises, however, the mayor has taken no action. A patient, repetitive request for a progress report every week or so may turn out to be very effective. The mayor may decide it is easier to do what you want than to have you come around and check on him every week. It's worth a try.

Fair Hearings, Grievances, and Complaints

Fair hearings and grievances are administrative procedures designed to ensure that clients or client groups who have been denied benefits or rights to which they are entitled get equitable treatment. In fair hearings, clients notify the agency that they wish to have a fair hearing concerning the decision-maker's actions. This means that an outside person (usually a state employee) is appointed to hear both sides of the argument. If the fair hearing examiner finds that the decision-maker has violated state or federal policies, the examiner will direct the individual or agency to comply with the rules and award the client his or her rightful benefits. This approach makes sense when a public agency has been

ADVOCACY IN ACTION

Mendel Hawkins knew that his support group for parents at risk for abusing their children maintained a tentative existence. Attendance was often spotty. Members could elect not to attend because participation was completely voluntary. However, Mendel did not think lack of interest was the barrier. It was true that parents often gave various reasons for their poor attendance, which made it difficult to identify the problem. Mendel's agency thought the group was important enough to assign him to lead it, but he wasn't sure whether they would continue to support it with its poor attendance. While Mendel and Annie, his supervisor, discussed the situation from time to time, they remained unsuccessful at figuring out the root of the problem.

Mendel proposed asking group members to help him problem solve. Annie, however, did not think it wise to ask clients for their ideas. "I doubt they can provide much insight," she said. "Most of them don't have experience solving their own problems. How do you expect them to solve ours?" Pushing the idea a bit, Mendel decided on his own to ask the parent group members about their attendance. It soon became clear that two factors were limiting attendance. First, most parents in the group were low income and had limited resources. They usually lacked reliable transportation and, if they owned a car, it was not in good shape. Frequent breakdowns made it impossible to plan for anything until you went out to see whether the car would start.

In addition, there was the problem of inertia, of just getting up and moving. Members of the parents' group said they would come regularly if they had transportation, especially if they knew someone was coming to get them. From this discussion was born the idea of having a group member provide rides, with the agency reimbursing the driver for gas. At least two of the group members said they would be willing to drive others to the group, picking them up on the way. However, they could not afford the cost of serving as a carpool. Mendel doubted the agency would like this idea, but elected to test the suggestion on his supervi-

sor. Annie laughed when Mendel made the suggestion. "Why don't we just send a chauffeured limousine for them?" she asked, only half kidding.

"Look," said Mendel "we have the chance to try a new idea at relatively little cost to reach a population this agency says it wants to reach. We told the United Way that we serve parents at risk of abuse and that we are truly interested in outreach. Well, here we have the chance to put our money where our mouth is and get some real results. Take the idea to Ben (the deputy director). Tell him we're only asking for an average of $10 per meeting to reimburse one driver for gas. That comes out to an average of $2 per person and reliably doubles the number of members who attend each week. We might even be able to use this idea, especially if it works, to convince the county board that we are a really innovative agency and should get money for a purchase-of-service contract for doing something the public agency should be doing."

"Right, and horses can fly" replied Ann. Nevertheless, she proposed the idea to Ben, who thought it was a marvelous and inexpensive way to get to a hard-to-reach client group. "Tell Mendel I'll allocate $500 to the project, but I want an evaluation. How many clients attended each meeting before and after we started to provide transportation? What was the average cost per client? And ask Mendel to take more time with his group to see if there are other things we can be doing that are low cost and creative. I'm going to approach the Aloyious Lutheran Church Women's Auxiliary about funding this idea on a continuing basis if it pays off. I don't think Mendel is realistic about the county picking up the tab, but I think the auxiliary is looking for an innovative way to help in the area of child abuse. That's their focus this year. I think we can get some help on this one. Now get out of here and let me eat my lunch."

With that, Annie bounced out of her chair and headed for the door. "Thanks, Boss," she called as she headed back to her office. Once again, Mendel's advocacy for clients had paid off.

denying benefits to a group or clearly violating rules they are required to follow.

Grievances and complaints are also mechanisms for dealing with a decision-maker who has violated policy. Grievance procedures may be part of an agency's own policies. For unionized workers, they are often part of the union agreement between employees and the employer. An example of how this might work comes from a public social work agency. The agency director decided that agency staff would no longer be permitted to take their fifteen-minute afternoon break. The director's goal was to increase the daily productivity of each staff member by fifteen minutes. However, the social workers filed a grievance under their union contract and won. The agency director was required to pay each employee for fifteen minutes worth of work each day for the entire period his silly policy was in place. The result, following the effective use of a grievance procedure, was an expensive embarrassment for the agency.

Complaints are similar to grievances but are provided for in certain laws. In a recent situation, a large restaurant chain was treating African-American customers with disrespect. They provided poor service, and generally discouraged the customers from eating there. A group of customers filed a civil rights complaint against the firm and forced the company to change its practices.

Similarly, people with disabilities must be granted reasonable accommodation by employers if that will enable the person to do a given job. Some employers, however, routinely refuse to hire the disabled. Complaints can be filed with the state and federal governments under the Americans with Disabilities Act (ADA) to force compliance with the law.

Sometimes just the threat of using the formal grievance or complaint process is enough to change an adverse decision. Other times, the agency has no policy for a fair hearing or appeal. Then other confrontational tactics can be employed. It is often possible to seek advice and assistance from an attorney. Not infrequently, an attorney's letter suggesting the possibility of legal action is sufficient to cause adversaries to change their position. Pursuing legal action is a major endeavor and will be addressed as a part of social action. It is important to keep in mind that tactics and approaches such as fair hearings, complaints, and grievances, which are often used in case advocacy, can be used just as effectively for cause advocacy.

Embarrassing the Target

Most of us like to think of ourselves as decent individuals who treat others with a reasonable degree of fairness. Consequently, it is upsetting when others point out that we are not what we hold ourselves out to be. This is also true of organizations that purport to be sensitive to their clients' needs. When opponents use the media to call attention to one's failings, the result is predictable. The embarrassment can either persuade the target to change in the desired direction or result in even greater intransigence. Thus, embarrassing the target carries a degree of risk.

Letters to the local newspaper may focus attention on a target, especially if enough people write. Picketing an organization or handing out flyers pointing out what the agency is not doing is another way of embarrassing the target. Sit-ins and demonstrations are also tactics designed to embarrass (and inconvenience) the target. Both involve ''massing or marching together in highly visible settings or picketing the entrances of buildings where the behavior that the demonstrators find objectionable is believed to be taking place'' (Barker, 1991, p. 59). In the case of sit-ins, you physically occupy the offices or hallways of the organization you are attempting to embarrass.

Political Pressure

Political pressure is the application of political power to force changes which would not otherwise occur. Not all agencies, organizations, or situations are susceptible to political pressure. Public (tax supported) organizations are more likely to be sensitive to the concerns of political figures. Elected officials may be contacted and asked to look into a matter that falls under their jurisdiction. Take the example of a neighborhood where a significant population of Native Americans live. The streets in the area are in terrible condition and the city never seems to repair them. In addition, the streets are never plowed during the winter, so many residents are stranded in their homes. How do you deal with the failure of the city to perform the same functions for this neighborhood and these residents that it does for others? You might contact a city council member and ask her or him to look into the situation. The council member could inquire why the street department does not sched-

---

HIGHLIGHT 11.8

EMBARRASSING THE TARGET

A residential treatment center serving predominantly Hispanic children was run by a director who encouraged staff to use corporal punishment, ignored needs of the residents, and generally did not provide effective training for staff. The emotional problems experienced by many boys were ignored and led to several attempted suicides, frequent runaways, and other problems.

After approaching the director and failing to convince her to make improvements, the staff decided to undertake a series of actions. One such step was informing the news media of the conditions at the center. Once the local television station and newspapers picked up the story, the situation was too embarrassing for the director and her superiors to sweep under the rug. The director was forced to step down and new policies were adopted at the center that recognized the physical and emotional needs of the residents. The decision to involve the media was difficult, but there was no other way of protecting the needs of a vulnerable population-at-risk.

---

ule repairs in this part of town. She or he might also ask for city records showing the snowplowing routes during the winter. Just having a political figure ask these questions may be sufficient to bring a change.

At the state level, a social worker can contact a member of the legislature about a persistent problem involving funding for the mentally ill, clearly a population-at-risk. The legislator may ask the head of the state division of mental health why chronically mentally ill clients are not being provided services mandated by state law. This usually will bring some action or response from the agency or its staff. Publicly funded agencies do not enjoy having legislators looking over their shoulders, especially when they are not doing things they should be doing. At the same time, political figures must respond to constituent concerns in order to get reelected.

Petitioning

Petitioning is the act of collecting signatures on a piece of paper asking an organization or agency to act in a specified manner. A social worker might help a neighborhood petition the city for better police protection to deal with drug use and gang violence. Gathering petitions can be done by going door to door asking each resident to sign, or by setting up in central location where large numbers of people normally congregate.

Thus, a local beauty parlor, bar, barbershop, or shopping area may be appropriate. Although petition signatures are relatively easy to collect, this is also one of their limitations. Because they are easy to gather, petitions may not have the desired impact on the target system. The target system might conclude that the people who signed the petition don't really feel very strongly about the matter.

It is perhaps most helpful to present petitions in a public forum. Thus, you might present the petitions to the city council at the body's regular meeting. Presenting them at a time when others can see what you are doing helps make your efforts a matter of public record. In the case that opened the chapter, the Neighborhood Association used petitions to support its case that there should be no overnight parking allowed in their area. Highlight 11.9 presents a possible petition form.

Blank petition forms are usually photocopied so that several people can collect petitions at the same time. Extra copies of the petition can also be placed at appropriate locations.

Social Action

In our earlier section on definitions, we said that social action is "a coordinated effort to achieve institutional

---

HIGHLIGHT 11.9

A PETITION FORM

As residents of neighborhoods along Bush Creek, we are outraged by the City of Paris's failure to stop the pollution in this waterway. Raw sewage wastes, including fecal matter, are being discharged into Bush Creek endangering the health of our children and ourselves. Waterford Park, the only playground in our area, is closed because the Creek runs right through the middle of the park. We, the undersigned, demand that the City Council bring an immediate end to the sewage discharge, clean up the existing pollution in Bush Creek, and reopen Waterford Park.

_____ _____ _____ _____

_____ _____ _____ _____

_____ _____ _____ _____

_____ _____ _____ _____

_____ _____ _____ _____

_____ _____ _____ _____

_____ _____ _____ _____

---

change to meet a need, solve a social problem, correct an injustice, or enhance the quality of human life''(Barker, 1991, p. 217). Social action usually involves more complex, complicated, and confrontational approaches to achieving goals than your usual day-to-day work entails. As a consequence, the use of some social action tactics raises difficult questions and produces differences of opinion about social work's obligation to use this approach.

Alinsky's Social Action Approach

Saul Alinsky (1971), a strong advocate of militant social action activities on behalf of the poor, offers some key perspectives on social action that still have great relevance a quarter century after they were articulated. According to Alinsky, *power* is essential to change the status quo. Those individuals and organizations with power can control their environment much more easily than those with little or no power. Power may come in the form of human or financial resources. When you lack money, you need people to overcome that deficit. When enough people are involved and concerned about something, even those with money can't stop progress. The civil rights movement in the United States involved so many people that it helped bring an end to laws discriminating against African Americans and other persons of color.

A corollary is that power is not the sum of what you actually have, but rather the sum of the *appearance* of what you have. To phase it differently, it matters less how much power you actually have than how much power others *think* you have. Social workers in many states were successful in achieving licensing for their profession despite that fact that the actual number of social workers is relatively small. Lawmakers assumed that a sizable group was interested in the legislation because they were hearing from so many people.

A third rule described by Alinsky is that power is not given to you. Rather, you acquire it by taking it from those who have it. Thus, the very act of acquiring power is potentially confrontational.

Alinsky's fourth guideline recommends that the methods used to achieve goals should be familiar to those seeking power (in your case, the action system) and unfamiliar to the target system. In other words, it is easier to be successful when your opponents are caught off guard by your methods. Consider the refusal of the city public works committee to recommend paving gravel roads in a low income neighborhood. The committee of seven individuals meets in a small room at city hall which has seats for an audience of fifteen people. Having all 150 members of your neighborhood group attend a public works committee meeting will undoubtedly catch the committee off guard. At the same time, the methods you use must be consistent with the interests, wishes, and needs of the group with whom you are working.

Fifth, Alinsky believed that all organizations have rules which they say they live by. The rules may be policies, laws, or other regulations that the organization must follow. By making them live within their announced policies and rules, you are asking nothing more than what they say they normally do. Since those rules are generally based on a set of high moral standards, by living within their own rules, an organization often becomes much fairer in dealing with others. An organization that refuses to hire people with disabilities despite laws prohibiting such discrimination can be forced to obey the rules.

A sixth rule is that people should be organized around issues that are vital to them. For example, if gay or lesbian teachers are being denied employment in the school system because of their sexual orientation, this is a significant issue. It makes more sense to use employment discrimination as the focal point rather than to highlight a concern with less impact on the group members. Stated differently, you will have much less success getting people involved in issues about which they don't care.

A seventh rule involves using political pressure. According to Alinsky, most people in power respond to political pressure. Whether this is right or wrong is immaterial. If you know which buttons to push, push them.

A more controversial eighth guideline suggests that successfully attacking a target requires a clear demarcation between good and evil, or haves and have-nots. It is much easier for people on the sidelines to take action if the differences between the groups are clear. This requires, however, that you paint your opponent as bad and yourself as good. Take the situation of an employer who refuses to hire women because the job involves exposure to chemicals that can cause birth defects. It is easy to portray the employer as sexist, guilty of gender discrimination, and a law violator. At the same time, you can paint yourself as concerned about sex discrimination and equal rights for women. This is the good-bad characterization of which Alinsky speaks.

Extreme positions like this can backfire, however, when others do not view your opponent in the same light. In the above example, some may think the employer is really concerned about women and does not want them exposed to substances that produce birth defects. Others may believe he is taking a reasonable approach to reducing his liabilities, since he could be sued for placing workers in an environment where they could be hurt.

Alinsky also suggested a ninth principle, namely, turning negatives into positives. He says you must expect to lose some fights, so you must always be prepared to salvage whatever is possible. This way you can learn from the negative and can perhaps figure out a more effective strategy next time. It is common for the losing party in a dispute to say that its real goal was to have its grievances heard or to draw attention to a particular problem. This is an attempt to turn a negative (losing) into a positive (spotlighting a problem). In political jargon this is called *spin*.

A tenth rule suggested by Alinsky is preparing yourself to propose an alternative. Ripping away at the enemy is fine until the time comes to propose a different solution. Be ready with that solution. Otherwise, you become identified as a crank or inveterate caviler (chronic complainer). If the city says it cannot provide sufficient additional police to patrol an area wracked by burglaries and assaults, perhaps you can propose that the police help organize a citizen patrol and neighborhood watch program to help reduce crime.

Concerns about Social Action

Zippay (1994) argues that some of Alinsky's principles are less useful today than when he first articulated them. For example, she notes that enemies are harder to identify and that the high tech world of today makes the role of the media much more influential in affecting ideas, perceptions, and actions. In addition, the tactic of mobilizing one group to attack another typically polarizes people while other approaches may accomplish the same end without the same side effects.

Zippay also argues that we need to connect people to existing sources of power both inside and outside the community. She emphasizes the role of external resources in solving community problems. The nature of many community problems precludes solution without outside funds, according to her perspective. By themselves, cities don't have enough money to solve such major problems as drug abuse and unemployment. She urges the need to work with business, civic, and community leaders to achieve goals instead of creating an us-against-them approach. The skills she believes are most important for neighborhood leaders include understanding bureaucracies and political systems; fundraising; legislative advocacy and lobbying; and working with local boards, business leaders, and committees. For the most part, these are much more collaborative approaches than Alinsky advocates. The debate about which strategies and tactics to use is likely to continue because both arguments have merit and both have proven effective in different situations. Perhaps the most important lesson from this debate is that to be effective generalists social workers must be flexible.

Legal Action

Legal action has been used for many years to force changes that would otherwise not have occurred. Women's right to an abortion was not recognized until the 1973 decision in *Roe v. Wade*. More recently, the courts have prevented states from placing severe restrictions on the right to an abortion.

The long-standing practice of having "separate but equal" school systems for African Americans and whites (which produced greatly inferior facilities and teaching materials for the former) was struck down in 1954 in a court case (*Brown v. Board of Education*). More recently, courts have been used to end practices that allow one school district to spend substantial amounts on each student while another poorer district spends a fraction of the amount. By doing so, the courts have acted to prevent some districts from continuing funding practices that discriminate against the poor.

Yet another example of using the courts involves Native Americans. Many tribes suffered major losses in the 1800s when tribal lands were stolen or acquired through exploitation. Court decisions have returned lands or required restitution to the plaintiff tribes. In these instances, the courts have been able to resolve disputes that had existed for a century.

Courts have also been a resource for powerless people to force organizations and institutions to abide by existing laws. The Americans with Disabilities Act has provided a means for courts to force an end to discrimination against people with disabilities. Legal action has also been used to achieve new interpretations of old laws.

Legal action is used when it appears that one party has not been abiding by generally accepted rules. Perhaps, your adversary has broken the law. Maybe the agency or organization has not operated in accordance with its own policies and procedures. Sometimes rights granted by the U.S. Constitution, such as due process, are not followed. Due process requires that organizations observe "rules, procedures, protections, and opportunities legally available" before depriving someone of liberty, property, or life (Barker, 1991, p. 68).

Taking legal action is definitely a form of confrontation. It is designed to threaten, embarrass, or otherwise coerce your opponents into doing something they would not otherwise do. Legal action may be taken against individuals, groups, agencies, organizations, companies, and governments. It can be taken on behalf of an individual person or organization, or on behalf of a class of individuals. Such *class action suits* argue that an entire group has been hurt and needs the courts' help to remedy the problem. Class action suits have been used on behalf of people who have certain things in common, such as race or gender. A suit could be filed on behalf

---

HIGHLIGHT 11.10

SOCIAL ACTION ON BEHALF OF THE HOMELESS: SOME CONSIDERATIONS

Social action strategies designed to help the homeless must recognize that the homeless are not a homogeneous group. Thus, the strategies for help may have to be different depending upon the needs of a particular subgroup. For example, North and Smith (1994) found that homelessness among nonwhite people was most often caused by socioeconomic problems (lower income, welfare system inadequacy) while whites were more likely to have problems caused by drug abuse or psychiatric illness. There were major differences within each group, however. Would these observed differences between the two groups suggest different types of programs?

There is substantial evidence that many homeless people are being sheltered by family and friends. Yet we have no policies or programs to assist these caregivers who are clearly helping the oppressed. Is this an appropriate goal for social action?

Homeless children are more likely to lack immunizations and at greater risk of failing in school according to Ziesemer, Marcoux & Marwell (1994). Which of these problems is the most pressing? Why?

Meeting the needs of the homeless may entail such varied strategies as stress management for problems associated with poverty; reducing the number of stressors impacting on people; reducing stress by such actions as having homeless shelters remain "open all day, by allowing older siblings and fathers to remain with their families, by providing day care and preschool programs, by providing supportive services during and after a shelter stay, and by allowing choice and control over daily living. Schools can reduce stress by removing barriers to enrollment, easing access to various programs, and "providing transportation, parent-student orientation, free breakfast and lunch, school supplies, and a safe place for possessions" (Ziesemer, Marcoux, & Marwell, 1994, p. 667). Depending upon the barriers to achieving these goals, appropriate strategies might range from advocacy to social action.

---

of men denied employment at a restaurant that has historically hired only women. While a single plaintiff may start the process, it is common for such suits to become class action suits, since all members of the group are affected.

Of course, you do not always have to use the more drastic step of going to court. Sometimes, the suggestion that one is ready and able to seek redress through legal action accomplishes the same purpose. Most people prefer to avoid lawsuits because of the cost, bad publicity, and time involved. Indicating to adversaries that you are seriously considering suing them can get their attention. Rubin and Rubin (1986) suggest that lawsuits are more effective threats against those who do not have their own attorneys. Agencies or organizations that have attorneys on staff have an advantage. They can simply assign that individual to deal with your case and it costs them little or nothing. Thus, the threat of a suit may be more credible against those who must acquire outside legal assistance. Even thinking about having to hire an attorney and go to court may be sufficient reason to reconsider one's position.

There are other benefits to using legal action to achieve the goals of your group. As Homan (1994) has indicated, finding that the courts will help you is an empowering experience for those long used to having no power. Moreover, lawsuits are a way of working through channels and using the system to accomplish your goals (Rubin & Rubin, 1986).

Another benefit is that courts tend to be more immune to the political process, so there is less likelihood that the judge will be swayed by contributions, letters, phone calls, or other tactics used in other circumstances. This can be to your advantage.

On the other hand, lawsuits can seemingly take forever to run their course, leaving you and your group waiting. The process of accepting delays, dealing with postponements, and the like can sap the strength of everyone involved in the process. Delays tend to favor those with the most resources and the most to lose when the case is settled. Thus, this party to the suit normally seeks delays. The tendency for things to be delayed can also work in your favor. Projects which are tied up in court may be abandoned as costs mount or deals fall through. Court delays can also lead to other tactics for changing the situation. A court delay might allow time for a change in the law to become effective. It might even allow you enough time to get a law changed or enacted. Delays may also encourage the other party to compromise rather than have the threat of the court decision hanging over them. Thus, delays should not necessarily be considered an evil. They can work to your benefit.

The attorney who will represent you in a court case should be consulted to determine typical concerns such as costs, how long it is likely to take before the case is resolved, and the probability of succeeding with your suit. Attorneys can also explain some of the formal procedures and terminology you will encounter in the court system. The very act of filing a lawsuit can give you information about your opponents that was not previously available. A legal step entitled discovery allows each side to see documents in the possession of the other. Let's say that a social agency is proposing to sell the homeless shelter they own to a developer who will tear it down to build an office building. You might learn through discovery that this sale violates the terms of the agreement under which a donor gave the agency the building to begin with.

When you decide to use legal action to pursue your claim, others may brand you as a troublemaker. Accept the label as a cost of dealing with people whose own behaviors are the real problem. If you are put off by being labeled, you will lose some of your ability to succeed. The other side counts on your wishing to be seen in a favorable light. They hope that by attacking you or your group, they can dissuade you from your lawsuit. Remind your critic that what you are doing is equivalent to calling the police to stop someone from committing a robbery. If the policies or actions of others were not violating the rights of your clients, the lawsuit would be unnecessary.

Courts are also a good place to deal with certain types of situations. Court injunctions, for example, are sought when immediate steps are needed to stop an impending action which, if allowed to proceed, could not be undone. Let's take the example of a university that plans to tear down houses in a low-income neighborhood adjacent to its campus in order to build a performing arts center. The residents have long maintained that the university is insensitive to the neighborhood's needs. Now the university wishes to further destroy their neighborhood. Filing a suit over the proposed destruction would take too long, and the university would go ahead with its plans while the suit was under way. But neighborhood residents can ask the court for an injunction to stop the university from any action which would destroy the neighborhood. If granted, the injunction allows the neighbors time to file a suit challenging the university's action because the injunction prevents the university from doing anything until the suit is resolved in court.

Legal action can be used for other purposes. Perhaps a law is so confusing that it is not being enforced or its enforcement is uneven. Courts can interpret a law to ensure a consistent perspective on its intent. Sometimes the court will rule that a law is simply unworkable because it is too broad or is poorly worded. Court suits can force people to do things they promised to do. Suing an agency for specific performance means that you want them to follow agreements into which they entered. Sometimes money can be sought from those whose actions have hurt others. Money damages might be demanded from an organization that wrongfully discharged minority workers or discriminated against women in the hiring process.

As you have seen, legal action can be employed for a great many purposes. Moreover, even the threat of legal action can be effective. Legal action can force organizations to follow the laws or their own rules, or to make them live up to their promises. Successful lawsuits can help empower a group. At the same time, legal action is expensive, time consuming, and may ultimately be unsuccessful. Like other methods, legal action should be pursued when it is the most appropriate way to resolve a problem.

Empowerment

As described earlier, empowerment suggests that people have "the right to power, ability, and authority to achieve self-determination.'' (Hartman, 1993, p. 365). Social workers generally observe the principle that clients have the right to self-determination. However, as Hartman notes, ''self-determination was a hollow promise sharply limited by lack of access to resources, to opportunity, to power'' (p. 365). The absence of alternatives, outright oppression, and exploitation all lower the opportunity to self-determine and can result in social and economic injustice. Though social workers might like to believe otherwise, power is unequal in the client-worker relationship—clients have less, we have more. Some of this power is vested in the agency through its resources. Hartman suggests that sharing power with clients may mean giving clients more role in deciding how agency resources are spent, organizing clients of the agency as a collective and dealing with them as a group, and creating alternative programs.

Other sources of power can inhibit client empowerment. For example, your expert knowledge is a form of power which can further distance you from clients. You also gain power over clients by your ability to persuade them. This power grows out of interpersonal skills such as empathy and your rapport with clients. When you say or do things that confuse clients, you reduce their power. When you use your power to make something happen to benefit the client, you are also increasing the power imbalance.

Demystifying what you do can empower clients. Rather than telling a client group, ''I talked to a friend of mine at city hall and he has agreed to meet your group to talk about what can be done,'' suggest that the group leader contact the official directly.

A fourth source of power is the legitimate authority vested in you by the state. Social workers who work for public agencies, such as protective services or probation and parole, have social control roles which can conflict with the profession's commitment to empowering people. Because of your role, client groups may tell you what they you want to hear rather than share their true feelings. Thus, this power can get in the way of client groups being honest and able to discuss their problems freely.

The strengths perspective, so important to generalist practice (Saleebey, 1992), assumes that power resides in people and we should seek it through such things as refusing to label clients, avoiding paternalistic treatment of clients, and trusting clients to make appropriate decisions. Group work tends to be empowering because

it emphasizes collaboration and collective problem solving. Macro practice that involves the use of client groups to achieve identified goals extends this empowerment.

In summary, empowerment of oppressed groups and of those experiencing social and economic injustice is a legitimate goal for generalist social workers. It is consistent with our commitment to improve social conditions, assist populations-at-risk, and restore the capacity of people to solve their own problems.

Legislative Advocacy[1]

Earlier in this chapter we discussed case advocacy and cause advocacy. In this section we will discuss *legislative advocacy*, which is similar to cause advocacy in that the social worker is working for a broad category of clients or citizens. Legislative advocacy specifically involves efforts to change legislation to benefit some category of clients. It is a macro-level intervention. At its most basic, it involves urging lawmakers to pass the laws you want. For simplicity, we will use the term ''legislators'' to refer to both state and federal lawmakers.

Legislative advocacy may also include efforts to defeat bills considered harmful in some way (Dear and Patti, 1987). A proposed reduction in funding for the Headstart program would mean limiting or cutting off Headstart services previously available to clients. Headstart is a ''federal program established in 1965 to provide preschool children of disadvantaged minority families with compensatory education to offset some of the effects of their social deprivations (Barker, 1987, p. 69).

Another example of harmful legislation is a proposed state bill to restrict access to reproductive health services such as Planned Parenthood. This agency provides information, contraception, counseling, and physical examinations, all directed at helping people (usually women) gain control over their own reproduction. Services are usually provided on a sliding fee scale. This means that fees are based on how much people can pay. Poorer people pay less. Richer people pay more.

Legislation limiting access might incorporate requirements such as forcing women under age eighteen

---

1. Material in this section is adapted from *Understanding Generalist Practice*, by Karen Kirst-Ashman and Grafton H. Hull Jr. Used with permission of Nelson-Hall, Inc.

to provide written parental permission before they can receive any services. This type of legislation has been introduced at both state and federal levels. Another inhibiting proposal might involve denying any state or federal funding if agency staff discuss abortion as a possible alternative to unwanted pregnancy. Both of these examples limit available services. The first places restrictions on the basis of age. The second limits the potential for informing clients of the options available to them.

Responsibility for legislative advocacy is part of being a social worker because so many decisions affecting social work programs, social workers, and clients are made in the legislative arena. Thus, it is impossible *not* to be concerned about and involved in legislative advocacy. Some workers may feel a bit awed at the prospect of trying to get laws passed and programs funded. Fortunately, legislative advocacy has one unique feature which makes this less difficult. The primary rule of legislative advocacy is that getting elected and reelected tends to be very important to most legislators (Dear & Patti, 1987). This means that most legislators want to know what their constituents want and, are therefore, susceptible to their constituents' influence.

In addition, most legislators must make decisions about many proposed bills based on very limited information. Bills are often complex. This increases the likelihood that a legislator will depend on others for information. As a consequence, legislators may very well be influenced by a small number of advocates or by a particularly persuasive argument about a given bill. In other words, you are encouraged to tell your state and federal senators and representatives what you think should be done about bills and issues. You can also mobilize other workers or clients to write or call in what they think. This is one means of gaining some power over which laws are passed or defeated in the political process.

Simultaneously, realistic barriers reduce the likelihood of getting new legislation passed. First, there is the fact that the majority of bills do not become law. At the state level, only about 20 percent of proposed bills receive legislative approval and are signed by the governor (Dear & Patti, 1981, p. 289). At the federal level, an even smaller portion become law. Moreover, most legislative sessions are somewhat short, lasting only a matter of months. Lawmakers might not even get to the bill you're interested in. This means that desired legislation may have to be reintroduced next year. Often

this involves starting the whole process of influence over from scratch.

Additionally, legislative bodies are unpredictable. Turnover in membership from session to session after elections, changes in control (from Republican to Democratic leadership or vice versa), and economic news (lower than expected tax revenues resulting in less available money) make the entire legislative process more complicated. People in power also make unpredictable decisions that affect legislation. In a recent race for president, the successful candidate pledged, ''No new taxes.'' However, within a short time he approved new taxes sought by the opposing party. His change in position became an issue when he ran for reelection. The unpredictability of the legislative process and the importance of compromise in the political environment also mean that a candidate's past positions are no guarantee of future actions. Social workers must be clear about this.

Complicating matters further is the fact that even bills that seem to benefit everyone may not become law. Patti and Dear (1975) note that even documented evidence strongly supporting a bill will not guarantee passage (p. 110). A number of factors can kill a potentially good bill. These include economic conditions and political positions taken by the lawmaker or a political party. In addition, the values and personal experiences of legislators can derail a bill. For example, the effort by the NASW to achieve licensure for social workers in one state was stymied for years because the speaker of the house was personally opposed to social workers. The point is that many factors may override logic and compelling arguments and defeat a bill.

To make matters more complex, even a legislator's agreement to support a bill may prove meaningless. Pet projects of legislators can end up buried or defeated in a committee. Legislative committees are smaller groups of legislators who evaluate the merits of each bill and decide whether to recommend it to the entire legislature. If a committee does send a bill to the floor of the legislature, it may still be defeated or returned to committee for further work. Finally, governors and presidents can, and often do, veto bills for their own reasons.

Factors Affecting Legislative Advocacy

Success as a legislative advocate requires an understanding of the factors influencing the legislative process.

The financial or fiscal implications of a bill are perhaps most important to its chances for success. Put simply, bills that cost a lot of money are less likely to be approved.

A bill's popularity is also a significant factor. The more people (whether the general public or legislators) who support a bill, the more likely it is to pass. In addition, a bill is more likely to pass if it targets a group or issue that is seen as a problem by the rest of society. Bills to increase the length of prison terms for certain types of crimes or to require mandatory sentences for drug pushers tend to pass more easily. At the same time, a bill to provide more money for drug-related education in the schools is less likely to be passed because it will cost more money.

Steps in Legislative Advocacy

State and federal legislatures follow a similar series of steps in the process of turning ideas into laws. These steps are also appropriate intervention points for social workers seeking input in the legislative arena. The steps for legislative advocacy include the following: developing a draft of the bill; figuring out who else will help you support the bill; getting specific legislators to sponsor the bill; asking your legislative sponsors to introduce the bill; educating the general public about the bill's value; trying to influence positively any legislative subcommittee members responsible for decision-making about the bills; and trying to influence other legislators to vote for the bill's passage.

Step 1: Developing and Revising the Draft Bill

Formulating an original piece of legislation may sound formidable. It requires both legal knowledge and a familiarity with existing laws, related policies, and programs related to the proposed bill. Consequently, most ideas for laws are sent to an already established unit (sometimes called a legislative reference bureau) which is responsible for writing the first draft of a bill. Reference bureau staff develop a synopsis of the bill to help legislators understand its intent. Once in draft form, the bill needs further refinement, including clarifications and changes to make the bill reflect its supporters' intentions. If your bill would establish funding for low-income day-care centers, you want to be sure the bill defines what low-income means.

Because legislative reference bureaus work for the legislative body, it is difficult for social workers to have much direct impact on their work. As a result, a bill can languish for a time before the reference bureau staff gives it the needed attention. One state bill strongly sought by social workers was buried in the reference bureau for eleven months and was released about a week before the legislative session ended. As a result, the bill died without ever coming before the lawmakers.

Influencing the reference bureau to develop, revise, and complete work on a law can often be more effectively done by a member of the legislature. Thus it may be appropriate to seek a legislator's assistance if a bill seems to be stuck in the bureaucracy.

In the process of pursuing a macro intervention in the legislative arena you will have to become something of an expert on the bill(s) in which you have an interest. Kleinkauf (1981, pp. 298–302) recommends that you adequately research any bill so that you know exactly what it says and what other bills or laws may be affected by it. Learn which other agencies and organizations have taken a position on the bill, who the sponsors are, and the history of this bill. After all, it would be most embarrassing to write a letter to U.S. senator asking for support of a bill funding family planning services when, in fact, that senator is one of its chief sponsors.

Step 2: Identifying, Obtaining, and Maintaining the Bill's Supporters

Every bill has some natural supporters. These are individuals or groups that are naturally interested in the bill's topic or will obviously benefit from the bill. Make a list of those individuals and groups. They are potential allies.

It is equally important to predict who will be neutral or opposed to a bill. If you hope to see this bill become law, you need to know who will work against it. Those who are initially neutral are potential supporters. Later, you may be able to persuade them to support the bill. Lists of supporters and opponents will include legislators, legislative staffs, external groups (for example, the National Association of Social Workers [NASW]), governmental agencies (for instance, the Department of Health and Social Services), social service providers, and those who will benefit from the bill.

Once you have identified potential supporters, it is essential to iron out any differences between groups that support the bill. It is not uncommon for people to support bills for vastly different reasons. As a result, each group may have ideas for improving the bill. One group may dislike a particular section or wording. These differing perspectives must be reconciled if at all possible. Modifying a bill to suit other groups is just one cost of keeping these supporters on board.

In many cases it is wise to meet with both supporters and opponents and go over actual copies of the draft bill. This permits all parties to detail their positions while giving you the opportunity to develop further allies. This process usually results in changes in the bill to appease and gain the support of neutral or opposing groups.

Whenever possible, it is wise to seek support from the governor or president as well as from federal or state agencies affected by the bill. A bill providing increased funding for education for prison inmates will be of great interest to the state bureau of corrections. Another bill outlawing employment and housing discrimination against lesbian and gay persons will be of interest to the departments of justice and labor.

State and federal agencies are more likely to be successful in getting bills they support approved. At the same time, an agency's opposition can be fatal to a bill because state and federal agencies administer bills passed by legislatures and Congress. This gives them status as experts on legislation affecting their respective areas of responsibility.

Step 3: Arrange for Sponsorship of the Bill

It is essential to identify legislators willing to introduce and work for passage of a bill. It is also important to seek the help of legislative or congressional staff members. Often, these individuals have great influence with the legislators. Modifying a bill to gain their support can be a wise move.

To get some ideas about whether given legislators will support your proposed law, look at their track records. Determine whether they supported similar bills in the past. Have they taken any public positions on this topic?

Another factor of importance is the ''safety'' of the legislator's seat. Legislators who easily win election (or reelection) can often take riskier positions than those who worry that they may lose the next election. ''Safe'' legislators may be more inclined to support a bill if they know it won't cost them their jobs. It is great to have the support of a legislator, but an individual who refuses to compromise is a potential danger. Compromise is the currency of politics, and those unable or unwilling to understand this are likely to be risky allies.

Whenever feasible, seek support from legislators in the majority party. The fact that they control the legislative process makes them important. It is even better to have bipartisan support. Obviously, it is also important to get as many sponsors for a bill as you can. Multiple sponsorship increases the likelihood that the bill will pass.

Step 4: Introducing the Bill

Once you have identified legislative sponsors for your bill, ask them to introduce it before the legislative session or as early in the session as possible. Early bills give you more opportunity for lobbying and, if necessary, amending the bill to attract supporters. Bills introduced too late in a session usually end up in the wastebasket and must be reintroduced in the next session. Lobbying involves seeking ''direct access to lawmakers in order to influence legislation and public policy. The term originated in the tendency of some people to frequent the lobbies of legislative houses in order to meet lawmakers'' (Barker, 1987, p. 90). Steps in the legislative process are shown in highlight 11.11.

Step 5: Work with Interest Groups to Broaden Support for a Bill

Because every bill has many possible supporters, it is important to determine which groups and individuals have an interest in your bill. Sometimes potential supporters are not aware that a bill has been introduced. Other supporters may lack confidence in their ability to influence the outcome even though they are very interested. Your goal is to reach as many of these supporters as you can. You will need all the help you can find. One benefit of involving people in your effort to get a bill passed is that they may become future players in the political process.

HIGHLIGHT 11.11

STEPS IN THE LEGISLATIVE PROCESS

Step One: Introduction of a bill in House/Senate

Step Two: Referral to committee

Step Three: Committee report to House/Senate

Step Four: Action by House/Senate

Step Five: Bill sent to other chamber

Step Six: Committee reports to the chamber

Step Seven: Debate and action by the chamber

Step Eight: Bill referred back to original chamber

Step Nine: Signing of bill by both chambers

Step Ten: Bill referred to President/Governor for signing

Step 6: Educate the Public

Although many bills of are of little interest to the general public, there are times when public education can be helpful. Repeated polls have shown that most people do not favor stringent barriers to abortion. Yet, state legislatures continue to pass bills (many of them vetoed) setting up various hurdles for women seeking abortion-related services. Public education can be used to rouse opposition to bills not favored by a legislator's constituency. This opposition may force a change in that person's vote. Public education can also take the form of writing letters to the newspaper, holding public forums on a topic, and going door to door with leaflets that explain a bill.

Step 7: Influence Legislative Committee Consideration

The specific committees that consider given bills are another potential focus of lobbying efforts. If, for example, all health-related bills are sent to the Health and Human Services Committee, this group can be a lobbying target. Committees are the bodies responsible for reviewing, modifying, and recommending action on a bill. Committee appointments are important sources of power for legislators and the leadership of the House or Senate usually makes these appointments.

Note that committees often appoint subcommittees

to deal with individual bills. An education committee might have subcommittees dealing with elementary and secondary education as well as with colleges and universities.

Because each bill must go through one or more committees or subcommittees, these bodies have a great deal of power. They can refuse to act on a bill or vote against sending it to the full body. The power of committees and their members makes them a logical target for lobbying. Obviously, a bill must have support of enough committee members to get reported out to the entire House or Senate. Since getting committee members' support is a critical goal for social workers seeking a bill's passage, it is important to evaluate and appraise the composition of the committee, noting each member's political party, identifying the committee leadership, and recognizing potential supporters and opponents on the committee.

Committees often hold public hearings on a bill. These hearings allow a broad range of people to express opinions. The hearings can be a forum for social workers and their allies to present arguments for or against a proposed law. Both expert testimony and the opinions of ordinary citizens are welcome at these hearings.

Kirst-Ashman and Hull (1993, pp. 489–90) provide suggestions for presenting testimony at public hearings. These suggestions include identifying those who will speak, in what order, and what they will say. People who testify should provide a written copy of any testimony to the committee members before speaking. The written statement should be able to stand on its own (that is, it should not need any additional verbal clarification). Additionally, it should be worded so that it is clear, straightforward, and readily understandable by any literate adult (Sharwell, 1982, p. 94). Jargon should be omitted. Don't use professional terms that only those in your field will understand. The statement should say specifically why this law is important and what particular benefits it will have. Argue the case on its merits. Certainly, do not preach. Use factual material and cite its source (for example, census data, specific government studies, or publications).

It is also permissible to use case examples to illustrate the impact of a specific bill. If you are lobbying for a bill that prohibits housing discrimination against gay and lesbian persons, give examples of how the absence of such a law has affected various people.

Use humor very carefully. It's important to be perceived as a serious professional person. What you think is funny may be seen as insulting, juvenile, or inappropriate by someone else.

Avoid hostility and focus testimony on the proposed legislation. Be brief, show respect for committee members, and be ready to answer questions, including hostile ones. Be ready to admit you don't have an answer rather than try to bluff your way through.

It is always best to prepare yourself in advance by practicing what you will say. Dressing professionally is expected and you should address members of the committee appropriately. Always maintain your demeanor. Remember, the way you present yourself can be just as important as what you have to say. Finally, afterward, thank the committee for the opportunity to speak. If you need to do any follow-up, such as sending additional data, do so immediately.

Thinking about testifying before a legislative committee may be very scary, but we must have the ability to get up in front of a group and describe a problem and a proposed solution, and ask others to support our position. At one level, this is not much more involved than participating in a multidisciplinary team staffing within an agency. There one must present information, answer questions, and sometimes defend one's assessment. In legislative hearings a judicious combination of hard data and case examples can be helpful in communicating the impact of existing or proposed policies. Of course, the social worker is not the only one who can testify on macro issues, clients can as well. In fact their perspective may be more useful than one provided by the professional relating someone else's story.

As we have indicated, your attempts to influence legislators regarding a bill are examples of lobbying. Lobbying is an effort to persuade someone else to accept your interpretation of events, facts, and evidence. Lobbying is consistent with social workers' responsibility to pursue such goals as social and economic justice for populations-at-risk. Calling or writing to a legislator asking for support is a form of lobbying. So is testifying before a legislative committee. Our status as amateurs may actually help us, since we are not paid lobbyists. Our conviction and values tend to drive our efforts. This is a relatively novel idea in a world where the paid lobbyists may outnumber the legislators several times over.

Step 8: Influencing Action on the Floor

Most bills are modified by legislators once they reach the floor of the House or Senate. You should expect this to happen and be willing to compromise by accepting amendments to the bill. Of course, you must also be willing to work outside the House or Senate by lobbying neutral legislators. This is an opportunity to educate them so that when they have a chance to speak or vote on the bill, they will do so with full knowledge of the facts. You can also seek media coverage of the bill and call legislators to remind them of your wishes just before a vote is taken. Remember that legislators on both sides of the issue can be lobbied, not just those supporting your position.

If at all possible, you and your supporters should be present for the debate on a bill. This is helpful in recognizing opponents' positions. It also can lay the groundwork for changes which will bring these lawmakers around.

Do not become discouraged when a bill is amended. Amended bills are much more likely to be approved than those in which changes have not been made.

Once a bill has received favorable action in one house of a legislature, a similar process occurs in the other chamber. Generally, a bill may be introduced in either house first, although some constitutions require that certain types of bills originate in one house or the other. The legislative process ends, hopefully, when the chief executive (president or governor) signs the bill.

Macro interventions in the legislative arena are not limited to legislative advocacy. It is often much easier to work with legislators who share our values. Therefore, an appropriate macro-level intervention is working for the election of candidates favorable to social work positions and issues. Working in a political campaign can be a very positive experience. Social workers with their various professional skills can play many roles in political campaigns. Everything from door-to-door campaigning, distribution of campaign materials, phone contacts with likely voters, fund-raising, locating and placement of yard signs, and office work are helpful activities. Those who receive your help during their campaigns are likely to remember you when you seek their support later.

Another way to become involved at the macro level is by joining Political Action for Candidate Election (PACE). Pace was established by the NASW to work for candidates who support social work values and ideals. Both state and national PACE activities occur each year and include providing financial support and other assistance to candidates.

Lists of your elected representatives can be acquired from the public library or by contacting your city hall. In addition, some states publish very detailed books listing all state officials. These may be found in your public library and can often be obtained for free from your state legislator.

Writing to lawmakers is relatively easy. Letters should be succinct and should clearly state the position of the writer. It should identify the bill or issue of interest and inform the legislator of the need or problem being addressed. The return address should be included on the letter so that the recipient can respond to your letter. Whenever possible, point to the results of evaluations of programs or policies which support your point of view.

HIGHLIGHT 11.12

COMMUNICATING WITH ELECTED OFFICIALS

Social workers often have reasons for writing to elected officials. It is important to use the correct form and address for such letters. Some common addresses and the accompanying salutation appear below.

Letters to the president:

> The President
> The White House
> 1600 Pennsylvania Ave. NW
> Washington, DC 20500

Salutation: Dear Mr./Ms. President:

Letters to U.S. Senators:

> The Honorable (full name)
> United States Senate
> Washington, DC 20510

Salutation: Dear Senator (last name):

*Letters to members of the
House of Representatives:*

> The Honorable (full name)
> U.S. House of Representatives
> Washington, DC 20515

Salutation: Dear Representative (last name):

Letters to Cabinet Members:

The Honorable (insert full name)
> Secretary of (insert name of Department)
> Washington, DC (correct zip code)

Salutation: Dear Secretary (last name):

U.S. Senator Barbara Mikulski, a social worker, is receptive to issues that deal with the impact of social policy on clients and services.

Haynes and Mickelson (1991) believe that social workers are especially well suited to know the impact of social policy on clients and services. After all, you are the ones most aware of what happens to clients as a result of a particular social policy. Yet, macro practice has assumed a decreasing role in social work practice if recent surveys are to be believed. Fortunately, there are examples of social workers who are using their social work skills in the political arena. U.S. Senator Barbara Mikulski began as a member of the Baltimore city council and eventually became the first social worker in the Senate. At the local level as a council member, she worked on issues of concern to neighborhoods such as potholes, education, and transportation.

Some of the skills that social workers already possess, such as the ability to compromise and bargain, are particularly useful in the political arena. The art of politics is the art of compromise since it is very rare that anything gets into law in its original form. A hard lesson for many social workers is that the political process does not operate on the same principles as other areas of social work. All political decisions are based on values and "competing political ideologies" (Haynes & Mickelson, 1991, p. 23). We must often present arguments for particular positions without providing the alternative perspective. Our normal tendency to present both sides of the argument is not usually effective in convincing political figures to take specific stands in favor of our legislation or policies. The tactic of using cases to illustrate need can have strong emotional appeal. It is an effective way to illustrate to decision-makers the impact of their previous actions or to point out how change would benefit a particular segment of the population.

Deciding whether to become involved in the political process also requires that you consider where the problem arises. Is the problem rooted in the legislative arena (such as absence of a law or existence of a poorly written law) or in the judicial area (as happens when judges misinterpret or narrowly interpret the law).

One judge continually sentenced sexual offenders to relatively minor prison terms and seemed to ignore the impact the offense had on the victim. A group of victim advocates organized a court watch program to ensure that in every court case involving a sexual offense, at least one court watcher would be present. Court watchers were usually identified by an arm band or other insignia. The goal of this program was to communicate to the judge that his actions were under scrutiny. Since judges must stand for election periodically, they are sometimes susceptible to the same political pressures as other elected officials. Later the same tactic was used with a district attorney who was considered too willing to plea bargain sexual offense cases or to request modest sentences for perpetrators.

Another potential source of a problem could be in the administrative area where rules are promulgated. Both governmental bodies and individual agencies develop rules to implement laws that have been enacted and to facilitate their ongoing enforcement. Perhaps proposed regulations or those already in place are having very negative effects on a particular group of clients. A regulation or rule which discourages clients from seeking help until they are in a financial crisis may make the situation much worse than if clients could apply for assistance before they had used up their very last dollar.

Of course, sometimes the problem is rooted in the ideologies of political figures themselves. In this case, the solution may be to replace the individual at the earliest opportunity. A local district attorney advocated that any victim of rape should put up the greatest possible amount of physical resistance, even if that resulted in her being seriously injured. He argued that such actions gave him a better case to take to court. Of course, he ignored how his philosophy might lead to the injury or death of the victim. Despite attempts by various groups to present their concerns about this dangerous approach, the district attorney refused to change his mind. Since he already had a poor reputation for sensitivity to issues involving women, he was targeted for replacement in the next election. Social workers, women's organizations, and others concerned about rights of the victims worked to ensure that he was not reelected.

Awareness of macro-level problems does not ensure that any action will be taken to address the problems. Often we must document the problem in terms that are understandable to others. This means we need information on many things. We need to know how many people are affected, how serious the problem is, and how the problem came about. This means we must analyze the problem to know whether it occurs in the legislative, political, judicial, or administrative realm.

Other Political Activities

Legislative advocacy is just one way of participating in the political process. There are other things the generalist social worker can do to influence macro-level change. You can, for example, get involved in registering voters. Clients are one of the groups with the poorest record of political participation. Yet voting is a basic way for clients to express their views. Clients can't do that, however, unless they are registered. Registering to vote is becoming increasingly easy and can be done in conjunction with registering a motor vehicle. In addition, social workers have been active in registering clients at their agencies.

At certain times of the year (usually just before elections), one can register in local shopping malls, on campuses, and in other public locations. Registration is encouraged and many sites are established. In some states, it may be possible to have an individual certified as a voter registrant. That person can then register others in accordance with whatever policies and procedures have been set by the state. Consider, for example, a recent referendum over a hotly contested state constitutional amendment which would have seriously damaged education, social welfare, and similar programs. University student government leaders were certified as reg-

istrants, set up a registration table on campus, and registered hundreds of new voters just in time for the election. The proposed amendment went down to defeat.

Thompson (1994), summarizing the impact of the Reagan-Bush administrations, noted that federal support for a number of social programs including housing went down while the size of the American population in poverty increased by almost one-third. Taxation of the poorest segment of the population went up. The ratio of funds spent on defense relative to housing went from 7 to 1 to 46 to 1 between 1981 and 1988. Deregulation of certain industries led to major financial disasters for which the taxpayer ultimately paid the price. Two examples include the savings and loan industry and the security and exchange industry. In the former case, the lack of adequate government oversight led to risky loans and bad financial decisions. It also allowed greedy executives of savings and loan firms to literally steal money from their customers. Because the federal government insured these firms, taxpayers ended up several billion dollars poorer.

These experiences and others suggest some of the reasons why social workers must become politically active. First, the very profession is at risk. Many conservatives see no role for social workers and resent the profession's identification with the poor, oppressed groups, and others traditionally at risk. In addition, most of the programs to provide economic resources and meet social and economic justice needs are derived from federal and state tax revenues. The social work "industry" of helping those damaged by the effects of a capitalist economic system is threatened by our failure to become involved in the political process.

Logical roles for social workers include running for nonpartisan political office (city council, school board) and seeking appointment to boards and commissions in your area of interest. Both state and local boards exist, and many times openings on these bodies are announced in the newspapers. Licensing boards for social work and social service advisory boards are typical. Citizen advisory boards often exist to help communities better meet the needs of the physically disabled. In addition, social workers can seek seats on police and fire commissions, park boards, and building commissions.

They can also become involved in local, state, and national campaigns as long as their activities take place outside the workplace. Possible activities include distributing campaign materials, driving voters to the polls, speaking on behalf of a candidate, and putting up yard signs. The Hatch Act, which prohibits some types of political activity on the part of government employees, rarely presents a real threat to social workers. However, in isolated cases workers have been criticized for confusing their official position and their off-duty roles. This can occur when a social worker writes letters to the editor, endorses a candidate, or otherwise participates in a political process while *simultaneously* identifying him- or herself as an employee of an agency. Most agency policies and common sense dictate that such action would be confusing to the general public and should be avoided. Whenever possible, you should avoid even the appearance of using your professional position to push for your personal goals. It is always wise to check your agency policies to see if they contain any other restrictions.

Chapter Summary

This chapter begins with definitions of four primary concepts: advocacy, social action, empowerment, and populations-at-risk. Populations-at-risk are described in terms of factors which contributed to the group's being at risk. The role of social workers in helping these populations is reviewed and several examples are provided. Advocacy as a major macro-level activity for generalist social workers is also considered in some detail. General observations about advocacy are made and principles of advocacy articulated. A set of guidelines for engaging in advocacy are provided along with some specific advocacy tactics. Social action including legal action is discussed amid the debate about what approaches to social action are most effective and appropriate in the current environment.

Empowerment and the role of social work in empowering oppressed populations is reviewed, along with a set of guidelines. The relationship between self-help and empowerment is covered.

Finally, legislative advocacy is described in some detail along with other political activities appropriate for generalist social workers. The importance of the political process for social work and social work programs is stressed.

CHAPTER TWELVE

Ethics and Ethical Dilemmas
in Macro Practice

The family services agency where you work has suffered significant budget cuts. It appears that the agency must totally eliminate some of its services in order to stay afloat. Potentially targeted programs include day care for working parents, sex education and contraception counseling for area teens, a treatment program for domestic violence perpetrators, and the thriving but expensive foreign adoptions program. Your community has depended on your agency's provision of all these services for many years. Thus, adequate alternate services to meet these respective needs do not exist. What is the ethical thing for you and your agency to do? From an ethical viewpoint, what services or programs should be abolished?

You have a professional colleague who is engaging in what you consider unethical behavior. Twice you have seen him out in the community on dates with women you know are his clients. It would be very uncomfortable for you to confront him about his behavior. Is it any of your business? Informing your supervisor seems like tattling. Shouldn't this colleague be responsible for his own actions? Why might you feel obligated to get involved? What is the ethical thing for you to do?

The private social service agency you work for does not have a formalized affirmative action policy. You have observed the agency director making lewd racial remarks and jokes. You cannot believe that he has gotten away with it. You have worked for the agency for only three months of your six-month probationary period, so you could easily be dismissed. The agency has no people of color on staff despite having numerous clients who are minorities of color.[1] You feel that recruiting staff who are minorities of color is essential to the agency's ability to perform the way it's supposed to. What should you do? Should you simply look away and pretend you don't know anything about the problem? Should you charge into the Director's office like a bull into a china shop and complain? How about talking to other staff to see what they think? Or should you call the press or a regulating agency and blow the whistle? Should you quit your job? How do you determine the most ethical thing to do?

The community in which you live and work provides no service for homeless people, despite the fact that their numbers are escalating. Every day on your way to and from work you pass at least a half dozen people roaming the urban streets. Many times you see children with them, dirty, probably hungry, and obviously not in school. Most people at your agency don't really want to talk about it. You get the feeling that colleagues think they have enough to do trying to accomplish their own jobs. Work demands continue to increase while funding resources shrink. Should you ignore these homeless community residents, or should you try to implement some macro change to provide them with desperately needed services? What is the ethical thing to do?

Introduction

As you know, this book is oriented toward practitioners who work primarily in micro and mezzo settings. However, the fact remains that you as a practitioner will always be working within the macro contexts of your organization and the community. Therefore, the surrounding macro environment will invariably impact decisions you make concerning what to do, what not to do, what is right, and what is wrong. Public laws and agency policies will regulate what you do and how you do it. That is all well and good. However, what about those times when what you consider the right thing to do seriously conflicts with these laws and policies? What about when the existing laws and policies ignore or don't allow for services your clients need? What happens when you see colleagues, administrators, or community leaders doing things you consider unethical? This chapter deals with making ethical decisions within macro contexts. It focuses on those decisions you must make when there is no absolutely clear *right* thing to do.

This chapter will:

- Explain the meanings of values, ethics, and ethical dilemmas.
- Examine the NASW Code of Ethics point by point.
- Appraise the significance of personal values.
- Formulate an eight-step decision-making model for conceptualizing and addressing an ethical dilemma.
- Discuss Reamer's in addition to Loewenberg and Dolgoff's suggestions for ethical decision making.
- Identify a range of ethical dilemmas commonly observed in macro contexts.
- Analyze these dilemmas, raise questions, and propose some solutions.

---

1. *Minority* is "one term for a group, or a member of a group, of people of a distinct racial, religious, ethnic, or political identity that is smaller or less powerful than the community's controlling group" (Barker, 1995, p. 236). The term *minorities of color* is used to denote "people who have minority status because their skin color differs from that of the community's predominant group. In the United States, the term usually refers to African Americans, Asian Americans, American Indians, and certain other minority groups" (Barker, 1995, p. 236).

Professional Values and Ethics in Macro Contexts

Along with knowledge and skills, professional values comprise the third basis for the foundation of generalist social work practice. Values are what you consider important and what you do not, what seems to you to have worth and what does not. They underlie your judgments or decisions about relative worth, what is more valuable and what is less valuable.

Ethics are sets of principles that specify what is good and what is bad. They clarify what should and should not be done. As you should know very well by now, social workers have a specific *Code of Ethics* based on professional values (National Association of Social Workers [NASW], 1993). Ethics and values are clearly related, although they are not the same thing. Loewenberg and Dolgoff (1985, p. 15) explain, "Ethics are deduced from values and must be in consonance with them. The difference between them is that values are concerned with what is good and desirable, while ethics deal with what is right and correct." Values deal with appropriate beliefs. Ethics address what to do with or how to apply those beliefs.

This hospital social worker cares about the well-being of her clients enough to register an angry protest when she gets word that one of them was mistreated by the nursing staff.

Social work values focus on "a commitment to human welfare, social justice, and individual dignity" (Reamer, 1987, p. 801). This frames the perspective with which social workers view their work with people. In other words, the well-being of people is more important than making a business profit or becoming a famous actor. Social workers care about other people and spend their time helping people improve the conditions of their lives.

Social work values address individual needs and concerns, those of communities, and those of society in general. Professional values are interwoven throughout micro, mezzo, and macro levels of practice. Professional values and ethics should guide your own decisions in micro and mezzo practice. Likewise, they should provide a macro perspective for how you view agency and community resources and constraints. For example, the individual well-being of a victim of child abuse is critical. Likewise, the way public services and laws generally treat child abuse victims is also critical.

Cournoyer (1991) clearly summarizes the momentous importance of social work ethics: "Ethical decision making constitutes the sine qua non of professional social work practice. Ethical responsibilities take precedence over theoretical knowledge, research findings, practice wisdom, agency policies, and, of course, the social worker's own personal values, preferences, and beliefs" (p. 43).

Superficially, this appears simple. The profession provides ethical guidelines for how to help people and work within agencies. Theoretically, then, all you have to do is closely adhere to those guidelines and ethical practice will follow. You are simply supposed to look out for the well-being of your clients, right?

It is a cliché to say that people are complicated, as is life in general. However, it can also be said that the application of ethics to actual decision making is often a tremendously complicated task. Many times the monster of ethical conflict will loom its hoary head. Adherence to one aspect of ethics will strikingly contradict adherence to another aspect of ethical conduct.

Reamer (1987, p. 804) cites an example of a typical ethical quandary: "The NASW Code of Ethics states that the 'social worker should not engage in any action that violates or diminishes the civil or legal rights of clients.' However, the code also states that the 'social worker should adhere to commitments made to the employing organization.'"

Suppose a client reveals that he has contracted AIDS. He has just been given the diagnosis. This condition is almost certainly fatal in the long run. The social worker knows that the client has been having unprotected sexual relations with several people over the past months. During their meetings the client has revealed these people's identities. After discussing options, the client refuses to tell his sexual partners about his diagnosis. Additionally, for a variety of reasons, the social worker doubts that the client will begin to use precautions against spreading the disease in the near future. Agency policy mandates that social workers not violate clients' confidentiality. This means that, according to policy, the social worker may not tell anyone about the AIDS diagnosis without the client's clearly expressed written permission. But the worker worries that if the prior sexual partners are not told about the AIDS diagnosis and their potential exposure, they (as well as the client) may continue to spread the disease. Which ethical concept is more important—the worker's commitments to her employing organization and its policy, or her ethical responsibility to the general welfare of society and the well-being of other people? What if the social worker discovers more and more clients in similar situations? Can the social worker ignore a policy that negatively (and critically) affects scores of people? Should the social worker assess possible initiation of a macro change process? Does she have time and effort to do this in view of her other job responsibilities? There is no easy answer.

There are numerous other ethical dilemmas. A law might dictate a lengthy procedure for removing the perpetrators in cases of alleged sexual abuse. What about the immediate, critical needs of the victims to be kept safe? Or suppose you work at a public assistance agency that requires applicants for resources to maintain residency for a specified time period before they become eligible for help. You know of several single parents who have come to your agency pleading that their children are starving. They are desperate for help but have not lived in the area long enough to satisfy the residency requirement. You can think of nowhere else in the community that these families can turn for help. What should you do? Should you let a family starve? Is it your ethical responsibility to pursue some macro change efforts on these families' behalf so that they can get the resources they need to survive?

The potential variety of ethical dilemmas is endless. Professional values and ethics do provide some basic guidelines, but many times, a social worker has to make hard choices about what is more ethical or more critical to do.

The NASW Code of Ethics

We have established the importance of ethics in guiding our professional behavior. Because of its significance, we will examine the code section by section. The NASW *Code of Ethics* addresses six aspects of professional responsibility. In other words, ethical guidelines for how to make decisions and practice social work are given in six general areas. These areas include the social worker's conduct and comportment as a social worker, and ethical responsibility to clients, colleagues, employers and employing organizations, the social work profession, and, finally, to society in general (National Association of Social Workers, 1993, pp. 1–2).

Highlight 12.1 features the detailed NASW Code of Ethics. Throughout the following section, which discuss the Code portion by portion, you can refer to highlight 12.1 for the exact wording.

The Social Worker's Conduct as a Social Worker

The first section of the NASW Code of Ethics refers to "the social worker's conduct and comportment as a social worker" (NASW, 1993). In other words, professional social workers' behavior should be appropriate and professional. This applies in micro, mezzo, and macro contexts. How should social workers behave? What should they do and not do as professionals? This could suggest what you should and should not say in your professional role and what decisions you make about how to act. It could even affect how you present yourself in public. The Code targets five specific areas of behavior in detail. They include propriety, competence and professional development, service, integrity, and scholarship and research (NASW, 1993).

Propriety

Social workers' conduct should be consistently proper and socially acceptable. Professional social workers "should maintain high standards at all times" (NASW,

HIGHLIGHT 12.1

THE NASW CODE OF ETHICS

superseded by 1996 Code

I. The Social Worker's Conduct and Comportment as a Social Worker

A. Propriety—The social worker should maintain high standards of personal conduct in the capacity of identity as social worker.

1. The private conduct of the social worker is a personal matter to the same degree as is any other person's, except when such conduct compromises the fulfillment of professional responsibilities.
2. The social worker should not participate in, condone, or be associated with dishonesty, fraud, deceit, or misrepresentation.
3. The social worker should distinguish clearly between statements and actions made as a private individual and as a representative of the social work profession or an organization or group.

B. Competence and Professional Development—The social worker should strive to become and remain proficient in professional practice and the performance of professional functions.

1. The social worker should accept responsibility or employment only on the basis of existing competence or the intention to acquire the necessary competence.
2. The social worker should not misrepresent professional qualifications, education, experience, or affiliations.

C. Service—The social worker should regard as primary the service obligation of the social work profession.

1. The social worker should retain ultimate responsibility for the quality and extent of the service that individual assumes, assigns, or performs.
2. The social worker should act to prevent practices that are inhumane or discriminatory against any person or group of persons.

D. Integrity—The social worker should act in accordance with the highest standards of professional integrity and impartiality.

1. The social worker should be alert to and resist the influence and pressures that interfere with the exercise of professional discretion and impartial judgement required for the performance of professional functions.
2. The social worker should not exploit professional relationships for personal gain.

E. Scholarship and Research—The social worker engaged in study and research should be guided by the conventions of scholarly inquiry.

1. The social worker engaged in research should consider carefully its possible consequences for human beings.
2. The social worker engaged in research should ascertain that the consent of participants in the research is voluntary and informed, without any implied deprivation or penalty for refusal to participate, and with due regard for participants' privacy and dignity.
3. The social worker engaged in research should protect participants from unwarranted physical or mental discomfort, distress, harm, danger, or deprivation.
4. The social worker who engages in the evaluation of services or cases should discuss them only for the professional purposes and only with persons directly and professionally concerned with them.

(continued)

HIGHLIGHT 12.1—(Continued)

5. Information obtained about participants in research should be treated as confidential.
6. The social worker should take credit only for work actually done in connection with scholarly and research endeavors and credit contributions made by others.

II. The Social Worker's Ethical Responsibility to Clients
F. Primacy of Clients' Interests—The social worker's primary responsibility is to clients.
1. The social worker should serve clients with devotion, loyalty, determination, and the maximum application of professional skill and competence.
2. The social worker should not exploit relationships with clients for personal advantage.
3. The social worker should not practice, condone, facilitate or collaborate with any form of discrimination on the basis of race, color, sex, sexual orientation, age, religion, national origin, marital status, political belief, mental or physical handicap, or any other preference or personal characteristic, condition or status.
4. The social worker should avoid relationships or commitments that conflict with the interests of clients.
5. The social worker should under no circumstances engage in sexual activities with clients.
6. The social worker should provide clients with accurate and complete information regarding the extent and nature of the services available to them.
7. The social worker should apprise clients of their risks, rights, opportunities, and obligations associated with social service to them.
8. The social worker should seek advice and counsel of colleagues and supervisors whenever such consultation is in the best interest of clients.
9. The social worker should terminate service to clients, and professional relationships with them, when such service and relationships are no longer required or no longer serve the clients' needs or interests.
10. The social worker should withdraw services precipitously only under unusual circumstances, giving careful consideration to all factors in the situation and taking care to minimize possible adverse effects.
11. The social worker who anticipates the termination or interruption of service to clients should notify clients promptly and seek the transfer, referral, or continuation of service in relation to the clients' needs, and preference.

G. Rights and Prerogatives of Clients—The social worker should make every effort to foster maximum self-determination on the part of clients.
1. When the social worker must act on behalf of a client who has been adjudged legally incompetent, the social worker should safeguard the interests and rights of that client.
2. When another individual has been legally authorized to act in behalf of a client, the social worker should deal with that person always with the client's best interest in mind.
3. The social worker should not engage in any action that violates or diminishes the civil or legal rights of clients.

H. Confidentiality and Privacy—The social worker should respect the privacy of clients and hold in confidence all information obtained in the course of professional service.
1. The social worker should share with others confidences revealed by clients, without their consent, only for compelling professional reasons.

2. The social worker should inform clients fully about the limits of confidentiality in a given situation, the purposes for which information is obtained, and how it may be used.

3. The social worker should afford clients reasonable access to any official social work records concerning them.

4. When providing clients with access to records, the social worker should take due care to protect the confidences of others contained in those records.

5. The social worker should obtain informed consent of clients before taping, recording, or permitting third party observation of their activities.

I. **Fees—When setting fees, the social worker should ensure that they are fair, reasonable, considerate, and commensurate with the service performed and with due regard for the clients' ability to pay.**

1. The social worker should not accept anything of value for making a referral.

III. **The Social Worker's Ethical Responsibility to Colleagues**

J. **Respect, Fairness, and Courtesy—The social worker should treat colleagues with respect, courtesy, fairness, and good faith.**

1. The social worker would cooperate with colleagues to promote professional-interests and concerns.

2. The social worker should respect confidences shared by colleagues in the course of their professional relationships and transactions.

3. The social worker should create and maintain conditions of practice that facilitate ethical and competent professional performance by colleagues.

4. The social worker should treat with respect, and represent accurately and fairly, the qualifications, views, and findings of colleagues and use appropriate channels to express judgments on these matters.

5. The social worker who replaces or is replaced by a colleague in professional practice should act with consideration for the interest, character, and reputation of that colleague.

6. The social worker should not exploit a dispute between a colleague and employer to obtain a position or otherwise advance the social worker's interest.

7. The social worker should seek arbitration or mediation when conflicts with colleagues requires resolution for compelling professional reasons.

8. The social worker should extend to colleagues of other professions the same respect and cooperation that is extended to social work colleagues.

9. The social worker who serves as an employer, supervisor, or mentor to colleagues should make orderly and explicit arrangements regarding the condition of their continuing professional relationship.

10. The social worker who has the responsibility for employing and evaluating the performance of other staff members, should fulfill such responsibility in a fair, considerate, and equitable manner, on the basis of clearly enunciated criteria.

11. The social worker who has the responsibility for evaluating the performance of employees, supervisees, or students should share evaluations with them.

K. **Dealing with Colleagues' Clients—The social worker has the responsibility to relate to the clients of colleagues with full professional consideration.**

1. The social worker should not assume professional responsibility for the clients of another agency or a colleague without appropriate communication with that agency or colleague.

2. The social worker who serves the clients of colleagues, during a temporary absence of emergency, should serve those clients with the same consideration as that afforded any client.

(continued)

HIGHLIGHT 12.1—(Continued)

IV. The Social Worker's Ethical Responsibility to Employers and Employing Organizations

    L. Commitments to Employing Organization—The social worker should adhere to commitments made to the employing organization.

        1. The social worker should work to improve the employing agency's policies and procedures and the efficiency and effectiveness of its services.

        2. The social worker should not accept employment or arrange student field placements in an organization which is currently under public sanction by NASW for violating personnel standards, or imposing limitations on or penalties for professional actions on behalf of clients.

        3. The social worker should act to prevent and eliminate discrimination in the employing organization's work assignments and in its employment policies and practices.

        4. The social worker should use with scrupulous regard, and only for the purpose for which they are intended, the resources of the employing organization.

V. The Social Worker's Ethical Responsibility to the Social Work Profession

    M. Maintaining the Integrity of the Profession—The social worker should uphold and advance the values, ethics, knowledge, and mission of the profession.

        1. The social worker should protect and enhance the dignity and integrity of the profession and should be responsible and vigorous in discussion and criticism of the profession.

        2. The social worker should take action through appropriate channels against unethical conduct by any other member of the profession.

        3. The social worker should act to prevent the unauthorized and unqualified practice of social work.

        4. The social worker should make no misrepresentation in advertising as to qualifications, competence, service, or results to be achieved.

    N. Community Service—The social worker should assist the profession in making social services available to the general public.

        1. The social worker should contribute time and professional expertise to activities that promote respect for the utility, the integrity, and the competence of the social work profession.

1993, p. 3). Social workers should obey the law. Situations involving deception and corruption should be avoided at all costs. Workers should be honest and present themselves and their ideas straightforwardly. Finally, social workers should carefully clarify the difference between their personal opinions and the views and ethics espoused by the profession.

Reflecting upon these requirements, it appears that the maintenance of proper and socially appropriate conduct at all times is a tough act to pull off. Which of us is prefect? Which of us never ever makes any mistakes? Which of us looks good all the time? I have often made fun of the term "socially appropriate." What exactly does this mean? To what extend can you exercise your legal right to say what you want and look the way you want? Should you make certain that your personal haircut is "conservative" or "conventional," whatever these words mean? Must you avoid wearing clothing that is hot pink or fluorescent orange to the office because darker blues and greys are more appropriate in the eyes of colleagues and administrators?

We could go on raising such questions ad nauseam. The central point is that professional social workers should consistently strive to be aware of how they appear to others in the organizational and community contexts. Propriety involves thinking about the best way to act in order to enhance the social work profession and do the best, most thoughtful job you can. Of course the basics of honesty and legality are always involved. These primary tenets are often sound guidelines for be-

2. The social worker should support the formulation, development, enactment and implementation of social policies of concern to the profession.

O. Development of Knowledge—The social worker should take responsibility for identifying, developing, and fully utilizing knowledge for professional practice.

   1. The social worker should base practice upon recognized knowledge relevant to social work.
   2. The social worker should critically examine, and keep current the emerging knowledge relevant to social work.
   3. The social worker should contribute to the knowledge base of social work and share research knowledge and practice wisdom with colleagues.

VI. Promoting Worker's Ethical Responsibility to Society

P. Promoting the General Welfare—The social worker should promote the general welfare of society.

   1. The social worker should act to prevent and eliminate discrimination against any person or group on the basis of race, color, sex, sexual orientation, age, religion, national origin, marital status, political belief, mental or physical handicap, or any other preference or personal characteristic, condition, or status.
   2. The social worker should act to ensure that all persons have access to the resources, services, and opportunities which they require.
   3. The social worker should act to expand choice and opportunity for all persons, with special regard for disadvantaged or oppressed groups and persons.
   4. The social worker should promote conditions that encourage respect for the diversity of cultures which constitute American society.
   5. The social worker should provide appropriate professional services in public emergencies.
   6. The social worker should advocate changes in policy and legislation to improve social conditions and to promote social justice.
   7. The social worker should encourage informed participation by the public by shaping social policies and institutions.

Source: As adopted by the 1979 NASW Delegate Assembly and revised by the 1990 and 1993 NASW Delegate Assemblies. Copyright 1993, National Association of Social Workers, 750 First Street, NE, Suite 700, Washington, DC 20002–4241.

havior. You know when you are telling the truth and when you are not. You know what is legal and illegal in most everyday circumstances. Thus, propriety involves thoughtfulness and sensitivity as well as decision making. Perhaps it would be in your best professional interest not to streak your hair in rainbow hues if such behavior turns off your clients, colleagues, and administrators. However, if you decide such behavior makes no difference, you certainly have your personal rights. People have often said that women look most professional and appear most credible when they wear skirts. However, some women dislike skirts and generally refuse to wear them. It is a personal choice that does not hamper performance as a professional social worker.

There are some personal values and opinions, how-ever, that might be in such opposition to the Code of Ethics that they are professionally intolerable. For example, a social worker boasting of membership in the Skin Heads or the Ku Klux Klan clearly is in opposition to professional values. Cox et al. (1987) conclude: "The private or personal behavior of a social worker should be regarded as exactly that (i.e., not subject to the Code), except insofar as such conduct might impinge on fulfillment of professional responsibilities. In a situation in which a member would be charged with breach of ethics stemming from private conduct, the critical question would be whether this interfered with carrying out professional responsibility. A jury of peers would have to decide that question, based on the facts of the particular situation" (p. 424).

Competence and Professional Development

Professional social workers should accept only positions of employment for which they are competent. They should never misrepresent their intent or their credentials. Additionally, social workers should strive to prevent any personal issues and problems—including substance abuse, mental illness, and emotional difficulties—from interfering with their professional performance. Furthermore, in the event that personal issues do interfere with his practice, a social worker is obligated to seek competent professional help immediately. He should take any steps necessary to prevent harm from occurring to his clients and/or agency.

At face value, these standards sound good, and, of course, their intent *is* good. However, they are not always so easy to follow. Suppose you joyously snatch up your very first professional social work position. What if you find that you really do not feel qualified to do the job the way you think it should be done? What if you lack some of the necessary skills, even though you are technically qualified for the job?

Essentially, here the Code addresses three issues. First, you should never mislead employers about your credentials. This adheres to the principle of professional honesty discussed earlier. The bottom line is that you get a job on the basis of honest and accurate qualifications. Now, if that job requires skills you do not currently have, the second issue concerns how you should plan to acquire such skills. If you need more advanced counseling skills, can you enroll in a family counseling program to enhance and extend your credentials? If you require a specific skill that you don't currently have, can you participate in a series of training programs to develop that skill? Many states have requirements that professional social workers undertake an ongoing program of postgraduate training, requiring a designated number of hours every one to three years. Perhaps you find that you need divorce mediation or child management skills. You might be able to find programs that educate professionals on these very issues. You can also continue your professional education by reading to acquire knowledge and skills you don't have. You may want to audit a course at a local university. Finally, you can seek help from your supervisor and others at your agency.

If, after some arbitrarily determined amount of time, you still feel you cannot fulfill your employment and professional responsibilities, then perhaps, it is time to look for another job. The key here is thoughtful consideration and honesty. What do you feel is the best thing for you to do for the profession, the agency, your clients, and yourself?

The third issue concerns personal problems. Everyone has them, as we know all too well. This, of course, includes professional social workers. Romf and Royse (1994) recently found "social work students more likely than a comparison group to report having grown up in families where there was psychosocial trauma" including alcohol or drug addiction and child maltreatment (p. 169). What do we as professionals do with our dysfunctions, especially when they become serious?

Once again, the answer is to try to maintain awareness of your own mental health and performance and to be honest about it. If you honestly feel that your own problems are interfering with your work, then do something about it. Get professional help. If the problems are so severe that you feel you cannot function adequately, then get into an inpatient treatment program, take a leave of absence, or quit and seek another job. Your professional work and your clients' interests come first. Later on in the chapter we will discuss how to deal with colleagues' mental health and performance difficulties.

Service

Two issues arise concerning social workers' ethical responsibilities in terms of service. First, social workers should be committed to providing high quality service. They should assume responsibility for their own work. This indicates that ultimately your work is your own responsibility, not that of your agency, supervisor, or agency administration. This implies that a professional social worker must strive for effectiveness even in adverse organizational environments.

The second service standard applies to workers' responsibility to thwart any cruelty, unfairness, or discrimination that they observe. Once again, this standard places the ultimate responsibility upon the individual worker, not the agency or agency administration, to make certain that service is provided fairly and people are treated justly. This doesn't negate the responsibility of agency administrators, but, individual professional social workers are also responsible for intervening when they see unfair things happening. Later, we will examine ethical dilemmas wherein colleagues and administrators, for a wide range of reasons, fail to meet this standard. We will explore what workers can do when others around them, often those with greater power, fail to fulfill their service responsibility.

Integrity

The Code explains integrity as having two parts. First, professional social workers should endeavor to identify and resist any influence or temptations that threaten to curtail or obstruct professional performance. Influences might include threats of harm or promises of reward. In other words, don't allow direct or indirect "bribes" that might affect you personally to interfere with your professional judgment and performance.

Suppose you are a public assistance worker. You notice that a number of your clients are not receiving the benefits they deserve. They failed to apply for these benefits purely out of ignorance. However, your public agency is suffering an extreme financial emergency. There is substantial public pressure to spend as little as possible. You take the issue to your supervisor, and she strongly discourages you from bringing the additional benefits to the clients' attention. She suggests that such "loyalty" to the agency will result in an enhanced annual performance review. A good review results, in turn, in a bigger raise. Your supervisor is interested in keeping paid benefits down because her own supervisor has told her that such compliance could lead to her promotion, which she fiercely seeks. According to the standard of integrity, what is the ethical thing for you to do? Of course, you should do what is best and right for your clients, not for yourself. The question is, what is the *most ethical* thing to do, not necessarily the *easiest*?

The second aspect of integrity involves not using professional relationships to your own personal advantage. For example, you as a worker should not pressure one of your field students to go out with you or become intimate with you. Likewise, your own supervisor should not pressure you just because he or she has supervisory power over you.

Scholarship and Research

Social workers participating in research should remain vigilant regarding the rights of their human subjects. Research should be undertaken openly and always with subjects' overt consent. People choosing not to participate should receive no punishment or censure of any kind. Nor should research participants be made to suffer any pain or damage. Any discussion of research and of subjects' participation in it should be limited to professional situations with involvement of other relevant professionals only. All information gained from subjects should be held in strict confidence. Social workers should assume credit only for their own endeavors, giving other participants in the research due credit.

Two themes that surface when reading these ethical standards are concern for the rights and needs of others and commitment to honesty and fairness. You should undertake any research endeavors only while holding the well-being of others, especially your research subjects, as your highest priority. Additionally, you should be honest with all involved regarding what you plan to do in conducting the research, who will have access to any information and findings, and who deserves credit for any findings obtained.

The Social Worker's Ethical Responsibility to Clients

We have reviewed guidelines for how professional social workers should appear and behave in public, for how they should generally behave as professional social workers. A second major ethical dimension is that of how social workers should treat their clients. The Code targets four ethical points in this category. These include the primacy of clients' interests, the rights and prerogatives of clients, confidentiality and privacy, and fees (NASW, 1993).

Ethical responsibilities to clients involve the individual decisions practitioners make in micro practice, but such responsibilities also concern agency policies and procedures about how clients should be treated as well as public laws under which practitioners function. Thus, ethical responsibilities to clients are both micro and macro concerns.

Primacy of Clients' Interests

The first principle guiding social workers' interactions with clients is simple and straightforward. That is, the client should always come first. Social workers should treat clients with respect, persistence, and dedication. They should consistently use their skills to the very best of their ability.

It is critical that any type of unfair treatment or discrimination should be avoided at all costs. In other words, if you see any discrimination or unfair treatment, it is your responsibility to initiate action to intervene on your clients' behalf. You should not simply ignore the problem, but should do something about it.

Social workers should never take advantage of clients for personal gain. Professional social workers should never enter into sexual relationships with clients. For example, a twenty-two-year-old student in field placement called about her temptation. She was working at a halfway house for young men on parole who also had substance abuse problems. She said she was totally enamored with one of her clients. She confessed that she had difficulty controlling her emotions. We talked about what effects inappropriate and unethical behavior could have on her reputation, her career, and her client. She had only four more weeks of placement at the agency. The agency had an established policy that no staff, including staff who left the agency, should enter into romantic involvement with clients for at least six months following the client's termination. This student knew that involvement with the client was wrong. We didn't even get into the other potential problems of entering into a relationship with a person who had been in jail and who was substance addicted. The student was struggling. As she didn't call again, we don't know what she chose to do. This is not an uncommon kind of situation.

The Code uses powerful language to emphasize that workers should not have sex with clients under any circumstances. Cox et al. (1987) comment: "Great damage has been done to clients who have been exploited by trusted physicians, therapists, and other helping persons, and to the professions (especially in the mental health field) which has seen public confidence in their motives, competence, and integrity steadily eroded" (p. 426).

Social workers should always let clients know everything about the services those clients will receive. This is related to the previous integrity example in which you, as a worker, were confronted with the choice of alerting a client to all available benefits or not. This tenet of the Code indicates that it is clearly your responsibility to do so.

When facing an overly problematic situation with a client, social workers should consult supervisors or appropriate others to help them deal with the case as effectively as possible. It is your ethical responsibility to get help when you are in over your head with a problem. It is inappropriate to adopt an "out of sight, out of mind" approach, that, if you don't think about it, the problem will cease to exist. Rather, it is your responsibility to tackle the problem to the best of your ability, including soliciting help.

Social workers should terminate relationships with clients when the relationship is no longer either useful to or wanted by the clients. Similarly, social workers should avoid abrupt withdrawal of services if at all possible. Such action should occur only after a matter has been given very serious thought. When a social worker is forced to initiate an abrupt termination or obstruction of service, that social worker should alert clients to the situation immediately and provide appropriate referrals.

It is typical for workers to seek new professional positions. Usually workers keep quiet about job searches at their current jobs in case they don't find an appropriate new position. Workers often start new jobs after giving their current employers two- or four-weeks notice. Two to four weeks is not much time to help clients work through a transition from one worker or service to another, especially if the clients have been with one worker for a long time or have unusually difficult problems. In these cases it is the worker's ethical responsibility to make the clients' transitions as smooth and agreeable as possible.

Rights and Prerogatives of Clients

Social workers should strive to support clients' *self-determination* to the greatest extent possible (NASW, 1993, p. 6). Barker (1991) explains that self-determination "recognizes the rights and needs of clients to be free to make their own choices and decisions. Inherent in the principle is the requirement for the social worker to help the client know what the resources and choices are and what the consequences of selecting any one of them will be" (p. 210).

When a client is found "legally incompetent," the social worker should do everything she can to make certain that the client's rights are not violated. When someone else is designated to act on the client's behalf, the social worker should keep her client's rights and well-being in mind at all times. Social workers should never participate in activities that infringe upon their clients' constitutional rights.

Confidentiality and Privacy

Confidentiality is the ethical principle that workers should not share information provided by a client or about a client unless that worker has the client's explicit permission to do so (Barker, 1991, p. 46). Within a professional context, social workers must keep confidential any information provided by clients or others who share information based on the premise that it will not be disclosed. Social workers should always hold clients' privacy in high regard. Social workers should share such client information only under extreme circumstances when they determine it is absolutely necessary. For example, a social worker's records about a client could be subpoenaed by a court. Issues involving the confidentiality of records will be discussed more thoroughly later in the context of ethical dilemmas.

Workers should provide clients with as much access to their own records as possible while being careful to maintain the confidentiality of others in their clients' records. Finally, social workers should always obtain clients' consent to share records with others or to record client interactions. A range of dilemmas related to confidentiality will be discussed later in the chapter.

The Social Worker's Ethical Responsibility to Colleagues

Two primary dimensions characterize the social worker's ethical responsibility to colleagues within the organizational and community macro environments. First, professional social workers should "treat colleagues with respect, courtesy, fairness, and good faith" (p. 7). Professional social workers should attempt to cooperate with colleagues in professional pursuits and practice, even when these colleagues are difficult to work with. Chapters 2 and 3 offer numerous suggestions for dealing with interpersonal conflict in a variety of contexts.

Respect, Courtesy, Fairness, and Good Faith

You should respect your professional colleagues and treat them courteously and fairly. You should keep any information they share with you concerning their work in confidence. You should aim to maintain a positive environment in which to work. You should respect their views, experience, and qualifications. If you have a disagreement with a colleague you should "use the appropriate channels" to achieve resolution (NASW, 1993, p. 7).

If you take another professional's place after he or she leaves, continue treating that person with respect. It is easy to criticize someone who has left for not doing a very good job or leaving you with some disorganized mess to clean up. Avoid such overt criticism. Likewise, do not criticize someone who has assumed one of your old positions.

Don't talk behind colleagues' backs or purposely try to make them look bad. Don't deceitfully manipulate conflictual situations to your advantage. Address issues openly and honestly.

For example, Charley is a social worker who does not treat colleagues ethically. He is interested in his own personal image and in having power within his agency unit. Typically, if he has a criticism of a colleague, he does not confront that colleague openly. Charley hates open confrontations because he can't always control them. Instead, he goes to Bob, the person who supervises them both, and complains about the colleague in question behind closed doors. Concurrently, he emphasizes how well Bob usually solves such problems. One colloquial term for this latter behavior is "brown-nosing." From Charley's perspective, he can achieve three goals from this action. First, flattering the supervisor can gain Charley greater power by strengthening his alliance with Bob who, because of his supervisory position, has greater power. Second, Charley makes himself look better by comparison when he criticizes his colleague. Third, Charley can solve an identified problem without doing anything about it himself. He can avoid uncomfortable confrontations. Unfortunately, Bob is not quite sharp enough to catch on. He inevitably follows Charley's suggestions, thereby reinforcing and perpetuating Charley's unethical behavior, despite the fact that most of Charley's colleagues have lost respect for him because of this very behavior.

The Code also instructs supervisors to "make orderly and explicit arrangements regarding the conditions of their continuing professional relationship" (NASW, 1993, p. 7). Supervisors should treat all staff fairly and share evaluations with them. In the example above, ethical questions can be raised about Bob's behavior. Is it ethical to react to Charley's informal accusations of his current target of criticism? Is Bob treating Charley like other staff, or is Bob giving Charley certain advantages? To what extent does Bob share with the criticized colleagues how he became aware of the alleged problem (that Charley reported on them)?

You should treat with respect not only other social workers but also colleagues of other disciplines. This coincides with respect for basic human dignity. Make it a point to treat janitors and others with relatively low-status positions with special respect. Everyone's job is important. Everyone needs to feel valuable.

Social workers should not use any power inherent in a position "such as that of employer, supervisor, teacher, or consultant, to his or her advantage or to exploit others" (NASW, 1993, p. 8). For example, a supervisor should not assign his or her own work to a supervisee and force that supervisee to work overtime to complete it.

Finally, one other aspect of respecting colleagues is helping them. If you find out that a colleague has a personal problem (such as substance abuse or depression) that seriously impedes his work, assist that colleague in getting help. You can give him feedback about his performance and help him review potential alternatives to solve the problem.

Dealing with Colleagues' Clients

At some point you might be in the position of "dealing with colleagues' clients" (NASW, 1993, p. 8). Don't take over or interfere with colleagues' clients "without appropriate communication with that agency or colleague" (NASW, 1993, p. 8). Consider a colleague's client who comes to you complaining about that colleague. Perhaps the client tells you how much better you are and that she would really like to be your client instead. This is flattering. Beware of flattery. What are your ethical choices? You can refer the client back to your colleague to give him feedback about whatever she disapproves of. Also, you can talk to your colleague about the issue and ask him what he wants to do about it.

Second, treat colleagues' clients as well as you treat your own. In the event of a colleague's illness, crisis, or other indisposition, you might be assigned that colleague's clients. They should not be treated as second-class citizens. You should provide them the same attention as you do your own clients.

The Social Worker's Ethical Responsibility to Employers and Employing Organizations

The Code states that you as an employee should abide by the organization's rules, regulations, and policies. It makes four specific points. First, work to correct and enhance agency policies and procedures in need of improvement. It is your ethical responsibility to assist the agency in improving its "efficiency and effectiveness" (NASW, 1993, p. 8). Sometimes it will be your ethical responsibility to pursue macro change on your clients' and agency's behalf.

Second, do not assume a job with an agency currently under NASW sanction for a breach of ethics. Likewise, do not place field students in a sanctioned agency.

Third, it is your ethical responsibility to try to "prevent and eliminate discrimination in the employing organization's work assignments and in its employment policies and practices" (NASW, 1993, p. 8). Earlier chapters more thoroughly addressed organizational change, including changing agency policy.

The Code's fourth point concerning your ethical responsibility to employers involves use of agency resources. It emphasizes that you should use such resources with "scrupulous regard" (NASW, 1993, p. 8) and only for those purposes designated by the agency. In other words, you should not bend the rules so that ineligible clients receive benefits. Nor should you pad your mileage expense account for home visits.

The Social Worker's Ethical Responsibility to the Social Work Profession

The Code addresses three issues for the social work profession. They include "maintaining the integrity of the profession," "community service," and "development of knowledge" (NASW, 1993, p. 9).

Maintaining the Integrity of the Profession

Social workers should "protect and enhance the dignity and integrity of the profession" (NASW, 1993, p. 9). You should not talk about social work disparagingly. Talk about your chosen field with due respect. Often,

Before social work became a recognized profession with a stringent code of ethics, women such as this one made regular visits to those in need. This "visiting nurse," as they were called, is working in the New York City slums in 1910.

when asked about their major or field of study, I hear students say something like, "I'm in social work. I know I won't make as much money as in business, but I like it." Don't do that. That's an apology. Social work is an honorable profession with a solid knowledge, skill, and value base. Social work values involve serious concern for the well-being of other people. What more virtuous value is there than that? Additionally, social workers like many other types of professionals, can carve out excellent careers for themselves and make more than adequate money.

A second dimension concerning the profession's integrity involves taking appropriate action against other professionals who violate professional ethics. The Code indicates that you are responsible for taking "action through appropriate channels against unethical conduct by any other member of the profession" (NASW, 1993, p. 9). Additionally, you "should act to prevent the unauthorized and unqualified practice of social work" (NASW, 1993, p. 9). The following example illustrates violation of both of these tenets.

Georgia, a unit supervisor, found out that Joanne

had applied for their state's Independent Clinical Social Worker certification. This was the highest level of practice certified in that particular state. Among other things, requirements included an MSW degree and at least two years of supervised post-MSW clinical experience. Georgia knew that Joanne did not have the required two years of supervised clinical experience. Joanne had taken time off to raise her children after receiving her degree and assumed a professional social work position only six months ago for the first time since graduation. Joanne had asked John, another social work colleague of hers, to indicate that he had been her supervisor for the required two years. He signed the required form to verify this "fact," even though he had never supervised Joanne in his life. Now, is this beginning to strike you as being a bit unethical?

At any rate, Georgia contacted the state certification office and informed them of the situation. They investigated and found out that Georgia was correct. Joanne was denied that certification. Georgia put a letter of reprimand in Joanne's personnel file. For whatever reason, John never suffered any consequences for his behavior. Two months later, Georgia left the agency for what she considered an even better job in another city. Joanne immediately applied for Independent Clinical Social Worker certification again and, shortly thereafter, received her certificate. The new supervisor who took over Georgia's old position never found out about the whole thing. Somehow, the letter of reprimand had mysteriously disappeared from Joanne's personnel file.

Georgia was ethically correct to "prevent the unauthorized and unqualified practice of social work" on Joanne's behalf (NASW, 1993, p. 9). However, other questions remain. Should Georgia have pursued the fact that John essentially perjured himself? Should the new supervisor have double-checked Joanne's credentials when Joanne applied for certification, or should she have respected Joanne's supposed integrity? Should Georgia have made certain that Joanne's new supervisor was informed of the situation, even after Georgia had left and was intricately involved in her new job? What do you think?

The final dimension of professional integrity states that you should never misrepresent your credentials, skills, or practice results. This is especially true concerning any advertising about yourself. Of course, this point coincides with the basic professional and human value of honesty.

Community Service

The Code emphasizes the value of "community service" (NASW, 1993, p. 9). We have already stressed the importance of working within the community context for the betterment of your clients and other community residents. A primary thrust of generalist practice is implementing needed changes on the macro level, including those needed by the communities with which you and your clients are involved.

The Code identifies two specific aspects of community service. First, you should invest time and energy in "activities that promote respect for the utility, the integrity, and the competence of the social work profession" (NASW, 1993, p. 9). Being an active participant in the national and state NASW is one means of doing this. Contributing financially to supportive funds such as the NASW Political Action for Candidate Election (PACE) fund is another means of promoting the profession. PACE "helps coordinate personnel and financial resources of interested membership to elect political officials" (Barker, 1991, p. 166).

Concerning community service, the Code also stresses that you should "support the formulation, development, enactment and implementation of social policies of concern to the profession" (NASW, 1993, p. 9). You can do this by becoming involved in election campaigns of political candidates supporting social work values. Even writing legislators to offer your opinions on a range of issues critical to social work and clients can have substantial impact on social policy development. You might even participate in an organized network of social workers, already established in some states, who contact each other when political pressure is needed to sway elected officials' votes and decisions.

Development of Knowledge

At one time I actually thought that when I finally received my bachelor's degree, I could simply quit working at learning. I found out that was and is certainly not the case.

Assimilating and using knowledge is an endless process. First of all, the Code requires that social workers base their practice decisions and actions on the knowledge that has already been accumulated. This assumes that you have a substantial foundation of knowledge already. Secondly, the Code requires you to continuously "critically examine and keep current with emerging knowledge relevant to social work" (NASW, 1993, p. 9). You can do this through reading professional journals. NASW members, of course, automatically receive *Social Work*, the field's most widely circulated journal. Additionally, practitioners often subscribe to journals more specifically directed at their own clientele or arena of practice. *Public Welfare, Affilia: Journal of Women and Social Work, Child Welfare, Journal of Community Practice*, and *Social Work with Groups* are among the many journals available. Books, of course, are another knowledge source. Conferences and in-service training provide more means of keeping current, increasing knowledge, and enhancing skills.

The Code also requires that you "contribute to the knowledge base of social work and share research knowledge and practice wisdom with colleagues" (NASW, 1993, p. 9). Therefore, even if you do not have a PhD, you can use your current knowledge to evaluate both your own practice and your agency's programs. "Practice wisdom" is an expansive term. Sharing this with others can involve informal communication with individual colleagues, formal presentations, or discussions during group supervisory sessions. The point is to keep thinking, evaluating practice, and improving service provision to clients.

The Social Worker's Ethical Responsibility to Society

Social workers are responsible for "promoting the general welfare . . . of society" (NASW, 1993, p. 10). That is a pretty broad statement. The general welfare of society can include just about everything. The Code highlights seven major themes identified below that should permeate your practice. They should provide the context for everything you do professionally, regardless of whether you are pursuing micro, mezzo, or macro targets of change.

1. *Elimination of discrimination*. The Code indicates that you should work to "eliminate discrimination against any person or group on the basis of race, color, sex, sexual orientation, age, religion, national origin, marital status, political belief, mental or physical handicap, or any other preference or personal characteristic, condition, or status" (NASW, 1993, p. 10). *Stereotypes* are "preconceived and relatively fixed ideas about an individual, group, or social status. These ideas are usually based on superficial characteristics or overgeneralizations of traits observed in some members of the group" (Barker, 1991, p. 227). A *prejudice* is "an irrational attitude of hostility directed against an individual, a group, a race, or their supposed characteristics" (*Webster's Ninth Collegiate Dictionary*, 1991, p. 928). *Discrimination* involves "the prejudgment and negative treatment of people based on identifiable characteristics such as race, gender, religion, or ethnicity" (Barker, 1991, p. 64).

The Code's intent in the matter of discrimination is pretty straightforward. Essentially, it tells you not to discriminate under any circumstances on the basis of potentially prejudicial group characteristics.

A problem is that none of us is perfect. We are all affected by stereotypes and prejudices. The best we can do is to continue striving to identify them and eliminate them. We can work to avoid acting on them which would

result in discrimination. This is an ongoing process. Highlight 12.2 poses some suggestions for addressing your own stereotypes and prejudices.

2. *Ensured access to resources*. The second theme underlying social work values and practice is the idea that all people should have fair and equal access to the "resources, services, and opportunities which they require" (NASW, 1993, p. 10). If people are not getting what they need, it is your responsibility to help them. For example, a social service worker who oversees financial planning and debt management services for community residents who qualify by a means test[2] might begin to notice that many homeless individuals and families are ineligible for such services. Agency policy mandates that a client must have a semi-permanent residence and a phone number where he or she can be contacted. The agency says it needs to establish client residency which qualifies community residents for services and resources. Homeless people by definition have neither an address nor a phone number. Ethically, it is your responsibility to consider addressing this issue. Can you become a change catalyst to initiate an alteration of agency policy? Can you share your concerns with others to begin a macro change process aimed at serving these homeless community residents?

3. *Choice and opportunity for all*. The third underlying theme in social work is the need to "expand choice and opportunity for all persons, with special regard for disadvantaged or oppressed groups or persons" (NASW, 1993, p. 10). If you are a school social worker at a school with no access for people requiring wheelchairs, you need to pursue the possibility of such access. Oppression involves "the social act of placing severe restrictions on a group or institution" (Barker, 1991, p. 162). Oppression by definition limits choice and opportunity. Therefore, when you identify a situation as marked by significant oppression, it is your ethical responsibility to do something about it.

4. *Respect for cultural diversity*. Being sensitive to and respecting cultural differences is the fourth theme

---

2. A *means* test is used to evaluate a "client's financial resources and using the result as the criterion to determine eligibility to receive a benefit" (Barker, 1995, p. 228). A social worker would typically assess all of a client's assets weighed against the client's debits or debts. If the client's total assets fell below a designated level, the client would be eligible to receive services or resources. In essence, a means test establishes that a client does not have the *means* to pay for these services or resources without outside help.

HIGHLIGHT 12.2

COMBATING YOUR OWN STEREOTYPES AND PREJUDICES

Combating your own stereotypes about and prejudices against various groups of people is an ongoing process. For whatever reasons, we all develop them even if we hate that fact. The important thing is to continue working to identify them and obliterate as many as we can. One problem is that we may think we have one taken care of and another one pops up.

For example, Danielle, forty-two, is a Caucasian social worker in a very Caucasian rural county in a Midwestern state. She is married to Gerhard, forty-five, a Caucasian engineer. Danielle engages in constant warfare with her own stereotypes and prejudices. She hates the fact that she *has* them. She knows she's not supposed to have any. She really doesn't want to have any. It is a constant struggle for her to identify them.

Gerhard's boss, Steve, invites both of them to a Christmas dinner party with Steve's other supervisees and their respective wives and husbands. Danielle thinks about the upcoming Christmas dinner. She pictures Steve, an African American, in her mind. She has never met him. She knows a few African-American people, but none are among her close personal friends. She'd never even met an African American until she went to college. She has done substantial reading about African-American culture out of genuine interest. In her living room she displays an entire wall of African masks and figures that a friend brought, at Danielle's request, when that friend once visited central Africa.

Danielle and Gerhard attend the dinner. By chance, they sit at the same table with Steve and his wife, Sue, also an African American. Whatever stereotypes and prejudices Danielle had harbored (and fought to get rid of) about Steve and Sue as African Americans soon dissipated, much to Danielle's relief. Steve and Sue were both from central Manhattan. They spoke concisely and fast, having

what Danielle considered strong "New York accents." What Danielle had studied about African-American culture had nothing to do with her interpersonal interactions that particular evening. Sue, as a matter of fact, had just spent two weeks participating in a dig in central France, (anthropology was one of her primary interests). Danielle found Sue a fascinating, good-humored individual and liked her very much.

So what exactly was the problem? Danielle found herself switching gears from fighting any remnants of prejudices and stereotypes about African Americans to identifying and combating her prejudices and stereotypes about New Yorkers. She thought to herself that if it's not one thing, it's another. She had a lot more attitudinal changes to work on.

A major difficulty in combating stereotypes and prejudices is that you're not supposed to have any in the first place, which makes it very difficult to identify them. If you admit that you sustain some stereotype or prejudice, you admit to a serious failure. However, before you can work to obliterate a stereotype or prejudice, you must be clearly aware that it exists. This is a catch-22 situation.

Following these steps is one means of beginning to combat personal prejudices.

1. *Carefully observe and monitor your thoughts when interacting with anyone belonging to a group with characteristics significantly different from your own.* Part of this involves acknowledging that you notice a difference. Are you especially aware that this person has Asian facial characteristics, red hair, speaks with an Italian accent, walks with a limp, or comes from western Tasmania? Does the awareness of the characteristic stand out in your mind? Are you making prejudgments to yourself about this person on the basis of this characteristic? True, it is important to recognize people's characteristics in general, to have good ob-

servational skills. However, the fact that you are paying special attention to some specific characteristic, some difference between you and the other person, may alert you to a potential prejudice.

2. *Identify exactly how you treat this person differently.* Are you monitoring the words you say? If so, in what manner? Do you treat this person differently? If so, in what ways? Begin to measure the difference between the way you treat this person because he or she belongs to some particular group against the way you treat people who are not very different from yourself.

3. *Gradually change your behavior toward the identified person, bringing it more in line with your behavior toward "nondifferent" people.* Of course, always be vigilant regarding cultural differences. That is, be sensitive to other people's potential cultural expectations. Respect cultural differences, but identify the differences in behavior that are based on your own prejudices. In effect, you can *normalize* your behavior toward this "different-group" person.

4. *Monitor your progress in combating your stereotypes*

and prejudices. To what extent have you managed to amend your behavior to the "different" person so that you now treat that person as "nondifferent"? To what extent do you no longer have to expend any effort to do this? When you no longer notice any difference when interacting with the person in question, you have probably made substantial gains in demolishing your stereotype or prejudice—at least insofar as this individual is concerned.

5. *Maintain a perspective that appreciates and respects both individual and cultural differences.* Being fair, open-minded, and impartial on the one hand, and sensitive, perceptive, and appreciative of differences on the other is far from easy. It requires an ongoing vigilance over your own personal perceptions and actions. You do not want to pre-judge others on the basis of their membership in some group. You want to interact and communicate with each client, colleague, or administrator as an individual. Yet you also want to be sensitive and respectful to the cultural differences that do exist.

---

undergirding social work. Part of this involves appreciation and celebration of differences. Another part concerns taking care not to impose your own cultural expectations and values on those from cultures different from your own.

5. *Emergency service.* Providing help to people in a crisis or an emergency is yet another theme of social work. When people suffer extreme circumstances, you are ethically committed to helping them. Remember the awesome flooding of the Mississippi River a few years ago? Or the collapse of a portion of the Los Angeles freeway in the 1994 earthquake? Or the famine in central Africa when thousands of families were starving? Or the April 19, 1995, bombing of the Alfred P. Murray Federal building in Oklahoma City? Whenever social workers are even peripherally involved, they are obligated to do whatever they can to help people in such dire circumstances.

6. *The improvement of social conditions and the promotion of social justice.* Whenever possible, social workers are ethically obligated to advocate for improved social conditions and the promotion of social justice. This may mean talking or writing to legislators asking them to change or improve unfair policies. It may mean marching to protest unfair treatment or practices. Likewise, it might concern educating voters

about social issues so that they can press for positive social change.

7. *Informed public participation.* The final theme underlying social work is that the public has the right both to be informed accurately about the issues and to shape "social policies and institutions" (NASW, 1993, p. 10). In other words, social workers should encourage all people to have access to information about how public decisions are made. People should have the opportunity to participate as much as possible in the decision-making processes that formulate social policies that, in turn, shape these people's very lives.

Personal Values

Values are "one's belief about how things ought to be (i.e., what is 'right')" (Sheafor, Horejsi, & Horejsi, 1991, p. 20). We all have the right to our personal values and to ideas about how we personally feel things should be. We have opinions about whether public finances should be used to build a new baseball stadium or to establish an ongoing jobs training program for women on public assistance. We have personal values and beliefs about religion, state and federal tax rates, and whether women should change their last names when they marry. We even have opinions about whether or not former football great O.J. Simpson murdered his ex-wife Nicole.

At this point in your social work education, you should have addressed the concept of personal values and how they must stand apart from professional values. You have probably done this within the micro and mezzo contexts. For example, how do you avoid imposing your personal values on your clients? How do you hold your own values in check when helping a family reach a decision? As you run a group, how do you prevent your own values from interfering with the values of group members?

It is just as important to separate your personal values from professional objective judgments in the macro context. When addressing macro issues such as potential agency policy change or development of a community resource, it is critical to work on the behalf of the client system's needs and beliefs, not your own.

Tropman (1995, p. 68) proposes several questions about which you may sustain strong personal opinions:

- How much should the government do for people?
- Does the government owe everyone an adequate income?
- Should people be allowed to work as long as they want?
- How much responsibility should the family take in caring for its older members?

When confronted with any macro situation, you must carefully identify your personal values and distinguish them from what is in your client system's best interest from that system's own perspective. Consider being in the position of supporting an agency policy relating to the last question posed above. What if the social service agency you work for implements a new policy that requires family members to care for elderly members in order for the family to receive any benefits? To what extent might your personal values and opinions differ from what is best for these elderly clients and their families? What would you do? Would you respond, "Okay, I'll go along with the policy?" Or would you try to inhibit and stop the policy's implementation? What would your professional values encourage you to do?

The answers to such situations are not easy. If a perfect answer existed, you would not even be contemplating the problem. It would already have been solved. We will discuss a wide range of ethical dilemmas and how you might address them in the macro context later in the chapter.

Types of Ethical Issues Confronting Agency Workers

Reamer (1983) describes three primary areas where ethical issues may confront social workers. They include those "in direct practice," "in social welfare policy and programs," and "among colleagues" (pp. 31–33). The issues addressed below reflect a combination of these three areas. As we have established, ethical issues in direct practice do not occur in a vacuum. Rather, they occur within organizational and community macro contexts. Social welfare policies and programs impose both responsibilities and constraints on your direct practice. Thus, they provide structures within which you must solve any ethical dilemmas confronting you. Finally, ethical issues arising among colleagues are different from those occurring with client systems, regardless of whether the system involves an individual, family, or group. Dealing with collegial and even administrative ethical issues requires a broader macro focus.

It is difficult to delineate clearly among the range of ethical dilemmas arising in micro, mezzo, and macro practice. Here we will assume a generalist approach, acknowledging that an ethical dilemma can involve two or three practice perspectives at once. Since this book's orientation is macro, however, we will emphasize ethical dilemmas within the macro context.

Ethical Absolutism versus Ethical Relativism

Two basic approaches exist for determining what is the right thing to do in any given practice situation (Loewenberg & Dolgoff, 1992; Reamer, 1990). One theoretical approach is that of "ethical absolutism" (Loewenberg & Dolgoff, p. 43). This perspective assumes that moral laws exist to govern ethical decision making in virtually any situation. In essence, decision making is not necessary because the answer should be clear to you. The assumption is that there is only one correct way of doing things. Perhaps you know people who espouse this view in other aspects of their lives. Their way is the only way—not only the right way but the only way—to approach a task or consider an issue.

Consider the view that there is only one way of stacking and arranging the dishes in a given dishwasher.

Any other way is totally wrong, inexcusable, and even reprehensible. Or the right time to wash dishes might be immediately after a meal. And they must be done by hand. People who use dishwashers are lazy and will never get anywhere in life. Dishwashers waste water and soap. They don't clean well enough. You have to scrape the used plates anyway before you put them in. If you don't, you have semi-permanent encrusted crud after the washing and drying cycles have ceased. The point is that people taking an ethical absolutism approach assume a black or white, right or wrong perspective on an issue. Other people's views are wrong. There is no flexibility here.

Reamer (1995, pp. 137–40) cites a further example that relates directly to social work practice.[3] He describes a Refugee Resettlement Center that provides a wide range of services to immigrants to the U.S. including "housing referrals, financial and job counseling, language tutoring, and concrete help with federal immigration officials" (p. 137). The U.S. Immigration and Naturalization Service (INS) begins exerting substantial pressure upon the center's director, Hernando Juarez, to report any illegal aliens coming to the center's attention. In actuality, a significant number of illegal aliens come to the center for help on a regular basis. Historically, the center's administration and staff have maintained that the agency's aspiration was to serve all immigrants in need, whether they were "legal" or not.

Hernandez approaches the staff during an agency meeting and asks them to reconsider their informal policy of not "snitching on" (the term used by many agency staff) illegal aliens who are desperately in need of help. Hernando raises two issues. First, the center is acting illegally by not reporting known illegal aliens. He fears the INS might initiate reprisals and even legal action against the center. Second, Hernando questions whether adherence to the non-reporting policy prevents center staff from reporting information about the illegal aliens for other purposes. What if center staff were aware of other reportable problems involving illegal aliens, such as child abuse or felonies? What if you were a social worker on staff at the center? What do you think the center should do—maintain its present nonreporting policy or not?

Ethical absolutism would dictate one of two clear-cut responses. First, an ethical absolutist could say that the law must be obeyed, no matter what. Therefore, the nonreporting policy must be rescinded. Center staff must report any illegal aliens who come to their attention. That is the law. There is no other choice.

On the other hand, ethical absolutists might assume the total opposite position. They might declare that, of course, staff must adhere to the informal nonreporting policy. That was part of the center's mission and its moral philosophy. Therefore, that was the only way to go.

What do you notice about the last two paragraphs? What do they have in common? They both assume an absolute approach and adhere to a principle unilaterally, giving no thought to appraising the issue from other perspectives.

The second approach to making ethical decisions is that of "ethical relativism" (Loewenberg & Dolgoff, p. 42). Here an ethical decision is based on the context in which the decision is made. Ethical relativism requires the evaluation of any particular action on the basis of its potential consequences. In other words, this perspective assumes that there are always a number of alternative choices in any situation involving ethics. It is up to you to determine what course of action is best. Which alternative will result in the most good and the least bad consequences? The emphasis is on *results* rather than on *principles*.

An ethical relativism approach in the case of the Refugee Resettlement Center would require giving careful thought to the situation and examining the problem from many angles. What action would produce the most desirable results? An ethical relativist might consider the arguments proposed for and against each alternative. On the one hand, changing the policy and requiring the reporting of all illegal aliens would comply with INS regulations. It would keep the center out of any potential trouble with the INS. It would also prevent U.S. citizens from subsidizing illegal noncitizens. The center receives its funding from a range of sources, several of them publicly financed.

On the other hand, changing the policy to report illegal aliens would deprive many people of services they gravely need and would directly oppose part of the agency's mission to serve any immigrants in need. To what extent would the INS really pursue this issue with the center? The INS has never done anything in the past. Both agencies value their positive relationship.

_____

3. The example as Reamer presents it is modified to comply with content employed here.

Reamer (1995) continues evaluating the situation, raising several points. If the agency begins reporting illegal aliens tot he INS, what will happen to its reputation? How likely will other immigrants be to utilize the agency services when they hear about the center's violations of confidentiality? The question for potential clients might be, could the center violate their own confidentiality and privacy?

One final point on the pros and cons of changing the policy deals with the difference between not reporting illegal aliens in general and not reporting illegal aliens who commit serious crimes. In the latter case, the center could implement a reporting policy without requiring universal reporting of illegal aliens to the INS.

The prior discussion does not settle on an absolute answer. It demonstrates an evaluative thought process by which a conclusion could be reached. Ethical absolutism maintains that there is always one correct answer. Ethical relativism, on the other hand, requires thoughtful review of the many variables involved in a given situation to determine the most advantageous result. From the preceding discussion, what is your own opinion regarding the center's best course of action? Would maintaining the current nonreporting policy or changing it to a reporting policy produces the best results?

As we have established by now, social work is not simple. Any profession involving such intensive work with people and their problems is complex, to say the least. Thus, we propose a blend of ethical absolutism and ethical relativism. Ethical relativism espouses no definite guidelines for addressing any situation involving ethical decisions. Each situation is unique, with a unique conglomeration of people and variables. Therefore, there are no consistently established values or rules to follow. Social work, however, does have recognized values inherent in its Code of Ethics upon which to base decisions. You might consider this a form of ethical absolutism. Yet as social workers you must look at many variables in order to come to a decision. You might think of this as ethical relativism. In summary, social work requires a blend of absolutism and relatism when coming to an ethical decision.

For example, what does the NASW Code of Ethics (1993) have to say about situations such as the Refugee Relocation Centers? Reamer (1995) makes several points. For one thing, the Code of Ethics never really requires social workers to obey policies and rules in so many words. Rather, he continues, several principles relate to the fair provision of services to those in need. Principle I.C.2. of the Code (1993) states that "the social worker should act to prevent practices that are inhumane or discriminatory against any person or group of persons" (p. 4). Principle II.F.1. requires that "the social worker should serve clients with devotion, loyalty, determination, and the maximum application of professional skill and competence" (p. 5). Principle II.G.1. continues that "the social worker should safeguard the interests and rights of . . . [the] client" (p. 6). Principle VI.P.1. states that "the social worker should act to prevent and eliminate discrimination against any person or group" (p. 10). Finally, principle VI.P.3. requires that "the social worker should act to ensure that all persons have access to the resources, services, and opportunities which they require" (p. 10). Reamer (1995) concludes that "as a group, these principles suggest that social workers have an obligation to assist all oppressed and vulnerable individuals regardless of their immigration status" (p. 139). In other words, what should the center do, change its policy or not? To what decision would this thought process, blending ethical absolutism and relativism, bring you?

Ethical Dilemmas

In social work practice one encounters a wide range of ethical dilemmas. The word *dilemma* has two primary meanings relevant to social work (*Webster's Ninth Collegiate Dictionary*, 1991, p. 355). First, a dilemma is "an argument presenting two or more equally conclusive alternatives against an opponent." Second, it can be "a choice or a situation involving choice between equally unsatisfactory alternatives." Your reaction to this might be, "Oh, great, you can't win in social work because you'll constantly be confronted with equally bad alternatives."

Ethical dilemmas involve problematic situations whose possible solutions all offer imperfect and unsatisfactory answers. In other words, your ethical guidelines conflict with each other. There is no one perfect answer that can conform to all the ethical principles in the professional code. You are stuck with deciding what to do.

When we reconsider, however, this is not really true. First of all, in social work we have professional values. *Ethical* dilemmas always involve values. Rarely, if ever, does an ethical dilemma face us with equally bad alternatives. Rather, we can use values to carefully examine and weigh alternatives to determine the best one.

In an ethical dilemma, then, we are faced with a situation in which a decision must be made under circumstances that set two or more ethical principles in conflict. Perhaps you cannot abide by both the social work ethic of confidentiality and the obligation to save a suicidal person's life at the same time. However, because we have professional values, we can formulate some guidelines for making tough choices. We can establish a hierarchy to decide what aspect of any particular ethical dilemma is more important than another.

Conceptualizing and Addressing an Ethical Dilemma: Decision-Making Steps

The first step in determining what to do about an ethical dilemma is to establish the fact that you actually have one. A series of variables can help you conceptualize the potential problem. This decision-making process involves the eight steps illustrated in figure 12.1.

Step 1: Recognize the Problem

The first step in confronting a potential ethical dilemma is to recognize the problem (Corey, Corey, & Callanan, 1993). The seed might be a gut reaction, an unarticulated emotional feeling that something is not right. Something does not fit or make sense. You must determine that an ethical dilemma exists before going any further.

Step 2: Investigate the Variables

The second step in the conceptualization process is investigating the complex matrix of variables that encompass the dilemma (Corey, Corey, & Callanan, 1993; Loewenberg & Dolgoff, 1992). What problems are involved? What people are involved? How are you yourself involved? What is your agency's involvement? How

Figure 12.1
Conceptualizing an Ethical Dilemma

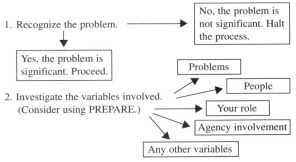

1. Recognize the problem.

No, the problem is not significant. Halt the process.

Yes, the problem is significant. Proceed.

2. Investigate the variables involved. (Consider using PREPARE.)

Problems

People

Your role

Agency involvement

Any other variables

3. Get feedback from others.

4. Appraise values that apply to the dilemma.

5. Evaluate the dilemma on the basis of established ethical principles.

6. Identify possible alternatives to pursue.

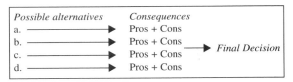

Possible alternatives	*Consequences*
a. ——————→	Pros + Cons
b. ——————→	Pros + Cons
c. ——————→	Pros + Cons
d. ——————→	Pros + Cons

Final Decision

7. Weigh the pros and cons of each alternative.

8. Make your decision about what to do.

might your agency be affected by resolution or lack of resolution of this dilemma? Roll the dilemma around in your mind. Think deeply about what it is and why it exists. What other variables might provide you with clues to a workable solution? You might follow the PREPARE process described in chapter 5 to stimulate your ideas.

Step 3: Get Feedback from Others

If at all possible, talk to other people about your concerns (Corey et al., 1993; Sinclair, 1993). Bounce your ideas off them to more firmly establish your objectivity. Brainstorm with them different ways of viewing and eventually handling the dilemma. A trusted supervisor or colleagues familiar with the dilemma's context could be helpful.

Step 4: Appraise the Values That Apply to the Dilemma

Assess and choose the values and ethical guidelines that best apply to the dilemma (Corey, Corey, & Callanan, 1993; Loewenberg & Dolgoff, 1992). What specific ethical aspects of the NASW Code of Ethics do you feel are being violated? You may discover that there is no ethical dilemma, only a more straightforward ethical problem. A problem can have a clear solution. A dilemma by definition has competing, imperfect solutions. If the Code provides you with a clear answer, use the Code's directives to follow steps toward the problem's resolution.

Step 5: Evaluate the Dilemma

It is possible to make conscious decisions about what values are more important than others. You can establish a hierarchy of principles based on values that can guide you through the process of confronting an ethical dilemma. Remember that ethical dilemmas always involve situations in which you cannot do all the right things. Each dilemma presents some conflict among ethical principles so that you cannot abide by them all. You might determine that staying alive is more important than telling the truth. Telling the truth is the ethical thing to do, but what if you are in a situation where it is impossible to both tell the truth and keep someone (perhaps yourself) alive at the same time? Your best course of action might then be not to tell the truth. Evaluating an ethical dilemma on the basis of ethical principles is the core of this chapter. We will review two approaches to the ranking of ethical principles and use one of them to elaborate on a wide range of potential ethical dilemmas that could confront you in practice.

Step 6: Identify and Think about Possible Alternatives

What can you do in your job to solve the dilemma? What creative ideas can you come up with? Finding a solution could employ the IMAGINE process to change a policy, initiate a project, or even develop a program.

Step 7: Weigh the Pros and Cons of Each Alternative

Weighting the pros and cons of each alternative is a common practice in social work. This approach is also useful in resolving ethical dilemmas (Corey, Corey, & Callanan, 1993). What course of action is best for the client? What alternative is most likely to succeed? How might you best proceed?

Step 8: Make Your Decision

Finally, make a decision about what is the best route for you to take. The IMAGINE process described in chapter 6 might apply here, depending on the alternative you choose. The main thing about confronting an ethical dilemma is to do some serious thinking about it.

Ranking Ethical Principles

There are various ways to address ethical dilemmas and make decisions on how to proceed. The following sections will review two of them. One approach to ethical decision-making pairs and ranks identified values against each other (Reamer, 1990). One value supersedes the other so that you know which one to choose in any conflict between the two. The second approach proposes a hierarchy of principles whereby those higher in the hierarchy consistently supersede those lower in the hierarchy (Loewenberg & Dolgoff, 1992).

Reamer's Guide to Ethical Decison Making

Reamer (1990) suggests examining an ethical dilemma on the basis of six ethical principles. He proposes six guidelines that rank one ethical principle against another. Each guideline can aid decision making in ethical dilemmas involving the principles.

A. Rules about Basic Survival Supersede Rules Governing Lesser Actions

Reamer poses that ''rules against basic harms'' or evils should supersede those against lesser harms. Thus, rules that ensure "health, food, shelter, [and] mental equilibrium" should supersede lesser rules concerning confidentiality, lying, or protection of goods or property (Reamer, 1983, p. 34). In other words, the most important rules protect people's right to survive. They reinforce people's ability to get what they need to continue living. Additionally, this principle "suggests that the expenditure of public funds to care for individuals whose lives or health are seriously threatened should take precedence over the expenditure of public funds for the arts and other recreational purposes when resources are limited" (Reamer, 1983, p. 34). Thus, ethical principles apply to interventions in both micro and mezzo practice, as well as in macro practice and policy.

B. One Person's Right to Well-Being Supersedes Another Person's Right to Be Free

The second principle in Reamer's hierarchy is that one person's right to "basic well-being" supersedes another person's right to be free (Reamer, 1990, p. 62). In other words, "this guideline suggests that individuals have a right to freedom and to act as they wish unless their actions threaten the welfare of others" (Reamer, 1990, p. 62). This principle once again emphasizes the importance of survival. It also ranks one person's survival and well-being above another person's personal freedom.

If a client tells his social worker that he committed an armed robbery for which another person has been incarcerated, the social worker, according to this principle, should report the confession despite breaking confidentiality with her client. The well-being of the person who is unjustly sitting in jail is more important than the client's right to privacy.

C. One Person's Right to Be Free Supersedes That Same Person's Right to Well-Being

The third principle in Reamer's ethical guidelines states that an individual's personal freedom and right to choose take precedence over that same person's right to well-being or even personal survival. This guideline emphasizes the individual's right to make her or his own decisions, regardless of whether such decisions are in that individual's best interest. Thus, a person has the right to participate in behavior that is harmful to her- or himself,

such as drug use, smoking, and even, potentially, suicide. We must stress, however, that this principle applies only if "the individual is making an informed, voluntary decision with knowledge of relevant circumstances and . . . the consequences of the decision will not threaten the well-being of others" (Reamer, 1990, p. 63). The individual making the decision must be of sound mind and totally aware of the potential consequences of the behavior.

Therefore, for example, a woman with a physical disability who is eating poorly, suffering health problems, and living in squalor has the right to do so if she is, indeed, capable of making informed, independent, conscious decisions (Reamer, 1990). This assumes, of course, that she is hurting no one but herself. On the other hand, if she has a dependent living with her, something will have to be done. Guideline B above indicates that one individual's (the dependent's) right to well-being takes precedence over another individual's right to be free (to choose to live in squalor).

D. Obeying Rules You Have Agreed to Support Supersedes the Right to Freely Break These Rules

Obeying rules and regulations takes precedence over the personal right to break them. Reamer (1990) specifically refers to those rules that you have already agreed to obey, such as the policies of the agency for which you work.

Another example involves NASW members. We have examined and explained NASW's Code of Ethics. If you are an NASW member you have agreed to follow NASW's rules and directives (Reamer, 1990). Therefore, NASW can censure members who do not obey those rules. The Code of Ethics forbids engaging in sexual relationships with clients. This ethical rule takes precedence over your personal right to enter into such an intimate relationship.

E. People's Right to Well-Being Supersedes Adherence to Rules You Have Agreed to Support

Once again, the individual's right to survival and well-being assumes precedence, this time over the rules you have agreed to support. This guideline indicates that the basic right to survival is more important than adherence to rules and regulations to which you have voluntarily agreed. If your agency adopts a policy denying services to people who are illiterate because they are unable to complete the necessary application forms, these people's well-being is more important than the agency rule. This guideline directs you to provide people with the services they need rather than follow the unethical agency rule.

F. Preventing Harm and Fulfilling Basic Needs Supersedes Withholding Your Own Property

This guideline indicates that people have the right not to suffer major harm, such as starvation, and to have basic needs met, such as housing and education, even if that requires others to sacrifice property (Reamer, 1990). This guideline relates to the government's right to levy taxes to provide the general populace with what they need. In other words, poor people have the right to have basic needs met even at the expense of wealthier people. Children, even if they are poverty-stricken, have the right to food, clothing, and lodging. It follows that the state has the right to tax wealthier people in order to accomplish this.

How does this particular principle relate to the thousands of impoverished homeless people wandering our streets? Does the taxation and social service structure as it now exists abide by this ethical principle? If so, why are the women, children, families, and single individuals still out there? If this principle does not apply, why doesn't it?

Postcript

You may or may not personally agree with Reamer's proposed ethical guidelines. They provide one example of an ethical guide to decision making in practice. They are solidly founded on the NASW Code of Ethics. Regardless of what ethical guidelines you use in practice, you will continue to be responsible for your own behavior and decisions.

Loewenberg and Dolgoff's "Ethical Principles Screen"

Loewenberg and Dolgoff (1992) propose a hierarchy of ethical principles with which to evaluate the potential

Figure 12.2
A Hierarchy of Ethical Rights:
ETHICS for U

Principle		Ethical Right–People Have the Right to:
1.	E	**EXIST** with their basic needs met.
2.	T	**TREATMENT** that is fair and equal.
3.	H	**HAVE** free choice and freedom.
4.	I	**INJURY** that is minimal or non-existent.
5.	C	**CULTIVATE** a good quality of life.
6.	S	**SECURE** their privacy and confidentiality.
7.	for U	**UNDERSTAND** the truth and receive available information.

courses of action in any ethical dilemma. A hierarchy is a ranked order in which a principle takes precedence over the principles below it. In other words, it is more important to abide by the first principle than by principles two through seven, by the second principle than by principles three through six, and so on. Thus, the "Ethical Principles Screen" is a prioritized list of seven ethical principles summarized in figure 12.2 (Loewenberg & Dolgoff, 1992, p. 60). The following section discusses these principles more thoroughly. Reamer's guidelines, on the other hand, contrast pairs of principles, and no pair has a clearly established relationship with any other pair.

ETHICS for U Principle 1: People have the right to Exist with their basic needs met

This principle stresses that people have the right to stay alive. As a social worker you should put this before any other ethical principle. When an ethical dilemma involves a life-or-death variable, you choose an action to save the life, even if this means breaking confidentiality with a client or suppressing the rights of others. Sustaining life takes precedence. You might note that people's right to survival also characterizes the most important consideration in Reamer's ethical principles.

ETHICS for U Principle 2: People have the right to *Treatment* that is fair and equal

The second ethical principle guarantees fair and equal treatment. You as a social worker should make decisions to abide by this principle except when life or death is involved. Ethical principle 1 is the only condition that takes precedence.

ETHICS for U Principle 3: People have the right to *Have* free choice and freedom

Ethical principle 3 maintains that people's right to be free is the third priority in addressing an ethical dilemma. We all know the value that social work places on the principles of self-determination. It is a person's basic right to make his or her own decisions. The Ethical Principles Screen indicates that only people's right to survival or their right to equal treatment takes precedence over their freedom.

ETHICS for U Principle 4: People have the right to experience *Injury* that is minimal or nonexistent

This principle states that people have the basic right to be protected from injury. In the event of potential injury, people have the right to experience the least injury possible, the least lasting harm or injury, and finally, "the most easily reversible harm" (Loewenberg & Dolgoff, 1992, p. 62).

ETHICS for U Principle 5: People have the right to *Cultivate* a good quality of life

People have the right to seek and attain a "better quality of life" than they currently have (Loewenberg & Dolgoff, 1992, p. 62). This applies to individuals, groups, neighborhoods, communities, states, and nations. Only principles 1 through 4 take precedence over this right.

ETHICS for U Principle 6: People have the right to *Secure* their privacy and confidentiality

Social workers should strive to secure people's privacy and confidentiality. People have the right not to have their private information made public. Confidentiality is the ethical principle that workers should not share information provided by or about a client without the client's explicit permission to do so (Barker, 1991, p. 46). Such information might include people's names, what they say, professional beliefs and findings about them, and anything written about them (Barker, 1991).

It is interesting that confidentiality is so strongly stressed in social work practice. Why, then, is it number 6 of 7 on the Ethical Principles Screen list? Later portions of the chapter focusing on ethical dilemmas will discuss this issue more thoroughly.

ETHICS for *U* Principle 7: People have the right to *Understand* the truth and receive all available information

Ethical Principle 7 states that people have the right to know and understand the truth. They have the right to accurate information. It would be nice to have the truth and nothing but the truth unveiled to you all of the time. When it is possible, this is an important axiom for social workers to follow. However, what if you are legally forbidden to disclosing information to clients? Should you be forced to tell them everything you think, even when your thoughts and ideas are negative? Must you always show people all your notes about them and the issues concerning them?

Discussion and Resolution of Ethical Dilemmas in Macro Contexts

There are endless types of potential ethical dilemmas that you can encounter in macro practice. It is beyond the scope of this text to address them all. However, we will address some of them, including: limited resources, community support (or the lack thereof) for service provision; relationships with colleagues; conforming to agency policy; breaching confidentiality; co-optation versus cooperation; fraud and illegal behavior; conflict of interest; potential harm to participants; and stigmatization tactics.

Distributing Limited Resources

Resources not only are consistently limited but also appear to be continuously shrinking (Reamer, 1987). Hard decisions must frequently be made regarding what is more and less necessary. Consider your own education. You pay tuition. Tuition, along with state and other funds, helps to pay for your educational process. There is a limited amount of funding to pay for potentially unlimited educational services. Suppose educational costs continue to rise and expenses increase. If you had controlled the budget at your educational institution and you had to make some hard spending choices, which of the following options would you choose to reduce spending?

1. Turn your classroom heat far down in winter (if you live in a cold northern state) or the air conditioning far down in fall and spring (if you live in a warm southern state).
2. Increase tuition by 12 percent.
3. Increase typical class size by 100 percent.
4. Increase parking costs by 300 percent.
5. Employ teaching assistants (not necessarily highly qualified) instead of full-time faculty as instructors.

If you had to choose one of these, none would be very appealing. Each involves giving something up. This is always the case with limited resources. You can't have everything you want or even need.

Reamer (1990) describes four variables to consider when trying to make the right distribution of scarce resources; they include the principles of equality, need, compensation, and contribution (p. 49). The principle of *equality* might seem simple at first. True equality means that all people "should have equal access to services, resources, and opportunities and be treated the same by all social, educational, and welfare institutions" (Barker, 1991, p. 76). Everyone should have equal access to resources, right? Isn't that fair? However, does the system really work that way?

Next, what about *need*? Needs are "physical, psychological, economic, cultural, and social requirements for survival, well-being, and fulfillment" (Barker, 1991, p. 153). Shouldn't people who have greater needs have better access to scarce resources? Why should people who need resources less than others get these resources anyway?

Then, there is the principle of *compensation*. Compensation refers to the provision of resources or treatment to pay for expenditures of effort or to make up for poor prior treatment. Should people such as African Americans, who have been discriminated against in hiring, be given some compensation in the form, for example, of preferential treatment? Should people who work hard be paid more than those who don't work hard or at all? Would you personally work for nothing? Would you work harder for more money? Would you work less enthusiastically for less money?

Finally, there is the principle of *contribution*. Contribution is giving or supplying, along with others, to a common fund or store (*Webster's Ninth Collegiate Dictionary*, 1991, p. 285). Should people who contribute more to a resource delivery system get more from that system than people who contribute less? Retirement funds are a good example. People who contribute more to their retirement fund by working longer and/or contributing a larger chunk of their paychecks get more at retirement than do those who work for shorter periods and contribute less. People who contribute nothing to a retirement fund get nothing from a fund. Is this fair? Is this ethical? The issues all these questions address are complicated. There are no easy answers.

Many times in practice you will be confronted by the need to make decisions about limited resources. Who will get the services and sustenance they need? Who will have to go without? Imagine a woman placed in a nursing home (Reamer, 1990). At age seventy-nine Hillary Krist had lived in the same home for twelve years. Supported by government funds, she had some difficulties with her sight and hearing. She also had severe arthritis. However, she was able to get around fairly well and care for herself.

A legislative committee was assigned to evaluate the state's overall costs for nursing-home care. The committee assessed residents' needs across the state, the level of assistance elderly people required, and the extent of services various nursing homes provided. The committee then performed a massive health-care evaluation on all nursing home residents, giving them scores for the amount of assistance they needed in their daily living care. The result for Hillary was not advantageous. The committee determined that she was living in a home that provided too high a level of support for her needs.

Higher levels of support meant more expensive support. Hillary abruptly received a notice in the mail saying that she would have to move to another designated nursing home in two weeks. Hillary was totally distraught. How could she leave her friends and the only home she had known for over a decade?

Hillary's nursing home social worker, Hannah Hefner, was seriously concerned about Hillary's well-being. Older people often adjust poorly to such major changes in life circumstances. Hannah was a direct service practitioner who focused on performing micro-oriented activities with individuals and families. However, a decision made on a macro level high above her and without her input now directly obstructed her ability to practice ethically and effectively.

Hannah recognized the problem. Her second task was to investigate the variables involved in the case. She called the committee and requested details about how decisions were being made. *She sought feedback from others* by talking to her supervisor. She also called other nursing home social workers she knew to discuss the situation with them and see if they were experiencing similar problems.

Next, Hannah appraised the values applying to the dilemma and evaluated the dilemma on the basis of the hierarchy of ethical principles involved. She could not be certain whether ethical principle 1 could be applied to the dilemma. Hannah was not certain how the move would affect Hillary emotionally and physically. She concluded that Hillary would survive the move. Concerning ethical principle 2, Hillary was being treated equally with other clients in similar situations. Hannah anticipated that many other clients would experience serious upsets as a result of the state committee's decision. Ethical principles 3 (the right to have free choice), 4 (the right to experience the least injury), and 5 (the right to cultivate a good quality of life) all indicated that it was unethical—that is, not in Hillary's best interests—to move her. Principle 6 (the right to privacy and confidentiality) does not clearly apply in this case. Principle 7 (the right to understand the truth and be privy to all relevant information) implies that Hillary should have been notified much earlier regarding the decisions that were being made about her and how they were being made.

Hannah identified and seriously considered possible alternatives to pursue. She weighed the pros and cons of each. First, Hannah pleaded with state committee representatives on Hillary's behalf. This could have resulted in macro change affecting a large group of elderly citizens. If committee members had listened, they might have been enlightened regarding their decision's possible affects on many people. However, the committee members remained firm in their decision. It was fiscally inefficient to allow Hillary to remain in a facility that, at this time, provided inappropriately expensive care. Ethical principle 2 (the right to equality) supports the stance that the state should treat all of its clients in the nursing home system equally. It was not justifiable to deny other clients the more intensive care they needed just because Hillary would be upset about being transferred.

Hannah determined that there was nothing she could do about the inevitable conclusion, that Hillary would have to be moved. *However, Hannah did decide what she could do for Hillary.* She could ease Hillary's transition as much as possible (Reamer, 1990). Acting on ethical principle 7, Hannah made certain that Hillary understood the reasons for the decision. Hillary could comprehend both the need to be fair to all citizens and the rationale of fiscal exigency. Hannah also investigated the new home and described it to Hillary. Because of the short time frame, Hannah was unable to take Hillary there for a visit. This would have allowed Hillary to adjust to the whole idea more slowly.

Hannah thought that the committee could have followed several procedures that would have aided residents' transitions to new homes (Reamer, 1990). It could have given both Hannah and Hillary much more notice so that they could have been better prepared for the adjustment. The committee could also have explained the process and rationale more clearly to residents, giving residents some choices about where they wanted to go instead of assigning them specific homes. Finally, the committee could have implemented an appeals process so that residents in truly dire straits would have somewhere to turn. But, alas, Hannah thought, it was too late to do much for Hillary. The only thing Hannah could do at this point was make Hillary's transition as comfortable and predictable as possible.

Yet Hannah might have decided that the ethical thing for her to do was to pursue this issue on others' behalf. Hannah could have resolved to assess the potential for a positive macro level change that would affect many people in positions similar to Hillary's. Hannah might have worked to improve the planning for, involvement of, and treatment of such people. Hence, Hannah could have become a change catalyst system and have begun to form an action system. The action system might then have decided what alternatives to follow. This might have involved the solicitation of voters' support for recommended changes by walking from house to house and encouraging them to sign a petition. Likewise, the chosen alternative might have been to undertake a major newspaper campaign focused on alerting the public to the fate of people like Hillary and on improving the quality of their treatment.

Community Support (or the Lack Thereof) for Service Provision

What if a service is useful and needed, but the community simply does not want it? This is one potentially serious dilemma in macro practice (Reamer, 1990). For example, Sara Newheart works for a private social service organization that runs a number of groups homes for people with developmental disabilities. Each home is supervised on a full-time basis. Sara is in the process of preparing six people to move into a duplex. These clients have been housed in a large institution for many years. Sara and other involved professionals have determined that these clients will fare and progress much better if they are mainstreamed into the community.[4] They have been unable to maximize their potential in this dull, sterile setting.

Suddenly, the agency receives a letter from the Neighborhood Organization stating that community residents are vehemently against this plan. They do not want a facility harboring "that type of people" in their neighborhood! Sara suddenly recognizes that she has a problem (step 1 in the ethical decision-making process).

Hence, Sara and her supervisor are faced with an ethical dilemma. Although Sara is not an administrator, part of her job is to help residents adjust in their transition from institutionalized to community-based group home care. The community's vehement resistance to

opening the facility is preventing Sara from doing her job and helping her clients. Sara has a direct service position, but she is confronted with a macro problem at the community level.

The first thing to do is to think more extensively about the situation and investigate the variables involved (step 2). What factors are involved? What variables should be investigated? What clients' needs are at stake? What is the ethical thing to do?

One issue is the entire concept of deinstitutionalization. Deinstitutionalization involves: "the process of (1) preventing both unnecessary admission to and retention in institutions; (2) finding and developing appropriate alternatives in the community for housing, treatment, training, education, and rehabilitation of [persons] who do not need to be in institutions; and (3) improving conditions, care, and treatment for those who need to have institutional care. This approach is based on the principle that . . . persons are entitled to live in the least restrictive environment necessary and lead lives as normally and independently as they can" (U.S. General Accounting Office, 1977, p. 1).

The merits of placing clients in a community-based setting instead of an institutional one must be clearly understood. Sara firmly believes that her clients will be much better able to function normally in a community than in an institutional setting. She foresees involving them in a nearby sheltered workshop. She thinks about teaching them how to travel on the city's transportation system. She see the community facility as much better for her clients' overall well-being than the institution. Therefore, Sara strongly feels it is in the best interest of her clients to enter the group home.

Sara gets feedback from and consults with other relevant people concerning the issue (step 3). She also consults with her immediate supervisor who, in turn, works with higher level administration concerning this matter. Additionally, she talks to colleagues at other group homes to see what they have done to address similar issues.

How does the hierarchy of ethical principles apply to this situation (steps 4 and 5)? The Code of Ethics does not supply a simple answer to her dilemma. Sara, thus, must consider the ethical principles, one by one. Principle 1 is really not involved. Life, the right to exist and have basic needs met, is not at stake. Principle 2 is related, in that people with developmental disabilities should have equal access to community living and the

---

4. *Mainstreaming* involves taking people with exceptional characteristics and placing them in environments where people without such exceptional characteristics live, work, and learn (Barker, 1991, p. 136). The intent is usually to provide these exceptional people with the same or similar experiences and opportunities that are available to everybody else.

rights involved, as anyone else in the community does. This takes precedence over principle 3, which might apply to the community members' right to make their own decisions.

Consider the community's perspective. Community residents don't know much about developmental disability. The unknown breeds fear and suspicion. People have unjust and untrue stereotypes about and prejudices toward people with developmental disabilities. One common myth is that people with developmental disabilities can't control their behavior. Perhaps another stereotype is that such people are violent. Sara needs to think about and empathize with the community resident's perspective.

Principle 2 also supersedes principle 4. The latter could relate to the community residents' right to protection from any injury or harm caused by the group home's residents. Principle 5 emphasizes the importance of pursuing a good quality of life. This is so, both for Sara's clients and for community residents. Principle 6, concerning privacy and confidentiality, does not clearly relate to this situation. However, principle 7, which addresses the right to hear the truth, can be related to the community's need for education. Community residents need to understand what Sara's clients are like and that they can become an integral part of the community.

In summary, principle 2, receiving fair and equal treatment, appears to take precedence over other concerns. Thus, Sara can work to resolve the dilemma with this principle in mind.

The group home's administration made the mistake of not educating and involving the community before initiating a new facility. What can Sara and the agency do now to remedy this? First, Sara mush identify and think about possible alternatives to pursue (step 6). Then, she must weight the pros and cons of each alternative (step 7). Finally, she must come to a final decision concerning what to do about the problem (step 8).

Sara works with her supervisor to develop a plan to educate the community and involve it in running the new facility. She develops a presentation and asks the neighborhood organization if she can come and speak to them at their next meeting. She brings a slide presentation with her to show the types of activities, projects, and accomplishments other clients have pursued in other agency group homes. (Of course, she does this only after getting their informed consent and that of their guardians.) She emphasizes how valuable the community experience is to these human beings. She answers questions, confronts myths and stereotypes, and allays fears.

Additionally, Sara discusses the possibility of inviting neighborhood residents to sit on the agency's board of directors. Agency administration thinks this is a great idea. The neighborhood organization is invited to recommend potential board members. In this way the agency can include the community in its program development process. The neighborhood organization, delighted by the offer, accepts and suggests specific potential board members. Understanding the issues involved and feeling that it has input into the program, the neighborhood organization no longer stands in the way of the program's development.

It would be nice if everyone lived happily ever after, never to confront an ethical dilemma again. However, this is not the case. After the agency opens the group home, one of the residents runs away and breaks into a neighbor's garage. He causes some minor damage that makes the neighbor and the neighborhood organization members irate. Meanwhile, organization officers demand to review residents' files. This, of course, creates another dilemma concerning confidentiality. And so it goes. Both the ethical decision-making process and the hierarchy of ethical principles posed here can be used to address each dilemma as it occurs.

Relationships with Colleagues

What if you find out one of your colleagues is doing something unethical? Maybe that colleague is skirting major responsibilities. Perhaps the colleague is even doing something you feel is actively harming clients. What if that colleague happens to be a pretty good friend of yours? Ethical dilemmas concerning colleagues are often among "the most difficult and dismaying" to deal with (Reamer, 1990, p. 223). They may pose some of the greatest obstacles to your work within the macro environment.

The NASW Code of Ethics dictates that professional social workers "should treat colleagues with respect, courtesy, fairness, and good faith" (NASW, 1993), but it also emphasizes that "the worker's primary responsibility is to clients" (NASW, 1993, p. 1). So what do you do when these two principles conflict?

Loewenberg and Dolgoff (1992) indicate that you

have six choices when dealing with colleagues' unethical behavior. First, you can simply ignore the behavior, the "out of sight, out of mind" attitude. If you don't think about the issue, it will cease to exist. Your second alternative in dealing with a colleague's unethical behavior is to approach the colleague yourself and share your concerns with him or her informally. This is an especially attractive alternative if you feel the colleague is inexperienced or ignorant about the scope and ramifications of the behavior, or if the problem is relatively minor.

The third possibility is to inform your supervisor about the situation. There may even be established agency procedure for dealing with such violations of agency policy. Fourth, in the event that the colleague is an NASW member, you can bring the unethical behavior to the attention of the local NASW chapter for censure. In this case, you must have definite proof that the behavior has occurred and be willing to testify about it.

The fifth thing you can do is to bring it to the attention of the State Licensing Board for professional social workers. In this case, as when reporting to NASW, you must have clear evidence to support your accusation. Your final alternative for addressing such unethical behavior is whistle-blowing, or bringing the issue to the public's attention. Highlight 12.3 addresses the issue of whistle-blowing.

If, indeed, you choose to make a colleague's unethical behavior known by following any of alternatives two through six above, a number of possible consequences may occur (Loewenberg, 1987; Loewenberg & Dolgoff, 1992). First, your colleague may decide or be forced to discontinue the unethical behavior. Second, your colleague may suffer punitive repercussions for his behavior. Third, your colleague may be publicly embarrassed for his behavior, thereby losing clients to more reputable peers. Fourth, your colleague may be cautioned not to continue such behavior in the future and threatened with some form of punishment. Fifth, the agency or an organization responsible for maintaining professional ethics and behavior may denounce such behavior publicly.

Always remember that negative consequences can also result from raising an issue outside your own agency by choosing alternatives three through six (Sinclair, 1993). These include "humiliation to the alleged violator; embarrassment to professionals associated with the agency; a diminishing of the stature of the agency within the community and a resultant compromise of the agency's effectiveness; [and] a reduction in its funding" (p. 390). Thus, taking issues outside the agency should be considered very seriously.

We will address three examples of potential issues with colleagues, including having sexual relationships with clients, failing to report child maltreatment (Loewenberg & Dolgoff, 1992), and allowing personal problems such as alcohol addiction to seriously impede professional performance (Reamer, 1990).

Engaging in Sexual Activities with Clients

The Code of Ethics straightforwardly states that engaging in sexual activities with clients is forbidden. Such behavior should occur "under no circumstances" (NASW, 1993, p. 5). What if you know of a colleague who is doing this (Loewenberg & Dolgoff, 1992)? You happen to be out with a friend at a local hotel bar and see your colleague checking into a room with a person you know is his client. You have always respected this colleague as a knowledgeable, competent, responsible practitioner.

What do you do? *You have already recognized the problem. The next step is to investigate the variables.* The fact is that this colleague is checking into a hotel room with a woman you know is his client. Agency policy and professional ethics clearly indicate that this is taboo. You respect this colleague but seriously question his judgment in this situation. If he is engaging in such behavior with this client, has he done so with others? Is he establishing relationships with other clients right now? Since you have seen him, have other people seen him too? How will this affect the agency's and the profession's reputation?

The next step is getting feedback from others. You have a good relationship with your supervisor. You trust her and feel she might be good to talk with about the situation, but, should you talk to her—or even to other colleagues—before confronting the colleague who appears to have gone astray? If you do directly confront him, will that necessarily change his behavior? In this situation you determine to reconsider feedback from others later in your decision-making process.

You proceed to appraise the values that apply to the dilemma and evaluate the dilemma on the basis of

---

HIGHLIGHT 12.3

WHISTLE BLOWING

Whistle blowing involves "alerting those in positions of higher authority in an organization about the existence of practices that are illegal, wasteful, dangerous, or otherwise contrary to the organization's stated policies" (Barker, 1991, p. 250). In other words, whistle blowing means taking the problem outside the organization and making it known to others, possibly the entire public arena.

Some organizations such as the federal government provide established means for whistle blowing while maintaining the anonymity of the person reporting the problem. Likewise, laws exist to protect the whistle-blower from retaliation by supervisory and administrative personnel whose positions are threatened by the whistle-blower's revelations.

However, despite the fact that there is some protection, whistle blowing is usually a risky business. Whistle blowing carries a degree of risk that varies in direct proportion to the seriousness of the allegations. This makes sense. Airing "dirty laundry" outside an agency can be very threatening to people who run the agency. All agencies have problems of one sort or another, just as all individual people have problems. However, people responsible for agency activity do not like the negative aspects of their activity to be displayed for all to see. Such exposure reflects badly on those who run the agency because the implication, perhaps rightly, is that the administration is at fault. As a result, whistle-blowers may be fired, reassigned to insignificant responsibilities at remote locations, or harassed into quitting. In short, administrators and other people in power can make a whistle-blower's life extremely miserable.

Whistle blowing's consequences can affect the whistle-blower personally. The organizational administration or others who resent the whistle-blower's allegations can attack him or her personally. Others can seek to pinpoint and emphasize the whistle-blower's faults. We know that *everyone* has faults.

Colleagues may ostracize the whistle-blower, so whistle-blowers often feel tremendously isolated and alone. They may receive threats to themselves or loved ones. They may even lose their jobs. Perhaps worse yet, they may be blacklisted as troublemakers in the professional community and find it virtually impossible to obtain new employment unless they undertake a major relocation.

Yet, sometimes whistle blowing is necessary, especially after other less extreme measures (such as working through the agency administration) have been tried and have failed. Sometimes, whistle-blowing is an ethical imperative "when the violations of policy or law seriously threaten the welfare of others" (Reamer, 1990, p. 219). Several recent movies come to mind in which nuclear power plant employees (including Meryl Strepp as Karen Silkwood) blow the whistle on unsafe practices after these employees' complaints to plant administration have been ignored. Unfortunately, however, the whistle-blower heroine usually dies mysteriously near the movie's end, with implications of murder, though the plants do get shut down. Subsequently, the community suffers major economic problems from the resulting unemployment and lack of resources.

Levy (1982) addresses the choice of whether to blow the whistle or not: "The choice must be based upon the seriousness and the consequences of the organization's failing; the relationship of the failing to the organization's obligations to others; and the relationship and responsibility of the social worker or both. Whistle blowing is not always justifiable, but it is often necessary in the interest of fairness and justice, and in the interest of institutional responsibility. Whatever it is that the social worker may offer in justification of the act after the fact—for example, in an adjudication of a complaint or a grievance brought under the Code of Ethics of the social

(continued)

---

work profession—the social worker should carefully consider before the act'' (p. 57).

Most cases involving potential whistle blowing are ambiguous; there is frequently a fine line between *breaking* the rules and only *bending* them (Reamer, 1990). Therefore, we continue to stress that the decision to act is very serious one. Before blowing the whistle on agency or colleagues, consider four questions (Reamer, 1990).

First, how great is the threat to the potential victims? Is it life-or-death? Or is it only a minor infraction of the rules? Is it worth the time, energy, and risk it takes to blow the whistle?

The second question to address before blowing the whistle is what type and quality of proof you have available that the wrongdoing has occurred or is going on. How solid is your evidence? Do you have written documentation? Do you have witnesses? Or do you have some ideas based on informal observations and hearsay?

The third question to ask yourself before blowing the whistle is whether less severe alternative measures might remedy the problem. Are there established agency channels through which you can work? How difficult would it be to navigate through these channels? How much resistance do you anticipate encountering? Can you confront the abuser personally before trying other more severe measures? Can you solicit support from colleagues? Will your supervisor help?

The final question to ask before blowing the whistle is whether or not you can assume the burden of risk. How much do you really have to lose? Is it worth it? Is whistle blowing really the only way to attack the ethical problem? Or are there other less risky alternatives you can pursue?

Frederica, a public assistance worker facing an ethical dilemma over a newly promoted supervisor, wonders whether to blow the whistle on this supervisor or not (Reamer, 1990). Frederica has been working for the agency almost two years and is becoming increasingly frustrated by the attitudes and work hab-

its of a number of her immediate colleagues. She sees that they spend as little time with clients as possible, even denying them needed and rightful assistance if the workers do not have time to complete all the necessary paperwork. At other times, workers bend the rules to give clients benefits to which they are not entitled. For example, workers might not report all the clients' income. Many clients work as domestic help, receiving cash from employers so no record of earnings exists. Workers make decisions solely on their own discretion. Additionally, Frederica notes that workers consistently pad the travel expense accounts that reimburse them for home visits. Frederica is appalled.

Although she doesn't like the thought of ''making waves,'' she finally confides her concerns to her friend and colleague Zenda. Zenda dismisses Frederica's concerns almost condescendingly, indicating that such violations are simply a means of bending rules that aren't very good to begin with. She explains that such worker discretion is really an informal agency policy and adds that padding travel expense accounts is universally accepted as a means of increasing workers' relatively meager salaries. Zenda tries to soothe Frederica and arrest her concerns.

It doesn't work. Frederica decides to keep her concerns to herself until she can figure out what to do about them. Suddenly, Frederica learns that Zenda has been promoted to unit supervisor. Frederica is stunned. How can Zenda maintain order and help supervisees follow agency and other regulations when she herself regularly violates them?

What can Frederica do? Should she ignore the whole situation? Should she confront colleagues about their behavior? Would such criticism cause her colleagues to ostracize her? Should she confront Zenda again, even though it did no good the first time? Should she report her concerns to someone higher in the administration? How will that make Zenda feel toward her? If Zenda considers Frederica a traitor, how miserable can Zenda make Frederica's life as an employee? Should Frederica report the problem to NASW or the State Licensing Board? Should she blow the whistle to the public? How long does she think she will keep her job if she takes the problem outside established agency channels?

There is no easy answer to Frederica's situation. How would you apply the hierarchy of ethical principles to her decision-making process? What would you do if you were she?

The decision to blow the whistle, whether to higher levels of administration or to someone outside the agency, is a tough one. It requires weighing the numerous pros and cons of your own individual situation. If the ethical dilemma literally concerns life and death, you ethically must attack the problem in some way. However, what way? Many courses of action are available to you. Whistle blowing is probably only one of them.

If you do choose to blow the whistle because you see no other choice, there are several recommendations to follow. First, be certain that you clearly define the variables and issues involved. What, specifically, is the problem? What documentation can you offer as proof of your allegations? What ethical standards or rules are being violated? In what ways are these standards and rules being breached?

The second suggestion for blowing the whistle is to know what your rights are. Do you work for a public agency whose policy sanctions employees' right to free speech? Is it agency policy to address procedural issues internally—and only internally? Is there an available grievance or complaint procedure to utilize? How easy is it for your agency to fire you? Do you belong to a union on which you could depend for help? Is the union strong or relatively weak?

The third recommendation for whistle-blowing is to be prepared for the consequences. What is the worst thing that could happen to you? Could your supervisor put a note of reprimand in your permanent file, barring you from future promotions? Would such a note work against your request for a positive letter of recommendation? Could you be fired as a result of your actions? Could blowing the whistle ruin your reputation in the professional community, branding you as a troublemaker no other agency wants to hire? If the worst does happen to you, what are you prepared to do?

The fourth suggestion for whistle blowing is to follow the chain of command. Earlier chapters have addressed power in organizations and formal lines of communication and supervision. Going over your supervisor's head almost always puts you at risk of his resentment and wrath. After all, you appear to have negated his authority and competence. This is usually very threatening to supervisors. In fact, it probably would be threatening to you, if you were in their position. At any rate, if at all possible, try to follow the agency's predetermined and sanctioned chain of command. If that doesn't work, then consider more extreme options such as whistle blowing.

Finally, the fifth recommendation for blowing the whistle is to establish a clearly defined plan of action. Whom do you plan to tell about the problem? In what order will you tell people? What will you do if they react positively? How will you proceed if they respond negatively? Whom can you solicit as allies? Are other workers and administrators willing to support you? Are there external organizations, such as NASW or licensing bodies, that would aid you or even advocate for your cause? Can you ask experts to support your case? What are your specific goals? What is your time frame for achieving them?

In summary, it is extremely important to consider the whistle-blowing alternative very carefully. Weigh potential gains against risks and negative consequences. There is no crystal ball. All you can do is act as your conscience dictates and do the best you can.

established ethical principles. Does this behavior violate ethical principle 1, the right to protect life and have basic needs met? No. What about ethical principle 2? Does the action involve the right to equal treatment? No, again. However, principles 3 (having free choice and freedom) and 4 (exposure to minimal injury) raise serious concerns. The reasons for the code's strong statement about sexual relationships is that such relationships often cause serious harm to clients.

There is also an unequal distribution of power. The social worker as the professional, in effect, has influence and perhaps even decision-making power over the client. This may impede the client's autonomy and right to have free choice.

So which of the alternatives mentioned earlier will you pursue? You *identify your various alternatives* and *weigh the pros and cons of each.* You decide that this is serious enough that you must do something. You cannot simply ignore your colleague's behavior. You decide that reporting your colleague to NASW or the state licensing board for censure, or whistle blowing to the public are too severe. You determine to deal with the issue closer to home, either by confronting your colleague directly or by talking it over with your supervisor. This is a difficult call. It would be easier to tell your supervisor and let her deal with the situation than to confront and scold your colleague. However, it might be more fair and effective to talk to your colleague first, find out all the facts, and observe his reaction. You *decide to confront him as soon as possible* and get it off your chest. Depending on your satisfaction with his response, you can tell your supervisor at a later time. You also decide that a series of in-services on proper professional conduct are in order. You will suggest this to your supervisor tomorrow. You can always share your specific reasons for your suggestion with her at some later time.

Neglecting Child Maltreatment

What if a professional colleague makes a misjudgment that has serious repercussions for clients? Consider a case of child maltreatment (Loewenberg & Dolgoff, 1992). Jimmy Beam, age five, is raced to the emergency room of Clemency Hospital at 2:00 A.M. He has suffered serious head injuries, a compound fracture of his left arm, and had several crushed bones in both hands. Jimmy's parents say their only child had been running and had fallen down three flights of stairs. He is bleeding profusely due to numerous abrasions. Clemma Zendt, the hospital social worker, is notified to Jimmy's arrival and called to his bedside the next morning. Physicians attending to Jimmy immediately suggest the possibility of child abuse. It makes no sense that Jimmy was brought into the hospital at that time in the morning after running and falling down flights of stairs. They ask Clemma to visit the family's home to gather more information before reporting suspected child maltreatment.

When she arrived at the Beams' apartment, the Beams refused to admit or talk to Clemma. They say they already have a caseworker at County Social Services, Fred Slintfone, who is providing them with family counseling. They say Clemma should talk to him.

Clemma contacts Fred immediately. Fred says he was seeing the family for a number of problems including wife battering and alcoholism. He strongly suspected that child maltreatment was occurring in the Beam home, but had said nothing about it. Fred feels that a breach of confidentiality would ruin his relationship with the family and his ability to help them gain control of their problems.

In Clemma's mind there is absolutely no question that Fred should have reported to Child Protective Services that he strongly suspected child maltreatment in the Beams' home. State law mandates that social workers and other professionals report any *suspected* child maltreatment. Clemma learns that Jimmy has suffered serious and irreversible brain damage. He will live, but will have to be institutionalized because of the extensive care he will require.

How should Clemma proceed? This is a difficult decision. There is no absolutely correct answer. She has already *identified the problem.* She proceeds to *investigate the variables.* Clemma feels that Fred made a serious mistake, essentially ruining Jimmy's life. Fred didn't do it intentionally, but the result is disastrous. However, what good will it do to report it? Jimmy is no longer in danger because he will no longer be living with his parents. The damage has already been done. But what about Fred's grim mistake? If he's not held responsible, will he ever make a similar mistake again?

Clemma *appraises the values that apply to this dilemma* and *evaluates the dilemma* on the basis of our proposed hierarchy of ethical principles. How do each of the seven ethical principles apply to this case? Which of the six alternatives for dealing with unethical behavior on the part of colleagues should Clemma pursue? *What alternatives* does Clemma have and *what are the pros and cons of each?* Should she ignore the dilemma and classify it as a nonissue? Should she sit down and have a serious talk with Fred? She works for an entirely different agency. What right does she have to intervene? What effect will her feedback have anyway? Should she tell someone else, such as her supervisor, the state branch of NASW, or the State Licensing Board? Is this case sad and extreme enough to blow the whistle on Fred and his agency? *What would you decide to do if you were in Clemma's place?*

HIGHLIGHT 12.4

NEGATIVE RESPONSIBILITY

This might be a good time to introduce the concept of *negative responsibility* (Reamer, 1990, p. 183). Positive responsibility is responsibility for your own behavior. Whatever you choose to do, you are responsible for your actions and their consequences. Negative responsibility means that you are also responsible for those actions you choose *not* to take. In other words, you assume some of the responsibility for any harm done because you knew about a problem and chose not to do anything about it.

Consider, for example, the woman whom a group of men raped and beat in an inner city neighborhood several years ago. Dozens of tenants looked on silently from the windows of their apartment buildings high above the scene. No one raised a hand to help the woman. They just watched. These watchers weren't hurting her. They had nothing to do with the whole thing. How much were they to blame? What was their negative responsibility for the woman's death?

Remember when a major portion of the San Francisco freeway buckled and collapsed during a serious earthquake a few years ago. Dozens of vehicles were crushed and people were trapped. Without hesitation, onlookers and community residents rushed to the earthquake victims' assistance despite that fact that these people lived in a very poor urban neighborhood and had serious problems of their own to face on a

daily basis. Nonetheless, these helpers cared. They turned their negative responsibility into positive action. Instead of standing on the sidelines watching the appalling scene, they jumped right in to help.

Reamer (1990) notes that issues of negative responsibility are relative. You can't rush into battle on every single issue every single time, especially at your own expense. You must weigh the pros and cons of your actions. He makes three suggestions. First, think seriously about the degree of impending harm to the people involved (in many cases, clients). Our hierarchy of ethical decision-making principles takes a clear stand on life-or-death issues as a number one priority for ethical action.

Your second consideration regarding the assumption of negative responsibility involves assessing the extent to which the potential victims can help themselves. To what extent is the problem their own responsibility? If the victims are children, they probably have little ability to help themselves without assistance. They probably need your help even more than adults do.

The third suggestion involves consideration of the extent to which your involvement endangers your own welfare. Is it a good plan to jump into a raging river to save a drowning person when you can barely swim?

Incompetence Due to Personal Problems

What if a colleague is inadvertently doing harm to or at least not working as she should with clients. What if her personal problems are keeping her from performing adequately? Once again, what if this colleague is a personal friend of yours?

Consider the following case, which involves alcohol problems (Reamer, 1990). Irma LaDouce is a social worker at a residential center for children diagnosed with both mental retardation and behavioral problems. She is responsible for her caseload's behavioral pro-

gramming, consultation with child care workers and teachers to implement the programming, and family counseling. Irma is good friends with Farrah Froemming, a colleague who has the same job description and supervisor. As a matter of fact, Farrah was initially responsible for getting Irma her job three years ago. It was Farrah's strong recommendation of Irma that convinced the hiring supervisor to give Irma the job. Irma owes Farrah a lot. Irma loves this job.

The problem is that Farrah is going through a really rough divorce. Irma, as her good friend, is trying to be as supportive as possible. She likes Farrah, appreciates all Farrah has done for her, and respects Farrah's competence. During these hard times, Irma makes a point of meeting Farrah after work for a drink and dinner. Irma notices that Farrah has increased her number of before-dinner cocktails from one mild highball to three stiff double Scotch on the rocks. Irma notices that more and more frequently Farrah slurs her words when Irma calls her at home. Finally, Irma notices that Farrah has liquor on her breath when coming to work two days in a row. At other times Irma notices an overpoweringly strong aroma of mouthwash or mega-breath mints. Irma suspects that Farrah is taking a few nips on the side from a bottle of vodka Farrah keeps in one of her desk drawers. Farrah's office door is closed now much more than it used to be.

The worst thing is that Irma sees Farrah handling one of her clients too roughly, in Irma's opinion, on two separate occasions. Another incident involves one of the child-care staff who casually mentions that Farrah slapped a child one day.

Irma *recognized and defined the problem* as Farrah's difficulty in dealing with personal situations that affect her ability to perform her work effectively. Regarding *investigation of the involved variables*, Irma already knows much about the situation from her many discussions with and observations of Farrah. Irma *considers getting feedback from others*, especially her supervisor. However, in this instance she first needs to decide whether she will approach Farrah before going any further with the issue.

Irma *appraises the values that apply to this dilemma*. Irma is faced with a conflict between respecting a colleague and treating her in good faith and maintaining the primacy of clients' interests. According to the hierarchy of ethical principles, clients have the right to be free from injury (principle 4) and to a good quality of life (principle 5). Farrah is failing to deliver on both of these principles. Treating the children with inordinate roughness and even slapping them is unethical as well as illegal. Failing to perform her job adequately deprives clients of the best possible quality of life in this setting and later in another less treatment-oriented setting.

As a result, *after evaluating the dilemma on the basis of established ethical principles*, Irma determines that primacy of clients' rights supersedes Farrah's right to make her own decisions. Irma *identifies the following alternatives*: ignore the behavior, talk to Farrah about her concern, talk to their supervisor about the issue, report the problem to NASW or the State Licensing Board, or blow the whistle to the public.

Irma *weighs the pros and cons of each alternative*. She decides she cannot ethically ignore the issue in view of the harm done to clients. Nor does she seriously consider contacting the state NASW chapter, reporting to the State Licensing Board, or blowing the whistle to the public. These would make the whole agency look bad. Additionally, she knows it is almost always best to try to work through the appropriate internal agency channels before going outside the agency. Otherwise, agency personnel might blame her for not following proper and potentially more effective channels to remedy the situation and help Farrah cope unobtrusively with her alcohol and personal problems. It is important to work within your own agency system whenever possible instead of fighting against it (Corey, Corey, & Callanan, 1993).

Irma *makes her decision* regarding what she will do. Because Farrah is her friend, Irma decides to confront her first. She will encourage Farrah to seek help and tell Farrah she is more than willing to help her do so. Depending on Farrah's response and what she does in the next few days, Irma decides to hold off briefly on sharing her concerns with their supervisor. Irma hopes that Farrah will seek help, possibly by admitting herself to the inpatient substance abuse program that their agency's health insurance will pay for. If Farrah fails to respond appropriately, Irma will talk to their supervisor. It will then be up to the supervisor to take action.

Irma knows that her decision might endanger her friendship with Farrah, and that she might regret her decision. However, she evaluates the potential benefits and risks, and determines her best course of action.

It must be emphasized that there is no best or easy solution to an ethical dilemma. You must weigh each dilemma on the basis of the circumstances, issues, and values involved. This and other examples of resolutions to ethical dilemmas are only that—examples. In your future practice experience you will have to take into account each unique situation involving an ethical dilemma and assess it independently.

Conforming to Agency Policy

A primary aspect of the macro environment in which generalist practitioners work are the agency policies that regulate their actions. The NASW Code of Ethics asserts that professional employees "should adhere to commitments made to the employing organization" (NASW, 1993, p. 8). Superficially, it might seem obvious that workers are supposed to abide by agency policies. Some policies are almost inviolable on an ethical basis. For example, workers should use the agency's resources only for purposes intended by the agency (NASW, 1993; Reamer, 1983). And to meet their own personal needs.

Thus, workers are paid for doing what the employing agency assigns them to do, right? The problem is that often an organization's goals are not totally consistent with professional values and ethics (Loewenberg & Dolgoff, 1992). Chapter 4 discusses common problems in agencies—especially large bureaucracies—such as goal displacement. A common form of goal displacement occurs when the agency places more importance on the process of getting things done (for example, completing paperwork on time) than on the effectiveness of results achieved. Thus, you as a worker may find yourself in an ethical quandary regarding whether to be loyal to your agency and its policies or to provide your clients with what they need most.

Reamer (1990) cites an example concerning a Big Brothers organization and its policy against having gay men act as Big Brothers. Long Chow, a worker for the Big Brothers organization, recruited and oversaw several dozen Big Brothers and their clients over extended periods of time. Axel, age twenty-nine, had been a Big Brother to Joe, age ten, for almost eight months. Long felt Axel was exceptionally good at this voluntary job. Joe, who a year ago had been a shy, passive, almost lifeless, boy, was now coming out of his shell. It was exhilarating to see a wide grin spread over Joe's face sometimes when he and Axel participated in games and activities. Axel usually spent one evening a week and a few hours during the weekend with Joe, taking him to movies, playing ball or miniature golf, or jogging in the park. Long felt that the two had established a very positive relationship. Axel was an excellent male role model and a partial support system for Joe. Also, Joe's mother liked and respected Axel. She felt he was a godsend to Joe at a very difficult time in Joe's life.

The problem was that Axel sat down with Long and, in a concerned tone of voice, told Long that he was gay. Axel felt that is was not right to deceive Long. He had known about the policy from the beginning of his involvement with Big Brothers, but felt that his sexual orientation had nothing to do with his relationships with children. Axel was in a secure, long-term relationship with his partner. He had absolutely no sexual interest in children. Indeed, Axel loved children and regretted that he would have none of his own. Therefore, he had volunteered to be a Big Brother. He felt that he could provide worthwhile experiences for a young boy and, at the same time, enjoy doing it. Subsequently, Axel was assigned to Joe.

Long suffered an ethical dilemma. It was clearly against agency policy to allow gay men to be Big Brothers. The policy had originated several years earlier when a boy accused a Big Brother who happened to be gay of sexually abusing him. Long believed that Axel was truly good for Joe. He understood that sexual orientation and sexual abuse were unrelated issues. Breaking Joe and Axel up would tear Joe apart, and Joe had already suffered too many other losses in his life.

Long had *identified the issue*. (The steps in ethical decision making are italicized.) He had *investigated the variables involved* by talking extensively with Axel, researching the history of agency policy, and becoming knowledgeable about the lack of relationship between sexual orientation and sexual abuse. Long consulted the agency director, his direct supervisor, to *get feedback from others*. The director, busy with many aspects of agency life, emphasized the importance of adhering to policy and offered no better solutions. Sometimes trying to get helpful feedback from others does not work. Long also evaluated the legal status of the policy, which turned out to be ambiguous in his particular state. In other words, he could get no definite answer regarding whether it was legal or illegal to discriminate against gay people in this manner.

Long *appraised the values that applied to the dilemma* and *evaluated the dilemma on the basis of established ethical principles*. This situation didn't seem to fit very well. Principle 1 in the hierarchy of ethical principles (the right to live and have basic needs met) really did not apply. Principle 2 (the right to equal treatment) applied to Axel, but not to Joe. Through no fault of his own, Axel was not being treated equally with other volunteers upon which the agency depended. However, Axel was a volunteer, not a client. Principle 3 (the right to have free choice) might also be applied to Axel. His sexual orientation was his own business. He should have the right to free choice concerning his own behavior when it harmed no one else. Although the policy implied a violation of principle 4 (the right to experience the least injury) in terms of protecting clients from sexual abuse, Long knew the assumption (that gay men sexually abuse children) upon which it was based was wrong. In actuality, removing Axel from the picture would probably harm Joe emotionally. Did Joe have the right to be protected from intentional harm according to ethical principle 4?

Long *thought about the alternatives available* to him. Long could ignore the situation and purposely disobey agency policy. However, he had voluntarily joined the organization and had agreed to abide by its policies, including this one against inclusion of gay men. Therefore, Long would be held liable and censurable for not heeding this policy (Reamer, 1990).

Talking to his supervisor, also the agency director, did not help. There was really no one else higher in the agency structure to whom he could turn. Reporting to someone outside the agency made no sense. By doing so, he would break confidentiality with Axel. Thus, Long could see no solution to be derived from that tactic. Long didn't want to quit his job. What good would that do? He loved his work, and it wouldn't help solve the problem at hand anyway.

One alternative was to attempt changing agency policy and establish better screening procedures for all Big Brother candidates, gay or straight (Reamer, 1990). Long felt that this might be the answer. He *made his decision* and began planning a strategy for going about accomplishing such a policy change. In effect, Long decided to assess his potential as a change catalyst system to address a macro (organizational) issue. If Long was successful, then the dilemma confronting Axel would disappear.

Reamer (1982) emphasizes that "it is as much an ethical responsibility—to assist the organization in reconsidering its policies and procedures, as it is to abide by those policies and procedures" (p. 54). Thus, Long made an appropriate choice. He would attempt going through agency channels before undertaking more drastic measures. At any point in the future, he could revert to one of the other alternatives or tactics. All would depend on his evaluation of the situation, its context, and the relative significance of ethical principles at the time. How do you think this scenario turned out?

Numerous other examples of conflicts between workers' professional ethics and agency policies exist everywhere. Organizations might cut corners and de-prive or even harm clients by cutting services under budgetary pressure (Loewenberg & Dolgoff, 1992).

Workers might even discover agencies undertaking clearly unethical practices in the name of greater efficiency. Consider a nursing home that supports the policy of drugging clients to keep them minimally active. If clients just lie in bed all day doing nothing, it costs the agency much less in terms of staffing for supervision and other activities.

What would you do if you were a social worker at such an agency? You know that it is obviously not in the clients' best interest to be drugged senseless until they literally die. These practices obviously violate at least ethical principles 2 (the right to equality and equal treatment), 3 (the right to have free choice), 4 (the right to protection from injury), and certainly 5 (the right to cultivate a good quality of life). There are also questions regarding whether the agency is in violation of principle 1 (the right to exist with basic needs met—essentially, the right to life). In this severe case of an agency's unethical behavior, what alternatives are available? What choices would you make? What would your plan entail? Once again, there are no easy answers to ethical dilemmas.

Breaching Confidentiality in a Macro Context

Confidential information includes "those personal facts or conditions pertaining to the client's life which he has communicated to the agency for definite purposes related to the service he is requesting or receiving from the agency. It is the client's right and expectation that such information will be respected and safeguarded by the agency and all of its personnel; professional, administrative, secretarial, and clerical staff; field-work students, volunteers" (Koestler, 1966, p. 33). Confidential information can include the client's name and demographic data, what the client says, what professionals observe and perceive about the client, and anything else that might be in the client's records (Barker, 1991).

In one way, confidentiality, then, refers to "safeguarding information about an individual that has been obtained by the . . . [professional] in the course of his teaching, practice, or investigation [and] is a primary obligation" of the professional (American Psychological Association, 1968, p. 358). The basic idea is that a professional practitioner is not supposed to divulge information about a client unless that client gives her explicit permission to do so. The maintenance of confidentiality is of major importance to the social work profession. The Code of Ethics stresses its importance by stating the social worker should "hold in confidence all information obtained in the course of professional service" (NASW, 1993, p. 1). However, it continues that the social worker should share such information only under "compelling professional reasons" (NASW, 1993, p. 6). The Code, thus, places the burden upon the worker to prove that any breach of confidentiality is indeed *compelling* (Cox et al., 1987). There are no clearly defined reasons provided (Reamer, 1987).

Absolute confidentiality refers to the perspective that the clients' confidence will not be broken no matter what. *Relative confidentiality*, on the other hand, is what the Code refers to. That is, professional practitioners may have to break confidentiality under compelling circumstances. Ethical dilemmas involve relative confidentiality. The hierarchy of ethical principles clearly emphasizes that there are numerous instances when confidentiality (involving principle 6) must be broken.

There are at least nine common reasons for breaking confidentiality (Huber & Baruth, 1987; Sinclair, 1993). First, when a court appoints a social worker to evaluate a person, that worker is obligated to provide the court with information about the client. Second, in the event that a worker determines that a client is a potential suicide risk, that worker should inform the appropriate helping body. Third, when a client sues a social worker, such as for malpractice, the worker may have to share information about the client. Fourth, when a client introduces "mental condition" as a claim or defense in a court action, the worker may be forced to respond to this claim. Fifth, workers must report confidential information in the event that a minor is being maltreated. Sixth, a worker must report information and get help for a client who the worker suspects has such a severe mental condition that she requires hospitalization. Seventh, workers must report if they find out clients are participating in criminal activities. Eighth, when otherwise confidential information is made an issue in court, a worker must respond. Finally, social workers must report to the appropriate authorities when a client reveals that she is going to commit a crime, harm someone else, or hurt herself. Chapter 13 discusses confidentiality within the legal context.

Confidentiality issues in a macro agency setting can be much more complicated than an individual practitioner's adherence to privacy principles. Loewenberg and Dolgoff (1992) emphasize this complexity by citing several contexts in which confidentiality becomes exceptionally difficult to maintain. These include communications with other professionals, administrative record-keeping requirements and access to information, relationships with insurance companies, and police needs. Each context can present problems either for the individual practitioner or for general agency policy.

To what extent is it the agency's formal or informal policy to talk to other professionals about your clients, their problems, and issues? Are all clients alerted to the fact that you may discuss their cases with others, including supervisors and interdisciplinary team members? What about multiproblem clients involved with a range of other services and resources? Must you inform your client about every other professional, even from other agencies, to whom you talk about that client? Isn't sharing information critical in many instances to coordinate services and provide the most efficient and effective intervention possible?

Then there are recording requirements. To what extent do your agency superiors have access to information about your clients? Virtually every agency requires record keeping for the sake of accountability. However, who exactly will have access to this information? Who will know about your client's intimate problems? In what kind of detail will others be able to investigate your clients and their lives? What about funding agencies? What client information should they have access to? Should you be certain to tell your clients about each and every person who will have potential access to their records? Should you get their signed consent for revealing this information? How does your agency's policy help or hinder you in trying to answer these questions?

The records issue is becoming increasingly complex because of the extensive computerization of information. Who exactly might have potential access to information about clients? One state automatically tests all blood donors for HIV. The blood donation centers forward the identities and demographic data of individuals who test positive to a centralized data bank. The blood centers also inform the designated individuals of their positive HIV status. However, they do not inform these people that their names will be added to the HIV-positive data bank. Nor do the blood centers inform donors that they will be tested for HIV in the first place. Who, then, has access to the names of people testing HIV-positive? Do administrative assistants or other employees working with and around the computers have opportunities to look at the list of names? If so, whom might they tell? Can insurance companies readily check this data bank for the purpose of denying people coverage if they have preexisting HIV-positive status?

What about insurance companies who reimburse for services provided clients? Should social workers always be totally honest and open concerning their records and services? What if you determine that an insurance policy is unfair? What if an insurance company will reimburse for six weeks of inpatient treatment for alcoholism only if the referring worker deems the problem "very serious"? What if the worker feels the problem is only "mildly serious"? This latter diagnosis will allow the client only four outpatient treatment sessions, which the worker knows will be insufficient to help the client. Should the worker report the problem as "very serious" in order to give the client a chance at solving her problem?

Finally, police often have the right to know about clients' problems, whether such problems are shared with workers confidentially or not. Many states require social workers to inform the authorities whenever the workers become aware of a felony or threatened felony. What if revealing such information will annihilate your relationship with your client? What if you hear about the supposed felony fourth-hand and from a relatively unreliable source? As you can see, the concept of confidentiality is fertile ground for ethical dilemmas.

Co-optation versus Cooperation

Co-optation refers to eliminating opposition to a cause, plan, or organization by assimilating opponents into the group favoring the cause, plan, or organization. Co-opting enemies makes former enemies look foolish if they disagree too much with the cause, plan, or organization because they are now members of the co-opting group. In other words, co-optation absorbs the opposition.

Cooperation, on the other hand, involves different factions working together to achieve some mutually agreed upon goal without either faction losing its own identity. The factions remain as separate groups.

Frequently, a direct service social worker trying to implement a change in an organization or community lacks adequate power and experience to do so. Higher level administrators or people with greater experience are much more accustomed to wielding power and to making changes or stopping them from occurring. It is relatively easy for people in power to "seduce" a worker into co-optation. Hence, people with more power often find it useful to co-opt, rather than cooperate with, a worker seeking some kind of organizational or community change.

Co-optation can assume several forms. Those with power may appear to befriend a worker by offering personal camaraderie or other social opportunities that the worker might not otherwise experience. Being invited to gatherings of important executives, community leaders, and other big names can begin to create a "we" feeling in the worker. She may begin to lose steam over what she had hoped to change or implement. It may become easier for her to believe what the people in power are telling her. After all, she might think, they do have greater experience and wisdom, not to speak of money. Co-optation can serve to awe an inexperienced, relatively powerless worker into agreeing with the status quo.

Another example is an eighteen-year-old undergraduate student who rode the city bus daily for an hour and twenty-five minutes from her home to her urban campus. Because it was a daily routine, she saw the same people on a fairly regular basis. Gradually, she struck up some conversations with these people to pass the time. One man, twenty-two, also a student at the same urban campus, amazed her. At one point the two were discussing national politics. The young man straightforwardly said that he was going to vote for the current (at that time) staunchly conservative, anti–social work president because his parents were going to vote for this man. The young man added that the conservative president must be good because he had already been elected and so many people must have known what they were doing. (It might be noted that the president eventually had to resign—after Watergate—or else risk impeachment.) The student could not believe her ears. She was stupefied that this young man seemed unable to think for himself to any extent. Instead, he had been co-opted into his parents' value system. Needless to say, that was the end of their convivial discussions. She decided she would rather study her ancient Spanish literature on the bus than participate in what she considered mindless chitchat.

Another means of co-optation concerns how decision-makers appeal to a worker's sense of reason. They may suggest that the worker simply—and naively—does not understand how difficult things are or how impossible it would be to accede to the worker's requests and goals. Again, people in power can co-opt by establishing a "we" feeling of solidarity and safety with the worker.

In the event that co-optation tactics are effective, the worker may find herself losing her perspective. She may also lose effectiveness in representing her clients' interests and weaken in her advocacy efforts. She may even be viewed by others, including clients who support positive change, as "selling out to the enemy" (the people in power).

Fraud and Illegal Behavior

Committing an illegal act does not sound like an ethical thing to do. However, it is amazing regarding what situations can arise in agency practice. Fraud is intentionally perverting the truth in order to receive something of value (*Webster's Ninth Collegiate Dictionary*, 1991, p. 490). For example, consider Horace, a half-way house supervisor for drug-addicted young adults. The agency administration charged him with purchasing appliances for a new group home. A local vendor prepared a bid on the appliances and offered Horace his choice of a new VCR to "thank" him for considering him as the potential vendor. Accepting this gratuity would clearly be unethical. Horace would present himself to the agency as evaluating all the vendors' goods on a fair and equal basis. The covert reality would be that receiving a bribe—the VCR—could significantly influence Horace's judgment. Such action might also be illegal, depending upon state or local laws.

Another example is an agency director who accepts a free turkey for his own family from a vendor who supplies food to the agency's summer lunch program for homeless children. This director runs a serious risk of having his judgment, or lack thereof, called into question on the grounds of showing partiality to this particular vendor.

Conflict of Interest

A conflict of interest is a situation in which personal gain conflicts with professional objectivity. Often it involves holding two conflicting roles with conflicting goals. Vita is a member of the Citizen's Disability Board, an advisory board charged with advocating for the needs of city residents who have disabilities. An advisory board is a group or committee that meets to supply data and information, expertise, and suggestions for achieving an organization's goals (Barker, 1991, p. 7). The city's mayor appointed Vita and the other four board members. The board had been trying to persuade the city to adopt a comprehensive ordinance requiring the city's rental apartment owners to make all units accessible to individuals with physical disabilities. As a social worker, Vita is acutely aware of the needs of the city's residents with disabilities. However, Vita was also part owner of an old apartment building that would be horrifically expensive to modify to accommodate residents with physical disabilities. When Vita's board debates this issue, what should she do? She holds two conflicting roles at the same time. Voting for what she thinks is right—making the entire city accessible—would affect her personally and financially in a very negative manner. Perhaps the best thing would be to remove herself from the board, and, thus, from this conflict of interest.

Another example of conflict of interest involves Alice, who is running for a seat on the city council. She is also a member of the city's Police and Fire Commission and has been very active in pushing both the police and fire departments to hire more women. Her community, however, is very conservative. Potential voters have little or no interest in recruiting more women or minorities for the police and fire departments. If anything, most voters are generally against this strategy. This community context sets the stage for a conflict of interest on Alice's part.

After Alice declares her candidacy for a seat on the council, she becomes much less vocal in her support of hiring women and minorities. She wants to get elected and, therefore, feels she must go along with what her voting constituency wants. By being silent on the issues, she is implying that the city needs the very best officers it can recruit regardless of gender or race. She no longer appears to support hiring women and minorities. Has Alice "sold out" her fellow police and fire commissioners in order to get elected to the city council? Has the possibility of getting elected made her agree with and become part of a constituency with little interest in expanding opportunities for female and minority personnel?

Potential Harm to Participants

What if doing the "right" thing causes more harm than good? Any attempt to bring about large-scale organizational or community change poses the risk of some negative consequences. A public assistance worker might nag a landlord (or "slumlord," as his tenants call him) to improve his dilapidated rental properties in order to bring them up to code. The landlord might decide that such upgrading is not worth it financially and abandon the property rather than fix it up. The clients then may face the serious problem of finding a place to live that is within their meager means.

Stigmatization Tactics

Stigmatization means identifying or describing someone or something in disgraceful, contemptuous, or reproachful terms (*Webster's Ninth Collegiate Dictionary*, 1991, pp. 828, 1158). In a confrontational situation, such as when trying to implement macro change, painting your opponent as bad or evil may permanently alienate that opponent. It is easy to criticize or stigmatize an opponent, especially in the heat of pursuing some marvelous cause. However, by doing so, you can make a permanent enemy on whom you can never again depend for help. Therefore, it is best to avoid a we/they or good guy/bad guy dichotomy.

It is probably in your interest to recognize realistically that there are few permanent friends, allies, or enemies in a professional context. Some issues, such as the right to adequate housing or ready access to quality education, may be permanent, but the perspective each player assumes toward these issues is not. It depends on each player's own interests in a particular macro scenario (agency or community). The cantankerous landlord today may become a member of the city council or your own agency's board of directors tomorrow. In summary, be careful. Stigmatizing the "enemy" may backfire later when you badly need his or her support.

Chapter Summary

This chapter discusses the NASW Code of Ethics, segment by segment. The significance of personal values and their relationship to professional performance is examined. The types of ethical issues confronting agency workers and the dilemmas involved in macro settings are introduced.

Decision-making steps for resolving ethical dilemmas are identified and explained. Steps include recognizing the problem; investigating the variables; getting feedback from others; appraising the values that apply to the dilemma; evaluating the dilemma on the basis of established ethical principles; identifying and thinking about possible alternatives to pursue; weighing the pros and cons of each alternative, and finally making a decision. Reamer's guide to ethical decision making is examined. Loewenberg and Dolgoff's "Ethical Principles Screen" is explained. The seven levels involved in the latter are identified by the phrase ETHICS for U.

A range of possible ethical dilemmas is appraised. They include distributing limited resources, lack of community support for service provision, problematic relationships with colleagues, conforming to agency policy, breaching confidentiality, co-optation versus cooperation, fraud and illegal behavior, conflict of interest, potential harm to participants, and stigmatization tactics.

CHAPTER THIRTEEN

Working with the Courts
Patricia M. Christopherson

Rita Moro, a social worker, is about to appear in court. She is to testify regarding the possible need for protective guardianship of her client, Alfred Garcia, age eighty-seven. Mr. Garcia has Alzheimer's disease and according to his family cannot function well alone. In Ms. Moro's[1] opinion, following an assessment process, this client is unable to care for himself and make realistic decisions about his own care. The presiding judge asks the worker to identify the "least restrictive" alternative or option available to the client. In order to function as a professional social worker, Ms. Moro *must* know the legal definition of "least restrictive care," assess the available options meeting the criteria in the community, and respond to the judge during a court hearing.

Archer Daniels, a child protective services social worker, has been subpoenaed into court, along with his client's agency records, regarding an alleged physical abuse incident. In his case notes, Mr. Daniels has written that the mother appeared "depressed." Upon cross-examination, the defense attorney asks Mr. Daniels to give a clinical definition of depression. He is unable to do so, which significantly reduced his credibility in the eyes of the judge. By failing to define the term adequately and to cite specific examples of depressed behavior or appearance in the record, Mr. Daniels looks as if he does not know what he is talking about. He is unable to help his clients as effectively as possible.

During cross-examination at a dispositional hearing, Mary Clark testifies regarding her experience in providing individual and family counseling to the defendant. The defendant has been found guilty of having sexual intercourse with a minor. The prosecuting attorney looks Ms. Clark directly in the eye and poses his final question: "Can you promise me, Ms. Clark, that the defendant will never have sexual contacts with minors again?" Ms. Clark recognizes that no one can assure the future behavior of another person. Confounded, Ms. Clark is at a total loss for how to respond to the question. She has no idea how to answer yes or no without being able to offer further explanation.

The Significance of the Legal System

The significance of the legal system for social work practice cannot be overestimated. We consider the court

Patricia M. Christopherson, ACSW, ICSW, is Chairperson of the Department of Social Work at the University of Wisconsin–Eau Claire. She wishes to acknowledge the help of numerous social workers and attorneys who suggested examples and topics for this chapter.
1. Unlike most other chapters in this book, in this chapter surnames are used intentionally and consistently to reflect the formality of the courtroom process.

THE ABILITY TO STOP CHILD ABUSE IS NOW IN ALL OUR HANDS.

Social workers are known for their advocacy of children's rights and their attempts to prevent and to stop child abuse.

system one of the primary macro arenas for generalist practice. Some of the most important progress in providing social services to vulnerable populations has resulted from legal decisions. Judges have expanded the rights of people with developmental disabilities and forced national, state, and local governments to confront discrimination in the school systems. Social workers and others serving as advocates for those denied social and economic justice have repeatedly asked the court system to intervene. Courts frequently force governments, organizations, and agencies to abide by their own rules, adhere to the U.S. Constitution, and honor the intent of legislation. For these reasons alone, it is important for social workers to understand the legal system, particularly those components most likely to be experienced by the generalist practitioner.

Additionally, social workers may speak before legislative bodies or testify in administrative or civil hearings. In each of these cases, the social worker is playing a role at the macro level in policy and program implementation. The process of presentation in such instances of macro practice is similar to testimony in a court of law.

The United States is becoming a more litigious society. In other words, to an increasing extent, citizens are asking our legal system to address moral, health, and social issues in addition to those in the more traditional areas of criminal justice (crimes such as theft or murder). For example, courts are now routinely asked to determine what medically constitutes the term "life." that is, society is asking the courts to decide if "life" is defined as heartbeat, brain activity, or meaningful interaction with the environment (consciousness). Another issue before the courts in some states is the age of majority. That is, what are the appropriate ages for drinking alcoholic beverages, driving motorized vehicles, or getting married? Values are becoming more diverse, and knowledge about human growth and development is expanding. It is arguable then that the courts will be asked to address increasingly complicated questions of fact and judgment.

Social workers have joined members of other helping professions in being asked to work more directly and more frequently with the legal system. The exchange between the social welfare and legal systems often produces situations in which social workers feel ill prepared. They may feel unable to serve the needs of clients, agencies, or the larger society. Additionally, they may feel unable to present themselves in the most professional manner. A 1988 national study of the educational backgrounds and work experiences of child welfare personnel indicated that although practitioners with baccalaureate social work degrees perceived their education as better preparation for child welfare work than other baccalaureate degrees, a significant number did not think they were adequately trained in "preparing/giving testimony in court" (Lieberman, Hornby, & Russell, 1988). This chapter will provide basic background information about the legal system and those legal circumstances in which social workers might be most likely to need further help in their efforts to benefit clients within this macro context.

Seven areas have been identified as basic to all social work practice and its relationship to the legal system. They include: confidentiality; clients' consent to intervention; legal rights of clients; documentation of evidence in the case record; legal authority for practice; testimony in court; and legal duties implicit in professional practice (Jankovic & Green, 1981). A review of the professional literature indicates that some of these topics more than others have received examination and discussion (for example, see Wilson, 1980, on confidentiality and documentation).

This chapter will focus on practical and general preparation for court and actual testimony regardless of practice area (for example, child welfare or working with elderly people). Social workers need to be educated about courtroom protocols and procedures to serve their clients more effectively. The courtroom is also open to public scrutiny in most cases, except those involving minor children. As such, it provides an arena for visibility and accountability that may seem unfamiliar and exposing to a social worker whose day-to-day practice is conducted under less scrutiny.

Many laws governing social work practice and the possible resultant grounds for testimony are legislated and regulated on the state level. It is, therefore, advisable for generalist practitioners to recognize that differences between states are likely. Workers need to educate themselves about appropriate state statutes governing their areas of practice. Likewise, it behooves any social worker facing courtroom testimony to learn what protection, if any, is available to him or her by state statute. Does the state where you will practice offer privileged communication with clients—that is, do state statutes protect from public disclosure any information shared between the client and another party? Many states do not recognize the confidentiality of communication between clients and social workers. In such circumstances, workers must be prepared to face contempt of court charges if they refuse to divulge information garnered during sessions when they assumed their privacy was protected.

This chapter will:

- Define key terms in the courtroom process.
- Describe general differences between social work practice and courtroom protocol.
- Discuss how to prepare for courtroom testimony.
- Examine the phases in the adjudication process.
- Explore various strategies in cross-examination.

Functions of Professional Terminology

Every profession utilizes words and expressions that are unique in usage or meaning. One of the functions of such specific terminology is to shorten communication and assure shared meaning. A doctor and a pharmacist can talk comfortably with each other about medicinal dosages and chemical equations. Each knows that the other has the necessary background to interpret similar meanings of the terms they use. Therefore, they can expect to understand each other.

A second function of professional terminology is to establish boundaries between users of such terms, such as the designated professional, and those who do not belong to these professions. In other words, the role of medical, legal, or social service provider becomes more clearly delineated from the role of service user because of this different use and understanding of terminology. The words clients or patients use are probably much more general than those used by professionals. Members of any profession must often be very specific in word choice and usage because of complex and/or adversarial situations they encounter.

Once a social worker consults with an attorney or steps into a courtroom to testify, she may recognize both of the above functions of legal terminology. When interaction with the legal system occurs, it is necessary for the social worker to learn to recognize and use key terms according to their legal definitions. This assures shared meanings and allows social workers to interact comfortably as full participants in the legal process.

Important Legal Terms

Some of the most relevant legal terms for social workers will be defined and discussed at this point. They include: violations, jurisdiction, allegation, court processes, due process, stipulation, burden of proof, standards of proof, evidence, witnesses, guardian *ad litem*, confidentiality, and privileged communication.

Violations

Violations are offenses that involve the breaking of a law or rule. Generally, the terms violation and offense can be used interchangeably. Violations of law can occur in three different ways. First, *criminal violations* are offenses penalized by fine and/or imprisonment. Usually, criminal offenses are deemed the most serious and are familiar to most members of a society.

Criminal violations are divided into felonies and misdemeanors. In most states, *felonies* are crimes considered serious enough to be punishable, in part, by imprisonment for a term of one or more years. Murder, kidnapping, and first degree sexual assault are typical felonies. *Misdemeanors* are less serious crimes punishable, in part, by confinement in a city or country jail for a period of less than one year. Misdemeanor violations

might include battery (bodily harm to another with intent and without consent), negligent operation of a vehicle, or carrying a concealed weapon.

The second type of violations are *civil offenses* for which the sole penalty is forfeiture of money or goods. Violations of state fish and game laws, malpractice suits, or product liability cases are examples. If found guilty of a civil violation, the defending hunter, professional, or company often has to make restitution and/or pay a fine.

The third type of violation involves *ordinance offenses*. Ordinances are civil (noncriminal) laws enacted by a local unit of municipal government. Conviction for a noncriminal offense can draw a fine but not incarceration of the offender. For example, local governments establish zoning regulations, require registration of bicycles, or limit ownership of handguns.

Jurisdiction

Jurisdiction means authority to act. A court can proceed and its findings be binding only if it is authorized by law to handle the case before it. Jurisdiction may be challenged based on age (adult vs. juvenile court) or location (site of the offense vs. place of arrest).

In all states, juvenile court has jurisdiction over most illegal acts committed by children (that is, people under age eighteen). However, there are exceptions. In some states, adult courts have exclusive jurisdiction over boating and vehicle regulation violations committed by those sixteen years of age and above. Therefore, sixteen- and seventeen-year-olds, although technically children, are prosecuted in adult court instead of juvenile court when they commit such violations. In other instances, often dependent upon the nature of the offense and the age of the alleged offender, adolescents can be waived into adult court. There, they face the stiffer consequences adult courts are authorized to impose. Some state legislatures are being urged to change the legal definition of childhood to include an automatic waiver into adult court depending on the nature of the alleged crime.

Social welfare agency personnel may, at times, have to ascertain geographic jurisdiction before proceeding legally. State or federal statute and/or case law precedent may determine jurisdiction where residence of the alleged offender and location of the alleged violation are different. In such cases, a determination of jurisdiction is necessary before determination of guilt or innocence begins. A social worker may be involved in the apprehension of a juvenile legally residing in one state who is alleged to have committed an illegal act in another state. Different circumstances and appropriate state statutes may dictate how the legal system would proceed. For example, attorneys and judges would consult the law to determine jurisdiction over a juvenile arrested for delinquent behavior outside the state of his legal residence. The alleged offender may be extradited (surrendered) to another authority for prosecution.

Social workers involved in cases where there might be jurisdictional disputes of procedures are well advised to consult with their supervisors or corporation counsel (that is, the attorney hired by the agency for legal services). Jurisdiction may not be straightforward and may require the advice of those with advanced legal training for interpretation of the appropriate statutes.

In addition to consultation with agency supervisors or corporation counsel, the district attorney may be called upon to help determine jurisdiction. The district attorney (sometimes called the prosecuting attorney) is an elected or appointed officer who acts as attorney for the people or government within a specified district, such as a city or county.

Allegation

A term heard frequently when violations are discussed, an *allegation* is the assertion of one side in a lawsuit setting out what that party expects to prove at the trial. More specifically, it refers to the protection and legal right of a defendant to be assumed innocent until determined guilty. Hence, in written and oral communication, the defendant is referred to as the "alleged" perpetrator of a crime. Until a determination of guilt has been legally obtained, the defendant has only been accused of committing a crime. Thus, social workers should develop the habit of calling the defendant involved in a legal case an "alleged" offender until such time as guilt has been legally determined.

Court Process

There are two phases of the court process. During the *adjudication phase*, facts are presented, and the charge is determined by a judge or a jury. This phase is quite

familiar to the average citizen. Both sides present testimony to the individual (judge) or group (jury) who bears responsibility for making the decision as to guilt or innocence. The second phase, *disposition*, occurs after adjudication and refers to the sentence determination. In most cases, laws provide a specified range of sentence for a given crime.

Often, the adjudication and disposition phases are separated by time. The judge may order a presentence investigation report or consult case precedents (that is, decisions made about similar cases decided earlier by other judges) before disposition. The judge is limited by law and precedent regarding the degree and nature of the punishment. In some cases, adjudication and disposition may occur sequentially on the same day.

Due Process

Courts are mandated to provide *due process* during the conduct of business. Specifically, law in its regular course of administration must document that it guarantees the protection of a fair trial. Specific procedure must be followed. Often, the expression "due process rights" is used to refer to the safeguards protecting the accused person. The bottom line is that each individual is innocent until proven guilty.

Since 1967, due process rights have been protected for juveniles as well as adults (*In re Gault*, 1967). Juvenile codes (that is, state statutes applying to persons under age eighteen) vary by state in the degree that due process rights are recognized and protected. In some states, social work practice is likely to be governed by the concept of "best interest of the child" (that is, decision making by any authority figure should reflect the adult's judgment as to the best alternative *for the child*) in conjunction with due process safeguards. For example, a social worker may recommend in a court report that the mother, instead of the father, get custody of their children in a divorce dispute. Such a recommendation would be based on the "best interests" of the children according to the assigned social worker's investigation and judgment.

Stipulation

Attorneys representing both parties can agree to *stipulate* to any matter pertaining to the proceedings or trial.

By so doing, they are, in effect, agreeing on the point of information or fact. In a murder trial, the attorneys could stipulate that the defendant had, in fact, shot the victim. The disagreement then might focus on whether the defendant was legally sane at the time of the incident. Usually, "sanity" in legal terms means the ability to recognize the implications of his or her behavior and to assist in his or her own defense. The defendant's social worker could testify at the trial about information pertinent to the client's sanity.

Burden of Proof

In the United States, the *burden of proof* rests on the prosecution or plaintiff (that is, the party making the complaint). It is the responsibility of that party to prove the allegations set out in the petition filed before the court. As previously mentioned, a defendant is innocent until adjudicated guilty. The defendant is the person against whom a claim or accusation has been brought in court.

Standards of Proof

Standard of proof pertain to the *level or degree of certainty* needed to prove an allegation in court. There are generally three different levels: beyond a reasonable doubt; clear and convincing evidence; and preponderance of the evidence.

Beyond a reasonable doubt is used in criminal or delinquency cases (*In re Winship*, 1970). It necessitates evidence that is entirely convincing to a moral certainty (sometimes referred to as 90 percent sure).

Clear and convincing evidence refers to approximately a 70 percent degree of certainty. Such a degree of certainty may, for example, be used in cases of child abuse or neglect. In other words, a social worker might be asked to state how certain he is that the abuse or neglect actually occurred.

Preponderance of the evidence (51 percent minimum certainty) is the standard of proof applied in civil (as opposed to criminal) cases; some states also use this standard for child abuse and neglect cases. In some agencies, the standard of proof used by social workers and supervisors *within* a child abuse case investigation is preponderance of the evidence. In other words, the

social worker would want to establish at least a 51 percent certainty that the abuse occurred before taking some remedial action. Generally, the more severe the charge, the higher the standard of proof required for a conviction.

Evidence

Evidence may take several forms: real, documentary, or testimonial. *Real evidence* consists of tangible objects such as weapons or photographs. *Documentary evidence* pertains to certified documents usually identified and authenticated by proper authorities. For example, x-rays or medical records are documentary evidence, and the authenticity of either would be stipulated to or testified about by an employee of the department responsible for such records. *Testimony*, of course, refers to the actual interviewing of a witness by the defendant or, more typically, his or her attorney.

Hearsay Evidence

The type of testimony typically most questioned by counsel during the court session is hearsay evidence. *Hearsay* refers to testimony about a statement made outside the courtroom. Such testimony is not placed in evidence because there is no opportunity to test its reliability through cross-examination. Generally, unless the person who is testifying saw or participated in the activity about which she or he is testifying, the testimony is inadmissible.

A social worker who is given information about an alleged child abuse incident by a neighbor during the course of that worker's investigation cannot testify in court about that story. If the case goes to court, the hearsay restriction limits the testimony the social worker can give about the incident learned from the neighbor. Instead, the neighbor might be subpoenaed to testify about his or her own observations.

In most instances, hearsay testimony is not admissible for several reasons. First, there is no opportunity to cross-examine the person making the original statement. Second, the original statement was not made under oath. Third, there is a problem of accuracy in repeating a statement made by someone else. A demonstration of such a problem is the game wherein a group of people sit in a row and each whispers to the person on one side what was just whispered to him or her by the companion on the other side. At the end of the line, the final person states out loud what he or she heard. Typically, significant distortion has occurred as information was perceived and passed along by the various people. The initial statement might be, ''The streamlined boat met its challenge on the high seas and, in the minds of all its crew, was on the brink of damage.'' After hearing the interpretation by a large number of people, the final statement might be, ''Goats lined the stream while they grew and died of brain damage while drinking Hi-C fruit drink.'' Although this example is a bit absurd, the point is that the courts acknowledge the possibility of distortion. Hence, hearsay information is generally not allowed.

The fourth problem with hearsay testimony is that there is no opportunity for the finder of fact (judge or jury) to observe the demeanor of the person making the original statement. To what extent does the witness's nonverbal behavior coincide with and support what the witness is saying verbally?

There are a number of exceptions to the hearsay rule too detailed or specific for presentation in this chapter. For further information you are advised to consult Caulfield and Horowitz (1987).

Quality of Evidence

To be admissible, usually all forms of evidence must have three qualities. First, the source must be *competent*, that is, qualified to make the observation. A witness must not have been legally intoxicated at the time of the event. Second, information must be *relevant*, meaning that is must bear on the proceeding at hand. Finally, information must be *material* and thus have important consequences for the case.

Witnesses

Courts of law define two distinct types of witnesses, namely, lay (that is, factual) and expert. The term *lay witness* refers to one who is limited in testimony to what she or he saw, heard, smelled, or touched. In addition, a lay witness can give her or his opinion about a perception, typically involving such factors as speed, intoxica-

tion, or insanity. Opinions on other topics by lay witnesses might also be requested and given, assuming there is no objection from opposing counsel.

In many states, social workers testifying about an investigation of child neglect might be limited to the above restriction. That is, they might be considered lay witnesses who could provide only testimony as identified above.

An *expert witness*, on the other hand, is rendered ''qualified'' by the judge to give opinions in a particular area of expertise. Expert witnesses typically have advanced degrees, training, credentials, continuing education, practice experience, and the like, cited in court to document their expert status. The status of expert is conferred only for the length of any one particular trial. In other words, it is possible for a social worker with a particular background to be judged an expert by one judge and not by another. The expert status is not transferrable from one court case to another. A judge could determine that an individual developmental psychologist is an expert in a specific neglect case. As such, she could testify about normal child development and its pertinence to the case before the court.

Judges vary greatly in admissibility of social workers as expert witnesses, and they have the authority to determine who will be admitted as an expert for the case before the court. In any case, the generalist practitioner must be prepared to defend his or her qualifications for the status of expert. Lengthy and detailed questions might be asked about the social worker's education and experience by either side's attorney to support or challenge the request for expert designation.

Guardian ad Litem

Under the laws of many states, all children and any adult who is adjudicated not to be legally competent (or is in court for that to be determined) may have a *guardian ad litem* appointed to represent that person's ''best interests.'' It should be noted that best interests are to be determined by the guardian *ad litem*, and not by what the client might identify as his or her preferences.

In some states, the guardian is mandated by law to be an attorney. In others, it can be any member of the community in good standing, including a family member, a professional, or any other citizen.

In the capacity of guardian *ad litem*, the appointed

party may question witnesses on the stand on behalf of the client. In general, this party represents a viewpoint distinct from those of either the plaintiff or the defendant and their respective counsels.

Confidentiality and Privileged Communication

Confidentiality and privileged communication are important terms for both the helping professional and the client. Both concepts involve the degree of protected disclosure of communication between professionals and their clients.

To many social workers, confidentiality is the more known and recognized term of professional responsibility. *Confidentiality* refers to the principle that information shared between the client and social worker is intended to be kept private. Social workers are advised to be very aware, according to state statute and agency policy, of what types of information can safely be labeled as confidential between client and helper. Of course, true confidentiality occurs rarely in a professional setting since secretaries, transcriptionists, filing clerks, supervisors, and, to a certain degree, colleagues in the same or contracting agencies have access to information. Such information can be shared orally or, more frequently, in writing via charts, social histories, progress notes, etc.

While many clients are aware of these policies regarding shared knowledge about agency records, it is often advisable to inform clients during the first meeting about what information they might share would or would not be held in confidence. Furthermore, the generalist practitioner needs to be aware of ethical obligations to report certain types of information, such as child abuse, mandated of all professionals identified in state law.

Confidentiality, as both a professional and a legal term, is seldom as pure as inexperienced social workers or clients might expect. The social worker must be aware of any and all restrictions that determine the confines of a "confidential" relationship. Confidentiality has always been an issue in matters important to the well-being of the general public. A physician is mandated to report births, deaths, gunshot wounds, or sexually transmitted diseases in many states. True confidentiality would prohibit such reporting.

Another example concerns confidentiality among

professionals. Doctors or hospitals may limit access to specific information (such as an AIDS diagnosis) for other health care providers based on a need-to-know criterion. In other words, to protect the patient, only those health care providers in jeopardy of contracting AIDS themselves from a particular patient "need to know" the diagnosis. The argument to limit disclosure of HIV status rests on the premise that, among health care professionals, precautionary procedures regarding transmission of deadly diseases should be standard operating procedure in all medical situations. Thus, there is no overriding "need to know" in any particular instance. This type of confidentiality restriction and discussion is relatively recent. Historically, professionals working in agencies under a binding contract and with the same client may have disclosed information to each other using a more general rule. For a more complete discussion of confidentiality, see Perlman (1985).

Privileged communication refers to information shared between the client and another party that is protected by state statute. Usually, the other party is a professional, spouse, or member of the clergy. In such instances, the professional is protected from disclosing information learned in the course of regular duties in a court of law. Only the client or patient (and not the professional) can claim privileged communication. This is a very important distinction. In other words, a professional is not exempted from divulging confidential information in the courtroom if the client has not claimed privileged communication. Likewise, if the client does claim privileged communication, the professional is barred from disclosing the information, regardless of the professional's preference. Additionally, it is important to note that the court protects the professional in privileged communication.

Privileged communication coverage by profession varies by state. In most states physicians, lawyers, spouses, and religious personnel are covered. Often, other professionals, such as social workers, may not be. In such circumstances, refusal by such an unprotected professional to share information would result in being held in contempt of court. Contempt of court refers to willful disobedience to or open disrespect for the rules of the court. Accordingly, the involved judge may punish with a fine or jail placement. Generalist social work practitioners must be fully informed of the definitions, coverage, and case law regarding confidentiality and privileged communication in the state where they practice.

HIGHLIGHT 13.1

LEGAL TERMINOLOGY IN YOUR AREA OF PRACTICE

We have established that mastery of legal terminology is important both to specify meaning clearly and to relate to other professionals. A third function of legal jargon relates to your need as generalist practitioner to know all professional terms in your area of practice. Most often, the specific definitions of terms and their relevance to your practice are defined and governed by state or federal statute.

In some instances, the legal definition might not be similar to the common sense definition or the one most frequently used in practice. Confidentiality between a professional and a client (disclosure to no one else, possibly not even written into the case notes) may or may not be protected by law. Social workers may have to break confidentiality to report child abuse, because this is legally mandated. In other words, reporting of suspected child abuse takes precedence over confidentiality. Dependent upon your area of practice, you may need to know the legal definitions of child abuse, child neglect, least restric-

tive care, restitution, diversion, permanency planning, or family-based services.

You are well advised to consult with supervisors or your agency's policy manual for the appropriate definitions at the beginning of employment. Such definitions are the basis for professional decision-making of all sorts. A social worker would need to know the various levels of sexual assault to make an accurate referral of a client to law enforcement officials.

Once on the witness stand, it is appropriate that you as a social worker be able to document your authority and expertise by citing legal definitions. Furthermore, your professional credibility will be greatly diminished if you cannot adequately define terms relevant to a case.

The legal terms listed and defined here are common to most social work practice, regardless of problem area. Familiarity with all of these terms assures increased comfort with the legal process generally and with testifying in particular.

Differences Between Courtroom Protocol and Social Work Practice

Social workers are trained to move and to act in a variety of systems. These range from one-on-one counseling with an abused child in a micro setting to participation in international conferences on shared global concerns such as world hunger in a macro context. As we have established, generalist practitioners take pride in the development of knowledge and skills that transcend system type and size.

Being effective in a system, however, necessitates not just an awareness of the commonalities shared by different systems but an equal awareness of the differences among systems that necessitate specialized knowledge and skills. Basic differences exist between social

welfare and legal systems. The following section addresses the common differences between standard social work practice and courtroom proceedings. Figure 13.1 introduces and summarizes the major points.

Adversarial versus Conjoint Problem Solving

Court proceedings in this country are based on one model of human problemsolving. This model proposes that truth and justice are more likely to be served if each side in a case presents information either beneficial to its own cause or detrimental to it opponent's. For the duration of the proceedings, plaintiff and defendant become adversaries. They singlemindedly pursue the pre-

Figure 13.1
Social Work Practice versus Courtroom Protocol

Social Work Practice	**Courtroom Protocol**
Process: Conjoint problemsolving	*Process:* Adversarial/gamelike; ritualistic
Informal atmosphere	*Formal atmosphere*
1. Dress: casual	1. Dress: formal
2. Name Usage: first name	2. Name Usage: "Your Honor"; last name with title
3. Deadlines: flexible; some dictated by law or administration	3. Deadlines: rigid; defined by law
4. Space: managed by nonverbals, furniture, culture	4. Space: managed by judge, furniture, protocols
5. Language: open; inconclusive (e.g., It seems ....)	5. Language: definitive, precise
6. Nonverbals: congruent with internal state	6. Nonverbals: may be incongruent with internal state
Client Rights	*Due Process Rights of the Defendant Procedurally*
1. Confidentiality	1. Right to be notified of charges and face accuser
2. Self-determination	2. Right to legal counsel
3. Consent to treatment	3. Right to cross-examine witnesses
	4. Privilege against self-incrimination
Outcome: Stoppage of abuse/Rehabilitation/Strengthening of family; Placement; Services	*Outcome:* Determination of charge/Disposition

sentation of fact and innuendo favorable to their respective cases. The finder of fact, be it judge, jury, or hearing examiner, can then make a reasonable decision. Decision-makers assume that each side has presented its most convincing information and argument.

Courtroom process appears to be game-like in comparison to typical social work interactions. In court each attorney presents a line of reasoning that might best persuade decision-makers. It is interesting to note that each attorney could just as easily present the opposing viewpoint using a contrasting line of reasoning. Interactions in court appear fixed and ritualistic. They are prescribed by conventions unfamiliar to the daily communications, activities, and routines of social workers.

Social work practice is much more likely to be based on a model of problem solving that stresses a conjoint solution. Such solutions emphasize the different parties' similarities, negotiations, and compromises. Attempts are made to reduce blaming and not to picture any given party as the sole culprit. The helping professional often tries to foster a sense of good will and common good among the differing parties.

When members of the social work profession, therefore, are subpoenaed to testify in court, they are entering a very different arena from the one in which

they typically conduct day-to-day business. The setting and the rules of procedure are vastly different. Generalist social workers may feel vaguely uncomfortable because of those differences. Consider a situation in which one of the attorneys has been hired, in part, to make the social worker's testimony less consequential and credible. Most social workers do not operate in a daily arena where it is someone else's job to discredit the perception of their professional competence. It is easy to feel uneasy and threatened under such adversarial conditions.

Formal versus Informal Atmosphere

A court of law is conducted according to historical precedents which dictate the setting, appearance of the participants, and rules of conduct. The space within the courtroom is managed by the arrangement of furniture and the physical proximity of the various players. Formal attire, including long robes for the judges, attests to the seriousness and significance of the proceedings. Language is circumscribed by law and age-old protocols. Judges, for example, are addressed as "Your Honor." Likewise, a witness must take a formal oath in a specific physical posture attesting to the truth of future statements.

Aspects of court procedure such as deadlines for document submission, filing of petitions, presentation of presentence investigations, and appearance for testimony are to be taken seriously. One's cause can be compromised severely if such deadlines are not met.

The practice of social work is typically more informal. Often, dress is casual and first names are used. Deadlines exist, but may not be rigidly enforced. Consequences for missing deadlines are usually much less severe than those courts may impose. Space in an agency is not mandated by strong external or historical precedents. Each worker is free to arrange furniture and decorate as desired within restraints imposed by space and consideration for colleagues' needs and well-being. Generally, there is more latitude in interpersonal interactions. Common courtesy dictates friendly or informal, day-to-day discourse. Social workers may or may not rise when greeting a client, for example.

The social worker coming from the social welfare environment will note the strong contrast with the atmosphere in a court of law. Social workers may feel they are on unfamiliar ground and present themselves much less comfortably as a result.

Practitioners are advised to prepare themselves for the differences in formality and to dress much more formally than usual for a court appearance. The suit with contrasting blouse, heels, and conservative jewelry a woman might wear for a court appearance would contrast sharply with the casual slacks and sweater worn for an average day in the office. When dressed for court, expect office colleagues to ask whether you're planning to attend a funeral.

Both the social worker and clients can become more comfortable with the proceedings by reviewing the physical layout of the courtroom. Many social workers stress to their clients the differences in formality between court and almost any other familiar setting. You as a social worker might take future witnesses to an empty courtroom to educate them on-site regarding layout, participants, procedures, and other details.

Legal Due Process versus Client Rights

In both a court of law and in the social work profession, rights and responsibilities of the defendant/client and the attorney/social worker are protected by historical precedent and by case law. Over time and based on the results of specific cases, certain roles of attorney and social worker in relationship to their respective clients have been defined and protected. For example, confidentiality has been honored both professionally and legally.

In a court of law in this country, the defendant is assumed to be the one most in need of safeguards protecting his or her rights. Potentially, he or she has the most to lose. Thus, the defendant has a number of procedural rights, including the right to be notified of all charges against her or him, the right to legal counsel, the right to cross-examination of all witnesses, and the privilege against self-incrimination. This last privilege assures defendants that they do not have to participate in any procedures that could suggest guilt. The *Gault* decision in 1967 assured these same rights to juveniles. All these safeguards are measures to prevent the government from arbitrarily usurping individual freedoms.

Client rights in professional relationships have evolved through time as both individual professionals and the profession as a whole have monitored compliance with recognized values and ethics. At other times, the rights of clients have been defined or protected by legal or legislative decisions. Many states now have statutes outlawing contact of a sexual nature between a client and a member of many professions.

Common client rights include: foreknowledge of confidentiality and its constraint, self-determination, and informed consent for treatment. Earlier, this chapter discussed confidentiality and its limitations. Basically, a client who shares information has the right to know if the professional is legally and ethically required to report any of this information (for example, child abuse). Likewise, if a client's social worker or other helping professional is called to testify in court about the client, the client has the right to invoke privileged communication. This limits what the professional can disclose. A client also has the right to select alternatives from the choices available to him or her (self-determination) without undue pressure from the helper. Lastly, a client has the right to be informed about the choices for treatment and the known consequences of each and every treatment. The client can, thereby, select and consent to one or any combination of choices.

Outcome: Determination of the Charge versus Rehabilitation

The ritualistic procedures of courtroom protocol result in a decision of guilt or innocence (adjudication phase). This is followed by the disposition phase (or sentence) which is usually determined by the judge. The end result is clear and unambiguous. The time frame is relatively short, and all efforts are directed to a specific conclusion.

In contrast, social work practice is much more ambiguous in process and, often, in outcome. Usually, client or system change is the goal. However, a case can be open for an indeterminate period depending on the circumstances and what the agency dictates. Social workers often work ''for the best interests of the child'' or for the ''preservation of the family.'' Yet such goals are open to varied interpretations and final results will vary. Social workers need to be aware of the difference in focus between their regular, daily practice and formal courtroom protocol in order to be more relaxed and effective courtroom participants.

Presentation in Court

So far, this chapter has described terms commonly used in courts and contrasted generalist social work practice with the more formal courtroom process. This sets the stage for how social workers should prepare to testify in court. The remainder of this chapter focuses on how social workers can best present their testimony in courts of law.

Preparation for Testimony

A number of issues are involved in preparing for court testimony. They include: appropriate documentation, review of other documents, establishment of expert witness status, review of testimony with the attorney, and preparation of witnesses.

Documentation

As a generalist practitioner prepares for an upcoming court date, the payoff of good documentation becomes obvious. Some experts argue that the best preparation for testimony lies in the assessment and case note documentation of the social worker's opinions or observations (Miller, 1980). Often the credibility or believability of testimony is directly related to the amount and accuracy of detail the worker has put into the case record. If opinions and facts are not well-documented in a case, the benefit of the doubt will often go the way of not taking any action. This means that whatever change was recommended by the social worker, such

---

HIGHLIGHT 13.2

COURT IS LIKE A STAGE

It is important for a social worker to remember that, unlike much social work practice, there is an element of drama or theater in the courtroom. Players move in assigned parts towards a specialized outcome that, hopefully, includes both truth and justice. The social work role is often of a secondary or supporting nature. That is, the professional has no primary responsibility for formulating arguments or making final decisions. A court is the turf of other professionals. Social worker participation is circumscribed by the dictates of the other key roles and the players in these roles. Typically, single pieces of information or testimony do not by themselves lead to a specific conclusion. Instead, it is how lawyers put the pieces together that establishes a theme. It is the accumulation of evidence that builds a case.

as removal of children from a neglectful or abusive home, will not occur because there was not enough documented evidence to support such a radical decision.

Documentation adequate for courtroom testimony typically includes acknowledgment of all contacts the worker has had with the client and others involved in the case. Contact dates, including the year, should always be noted. (It is amazing how fast years fly by and how difficult it is to remember what year you wrote what note.) It can also be important to cite ''no shows'' or cancellations of appointments, which may demonstrate a client's lack of commitment and inability to assume responsibility.

Another important factor to remember about documentation is to avoid value-laden terms such as ''egocentric,'' ''callous,'' or ''obnoxious.'' More neutral terms plus one or two behaviorally specific descriptions enhance the record's and the worker's credibility. A parent might be described as ''inattentive'' if his toddler were sitting nearby sticking hair pins into an electrical outlet. It should be emphasized that any observation needs the support of such specific examples.

Positive, as well as negative, observations should be included in the record. Such impartiality in the record establishes that the worker is objective and has good observational skills. Lastly, subjective professional impressions should be clearly separated from behavioral observations and facts. Impressions should be clearly labeled as such. For example, you might state, ''It is my impression that . . . ,'' ''My impression is . . . ,'' or ''My opinion is. . . .'' If you can provide documentation of a statement made by a client or another person, you might indicate that in the record as well.

Following these suggestions is likely to have a strong bearing on the credibility of your testimony should you be called into court. It is not unusual for practitioners to be summoned into court years after terminating with a client and closing the case record. Specific and detailed case notes may be the only link with the information necessary for a credible performance (Howard, 1982).

Review of Other Documents

After reviewing the record, the social worker may want to review several additional documents. These include the agency policy and procedures manual, relevant state statutes for key definitions or outlines of procedures, and pertinent case law (if applicable).

An agency policy manual may document that the social worker was following recognized procedures in the investigation of the elder abuse case before the court. Or while testifying in court, the professional may be asked to provide definitions of client populations from an agency manual. You as a professional practitioner will appear much more knowledgeable if you can either recite from memory or readily find in the manual the section under discussion.

Appropriate state statutes can help substantiate the choice of out-of-home, independent, supervised apartment living as ''the least restrictive'' alternative in an adult protective placement hearing. In such cases, the worker has to demonstrate in court that some limitation on mobility, housing, or finances on the part of an elderly client necessitates intervention for her safety. As a worker on the witness stand in this instance you might be asked to define ''least restrictive'' and describe how your choice of supervised housing fits the criteria of the definition. Credibility on the witness stand will be greatly enhanced if you can cite definitions, procedures, or exceptions from the governing statutes.

Some recent legal decision may confirm the appropriateness of an intervention chosen by a worker in a particular case. Application of law in one state may have implications for care nationwide. Standards of care may be cited as an ethical obligation, substantiated by another state's laws. The well-informed social worker can strengthen his or her testimony by knowing and citing other states' standards or precedents. In other words, it pays to be as well-informed as possible as to the context of the case before the court. Relating the details of any specific case within the context of agency procedures, current professional literature, or recent case law can only strengthen anyone's testimony, including yours.

Establishment of Expert Witness Status

Once on the witness stand, you as a professional practitioner may be asked several questions relevant to your professional and personal history. An attorney might raise such questions in order to build a case for expert witness status or to increase the credibility of your future testimony. If you anticipate being called to the stand, it is a good idea to refresh your memory regarding educational background, previous professional experience, continuing education, published works, professional memberships, and the number of similar cases you have handled in the agency.

Review of Testimony with Attorney

Prior to the court date, you as the involved practitioner should meet with the attorney regarding your role in the court presentation. The attorney regarding your role in the court presentation. The attorney may have developed a theme or orientation to the case that necessitates specific information from you to complete the argument. For example, your testimony regarding a series of abuse reports over several years in a family with several children would strengthen the prosecuting attorney's theme of chronically poor and risky parenting skills.

You may want to discuss the strengths and weaknesses that you see in the case as it would be presented in court. Additionally, you and the attorney may want to develop strategies for its presentation. You might want to suggest a specific line of questioning to document certain background information. You should also share with the attorney any documents or information he or she is unaware of. It is also appropriate to discuss the opposing counsel and the judge in terms of known personal preferences, prejudices, or prior decisions. Some judges and attorneys develop reputations for specific questions, attitudes, or behavior in the courtroom. You may have to press the lawyer for such a pretrial meeting. However, it is usually well worth the effort. Such prior planning can enhance your professional credibility and provide for a much more coordinated effort.

Preparation of Witnesses

It is very important for any future witnesses to address their own verbal and nonverbal presentations of themselves. Remember the formality of court versus the informality of the social work agency! You as a future witness may decide to consult the attorney on a wide range of issues including appropriate dress, eye contact, and the language you should use.

In preparation for a court appearance, you may also want to discuss these same issues with your client. In particular, you may need to educate clients about the importance of nonverbal communication during testimony. The witness stand is not an appropriate place for chewing gum or wearing sunglasses. It is well documented that nonverbal behavior can be very persuasive, either positively or negatively. All parties involved in the courtroom drama need to be aware of self-presentation as credible presenters of fact or opinion.

Phases in the Adjudication Process

Major phases in the adjudication process involve direct examination of witnesses and subsequent cross-examination. Re-direct and re-cross-examinations are also possible. The following section will discuss specific techniques for effectively responding to questions in both major phases. Approaches and tactics frequently employed by opposing counsel during cross-examination will be explored as well.

Direct Examination of Witnesses

The purpose of direct testimony is to communicate as persuasively as possible the truthful facts pertinent to a case. The plaintiff's attorney or the district attorney's staff uses direct examination to get to the facts of the case. At this point the attorney questioning the plaintiff is likely to be on the plaintiff's side in the adversarial process. Thus, questions will most likely be relatively benign and straightforward.

The social worker as a witness is allowed to use notes during testimony. Using notes is especially recommended when there is a large amount of specific data relevant to the case. Likewise, notes are useful when a social worker suspects that his anxiety may hamper recall.

Memorizing data is not recommended because it sounds robotic and less persuasive. Additionally, the witness may block on memorized information and appear evasive or unnecessarily rattled. If there is a possibility that you as the worker will be called upon to consult the case file, it is advisable to review the file prior to testifying. In this way, you can more easily locate relevant information. It can be disconcerting to have a roomful of people waiting quietly while one is shuffling

---

HIGHLIGHT 13.3

SUMMARY:
YOUR ROLE IN COURT

Overall, it is important to remember that the primary mission of a professional social worker testifying in court is to *inform* or *educate* the finder of fact. Social workers are generally advised to present themselves as "friends of the court." As such, the generalist practitioner does not have an overinvestment in the outcome of the legal process. The professional's role in the legal process is to educate and inform, not to pass judgment.

As part of the educational effort, you as a social work practitioner need to refresh your own memory regarding the details of the case. Learn as much as

possible about the policies and state statutes governing such cases. Review your own professional credentials and be able to articulate them clearly. Finally, meet with the attorneys involved to learn of any information that can increase your credibility and comfort on the witness stand. Additionally, defendants need to be advised regarding the importance of their appearance and demeanor in court. It is arguable that the more serious the charge, the more important it is that defendants be aware of how they present themselves.

---

through a large volume of papers looking for one specific fact.

All testimony is recorded by a court reporter who transcribes the comments of all parties as they occur. It is thus important that all questions be answered clearly in words. Nonverbal behaviors such as hand or head gestures are inappropriate. Word choice and usage should reflect awareness of the audience, including judge, jury, attorneys, and observers. The finder of fact, especially if a jury, may be unfamiliar with professional jargon. If, for example, you describe a child to a jury as "acting out," you must be prepared to elaborate upon the behaviors and attitudes reflective of the term in lay language (that is, language that can be clearly understood by nonprofessionals).

When asked a question while on the stand, the witness should answer the question and only the question. Try to stay away from the hypothetical and the passive voice. In other words, try to talk directly about the person or situation being discussed and avoid conjecturing about possible causation or explanation. Furthermore, language is more lively and forceful if the *active voice* is used ("John *pointed* the gun at Tim," not "The gun *was pointed* at Tim by John").

If counsel asks, "Do you have an opinion on

whether Mr. Smith can manage his own money?" simply reply, "Yes" or "No." Do not elaborate on your opinion of Mr. Smith's financial management abilities. Instead, wait for the next question. The attorney might then ask, "What is your opinion of Mr. Smith's ability to manage his own money?" Subsequently, limit your answer to address only Mr. Smith's ability to manage finances. Do not elaborate on any other topics such as his work performance or personal relationships.

If necessary, ask to have a question repeated or reworded. If the question is still not understandable, it is appropriate to say so. Credibility is not seriously hurt if you simply do not know the answer to one or even several questions. If the answer is an estimate, indicate this. Do not allow an attorney to force you to give a more exact put possibly, inaccurate figure.

Witnesses may refresh their memory, too, by consulting exhibits or personal notes. *Exhibits* are tangible articles such as weapons or copies of documents that have been collected, identified and made available to the court for a particular case. While still on the witness stand, it is possible to correct information in previously given testimony. However, it is more advisable generally to limit such clarifications and to speak accurately the first time.

When social workers act as witnesses in a courtroom, they are permitted—even encouraged—to use notes to help them recall specific data. The worker pictured here without notes looks as though she could use some help.

Remember that you can say, "I don't know." All courts recognize that there are limits to a professional's knowledge or experience.

At times a question may be quite complicated. Then it is entirely appropriate to pause and think about a response before proceeding. Obviously, the practitioner does not want to appear to be manufacturing an answer on the spot. However, such pauses allow time for contemplation and increase the social worker's control of how questions are *paced*. It is recommended that the witness maintain control of the question and answer process. Otherwise, the attorney can rush and possibly confuse the respondent.

We have already stressed the importance of a pretrial conference with one's attorney. At that time, it may be wise to establish some nonverbal sign language, in this way, the attorney will know when you wish to follow up on previous testimony, consult data not immediately available, or even take a break.

Witnesses are totally responsible for their own answers while on the stand. Witnesses must answer all questions directed at them to which the opposing counsel does not object. Always address answers to the finder of fact, usually the jury or the judge. There is no need

to establish eye contact with opposing counsel or the defendant, especially if that is uncomfortable. Most often, the witness should stop instantly, in mid-sentence, if the judge interrupts or the opposing counsel objects. At times, it might be advisable to finish a sentence if one's attorney has decided that sharing such information is pivotal to the case.

Direct examination offers the opportunity for the district attorney or the plaintiff's attorney to present evidence supporting a decision of "guilty." The evidence is accumulated incrementally with testimony, depositions, and exhibits. All this substantiates the presentation of fact as the plaintiff knows it. Your testimony as a social worker is one piece of a jigsaw puzzle. There will be opportunities for you to provide information in the case-building process. Typically, you are given enough time to answer each and every question. Each question will usually build upon one of its predecessors.

Cross-Examination of Witnesses

Cross-examination is the step in the courtroom process that is most likely to show the adversarial nature of the proceedings. The goal of cross-examination is to decrease the likelihood that the finder of fact will believe the information provided during direct examination. The goal of cross-examination is not usually to seek objective information. In other words, cross-examination is that portion of the courtroom drama wherein the witnesses' personal and/or professional credibility is most often challenged.

Defense attorneys are hired to advocate for their clients' positions. To do so, they need to weaken testimony that is harmful to their clients. The idea is that this process serves truth and increases the likelihood of a just outcome. First, the plaintiff and counsel attempt to build a strong case for themselves. Then, the defense follows with a more critical, or even hostile, cross-examination of the same person.

Often, this process feels foreign to social workers on the witness stand. It is easy to take the probing questions of the opposing attorney personally. In reality, these questions have nothing to do with an attack on you personally. They are simply a means for opposing lawyers to strengthen their respective cases.

Attorneys conducting cross-examinations adhere to several general principles. First, a cardinal rule of opposing counsel is never to ask questions to which they do not already know the answer. Cross-examination is not the time to accidentally discover new information pertinent to the case. Thus, often, cross-examination is designed to trick the witness into saying what the attorney wants to hear. Examples of such leading questions include:

Does it not seem likely that . . . ?
Wouldn't you agree that . . . ?
Is it not the case that . . . ?

Many of these questions are phrased in the negative or worded so that agreement with them provides answers opposite to those that the witness intended to give. One could be asked, "Does Mr. Smith still beat his wife?" Any direct answer indicates agreement with the fact that Mr. Smith does, or once did, indeed physically assault her. Opposing counsel listen very closely to the respondent's answers. They look for any additional information that the social worker might accidentally volunteer that could provide a lead for further questioning or raise a doubt about the testimony given thus far.

Another tactic employed by defense attorneys is to prohibit witnesses from repeating their direct testimony.

The more frequently finders of fact hear the same testimony, the more likely they are to believe it. Questions asked during cross-examination are often limiting. The opposing counsel may not want to permit a witness to explain or elaborate.

A final ploy used by opposing attorneys is "saving" their ultimate point for the closing question. This deprives witnesses of opportunities to soften the impact of their responses. Remember the disposition hearing described at the beginning of the chapter? A social worker was asked whether a man found guilty of sexual assault would ever sexually assault again if the opportunity arose. By asking the worker, "Can you promise me, Ms. Clark, that the defendant will never have sexual contact with minors again?" the attorney attempts to limit Ms. Clark's response. The obvious reply is, "No, I cannot promise that." The opposing counsel would then close the questioning. This would prevent Ms. Clark from elaborating on what she really meant. A more effective response might be, "I cannot speak in terms of promises. That is outside the boundaries of certainty recognized by anyone in the mental health field." Another strategy for a witness might be to say, "I can't answer that with a simple yes or no.

Strategies in Cross-Examination

There are four strategies of attack in the cross-examination of a witness, all involving confrontation. They include confrontation of direct testimony, of the credentials of the witness, of the person him- or herself, and of the profession represented (McGoverns & Peters, 1985; Dept. Of Health, Education, and Welfare, 1979). Attacking a profession indicates more desperation on the part of the opposing counsel than attacking any of the other three.

Attacking Direct Examination Testimony

Common attacks of direct testimony focus on several issues. First, opposing counsel will address any discrepancies between records and testimony. Second, any discrepancies between direct and cross-examination on the part of any witness will be further examined. Any such differences will likely be addressed if the result looks advantageous to the opposing counsel.

There may be an attempt to show that the social

worker disliked the plaintiff and is, therefore, biased. This ploy can succeed if indeed the worker made a comment to that effect and was overheard. However, it can be deflected by indicating that personal reactions were not a part of the professional exchange between the social worker and the defendant.

Attempts may be made to show that the social worker is inexperienced. Opposing counsel might try to prove that real assistance was not offered as mandated by the law. Questions may address whether the social worker made out-of-court statements inconsistent with statements made in court. Lastly, the worker's accuracy of observation or even his or her memory might be questioned. Opposing counsel may also solicit contradictory evidence not heretofore in the record.

Questions that weaken or impeach previous statements made during direct examination provide the opposing counsel's strongest opportunity to help the finder of fact doubt the witness's testimony. Thus, it behooves all witnesses to review direct examination statements and be prepared for questions on any obviously unclear or ambivalent statements.

Attacking Credentials

Attacking credentials includes posing questions regarding a worker's professional qualifications. This might involve the worker's formal education, continuing education, training, or virtually any other element that could help counsel build a case. There could be questions regarding specific coursework, membership in professional organizations, history of publication, and previous testimony for either side of similar cases.

New social workers are often self-conscious about their perceived lack of experience. However, it is generally accepted that members of any profession were novices at some point in their careers. Simple acknowledgment of length of employment or type of professional experience is appropriate. Such straightforward truthfulness is usually not to your disadvantage. You need not be defensive. As a professional, you may be quizzed about previous testimony. This would include whether you had ever been paid to testify or whether you had testified for either side in similar cases.

If you as a professional have been established as an expert witness, you should be prepared to answer all questions involving your areas of expertise. Otherwise,

your credibility will be seriously eroded before the court.

Attacking You as a Person

Resorting to personal attacks indicates that the examiner thinks neither your testimony nor your credentials is vulnerable. Questions involving personal attacks include:

Do you believe in corporal punishment?
Wouldn't you personally like to see Mr. Davis get custody of the children?
How clean do you keep your house?
How many children do you have?

The intent of these questions is to demonstrate that the professional's personal beliefs or experiences bias her work with the client involved in the court case. Such ploys are common among those familiar with courtroom proceedings. If an attorney asks you such questions while you are on the witness stand, you must decide either to answer or to dispute their relevance to the current situation. Again, a nondefensive stance is recommended.

Attacking the Profession

Attacks on the witness's profession reflect last-resort efforts to discredit damaging testimony. Questions might include:

Is social work a licensed profession?
Can just anyone be a social worker?
How many continuing education credits are mandated yearly for social workers?

The intent of such questions is to subtly or not so subtly eat away at the profession's value and credibility. There is no need to be defensive about the profession of social work. The courts recognize its body of knowledge and professional expertise.

Other Confrontational Tactics

Other tactics used by opposing counsel usually relate to three variables. The first concerns the type of question asked. Attorneys may demand "yes or no" answers. Or they may reverse word order to confuse the witness.

A second confrontive tactic involves the general pacing of questioning. Attorneys may fire questions at the witness in rapid succession, or a set of questions answered in the affirmative may be followed suddenly by a question that the worker, with forethought, would answer in the negative.

A third manipulative tactic involves the attitude opposing counsel projects during cross-examination. A condescending attitude may be used to make the witness appear inept. A friendly attitude may be an attempt to lull the witness into a false sense of security and well-being. In general, it is best for a witness to project a calm and competent exterior. Answer questions in a pleasant and firm voice. The display of any emotional reaction may feed into the attorney's game plan and/or reduce your air of professional objectivity.

Suggestions for Cross-Examination Testimony

Cross-examination can address any information covered earlier in the trial. Thus, all information is open for review and reversal during this portion of a trial. The social worker should prepare for possible questions in any area cited. As the questioning begins, the professional needs to focus carefully on the content of previous direct testimony. Many social workers with much courtroom experience also keep in mind weaknesses in previous testimony. In preparation, they try to formulate the strongest responses possible. To repeat, the witness should make every attempt to control the pacing of the questions. This can be done by using pauses, asking for clarification, or repeating the question silently to oneself before responding.

It is generally advisable not to answer questions that are ambiguous or unclear. Such ambiguity may be purposeful and might reflect an attempt to elicit additional information helpful to the opposition.

Social workers have excellent training in listening skills. Cross-examination is an opportunity to practice listening with immediate and practical results. It is advisable to listen carefully and to answer completely and honestly. Speculation, admitting errors, and admitting you cannot totally remember generally do not cause problems unless such answers are repeated frequently.

Listen carefully to any objections from the attorney representing the side for which you are testifying. Such objections may provide clues about how to answer. If the objection is overruled, answer the question to the best of your ability. Have it repeated if necessary. During the process, be polite at all times.

If you are distracted by your own emotional response to the attorneys or to the questioning, the attorneys have taken control of the process. They are then more likely to successfully challenge your direct testimony. Be aware of personal styles or gimmicks used by attorneys to make a witness anxious or distracted.

After cross-examination, a witness may be called back to or asked to remain on the stand for re-direct examination or re-cross-examination. In such cases, you can assume that your testimony plays a pivotal role in the outcome of the case. Further clarification, damage control, or additional information are often discussed at this point. For example, the attorney may want the jury to hear again some specific detail of the witness's testimony in light of cross-examination. A social worker may also be recalled to clarify timing of interventions.

Chapter Summary

This chapter identifies the need for social workers to be educated concerning courtroom procedures. The importance of understanding relevant legal terms is stressed, and a variety of such terms are defined and discussed. These include: violations, jurisdiction, allegation, court process, due process, stipulation, burden of proof, standards of proof, evidence, witness, confidentiality, and privileged communication.

The major differences between the social work practice arena and the significantly more formal courtroom environment are examined. Specific dimensions of difference include process, atmosphere, client/defendant rights, and potential outcomes.

Numerous specific suggestions for responding during the direct and cross-examination processes are explained. Strategies frequently used by opposing counsel are described. These include those that attack a worker's direct testimony, professional credentials, the person (you) as an individual, and the profession of social work itself.

CHAPTER FOURTEEN

Developing and Managing
Agency Resources

"But where will we get the money?" asked Heather Jones, a social worker in the regional office on aging. Heather and two of her social work friends, Tina Lax and Wolf Jackson, were discussing the plight of family members caring for Alzheimer's disease patients. Few of these family members had any time off from the stress of caring for loved ones suffering from this dreaded disorder. Alzheimer's is a mental disorder which can leave its primarily elderly victims confused and with significant memory loss. Eventually it produces dementia, and victims may require help with such simple tasks as putting mashed potatoes on their plates or going to the bathroom. Unable to remember who or where they are, and often unable to manage the simplest self-care tasks, Alzheimer's sufferers place a fantastic burden on the family members who take care of them. The three friends had been sorting out ideas and had hit upon a possible solution. "Look," said Tina, a social worker for a local agency serving Alzheimer's patients, "what we need is a place for caretakers to bring their family members for a few hours each week so they can get some time off from such onerous responsibility."

"Well, you know the Senior Centers in each country rarely have anybody there in the afternoon after the luncheon meal" said Wolf Jackson, a social work instructor at a local college. "What if we could use the centers to provide respite care for people with Alzheimer's or related disorders?" *Respite care* is "the temporary assumption of responsibilities of a person who provides for the home care of another. The goal is to give the caretaker a break from the responsibilities to that tensions are minimized, so the caretaker can have some other interests or take care of personal crises, and so the client can stay out of institutional care" (Barker, 1991, p. 202). Wolf had learned about the unused centers while evaluating the effectiveness of some aging programs.

Soon the three were spinning out related ideas. "What if we could get a social worker to direct the program along with a Licensed Practical Nurse (LPN) and perhaps an activity director at each location? We could provide a great service and give these caregivers a rest," said Tina.

"Yea!" chime in Wolf. "We could offer respite care for enough hours each week that caregivers could reserve a set time for their family member. We might even be able to coordinate this care with other community services such as blood pressure screening and glaucoma testing."

Heather's question about financial resources slowed them down only temporarily. "What about the county or state picking up the cost?" asked Wolf.

"Nope," said Heather. "They already told me they will be short of funds for existing programs. But the Governor has promised more money for programs for the elderly in the next budget." "That's too long to wait," said Tina. "We

have people ending up in nursing homes because their caregivers can't get a break each week from this burden. That's a terrible waste of money and devastating to many of these families."

"The latest issue of the *Alzheimer's Newsletter* (a monthly publication about the disease) had a notice about possible grants from a national foundation. They're particularly interested in funding innovative ideas for serving the elderly in rural areas," Heather enthusiastically suggested.

"Do you still have the newsletter?" asked Wolf.

"Yes, if I can remember where I left it," replied Heather. When Heather tracked down the missing newsletter (under the couch pillow where her golden retriever, Prince, sleeps), the three friends plotted their course of action.

"Let's try for one of these grants," said Tina. "We have nothing to lose and a lot to gain if we can pull it off."

Introduction

This chapter will discuss creating and maintaining various agency resources. These resources include the agency's reputation, which is important because both agencies and services require good public relations to keep the support of taxpayers and contributors. Specifically, we will look carefully at the topic of working with the media to help ensure that your agency receives the most fair and positive treatment possible from the news media serving your community. We will also consider the use of technology to manage resources and assist in an organization's operation. Technology, particularly computers, is becoming an everyday reality in most social agencies.

In the last two sections we will introduce you to several important aspects of resource development with a specific focus on fundraising, grants, and contracts. Fundraising is a primary concern for all nonprofit and many public agencies. Learning how to raise money to pay for existing services, to develop new ones, or to test creative ideas is an important skill for social workers. This chapter will look at several fundraising ideas that have proven effective for a variety of agencies and organizations.

Because most agencies and social workers at some point end up involved with grants or contracts, the last portion of the chapter will discuss these topics in great detail. Most private nonprofit agencies receive grants or contracts to provide services and many public agencies do as well. In addition, many public agencies contract with private agencies to provide services the former cannot or choose not to offer. Thus, it is difficult to function in the field of social work without some familiarity with grants and contracts.

This chapter will:

- Discuss several aspects of developing and managing certain resources for your agency.
- Discuss how you can help build and maintain the agency's reputation by working with the media.
- Consider how agencies are using technology to manage resources, facilitate service delivery, and evaluate the effectiveness of agency practices.
- Discuss fundraising, grants, and contracts.

Working with the Media

The term "the media" refers to television, radio, and newspapers that deliver news and information to the public. Obviously, the purpose of the media is not just to paint you or your agency in a favorable light. Yet, the potential value of the media to your agency or organization is awesome. There are at least four ways in which the media can be beneficial to an agency.

First, skillful use of the media can make the public aware of your organization. This is important because public awareness creates a potential source of new clients, alerts potential donors to your existence, and can create a favorable impression of your organization and the services it provides.

Second, the media can be helpful in fundraising. Individual fundraising activities (such as a pancake breakfast or raffle) can be highlighted in the media. The need for specific items or services can also be announced. Equally important, the media can encourage the public to contribute much needed money to your agency.

Third, an effective media-relations effort can prevent minor problems from becoming more serious. Concerns or problems which arise and become known to the public can be countered more easily when the public has a positive perception of your agency.

Fourth, the media can also be helpful in publicizing problems and influencing decision-makers. Media attention can focus the public's awareness on a problem such as lack of service to a particular group. It can help expose unfair treatment by government officials or other individuals.

General Guidelines for Using the Media

Church (1981) has provided some general guidelines for working with the news media. First, *make it your policy to maintain ongoing relationships with media personnel.* Your contacts with the media should begin as early as possible. Don't wait until a problem arises before contacting the media. Having an existing relationship with members of the media makes it much easier to work with them when you require their assistance. Remember, the media exist to provide news and information to the public. That means the material provided to the media should be of interest to others. Reporters appreciate people who help them by providing possible story ideas. Is there a critical service that does not exist because there is no money? Are children or the elderly being hurt because of the actions of a particular agency or government department? Is there a particularly successful program serving the needs of chemically dependent individuals? Has your agency decided to provide service to an underserved population such as displaced homemakers? Generally speaking, if an item interests you and you alone, the media won't touch it with a ten-foot pole.

Second, *nurture a variety of contacts within the media.* All of the various media can and should be viewed as potential resources for your agency. Too often, social workers rely on a single individual (one reporter) or one medium (a newspaper) rather than using all of the media available. Any agency needs a variety of resources to which it can turn when in need. Consider the media among those resources.

If you happen to be a local expert on a subject, let the media know this. Your expert perspectives on health care might be sought by local media when the national media focus on this subject. Once you have developed a relationship with media personnel, maintain regular contact with them.

Third, *if you are speaking for an organization or agency, be certain you have sanction, or permission, to do this.* Agency administrators don't like to see their workers quoted as speaking for the agency when they have not authorized such action.

Fourth, *make it easy for the media representatives to contact you.* Providing home and office numbers and addresses is helpful. Also give them the names of others they can talk to about your agency or issue if you can't be reached.

Fifth, *learn the media's time schedules.* All the media have deadlines for their reports and stories. Learn these time frames and give media representatives timely notice of newsworthy events. If you miss the deadline for tonight's local TV broadcast, your story may get lost tomorrow. Some big news item such as a major fire, earthquake, or other sensational event may dwarf your particular news.

Sixth, *avoid playing favorites among the news media.* Don't give a press release to one media representative without also providing it to the others. The only exception to this guideline is the exclusive interview. An exclusive interview means you are giving a single reporter a story and she or he is the only one who has the information until it appears in the media.

Seventh, *recognize that the media can and do make mistakes.* When they do, be careful how you react. If a serious error requires correction, handle this diplomatically. Tactfully explain the reasons for your request and ask for a correction. Don't fool around asking for corrections of minor errors. On the other hand, praise reporters who produced a good story. Praise and support work about as well with media representatives as the public. Most of us like to know others think we do a good job. Never be afraid to compliment a reporter on an exceptional article or report.

Eighth, *don't be disappointed if a story you hoped would appear does not.* This is the nature of the news business. Perhaps your story got cut to provide room for a train wreck or the arrest of the local ax murderer. That's life in the big city, as they say. Recognize that reporters are not any happier about this than you are because they like to see their names in print (or be on camera). If your news item happens to disappear, thank the reporter anyway and tell her you look forward to working with her again.

Homan (1994) reminds us that anything you say to the media can, and often does, end up in print. Even specifying that something is "off the record" does not guarantee that it will not become part of a story. In theory, off the record comments are intended to help reporters better understand a story or point of view and are not intended to show up in their report. However, reporters are interested in news items and the off-the-

record comment may be truly newsworthy to them. Their sense of obligation to their employers and the public may supersede your wish for something to remain off the record.

Contacts with the Media

Contacts with the media can come about in a variety of ways. First, the media may contact you. If media personnel have heard about you or think there is a news story in something with which you're connected, they may make the first move. Second, you can call the media yourself and explain that you have what you believe is a newsworthy item. If it shows promise, the media representative will probably set up an appointment to meet you. Third, you may contact the media through a news release. This is a written announcement of some event that you believe is of interest to the public. Highlight 14.1 offers an example of a news release.

Media Interviews

If you are going to be interviewed by the news media, prepare well in advance. This means thinking carefully about what is most important to get across. Newspaper reporters usually spend several minutes to an hour on an interview. They try to allow time for you to expand on an idea. On the other hand, television interviews often last only a minute or two, which allows you little time to come up with your answers. Watch the local news programs to observe how little time on the air any story actually gets. Time the taped interviews to get an idea of what can be said in a minute or two.

Practice going over the important "sound bites" that carry your primary message. Sound bites are the short passages that people tend to remember from an interview. For example, Diane might have much she would like to say, but the important message is: "The city is putting our children in danger. No child should be at risk of getting shot just walking to school. A mayor and police chief who won't do their jobs should be replaced. We have tried to meet with Mayor Doublespeak and Chief Nightstick and they refuse. We are tired of the runaround and sick of hearing rescue squad sirens in our neighborhood. The association has no choice but to ask the court to intervene." Amazingly, just this little statement takes almost thirty seconds to say. This sug-

HIGHLIGHT 14.1

EXAMPLE OF A
NEWS RELEASE

Fremont Street Neighborhood Association
1234 Fremont Street
South Swampland, Missouri 65803
417-863-1000

For Immediate Release

Neighborhood Association Pushes City for Action
South Swampland, MO—August 1, 1995

The Fremont Street Neighborhood Association has threatened to sue the City of South Swampland for failing to adequately protect children waking to school along East Doyle Avenue. Association president Diane Chambers said that two children were hurt in drive-by shootings during the past four weeks while the city does nothing about the problem. The Neighborhood Association Board of Directors voted yesterday to sue in Circuit Court, charging the Mayor and Police Chief with discrimination against the predominantly African-American neighborhood along Fremont Street. The association is calling for increased police patrols and arrests of the gang members who frequent the area, brandishing weapons and selling drugs to children. They also demand the city close the south end of Fremont Street to prevent drivers from racing down the street. "If the city fails to take action to alleviate the problem, we will then take them to court," said Chambers. "We are also considering filing a discrimination complaint with the state Office of Civil Rights," she said. Chambers said a rally is scheduled for 10:00 a.m. Monday. Former Fremont Street resident and professional ballplayer Sam Malone will hold a news conference along with Association officers.

For further information contact Diane Chambers 863-1000 or 883-5060.

###

Note: A news release should be typed double-spaced, with margins of at least one and one-half inches all around.

gests how little information really appears in television interviews. Prepare yourself for this strict time limitation.

Respond to questions clearly and candidly. Don't take offense if reporters ask probing or difficult questions. That is their job. Offer to answer any other questions they have that may come up later. If you don't have information they need immediately, try to get it quickly. Remember, the media work under tight deadlines. If you are seen as a credible, cooperative, and helpful interviewee, media representatives will value your contribution to their work and jobs.

Other Media Communications

We have spoken mainly about dealing with the media through interviews and news releases. Obviously, these are not the only ways in which we can work with the media. For example, every newspaper has a "Letters to the Editor'' section where interested readers share their views on various topics. Such sections provide ample opportunity to have your say along with the other respondents. Note that most papers limit the length of what they will print and expect you to identify yourself, including your name and address. Some papers will withhold your name and address if desired. However all newspapers want this information to prevent anonymous misuse of the media. Since anonymous letters cannot be traced to anyone, they are always suspect.

Expect editing or shortening of your letter if it is too long. Don't get excited if it doesn't appear at all. This can happen from time to time. Newspapers may receive lots of letters and often can't print them all.

Letters to the editor should not contain libelous (defaming) statements that can get you and perhaps the paper sued. Of course, the best defense against an accusation that you have said something damaging about another is that the statement was true.

When you write to the paper, reference something that was in the paper recently. This orients both the paper and its readers to why your item is relevant. After all, the purpose of the letter section is to let the reader have his or her say about things that appear in the paper, not to tell everybody that your neighbor has an obnoxious, constantly barking Doberman Pinscher.

Sometimes you can entice the newspaper editors to write an editorial on a particular topic. Editorials are the newspaper editor's views on issues of concern in your community. Editorials can cover everything from the editors' position on local elections to concerns about problems in city government.

You will probably need to meet directly with editorial staff and ask if they would consider an editorial about your cause or agency. Be prepared to give them background information and facts that they will need to support their position. Homan (1994) suggests that you emphasize the logical relationship between your issue and their past stand on similar matters. Highlight 14.2 presents a typical newspaper editorial.

Using Technology in Your Agency

Few, if any, social agencies operate without extensive use of various forms of technology, most commonly computers. Computers have joined various other technological advances (telephones, dictation equipment, FAX machines, photocopiers, and voice mail/answering machines) as indispensable facets of our professional lives. Essentially, all these items are tools helping us to do our jobs better. While most social workers have

---

HIGHLIGHT 14.2

EXAMPLE OF AN EDITORIAL COMMENT

County Needs New Juvenile Facility

The proposed county juvenile detention facility will be discussed by the board of supervisors at its meeting tonight. The number of juveniles detained for a week or longer in the county has increased threefold in the past two years.

Keeping juveniles in the county jail, even when the jail is not busy, is, in our opinion, a poor practice. Depending upon their situation, juveniles housed in the county jail need various amounts of supervision. Few require the same level of security as adult inmates. We see no way that keeping adult criminals with juveniles (many of whom aren't even charged with a crime) can benefit anyone. We strongly urge the board to consider funding a separate facility for our community's juveniles who need temporary detention.

contact with computers at some point in their college careers, often this experience is limited to word processing. While word processing is an important role for computers and is routinely used in most agencies, it is only one of several available technological functions. In this section we will describe some typical uses you and your agency will have for computers.

Understanding Computer Hardware

Large agencies have used computers for decades to perform certain functions such as printing payroll checks for workers, client public assistance checks, and checks to pay agency bills. Before the arrival of personal computers in the early 1980s, outside companies performed this work for a fee. Often the computers used for printing checks were what is known as mainframes or minicomputers. In those days, computer use required a high degree of training and substantial knowledge of computer systems. Some agencies operated their own computer systems. However, for many the closest they came to modern technology was the use of typewriters with memory for printing out form letters.

With the beginning of the age of personal computers, a major transformation occurred. Personal computers became commonplace in most agencies, first with secretaries and administrative personnel and later with other staff. This did not mean the end of larger computer systems. Many agencies still use these for a variety of purposes, especially when large volumes of data must be maintained. It does mean, however, that many agency technological functions can be performed by nonexperts with boxes on their desks and the right computer software. Software includes the special programs that make the computer do what we want it to do. Most software available today can be used by anyone willing to take the time to learn the operating rules. Specialized training is not normally needed.

The personal computer found in most agencies consists of a *central processing unit (CPU)*, monitor, keyboard, and printer. The CPU is the "box" which contains the electrical, electronic, and mechanical components that make the computer function. Among these components are computer chips containing the "memory" of the computer. To be accurate, this is the computer's short-term memory, since whatever is in memory when you turn the computer off is forgotten immediately. This is similar to my ability to remember a phone number I've just looked up in the telephone book. As long as I'm paying attention to the number, I can recall it. Five minutes later, when I've switched off my interest, the number is gone. Despite the limited nature of this form of memory, it is important since it affects how well various software programs work. CPU memory is typically measured in megabytes with four, eight, or more megabytes common in most newer computers. Bytes are part of the measurement system used in computers. Each byte represents a character (such as the letter "a." A megabyte holds 1 million characters. As a rough comparison, one double-spaced page of type contains roughly 250 words or 1,273 characters. A megabyte represents something over 775 pages of double-spaced text.

Also included in the box are several data storage devices such as *hard drives* (sometimes called fixed or high density disks), and one or more "floppy drives." The hard drive is located inside the box and is similar to a small compact disk upon which data is easily stored and retrieved. It normally has a very large memory capacity allowing significant amounts of data to be stored on the disk. This is effectively the long-term memory of your computer. Hard disk drives come in many sizes commonly measured in megabytes (for example, 250, 500, 1000 and so on). Older hard drives were smaller and held only twenty or forty megabytes of data. Data on the hard drive does not go away when the machine is turned off. Hard drives are usually used to store the computer operating system, primary software programs, and any other information to which you want quick access.

The *floppy drives* are devices that use small, flexible (hence, the term floppy) disks used for storage and retrieval of data. Typical floppy drives are of two sizes, five and one/fourth inches and three and one-half inches. The larger disk is very thin and truly is floppy or bendable. The smaller disk is more rigid and holds more data than its larger five-and-a-quarter inch sister. The smaller disk is becoming the standard for new computers. Some computers have both size drives (plus the hard drive), while others have only the hard drive and the smaller floppy. The amount of data which can be stored on a floppy disk varies depending upon whether the disk is double-sided (data can be stored on both sides) and on the "density" of the disk. Density is denoted in one of three categories (regular density, double density, and high density). Higher density disks compact the data more than lower density disks. Three-and-one-half inch disks are currently rated at 1.55 megabytes or about 1100 double-spaced pages of type. As on the hard disk, items saved on the floppy disk do not disappear when the computer is turned off. Typically, you save data on both the hard drive and the floppy disk.

Personal computers typically operate under one of two standard operating systems—Apple or DOS (Disk Operating System). Apple is the trademark for computers produced by the Apple Computer company. DOS-based systems (sometimes called IBM-compatible) are based on an IBM Corporation standard format. To confuse matters even more, the DOS system may be manufactured by different companies (for example, Microsoft and Compaq). Until recently, software programs (such as word processors and spread sheets) that worked on one type of system (Apple) would not work on the other (DOS). More recent advances allow a greater degree of sharing between these two operating systems. In other words, programs are available that allow for translation from one format to the other and some machines can run both DOS and Apple-based software.

IBM-compatible computers continue to go through a series of metamorphoses in sophistication, speed, and capabilities. It is not uncommon to see computers listed as 386, 486, and pentium (equivalent to 586) units, sometimes with suffixes such as SX or DX. These designations simply indicate the relative speed and capability of each computer. As one might expect, a 486 is faster than a 386. Similar changes have occurred in the Apple machines. It is the nature of this technology that whatever hardware and software are in use today will be replaced, upgraded, or otherwise improved in a very short time.

While the "box" on your desk is important, it is impossible to operate a computer without two other key components. The first is the *keyboard*. The keyboard allows you to input data through a standard set of keys that resemble those on a typewriter. In addition, all keyboards have a series of special keys (sometimes called function keys) that have other uses. Depending upon the vintage of the keyboard (and on the manufacturer), these additional keys may be located on one side or the other of the basic alphabetical keys, or along the top of the keyboard. These keys, alone or with other keys, allow the operation of the software programs which are essential to completing our tasks (e.g., word

processing, database). For example, pressing the Fl key in many programs gives you access to the software's help screen. Pressing F12 in WordPerfect for Windows calls up the screen for setting up tables. Many keyboards also have a separate number pad on the right-hand side of the board to allow for quicker entry of numerical data.

The *monitor* is also an essential part of the computer. Monitors are television screens on which your keystrokes appear and which the computer uses to send you messages. Monitor screens may be in full color or in one color. They also come in various sizes and with different degrees of clarity and preciseness.

Along with most computers you will have a *printer*. Printers allow you to print information from your computer onto paper. Printers come in different types and styles as well. Dot matrix printers use tiny dots produced by a series of pins to print data on paper. The printer hammers the pins onto a ribbon which prints the data on the piece of paper. These printers are less expensive and relatively slow. The quality of print appearing on your paper is also generally lower than other printer systems because items are printed as a series of tiny dots instead of as solid type.

Some printers use a variation of this hammer method in which a wheel containing the characters imprints the data on paper. So-called daisy wheel printers produce a very good quality of print but are very slow. In many ways they resemble the current office typewriters in operation and quality of print.

Ink-jet printers use a different technology to produce data on paper. Ink is sprayed on paper from a small cartridge producing a very good quality of print. Ink-jet printers are typically more expensive than dot matrix or daisy wheel printers and much faster.

Laser printers are really an adaptation of photocopier technology. They produce images on paper in the same way as a copy machine, using laser light and operating at fairly high temperatures. They also are the fastest printers, come in different rates of speed, and are the most expensive.

Understanding the Software

Software is the term used to describe the various specialized programs which produce the results we want. Most of us are familiar with word processing programs. These

Figure 14.1
Information in a Database

Name	Street Address	City, State, Zip	Telephone	Last Appt.
Abbott, Lois	1234 Hollywood Dr.	Los Angeles, CA 19876	835-4578	2-12-96
Costello, Bud	4321 Mudslide Rd.	Los Angeles, CA 19876	835-8754	3-24-96
Hardy, Stanley	3454 Bonk Circle	Huntington Beach, CA 19874	458-2345	3-12-96
Laurel, Olivia	987 W. Hartburn Lane	Huntington Beach, CA 19874	458-9345	3-18-96
Mangreen, Newt	1776 Idea Street	Los Angeles, CA 19876	777-6666	7-4-96
Peru, Rosina	1890 Money Boulevard	Los Angeles, CA 19876	345-1945	11-3-92

programs are made by many companies and allow the computer to operate as a typewriter. We can type data that appears on the screen, print it using our printer, and/ or save it for later retrieval. Agencies use word processing software to enter data in client files, keep worker records of client contact, send letters, and the like.

Software may be designed for a single purpose such as word processing or be "integrated," allowing several functions to be accessed within a single program. An integrated system might allow you to type a letter to a client, look at the client's record to find her or his address and your last contact with them, and even schedule an appointment on your first open date next month. With single purpose software, it is generally necessary to exit or turn off one program before going into another.

Software exists for an infinite variety of purposes. We have mentioned word processing. *Database software* allows us to maintain extensive records and retrieve that data quickly. We might like to know which of our clients we have not seen in the past three months. We can easily get a list of those clients and their addresses. If we want to know for which clients a report to the court is due this month, the database will tell us. Just about any piece of information can be entered into a database system. Figure 14.1 shows the way information might be displayed in a database.

Of course, a great deal more information can be contained in a database than what is represented here. We could list the presenting problem, names of family members, and any other data. At the same time, databases are useful for purposes other than maintaining

client records. We could, for example, use a database to keep membership records for a community association or organization, to maintain a record of contributors to a political campaign, to save a list of social workers and their agencies, phone numbers, and other information. You can also have the database reorganize information into reports. You might want a report on all members of your organization who have not paid their dues. As you can see, a database can be a useful piece of software whether you are working with macro, mezzo, or micro problems.

Spreadsheets are software packages that allow us to maintain various kinds of financial or numerical information. Spreadsheets are essentially electronic accounting ledgers into which we type the same type of information we would write into an accountant's ledger. All software spreadsheets allow us to keep track of what we spend on various projects. They allow us to add up costs just as we might do in a ledger book, except that every change in a figure can be automatically reflected in the changed total. Figure 14.2 displays a typical spreadsheet.

A real spreadsheet could have many more columns and rows, depending on the financial information you were keeping track of. Spreadsheets allow you to build formulas and automatically recalculate totals. This way, as the number of purchases you make increases, the total spent at the bottom changes along with it. The $700.22 would keep changing as new items were entered into the spreadsheet. You can also calculate what a 5 percent increase in your organization's income

Figure 14.2
A Spreadsheet

Date	Item	Cost	Category
1-3-96	Postage	14.56	O1
1-5-96	Desk	456.00	E3
1-5-96	Chair	134.00	E3
1-7-96	Paper	95.66	S2
Total		700.22	

would do in various categories such as operating expenses, equipment, supplies, and personnel. The codes 01, E3, and S2 are a means of categorizing items as equipment, operating expenses, or supplies. Users tend to develop their own systems of categorization based upon the needs of their agency.

Besides these broad categories of software, there are many other types of software in use. Agencies use financial packages to do payroll, pay bills, and update financial records. Some larger agencies may even have special programs written to perform tasks unique to the agency or reflecting the agency's specialized needs.

Agency Software Usage

Computer software usage varies by agency. Besides the general types of software packages referred to above, many agencies will use software specifically designed to meet social workers' needs. Specialized software packages now exist for many social work purposes. These include: ''keeping client records and notes readily available (even from varied sources); administering social histories and many other types of clinical questionnaires and screening devices; conducting clinical interviews; administering and scoring mental status tests and other evaluative examinations'' (Nurius & Hudson, 1993, p. xv).

The thought of making an assessment based upon symptoms typed into a computer is challenging. However, the software already exists to do this with relative ease. The ability to refer a client to an appropriate service can be enhanced if a list of available agencies and resources exists in a database. One can enter, say, a

problem like lack of transportation for medical care and get a listing from the databases of all agencies and organizations which might provide this service. Di Benedetto and Pirie (1980) have also described how computers can be effectively used for information and referral.

Of course, the potential to determine eligibility for various financial assistance programs is obvious. If data on a client can be entered into a software program, it can easily be determined whether the person meets the guidelines for a given program such as AFDC.

Databases can also be used to match clients with services. Schwab and Wilson (1989) describe the successful use of computers to match children needing various types of temporary care (foster care, group homes, etc.) with the availability and service provided by each of these resources.

Client data entered into case records are part of agencies *management information systems (MIS)*, methods for gathering, analyzing, and evaluating data in an agency or organization. The data collected on a client through the use of application forms and other agency records is also part of the management information system. Other facets of the management information system could be data on employees, their training, level of experience, and agency assignments. Much of this information can now be computerized and allows administrators to better manage their agencies. An agency administrator can use such data to analyze and understand what kinds of problems clients experience and what types of services are provided by the agency. This information becomes invaluable when deciding which programs should receive additional funding or where improvements are needed in service to clients. An analysis of agency workload might reveal that the unit providing child neglect and abuse services is getting twice as many referrals as in the past, although the staffing has not changed. This might well justify adding staff to the unit, especially if another unit was underutilized. Highlight 14.3 gives another example of how management information might be used.

Management information systems also help agencies identify problems not being met by existing resources. Perhaps many clients are in need of emergency housing but the agency does not provide this service. Or perhaps, there are specific services that the agency offers that no one is using. Such a situation might suggest that agency resources be redeployed where they are most needed.

HIGHLIGHT 14.3

MANAGEMENT INFORMATION SYSTEMS

Chris Vlahoulis was new at his job as deputy director of the Mapleton Service Agency. Mapleton provided a variety of outpatient mental health services to clients, ranging from marital counseling to children's groups. The agency director had asked Chris to prepare a report on clients seen in the previous twelve months. Chris knew quite a bit about computers but little about the system of data gathering employed in his agency. He quickly discovered that all client data were entered into a database that allowed him to ask specific questions about the information contained therein.

Chris asked the database to list all presenting problems reported by clients in the past year. The computer gave him a list that showed how many people had what diagnoses. Interestingly, Chris discovered that many clients presented problems with substance abuse. What was most interesting, however, is that no workers in the agency had any certification as substance abuse service providers. Only a couple had any specialized education for working with this client group. Chris could use the data to show the number of client problems and also to recommend that workers receive additional training in helping chemically dependent clients.

Evaluation of outcomes can be enhanced by an effective MIS. Outcomes, you will recall are quality-of-life changes resulting from social work interventions. It should be relatively easy to see what percentage of clients report satisfaction with the services they receive It should also be possible to see how many cases are closed, thus showing that client goals have been achieved. Chapter 10, "Evaluation in Macro Practice," described some of these scenarios.

Depending upon the agency, each computer may be provided with its own software or the agency may be "networked." Networking just means that several computers have access to the same software. Networking is economical and allows people to share data. Thus, the secretary typing a letter to a client, the billing department preparing a monthly statement, and you may simultaneously get information from the client's record. It also means you can leave a message for your supervisor on her computer such as "I'm taking a six-month vacation in Fiji. See you in May. Please hold my calls."

While we have talked mainly about the use of computers in agencies, there is no limit to how this technology can be used in other environments. Bernstein (1991) describes the use of several common software packages, primarily spreadsheets and databases, to manage a political campaign for a presidential candidate. Software was used for everything from keeping records of donations and expenditures to identifying likely voters, preparing campaign reports, and analyzing voting trends.

Cordero (1991) reported on the use of crime reports to identify neighborhoods with high crime rates. Citizen patrols and police were then concentrated in those neighborhoods, thus helping to reduce criminal behavior. The computer's ability to aggregate data like this can be very helpful in revealing common problems that otherwise appear to be isolated. A computerized database of problems might show that a neighborhood school has expelled twice as many students this year as last. One might then look at possible explanations for such a dramatic increase in punitive actions taken by the school principal or school board.

Computers can also be used to publish newsletters and other public access documents such as brochures describing agency services. These can be done on regular word processing software or with greater ease on software designed for "desktop publishing." This type of software was developed to help lay out pages of documents, move pictures around, and perform the kinds of tasks that used to be done only by professional print shops. The availability of this software can reduce the cost of producing a document. Because it is tailored specifically to developing such documents, it also makes the task easier than using a regular word processor.

General Observations about Computers

As we said earlier, computers are just one of several tools we use regularly in practice. Like any tool, they can be misused. Sometimes people use data in computer files without authority, thereby endangering confidentiality.

Computer mistakes can be annoying, damaging, and difficult to correct. Whether for good or evil, computers generally do exactly what we tell them to do. If we err and tell a computer to enter data into the file of John R. Smith when we really meant John T. Smith, the computer does what we tell it to do. It doesn't know that we made a typing error and meant to hit an adjoining key. Similarly, if we say we saw the client first on 8–15–95 but typed 8–15–94, the machine does not know what we meant, only what we told it to do.

Like any new skill, computer use requires learning time. Sometimes it seems as if the learning curve for computers goes straight up before it levels off and we feel some degree of comfort. Initially at least, it may take us longer to enter data using the computer than it did the old-fashioned way. This phase passes, however, and we all get better and faster at entering information. As Nurius and Hudson (1994) point out, there is increasing evidence that computers can be used very effectively by social workers and their clients for many purposes, from record keeping to evaluation.

Learning different software packages for different purposes (for example, word processing, or establishing a database) requires mastering different commands and keystrokes. Most computer software comes with sufficient information to learn the basics very rapidly. Some more sophisticated programs are difficult to learn. Classes may be available at nearby colleges or technical schools to help those desiring formal instruction. In addition, books are available for most major programs to help you learn your new software. Many software programs come with detailed workbooks and on-line help menus to teach the user how to implement the software.

One of the nicest things about using a personal computer is that you are the boss. If you make mistakes, you can usually correct them easily. If you get frustrated with your progress, you can turn the darn thing off and start another time. Once mastered, computer skills will enhance your effectiveness as a generalist practitioner.

Fund-Raising

Few social workers begin their careers with the clear goal of becoming fund-raisers. The frequently expressed motivation for a career in social work—"I want to help people"—does not often extend to raising money. A failure to mention fund-raising as a goal is not particularly surprising. First, raising money is not seen by the novice as a social work task. Second, many of us lack confidence in our ability to raise money. Finally, compounding the lack of both an understanding of the importance of this role and the confidence to fulfill it is the absence of much education or preparation to be a fund-raiser. Yet, all social agencies require financial resources (money) to operate.

Raising the funds to run an agency can be a daunting task. While public agencies often receive most of their funds from tax money, many other agencies and organizations must rely on a variety of sources to provide services. These agencies are frequently called nonprofit or not-for-profit organizations. Most such programs use a combination of public funding and private donations to help meet the need. As a result, the division between nonprofit and public agencies has blurred substantially over the years due to the need to raise funds. Most private nonprofit agencies receive grants or contracts from public sources (that is, tax money). A private agency might receive a contract or grant from a public agency to offer a service the public agency cannot afford or does not wish to offer. Similarly, many public agencies accept donations and grants from private individuals, foundations, and organizations. In the last section of this chapter we will examine the use of grants and contracts, two common methods of raising money for program operations.

Often, however, neither grants nor contracts by themselves are sufficient to fund agency programs. Possibly, no grant or contract is available for what we want to do, but even if one is, the amount of money offered is insufficient. Grants are generally used for one-time projects and rarely is grant money available on a continuing basis. Raising money, even for causes we deem worthy (such as social programs), is not an easy task. As social workers most of us find asking for money very difficult. Perhaps this is because we have little or no preparation for fund-raising. Perhaps, it is because we don't feel comfortable asking others to help us. After all, as social workers we are usually the ones giving

---

HIGHLIGHT 14.4

FUND-RAISING

Fortuitous Crunk didn't know how many friends she had until disaster struck. Her house, on the edge of the inner city, was a bit rundown, but provided shelter for her family of four children. One of these children was a foster child with severe developmental disabilities. One frosty fall evening, Fortuitous awoke to hear the neighbor's dog barking. It turned out to be a lucky break. When she awoke she smelled smoke and managed to get all her children out of the house before it was completely engulfed in smoke and flames.

Because of her poverty, Fortuitous had never carried fire insurance on her property. Thus, when her house burned down she faced the possibility of joining the other homeless persons living in the public park six blocks away. Her neighbors, however, would not let this happen. They immediately began to raise money to repair her home. First, they alerted the news media to the neighborhood's efforts to help one of their own. Such public interest stories often appeared in the "Friends and Neighbors" section of the local paper. The neighbors also held a series of fundraising events including a pancake and sausage breakfast at a neighborhood church. This event not only raised funds through people buying their breakfasts, but also brought in donations. A local builder offered to assign a crew of carpenters and plumbers for one day to help with the rebuilding. A large lumberyard in town donated lumber, nails, and sheetrock for walls and ceilings in the badly damaged structure. Finally, the neighbors picked a weekend to pitch in and put the finishing touches on the house. They had successfully raised $6,000, not including the value of donated materials and labor. The money purchased furniture to replace what was destroyed in the fire. The entire process from the night of the fire until Fortuitous was back in her home took exactly thirty-nine days.

---

help. Whatever the reason, fear of fund-raising is a hurdle we must overcome.

Not only is money needed to operate basic programs, but funds are needed to support new civic and political causes (including political candidates). Money is also necessary for campaigns to convince voters to support bond issues, tax increases, or help for disaster victims. Highlight 14.4 gives an example of fund-raising to help an individual deal with a calamity.

Sources of Funds

Social workers are frequently asked to help raise funds for a variety of causes ranging from ongoing operation of an agency to political campaigns. Thus, we must be aware of the potential sources of fund-raising. Fortunately, there are many possible avenues for fundraising. Flanagan (1980) and Homan (1994) identify several alternate sources of funds. These include individual donors, benefits, corporate donors, membership due, and foundations. In addition, church organizations and service clubs often provide funding if the area to be supported falls within their sphere of interest. We will address each of these sources in the following pages. We discuss foundation and corporate sources in the last portion of the chapter under the topic of grants and contracts.

Individual Donors

Individual donors are people who dig into their own pockets for money to help a project or activity. There are many motivations for individual giving. Some people give because they are getting something they value in return. People who buy raffle tickets hope to win a prize. Likewise, those who buy a ticket to a concert or church-sponsored chicken dinner are getting something concrete in return for their contribution. Others give

Service organizations such as the Salvation Army often provide funding if the area to be supported falls within their sphere of interest.

from a sense of personal or civic obligation based on their own values. Some give because they devotedly believe in your cause, project, or activity. Still others contribute, expecting recognition for their goodwill. In fact, most people probably give for a combination of reasons. We are likely to be more successful in our fund-raising efforts if we can provide potential donors with multiple reasons to support our cause or activity. Let's consider some of the different ways of raising money from individual donors.

Benefits

The pancake and sausage breakfast her neighbors used to raise funds to repair Fortuitous's home (see highlight 14.4) is one example of a *benefit*. Benefits are activities and events held to raise money for a worthy cause. Examples include concerts, dinners, and sporting events. When musicians hold a concert and the proceeds go to charity, that is a benefit. Every year some sporting events (for example, professional football games) are held to benefit specific charities. Of course, benefits can be much more modest, say, a giant neighborhood garage sale with the funds going to pay for an operation for a neighborhood child.

There are several challenges in raising funds through holding benefits. First, there is often a great deal of work to plan and carry out a benefit. Let's look back at the situation with Fortuitous and think of the things that were needed to get a pancake breakfast off the ground. Fortuitous's neighbors had to choose a location and date. They had to acquire sufficient food (purchased or donated) to meet the anticipated need. (They didn't want to run out too early or to have too much left at the end.) Fortuitous's neighbors needed to ensure that cooking facilities for a large group as well as adequate supplies of plates, utensils, cups, and glasses, were available. In addition, servers were needed to prepare and serve food and to clean up the breakfast's aftermath. Planning and arranging all of this took time. Still other help was required to advertise the breakfast, prepare posters, tickets, and news releases.

Whether a group gets items donated for a benefit or pays for them, the task is formidable. We also need people to sell tickets to the event. Tickets sold in advance are generally more profitable to a benefit than those sold at the event itself because many people and organizations buy tickets to events but don't plan to attend. This actually works out quite well. At events where something concrete is provided (such as food), the value of the food not consumed increases the total contribution. In other words, if you don't have to make five-hundred pancakes but someone paid you for that many, you come out ahead. Sometimes organizations and businesses buy blocks of tickets that they distribute to employees or customers. Again, not all those who receive tickets will necessarily attend. Therefore, benefit sponsors profit from unused tickets because food is paid for but not actually consumed.

It is important to encourage media attention to your event by showcasing those who contributed their time and money to make it happen. This is also a way of saying thanks to those who helped and, for businesses, of giving them free publicity. Additionally, you should announce the event to other community organizations and groups. Send notices to service clubs, such as Lions and Rotary, and to groups such as Parents Without Partners.

Of course, benefits work best when people find the event attractive and want to come. Making the event attractive can be managed in a variety of ways. Perhaps the cost-to-benefit ratio is quite good (that is, donors are getting a very good deal—all you can eat for $4 or a chance to meet a famous person for only $5). Perhaps this event is the place to be (because all the important people in town are likely to come). Maybe the benefit is attractive because participants really want to support the cause. Ideally, we would like our event to have several of the aforementioned characteristics. Held every year, benefits can become very successful. They can even develop into ongoing sources of funding.

Some churches and other organizations have adopted an interesting variation on the benefit. They solicit donations from their members or the public to avoid holding a benefit. Since the work involved in benefits and activities can be great, members are often enticed into contributing cash rather than having to work the event. There's always an angle if you really want to raise money.

Corporate Donations

Another variation on the benefit idea is joining forces with another organization such as a business. Each year some businesses donate part of their proceeds or a day's receipts to a community charity. This charity or cause could be yours. Perhaps Shady Sam's Shine Shop could make a donation for every car washed. Each person who had a car washed last Saturday represented a donation of $1 to your organization. Such events and activities benefit both you and the business. Because of the extra publicity and good will, more people may patronize the business on that special day.

Finally, there are other variations on the benefit theme. Rather than hold specific events, such as breakfasts, fundraisers can sell a product or service—car washes, candy, Christmas cards, and cookie sales (remember the Girl Scouts). Often it seems that most people who make these purchases are parents or relatives of those selling the goodies, but that doesn't matter to those receiving the funds).

The primary limitation to benefits and other such activities is the relatively limited amount of money that can be raised. If your needs are small (under $10,000), these events can be quite useful. Unfortunately, they do not produce the tens of thousands of dollars needed each year to pay for major services. Except for annual events that evolve into major community activities, benefits don't usually provide substantial ongoing sources of money.

One well-known way of raising money is to sell a product or a service. The Girl Scout annual cookie sale is a particularly successful example of this fund-raising method.

Direct Solicitation

Direct solicitation of gifts means asking others to contribute. Instead of selling raffle tickets, chicken dinners, or rock concerts, we say straight out, "We need your money.'' Of course, we can't do this without paying attention to some basics. It makes no sense to ask people to give more than they can afford. Individual requests for money must be based on the gift giving potential of donors and their possible motivations for giving to your cause. We discussed some common motivations earlier. Assessing how much someone can give is not always easy. It helps if you know what this person has contributed to other activities. If you don't know, make an educated guess. Unless you are asking hundreds of people each to give $10, you might wish to focus on those individuals who are capable of larger gifts. Asking two hundred people to give you $10 each could net you $2,000. Asking four people with sufficient incomes to give you $500 each seems like a simpler task. Of course, asking one person to give you the entire $2,000 is not out of the question. Many individuals regularly contribute this much and more.

Some gifts are reported publicly so it is possible to anticipate a donor's potential contribution. People running political campaigns must identify donors and contribution amounts. This information is often published in the newspapers. Additionally, newspapers publish a wide range of other articles describing contributions for various causes. Recently, a paper credited a donor who gave $13,000 to build a new animal shelter. Another paper named an individual who contributed $20,000 to a campaign opposing the building of an urban entertainment park. Local universities publish lists of donors, often with the actual amounts or the general category of contributions. Other civic organizations, such as the theater or symphony, list major contributors in their programs for attendees. It is possible to cull these various lists to identify individuals who have the potential for larger donations. If your responsibilities routinely involve fund-raising, you should develop your own personal list of possible donors and of the range of their contributions.

Once you have done your homework, you are ready to ask for the contribution. Make an appointment with the designated donor, carefully rehearse what you are going to say, show up on time, and make a pitch that you have carefully developed. What you say depends upon what you and the donor have in common. Do you share ideas about what is good for your community? If so, share this in your pitch or proposal. Are your opinions the same on political issues? Then include that fact. Are you both concerned about a particular problem that

this donation can help resolve? Then emphasize that point. If you can identify any commonality with a donor, at the very least you can clearly articulate the value of your project and how the donor's contribution can help the cause.

Some fund-raisers recommend asking for a specific amount from a donor, while others suggest the donor should make that determination. If you ask for too little, donors might think you didn't believe they had the potential to give much—a possible insult. If you ask for too much, you might flatter them by implying that they're wealthier than they are. In that case, they might give a bit more than they normally would to avoid looking stingy. The final decision about whether to ask for a specific amount is yours.

When the donor offers an amount, it is best to solicit the donation at once. Donations promised for later sometimes don't appear. If you can't get the money immediately, ask for a specific time you can return for it. Remember the old adage, a bird in the hand is worth two in the bush. It's still true.

Seeking Group Giving

Every community is filled with dozens (sometimes hundreds) of groups, organizations, and associations with potential for contributing to any given cause. Every social or fraternal organization (Rotary, Elks, Kiwanis, Junior League) gives substantial amounts to their respective communities. They exist, at least ostensibly, for this very purpose. Thus, you will be missing a beat if you ignore these organizations.

Finding a list of these organizations is usually easy. Check either the local library or the chamber of commerce for a list of all civic organizations. Normally, you will be given a list (often slightly out of date) which will include each organization's name along with that of its president or chairperson. If you don't know whether the organization supports your kind of project, try to talk with a member or even the president about your idea. Find out how other causes solicit gifts. Typically, you must provide a written request. Many organizations also expect a presentation. Perhaps you can get on one of the organization's agendas. Most such groups have a planned speaker or program at each meeting. This is a wonderful opportunity to get your ideas across to the membership and to drum up enthusiasm for your project.

The organization's board of directors or steering committee may make the actual decision about whether or not to make a donation. Thus, you should write a proposal describing the need and the amount you would like the organization to contribute. Sometimes it is best to ask for specific items, such as a computer and software package for a group home or playground equipment for a day-care center. Perhaps you would like the group to underwrite the monthly cost of sending a child to summer camp. Generally, such organizations will give to causes that are consistent with their own purposes and history. For example, Lions clubs are often very in interested in issues dealing with vision and eyesight. The Kiwanis are interested in children.

While financial contributions are always welcome, perhaps the organization can help you in some other way. Some organizations undertake projects that combine donations of money with donated efforts from their members. One women's organization donated money to buy furniture and draperies for a group home, and then contributed members' time to paint and decorate the home. A Kiwanis club contributed both money and labor to build a park shelter. Both kinds of help, money and volunteer effort, are welcome.

Creating Your Own Organization

Another way to raise funds is to ask people to join an organization and pay dues. The membership dues are then available for various projects. Civic organizations often raise funds for their own projects in this way. Belonging to a group and paying dues helps raise one's sense of commitment to the organization. Many of us belong to organizations whose purposes we support to varying degrees. One individual might belong to a civic club, a church group, a parent-teacher association, two or more professional associations, a neighborhood association, and a recreational organization.

Each of these organizations collects membership dues and uses them for various purposes. Some organizations, in turn, donate the money to other worthy causes. Others use the funds purely to operate their organization. If you think about the membership organizations you know of (or belong to), you can get an idea of the potential money these groups can raise.

Of course, the decision to start a membership group must be well-thought-out. The reason for starting a membership group should be clear. It is easier to ask people to join a group than to contribute money. By joining, they get something in return for their money. Belonging to a group is a way for a person to feel connected. Many social work students join student organizations for this very purpose.

Potential members include everyone with the slightest interest in the group's purpose. If dues are low enough, as Homan (1994) recommends, it is easy to ask people to join. Develop a membership application that is short and easy to complete. Typical information on the application should include name, address, and telephone numbers for home and work. You may decide to request other information, such as name of employer or of other organizations to which the prospective member belongs. Whenever you come across people with an interest in your cause, invite them to join. Subsequently, provide members with benefits. These include membership cards and periodic newsletters that inform members about the organization and issues of concern to them. Most organizations also make regular (at least annual) requests for additional contributions to support special projects.

One benefit of membership as a source of revenue is that dues are generally free of the restrictions associated with other kinds of donations. Because the total amount of dues you can collect depends upon the membership, size of the member pool becomes important. Membership dues provide continuous funds although usually not nearly the amount available from other sources, such as grants and contracts.

Other Fund-Raising Techniques

You can raise money in various other ways beside those described above. Homan (1994) points out that telephone and mail solicitations are sometimes used to raise money. Both methods work best if you target individuals with proven track records of supporting your cause or causes similar to yours. Cold calls, in which you simply dial a number and hope for a favorable response, are very unproductive in terms of dollars generated. While they can eventually result in a list of potential contributors, much money and time must be spent in the effort. If your organization happens to be famous or everyone automatically knows why you are calling, the task is easier. When Girl Scouts go door-to-door selling cookies, they are essentially making cold calls, but this is rarely a problem. Almost everybody knows why they are there, knows about the product they get in return for their "donation," and feels good about contributing.

Whether you are using the phone or the mail to raise money, develop your plan very clearly. Your approach should indicate who you are, why you're calling (or writing), and why the targeted donor should support your organization. If you are phoning, do so from a location where you won't be disturbed. Often it helps to have multiple phones available and have several people calling at once. This can even be fun (you might serve pizza during the session to make it a social event for participants). You can also send a mail solicitation and follow up with a phone call. This alerts people to your cause and gives them time to think about it before they pledge an actual donation.

Raising money using the mail alone often expends much effort for very little money. Preparing envelopes, stuffing, and stamping them can be boring tasks. One alternative is to make the mailing activity festive by having food or music so that people can chat and relax while they are working. Another alternative is to hire people to do such tedious tasks for you. However, since we assume you don't have much money to start with, we suggest you use volunteer help whenever possible.

No matter what method you use, keep focused on a professionally produced product. Your mailed materials should be of good quality and present a very positive image of you and your cause. Proofread everything and then do it again. A campus women's programming committee chaired by a social work professor once undertook a fund-raiser to enhance opportunities for student education about date rape. The idea was to solicit funds to bring in outside speakers who were experts on the subject. A graduate student (in counseling and guidance) and member of the women's programming committee assumed leadership of the project. This student developed a mailing that described the fund-raiser and solicited donations. She subsequently sent it to almost every student, faculty member, staff, and administrator on campus. So far, all of this sound good. However, the graduate student spearheading the event spelled the word "assault" as "assult" on the flier *nine* times. Worse yet, the student sent the flier out on university letterhead. Needless to say, the social work professor chairing the committee that sponsored the fund-raiser received calls from the chancellor, the vice chancellor,

almost all division heads, and its seemed every other administrator on campus, all complaining about the flier and how ignorant and foolish it make the entire university look. The social work professor was mortified. She would never again allow anything to do with her be circulated unless she had carefully scrutinized, proofread, and edited it. Additionally, she never again assumed that graduate students could spell. The sad thing is that the student had volunteered her time and effort. She had only the best of intentions. Such a simple mistake ruined the entire project.

If you are telephoning your solicitation, rehearse what you will say and perhaps write out your "spiel" in advance. Role play some typical responses you might encounter. And, as the Boy Scouts say, "Be Prepared."

Grants and Contracts

Social work programs are almost always in need of additional resources, and macro change efforts often require funds not already in any agency budget. Geri's agency (the domestic violence shelter mentioned earlier in the book) had no money to renovate its building. It also received no support from other agencies for the services it provided to survivors of domestic violence. Each of these problems was resolved, one as a result of a state grant and the other through a contract with public human services agency.

Most social workers will deal with grants and contracts at sometime in their work experience. Indeed, many of you are already familiar with grants. Pell Grants and other grants are often part of the financial aid package provided to students attending college and universities. According to Barker (1991), a grant is "a transfer of funds or assets from one government, organization, or individual to another for fulfilling some broadly specified function or purpose" (p. 95). Contracts are agreements between two organizations or bodies which specify that one will provide certain services in exchange for payments from the other (Coley & Scheinberg, 1990). In other words, one organization is buying the services of another.

In social work parlance, grants and contracts are nothing more than the moving of resources from one entity to another. Typically, grants and contracts are given for specific purposes such as providing services to a certain target group. A family service organization might receive a grant from the United Way, a local private foundation, to provide special services for survivors of sexual abuse. A contract agreement might be arranged between the county Department of Social Services and a private inpatient drug treatment program whereby the county agency agrees to pay the other program a set amount for each client served.

Grants may fund a new service in total, or they may be combined with other funds (other grants, contracts, fees for service, and tax revenues). They may provide funds to operate a single program or a series of programs. The granting agency or organization provides the grant because it believes in and supports the cause of purpose for which funds are sought.

Normally, the agency seeking a grant or contract prepares a written proposal for the organization that has the money to give. That proposal describes what the agency will do with the money if the grant or contract is approved. The funding body reviews the proposal and may: (1) accept the proposal and fully fund it, (2) accept the proposal and partially fund it, (3) request that the proposal be modified in some way, or (4) reject the proposal. Because the funding organization is under no obligation to give anyone the money in the first place, it often has the right to reject an application without explanation. Frequently, however, granting agencies offer information about why a proposal was not funded. They may also suggest changes in the proposal that would increase the likelihood of future funding.

The following section covers various sources of grants and contracts, describes the contract and grant application process, and provides tips on writing good proposals.

Finding Out about Grants and Contracts: Where Are They?

There are several major sources of grants and contracts in the United States. One source is government agencies including federal, state, and local units of government. Various divisions of the federal Department of Health and Human Services provides grants to fund experiments with promising new approaches to solving specific human problems. They might provide money to a program seeking to prevent drug abuse among rural adolescents. Geri's agency received a state grant to rehabilitate its new building.

A second major source of grants includes foundations, private organizations set up explicitly for gift giving. Generally, the money given by the foundation comes from a business or commercial activity or company. The Ford Foundation is one example.

The third major source of funds is businesses and corporations. Rather than funneling the money through a foundation, a corporation will provide the grant or contract directly. Grants and contracts from each of these sources annually total in the billions of dollars. Each granting or contracting source has specific advantages and disadvantages for those receiving funds. Government grants and contracts are often restrictive in nature, limiting funding to only those purposes approved by the particular legislative body (Congress or a state legislature). This might mean, for example, that money can only be spent on drug treatment services to people who fall below the poverty line. Private foundations and corporate sources are often more flexible in what and when they may fund. Consequently, they might be more willing to support creative new programs or to respond quickly to a funding request. Private foundations and corporate sources may more readily give money to an untested, but promising, program aimed at stopping gang violence in urban neighborhoods.

Gathering information on sources of grants and contracts is not difficult. Public and university libraries usually have material on granting sources. Libraries typically have reference books, such as the *Foundation Directory*, that describe private foundations. The *directory* contains information about each foundation, including the type of programs or purposes for which it provides support. The *Annual Register of Grant Support* is another source that is updated annually. It is more comprehensive because it lists not only foundation grants but also those provided by governmental and business organizations.

These resources typically provide enough information about the granting agency to allow the reader to decide whether a specific grantor is an appropriate organization to approach for funding. They usually indicate deadlines for submitting proposals and provide mailing addresses.

It is very important to accurately establish the granting agency's title and address before sending in an application. A faculty colleague once applied for a grant. She was not renowned for her attention to detail. She heard about a grant that could provide her with some research funding. However, she somehow lost the accurate title and address of the granting agency. She wrote up a grant proposal anyway and sent it in. Believing that she remembered part of the agency's title, she combined the words she thought she remembered and sent the proposal. She could not exactly remember the agency's address either, but she thought she remembered part of it. She addressed the package, combining the parts of the address she thought would direct her proposal to the Washington, D.C., governmental department she thought was funding the grant. Worse yet, she rushed to make the posting deadline and missed it by three days. She was so late she had ''no time'' to make a copy of the material. So she sent the only copy of the proposal to someone she wasn't sure of at a place she wasn't sure of. Needless to say, she neither received the grant nor heard from the intended agency.

The lessons from this example are threefold. First, verify the name and address of the agency. Second, make a copy of the document for your own records. You never know when a document requiring dozens of hours of labor, will get lost in the Twilight Zone. Finally, meet the deadline specified in the agency's announcement of grant availability. Getting a proposal in late can be the same as not sending it at all.

Other resources available in the library are publications such as the *Chronicle of Higher Education*, *Foundation News*, and the *Foundation Center Information Quarterly*. These publications include information on sources of grants, describe recent grant recipients, and generally give current information about grant giving in the United States.

Other possible sources of information about granting agencies include research and grant offices operated by universities and large nonprofit organizations such as NASW. In addition, there are subscription services (providing periodic reports on specific types of grants) and workshops on grants. Both colleges and private agencies often offer grant-writing workshops that help the novice grant writer put together a convincing proposal.

Finally, you can learn of grant opportunities by talking to other social workers about their respective experiences and ideas. Often, talking with those who have been successful grant writers offers insight into both potential sources of grants and tips for writing better proposals. The goal in this process of reviewing possible funding sources is to eliminate those unlikely to fund your proposal and to focus efforts on the likely

ones. In addition, discussions with experienced grant writers at a college or university may lead to a collaborative grant. Such a grant would involve both your agency and the academic institution, combining the expertise of social work faculty with that of agency personnel. A grant might be available to help reduce substance abuse among homeless adolescents. Your agency is interested in receiving a grant to help homeless adolescents in your community. The university social work faculty might help with the grant and take responsibility for evaluating the success of your proposed program.

Government Grants

Certainly the largest source of grant funds in the United States is the federal government. Federal programs are listed in the *Federal Register* and the *Catalog of Domestic Assistance*. State programs are often announced in the *State Contract Register*. Such sources describe hundreds of programs covering such divergent area as space and energy or health and education. Granting agencies include, the National Institute for Mental Health, the National Institute on Aging, and many other federal units of various sizes.

Typically, these agencies announce the availability of grants and send out requests for proposals (RFPs) These RFPs describe the type of program that the agency expects to fund and the dollar amount available. They contain the deadline for submission and other information useful to the prospective grant writer. Many RFPs ask you to send for a grant application packet which is to be completed and returned. Again, it is important to read the RFP carefully. Everything you need to know about the grant is likely to be in there.

Sometimes a government grantor will hold a meeting called a bidder's conference where grantors provide more information to interested parties (Coley & Scheinberg, 1990). These conferences help you understand the grantor's needs, and, in turn, assist grantors to learn about you and others who are applying for grants.

Foundation Grants

Foundations range in size from those with assets in the billions of dollars to those with extremely modest endowments of a few thousand dollars (White, 1975). While some foundations carry famous names (e.g., Rockefeller, Ford, Carnegie, and Kellogg), many are named for individuals or families with only local reputations. All foundations are governed by boards of directors that often decide which grant applications to fund. Larger foundations usually have professional staff, while many smaller ones operate very informally. In the latter foundations, a single staff member may have responsibility for reviewing the grant, deciding whether to fund the request, and determining the amount of money to be provided. An example of one small foundation with which the author is familiar was established by a local family to help address various community needs. They provide small amounts for worthy causes, including money for an annual dinner honoring foster parents for working with neglected and abused children.

Most foundations have identified specific areas where they concentrate their grant giving. They may focus on grants for social service activities, for community betterment, or for beautification. Other foundations give only to those in specific geographical locations such as certain cities, counties, or states. Some will fund capital improvements (buildings) while others will not. Finally, some will provide money for beginning programs, but not for continuing them.

Getting accurate information about foundations is not particularly easy. Unlike government grants for which information may even be available in libraries and through public announcements, many foundations do not advertise their existence or suggest what types of grants are available. They typically do not issue RFPs. The Foundation Center is a most helpful source of information about private foundations. The center maintains offices in New York and Washington, D.C., under its own name and in Chicago where it is called Donors' Forum. Many states also maintain reference centers where information about foundation grants is readily available. Usually, there is no charge for using the reference center, although customized computer searches for information may carry a fee.

Fortunately, assistance in locating information about foundations is available. The *Foundation Directory* lists the largest foundations to help readers locate appropriate grantors. A copy of this directory is often available in public and college libraries. Unfortunately, this resource does not provide information on smaller foundations. Sometimes foundation resource books are available for specific states (such as California, Maine, or Michigan). These listings contain information on each foundation, including its purpose, such as aiding "distressed bowlers and families" (White, 1975, p. 145–46) and its grant-giving record for the previous year. Most listings show restrictions foundations have placed on their giving and the grants they have available.

For those whose activities include frequent grant writing, several organizations provide periodic listings of granting agencies. To receive such listings, you must pay for a subscription, so these are normally useful only for larger organizations that can afford the cost. They are typically expensive and cover only the largest foundations. Examples include the Foundation Research Service and the Taft Information System.

Colen and Scheinberg (1990) suggest that foundations are willing to accept unsolicited proposals about four times a year. Unsolicited proposals are ones that the foundation has not previously indicated an interest in. The grant writer has simply put forward an idea and asked the foundation to consider it. Colen and Scheinberg (1990) also recommend sending a letter showing the intent of your proposal before preparing the full document. This makes sense because you don't want to put a great deal of work into a proposal that simply does not fit the granting organization's interests. Larger foundations with sufficient staff may discuss your ideas with you to help you learn whether your proposal is fundable. Most smaller foundations have no such staff. Thus, it is very difficult to get significant amounts of information from them.

Business and Corporate Grants

Many large businesses have established charitable arms or divisions (often called foundations) to dispense funds for various purposes. Usually these granting bodies give money to nonprofit agencies or organizations. Nonprofit organizations are those that do not intend to produce revenue over their costs of operation (Family Service America and NASW are both nonprofit organizations). Grantors typically evaluate both the proposal and the organization to ensure that the money will be used as intended. Corporate foundations usually specify the purposes for which they will donate funds. Typically, it is possible to discuss an idea with the corporate foundation representative before submitting an application.

HIGHLIGHT 14.5

MY FIRST GRANT

On my first day on the job with a county human service agency, the deputy directory dropped a folder on my desk and said she wanted me to finish writing a grant. Not wishing to appear completely ignorant, I stifled my initial inclination to say, "What's a grant?" Looking through the folder, I quickly discovered the grant proposal was designed to solicit money from a state criminal justice agency. The purpose of the grant was to create a group home for delinquent boys. Well, at least now I knew what the deputy director wanted me to do and why.

I quickly saw why my predecessor had not completed the grant application. Under the section on Need for the Grant, the first writer had provided three case examples designed to illustrate the type of kids for whom the group home would be designed. These examples were certainly interesting, but would not offer a compelling argument for a public granting agency. The application was long on stories but very short on specifics. There was, for example, no indication of how many adolescent males might need this type of facility. The number of "beds" in the facility had never been considered. Nor was there any com-

parison of costs to show that this proposal would reduce costs to the county by allowing youth to be treated and reside in their home community.

After I looked through the forms and information provided by the granting agency, I had a much better sense of what needed to be done. In about a week the proposal was done in draft form for review by agency administrators. A modified copy was provided to the county social services board (a body which oversaw operations of the human services agency). That group agreed to continue funding the group home after the grant ran out, providing that the project proved successful.

Three weeks later I explained and advocated for the proposal before the regional criminal justice board which subsequently approved sending it through to the state board. Within the month the state board approved the proposal, and we were able to open our group home. Finally, I knew what a grant was and my success with this would later give me the confidence to prepare other grant proposals. Unfortunately, I could never again claim a 100 percent success rate for my grant applications.

We recommend this step whenever possible. To get initial information, you might turn to the community relations departments of corporations in your communities to learn whether they have grants available. Building relationships by meeting and talking with staff of these departments and other employees in these corporations is a recommended method for strengthening your proposal (Coley & Scheinberg, 1990).

Many business foundations exist to support research in areas that indirectly benefit the corporation. Still others fund areas not at all related to the needs of the particular company. Unlike other sources of grants, there are no universally helpful resources identifying the purposes and grant-making history of corporate foundations. This information is best gleaned from talking with others who have successful track records in

obtaining corporate grants. Corporations may find proposals that cast them in a favorable light very attractive, especially when such proposals' intent merges with a corporate image or interest. A corporation that sells medical equipment used with elderly patients may be very interested in a proposal for serving the elderly through a new adult day-care center named after the company.

Unlike most government granting agencies, private foundations and corporations may make a site visit to your agency. There they will talk with staff, examine your physical facility, and study your programs. While this step may seem bothersome, it is wise to recognize that many of these organizations do not require a lengthy proposal. On-site visitation replaces endless writing. Fewer than ten pages may be required compared to a government grant proposal which may run to dozens of pages.

How to Apply for a Grant

Getting grants is neither mysterious nor particularly difficult. Being successful requires the same kind of preparation and care you would give to other important projects. The project can be divided into three steps—the pre-application phase, the application phase, and the post-application phase (figure 14.3).

Pre-Application Phase

In the first stage you must identify potential grant sources. Using the resources described above should help you in this part of the project. Your list of potential sources should focus on those that sponsor activities like yours. Exclude those that have shown no interest in your particular field, do not grant funds for projects in your locale, or have other unacceptable limitations.

In this stage you will also make preliminary contacts with likely grantors to identify deadlines and discuss their organization's interest in proposals such as yours. You probably should write to grantors for further information about their goals and purposes. When you have

Figure 14.3
Steps in Applying for a Grant

Pre-Application Phase

- Identify potential grant sources
- Contact potential sources

Application Phase

- Develop draft proposal
- Consult with potential grantor

Post-Application Phase

- Review of grant proposal
- Revise grant if requested
- Plan for ending of grant

received the necessary information, the first rule is to read everything with great care. For example, there may be length or budget limits to the application that, if not observed, will doom your proposal to the circular file.

Application Phase

Next, develop a draft of the proposed grant. This should describe what you intend to do, why it is worthy of funding, and the approximate cost of the project. Your draft should state who will do what, and what goals or objectives are to be achieved. Don't forget to include the project director's or applicant's resumé.

Generally speaking, granting agencies don't like giving funds to individuals. Thus, any proposal is more likely to be funded if an organization rather than an individual applies. This means that you should fully discuss any plans to apply for a grant with your administration and board of directors, assuming that your organization will receive the funds. Topics that must be decided include who will administer the grant, what facilities or staff will be required to carry out the purposes of the grant, and what services the organization must provide (clerical, janitorial, or equipment). What expenses or costs will the organization incur? Are there any special precautions which must be taken to protect human subjects or keep project records safe for an extended period? These items are described in more detail in highlight 14.6.

Spending the necessary time at this stage to "work the bugs out" will bring greater benefit once the grant is received. You do not want to be in the position of receiving a grant and then having to spend weeks figuring out who will do what. This sort of catch-up planning after receipt of a grant often means your program can't be carried out as quickly as possible. This delay often comes at the expense of clients who should be receiving services.

Writing a Grant Proposal

Before writing a grant proposal, it is important to consider the different kinds of proposals you could write. It is also necessary to consider carefully what goes into a good grant proposal. We will look at items that must be addressed in most, if not all, grants. This next section

---

HIGHLIGHT 14.6

CRITICAL TOPICS REGARDING GRANT APPLICATIONS

Who will administer the grant?

Deciding who will administer the grant is important because someone in the agency will need to take overall responsibility for ensuring that deadlines are met, goals are achieved and financial records are maintained. Previous experience in administering grants is helpful.

What facilities or staff will be required?

Decide what staff and space will be needed to achieve the purpose of the grant. Identify specifically the individuals and physical plant areas to be used. If people will be hired to carry out the project, identify the qualifications of those individuals.

What services must the organization provide?

Decide what clerical support, bookkeeping, and related services your organization will provide. Both the types of activities and the costs of providing them are important. If your organization will contribute equipment, computer analysis of data, or other items or services, these should be described.

What expenses or costs will the organization incur?

Identify the nongrant money to be spent by your agency to carry out the grant. Describe any other expenses for personnel, equipment, and/or services that the agency will pay for.

What precautions are needed for record keeping or protecting human subjects?

In some situations involving sensitive information about clients, the records must be kept under lock and key. Sometimes a granting agency will require that records be kept for a specific period of time, such as five or ten years. In addition, you must describe any special precautions needed to protect from possible harm clients served by the grant. This is not a major concern in most grants to provide human services because clients are not exposed to experimental methods that may endanger their lives or health. At the same time, clients should be informed about any possible risk.

---

will review the following topics: description of a grant proposal; kinds of grant and contract proposals; what goes into a good grant proposal; and specific things to consider about every grant.

Description of a Grant Proposal

White (1975) says that the most important ingredient of a grant proposal is ''a good idea.'' Ultimately, it is the soundness of your idea that influences granting agencies to fund a particular proposal. Of course, rejection of a proposal can occur for a variety of reasons:

1. *The proposal was poorly written.* Proposals with misspellings, grammar errors, or typos are likely to be re-

jected. If it looks as if you did not put effort into doing a good job now, granting agencies may not believe you will carry out the grant project either.

2. *The competence of those who would carry out the proposal was not clearly documented.* A track record or other evidence that you can do what you propose is important. Granting agencies don' t like to think they're giving the money to people who can't do the job.

3. *Inadequate planning was evident in the application.* A proposal which does not include critical information or leaves out important activities (such as evaluation) is less likely to be funded.

4. *The application itself was not carefully prepared.* Missing deadlines or not addressing parts of the application required by the grantor indicate you did not prepare the application with diligence.

5. *The proposal was good but needed revisions, and there*

was insufficient time to modify it. Grant applications often seem to be done at the last minute. If you have a good idea, but there is not enough time to revise your proposal to meet the grantor's wishes, you may find your proposal rejected.

6. *The problem being addressed is not significant.* A problem may not be significant from at least two perspectives. First, the problem may be of no interest to the granting agency because it falls outside the area for which they usually provide grants. A problem may also be insignificant because it proposes to help a very limited number of people or because the problem upon which it is focused is relatively unimportant. Asking for $175,000 to help six people overcome fear of bats would likely be a loser on two counts: Too few people are being helped, and being afraid of bats is rather trivial compared with the needs of homeless populations, crack babies, and AIDS victims.

7. *The proposal does not make clear how funds will be used.* Unclear details about how you intend to spend the grantor's money is a serious problem. You should indicate clearly what the money will be used for, such as hiring staff, renting office space, or providing transportation for clients.

8. *The means proposed for dealing with a problem don't make sense.* The grantor expects that the solution you propose is logical and related to the problem at hand. Offering family therapy to homeless people may not be seriously considered in light of the more pressing needs of this population.

9. *Objectives cannot be adequately assessed.* Objectives that are not measurable or are too vague are likely to cause the grantor to turn your proposal down. A proposal to offer services to the homeless without specifying what those services will be, how many people will be helped, and in what time frame the help will be delivered is not likely to be viewed favorably.

10. *The grant seeker has no past record of dealing with the proposed problem.* Granting agencies must have faith that you can do what you propose to do. If you don't seem to have experience with the services you propose to offer or the problem you seek to solve, the proposal is not likely to be successful.

Talking with a granting agency representative before submission of a proposal can help reduce these problems. Applications received early might allow feedback from the grantor agency's staff requesting modification before final submission. Funding bodies tend to be more supportive of proposals that are innovative yet have strong potential for success. They also support fiscally sound proposals. The extent to which an agency is perceived as hard working and dedicated can also be an asset.

A grant proposal is nothing more than a good idea articulated in written form. Many, but not all, granting agencies have a specific format for applicants to follow. There may be required forms, especially budget forms.

Whatever the format, however, a good proposal has certain characteristics. First, *the proposed activity must relate to the interests or purposes of the funding agency*. For example, a proposal to provide services to help women escape prostitution should not be sent to a foundation interested in funding medical research. It makes no sense (and wastes everybody's time) to prepare proposals that do not meet the funding body's objectives.

A second characteristic is that *the proposed activity will, in some way, promote a desirable end*. The proposal might allow service to a previously unserved population or test a new method of preventing recidivism among delinquents. Perhaps it promises to develop a more efficient system of linking the services provided by multiple agencies. In short, the idea itself should sound promising.

A third characteristic of a good proposal is that it shows *the proposer knows the territory*. That is, the applicant is already familiar with the literature in this field and knows what has previously been tried and found effective. Grant proposals incorporating approaches that previous research has proven ineffective are likely to meet with failure.

A good proposal's fourth characteristic is that *the people carrying out the project are competent to do so*. They have experience in this area and the credentials to achieve the proposal's objectives. A resumé detailing this information should be included with the project application.

A fifth characteristic is that *the expected results justify the costs involved*. Grant applications involve both time and money. The granting agency must be convinced that the outcomes are sufficiently important to warrant expending the necessary time and money.

The length of a good proposal varies tremendously. Some grant applications are only a few pages long while others may run to hundreds of pages. A lengthy proposal is not necessarily a good one. You must convince the application's reviewers that you have a good idea. A clear explication of your idea is much more important than the actual length of your proposal.

Kinds of Grants and Contract Proposals

Grant and contract proposals frequently fall into several categories (Lefferts, 1978). They include the following:

1. Program proposals. Program proposals are designed to provide a particular service to some size system—individual, family, group, organization, or community. A shelter for battered women applied for and received a grant to open a transition facility for women who were moving out of battering relationships. The facility, a multi-unit apartment building, was designed to provide low-cost housing for shelter residents needing a place of their own. The transition facility represented an extension of services already provided by the domestic abuse shelter.

2. Research proposals. Research proposals typically involve studying a particular problem or testing a specific intervention approach. They can be used to evaluate new programs or approaches. They can also be used to gather information leading to new programs or services. A proposal might be developed to study the needs of homeless children or adolescents. The findings could then suggest appropriate services to offer these groups.

3. Training proposals. Training proposals, as the name implies, are requests for funds to train or educate a specific group. This might be agency staff, volunteers, laypersons, or others. A training grant could be written to provide workshops on a new juvenile code for county agencies that must administer the new law. Training funds could also be used to educate staff on how to work more effectively with AIDS patients or other clients.

4. Planning proposals. Planning proposals are designed to allow an organization or agency to plan for a new program. Planning proposals are often the first step to setting up a program. Thus, you might request funds to begin planning a new juvenile shelter facility and later apply for funds to operate the shelter during its first year.

5. Technical assistance proposals. Technical assistance proposals provide for specialized help, allowing organizations or individuals to carry out a program. You might apply for a technical assistance grant to hire experts who would design a program to rehabilitate a block of historic buildings into low-income apartments. Usually such funds are used to hire people with special skills who would not normally be available to the agency or organization.

6. Contract for services. A contract for service is simply an agreement between two agencies or organizations for one to provide services to be paid for by the other. Public agencies often engage in contracting for services instead of providing services themselves. Sometimes this is called *privatization of services.* The services may be required by law, so they must be provided. However, the agency may find that it can purchase services from another organization for less than it would cost the agency itself to provide the service. Contracts for service generally involve an agreement to provide designated services in exchange for a specified dollar amount. Sometimes these proposals call for a per person charge, such as $3,000 for each person served by an agency. A public agency might pay another agency to provide outpatient treatment for substance abuse. At other times, an agency agrees to provide services for anyone who want them. A shelter for battered women might agree to take any women needing its services without limiting the number of clients it would accept per night or per year.

What Goes into a Good Grant Proposal?

We have already discussed some characteristics of a good proposal. As discussed earlier, the length of proposals varies greatly. Longer applications include the following specific sections: cover page; abstract or summary; narrative section; budget section; staff credentials; certifications of compliance; and agency or institutional endorsements. In shorter applications, some of these items are combined.

COVER PAGE. A cover page or letter should accompany the proposal. Often the granting agency provides such a sheet, possibly requiring specific signatures. The cover page should include information about the agency and persons who are applying for the grant (names, addresses, and phone numbers). It should detail the subject of the proposal (a group home for delinquents). The document should state the starting and ending times for the project and the amount of money requested. Finally, the date of application should be included. Highlight 14.7 shows a cover page.

TABLE OF CONTENTS. The table of contents will be a separate page identifying each distinct section

---

HIGHLIGHT 14.7

EXAMPLE OF A COVER PAGE

Application for Training Grant

Grantor:	Waterman Foundation 1234 Left Bank Road West Pavilion, Georgia 33333
Applicant:	Waterworld Family Planning, Inc. 2372 S. Suprema Boulevard Springfield, Missouri 65807
Principal Investigator:	Mary Hadalamb, ACSW 417 883-5060
Subject:	Training of social workers to provide family planning information and service to low-income clients living in Waterworld county.
Dates:	July 1, 1997–June 30, 1998
Amount:	$130,579.00

_____   Date: _____
Signature of Principal Investigator

_____   Date: _____
Signature of Agency Director

---

of the proposal. It should include page numbers so that readers can locate information quickly.

ABSTRACT OR SUMMARY. There should be a brief summary of the project. A limit of two to three-hundred words makes it easier for the reader to get a quick overview of your proposal. Complete this portion only after the rest of the document has been finished so that it captures exactly what the full proposal says. Abstracts include a short narrative highlighting the objectives, methods, results, and value of this proposal. Write the abstract carefully because some agencies may use this portion alone for evaluating your proposal. Highlight 14.8 shows a possible summary.

NARRATIVE SECTION. Next, include a narrative section describing the problem and what you will do about it. Provide more detail in this section. Some agencies may specify a length limitation for the narrative section. Be sure to follow their instructions. Topics addressed include a statement of the problem, goals and objectives to be achieved, methods to be employed, and evaluation. Provide separate headings for each of these sections.

1. Statement of the problem. The problem statement should not only summarize the issue being addressed but also identify causative factors and past efforts to solve the identified difficulty. This shows the grantor that you understand the problem and are aware of prior attempts to alleviate the situation.

HIGHLIGHT 14.8

EXAMPLE OF A SUMMARY OR ABSTRACT

Summary

The devastating effects of Alzheimer's Disease and Related Disorders (ARD) on the victim and caregiver are now part of the public consciousness. The burden of caring for a loved one who has ARD can be awesome. The number of support groups for caregivers has continued to expand around the country along with the rise in number of people with the disease. Support groups are essential for the physical and mental health of caregivers; however, support groups are not enough. As noted by the Alzheimer's Disease and Related Disorders Association, the most needed service to enhance the quality of life of ARD victims and their caregivers and prevent early nursing home placement is available, low-cost, effective respite care.

As pressing as the need for respite care is in urban areas, the need for respite care in rural areas is desperate. Every aspect of the health-care system in rural areas is in short supply: physicians, home care, homemaking services. Add to this reality the long distances that must be traveled for the most basic necessities and the isolation of people with ARD, and you can begin to appreciate their caregivers.

The purpose of this project is to enhance the quality of life for people with ARD and their caregivers living in the rural areas of Southwest Missouri. In order to accomplish this goal, a partnership will be established between the local area agency on aging, the Alzheimer's Association, and the regional university to provide scheduled, low-cost, effective respite care.

Specifically, this project will employ existing but underutilized Senior Centers in six rural Southwest Missouri communities as sites for respite care for people with ARD. Under the general direction of a social worker, an LPN, and an activity director at each location, respite care will be provided to approximately ten people a day three days a week at each center—a total of 37,440 hours of respite-care hours per year. This will be an extraordinary addition to the service base in the rural areas of the state.

Caregivers will be able to reserve a time each week for their family members. The centers will offer these services in conjunction with existing community resources such as churches, schools, and other health-care systems.

In short, this respite care program for people with ARD and their caregivers in rural areas will fill a gap in service. In so doing, it will reduce the awesome burden of this terribly debilitating condition for all members of the family.

Include appropriate data and documentation on the problem area. Provide specific statistics on the number of people affected by the problem or the number of communities dealing with the difficulty. Describe the age, gender, or other demographic information that may be useful in clarifying the problem. Provide citations and references for your data. Sources of data have been addressed in previous chapters. It is important that your data presentation show a thorough understanding of the problem. Beyond hard data such as statistics, it is also permissible to include qualitative information such as opinions of community leaders and case examples to illustrate typical problems. You might also provide a description of current services addressing the problem. You should indicate who is providing what services with what results.

Highlight 14.9 displays an example of the statement of the problem in a successful grant. The problem state-

HIGHLIGHT 14.9

EXAMPLE OF A PROBLEM STATEMENT OF A SUCCESSFUL GRANT APPLICATION

Responding to Caregivers of People with Alzheimer's Disease: Respite Care in Rural Areas

Problem Statement/Needs Assessment

The awesome burden of caring for a loved one with Alzheimer's disease is well documented (Mace & Rabins, 1991; Pruchno & Resch, 1989; Motenko, 1989). Nevertheless, in America today, it is estimated that over one million people are full-time caregivers to family members with this degenerative, consuming condition. Demographic projections suggest the caregiving population will increase dramatically in the next twenty-five years and the need to provide care to a loved one will become the norm.

Often, caregivers themselves are elderly, sometimes frail, and always overwhelmed. Yet they continue to provide the necessary intimate care of feeding, bathing, toileting, and dressing in the home rather than institutionalize their loved one. Unfortunately, while performing these tasks for many years, the caregivers also lose their identity, their sense of personhood, and their will.

Statistics augmenting these general statements are telling. Working women caring for elderly family members have a typical work week of 70–80 hours. In some cases, these responsibilities are equivalent to three full time jobs. Most caregivers provide care for one to four years including 60 percent who provide full-time care for at least three years. Most caregivers have few, if any, resources to help with their responsibilities. One-third of families with an Alzheimer's victim live below the poverty line.

The effects of this unrelenting condition on caregivers are predictable: poor emotional and physical health. Family caregivers suffer stress-related illness resulting from exhaustion, lowered immune functions, and injuries than the general population. One third of caregivers self-report their health as fair or poor, a much higher percentage than others in their age cohort. Caregiver depression is reported at 43–46 percent, about three times the national average. These factors are exacerbated by the fact that 36 percent of the caregivers are at least sixty-five years old. Alarmingly, 12 percent of caregivers for people with Alzheimer's report becoming physically ill or injured as a direct result of caregiving.

To cope with this tremendous burden, caregivers need assistance with caregiving responsibilities. Unfortunately, the kinds of services helpful in caring for a person with Alzheimer's are either too expensive or nonexistent.

For many people, the single most frequently expressed need is the opportunity to reduce their burden for short periods of time. It is the constancy and ubiquitousness of caregiving that is so oppressive, not the caregiving itself. They voice a uniform desire to have some time away from their caregiving.

Respite care, a time-out from caregiving, has become a universal response to the burdens of these people in need. Respite care can be offered in a variety of forms and models, but in whatever form, it makes a difference in the lives of caregivers. Over the past four years, the Alzheimer's Association has operated a National Respite Care Demonstration Program to establish and evaluate model respite care programs. In

(continued)

HIGHLIGHT 14.91—(*Continued*)

1990, some fifty local Alzheimer's chapters provided respite care services to an estimate three thousand families in twenty states, through programs as varied as the families they serve. While the outcomes of this and other demonstration respite-care programs are not quantitatively definitive, caregivers needs for respite at home are predictable. It is also predictable that all of the problems experienced by caregivers are amplified for those in rural areas. It is often assumed that in rural areas an informal helping network of friends, neighbors, and volunteers assists family members in need (Collins & Pantcoast, 1976). However, research with caregivers living in rural areas (Wolk, Pray, Kalkbrenner & Propp, 1987) indicates that the nature of Alzheimer's disease is so oppressive and foreign that informal networks are insufficient to meet their needs. Still, the harsher existence related to caregiving in rural areas remains. Basic health care, including the presence of physicians, is often unavailable, necessitating long-distance travel for routine health care. In the case of caregivers, this problem is complicated because of their own health needs, as well as those of the person with Alzheimer's.

Beyond basic health care, many ancillary health services in rural areas are in short supply. Support groups, in or out of home respite care, mental health services, and hot meal programs are limited or absent. Transportation problems, higher poverty levels, and the general underfunding of human services by federal agencies is a prescription for isolation and frustration.

Southwest Missouri, a catchment area encompassing twenty-seven counties, is by any accepted definition of the term predominantly rural. Problems encountered in this part of the state are comparable to rural problems everywhere. Moreover, the rate of Alzheimer's disease for the twenty-seven counties is high because the population is older than the national and state averages.

For this project, four counties in Southwest Missouri are targeted for services: Lawrence, Polk, Barry, and Wright. The Missouri Division of Aging uses a formula that estimates that 11 percent of people between sixty-five and eighty-four and 50 percent of people eighty-five and over have Alzheimer's disease or related disorders. Applying this formula to the sixty-five-and-over population in the four counties produces these estimates of people with Alzheimer's disease: Lawrence—795; Polk—594; Barry—661; Wright—434; total—2,484.

Most of these people live several miles from town. In previous research, a high percentage of rural caregivers had little or no respite from their responsibilities for months or even years (Wolk et al., 1987).

---

ment describes the number of those affected by the problem (in this case Alzheimer's disease) as well as the general purpose of the project.

2. Goals and objectives. Goals and objectives are end products of your grant project. They should be worth pursuing and should be limited in number and scope. Objectives that seem of little importance to the granting agency will probably eliminate your proposal form consideration. At the same time, trying to do too much or failing to establish measurable goals are equally bad. Goals are generally stated broadly and cannot be directly measured. Your objectives, on the other hand, should be as specific as possible. Highlight 14.10 gives

an example of both goals and objectives. If you plan to provide prenatal care to two hundred low-income women in the first year of operation, state this as an objective. Reducing by one-half the incidence of repeat delinquent acts by juveniles living in the Orange County Housing Authority is another measurable objective. Objectives should show a time frame by which changes are to occur.

Grant proposal objectives include two types: outcome and process (Colen & Scheinberg, 1990). Outcome objectives show what the result will be of our change efforts. A useful outcome objective might be providing immunizations to all children over the age of

In Southwest Missouri, a number of agencies have responsibility for providing services to the people in these counties. Specifically, the Alzheimer's Association of Southwest Missouri offers support and education in this region of the state. However, the office is staffed with only an Executive Director and volunteers. Realistically, the capacity to provide extensive support and education in so broad an area is limited. Regardless, the Association is engaged in providing the following services: support group development, advocacy, fundraising, community awareness, and staff training.

Another organization serving this geographic area and the elderly population is the Southwest Missouri Office on Aging, a designated Area Agency on Aging. This agency receives most of its funding from the Older Americans Act and Social Service Block Grant Funds. The Southwest Missouri Office on Aging is centrally administered, but each of the seventeen counties in its catchment area operates a Senior Center. These centers offer the range of services from developing a meeting place and providing congregate meals to the full complement of services to the elderly. Several centers operate in-home Companion Programs intended to reduce the burden of caregivers caring for frail elderly, though not elderly with any sort of dementia.

Some counties have augmented the funding for services by passing a county option tax. Some have additional transportation dollars from the local city government to help people get to the center. Although the centers remain open throughout the afternoon, not all have scheduled events or active participation after lunch. For the most part, none of the centers are readily accessible or staffed to accommodate people with Alzheimer's disease or their caregivers.

It is now common knowledge among specialists in the field of aging that when a family member cares for a loved one with a chronic physical or mental condition, and in particular, Alzheimer's disease, two lives are altered. The burden of caregiving, without sufficient support services, becomes oppressive. Clearly, caregivers in the rural areas of Southwest Missouri want to keep their family members in home and out of institutions as long as feasible. However, as they toil to accomplish this goal, the caregivers become entangled emotionally and physically in this debilitating disease. Caregivers need periodic and predictable relief from their responsibilities.

The primary purpose of this project is to assist in the reduction of the burden on caregivers of people with Alzheimer's disease and related disorders (ARD) in rural areas of Southwest Missouri. A significant aspect of this proposal will be the cooperation of several community agencies employing existing but underutilized resources to accomplish its primary purpose.

Source: Grant application adapted with permission from James Wolk, June Huff, and Lou Ann Trent.

three living in the Woodland Park neighborhood. This type of objective says specifically what you will do—give kids immunizations. You may also, however, want to include process objectives which describe the steps you will take to accomplish the outcome objectives. A process objective might be conducting a door-to-door neighborhood education campaign focused on encouraging parents to immunize their children. In other words, it is a step in the process of getting all kids in the neighborhood immunized. Keep objectives as brief and clearly stated as possible, whether they are outcome- or process-oriented.

3. Methods. The narrative section will also discuss the activities you will use to accomplish your objectives. Ideally, you would like to describe the tasks you will complete before and after the funds are provided. You might wish to describe staff to be hired, space to be acquired, equipment to be purchased, and services to be provided.

Details about your organization and how it is/will be organized to carry out your proposal might be discussed next. Will this project be carried out by an existing unit, or will a new structure be established? Will you need to create a new unit to house your project? What staffing needs exist? What duties and tasks will those involved in the project perform? You might include a job descrip-

---

HIGHLIGHT 14.10

EXAMPLES OF GOALS AND OBJECTIVES

Goals and Objectives

Goal 1—To reduce the physical, emotional, and financial burden on caregivers of people with Alzheimer's disease living in five rural areas of Southwest Missouri.

Objective 1—By the end of the first year, participant caregivers will experience a 25 percent reduction in their use of stress-related medication.

Objective 2—By the end of the first year, participant caregivers will experience a 25 percent reduction in their level of stress.

Objective 3—By the end of the first year, participant caregivers will reduce their number of physician's visits by 25 percent.

Objective 4—By the end of the first year, there will be a 50 percent increase in the number of caregivers involved in support groups.

Goal 2—To improve the quality of life of people with Alzheimer's disease living in rural areas of Southwest Missouri.

Objective 1—Within three months, participating people with Alzheimer's will increase their social interactions by 25 percent.

Objective 2—During the first year, progression of the disease will be 25 percent slower compared with a matched group of people with Alzheimer's.

Goal 3—To increase rural community awareness, knowledge, and interdependence regarding Alzheimer's disease.

Objective 1—By the end of the first year, 50 percent of the caregivers of people with Alzheimer's disease and related disorders will have knowledge of the support services available.

Objective 2—By the end of the first year, 80 percent of the health-care providers will have referred at least one person to supportive services.

Objective 3—By the end of the first year, at least one school in each community will be participating in services to people with Alzheimer's and their caregivers.

---

tion in the appendix to provide greater detail or to support the narrative. Highlight 14.11 describes the method used in the Alzheimer's grant.

4. Evaluation. The evaluation section requires that you think carefully about your ultimate goals and exactly how you will prove that you have been successful. Make certain that your identified objectives are measurable. Generally speaking, if your objectives (which are really more definitive and specific parts of the goal) are achieved, you have probably reached your goal too. Address the question, "How am I going to evaluate whether my objective has been achieved?" An objective

HIGHLIGHT 14.11

EXAMPLE OF A DESCRIPTION OF THE METHOD

Description of the Method

Caregivers of people with Alzheimer's Disease and Related Disorders (ARD) in rural areas of Southwest Missouri experience profound burdens in order to keep loved ones in the family home. It is clear that there is a dearth of available support services for caregivers in those rural areas of the state. Moreover, the informal networks in those rural areas are insufficient to meet the expressed need. Therefore, what is needed in the rural areas of Southwest Missouri is some type of formal agency service to help reduce the burden of caregivers and improve the quality of life for people with this disease.

In order to accomplish the stated goals and objectives of this proposal, several conditions seem paramount. First, any response to these complex problems and to the unmet needs extant in rural areas should be an interagency effort and not a unilateral organizational activity. An interagency effort will maximize the strengths of the existing formal and informal networks. Second, any response should capitalize on existing but possibly underutilized resources in these rural communities. Third, there should be centrally located administration and professional support but the services should be decentralized, incorporating the strengths of existing resources. Fourth, the model of service should be replicable in other rural areas of the state and nation.

The goals and objectives of this project and the conditions for service delivery can most effectively be met through a model of respite care provided at several locations throughout the Southwest Missouri area. This model is consistent with the stated conditions for service delivery to achieve the outlined goals and objectives.

Under the general auspices of the Southwest Missouri Office on Aging, coordinated with the Alzheimer's Association of Southwest Missouri and Southwest Missouri State University, weekly respite care will be provided to people with ARD in rural counties. Specifically, six communities located in four counties in rural southwest Missouri operate Senior Centers under the administration of the Southwest Agency on Aging: Monett, Cassville, Aurora, Mount Vernon, Bolivar, and Mountain Grove. These Centers operate Monday through Friday, but usually end their activities after the congregate lunch is completed. For the rest of the afternoon, numbers of participants at centers are limited.

It is planned that each of these six centers will be available for respite care to people with Alzheimer's three afternoons a week each. The days of the week will be staggered in order to allow central administration to be on-site when necessary. Operating hours will be 2:00 to 6:00 P.M. Each center will be able to serve up to ten participants per shift. Caregivers would be able to schedule fixed time each week that their family member can be brought to the Center for Respite Care. Once the program is fully operational, 180 people with ARD will be served, with caregivers receiving a total of 720 hours of respite care per week. Moreover, the Center will provide support groups for the caregivers. The structure of the respite care will provide an accessible opportunity for caregivers living in rural areas to participate in these groups. Also, every effort will be made to bring indigenous resources to the Center. The local schools, churches, and Senior Center participants will be organized to contribute to the services for people with ARD and their caregivers. Finally, it is generally acknowledged that caregivers often need assistance beyond respite. Professional help in acquiring

(continued)

important and necessary services will integrate with the provision of respite care. On-site assistance will be available to help caregivers access services for themselves or their family member.

To deliver the services of this rural respite care program, staffing must be professional in nature. The six sites will be coordinated by a person with a Bachelor's degree in Social Work housed at the Southwest Missouri Office on Aging, Springfield, Missouri. A social worker has skill in working with individuals as well as communities. Moreover, the social worker will travel to each Center on a regular basis to meet with caregivers around their social services needs.

Each Respite Care program will be managed by a Licensed Professional Nurse. It is felt that medical skills will be necessary in working with this client group. Even though these Centers will be in rural areas, it is believed that recruitment of LPNs will be possible. It is planned that the pay will be higher than current home health hourly wages and that predictable part-time work will be a desirable option. The LPNs will be responsible for implementing the program, controlling admissions, collecting fees, supervising other staff and volunteers, and coordinating activities with the Senior Center Director. It is expected that the person will be employed twenty (20) hours per week. This schedule will permit approximately eight hours a week for community coordination and administration without clients.

Because the days of the week will be staggered by Center, it is assumed that the various respite managers will provide temporary coverage for each other.

In addition, each center will have a twenty-hour-a-week activity director. This person will have experience in developing level-appropriate activities and exercises for people with Alzheimer's disease. They will have primary responsibility for carrying out the activities.

The nature of Alzheimer's disease requires ongoing training. The Alzheimer's Association of Southwest Missouri will provide this training for staff as well as volunteers.

---

of providing family planning service to one-hundred adolescent girls is fairly clear-cut. You either provided service to at least one hundred girls or you did not. Service provision to ninety-nine girls indicates that you have not met your stated objective.

You might also wish to know which of two service methods worked the best. If some girls received individual service while others were given group counseling, which method was most effective? Did the group method result in more or fewer of the adolescents avoiding pregnancy?

In addition, process evaluation may be important. It focuses on the process of giving service and should not be confused with outcome evaluation. Process evaluation is concerned with such factors as whether staff provided the service intended, whether the cost of service provided was reasonable, and whether clients were satisfied with the service provided. It is entirely possible that the staff provided the service indicated, clients were

satisfied or happy with what occurred, but the results (outcomes) of the project were not satisfactory. Perhaps all of the girls who received the family planning service praised their workers and thought the cost of service was fair, but 90 percent ended up pregnant anyway. Here the process was carried out well, but the outcome objective was not achieved. You need to decide what data is important to your evaluation. Obviously, you want basic demographic information such as age, gender, race, and other similar items. You may discover that the outcomes were different for men and women, or that younger children were affected differently by the project. The number of hours of service provided to each client may be an important variables, so you may wish to gather this information. Numbers of clients served and data from workers and clients may be useful.

Colen and Scheinberg (1990) suggest you incorporate several steps into your evaluation plan. First, they suggest specifying the purpose of the evaluation, de-

It will also be necessary to cultivate relationships in the communities with a number of people who will assist in encouraging family members to participate in the respite care program. In particular, physicians who treat people with Alzheimer's disease and clergy who minister to families will be invaluable sources of support and strength for caregivers who may be reluctant to abdicate total control over their loved one. The social worker as well as the LPNs will be networking with these important community resources.

In addition, contacts will be maintained with the existing Senior Center participants to encourage them to volunteer in the respite care. Moreover, they will be called upon to assist in helping the caregiver become involved with the Senior Center or other appropriate community services in preparation for the time when their family member cannot be cared for in the home.

Too, the staff will capitalize on existing transportation services available in some of the counties. Where no transportation is available, "Good Neighbor" programs will be developed that reimburse people who provide needed transportation. Finally, the respite care staff will attempt to develop positive working relationships with the local schools. The students can provide a resource and a perspective that will add to the community nature of the program.

In summary, the respite care program will be offered at six rural sites in existing Senior Centers. Each program will be staffed by an LPN and an activity director with the entire program coordinated by a BSW. Each center will be open three days a week for four hours a day and caregivers will have fixed scheduled time each week. As much as feasible, community resources will be integrated into the program and the caregivers will be provided services as needed beyond the respite care in the form of support group and social work services.

The purpose of this proposal is to provide respite care services for people with Alzheimer's and their caregivers in rural areas. During the first year of the program, it is the intent to provide this service for free or at low cost. However, it is also recognized that if this service proves valuable, it will need to be funded on a continual basis. To that end, there will be a minimal fee scale developed for the families. Prior to beginning the second year, all aspects of this revenue collection effort will be analyzed to determine its feasibility as a significant future revenue source.

scribing the design to be employed, and detailing what will be measured. They also recommend that you detail the data that needs to be collected and decide whether your evaluation uses a sample of the population or the entire population of persons served. You may recall that we discussed the terms population and sample in chapter 10. For our purposes, we refer to all of the participants for whom we provided service as the population. A sample would simply be a subset of the population. The timetable for data collection should be specified. In some situations the evaluation component is performed by someone or some organization hired specifically for this purpose. If the evaluation is going to involve significant costs (which might be the case if it is done by an outside group), a budget for evaluation should accompany the proposal.

There is yet another important consideration to address in the proposal—what happens when the grant period is over and the money is gone? What plans are there for carrying out the project after this point? Many funding agencies want some assurance that a good idea developed through a grant project will continue when the grant expires. Often the grant writer will need written assurances from agency executives or board chairpersons that the project will be continued if it proves successful.

5. Bibliography. Of course, like the papers you do for class, your grant proposal should include a bibliography. This should list the references to which you referred in your proposal. Highlight 14.13 illustrates the bibliography used for the Alzheimer's grant.

As you can see, the narrative section must address several areas and is extremely important. You must include sufficient detail so that reviewers do not become confused about your purpose or doubt your ability to carry out the project.

BUDGET SECTION. A budget section with explicit detail is essential. The most common type of bud-

---

HIGHLIGHT 14.12

EXAMPLE OF AN EVALUATION SECTION

Evaluation

An outcome evaluation will be conducted by the Center for Social Research at Southwest Missouri State University. In order to evaluate the objectives under first goal, an extensive social history will be completed upon admission of a family member. This history will include information related to the health and mental health of the caregiver. At the end of the first year, a follow-up interview will be completed to ascertain the changes that have occurred in those aspects of the caregiver's life. Also, a 10 percent random sample of caregivers will be personally interviewed in depth to ascertain a more subjective understanding of goal completion. Finally, the Burden Scale developed by Zarit et al. to determine the stress experienced by caregivers will be administered on a pre- and post test basis.

In order to evaluate the objectives under the second goal, all participants in the respite care will be administered the mini-mental scale that assesses their level in the progressive nature of Alzheimer's Disease. The scale will be readministered every three months. Scores of participants will be compared against a control group of people with ARD who are not participating in the respite care program.

In order to evaluate the objectives under the third goal, a series of interviews with key actors in the community will be conducted regarding their knowledge and behaviors related to ARD. A follow-up set of interviews will be conducted at the end of the grant year to ascertain changes. Additionally, a 10 percent random sample of known people with ARD and caregivers will be surveyed by questionnaire at the onset of the project and then again at the end of the first year.

---

get for proposals is what is known as a *line-item budget*. Line-item budgets identify personnel costs, operating costs (such as supplies, rental of equipment), travel, and capital costs (such as building costs or the cost of purchasing equipment). They tell the reviewer specifically what the grant covers. However, they do not separate individual portions of a program or, for that matter, specific programs. Highlight 14.14 shows a typical line-item budget taken from the Alzheimer's grant. Many programs or functions might be included in a budget such as this. The proposal might include training for peer counselors in a local high school and a drug-abuse prevention program in the same high school.

In contrast to line-item budgets, *functional (or program) budgets* depict costs based upon specific proposed program elements or functions. Thus, the proposal for training peer counselors and creating a drug education program described earlier would be separately bud-

geted. This means the cost for each of the two components would be shown individually rather than lumped together as in line-item budgets. Highlight 14.15 shows a functional or program budget.

Both line-item and functional budgets require similar attention to detail. You should include both salaries and fringe benefits (such as health insurance, social security, retirement) when calculating personnel costs. You must also decide how much of each person's time will go into performing the functions associated with the proposal and what proportion of time is allocated to work unrelated to the grant proposal. If your grant proposes using 100 percent of two people's time it is easy to figure the salary and benefits to be charged to the proposal. Simply include both person's total salaries including fringe benefits. However, if your grant proposal funds only 15 percent of one person's time, 25 percent of another's time, and 65 percent of a third

HIGHLIGHT 14.13

EXAMPLE OF A BIBLIOGRAPHY

Bibliography

Collins, A.H., and Pancoast, D.L. (1976). *Natural helping networks.* Washington, DC: National Association of Social Workers.

Mace, N.L., & Rabins, P.V. (1991). *The 36-hour day: A family guide to caring for persons with Alzheimer's disease, related dementing illness, and memory loss in later life.* Baltimore, MD: Johns Hopkins Press.

Motenko, A.K. (1989) The frustrations, gratifications, and well-being of dementia caregivers. *Gerontologist,* 29 (2): 166–72.

Pruchno, R.A. & Resch, N.L. (1989). Husbands and wives as caregivers: antecedents of depression and burden. *Gerontologist,* 29 (2): 159–65.

Wolk, J.L., Pray, J.E., Kalkbrenner, L., & Propp, J. (1986). Alzheimer's disease in rural areas: Can informal networks meet the needs? *Human Services in the Rural Environment,* 10 (3): 8–13.

person's time, the calculations become more complicated. You need to multiply the various percentages for each person times their annual salaries and benefits to arrive at the costs to be charged to the proposal.

The same is true for use of space. If you are renting or using an entire building, it is easy to calculate the cost. However, if you are using only 25 percent of the space for your grant project, you can only request funds for the value of 25 percent of the space. Highlight 14.16 shows an example of these calculations. As you can see, we are using a portion of four person's time and a corresponding portion of their assigned office space.

If you are going to be operating several programs in your agency (most agencies offer a variety of services and programs) you will also need to estimate how much total space each program will require. For example, if the total space needs of the peer counselor program is 500 square feet and the drug education program requires 250 square feet of office space, you will require a total of 750 square feet. If the agency has a total of 7,500 square feet of space available, it is clear your two programs will use 10 percent of the space available space in your building (10 percent × 7,500 square feet). This generally means that 10 percent of the rent and utilities

will be charged to the grant because these are also expenses of offering the program. If the building is rented for $65,000 per year this means that the grant will pay for 10 percent of that amount, or $6,500. In other words, if a grant proposal indicates it needs 10 percent of an agency's space, then you need to include in the grant budget 10 percent of other agency costs across the board.

Describe operating costs such as travel with an explanation of how much is allowed per mile as well as costs of other individual items such as hotel and meal expenses. This helps show that the amounts budgeted are reasonable and appropriate. Similarly, personnel costs should be broken down to show how much each person or group is being paid.

Make budgets realistic. Sometimes, applicants minimize the costs of certain elements hoping that a lower dollar amount will increase their funding chances. However, unrealistically low budgets may flag a proposal as poorly conceptualized.

Similarly, bloated budgets with unnecessarily high estimates are suspect. Of course, it is always difficult to forecast costs for even one year periods, let alone multi-year periods. It is sometimes helpful to show a

---

HIGHLIGHT 14.14

EXAMPLE OF A LINE-ITEM BUDGET

Budget

Expenses

Personnel Salaries

Baccalaureate Social Worker @ 100%		25,000
Six LPN's @ $8.00/Hr × 20hrs/wk		49,920
Six Activity Directors @ $5.00 × 12hrs/wk		18,720
Executive Director Alzheimer's Association @ 5%		1,500
Project Director Area Aging Agency @ 5% Benefits		1,500
15% of employees' salaries (fringes)		14,497
	Sub total	$111,137

Operating Expenses

Telephone (One line @ $90/month)		1,000
Supplies ($100/month)		1,200
Employee Travel ($.22/mile × 5000 miles)		1,100
Public Awareness Material		800
Office Equipment		1,000
Copying and Postage		2,000
Good Neighbor Travel (8,000m @ .25/m)		2,000
	Sub total	$9,180

Evaluation

Contract/Outside Evaluator	Sub total	$5,000

Indirect Costs

5% of personnel costs	Sub total	$5,557
	Total	$130,874

Revenue

37,440 hrs Respite/Year @ 50% billable hrs × $2.00/hr	$37,440
Total grant funds requested	$93,434

---

budget to others to see if you have missed anything or whether your estimates appear reasonable. In fact, acknowledge that you will usually forget something and plan for this eventuality with the agency which will receive the grant. Sometimes this means building in a slight overestimate of costs or asking the agency to set aside a contingency fund for costs not covered by the grant.

Items that might appear unusual or questionable to others should be discussed in an accompanying budget

HIGHLIGHT 14.15

EXAMPLE OF A
FUNCTIONAL OR PROGRAM BUDGET

Category	Peer Counselors	Public Education
Personnel	$50,000	$20,000
Operating expenses	$15,000	$ 6,000
Equipment	$ 1,500	$ 3,500
Total	$66,500	$29,500
Grand total	$96,000	

narrative. Here you should justify and explain the costs within the context of the proposal. Large cost items should be clearly explained. Highlight 14.17 provides an example of a budget narrative for the Alzheimer's grant.

CREDENTIALS OF STAFF. A section should be developed that describes the credentials of staff members carrying out the activities proposed in the grant. This includes resumes that clearly illustrate each person's qualifications. The purpose is to strengthen your credibility; you want to emphasize that your staff are capable of accomplishing what your grant proposes to do (Coley & Scheinberg, 1990) . Generally, a one page summary of each person's work experience and education is sufficient.

CERTIFICATIONS OF COMPLIANCE. If required, add a section to the proposal discussing compliance with civil rights laws and protections for human subjects. Most governmental grants require specific assurances that people will not be hurt by your project and that your agency obeys federal, state, and local laws and regulations. Federal law protects human beings from being subjected to treatment that endangers their physical or mental health. Activities that expose people to stress or that are deceptive will probably not be funded. If appropriate (if the proposal involves research respondents), address subjects' confidentiality. Explain how you will gather information in such a way as to maintain subject confidentiality. Additionally, describe

how you will obtain subjects' informed consent. Generally, projects that carry low risk to human beings are easier to justify. Recent revelations indicate that researchers in some medical studies subjected participants to risks including crippling disease and death. These incidents have made it more important than ever to guarantee protections, and funding agencies may not want to get involved in something that carries risk to the subjects.

COST SHARING, MATCHING FUNDS, AND INDIRECT COSTS. Another important budgetary concept is that the total amount of funding needed for a proposed project may come from different sources. Cost sharing is an arrangement whereby both the agency receiving the grant and the organization dispensing the grant contribute to the proposed project. Cost sharing methods include indirect costs and matching funds.

Indirect costs are often referred to as "overhead." If you glance back at highlight 14.14, you will see a line item labeled Indirect Costs. Indirect costs are so named because they are only indirectly related to the grant proposal. Indirect costs compensate your agency for its expenses in operating the grant activity. An agency seeking a grant of $500,000 to operate a homeless shelter for two years needs that money for direct expenses such as personnel, rent, utilities, and equipment. However, the agency will do the bookkeeping, pay salaries, and supervise the staff of the shelter. These activities and their related expenses represent indirect costs. These costs are usually included in the grant appli-

---

HIGHLIGHT 14.16

EXAMPLE OF ALLOCATING
TIME AND SPACE COSTS

Individual	Percent Assigned to Project	Salary	Project Cost
Lorraine Breitbarth	15%	$20,000	$ 3,000
Alice Fay	25%	$28,000	$ 7,000
Mike Miller	65%	$35,000	$22,750
Bob Lillegard	100%	$37,250	$37,250

Four offices @ 100 square feet per office = 400 square feet total.

Office space used: (15% + 25% + 65% + 100%) / 400 = 200 square feet

Office space rent is $30/sq. ft. per month

Office space cost of project: $6,000.00 ($30 × 200)

---

cation and listed in the budget. The Alzheimer's grant listed an indirect amount equal to 5 percent of personnel costs. Among the expenses which might be charged to indirect costs are such things as clerical support for projects, operation and maintenance of a facility, and administrative cost. Many organizations charge a set amount to cover these ''overhead or indirect costs.'' This amount is usually figured as a percentage of the total grant and may equal 20, 30, 40 percent or more. Thus, a grant to provide a new program costing $100,000 might have additional indirect costs of 30 percent. The granting agency would then be asked to pay $130,000 ($100,000 plus the $30,000 overhead).

To keep expenses as low as possible, not all granting agencies allow indirect costs to be charged to their grants. Instead, they expect the agency receiving the grant to absorb the indirect costs. Some granting agencies accept indirect costs but limit the amount of indirect costs you may charge to the grant. However, if a granting agency does allow indirect costs to be charged to a grant, this money goes directly to your agency. You might consider it a bonus for the agency.

Matching funds or cost sharing grants assume that the receiving organization will contribute part of the total project costs. The principle behind cost sharing is that an organization contributing some of its own resources to a project is more likely to operate efficiently and effectively. Grantors that do not let your agency charge indirect costs to the grant are forcing your agency to share the costs of the project.

Matching of funds or cost sharing may be handled in one of two ways. First, some agencies are expected to contribute actual cash to the grant project. This is often referred to as a *hard match*. If a grant requires an agency to provide a 10 percent cash match, a grant project costing $100,000 would be financed by $90,000 (90 percent) from the grantor and $10,000 (10 percent) from your agency. Generally speaking, agencies do not like to apply for grants when cash matching is required. Agencies simply do not have unallocated money available for such projects.

The second method of matching (a *soft match*) allows an agency to provide its share of the costs through contributed services or activities. An agency might contribute the cost of space (as in our example of 10 percent of the total agency space being allocated to a grant project). If the space is already being paid for by the agency, it is an easy contribution for the agency to make. Figure 14.4 gives an example of how such a calculation might be made.

HIGHLIGHT 14.17

EXAMPLE OF A BUDGET NARRATIVE

Budget Narrative

The salary for the BSW Director is consistent with salaries of experienced social workers in the area with administrative responsibilities.

The hourly wage for the LPN is higher than the prevailing rate. However, in rural areas, especially for part-time work, the salary must be competitive with home health agencies in order to attract competent personnel.

The hourly wage for the activity directors is about the rate for personnel of this training in the area.

The 5 percent buyout of administrative time from the Alzheimer's Association and the Southwest Missouri Office on Aging is necessary to augment the work these agencies will be performing in support of the respite care program.

The outside evaluation will be conducted by the Center for Social Research at Southwest Missouri State University. The Center has considerable experience with process and outcome evaluations. The figure of approximately 5 percent of the total grant costs is consistent with other center contracts.

Plans for Continued Support

Though none of the following funding possibilities are absolute, taken together they provide a package of financial options for future support.

First, as noted in the description of services section and the budget, the project plans to collect in fees $37,440 during the first year of operation. While the project will always allow participation of people who are unable to pay, it is believed that the projected amount is modest and can be increased in the future.

Second, several of the communities have passed mill taxes to pay for certain types of human services. A project such as the respite care program fits well with the intended purposes of that type of tax.

Third, the state of Missouri has in the past made resources available through block grant funding for innovative programs. The success of this project, especially as it demonstrates networking with other institutions in the community (such as schools and churches) will be highly regarded.

Fourth, the participating agencies in the initial grant, as well as other agencies, might increase their in-kind contributions. Specifically, as needs change within the human service field for the elderly, positions could be reallocated to meet more pressing issues.

Because it is much easier for agencies to contribute services than cash, most prefer the "soft match" arrangement. Soft match is also sometimes referred to as *in-kind contributions*. In-kind contributions are expenses that the organization will incur whether the grant is received or not. In some situations, the grant-seeking agency may seek to increase the amount of its in-kind contribution. A local business might be asked to donate a van to the senior center, and the value of the van would be used as match to help the senior center obtain a grant for outreach services to elderly citizens in the community.

Figure 14.4
Calculating a Soft Match

Total cost of operating child abuse prevention program	$40,000
Grantor will provide up to 80% of program costs (.80 x $40,000)	$32,000
Grantor requires 20% match for all grants (.20 x $40,000)	$8,000

Agency will provide its "match" of $8,000 through contributed services as follows:

a. 10% of one supervisor's time
   (annual salary of $40,000 x 10%)   = $4,000

b. 10% of supervisor's office space
   (annual cost of $2,000 x 10%)   = $ 200

c. 100% of new worker's office space
   (annual cost of $1,500 x 100%)   = $1,500

d. 15% of secretarial staff's time
   (annual salary of $15,333 x 15%)   = $2,300

                 Total $8,000

AGENCY OR INSTITUTIONAL ENDORSE-MENTS. The last portion of the grant application should include a signature page for executives of the receiving agency. Relevant signatures might include those of the agency director, chief elected official, or others who will accept ultimate responsibility for administering grant funds. These signatures reflect the agency's support for the grant's proposed project. Both administrators and involved staff commit themselves to the grant via their signatures. Ironically, as the grant writer you may not be required to sign the grant although you did all the work of preparing it.

In addition, you may sometimes request letters of support or endorsements from other agencies or individuals. This is especially important if several agencies are expected to work together on a project. The juvenile court judge may be asked to provide a letter requesting grant money for a juvenile detention center. If it is important that the supporting letters contain specific information, you may actually draft the letters. You then send the draft to the endorsing agency where administrators will modify or adapt it and return it to you. These letters indicate that other organizations support your proposal (Coley & Scheinberg, 1990).

Post-Application Phase

Many grant sponsors require that the grant application be received or mailed by a specific date. Proposals not received by this date are very likely to be ignored or returned to the sender. It is often wise to mail materials so that you are notified of their receipt. This prevents problems when a proposal gets lost.

Once received, grants are reviewed. The reviewers vary depending upon the type of organization. In private foundations either a single individual or a committee may review proposals. With government grants a committee is more likely to function as reviewer. Committee members will then give points for various portions of the proposal, such as budget and statement of problem. Those proposals receiving the highest points are usually funded. The number of proposals funded depends on the amount of money available. Sometimes, although a proposal receives fewer points, the agency believes it has merit. In some of these cases, the grantor will ask for revisions in order to address their concerns. The grant writer can then resubmit the revised proposal for reconsideration.

When the grantor is a foundation, there may be additional considerations. Colen and Scheinberg's research (1990, pp. 35–36) suggests that the following positive factors are important in determining whether an agency receives grant funds or not. Ideally the agency:

1. Shows a cost-effective operation. This means the cost of the intervention is reasonable given the expected outcome.
2. Supports other organizations in the community. Cooperative endeavors and collaborative activities tend to be more highly rated.
3. Reflects cultural sensitivity and diversity. Services provided should be sensitive to client differences especially in relation to culturally diverse populations.
4. Focuses on primary prevention of the problem. Prevention of a problem tends to be more effective than intervening after the problem has already arisen.
5. Has a proven track record. Foundations like to go with winners who have demonstrated they can do the job. A record of past grants received can be helpful.
6. Establishes new, innovative programs. Foundations prefer to encourage the development of new approaches rather than replicate something tried elsewhere.
7. Receives funding from other sources. Funding from other sources indicates wider support for a proposal and enhances its chance of being funded.

8. Has a previous relationship with the foundation. A past record of dealing with a foundation is helpful.

9. Has a reputation that is not too radical. Foundations can be somewhat conservative and may not be willing to have their names linked with radical proposals.

10. Has a competent and professionally trained staff. Competence of the people who will carry out the grant project is important. It is risky to give money to people who don't have the experience or education for the task.

Less Funding Than Requested

Frequently, grants will be funded but at a lower amount than originally requested. This generally requires major rethinking about whether the project is workable with the smaller amount. Don't assume that it is easy to "just cut corners a bit" and still serve the same number of people or operate on the same scale. A realistic conclusion is that less money means less program.

When the Grant/Contract Runs Out

Almost all grants run for a specified period, typically a year or two. After that time, the grant money will be gone. You must plan either to continue the program by finding other sources of funds or to terminate it. It is easy not to think clearly about this eventuality and neglect to plan for the post-grant period. Some granting agencies will require that you address this matter in your grant application. Highlight 14.17, the budget narrative example, includes a section on funding the project after the grant is over. The purpose of this requirement is not to commit the agency to continue a poor or ineffective program. Instead, it is to ensure that sound programs meriting continuation have some chance of surviving after the grant money runs out. Preparing for this period is part of the responsibility for good planning that any grant application project demands.

Chapter Summary

This chapter describes a variety of activities associated with developing and managing agency and organizational resources. Working with the media is addressed first. General guidelines for working with news media are included and an example of a news release is provided. Media interviews are discussed along with other forms of media communication.

The second section of the chapter covers the use of technology in agencies, focusing primarily on the use of computers. Information is presented on computer hardware components including the central processing unit, keyboard, monitor, and printers. Software, both general purpose and specific to social work, is also discussed. The importance of management information systems is stressed along with an accompanying case example. This section concludes with some general observations about the use of computers.

Fundraising methods comprise the third section of this chapter. Topics covered include sources of funds and various fundraising mechanisms. Options include individual donors, benefits, corporate donations, direct solicitations, group giving, and creating membership organizations.

The chapter's last section covers grants and contracts, two major sources of funds for many agencies. Included information details how one finds out about grants and contracts, and describes government foundation, business, and corporate grants. Instructions are given on how to apply for a grant including preapplication, application and post-application phases. Included in these phases are guidelines on writing a grant proposal, descriptions of different types of grant and contract proposals, and detailed information on each section of a grant application. A successful grant application is included as an example.

CHAPTER FIFTEEN

Stress and
Time Management

Consider this scenario. You are a social work practitioner for a county department of social services. It is now 8:00 A.M. By 4:30 P.M. today you are supposed to accomplish the following tasks:

- Meet with your supervisor for your weekly supervisory rendezvous.
- Complete appointments established with six clients as noted on your weekly calendar.
- Call to schedule a dentist's appointment as soon as possible. You cracked a molar and it hurts like all get out.
- Make return phone calls to the following clients about crisis issues: Ms. Hermanez, Ms. White, Mr. Scissorhands, Ms. Trashcan, Mr. Beauregard, Ms. Leinenkugal, Ms. Bloodred, Mr. Handmade.
- Find the homeless Shaver family a place to stay.
- Enroll Tina Tuna in an alcohol treatment program.
- Decide what to get your mother for her birthday (it's tomorrow and you already forgot to send her a card on time).
- Try to stop thinking about your fight with Honey this morning.
- Have lunch.
- Use the restroom, probably twice.
- Prepare an agenda for tomorrow's 8:00 A.M. staff meeting.
- Help Ms. Loophole place her critically ill father in a hospice.
- Drop your car off to get your leaky tire fixed.
- Complete your two weeks worth of progress notes before your supervisory meeting.
- Call Irma about riding together to the state social work conference next Thursday.
- Talk to your colleague Horatio about the minor conflict you had yesterday.
- Make appointments with eight clients for next week.
- Drive the Hanratti family to the doctor.
- Take your client Pauline Prudo to Planned Parenthood for contraception counseling.
- Check up on your client Merhan Birmquach who you believe is seriously depressed and potentially suicidal.
- Work on that grant application that's due in two weeks.

What would you do?

a. Cry
b. Take a sick day
c. Use good time-management skills
d. Update your resumé

What do you do when you have scores of tasks to complete right now? How can you handle the stress from the demands of clients who you feel desperately need your help? How can you keep your own personal concerns from interfering with your ability to accomplish your work? How can you keep from going absolutely crazy with all the pressure?

Two practical means of coping with professional and personal stress are recognizing and utilizing established stress- and time-management techniques. You can't necessarily get rid of all the pressure in your life, but you can begin to control it.

Introduction

Two variables are critically important in terms of conducting your professional life effectively and efficiently. They are stress and time. Both can and will affect your ability to do your job. They exist whether you like it or not, and they are related. Failure to manage time well can become a major stress producer. However, you can begin to get control of them. Stress and time management techniques allow you to maximize your time both professionally and personally.

Stress and time are addressed here because they are two critical facets of your macro environment. They are integrally involved in everything you will be doing. In order to fulfill your job responsibilities with clients, comply with supervisory directives, and make decisions concerning your macro objectives, you will need to get control of both your time and stress level.

This chapter will:

- Describe the dynamics of stress and explain the General Adaptation Syndrome.
- Discuss how stress occurs within an agency context.
- Explore the physiological, psychological, and behavioral problems that stress can cause.
- Propose a broad range of techniques for managing stress.
- Explain how poor time management causes stress.
- Identify various personal styles for dealing with stress.
- Propose approaches for establishing and prioritizing goals for managing time.
- Examine a variety of techniques for managing your time.
- Assess the dynamics of procrastination and suggest means for combating it.

Stress and Stress Management

Stress is "any influence that interferes with the normal functioning of an organism and produces some internal strain or tension'' (Barker, 1991, p. 228). Most of us recognize certain situations as causing unusual stress. For example, abruptly losing your job or hearing of a significant other's catastrophic death will usually cause stress.

Even positive events can be stressful. They, too, can force you to deal with new circumstances and expend energy pursuing unfamiliar or different activities. Getting married or receiving a promotion, desirable events for most people, still cause stress.

Environmental situations can also create stress. For example, expending time and effort to change an agency policy may add to the pressure you already feel from fulfilling your everyday responsibilities to clients. Or the abrupt shutdown of a major industry in the town where you work leaves thousands of people unemployed. Your client caseloads soar. You see the need to develop a range of new services, from job retraining to relocation planning to food pantries for hungry newly-unemployed workers and their families.

Likewise, personal characteristics such as perfectionism can magnify stress. Most of us, however, can withstand significant amounts of stress and survive. When we are exhausted, we go to sleep. When memories are too painful, we forget. In effect, we have developed coping mechanisms to keep our stress levels under some control.

Certain factors are associated with stress. Rigid, authoritarian attitudes and so-called "Type A" personalities appear to be more prone to stress. The "Type A" personality is frequently fighting the clock to squeeze more work into smaller and smaller time frames. Likewise, irrational thinking can cause stress. Believing that your intimate other can satisfy all of your needs, which, of course, is impossible, can produce stress.

Cultural factors such as gender role expectations may also play a role. The pressures many women feel to be supermoms (doing an outstanding job both at work and at home) can increase their stress levels. Belle's (1991) review of the literature suggests that there are important gender differences in how men and women construct their networks. These differences also affect the way each gender uses personal networks in times of stress. Such contrasting relationship styles apparently have consequences for our overall well-being. However, more research is needed before we can fully understand such gender differences. Belle concludes that

This woman is experiencing job-related stress. The tension she has been experiencing for several weeks has brought on a dreaded migraine.

women maintain more emotionally intimate relationships than do men. Therefore, they mobilize more varied social supports in times of stress. Women also provide more frequent and effective support to others than do men.

The General Adaptation Syndrome

Your body appears to respond to both negative or positive stress in the same way. Seyle (1956), one of the foremost authorities on stress, found that the body reacts to all stressors in the same way, regardless of the source of stress. This means that the body reacts to positive stressors (a romantic kiss) in the same way it reacts to negative stressors (an electric shock). Seyle found that the body has a three-phase reaction to stress: (a) the alarm phase, (b) the resistance phase, and (c) the exhaustion phase. Selye labels this stress response process the General Adaptation Syndrome (GAS).

in the alarm phase the body recognizes the stressor and responds by preparing for fight or flight. A stressor can be "any stimulus that causes stress" (*Webster's Ninth Collegiate Dictionary*, 1991, p. 1166). The body's reactions to a range of stressors are numerous and complex. Therefore, we will summarize them only briefly here. The body sends messages from the hypothalamus (a section of the brain that regulates a range of physiological functions) to the pituitary gland to release its hormones. These hormones trigger the adrenal glands to release adrenaline.

The release of adrenaline and other hormones results in:

- Increased breathing and heartbeat rate
- A rise in blood pressure
- Increased coagulation of blood to minimize potential loss of blood in case of physical injury
- Diversion of blood from the skin to the brain, the heart, and contracting muscles
- A rise in serum cholesterol and blood fat
- Gastrointestinal tract problems
- Dilation of the pupils

This range of changes results in a massive burst of energy, better vision and hearing, and increased muscular strength—all changes that increase our capacities to fight or to flee. A major problem of the fight-or-flight reaction in modern times is that we often cannot deal with a threat by fighting or by fleeing, especially in agency life. In our civilized society fighting or fleeing generally runs counter to codes of acceptable behavior. The fight-or-flight response was functional for primitive humans. Now such a response rarely is.

In the resistance phase (the second phase) bodily processes seek to return to homeostasis. The body strives during this phase to repair any damage caused by the stressors. The body can adapt itself to hard physical labor, a serious stressor. In handling most stressors the body generally goes through only the two phases of alarm and repair. Over a lifetime a person goes through these two phases hundreds of thousands of times.

The third phase, exhaustion, occurs only when the body remains in a state of high stress for an extended period of time. If such stress continues to impact the body, it is unable to repair the damage. If exhaustion continues, a person is apt to develop a stress-related illness or even to die.

The Macro Context for Stress

Social workers often consider themselves, their profession and the agency work environment to be highly stressful. Certainly, dealing with the complicated needs of multiple clients, confronting the huge amounts of paperwork and documentation required for accountability, and operating within bureaucratic systems can produce significant stress.

Among human service workers, Farmer, Monohan, and Hekeler (1984) found that at least 25 percent identified seven major sources of serious or very serious job stress. Workload and job expectations, conflicting demands placed on the worker, and administrative ambiguity (such as confusion about rules and how agency administrators wanted them implemented) were all cited. Other variables related to stress included overinvestment in clients, larger caseload size, and lack of possibilities for advancement (p. 44).

One of the greatest dangers in social work practice is burn-out (Simpson & Simpson, 1992). Burn-out is "a nontechnical term to describe workers who feel apathy or anger as a result of on-the-job stress and frustration" (Barker, 1991, p. 27). Burn-out can occur when you have too much work and feel that you have too little control over getting it all done. Obviously, social work usually addresses problems. Constant confrontation with problems is also stressful.

On the other hand, Simpson and Simpson (1992) explain: "Words cannot convey the satisfaction of having successfully intervened in someone's life. It is a good feeling to know that you have made a difference. And although the work can be grueling, it is rarely dull because people are rarely dull. Only the paperwork is tedious, and you will find that the case in every profession" (p. 18).

To avoid burn-out and enhance your usefulness, good stress- and time-management skills are essential. The following sections will explore stress-related problems and techniques for changing your perception about, and managing, stress. Because time management is so critical for effective control of stress, we will extensively explore the issues concerning time and techniques recommended to manage it.

Perceptions of Stress

Stress becomes a problem only when the stressors are so great that your adaptive system is overwhelmed. This can happen either from too much stress in a short time or from the cumulative effects of stress over an extended period. It is typically the chronic or long-term stress that causes us the greatest concern. Because of the prolonged time involved, you can develop both physiological and psychological problems. Interestingly, it is not often a single major event that triggers stress-related problems. Rather, it is many trivial occurrences and factors that add up.

Roskies (1991) says stressors can be better understood if we recognize that they differ in quality, duration, and quantity. That is, some stressors are harmful because of their importance (seriousness). Others are detrimental because of the length of time they work on us or because of the large number of stressors occurring at one time. What one persons considers stressful, another may not. Individual judgment defines just how stressful an experience is. Individual judgment also determines how effective we perceive our coping mechanisms to be (Roskies, 1991, p. 419).

Thus, both the type of problems you encounter and your perception of how well you can cope with them affect the stress-related problems you experience. If you feel you simply cannot cope with a particular problem no matter what, this perception can lead to increased anxiety. The anxiety increases stress and there is a snowball effect. The consequences of stress, thus, can include physiological, psychological, or behavioral problems.

Physiological Stress-Related Problems

Often the first recommendation for coping with stress is to recognize its existence and magnitude. *Physiological* problems of stress include headaches, stomach upset (such as colitis), and skin rashes or hives. They also can include high blood pressure which, of course, can be life-threatening (Farmer, Monohan & Hekeler, 1984). While most of us have some of these symptoms from time to time, you should recognize that chronic, long-lasting symptoms are warning signs that your stress level is out of control.

Psychological Stress-Related Problems

Psychological difficulties from chronic stress include anxiety and depression. Anxiety is "painful or apprehensive uneasiness of mind usually over an impending or anticipated ill" (*Webster's Ninth Collegiate Dictionary*, 1991, p. 93). Depression entails "a group of emotional reactions frequently characterized by sadness, discouragement, despair, pessimism about the future, reduced activity and productivity, sleep disturbance or excessive fatigue, and feelings of inadequacy, self-effacement, and hopelessness" (Barker, 1991, p. 60). Attempts to cope with psychological stress vary. Some people turn to excessive intake of alcohol or drugs, or to overeating. Others smoke or even consider suicide.

Behavioral Stress-Related Problems

Behavioral correlates of stress include any behaviors resulting directly from excess stress. A father might hit his five year-old daughter when he's had a hard day at work. Or a wife might argue incessantly with her husband when she's under extreme duress. Other people withdraw inward and isolate themselves.

Figure 15.1 illustrates an example of the stress process in a macro context, reacting to pressures at work. First, a stressor occurs. In this case the problem stressor is too much paperwork. Second, a person's perception of the problem shapes that individual's reactions to stress. Figure 15.1 illustrates that the person, depending on her individual make-up and perception, may experience: physical symptoms such as stomach aches, headaches, or hives; psychological symptoms such as anxiety or depression; or behavioral symptoms such as uncontrollable emotional outbursts. Depending on the individual, the environmental context, the problem, and the person's perception of the problem, each individual will react differently to stressors.

Confronting Stress: Flight or Fight

People react to stress in highly individualized ways. We have mentioned that some people react to extensive

Figure 15.1
The Stress Process

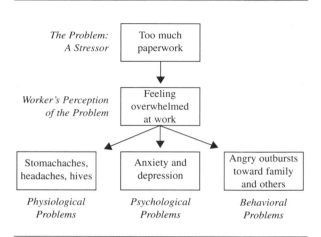

stress by *fleeing* it, pursuing activities to avoid confronting the stress. We have already mentioned that they might drink to excess or use drugs. They may overeat. Perhaps they will smoke.

Other people react to serious stress by *fighting* it. Positive ways to handle stress include the various stress management techniques we will discuss below.

Managing Your Stress

Managing stress often means reducing it or finding ways to keep it under control. Fighting stress to control it is more effective in the long run than fleeing from it. The latter only can result in physiological, psychological, or behavioral problems.

There are three primary approaches to stress management. This is true both in your macro setting at work and in your personal life. First, you can change the stressful event. Second, you can change the way you think about the stressful event. Third, you can adapt specific strategies and techniques to help control your stress level.

Changing the Stressful Event

There are at least five problem areas in a work context that can cause you undue stress (Sheafor, Horejsi, & Horejsi, 1991). These include inadequate or distressing work settings, frequent urgent deadlines, too much work to accomplish in the time allocated, deterrents to accomplishing work such as frequent interruptions, and problematic relationships with other staff. Sometimes you can change such stressful events. Other times you can't. The following will explore the possibility of implementing changes to control each type of stressful event.

INADEQUATE SETTING. Is your work environment helpful for getting your work done? Do you have sufficient privacy? Or do you have to work in a tiny cubicle separated only by paper-thin partitions of shoulder height?

A social worker we know once held a job as counselor at a mental health center. She was supposed to do counseling in an office located in a large room with paper-thin, dividing walls. It was virtually impossible to maintain confidentiality or to avoid distraction from other therapists going about their jobs. The answer was the purchase of a "white-noise" machine for each therapist. These machines blurred noise in the external environment so that workers could not understand what was being said outside their office cubicle. This minor change in work environment—acquisition of the white-noise machines—made all the difference in the world in the worker's ability to do her job.

There are other ways to evaluate and improve your immediate work environment. Can you make your office more pleasant? Can you put up pictures that appeal to you? Can you paint your office some tantalizing color? Or would music help? Does music relax you and thereby assist you in getting work done? Would it be appropriate to use earphones so as not to disturb others around you? These are only a few of the many questions you might ask yourself about improving your work environment.

URGENT DEADLINES. Do you feel that you can never catch up, no matter what you do? Paperwork is an ongoing problem for many workers. You have to complete your paperwork for the sake of accountability, but it's often excessively demanding and time-consuming.

How might you assume greater control of deadlines and paperwork? Is there any way you can decrease the urgency of deadlines? Can you decrease the amount of paperwork you must do? Can you record less? Are you incorporating too much detail? Are there ways you could be more efficient in completing your paperwork?

Is there any way that you can gain more lead time for accomplishing tasks and goals? Is there any way you can better manage your time? (Time management is discussed more thoroughly later on in the chapter.)

Do you clearly understand your job, or are you trying to accomplish too much? You might discuss with your supervisor the appropriate expectations of your role (Cooper, 1981): "Encourage your boss . . . to provide three separate lists of what he thinks (1) you should do more of or better of, (2) do less of or stop doing, and (3) keep on doing, or maintain unchanged in your job. In the meantime, you should prepare the reverse list of what you think he should be doing (1) more of or better of, (2) less of or stop doing, and (3) keep on doing in respect of you" (pp. 185–86).

TOO MUCH WORK AND TOO LITTLE TIME. The problem of an overly heavy workload is related to the discussion of urgent deadlines, above. Do you clearly understand your job role? Are you spending your time on the tasks that are most significant? Or are you wasting time on tasks that should not have priority?

As mentioned earlier, you might discuss your role with your supervisor. She or he might be able to help you better define your responsibilities and prioritize your job tasks. Are you wasting time trying to accomplish repetitive tasks? Can you better manage your time? Can you develop a form or procedure for accomplishing repetitive tasks to decrease the amount of time you have to spend on them? You might also examine your expectations for your performance. We will discuss this in more depth when we discuss changing how you think about stressful events, the second approach to stress management.

CONTROLLING DISTRACTIONS AND INTERRUPTIONS. Are people constantly popping into your office? Does the phone ring incessantly? Do you feel you never have an opportunity to think? How can you get better control of your time (once again, this refers to time-management techniques to be discussed later)? Can you shut your door during certain times of the day? Can you put a "Please do not disturb" sign on your office door? Can you possibly set aside some predetermined time to finish your paperwork? Can you

have an administrative assistant or secretary hold your calls and take messages or record them on your answering machine or voice mail so that you're not constantly distracted?

PROBLEMATIC INTERPERSONAL RELATIONSHIPS. Usually, problematic interpersonal relationships at work involve one of two scenarios (Cooper, 1981). First, you have a colleague, supervisor, or administrator who has poorly developed interpersonal skills. Such people have difficulties effectively interacting and communicating with others. Second, you alone have a "personality clash," for whatever reason, with a specific individual. If so, examine whether it is possible to resolve the conflict. In the first case, the person with generally poor social skills, can you and other colleagues talk to your supervisor about the problematic staff member? Can this person's own supervisor help him improve his interpersonal skills? Can the agency send him to receive some training to improve social and communication skills?

If you have a personality conflict with someone else, can you approach this person and straightforwardly try to resolve the conflict? Can you ask your supervisor to function as a mediator? Chapter 2 discussed some specific techniques for dealing with conflict, enhancing assertiveness, and gaining help from supervisors. If you don't think resolution is realistically possible, can you minimize your involvement or interaction with the individual without interfering with your own ability to do your job?

Change How You Think about the Stressful Event

If you can't change the stressful event or situation itself, can you pursue the second avenue of stress management? Can you change how you think about the stressful event?

The following are some suggestions to consider:

1. *Accept that some stress cannot be avoided.* Do you have to worry about every stressor? Or can you accept the fact that some stressors will exist regardless and put them out of your mind as much as possible?
2. *Realize that the primary changeable element in your life is you.* Appreciate the fact that you can control your thinking and your behavior.

3. *Separate insoluble problems from others.* If you can't solve the problem, can you put it out of your mind and stop worrying about it?

4. *Examine your expectations.* Put plainly, dump the unrealistic ones. Both positive thinking (reframing a negative event to make it more positive) and talking to others about your expectations can be helpful. Recognize that some things are not worth getting upset about.

5. *Avoid should/should not thinking.* This limits your options. Are you wasting time worrying about what you should be doing while you're not doing it? Either do it or don't, but don't waste time worrying about it. Thinking differently really can reduce your stress level.

6. *Analyze your needs.* What do you really need? How much does the stressful event really affect you? To what extent should you let it bother you? Are you wasting your time and energy thinking about it?

7. *Emphasize your strength—physical, emotional, and spiritual.* Could your time be better spent placing greater emphasis on positive aspects of your life instead of dwelling on stress-producing negatives?

Adopt Stress-Management Strategies

We have discussed controlling stress by either changing the stressful event or changing the way you think about it. The third way to manage stress is by adopting specific strategies and techniques to help subdue your stress level. There are at least three types of stress-management strategies. They include relaxation approaches, exercise, and "pleasurable goodies."

RELAXATION APPROACHES. Deep breathing relaxation, imagery relaxation, progressive muscle relaxation, meditation, and biofeedback are effective techniques for reducing stress and inducing the relaxation response (becoming relaxed). Making yourself comfortable and at ease, avoiding distractions, and closing your eyes are helpful for each of these approaches.

Deep breathing relaxation helps you stop thinking about day-to-day concerns and concentrate on your breathing process. For five to ten minutes, slowly and gradually inhale deeply and then exhale. Meanwhile, tell yourself something like, "I am relaxing, breathing more smoothly. This is soothing, and I'm feeling calmer, renewed, and refreshed." Regular practice of this technique will enable you to become more relaxed whenever you're in some tense situation—such as prior to giving a presentation or running a meeting.

Imagery relaxation involves switching your focus (for ten to fifteen minutes) from your daily concerns to your ideal relaxation place. It might be lying on a beach by a scenic lake in the warm sun. It might be soaking in a frothing hot tub while relishing your favorite magazine. It might be looking down on a vast wilderness landscape from the top of some picturesque mountain. Regardless, savor all the pleasure, the peacefulness. Focus on everything that you find calming, soothing, and relaxing. Sense your whole body becoming refreshed, revived, and rejuvenated.

Progressive muscle relaxation is based on the principle that people cannot remain anxious if their muscles are relaxed (Jacobson, 1938). You can learn the technique by tightening and relaxing muscles, set by set. When relaxing each set of muscles, you should concentrate on the relaxed feeling and the fact that your muscles are becoming less tense. Watson and Tharp (1973) provides a brief description: "Make a fist with your dominant hand (usually right). Make a fist and tense the muscles of your (right) hand and forearm; tense it until it trembles. Feel the muscles pull across your fingers and the lower part of your forearm . . . Hold this position for five to seven seconds, then . . . relax . . . Just let your hand go. Pay attention to the muscles of your (right) hand and forearm as they relax. Note how those muscles feel as relaxation flows through (twenty or thirty seconds)" (pp. 182–83).

The procedure of tensing and then relaxing is continued three or four times until the hand and forearm are relaxed. Next, other muscle groups are tensed and relaxed in the same manner, one group at a time. These groups might include: left hand and forearm; right biceps, left biceps; forehead muscles; upper lip and cheek muscles; jaw muscles; chin and throat muscles; chest muscles; abdominal muscles; back muscles between shoulder blades; right and lest upper leg muscles, right and left calf muscles; and toes and arches of the feet. With practice, you can develop the capacity to relax simply by visualizing your respective sets of muscles.

A variety of *meditative approaches* are also being used today to decrease stress and tension. (Deep breathing relaxation and imagery relaxation are two forms of meditation.) Benson (1975) has identified four basic components common to meditative approaches that induce the relaxation response: (1) being in a quiet environment free from external distractions; (2) being in a comfortable position; (3) having an object to dwell on, such as a word, sound, change, phrase, or image (since any neutral word or phrase will work, Benson suggests repeating silently to yourself the word *one*); and (4) having a passive attitude so that you stop thinking about day-to-day concerns. This last component, Benson asserts, is the key element in inducing the relaxation response.

Biofeedback equipment provides mechanical feedback to people about their stress levels. Such equipment can inform people about increasing stress levels of which they may be unaware until markedly high levels are reached. A person's hand temperature can vary ten to twelve degrees in an hour's time, with an increase in temperature indicating an increase in relaxation. Similarly, biofeedback equipment can measure the functioning of numerous physiological processes. These include blood pressure, hand temperature, muscle tension, heartbeat rate, and brain wave activity. With biofeedback training a person is first instructed in recognizing high levels of anxiety or tenseness. Then the person is instructed on how to reduce such high levels by either closing the eyes and adopting a passive "letting-go" attitude or by thinking about something pleasant or calming. Often, relaxation approaches are combined with biofeedback to elicit the relaxation response. In summary, biofeedback equipment provides a person with immediate feedback about the kind of thinking that is effective in reducing stress (Brown, 1977). Information concerning biofeedback equipment and other methods of professionally supervised stress management may be found in a large city's yellow pages under "biofeedback equipment and systems" or "stress-management services."

EXERCISE. Since the alarm phase of the General Adaptation Syndrome (GAS) automatically prepares us for large muscle activity, it makes sense to exercise. Through exercising, we use up fuel in the blood, reduce blood pressure and heart rate, and reverse the other physiological changes set off during GAS's alarm stage. Exercising helps keep us physically fit so we have more physical strength to handle crises. Exercising also reduces stress and relieves tension, partly by switching our thinking from our daily concerns to the exercise we are involved in. For these reasons everyone should have an exercise program. A key to making yourself exercise daily is selecting a program you enjoy. A wide variety of exercises are available including walking, jogging,

Yoga is an excellent stress-management technique. It combines physical exercise with soothing meditation. Yoga can be practiced alone or, as shown here, in a class.

isometric exercises,[1] jumping rope, swimming, lifting weights, and so on.

PLEASURABLE GOODIES. "Pleasurable goodies" are key to what we might call *personal therapies*. They relieve stress, change our pace of living, are enjoyable, and make us feel good. What is a goody (pleasurable experience) to one person may not be to another. Common goodies are: listening to music, going shopping, being hugged, taking a bath, going to a movie, having a glass of wine, taking part in family and reli-

---

1. Isometric exercises involve those in which "opposing muscles are so contracted that there is little shortening but great increase in tone of muscle fibers involved" (*Webster's Ninth New Collegiate Dictionary*, 1991, p. 642).

gious get-togethers, taking a vacation, going to a party, singing, and so on. Such goodies add spice to life and remind us that we have value. Personal pleasures can also be used as payoffs to ourselves for jobs well done. Most of us would not seek to short-change others for doing well; we ought not to short-change ourselves. Such rewards make us feel good and motivate us to move on to new challenges.

Enjoyable activities outside our work and family responsibilities are pleasurable goodies that relieve stress. Research has found that stress reduces stress; that is, an appropriate level of stressful activity in one area helps reduce excessive stress in other areas (Schafer, 1978). Getting involved in enjoyable outside activities switches our negative thinking from our daily concerns to positive thoughts about the enjoyable activities. Therefore, it is stress-reducing to become involved in activities we enjoy. Such activities may include golf, tennis, swimming, scuba diving, taking flying lessons, traveling, and a host of others.

Managing Your Time

"I can't do it, I just can't! Oh, if only I had more time." How often have you thought something like this (not in so many words, perhaps, but with the same gist) or heard others complain this way? So often it seems that there is simply never enough time to finish everything you absolutely must get done. If you don't have three exams to study for, you have four papers due next week. If you don't have papers due next week, then you have to work at your part-time job for thirty-five hours, do the laundry, clean the apartment for friends coming over next weekend, have the car fixed, and keep up with your regular homework.

People who are disorganized with their time usually feel that they're living on the brink of imminent catastrophe. The key is that they feel out of control. They are swept this way and that by the torrents of time demands. Time-management techniques can help people acquire a sense of control over their lives.

As a social worker you will be faced with the need to juggle many responsibilities. Your macro environment is saturated with demands and potential stressors. We have emphasized that the ability to successfully manage your time and your workload is essential for an efficient, effective generalist social worker. Learning specific ways to use your time more effectively and efficiently will help you manage your workload better. This section will identify a variety of techniques to help you manage your professional (and personal) time.

How Poor Time Management Causes Stress

If you are not managing your time efficiently, then you are probably not being nearly as effective as you could be. There are at least six reasons why insufficient or total lack of time management results in stress. These include "preoccupation" with the myriad tasks you're supposed to accomplish; poor task "pacing"; "stimulus overload"; stimulus underload; and "anxiety" (Curtis & Detert, 1981, pp. 190–91).

Preoccupation

Have you ever had so much on your mind that you felt totally overwhelmed? Perhaps, it seemed you had so much to do that you couldn't possibly finish it all anyway, so why even try? Did you end up "dead in the water"? Maybe the problem was that you were worrying about all the things you needed to do instead of paying attention to the task at hand. If you don't keep your mind on what you're doing, how can you expect to do a good job? Preoccupation with a huge throng of tasks is overwhelming and distracting. It adds to your overall level of stress.

Poor Task Pacing

It's interesting that academia, in some ways, is so very different from "the real work world." Specifically, academia bases itself on a series of escalating peaks of stress. In other words school starts. It's probably not too bad in terms of workload for a while, but soon enough midterm or trimester exams come up. Then you have three exams on one day or two twenty page papers due in the same week. During these periods, pressure escalates, and you probably feel some degree of stress. People with no stress doubtless drop out for lack of motivation. Then, finally, there's semester break when you have almost total respite from the seemingly unending flow of assignments, exams, research papers, and

HIGHLIGHT 15.1

TIME "TROUBLERS" AND CONTROLLERS

There are a number of elements that cause you and just about everyone else to waste time. Review the time "troublers," likely reasons, and possible options listed below. Then answer the questions.

Time Troubler	Likely Reasons	Possible Options
What a mess	Confusion, disorder	Throw out, reorganize file
Hurry, hurry	Doing too much too fast, too little attention to detail	Undertake less, allow more time, just say no
I just can't decide	Terror at making mistakes, cowering at responsibility, can't prioritize and set goals	Use decision-making, problem-solving, and goal-setting skills
Oops, forgot to plan	Just didn't think, things happened too fast	Take time to think things through ahead of time, allow time for thought
There's just too much to do	Unable to say no, too much pressure to perform, can't prioritize	Prioritize goals, just say no, evaluate what is possible to accomplish
I'll do it later	Overwhelmed, don't feel like it, it's too hard	Prioritize tasks, plan how to accomplish the most significant
There's that phone again	Can't resist answering, too nonassertive to not answer or to speak briefly, can't control yourself	Talk briefly, stick to the main points, offer to return call later
Unwanted guests	Just can't say no, talking is fun, allows you to avoid work	Limit easy access and availability, be assertive

Now Answer the Following Questions:

1. What is your number one time troubler? _____
   What are the likely reasons for this troubler? _____
   What are your potential options for controlling this troubler? _____
2. What is your number two time troubler? _____
   What are the likely reasons for this troubler? _____
   What are your potential options for controlling this troubler? _____

Source: Adapted from Mackenzie (1972).

other academic responsibilities. Finally, you may have a summer break, when you probably have to work, but not in school.

Hence, school creates an environment where stress levels escalate to a pinnacle, then abruptly fall away. In your working environment you should ideally try to maintain more even stress levels, avoiding such drastic, upsetting variations. In other words, it is important to pace yourself on a more regular basis so that you can both accomplish your tasks and control your blood pressure.

Stimulus Overload

Stimulus overload is having too much to do. No matter how you utilize management skills, you cannot possibly complete all of your assigned tasks. Stimulus overload is similar to preoccupation in that both can lead to stress and dissatisfaction with your work. It seems there is no possible way for you to do a good job.

Stimulus Underload

Stimulus underload is the opposite of stimulus overload. It occurs when you don't have enough to do to maintain your interest. Either there are not enough tasks or the tasks are numbingly dull. Have you ever spoken to someone who retired or quit working outside the home? Have you heard such a person comment that he can't get anything done, despite having significantly more time than he had before? An old cliché comes to mind, "Work expands to fill the time available." With fewer, or not enough, things to do, it is easy to become lethargic, to move slowly and sometimes pointlessly. Stimulus underload can cause stress if you can't get done the tasks you feel you should. Time-management skills can reduce stress by helping you analyze how you spend your time and plan to spend the time you have more productively.

Anxiety

Anxiety is "a feeling of uneasiness, tension, and sense of imminent danger" (Barker, 1991, p. 14). Anxious people may appear nervous, skittish, and edgy. They may have difficulty both controlling useless move-

ment," (pacing back and forth or tapping their fingers annoyingly on the table) and redirecting their energy and attention to completing tasks at hand. Anxiety can result in lack of attention to time management. The probable consequence is stress.

Anxiety can result from any number of causes. These include personal problems, such as not being able to pay your full phone bill this month or a fear that your significant other is being unfaithful. Anxiety can result from worries about work or school. It can arise from subjective feelings of failure or low self-esteem. Whatever it causes, anxiety detracts from your ability to perform any task, thus resulting in stress. As we will see, good time-management skills can help you control both your anxiety and your time. (Note, however, that chronic, long-lasting anxiety that cannot be controlled may signal the need for counseling.)

Styles in Dealing with Time

Different people have divergent approaches to dealing with time. Filley (1978) cites at least five styles, or ways people view and handle their time. First, there are people who are just bored. They are bored with work. Actually, they are lazy and don't like to expend any energy. They are bored with leisure time, too. They are critical of everything and complain a lot. Many are whiners. Essentially, they're just sitting around waiting to die. You probably don't like these people very much.

Second, there are people who are happy-go-lucky. They love their leisure time and would just as soon spend all their time playing and relaxing. They probably should be extremely wealthy because they don't like to work. They usually do work when they have to, but feel it is a waste of their precious leisure time. They are the people the boss frequently has to tap on the shoulder and ask not to read the newspaper for the first forty-five minutes of their workday.

The third type of people are the "nose to the grindstone" type (Filley, 1978, p. 117). They work, work, work to get ahead, ahead, ahead. They hate having fun because they don't really know how to. Sometimes other people refer to them as drudges.

In the fourth style, people perceive time as invaluable. Such an individual sees time "as a precious commodity, and feels guilty if it is wasted. Such people seem to be active and productive, both in their work and their leisure'' (Filley, 1978, p. 117). These people differ from the ''nose-to-the-grindstone'' type in that they place value on *time* rather than on *work*. They place equal emphasis on leisure time. They usually can't sit still. Other people often refer to them as busy bees, and they can drive these other people crazy.

Finally, the fifth time style is that of people who look at time as something they can choose to manage. They think in terms of priorities and goals. They make conscious choices concerning how to spend both their work and leisure time. In essence, they control time rather than letting time control them. These people are time managers. The following sections discuss the skills time managers use.

Issues Involved in Time Management

At least three issues are involved in time management. All involve expending some amount of effort to learn new approaches to handling time and changing old behavior patterns. They include planning, controlling your own behavior, and dealing with procrastination.

Planning Your Time

Planning your time involves four primary steps. First, figure out how you currently spend your time. You can't make changes until you know what you need to change. Second, establish goals for yourself. How would you ideally like to spend your time? What would you really like to get done? Third, prioritize your goals. What goals are the most important? What do you need to accomplish first, second, and so on? The fourth step is to specify the tasks you must accomplish in order to attain each prioritized goal.

STEP 1: FIGURE OUT WHERE THE TIME GOES. The first step in time management is to figure out where all of your time goes. Are you spending too much time on some activities and not enough on others? Are you avoiding unappealing tasks you know you should be doing? Do you dawdle? Do you spend more time than you think you should watching *General Hospital, One Life to Live, Beavis and Butthead,* or *Wheel of Fortune?*

Your first task in time management is to figure out

how much time you spend pursuing or not pursuing various activities. Figure 15.2 illustrates one method for achieving this. First, draw a circle representing a typical twenty-four-hour workday. Estimate exactly how you spend your time during that day. How much time do you usually spend sleeping? Studying? Working? Lying around doing nothing? Circle A in figure 15.2 shows how one individual illustrated approximate time spent on various activities (or lack of activities).

After completing your visual depiction of how you actually spend a day, draw another circle of the same size. Divide this circle to illustrate how you would ideally like to spend your day. Would you like to spend more time studying and working? Would you prefer to decrease your lazy time? Circle B in figure 15.2 demonstrates how the same individual would ideally prefer to spend his time. He deletes being lazy and watching television. Instead, he increases studying and working time and adds a shorter relaxing category. In a similar manner your own circle should provide a rough idea of how you spend your time and how you would like to. You should be able to identify both how you waste your time and how you ideally want to spend it.

Another more detailed and time-consuming technique for analyzing how you spend your time is keeping an hourly, half-hour, or fifteen-minute segment record of how you spend your time. Keeping such a log, (many professionals such as lawyers typically do) allows you to ''keep a record of what you do and how long each task takes'' (Filley, 1978, p. 126). Highlight 15.2 depicts a format for accomplishing this. You might choose to track your time for only one day or for several days. Depending on how detailed you want your findings, you could record how time is spent for fifteen-minute, one-half hour, or hour periods. Highlight 15.2 shows how to begin tracking fifteen-minute blocks. You would then continue this process to cover a twenty-four-hour period. You probably would simply block out whatever period or periods of time you spend sleeping. In any event, this approach should provide you with a fairly accurate picture of how you spend your time. It should pinpoint for you those periods when you waste time. Subsequently, this information can be a guide to those time periods over which you want to gain greater control.

We assume here that you are a student. Therefore, your time-tracking will be substantially different than if you were working in a full-time professional social

Figure 15.2
Where Does All the Time Go?

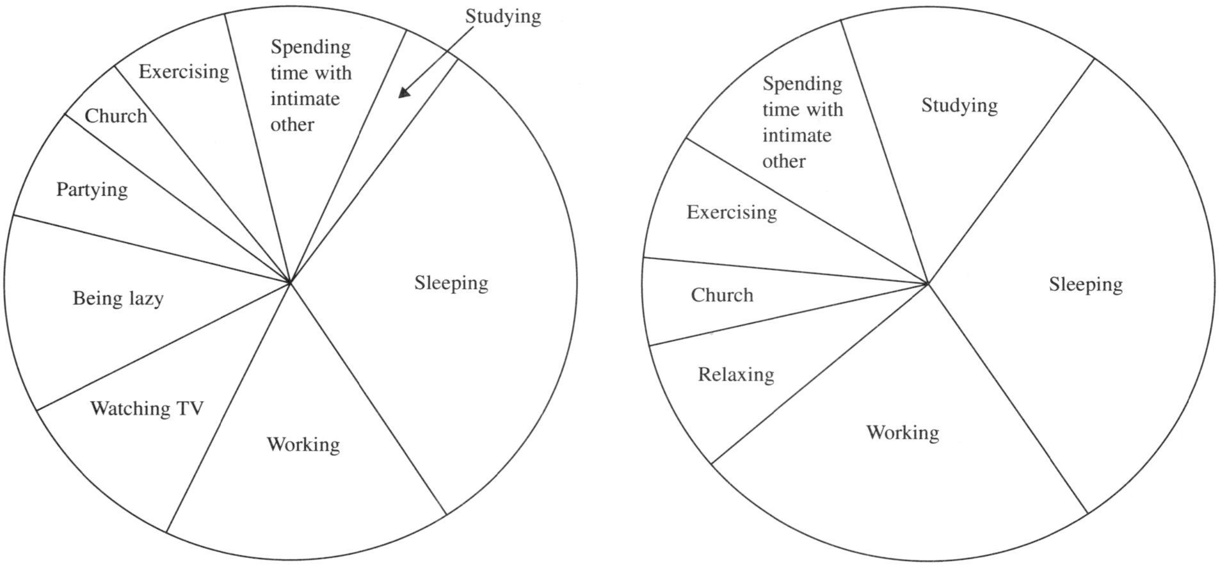

**Circle A: An Example of Unmanaged Time
Spent in a Typical Weekday**

Circle B: An Example of an Ideally Time-Managed Day

Source: Kirst-Ashman, K., & Zastrow, C., *Student Manual of Classroom Exercises and Study Guide for Understanding Human Behavior and the Social Environment*, 2nd ed. (Chicago: Nelson-Hall, 1990), pp. 133–35.

work position. However, many of the methods used to gain control over your time at this period of your life are identical to those you can use to gain control over your agency work time.

STEP 2: ESTABLISH GOALS FOR YOURSELF. One reason that people fail to use time wisely is that they simply do not set goals for themselves. They drift in time from day to day, maybe getting things done and maybe not. Therefore, one of the primary steps in time management is to establish goals.

You have already begun to explore how you actually spend your time. You should also have begun to think about how you might improve your time management. At this point it is helpful to establish specific goals for how you would like to spend your time. In this context, "goals are statements about what you want to accomplish with your time" (Curtis & Detert, 1981, p. 193).

Arbitrarily, we will divide time up into daily units. The point is for you to get a perspective of what you would like to accomplish on a short-term basis. Of course, you can use the same technique to establish longer-term goals of a week, a month, three months, a year, two years, or whatever. You can set goals for virtually any period of time. The intent of this exercise is to teach you the goal-setting and decision-making procedure. Highlight 15.3 gives you a format for doing this. Identify your goals using this format. An earlier chapter discussed the importance of establishing measurable goals. This is a good thing to keep in mind when establishing any type of goal, ranging from your own personal time management to major macro goals. For example, a goal stating "improve my personality" is pretty difficult to measure, but a goal to "give a genuine compliment to two colleagues today" is easier to monitor.

Note that your goals as a student will be different than your goals as a full-time professional social worker. However, once again, you can use these same proce-

---

HIGHLIGHT 15.2

TIME-TRACKING

Day: _____

Time Segment	**How Time Was Spent**
6:00 A.M.	_____
6:15 A.M.	_____
6:30 A.M.	_____
6:45 A.M.	_____
7:00 A.M.	_____
7:15 A.M.	_____
7:30 A.M.	_____
7:45 A.M.	_____

(Continue this process in a similar manner to account for your time during a full twenty-four-hour period.)

---

dures to manage your work time and workload in the future. Highlight 15.3 lists spaces for ten possible goals. The number of goals is arbitrary. You could list two, ten, or whatever number you wish.

STEP 3: PRIORITIZE YOUR GOALS. We have discussed some of the stress-producing situations that occur when people don't effectively manage their time. Some lead to people becoming overwhelmed and immobilized when confronted with a cluster of goals all at one time. Therefore, after identifying goals, prioritize them according to their importance. One common method of prioritizing is the ABC method (Curtis & Detert, 1981; Lakein, 1973). This method directs you to assign a value A, B, or C to each goal you cite. "A" goals are those you absolutely want to get done no matter what. These are top priority goals.

"C" goals on the other hand, are unimportant goals. They might be things that you would like to accomplish, but in all likelihood never will. You might want to write the first forty pages of the great American novel today. Or you think it would be nice to call your four best friends from high school by tonight. If you don't really think a "nice" goal is important or don't really think you'll get around to it today, drop it. Don't waste precious time worrying about things that you cannot or will not do. "C" goals often get relegated to the circular file.

"B" goals lie between "A" and "C" goals. You think you do need to get them done pretty soon, but you really do not think you'll have time to do them today. Frequently, today's "B" goal becomes tomorrow's "A" goal. This happens as a deadline approaches or your anxiety increases. If you can't decide whether a goal should be "A" or "B," automatically assign it a "B" (Curtis & Detert, 1981). If you're not certain that it's critical enough to be an "A" goal, it probably isn't.

Now, further prioritize each category of goals. Among the "A" goals that you absolutely feel you must get done, determine which one is the most critical life-or-death goal to attain today. Make this goal "A1."

HIGHLIGHT 15.3

PLANNING TIME-MANAGEMENT GOALS

Identify up to ten things you would like to accomplish today. (Remember that goals don't have to be set up on a daily basis. They can be for weeks, months, or years, depending on the unit of time over which you wish to gain control.)

1. _____   6. _____
2. _____   7. _____
3. _____   8. _____
4. _____   9. _____
5. _____   10. _____

Continue through your "A" goals, numbering them in order of priority. When finished, do the same thing first with your "B" goals, and ultimately with your "C" goals. This should provide you with a clearly prioritized plan for how to go about your day. First, pursue goal "A1," then "A2," and so on down the line. Highlight 15.4 illustrates one person's goal planning for one day.

Note that you can prioritize goals in at least three major life areas including "self, work, and family" (Curtis & Detert, 1981, p. 199). You can do this either separately or on one prioritized list. Highlight 15.4 includes goals in all three areas. Priorities are arbitrary depending on the individual's value system. The goals specified here would probably significantly differ from those you would formulate for yourself. But then again, maybe not.

Highlight 15.5 illustrates a potential prioritized goal list for a professional social worker working in a health-care center for the elderly. As we discussed, you can establish goals for virtually any area of your life.

STEP 4: SPECIFY TASKS FOR EACH GOAL. After prioritizing your goals, it is helpful to list the specific tasks needed to accomplish each goal (Curtis & Detert, 1981; Filley, 1978). A hospital social worker might identify the goal of arranging Ms. Jones's transfer from the hospital to a nursing home. She arbitrarily labels this goal "A1." Specific tasks to accomplish this

particular goal might include notifying Ms. Jones's son and daughter, locating an appropriate nursing home, arranging transportation, working out financial arrangements, and notifying the nursing staff that arrangements are complete.

Obviously, these tasks need to be accomplished in a particular order. For example, you arrange transportation only after you know the nursing home in which the client will be placed. Thus, it is probably wise to assign numerical priority to each task to guide your progress from one task to the next.

It is also important to leave sufficient time to complete each step. Think ahead and try to estimate how much time each step will most likely take. Do not allow one half hour to transport Ms. Jones to the nursing home if the hospital is forty-five minutes from the home—forty-five minutes, that is when there is no summer road construction and you aren't traveling during rush hour. In this case, it would be better to allow an hour and a half for the task.

Get Control of Your Own Behavior

What do we mean by controlling your own behavior? Doesn't everyone automatically control what he or she does everyday? The answer is no.

We have already discussed why planning is neces-

HIGHLIGHT 15.4

PRIORITIZED PLAN FOR
"A DAY IN MY LIFE"

The following is an example of one individual's daily goals, listed in an unprioritized order. They are followed by their designated "ABC" and numerical assignments.

Day: Monday

1. Finish Statistics assignment due Tuesday for class A3
2. Take Harry to the doctor A1
3. Go to aerobics class B5
4. Talk to Professor Tuffgrade regarding research project B1
5. Work at Wal-Mart for four hours A4
6. Write Myrtle C3
7. Play poker B3
8. Clean the bathroom B4
9. Clean the refrigerator C2
10. Go to class A2
11. Buy beer for poker game B2
12. Watch *The Young and the Restless* C1
13. Call Mom B6

---

sary for effective time management. However, time management involves more than planning daily goals. It requires following a number of principles that guide your choices for goal-planning. These principles include, committing yourself to the time management process; evaluating your actual job requirements; clustering similar activities together; using a calendar; handling each sheet of paper only once; delegating any tasks you can; avoiding doing other people's work; bringing order to your desk; developing time management systems; planning time for contemplation; designating leisure time; managing meetings effectively; managing your correspondence appropriately; using the phone efficiently; and reviewing your weekly progress.

LOOK AT YOURSELF. Develop a time management perspective. Instead of falling prey to the various stresses discussed earlier, look yourself right in the eye and commit to time management. Sheafor et al. (1991) suggest: "Come to terms with your 'inner rebellion'

toward the use of time management principles. Do not hide behind the claim that you are too busy to get organized, and do not mistake motion for work. Some people appear extremely busy because they are always in motion. But activity does not always mean that something is being accomplished. Clear goals and an understanding of the tasks to be achieved must precede the activity" (p. 109).

UNDERSTAND YOUR JOB. If you have a job, of course, you understand it, right? Not necessarily. We have established that most positions typically have job descriptions indicating what you are paid to do. However, many social work jobs are complicated. They involve not only your micro and mezzo obligations to clients, but also your macro responsibilities to your agency and community. They involve a lot of discretion regarding what you should do and how. Discuss with your supervisor what your job description really is: what are your specific responsibilities (Sheafor, Horejsi, &

```
┌─────────────────────────────────────────────────────────┐
│                    HIGHLIGHT 15.5                         │
│                                                           │
│              PRIORITIZED PLAN FOR                         │
│            A PROFESSIONAL WORKDAY                         │
└─────────────────────────────────────────────────────────┘
```

The numbered items to the left below comprise a nursing home social worker's unprioritized goal list for one workday. The arbitrarily prioritized "ABC" and numerical standings are depicted to the right of each goal below.

Day: Monday

1. Finish last week's progress notes C1
2. Call Sybil about Ms. Sicperson A1
3. Meet with supervisor B1
4. Get resources for Mr. Ed B2
5. Take Ms. Harrington to her daughter-in-law's A2
6. Complete resource file C2
7. Attend two-hour in-service B3
8. Run social support group A3

Horejsi, 1991)? Allow her or him to help you make decisions regarding how to prioritize goals and the respective tasks necessary to achieve them.

BUNCH SIMILAR ACTIVITIES TOGETHER. Sometimes, it is helpful to block portions of time for completing similar types of tasks (Filley, 1978). Some social workers set aside a specific day for doing paperwork. Others identify a portion of each day for tasks such as returning all phone calls. Concentrating on completing a cluster of similar tasks often saves the mental energy of switching from one orientation to another. It would probably be inefficient for you to spend every other fifteen minutes switching from studying policy to studying research. Focusing on one until you have completed your assignment and then moving on to the other is probably a much more coherent approach.

USE A CALENDAR. Using a calendar does not mean just writing your appointments down. Employing a calendar means establishing a whole new perspective on time. Instead of trying to keep everything in your head, look at your calendar and let it guide you. It can tell you whether or not you have time to assume additional responsibilities. When someone asks you if you can do something, consult your calendar to see if you have sufficient time to undertake whatever tasks the new responsibility involves. Consider such factors as the time it will take to go from one responsibility to another. Agreeing to do something for which you do not have sufficient time results in overscheduling, a source of stress for many people.

Calendars come in many formats including daily, weekly, or monthly. It doesn't matter which you choose. Select whatever format suits your needs and preferences best. Use your calendar as a record of your work. Check off appointments which have been kept. Jot down mileage to and from appointments. Insert notes that will save you time, such as the room number of a hospitalized patient or the directions to your client's house.

The goal is to make your calendar an indispensable tool for managing your time. The calendar should go with you everywhere, along with an address book. In emergencies you will have at your disposal both a means to reach people and your calendar. If you find yourself running behind, take a minute to call and notify your next appointment. If you do this, you will feel less pressure to race to your next stop. Both clients and colleagues will appreciate knowing your reasons for being late.

HANDLE EACH SHEET OF PAPER ONLY ONCE. Handle each sheet of paper only once? What do you mean only once? Many people might respond to this suggestion in a similar manner. However, think about it. How much time can you waste reading a sheet of paper, putting it on your desk, losing it, thinking about it again, finding it on your desk, reading it again, and so on? Generally, if you don't have time to focus your attention on that piece of paper right now, keep it until another period in your day when you will have time to address it. You probably should take some time as soon as possible because the letter or memo might be important. It might be a deadline notification from your supervisor or possibly a termination notice. Who knows? Making time for such activities highlights the importance of planning time for thinking and for responding to relevant correspondence.

An example of a colleague comes to mind. Sam is an avoider. If he is forced to take notes, they are typically brief and vague. Sam feels it's too difficult to both take notes and pay attention to what's going on. In one particular situation, he was recording the recommendations made at an important staff meeting. It was his turn. All other participants had already assumed similar responsibilities at other meetings. After the meeting, Sam got up, said he would finish the notes later, and left for his office. Days passed. Weeks dragged by. Meanwhile, in Sam's office, his sketchy notes drifted among the mounds of other paperwork on his paper-strewn desk. Occasionally, the notes surfaced, Sam looked at them, and then he put them down to submerge themselves once again. Finally, after several other staff members reminded Sam about his task, he finished the notes. He complained energetically about how difficult this task was. He whined about how hard it was to remember what occurred weeks ago. Sam's notes were vague and, in essence, altered. Sam wrote down what he thought he remembered from the meeting held weeks ago. The record was so bad that staff had to hold the same meeting all over again. This time participants did not ask Sam to assume any note-taking responsibility.

Sam is also a procrastinator. A later portion of this chapter discusses procrastination in greater depth including what to do about it.

DELEGATE. Too often, it is easy to feel that in order to get something done right, you have to do it yourself. Instead, if at all possible, delegate (Filley, 1978). Delegating simply means assigning responsibilities to someone else. We have discussed delegation in the context of supervision, as a critical supervisory skill. Although it is probably easier for a supervisor to "assign" tasks to someone else, you can still watch for your own opportunities to do so. Is there some repetitive task that your secretary (or administrative assistant) might be able to do as part of her or his job? Are there volunteers or students available to help you?

Delegating of course, requires defining what needs to be done with sufficient clarity that another person can complete the job. Next, leave the initiative with the delegates. If you tell people exactly how to do a job, you limit their creativity and further involve yourself in details that should be left to others. Don't forget to thank people and reward them for doing the job right. Like you, most people appreciate praise, acknowledgment, and other forms of recognition.

DON'T DO OTHER PEOPLE'S WORK. In time management, the flip side of delegating is making certain you do your work and your work only, not that of other people (Sheafor et al., 1991). Consider Sam, the procrastinator mentioned a few paragraphs ago. People who regularly fail, do a poor job, or never really learn how to complete a task can be very manipulative. Others learn that they are not dependable. Therefore, they get out of a lot of work. Colleagues no longer ask Sam to take notes at meetings because he inevitably "screws it up." Thus, he does less work, and his colleagues take up the slack and do more.

If you tend to have high expectations for the quality of work, be vigilant that you do not end up doing other people's work because you do it better or more effectively than they do. Think in terms of each individual being responsible for her or his own tasks and failings.

BRING ORDER TO YOUR DESK. Remember the adage, "A messy desk reflects a messy mind." No one knows if this is really true. However, organizing items on your desk so you can find them easily is a time saver (Sheafor, Horejsi, & Horejsi, 1991). Additionally, if you follow the prior suggestion of handling each sheet of paper only once, organizing your desk will be easier. Instead of allowing documents to drift amid an ocean of paper, you will deal with each paper once and put it in its resting place.

Another aspect of bringing order to your desk is making sure the information you use frequently is readily at your disposal (Sheafor, Horejsi, & Horejsi, 1991). You might have your telephone and address book with frequently used contacts in an obvious place. Likewise, you might retain certain forms, files, or manuals that you find particularly useful in a manila folder in your top stacking file or your top desk drawer. Saving time involves wasting as little as possible on useless activities like looking for lost or hard-to-find information.

DEVELOP A SYSTEM. Develop some kind of system whereby you can keep track of your deadlines (Sheafor, Horejsi, & Horejsi, 1991). You can note deadlines on your regular monthly calendar. Perhaps what works best for you is to have a large monthly calendar as a desk pad or hanging over your desk. Your system might be more sophisticated, using a computer program. Try various methods. Whatever works for you is the best system.

LEAVE TIME FOR COMPTEMPLATION. Even with an ever so busy schedule, allow yourself some "down" time each workday (Filley, 1978). You need time to organize your thoughts and evaluate your progress toward your designated goals. If you are constantly harried and distracted, you can't focus as well on the tasks and goals at hand.

DESIGNATE LEISURE TIME FOR YOURSELF. Workaholics often burn out and have heart attacks at young ages. Incorporate some leisure time into your schedule on a regular basis. What happens when you don't do this? Have you ever forced yourself to complete task after task after task with no relief in sight? Did you, perhaps, finally find yourself saying, "To heck with it" and end up doing nothing at all?

It is important to gain a realistic perspective on your time. Time with friends, family, and yourself alone are all important facets of life. If you control this and use such good time to reward yourself for work, you may find yourself working much more eagerly and effectively.

For example, we knew a student who would study like crazy virtually all day—in addition to going to class, of course—from about 9:00 A.M. to 9:00 P.M. However,

unless she had an exam the following day, at 9:00 P.M. she would abruptly stop whatever she was doing and go off either to play sheepshead (a card game unique to Wisconsin and Minnesota) or to party until about midnight. She made a point of not feeling guilty about having fun because she already had put her work time in. She felt she deserved some reward and relief.

MANAGE MEETINGS EFFECTIVELY. Most social workers have many chances to arrange, conduct, and participate in meetings, which occur any time two or more people come together for some designated purpose, usually to pursue some type of goal. Meetings involving social workers can range from staffings, where particular clients' progress is discussed, to task groups, where a variety of professionals get together to do something (such as propose amendments to social work certification requirements), to large political meetings, where political tactics are discussed. Regardless of the meeting type, there are numerous ways to use the time more efficiently and productively. Filley (1978) suggests using the following time management techniques regularly when participating in meetings.

1. *Start meetings on time.* Don't wait for stragglers. If you set the time for the meeting at 3:00 P.M., start promptly at 3:00 P.M. Doing this rewards those who are on time and teaches latecomers that you are serious about the schedule of the meeting. Time is important. Don't waste the time of people who have taken the trouble to arrive on time. Only the hardcore dalliers continue to arrive late once they learn that your meetings start on time. If you are a group member instead of the leader, suggest assertively to those in charge that they begin the meeting as scheduled. In this way you can help to modify and improve their behavior as well.

2. *State the ending time at the start.* Right at the beginning, let people know when the meeting will end. If you stick to that time, you are more likely to stay on task. Structuring meeting times establishes time boundaries. Participants should have a clear idea of how much time they have so that they can pace the meeting and achieve its goals. Establishing a time frame also makes it easier for you to conclude the meeting, since participants automatically anticipate the meeting's end. Conversely, don't allow meetings to go on endlessly. Do not be afraid to end a meeting early if your work is done. Some of the most productive meetings dwindle off to a vague

conclusion because no one suggests ending them when the real business is completed.

3. *Preschedule regular meetings.* Set your meeting times far in advance so people can plan their schedules around them. This increases the likelihood of good attendance. It also communicates to others that you realize they are busy and respect their time.

4. *Distribute printed matter well before the meeting.* Never expect meeting participants to read and understand lengthy written material handed out at the start of a meeting. Send any relevant material to meeting participants well in advance. Also, make sure they receive an agenda along with any other material so they know in what order the meeting will address this material.

5. *Hold meetings in meeting rooms—not in your office.* The setting of meetings is important. Hold meetings in locations that enhance participants' ability to discuss and get things done. There should be plenty of room, and chairs should be comfortable, if at all possible. All participants should have adequate space to write and organize their materials. Considering these suggestions, your office is probably not an ideal place to meet, unless you are a large agency's director with a meeting room attached to your office. Another bad thing about meeting in your office is that it becomes more difficult to terminate the meeting. Telling people to "get out" isn't very nice, and you can't simply say, "Well I have to go to my office now. See you later." In addition, office meetings can be interrupted more easily by phone calls and people who drop by to chat.

6. *Don't hold meetings and eat simultaneously.* Trying to conduct meetings over meals is not productive. Most people find it difficult to concentrate on eating, talking, listening, and thinking, all at the same time. Either eat first and get on with business, or schedule the meal following your work session. This may serve as a reinforcer for completing the work on time since people will look forward to finishing the task and then eating. Besides, as soon as I eat, I feel like taking a nap. Therefore, eating first doesn't help my concentration. Sometimes, refreshment "breaks" can help people get through exceptionally long meetings.

MANAGE YOUR CORRESPONDENCE. Since correspondence (letters, memos, announcements, and advertising) can consume a major portion of our busy time, it is appropriate to consider ways to manage this efficiently. Filley (1978) makes a number of suggestions to facilitate the efficient handling of paperwork.

1. *Use handwritten replies.* Write out short replies, if possible, instead of wasting time having such replies dictated and typed. Making replies on the original correspondence and returning a copy of it to the sender also saves time and paper, and reduces filing space. This latter technique makes certain that the original letter and the response are always together. However, *always* keep a copy of what you send. Many office correspondence forms have several layers allowing the sender to keep a copy of her reply. However, if yours do not, make a copy, even if that delays your response. Otherwise, especially if a deluge of paperwork typically crosses your desk, you may not remember what you said or, worse yet, whether you responded to the correspondence at all.

2. *Use form letters for standard correspondence.* If you routinely receive requests for similar information or need to send many people the same message, consider using form letters. A form letter is a prewritten correspondence. It usually either addresses answers to questions commonly asked or provides information frequently requested. Instead of "reinventing the wheel" and writing a totally new response each time, use form letters. You can even put a group of such form letters in a loose-leaf notebook. This way you can easily give your secretary a copy of the appropriate form letter. Of course, if you have your own office personal computer, you have ready access to consistent response formats. You can easily tailor each one to the individual recipient if you want to.

3. *Don't reread and sign your correspondence.* This suggestion applies to work contexts where secretaries or typists complete final drafts of correspondence, not where workers use their own personal computers. Don't waste time rereading your correspondence and signing it yourself. Much of the time saved by dictating correspondence is wasted when the document is proofread and signed. Make it clear that you expect the typist to proofread the document for clarity, spelling, punctuation, and similar items. The typist should then sign for you. Only when the typist is confused about something you have dictated should she consult you. If you're typing your own correspondence, spell-checker programs are great.

4. *Open second and third class mail once a week.* Second and third class mail includes the "junk mail"

we get at home and at the office. It is probably not important enough to make a real claim on our time. You should either immediately throw it out without opening it or bunch it together and save it until you have a small block of slow time. Such slow time might include lunch if you're having it at your desk, time waiting for an appointment to appear, or time at the end of the day when you are simply too "bushed" to do anything more difficult and productive.

If you doubt the efficacy of these suggestions, try this experiment. Save all your junk mail in a box for a week or two. When you open it, count the items you think are important. How many of them affected your day-to-day work as a social worker? How many of them had any importance in your personal life? The chances are good that most, if not all, of this material is of limited or no value.

USE THE PHONE EFFICIENTLY. Consider using conference calls instead of holding meetings. Conference calls are especially effective if the main reason for the meeting is to consult or to give information. Meetings take travel time, and much time is wasted getting started. Conference calls can be set up by the phone company and managed at much less cost than many meetings.

Outline your phone calls before dialing. Think about what you want to say and note the most important points on a piece of paper. This will help you use your phone time efficiently and ensure that you cover everything you had planned to.

REVIEW YOUR WEEKLY PROGRESS. At each week's end, review the extent to which you actually achieved your time-management goals. Were you on target? Or, did you overestimate (or underestimate) what you could accomplish for the week? How did this past week and the progress you made relate to your longer-term goals? Should your goals for next week be higher, lower, or about the same?

To get a perspective on time management for life, it is sometimes helpful to stop and ask yourself, "Is this the very best way I can be spending my time right now?" Periodically addressing this issue can help orient you to your life's broader picture. You might find yourself working two hours overtime to get those rotten progress notes done while you are missing your ninety-one-

year-old grandmother's birthday dinner. At such times, what really is most important to you? Does your quest for effective time management overshadow something else you might be doing that is really more important to you?

A related question to ask yourself occasionally is, "If I were faced with death this very moment, what would I regret?" Is there someone close to you that you haven't contacted for too long a time? Have you managed to avoid making your will? Whatever your concerns might be, confronting yourself like this can help you manage major life priorities. Perhaps people in your family are important to you. The old cliché is that time passes too quickly. Small children quickly grow up and move away. Old people get older and die. Is there time you should be spending with someone now—or soon—before it's too late?

POSTSCRIPT. Following these suggestions will help you use time more effectively. Since we can't manufacture time, we have to ensure that we use it as efficiently as possible. The multiple responsibilities of social workers require that we adopt strategies to help us do our jobs better. Time management is just one of those strategies.

Procrastination

We have established that time management involves both planning and getting control of your own behavior. The third major time-management dimension is fighting the tendency to procrastinate. To procrastinate simply means "to put off intentionally [and, sometimes, habitually] the doing of something that should be done" (*Webster's Ninth Collegiate Dictionary*, 1991, p. 938). Most of us, perhaps all of us, put off what we're supposed to do at some time or another. No one is totally faultless. However, when procrastination interferes with your ability to accomplish your goals in a significant or ongoing manner, then you are no longer in control. To gain control of your time you can implement a number of techniques for fighting procrastination.

REASONS FOR PROCRASTINATION. There are at least three reasons for procrastination. First, there is the quest for flawlessness. Some people cannot tolerate being anything but 100 percent perfect. Since no one is that perfect, this sets people up for failure. If you can't do it perfectly, why do it at all? Such an attitude prevents people from accomplishing their goals. Another aspect of the quest for flawlessness is putting the task off until another time. Perhaps you know that you will have to complete the task sometime. However, it is so aversive right now (because you want to do it flawlessly) that it's easier to worry about the whole thing later.

A second reason for procrastination is "fear of failure" (Curtis & Detert, 1981, p. 205). It is no news flash that our society places extremely high value on success. We generally do not want to fail, no matter what. If you feel that you may fail to accomplish a task, it can be easier to avoid the task altogether.

A third reason for procrastination is feeling overwhelmed. If you perceive a task as awesomely difficult, and perhaps even scary, it may be easier for you to avoid it altogether than to do it and get it over with. A fourth reason for procrastination is nonassertive overacceptance of responsibilities. People who just can't say no to requests can easily overextend themselves. Trying to get too much done can distract you from getting anything done at all. We have discussed how easy it is to become overwhelmed, unable to focus on anything adequately, and immobilized.

The fifth reason for procrastination is idling away your time with useless "busy-ness." You can avoid completing a task by doing something else and keeping busy. Busy-ness can provide you with an excuse for not doing what you're supposed to. For example, you might have to complete a research paper for one of your classes, and you hate doing research papers. You can avoid the actual writing of the paper by spending scores of hours in the library searching through literally stacks of articles.

THE CONS OF PROCRASTINATION. Sometimes it seems that procrastination is your best choice. It allows you to avoid some unpleasant work. However, there are at least four reasons why procrastination is unappealing (Lakein, 1973). First, it's probably best that you complete your own task rather than passing it on to someone else. Shirking responsibility is irritating to people. Others may not do the task the way you want it done or know it should be done. Additionally, you

can get a bad reputation as someone who cannot effectively complete assigned work.

A second con of procrastination is that unappealing tasks probably won't go away. They usually remain wedged in your consciousness, nagging you to get at them. Doing the task and getting it over with stops this bothersome nagging. The third procrastination con is the unfortunate fact that unappealing tasks rarely get any easier. If anything, the longer you put off a task, the harder it gets. Maybe you will forget some of the details. Possibly the task will increase in complexity as time goes on. The fourth and perhaps worst thing about procrastination is that the longer you put something off, the more aversive it becomes. If it seems like it's bad to start out with, it will only get worse.

BATTLING PROCRASTINATION. We have established that procrastination is a common problem plaguing most of us at some time or another. So, what exactly do you do about it? There are several suggested techniques including the "swiss cheese" approach, doing the worst job first, and doing whatever it is right now.

1. *The "swiss cheese" approach.* Lakein (1973, p. 71) suggests that you can often drastically reduce procrastination when you break up a large threatening task into a number of smaller, more manageable tasks. Even if you start doing a task for only five minutes, you are still combating procrastination and getting greater control over your time.

Suppose you have to write a twenty-page term paper. Thinking in terms of the entire gigantic paper—including all the research, thinking, and typing involved—can be paralyzing. Instead, divide the process into smaller, more doable pieces. First, go to the library and find some sources. Second, take notes on notecards from these sources. Third, make an outline of topics as the skeleton of your paper. Fourth, arrange your notecards in the order that you think you will use them. Fifth, sit down and type a rough draft. Sixth, edit that draft. Seventh, type your final draft. When thinking about these seven smaller tasks, don't envision yourself doing them all at once. Picture yourself doing them on different days at various times. As you complete each task, you will gain the satisfaction that task completion can give you. At the same time, you will be chipping away at completion of the final project.

HIGHLIGHT 15.6

SELF-ANALYSIS
OF PROCRASTINATION

1. What tasks do you procrastinate over?
2. What are your reasons for procrastinating over them? Why do you find them aversive?
3. What tactics can you use to control your procrastinating behavior?
4. When will you begin implementing these tactics?

---

2. *Do the worst job first.* Often anticipating a tough job keeps you from ever getting it done. Doing the job immediately means that other, less unappealing tasks will look better and easier in comparison. The other advantage of doing tough jobs first is that it ensures sufficient time to see the job through to completion. Saving the hard jobs until the end of the day often means that they don't get done.

3. *Complete whatever it is you start* (Filley, 1982). Coming back to an old project or task requires taking the time to get oriented to it again. You will probably need to waste precious time rethinking what you have already done. If you pick up an article to read, finish reading it. If you put it down and pick it up again later, you will probably have to reread the beginning to get yourself oriented again. If you begin working on a letter or social history, finish it before turning your attention to other tasks. If you don't build the habit of doing this, you will find your desk full of half-finished projects, most of which are probably overdue. Be persistent, even dogged, about finishing a task.

4. *Do it right now.* How many times have you heard friends say that they're going to quit smoking, lose twenty pounds, stop drinking, or study harder—some day? What have you noticed about these comments and these people's plans? Well, for one thing when they say they're going to do something, they obviously have not done it yet. Framing plans in the *going to* perspective is a good way to procrastinate.

We have a friend who is going to write a novel someday. She barely writes letters, but she is going to write that important novel. She's been going to do it for about fifteen years now. One minor related problem is that she can't spell very well and needs a lot of help with her grammar. A suggestion for becoming a good writer is to write—write a lot. Write right now. It need only be a page or two a day, but do it. Forcing yourself to do whatever your task is right now can save you a lot of wasted energy and worry (Curtis & Detert, 1982).

Chapter Summary

This chapter focuses on both stress and time management. Both are addressed here as they are integrally involved with how you will function in the macro environment. The General Adaptation Syndrome is explained, as is the agency context for stress. Stress-related problems including physiological, psychological, and behavioral are reviewed.

Three primary approaches to stress management are proposed and discussed: changing the stressful event; altering your thinking about the stressor; and utilizing any or all of a variety of specific stress management techniques. The latter include relaxation approaches, exercise, and seeking out pleasurable goodies.

The relationship between poor time management and stress is explored. Personal styles in dealing with time are identified. Three approaches to time management are proposed. First, planning your time involves assessing how you spend time, establishing goals for yourself, prioritizing these goals, and specifying necessary tasks to complete each goal. Second, getting control of your own behavior entails implementing a wide variety of specific techniques including: examining your own behavior and motivation; understanding your job requirements; bunching similar activities together; using a calendar; handling each sheet of paper once; delegating work appropriately; avoiding other people's work; organizing your desk; developing a system; allowing some time for thought; designating leisure time; managing meetings effectively; handling your correspondence appropriately; using the phone efficiently; and reviewing weekly progress. Third, combating procrastination requires understanding the reasons for and problems involved in procrastination. Specific suggestions for battling procrastination are proposed.

CHAPTER SIXTEEN

Resumés, Interviewing, and Getting the Job

Should your resumé be one or two pages long, or perhaps even longer?

Should you include nonprofessional, minimum- or near-minimum-wage jobs on your resumé?

Should you identify a career objective on your resumé?

How should you incorporate your field experience into a resumé? For instance, what should you call it?

What headings should you use for various sections in your resumé?

What kind of personal data, if any, should you include in your resumé?

Who should your references be?

How many references should you include?

Should you list all of your references or not?

What should a cover letter say?

When should you send cover letters?

Where do you find out what jobs are available to begin with?

How can you best prepare for an employment interview?

How should you dress for an employment interview?

How should you respond when a potential employer asks you what your greatest problem has been in a work environment?

What kind of salary should you ask for when you interview for a job?

How can you respond when asked what kind of supervision you prefer?

What can you say when an interviewer asks you to describe your primary weaknesses? What about your strengths?

How might you answer when an interviewer asks you what you want to be doing in five years?

What can you reply when asked how long you hope to stay with the agency?

Introduction

The answers (or lack of definite answers) to the questions posed above are all in this chapter. You will probably put your whole heart into seeking professional social work employment just before or immediately after graduation. This chapter addresses content relevant to getting a job. Specific sections address the assessment of your own capabilities and interests, the investigation of potential job possibilities, resumé preparation, writing of cover letters, preparing for and participating in job interviews, and follow-up on job possibilities. We address this content here in the last chapter of a macro textbook because we anticipate that you are approaching graduation. We assume that macro skills are built upon a foundation of micro and mezzo skills respectively.

Therefore, we also assume that you are nearing completion of your practice skill acquisition, at least in a formal educational setting.

This chapter will:

- Assist you in assessing your own capabilities and interests in preparation for seeking out professional employment.
- Explain how to identify and investigate professional employment possibilities.
- Propose principles for formulating your resumé.
- Respond to a range of specific questions concerning what makes the best resumé for you.
- Discuss the contents of cover letters.
- Propose suggestions for job interview preparation.
- Prepare you to answer a wide range of questions commonly asked in job interviews.
- Propose ways to follow up on job applications and interviews.
- Address briefly the appropriate manner of leaving a job.

Getting a Job

Like much of social work practice, successful job-finding is a combination of hard work and good luck. There are, of course, several steps you can take to enhance your credibility as a candidate. A document published by the National Association of Social Workers (Professional Advancement Fund, undated) suggests following six steps in the job-finding process. These include assessing your own capabilities and interests, investigating actual job possibilities, constructing a resumé and cover letter, preparing for interviews, and following up on contacts.

Typically, students not already employed in a social work position locate new positions within three months of graduation. Only about 10 percent of graduates take longer than six months to find a position. The medium length of time before locating a position is 1.40 months (Hull, Ray, Rogers, & Smith, 1993).

Assessing Your Own Capabilities and Interests

At least five areas are critical in the assessment of your own capabilities and interests (NASW Program Advancement Fund, undated). They include your competencies, accomplishments, job preferences, employ-

---

HIGHLIGHT 16.1

ASSESSING YOUR CAPABILITIES

The following areas may reflect your professional knowledge, skills, and values:

- Assessment of individual, family, group, community, and organizational problems and functioning
- Communication
- Understanding people
- Problem solving
- Decision making
- Planning
- Organizing
- Recording
- Clear thinking
- Acceptance of responsibility
- Dependability
- Pacing your efforts
- Coordination

- Case management
- Conducting meetings
- Advocacy
- Creativity
- Initiation of ideas
- Undertaking action

These concepts reflect the beginning of your capability assessment. The potential is unlimited. These are just supposed to give you some initial ideas. After giving your capabilities serious thought, write several paragraphs summarizing and prioritizing your greatest strengths. This can help you articulate for yourself (and later for potential employers) the reasons why you are and will be a capable professional.

---

ment goals, and personal attributes (pp. 2–11). You must be able to articulate these in order to construct an effective resumé and portray yourself as competent to potential employers.

What Are Your Competencies?

Competencies are your skills and abilities. What are you good at? What skills have you mastered that would enhance your performance in a professional social work setting? Think about the social work knowledge and values you have acquired and the skills you have mastered. Highlight 16.1 identifies some competencies you might consider.

What Are Your Accomplishments?

What have you achieved professionally that makes you most proud? Try to think of at least five such accomplishments. When thinking of your achievements and choosing words to use later in a resumé, it is helpful

to think in terms of clear, vivid, vibrant verbs (Bloch, 1991). Highlight 16.2 suggests a range of such words. For example, have you formulated case plans? Did you supervise volunteers? Did you initiate and implement a new policy? Did you lead a support group? The possibilities are endless.

What Are Your Job Preferences?

Ideally, if you could have the perfect job, what would it be? Think in terms of four areas: (1) the types of professional activities you would most like to pursue; (2) your preferred client population; (3) the problems you are interested in addressing; and (4) the type of agency setting in which you would like work. Answer for yourself the questions posed in highlight 16.3, which illustrates examples of each category. Note that simple identification of your preferred job characteristics does not mean that you will get that exact job or even a very similar one. However, the intent here is to help you seriously consider your own goals and career objectives. The better you know yourself, the more capable you

---

HIGHLIGHT 16.2

VIBRANT VERBS TO CAPTURE YOUR ACHIEVEMENTS

Assess	Formulate	Develop	Manage
Develop	Appraise	Supervise	Counsel
Organize	Achieve	Employ	Construct
Propose	Implement	Direct	Demonstrate
Assemble	Create	Improve	Initiate
Negotiate	Research	Analyze	Lead
Write	Design	Establish	Present
Teach	Administer	Revise	Coordinate
Plan	Evaluate	Solve	Examine

---

will be of presenting yourself to others (such as potential employers) and of making decisions about what job to pursue and accept.

What Are Your Employment Goals?

This question concerns the context of employment. What aspects of work are important to you, not including the type of social work skills you use or population you serve? You might put this another way: what aspects of your working environment would motivate you to perform and encourage you to like your job? Highlight 16.4 lists a range of work dimensions that may be of varying importance to you.

What Are Your Positive Personal Attributes?

The final critical area in the assessment of your own ability is that of your personal attributes. What qualities do you manifest that make you an excellent job candidate? Figure 5.7, ''Evaluating Personal Characteristics for Macro Practice'' (see chapter 5), provides a format for looking at and evaluating yourself.

Are you dedicated, hard working, responsible, ar-

ticulate, punctual, assertive, active, or helpful? Are there other positive qualities you can describe? What are your weaknesses? When beginning a job search, it is extremely important to know yourself well. You will have to write honest, straightforward cover letters, answer pointed questions posed by potential employers, and make hard decisions about whether some job really is right for you or not.

Investigating Actual Job Possibilities

Finding out about possible job openings can be easy or difficult, depending upon several factors. Many of these factors are beyond your control. Some states prepare lists of county and state social work openings and update them periodically. Other states have no centralized registry for jobs. There, students probably search for openings in local newspapers. Some state NASW chapters advertise positions in their monthly bulletins or newsletters. Sometimes these chapters advertise, primarily for MSW positions. In still other states, licensing or certification laws may require that graduating students pass a test before being eligible for appointment as a social worker. States' lack of uniformity makes it exceedingly difficult to give anything but general advice to you as the job seeker.

Identifying your job preferences is important to your career satisfaction. The social worker pictured here always wanted to work with the elderly.

Using Newspapers

According to an ongoing study by one of the authors, many social work graduates find jobs through newspapers and other news media. Thirty-three percent of graduates from large BSW programs located jobs through the news media (G. H. Hull, Personal communication, April 21, 1995). This figure is not uncommon for one simple reason. Most public and private social work openings appear in local newspapers even if they're also listed in other job publications in the state. Thus, you would be wise to target this source first. Since many smaller communities lack a newspaper or have papers with more limited audiences, administrators often advertise in the newspapers of nearby larger cities. So, for example, a social work position in Fort Atkinson, Wisconsin (a small town near Madison, the state's capital), might be advertised in the Madison newspapers. Similar arrangements abound throughout the United States.

Most university and college libraries have a collection of newspapers from various areas within the state or region. So do many public libraries. Locating this resource is a useful step toward collecting information about available openings. This is an excellent source of information about jobs in other states in case you are interested in relocating to another geographical area.

Once you have identified the appropriate newspapers, look carefully for job announcements under a range of categories. A given paper might have no listing under the title "social worker." Instead, these positions might be found under such labels as Counselor, Group worker, Case worker, Probation and parole officer, Youth worker, Medical social worker, Alcohol and other drug counselor, Case manager, Protective services worker, Youth counselor, Juvenile court intake worker, Job coach, Community support worker, Cofacilitator, Residential counselor, Surveillance officer, Public health advisor, or Director. Be creative when

---

HIGHLIGHT 16.3

JOB PREFERENCES

1. What types of professional activities are you most interested in pursuing? Prioritize the following.

_____Counseling	_____Supervising volunteers
_____Brokering resources	_____Writing grants
_____Running groups	_____Case management
_____Management	_____Supervising staff
_____Community organizing	_____Lobbying
_____Program evaluation	_____Research
_____Public relations	_____Fundraising
_____Running meetings	_____Training staff
_____Budgeting	_____Policy development
_____General administrative activities	_____Advocacy
_____Other _____	

2. If you had your "druthers," what client population would you prefer to work with? Prioritize the following.

_____Children	_____Other client populations (specify)_____
_____Young adults	_____Teenagers
_____Elderly people	_____Middle-aged adults
_____Women	_____Married couples
_____Intact families	_____Men
_____Minority groups (specify)_____	_____Single parents

---

you think about the wide range of specific job titles social workers can have.

Since the titles are often of little help in revealing exactly what the job entails, you are better off to read the entire announcement before deciding whether you are interested. Since classified ads in many larger newspapers are divided into subsections (such as professional, general, and sales), it is important to search each section carefully. One social work position might be advertised under the "Professional" heading and another under the "Health Care" section. Don't take chances. Scrutinize each section closely.

One suggestion for responding to an ad is to delay for a few days after the ad appears. Sunday newspapers usually carry the most extensive array of job possibilities. Sending in your resumé and cover letter a few days

after the employer receives the bulk of responses may make yours stand out. The employer may then be in the position of reviewing yours along with other more attractive applications. She would already have had the opportunity to review most of the applications and cut the less appropriate ones.

State Merit System Lists

Some state merit systems produce periodic listings of social work openings. You can probably find the address and telephone number of the division advertising jobs in the state capital's phone directory. Look under the listing for governmental agencies. Making a phone call to this agency will quickly tell you whether such a listing

3. What problems and issues are you interested in addressing? Prioritize the following.

_____Community development	_____Crime in communities
_____Alcohol and other drugs	_____Teen pregnancy
_____Child maltreatment	_____School problems (e.g., truancy)
_____Battered women	_____Financial resource acquisition
_____Probation and parole	_____Prison
_____Mental illness	_____Couples conflict
_____Family problems	_____Unemployment
_____Vocational rehabilitation	_____Suicide prevention
_____Developmental disability	_____Physical challenge
_____Health	_____HIV/AIDS
_____Eating disorders	_____Homelessness
_____Other_____	

4. In what type of agency setting would you prefer to work? Prioritize the following.

_____Private	_____Close, directive supervision
_____Public	_____Supervision primarily on a
_____Large bureaucracy	consultation basis
_____Smaller agency	_____Hospital
_____County social services	_____School
_____Institution	_____Community organization
_____Group home	_____Prison
_____Primary social work setting	_____Family planning agency
_____Primary medical setting	_____Mental health center or counseling
_____Primary educational setting	agency
_____Serving clients with a wide range	_____Hospice
of problems	_____Shelter (for example, for homeless
_____Serving clients with specialized	people or survivors of domestic
area of problems	violence)

is available in that particular state. Any state listings are also likely to contain detailed job descriptions and other information about the jobs, such as whether a test is required for the position and when such a test will be given.

NASW Publications

Positions for MSW graduates are often included in the *NASW News*, published by the National Association of Social Workers. This newspaper, published almost monthly, lists positions by state. Occasionally, BSW positions are mentioned, but only rarely. We have already said that many state NASW chapters publish newsletters that may advertise available positions.

The secret to locating a good job position is to exercise patience in your job search and be as thorough as possible. Some people use only one source (for instance, newspapers) and then give up. They whine that they can't find anything. Job finding is work. Remember, you only need one position announcement to get that particular job. You can't necessarily know in advance where you'll find it.

Networking

Networking in the job-finding context involves establishing and nurturing linkages with other social work professionals you know. An obvious linkage is with that of colleagues at your field placement agency. Some-

---

HIGHLIGHT 16.4

EMPLOYMENT GOALS AND WORK CONTEXT

What aspects of the work environment are the most important to you? Prioritize the following.

_____Salary
_____Sick leave
_____Hours of work
_____Social work supervision
_____Geographic location
_____Potential for advancement
_____Substantial discretion in decision making
_____Low stress levels
_____Realistic recording requirements
_____Being rewarded for achievement
_____Little travel
_____Potential for new skill development
_____Competent colleagues
_____Good office

_____Vacation time
_____Health care benefits
_____Not being "on call"
_____In-service training opportunities
_____Clear job description
_____Opportunity to function independently
_____Challenging environment
_____Good relationships with colleagues
_____Working as part of a team
_____Potential for travel
_____Respect from other staff
_____Clear rules and regulations
_____Responsive administration
_____Time flexibility

Is there anything else that would be motivating to you? If so, specify.

---

times, if the opportunity exists and a student works out exceptionally well in an agency, the agency will hire her right after placement. Nineteen percent of BSW graduates located their positions through these contacts (G. H. Hull, Personal communication, April 21, 1995). However, don't depend on this, since so many variables are beyond your control. The agency may simply have not openings when you need a job. Funding cuts may prevent hiring replacements for people who leave. An agency may have a policy against hiring students. There is nothing you can do about any of these variables.

You might keep in contact with your field placement supervisor or others whom you know in your field agency. The social work community in any particular area is usually pretty tight. People in the field are often the first to find out when an agency is hiring or about to hire. Keeping in touch with other professionals makes you privy to fresh job information.

People in your field agency are not the only primary contacts you might establish. Primary contacts are people whom you know personally. Perhaps you've met professionals from other agencies during meetings or in-services. Maybe you've worked in the field before and can contact former colleagues. Membership in state and local NASW branches can also help you form relationships with other social workers. Such membership may provide a means of linking you to the social work community's communication network.

Families and friends might also serve as part of your potential job-finding network. They, hopefully, are especially interested in your welfare and might expend substantial effort to help you find a job. Friends who are social work majors may hear of jobs through the grapevine and may share their own job-search ideas and findings with you. Thirteen percent of graduates learned of their subsequent job positions through either family or friends (G. H. Hull, Personal communication, April 21, 1995).

HIGHLIGHT 16.5

USEFULNESS OF PROFESSIONAL ORGANIZATIONS

You might ask yourself, "Why spend $50 to $180, or even more, to belong to professional organizations?" The primary social work professional organization is the National Association of Social Workers (NASW). Belonging to the national organization automatically entitles you to membership in your respective state's organization and its regional offices.

There are at least four good reasons to join NASW. First, membership in a professional organization lends you credibility (Simpson & Simpson, 1992). Most, if not all, established professions have an organization to which members can belong. Such membership helps to bolster your professional identity. It associates you with other social workers. It provides visibility for social work as a profession.

A second reason for professional membership is the opportunities it offers for networking. You can choose to attend regional, state, or national meetings where you can talk to other professionals. You can find out what is going on in your specific area of interest and in the field generally. You can also attend seminars relevant to your practice. You can even find out about potential job openings.

A third incentive for professional membership is receipt of professional information and material. National NASW membership entitles you to national newsletter published almost monthly, state newsletters when available, and the journal *Social Work* which has the largest circulation in the social work field. This can help you keep current on issues and techniques. You also have access to group liability and life insurance that costs significantly less than it would if purchased individually.

A fourth purpose for joining NASW concerns being a part of its national lobbying efforts (Simpson & Simpson, 1992). It exerts influence on behalf of causes and political agendas concurrent with professional social work values.

Costs for regular NASW membership is $130 annually. It is significantly less if you join while you are still a student.

There are numerous other professional organizations that you may choose to join. National groups emphasizing working with groups, administration, child care, suicide, sex education, and any number of other special areas. They can provide a useful source of information in a specific area of interest. Many social workers join those with which they most identify. Virtually all have membership fees.

A way to carry networking even further is to expand your primary contacts to secondary contacts. You can ask your primary contacts to refer you to other professionals you don't know personally. This can radically expand the number of contacts in your network. Every primary contact probably knows several secondary contacts for you. When contacting these secondary sources, you can cite your primary contact's referral. Any positive feelings your secondary contact has about your primary contact might "rub off" on you. Figure 16.1 illustrates how you can expand your network through

primary contacts who, in turn, can provide you with secondary contacts.

When you call primary and secondary contacts and there is no specific job opening, do *not* ask the contacts directly if they have a job to offer you. This puts them on the spot. Rather, try a two-pronged technique that can be quite effective. First, give the contact a truthful compliment about his professional status. You might say, "I know that you know many professionals in this area and have held offices several times in the regional NASW." You are calling this contact for a reason, to

Figure 16.1
An Example of Primary and Secondary Networking

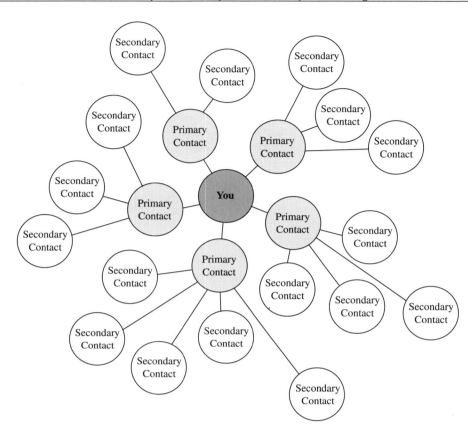

help in your job search. Therefore, it can be assumed that the person is relatively well-known, skilled, and well-connected.

The second prong of this technique is to ask your contact for advice, suggestions, or referrals to help you in your job search. You might emphasize that you know your contact probably has no job available at his agency. However, he might have a good suggestion. This takes the pressure off the contact to help you himself and also flatters him, because you are consulting him for help. You might also ask your primary contacts if you can use them as references. This may make them feel that they are "on your team."

Contacting people you haven't spoken to for a while can bring their memory of you out of the mists of memory and back into consciousness. If in the future they hear about a job opening via their own informal communication net, they are more likely to remember you. Thus, they may either give a potential employer your name or notify your directly about the job possibility.

Keep written track of contacts, both primary and secondary. Time can pass quickly. Briefly noting the contact's name, number, and what was said can help you plan your networking. You don't want to forget that you've already called a contact and then call her again. Also, keep track of how frequently you use a contact. You don't want to overdo it.

Finally, always write a brief thank you note to contacts for their time and help. Keep it short, writing only a paragraph or two on one page. You simply want to show them that you are grateful—and that you are responsible in terms of your follow-up ability.

Consult Your College or University Resources

Many, perhaps most, colleges and universities have some type of career placement service. You might contact yours to see what is available for job search recommendations in your area. Note, however, that only 2.2 percent of graduates found jobs through this route (G. H. Hull, Personal communication, April 21, 1995). Your social work department at school may also have job announcements. Many agencies seeking employees send announcements directly to social work programs. Check to see if there is a job board where the program posts such notices. If you are hoping to move to another state following graduation, you might ask the head of your college social work program for the name of a colleague in that state. Often a phone call to a social work educator in the state of interest can elicit the necessary information as well as other useful tips.

Using New Technology

More and more information is becoming available via computer technology. Many colleges and universities have access to programs that identify available jobs in various areas. To investigate what is available on your campus, contact either your career counseling and placement services or your computer center for on-line information.

Preparing Your Resumé

Unfortunately, preparing your first resumé is often a fairly miserable task. You must carefully scrutinize yourself and your experience. Then you must summarize this information using a virtually "perfect" format to present yourself as positively as possible. Since most potential employers first see your resumés as you, the resumé should always put your best foot forward. What is the "perfect" format for a resumé? No one really knows. Each individual has an opinion about what should be in a resumé, how long it should be, what color is best, and what contents must be included. Therefore, my advice to you is to ignore anyone who tells you exactly how your resumé has got to be. The number one rule of resumé writing is to make independent deci-

sions about what to include. Every piece of information you include in your resumé—indeed, every period and comma—should be there for a clearly defined reason.

The other thing to keep in mind is what you think an employer is looking for in an employee. What do you think is important in an employee? Dependability? Neatness? Good writing skills? Your resumé should reflect to the best of your ability what you think employers are looking for in you.

We will review a wide range of issues concerning resumés, not necessarily in any prioritized order. Each is important in its own right. The main intent is to raise questions and to give you new ideas about how to present yourself. However, the final decision regarding what belongs in your resumé rests with you alone.

Content

What should a resumé contain? Obviously, a resumé must give your name, address, and telephone number. Your name should be prominent. However, it doesn't have to be two inches high. You don't want to look arrogant. Some people prefer to label the document "Resumé" or "Vita," others do not. It is up to you. As a student it is often appropriate to note both your temporary and your permanent addresses.

Bloch (1991) suggests incorporating at least eight dimensions of content. The first is *education*. This is usually incorporated early in the resumé, before work experience. The first thing an employer will want to know is whether you are qualified for the job. Otherwise why should she waste her time reading any further? In the event that you have attended various campuses over your social work career, you may or may not want to list them all. The rule of thumb is to list them only if there is some specific reason, such as having earned an Associate's Degree. Otherwise, the school where you got your degree, the year the degree was obtained, and the fact that it is from an accredited social work program are the crucial points. Don't include high school information unless you have some specific reason, such as having received a major honor or scholarship. It is assumed that you graduated from high school in order to be accepted at college.

The second dimension of resumé content involves *certificates* or *licenses*. All states now have some kind of licensing or certification for social workers. However, not all states have licensing or certification at the baccalaureate level. (Iowa, for example, does not.)

You might choose to indicate, after citing where you received your social work degree, that it was from a program accredited by the Council on Social Work Education, the field's official accrediting body. If you have other certificates or licenses, you can list them at this time. If you happen to have a broad range of background experience and are a certified alcohol and other drug counselor, you will probably want to include this fact.

The next three content dimensions are *work history*, *related experience*, and *volunteer experience*. These three are addressed together because there are a number of ways to include this information. Which way depends on what is best for you. It is probably appropriate to put your social-work-related experience first. You may have years of such experience, or it may consist primarily of your field placements. You can use a variety of headings for this content including "Social work experience," "Social work-related experience," "Job experience," "Paid work experience," or the like. It is appropriate to include your field experience under the first two categories that emphasize the experience aspect. After all, that's exactly what your field experience was. However, do not imply that you were paid when you were not.

If you have substantial volunteer experience, you may choose to place this under a separate "Volunteer experience" category in order to emphasize it. Or you may feel it is better to include it in your "social-work-related experience" section. This is an arbitrary distinction. Think it through and decide what is best. Make sure you can articulate your reason for the placement.

Don't necessarily exclude other work experience, even if it's waitressing or flipping burgers at a fast-food restaurant. The fact that you worked is significant. It illustrates that you have assumed financial responsibility. If you financed some portion of your college career yourself, you may want to indicate that. What does this tell an employer? It implies that you are motivated and responsible. However, in jobs that are not very closely related to social work, you might not want to waste time and space on details.

If you have assumed job positions of significant responsibility, you may choose to elaborate upon them a bit. For example, handling budgets, supervising workers or volunteers, or planning activities all reflect skills

When this worker prepares her resumé, she should include her counseling experience with urban youth.

related to those used in social work. You want to emphasize this fact. When thinking about your various areas of experience, it is helpful to write down specific dates, job title, correct name and address (probably city and state will suffice) of the place, primary responsibilities, and special skills required. You can use this rough draft as a beginning to summarize your experience in that particular setting.

The sixth content dimension is *special work-related activities or accomplishments*. Is there anything in particular that you want to emphasize about your skills? What makes you special? Do you have a Spanish minor? This is an advantage when competing for jobs working with Hispanic populations. Or do you have a specialization in health education or recreation? Such skills might be useful in working with youth. Likewise, a women's studies minor might highlight your depth of understanding of women's issues such as sexual assault or domestic violence. Agencies addressing such areas might look on this experience very positively. Are you particularly adept at using certain computer programs? Include any aspect of your prior accomplishments that may make you stand out and look special.

Even if you have little or no work experience, emphasize activities such as work on a school paper, service on a committee, active participation or leadership in the social work club or organization, winning a writing award, and any other participation and leadership in clubs, activities, and events that you can think of. Be creative and give yourself credit.

The seventh content dimension involves *publications and presentations*. Do not be scared off by this. Very few people (including many college instructors) have published much, if anything. However, if you have published something, include this fact. You might have had the opportunity to put together a community resource directory as an independent study or to work on writing an improved agency policy manual as part of your field placement requirements. Any such activity counts.

Presentations are also impressive. Have you developed some minor expertise or interest and presented a training session to a class? Or were you able to put on an in-service training session at your agency? Even if you were not the only staff member participating in the presentation, you can still credit yourself for your involvement. Writing for agency newsletters is also significant. Writing is such a major part of social work practice that any evidence you can provide of competence in this area is relevant.

Other Possibilities

There are a number of other content areas that you may choose to include in your resumé. Some people suggest including a clearly stated *job objective* in addition to the other information discussed above (Parker, 1989). Evaluate the pros and cons of this tactic. If you state a specific objective (for example, "Position working with children having a developmental disability in a group home setting"), you may limit your opportunity. A potential employer with an opening that does not exactly fit this objective may automatically eliminate you. If you state a very general objective ("Gain a professional social work position"), what good is it? Isn't this fact assumed? In this case a potential employer may feel your interest is not specific enough to fit into her particular agency.

Some resumés also include a "Qualifications Summary" or "Highlights of Qualifications," usually at the resumé's very beginning, immediately following your name and address (Fry, 1992; Parker, 1989). However,

this approach is probably best if you have a substantial amount of experience to highlight. Later we will discuss how to tailor a cover letter to include a job objective related to a specific agency. The additional inclusion of a job objective in your resumé may then be unnecessary. Think about it. It is up to you.

Another suggestion sometimes made for content to be included in a resumé concerns *personal interests* and *hobbies*. We think this is a bit on the adding-useless-fluff side. However, a student once gave the rationale that such information might help a potential employer, especially one with poor interviewing skills, move on with the conversation in the interview. Another student indicated that her father had once gotten a good job mainly because he had cited on his resumé that he was a recreational pilot. The employer, also a recreational pilot, found that he had so much in common with my student's father that he gave the latter the job. Of course, the father was basically qualified for the job and had relevant work experience. But so, probably, did the other applicants. This subjective information pushed the employer's decision-making discretion over the edge into an almost immediate hire.

Some people include additional *personal information* in their resumés. For example, they might indicate that they're married or single. If you choose to do so, make certain that you have a clear reason why. A problem with including subjective, non-work-related content is that you may strike a potential employers' negative biases. It is important to emphasize the existence of personal discretion on an employer's part. You neither know of nor can control an employer's personal biases.

An employer might interpret a single female applicant as not being very stable. Who knows, she might run off and get married within six months. Granted, the latter is a very unfair, inappropriate, unwarranted response. However, you have no control over such biases. Or the employer might view a married female as one who will devote most of her time and energy to her husband and family, not to her job. Perhaps she will refuse to work nights if she can't get a baby-sitter. These biases are also unfair. However, once again, whenever you include subjective information, you run the risk of striking someone's negative biases. Such biases have nothing to do with your actual ability to do the job. Legally, employers are not supposed to ask you anything personal that is not clearly work-related. (Highlight 16.9 at the end of this chapter identifies a range of illegal questions that an interviewer might ask and suggests potential responses and their consequences.)

You might choose to include your date of birth on your resumé. Positively, this provides your employer with a frame of reference regarding how you have spent your time. Negatively, it might strike an employer's age bias. Maybe you're too young. On the other hand, maybe you're too old in the employers' eyes. We have seen resumés that included applicant's height and weight. Why?

Other people include their pictures on their resumés. Maybe it's nice if you take really attractive pictures. However, what if an employer sees your picture and thinks you're too young, or too old, or too fat, or that you have hair that's cut too conservatively or too punk? One student, who happened to be an art minor, felt that resumés like those described above were extremely dull. Apparently, her fellow art students were designing resumés with bold lines, artsy circles, and everything but holograms. It was her choice to have a similarly demonstrative resumé.

Another student brought in an example of a resumé done in a folder format with the actual resumé enclosed in a matching outside folder. The paper was parchment and the type was set in gold leaf. This student said her mother hired the individual for a sales position immediately upon receipt of the resumé. That particular resumé was exceptionally impressive.

Be aware, however, that artwork or fancy folders may "turn off" prospective employers. You never know when you might hit an employer's negative bias. Even something you feel is positively innocuous can append or annoy a potential employer. This is not fair, but true. Once a male student placed the words, "Every man in his place can perform miracles. The primary duty is to put all energy into it," right below his name on his resumé. To some people this sounds fine, like he's an energetic kind of guy. However, others immediately focus on the masculine emphasis of "every *man* in his place." What might this convey to some people about the applicant's potential sexist bias?

Personal information that you might consider including on a resumé is "Health: excellent," if that is, indeed, the case. It implies that you are not likely to take many sick days, which is positive.

There are almost endless categories of information you may choose to include in your resumé. If you want to, for brevity's sake you can combine categories that have little of nothing to do with each other. You might have a topical heading, following information about your education, entitled "Honors, Scholarships, and Committees." These three do not necessarily have anything to do with each other. However, they all relate to educational experience. It saves valuable space to group them together instead of citing them separately.

References

Some resumés include *current references*. Others do not. An advantage of inclusion is that an employer has the information right in front of her. If she's rushed, she can make a quick call to references cited. If she knows any of them, she may associate her positive feelings about them with you. However, if you anticipate your references getting dozens of annoying calls as a result, then maybe you shouldn't include them.

One advantage of not including reference information is a shorter resumé. If you choose not to include such information, you should always bring a copy of your references along to an employment interview. At the end of the resumé where references are typically cited, always include a statement such as "References Available Upon Request." This alerts the employer to the fact that you do have some. Always ask your references for permission to include them as such.

How many references should you include? The most typical number appears to be three. Sometimes public regulations require the inclusion of three references. However, you might include as many as five or six with the rationale that you are not "hard up" for references.

Always include a reference's full name, degree (if appropriate), full agency address including zip code, and full telephone number including area code. You may also want to include your reference's job title. This helps the employer know who he or she will be contacting. Make sure all the information is accurate. You don't want to offend either references or employers by making a mistake.

Who should your references be? Well, logically, who do you think would have the most credibility from a social work employer's point of view? Probably social work references are the most valuable. Perhaps your field instructor would write you a good one. Social work faculty are other potential references. Have you worked especially closely with any of your instructors? Have they gained a special appreciation for your abilities and skills?

Employment references are also appropriate. Good work skills such as responsibility, dependability, decision making, and the like apply to virtually all work settings including social work ones. Professional references probably gain more credence than do personal ones (Berk, 1990). A good employment reference from Ms. Hardibar probably carries more weight than one from Auntie Hildegarde or Uncle Morgan. In any case, a good reference assumes more importance than a bad one. It's better to include a positive personal reference than even a mildly negative social work one. Likewise, a detailed reference from a less "important" person who knows you extremely well is probably more effective than a vague, saying-not-much-of-anything reference from someone very important.

A note about prior supervisors: Do not feel obligated to list all of them as references. Supervisors come and go. No employer would expect to contact each and every one. Cite only your best. In the event that you would like a reference from a certain job or agency, but you didn't get along well with your supervisor there, this is not a problem. Simply ask another staff or colleague to write the reference for you. Once again, it is impossible for you or potential employers to keep track of the career paths of all of your prior supervisors. Other staff who know you and your performance will suffice. The bottom line, once again, is to choose each of your references for a designated reason. What can each say about you that will make you look as good as possible to potential employers?

Some people send copies of reference letters along with their resumé and cover letter. An advantage of this is that the reference information is readily and easily available to the potential employer. Another advantage may be that it makes you look thorough and conscientious. If you send copies of letters, make sure your reference has given you permission to do so. Also, make certain that you state in your cover letter something like: "Please feel free to contact my references for verification and further information." You don't want to give the impression that you've sent forgeries.

Length

How long should a resumé be? Some administrators prefer resumés no longer than one page. Other employ-

ers appreciate more detail. You can use your resumé to indicate to your employer how conscientious you are. You can use specific concepts to illustrate good communications skills and incorporate professional terms (even jargon, if you will) to emphasize your involvement with and commitment to the field.

It is important not to clutter a resumé with useless "filler" that can only annoy potential employers. They are busy, too. If you choose to write a resumé longer than one page, make sure that it is organized, clear, and easy to wade through. Later, we will discuss how using capital letters and underlining can format your resumé for easy reading. You want the reader to find different types of content (for example, educational and job experience) easily and quickly.

We still haven't answered the question of how long a resumé should be. That's because it's not important what I think. It is important what you think. Most resumés written by people new to the field seem to be one or two pages long. Many sources stress that resumés should be no longer than that (Fry, 1992). However, there are also excellent three- or four-page resumés written by students who gained substantial experience prior to returning to school for their social work degrees. You need to determine what will make you look your best.

Spacing

Allow ample space in margins and between entries. You want to provide "breathing" room so the information is clearly presented. On the one hand, your resumé should not look squished, but on the other, you should not waste any space.

Reverse Chronological Order

Always cite your educational and work experiences in reverse chronological order. Your employer wants to know what you have been doing most recently first. If you list an experience with which you are still involved, do not list a cut-off date (NASW Program Advancement Fund, undated). Rather, cite something like "May 1994 to present." Locate dates so that they are easy to find. One common format is to place them along the left-hand side of the page with the respective experience immediately to the right. You can use either months and years, or years only.

Don't Say Why You Left a Job

Never list why you quit a job or left a place of employment. However, at a job interview be prepared to explain your reasons. Employers assume a wide range of reasons for leaving jobs. Almost everyone has left a job at one time or another for one reason or another. This is why you have references. They are supposed to explain the good things about your work performance.

Use Vibrant Active Verbs

When discussing your job responsibilities, make them sound as exciting and relevant as possible. Try to use words like develop, formulate, lead, explain, run, or counsel. All of these words imply professional action. Highlight 16.2, which addresses the identification of your own competencies, offers additional good examples of words to use.

Use Parallel Structure

To facilitate the reader's comprehension of the resumé, cite items in a similar manner. For example, you might state your job title and place of employment for a series of positions, each followed by a section labeled, "Responsibilities" (see figure 16.2). That portion of your resumé may read, "Responsibilities: Develop programming for youth; lead groups; counsel pregnant teens." In this case each job description should have the same format. The word *responsibilities* should be capitalized and followed by a colon. Subsequently, each job summary should list responsibilities using present tense verbs.

There is no need to use complete sentences in description of education, jobs, or duties. However, it is important to use parallel structure so that each section reads like the previous one.

Time Gaps

Some people have gaps of time when they did not work. Perhaps they were going to school. Maybe they stayed home to raise children. They may even have been involved in some treatment experience. It is difficult to incorporate such content into a resumé structure. Some people have included their time not working outside the home by stating that they were homemakers for the period of time involved. Some have described community activities participated in during this times, such as scout leadership or church involvement.

If you choose not to comment on any gaps you may have, be prepared to address them during the interview. You may also briefly explain gaps of time in your cover letter. At any rate, don't worry about it. Many people, especially women with children, are outside the full-time work force for some period of time. If this is the case with you, it is not a problem. Stress your good points. Raising children requires time, attention, and assumption of serious responsibility. You may have learned effective child behavior management techniques. Frame your gaps, if you have them, within a positive perspective.

How Many Resumés?

A fairly common question involves whether to make one resumé or several slightly different ones. Should different resumés state different job objectives depending on the job you are applying for? Probably not. Completing a variety of resumés can become extremely confusing. Instead, you can use your cover letter to explain why you are as "perfect" as possible for the particular job.

Paper and Printing

In the past, conscientious resumé writers would take their resumés to a professional printer to have it typeset. Perhaps they would also pay professionals to have the resumés formatted. This is no longer necessary. Laser printers do excellent jobs. Additionally, formatting your own resumé on disk allows you to make ongoing changes and keep the resumé current. The danger of having someone else design and prepare your resumé is that he will probably not understand social work jargon and values. Social work resumés can vary significantly from other business resumés. The moral here is to be wary of strong suggestions from your business major friends (such as, a resumé *must* be one page long).

You probably should purchase some good quality

Figure 16.2
Examples of Resumés

Sample Resumé A

LYNN GWEENY

Permanent Address:
1950 Rock Knoll
Elvisville, Wisconsin 55894
Telephone: (714) 247-7526

Temporary Address
515 Skid Road, Apt. #235
Happyville, Wisconsin 23584
Telephone: (313) 786-6357

EDUCATION:

May 1995
Bachelor of Social Work (Accredited Program)
Improveyourself University, Happyville, Wisconsin

HONORS:

Spring 1995
Dean's List

SOCIAL WORK AND RELATED EXPERIENCE:

January 1995
to Present

Social Work Intern
Justincase County Mental Health Center
Porta Bella, Wisconsin
Responsibilities: Counsel individuals and groups; assess resource needs;
serve as liaison between community residents and resources; record case
histories and progress notes.

June 1994 to
December 1994

Co-Coordinator
(Volunteer)
University Women's Center
Improveyourself University
Happyville, Wisconsin
Responsibilities: Plan programming; run support groups; assist students
in information retrieval; plan and administer budget.

EMPLOYMENT:

May 1994 to
September 1994

Waitress
HeeHaw Truck Stop
Countrywestern, Wisconsin

May 1993 to
September 1993

Computer Assistant
Stellar Aeronautics
Havemercy, Wisconsin

Responsibilities: Enter data using Wordstar 5, Wordperfect 5.1 and
Quatro; assist in document preparation; file; type.

REFERENCES FURNISHED UPON REQUEST

Discussion of Resumés A and B

Resumés A and B reflect the same person's experiences. Note that Lynn Gweeny is a recent graduate with little experience. The intent of these documents is to illustrate that you can choose various ways of formatting your resumé. Resumé A includes both permanent and temporary addresses. Resumé B includes the permanent address only. The information on each resumé is provided under different headings. Resumé A begins with education and honors. Resumé B begins with objective and qualifications. Both honors and objective are optional items to include on a resumé. Depending on how you want to portray yourself, you may choose to include both, only one, or neither.

Work, social work, and volunteer experience are treated differently on each resumé. Resumé A clusters social work and volunteer experience together and employment separately. Resumé B, on the other hand, groups both social work and other work experience together. Volunteer experience is cited separately, thereby emphasizing it.

Figure 16.2
Examples of Resumés (continued)

Sample Resumé B

LYNN GWEENY

1950 Rock Knoll
Elvisville, WI 55894
Telephone: (747) 247-7526

OBJECTIVE:	Social work position counseling children and families.
QUALIFICATIONS:	Bachelor of Social Work, Improveyourself University, Happyville, WI, 5/95.
EXPERIENCE:	*Social Work Intern*, Justincase County Mental Health Center, Porta Bella, WI, 1/95 to present.

  • Counseled individuals and groups;
  • Assessed resource needs;
  • Acted as liaison between community residents and resources;
  • Recorded case histories and progress notes.

Waitress, HeeHaw Truck Stop, Countrywestern, WI, 5/94 to 9/94.

  • Served food and communicated with customers.

Computer Assistant, Stellar Aeronautics, Havemercy, WI, 5/93 to 9/93.

  • Entered data using Wordstar 5, Wordperfect 5.1, and Quatro;
  • Assisted in document preparation;
  • Typed and filed.

VOLUNTEER
EXPERIENCE: *Co-Coordinator*, University Women's Center, Improveyourself University, Happyville, WI, 6/94 to 12/94.

  • Planned programming;
  • Ran support groups;
  • Assisted students in information retrieval;
  • Planned and administered budget.

REFERENCES:

Frank Bizarre, Ph.D.	Sheila Weber, MSW
Associate Professor	Supervisor
Social Work Program	Justincase County Mental
Improveyourself University	Health Center
Happyville, WI 54908	Porta Bella, WI 52765
(747) 298-4333	(747) 256-9860

Myrtle Bureaucrat
Computer Analyst
Stellar Aeronautics
Havemercy, WI 57362
(747) 243-7987

Resumé A indicates that references will be furnished upon request. Resumé B provides the references.

Both resumés attempt to demonstrate a balanced appearance. Both are, obviously, single-paged resumés. Resumé A uses a "responsibilities" format for describing work experiences. Resumé B uses a series of bullets below job titles and locations. You can choose any way you feel is best to format your resumé. The important thing is to be consistent throughout. In other words, don't combine and mix both the "responsibilities" and the bullet formats in the same resumé. That would be confusing and look disorganized.

Pay careful attention to detail. Even the way dates are illustrated differs between the two resumés. Resumé A spells the months and years out in full. They are listed consistently at the left-hand side of the page. Resumé B, on the other hand abbreviates the dates to numbers (for example 5/94 for May 1994) and cites them consistently following the places of employment or receipt of degree.

Figure 16.2
Examples of Resumés (continued)

Sample Resumé C

RESUMÉ

Name: **Notfarg Lluh**

Address: 2732 N. Inferiora
Autumnfield, NE 70856

Telephone: Home: (714) 388-0506
Office: (714) 638-2545
Car: (714) 168-9002

Formal Education:

Bachelor of Science, Social Work
University of Nebraska, June, 1982

Master of Social Work
Florida State University, May, 1985

Professional Experience:

December 1991 to present	*Social Work Supervisor I*, Cowotinam County Department of Social Service, Cowotinam, Nebraska.
	Responsible for supervision and direction of Foster Care Unit, Delinquency Rehabilitation Unit, Group Home Project, and Day Care licensing.
May 1988 to December 1991	*Social Worker IV, (Foster Home Coordinator),* Cowotinam County Department of Social Service, Cowotinam County, Nebraska.
	Responsible for home finding, study and licensing.
June 1986 to June 1987	*Captain, Medical Service Corps, U. S. Army (Assigned as Chief of the Social Work Section)* Mental Hygiene Consultation Service
	Responsible for providing clinic's outpatient and outreach services.
July 1985 to June 1986	*Group Home Director*, MGM Group Homes, Inc., Lazybeach, Florida.
	Responsible for staff supervision and scheduling, treatment planning, case management, budgeting, and serving as community liaison.

Discussion of Resumé C

Sample Resumé C reflects the experience of a person obviously more experienced than the individual writing Resumés A and B. Notfarg Lluh has both a BSW and MSW. This resumé provides another example of how formats may differ. He includes more dimensions of content including grants, seminars attended, miscellaneous service, and professional memberships. He also includes five references, most of whom are from the agency where he is currently employed. Apparently, he decided that it was more important to have a longer resumé that provided greater detail. He could not include all the facts he wanted to if he tried to limit the format to a single page.

Figure 16.2
Examples of Resumés (continued)

Notfarg Lluh
Page 2

June 1982 to August 1983	*Social Worker I*, Children's and Adolescent Units Southwestern State Hospital, Buffalo Chip, Nebraska.
	Responsible for providing direct social work service, both individual and group for two units.

Grants

1991	Independently wrote and presented successful National Institute of Mental Health grant proposal to establish and fund a group home for delinquent boys.

Seminars Attended (Recent):

1994	Human Services Management Institute: Needs Assessment: Supervision Seminar; NASW National Conference
1993	The Dynamics of Childhood Sexuality; Adolescent Diagnostic and Treatment Issues; Total Quality Service; NASW National Conference
1992	Family Therapy in the 1990s; Quality through Accountability; Alcoholism and Adolescence
1991	Gangs in America; NASW National Conference
1990	Just Say No to Drugs; NASW National Conference

Miscellaneous Community Service:

Member, Cowotinam City Council (elected), 1992 to 1994

Member, Cowotinam Landmarks Commission, 1990 to present

Member, Board of Directors, Comehome Refuge House, 1990 to present

Memberships in Professional Organizations:

National association of Social Workers
Academy of Certified Social Workers
Delinquency Prevention Council of America

Note that his resumé indicates Notfarg received a promotion from Social Worker IV to Social Work Supervisor I. He emphasizes this difference even though both positions are in the same agency. Being promoted to a position with greater responsibility reflects the agency's respect for Notfarg's competence.

Figure 16.2
Examples of Resumés (continued)

Notfarg Lluh
Page 3

References:

Mary Poppins, MSW
Director
Cowotinam County
    Department of Social Service
Cowotinam, Nebraska 43789
(714) 638-8990

Kari Meeback, MSW
Social Work Supervisor I
Cowotinam County
    Department of Social Service
Cowotinam, Nebraska 43789
(714) 638-1135

Gene Yuss, MSW
Unit Supervisor
Foster Home Placement
Cowotinam County
Department of Social Service
Cowotinam, Nebraska 42789
(714) 638-4982

Minnie Series, Ph.D.
Executive Director
MGM Group Homes, Inc.
Lazybeach, Florida 34879
(908) 353-5713

Harry Kari
Social Worker
Cowotinam County
    Department of Social Service
Cowotinam, Nebraska 43789
(714) 638-2321

Another divergent feature from the other two resumés is the fact that Notfarg labels the resumé right at the top. Also note that at the tops of later pages he indicates both his name and the resumé page number. In case the employer misplaces pages she can easily replace the pages where they belong.

paper. This will help to make your resumé stand out among the scores of papers on an employer's desk. Select a color you feel comfortable with. My favorite is buff. It's neutral enough to avoid being offensive, yet different enough to stand out amidst white. Light blue, ivory, or light gray are other possibilities.

Be wary of excessively bright colors. If possible, print your cover letter on the same paper as your resumé. Matching envelopes are also impressive. If you have more than one sheet for your resumé, do not staple them together. For whatever reason, it is considered tacky and is simply not done. Never staple your cover letter to your resumé.

Do Not Make Mistakes

Do not make mistakes. This cannot be emphasized enough. If your resumé has a spelling error (when the resumé is supposed to be the ultimate reflection of your ability and near perfection), what does that tell an employer about your writing ability and competence? Proofread your resumé very carefully. It is also helpful to ask others to read it and share their opinions. Remember, however, that all they can give you are opinions.

Becoming Outdated

A resumé can easily, and most often does, become outdated the day after you complete it. This is to be expected. Inevitably, you will win some award, attend an exciting in-service training session, or assume some new work responsibility that you feel you must include in the resumé. You might choose to put the date of your resumé at the top. This will help orient you and your potential employer to when it was written and what time has elapsed since it was written.

The Application Cover Letter

Always send a cover letter with your application. The cover letter tailors you and your experience to fit the particular job you're applying for and also emphasize your greatest strengths.

NASW (Program Advancement Fund, undated) makes a number of suggestions for writing good cover letters. First, *write only one page*. A cover letter's purpose is to grasp your potential employer's attention. It should be short and to the point. Second, *each cover letter should be individualized for a particular job* at a specific agency. One purpose of a cover letter is to individualize and personalize your more generic resumé.

Third, *try to establish "a picture frame" effect* (p. 22). The letter should look good. Type should be centered with wide margins. Fourth, *use straightforward, understandable language* in fairly simple, direct sentences. Make certain what you say is grammatically sound. Fifth, *let your letter reflect your individual personality*. This is tricky. On the one hand, the letter should clearly be yours and only yours. On the other, be careful to "avoid being too aggressive, overbearing, cute, or humorous" (p. 22). It probably is better to err on the conservative side to avoid offending the reader.

Sixth, make sure you *sign the letter above your printed name*. Leave adequate space for your signature. Seventh, it is best to *address a letter to a specific individual*, perhaps the supervisor or department head doing the hiring, or the personnel director, if there is one. You can often call and find this out. Such personalization indicates that you expended the time and effort to find out to whom the letter should be sent or, at least, read the ad accurately. It is best to use the title preferred by the individual such as Ms., Mrs., Dr., Pastor. If you cannot find this information, you can address the letter To Whom It May Concern or Dear Sir or Madam followed by a colon.

Eighth, *get feedback from other people about your cover letter*. Is it worded as concisely as possible? Does it get your points across clearly? Ninth, *never send a cover letter out without keeping a copy*. In the event the employer calls you and refers to the letter, which might well be the case, you need to know exactly what you said. You do not want to look like an idiot.

Contents

NASW (Program Advancement Fund, undated) recommends using four paragraphs in your cover letter. The first should explain why you are sending the letter in the first place. Are you responding to an ad in the Sunday *Benjamin Key*? Or, were you referred by a colleague at another agency. Specify what job you're interested in. Make it clear how you found out about the job. For example, you might write something like: "In response to your advertisement for a Social Worker published in the October 20, 1996, *Jacksonville Journal*, I would like to submit my application for your consideration." (Please note that these phrases are simply examples for you to think about. These are not necessarily the best or worst ways to present yourself and get your points across. Their intent is to stimulate your ideas about how to say what you want to.) Or you might state: "Dr. Bill Ding, Director of County Social Services, has indicated to me that you have a Social Worker position available in your agency. My strong interest in this position has prompted me to apply."

The second paragraph should explain why you're perfect or almost perfect for the job. Briefly and succinctly, what interests, accomplishments, and qualities do you have that qualify you for this particular job? For instance, you might indicate: "My undergraduate social work degree, volunteer experience, and strong interest in working with youth contribute to my qualifications for the position. Additionally, my elective coursework has focused in that area which is, by far, my preferred area of employment."

The third paragraph should refer to the fact that a resumé is enclosed. If you are also sending an application form or copies of reference letters, mention that they are enclosed. You might say something like: "Please refer to the enclosed resumé for further details. It identifies some of the specific skills I have mastered during my field and volunteer experiences. They include planning and running small groups, providing basic counseling to enhance clients' decision-making ability, making treatment recommendations, writing grants, and using a wide range of recording formats for accountability." For the sake of brevity, you may choose to combine the second and third paragraphs into one. This is my personal preference.

The last paragraph should reemphasize your interest in the position. Additionally, thank the reader for her or his time, consideration, or attention. There is a range of opinion regarding what else should be said in this final paragraph. Some suggest expressing avid enthusiasm by indicating that you would like to have an interview or would appreciate it if the employer would call you. You might indicate when you will be in town and available for an interview. On the other hand, a potential employer might view this as being pushy. Decide what sounds right to you, and say it.

For example, your closing paragraph may resemble the following: "Thank you so much for your time and attention. I would welcome the opportunity to interview with you. I eagerly look forward to hearing from you."

Another closing might be: "I would like very much to discuss with you how my skills could contribute to your agency and your clients. The skills you require seem to match my professional strengths and personal qualities. I would be happy to schedule an interview with you at your convenience. Thank you for your consideration."

Formatting the Letter

Your letter of application and resumé are the first contacts an agency administrator will have with you. Make them pay off. Cover letters should always be typed, preferably on the same quality and color of paper used for the resumé. We have already indicated that the letter should not exceed one page in length.

Using block style for your letter is often easiest. Cover letter 1 in highlight 16.6 reflects this style. You position the date at least one inch down from the top of the paper (more if the letter is short). After the date, leave at least five spaces before the name, title, name of agency, and agency address. All sentences can begin at the left margin with no indenting required. Single space and leave a blank line between paragraphs.

Always include your full address in the letter. You want the employer to be able to reach you quickly and easily. You might also want to include your telephone number, as cover letter 1 illustrates, even though it is already included in your resumé. You can use any of a number of closing salutations. These include Sincerely, Very sincerely, Truly yours, or Very truly yours. It seems that people select the one they like the best and then use it pretty consistently thereafter.

Highlight 16.7 is cover letter 2, which contains several differences from cover letter 1. One variation is placement of the letter's date, the applicant's address, the closing salutation, and signature. All of these are indented to the right. They should align themselves approximately with the right-hand margin.

Another difference between cover letters 1 and 2 is that the latter incorporates four instead of three paragraphs. Cover letter 2's second paragraph elaborates upon some personal qualities, whereas the third para-

---

HIGHLIGHT 16.6

COVER LETTER 1

May 28, 1997

Russ T. Hinge
Social Services Director
Kneebend County Social Services
Kneebend, NY 98576

Dear Mr. Hinge:

I am responding to the advertisement for Case Manager published in the *Kneebend News* on January 17, 1995.

As my enclosed resumé reflects, I am well qualified for the position. I received my social work degree from an accredited program and have applied for state licensure which should be forthcoming. My field practicum at a child welfare agency has provided me with experience in case management. My work experience includes serving as care counselor for adult clients who have a mental illness in a group home setting. My volunteer experiences include visiting elderly adults living in health care settings. These experiences have provided me with a well-rounded exposure to a variety of social service settings that, I feel, have prepared me well for the case management position.

Thank you very much for your attention. I hope to be hearing from you soon.

Sincerely,

[Signature]

Ernest Endeavor
4995 Truthful Avenue
Wholesome, Massachusetts 48069

Telephone: (401) 859–4833

---

graph focuses on information included in the resumé. Cover letter 1 combines information about assets and resumé into only one paragraph and includes less content about personal characteristics.

The ''(C94 Penguin Press)'' in cover letter 2's first sentence is the ad's reference number. Newspapers usually use some kind of reference code so that they know to which blind ad an applicant is referring. A blind ad is one where the employer does not provide the agency's name and contact information, perhaps because the em-

HIGHLIGHT 16.7

COVER LETTER 2

84 Hot Street, Apartment #1
Boiling, New Mexico 48300
January 13, 1997

The Penguin Press
Box 8888
Frigid, Alaska 68349

To Whom It May Concern:

This letter is in response to the advertisement published in your June 1 edition for the position of Social Work Counselor (C94 *Penguin Press*).

My primary interest and career goal is to work with people who have developmental disabilities. I am hardworking and committed to enhancing people's well-being. I am open to constructive criticism and consistently strive to improve my skills. My intent is to become the best social worker I can be.

My resumé is enclosed. It reflects my accomplishments which include: a field internship at a sheltered workshop; volunteer experience with the Special Olympics; and a concentration of coursework related to developmental disability. Thank you for your consideration. When might I expect to hear from you?

Very truly yours,

[Signature]

Burr Bank

Enclosure

---

ployer prefers to review applications anonymously first and select the best qualified candidates. Otherwise, if applicants know whom to contact about the job, they may inundate the employer with phone calls and letters.

Cover letter 2 contains the word "Enclosure" at the bottom left. This refers to the enclosed resumé. You can also use the terms "Encl." or "Enclosure: Re-

sumé" to reflect this. However, since you have already stated in the letter's body that the resumé is enclosed, this is not absolutely necessary. Nonetheless, many people include it.

Cover letter 2 concludes with a question, a technique suggested by NASW. The rationale is that "it encourages a response" (Program Advancement Fund, undated). Our impression is that it's too pushy, but it is up to you to decide. What do you think?

Make No Errors

Proofread the letter carefully. An employer will likely throw out any letter with typing, spelling, or grammatical errors. If you make mistakes in your letter now, what can an employer expect later when you are on the job? Then you will be carrying a full caseload and trying to get such documents as court reports, social histories, and referral letters acceptably completed on time.

The Job Interview

Sooner or later one of your applications will result in an invitation for a job interview. This is often a bit scary even for the person who has successfully completed a four hundred-hour field placement or has additional social work experience.

Find Out about the Agency

To prepare for the interview it is often helpful to learn something about the community and the agency. Sometimes, your social work faculty can provide this information. At other times you will need to consult the telephone book and look up information about the city. Or you can consult government documents listing such information as population, ethnic diversity, and type of government. Try to find out what you can about the agency. What kind of clientele does it serve? What specific services does it provide?

Prepare Questions to Ask

Knowing some specific information about an agency can form a foundation for asking more thoughtful, and, in effect, impressive questions during an interview. Always think of questions you can ask (NASW Program Evaluation Fund, undated). Remember that the interview process is a two-way street. The employer is finding out whether you are right for the agency, but you are also finding out whether the agency is right for you.

Prepare for Potential Questions

You might want to prepare a list of questions to ask your interviewer. These could include duties/responsibilities of the position, date the agency would like the new employee to start, what other agencies you might have contact with on the job, and characteristics of the client population. Anticipate questions that might be asked and rehearse your responses. Highlight 16.8 illustrates some typical questions you can expect that an employer might ask.

Many of the questions posed in highlight 16.8 are tough, really tough. That's why it's important for you to give them serious consideration ahead of time. You should sound strong and definitive, and yet frame answers that sound as positive as possible. Let's consider potential answers. For example, how might you respond when asked what your major weaknesses are? Replying that you have none is probably not the truth. What about sharing a weakness that can also be viewed in a positive light? You might say something like, ''I tend to take my job too seriously'' or, ''I have some trouble letting go of cases I really care about.'' Both imply weaknesses in the context of a strong willingness to work and do an effective job.

Another question involves how long you think you will remain with the agency. How can you answer this honestly, yet positively? You might say something like, ''That's a tough question because it's hard to see into the future. I would like to remain with your agency as long as I feel the work is challenging and I am doing a good job.''

A related question can be posed to applicants who have a BSW about whether, and subsequently when, they plan to return to graduate school for their MSW. You might reply, ''I would be committed to working here in this position for several years. Yes, at some point I would like to go back to school. However, I want to get firmly established in the field first. Additionally, there's always the possibility of going back part-time.''

Other questions involve prior problems in supervision or being let go from some job position. Never lie. You will destroy your credibility forever. The social work community is a relatively small one. Word spreads. However, you can couch what you say in as positive a light as possible. For example, you might respond, ''I had difficulties with one supervisor. I was young and inexperienced. At that point in my career,

---

HIGHLIGHT 16.8

COMMON INTERVIEW QUESTIONS

1. We would like to get to know you a little better. Could you tell us about yourself?
2. What made you choose social work as a major? Who influenced you the most in choosing social work and in continuing in the major?
3. What interests you about this agency and position?
4. What are your major strengths? What are your major weaknesses?
5. With what type of clients would you like to work?
6. Are there any clients with whom you may have difficulty working?
7. What makes you the best candidate for this position?
8. What is your definition of a "family system"?
9. What kind of information would you collect on a new case?
10. What can you bring to this agency?
11. What are your long-term goals?
12. How will you work under pressure?
13. How do you deal with criticism?
14. What experiences have you had that might help you in our agency?
15. With what type of supervisor do you work best?
16. What do you do to unwind?
17. What motivates you the most?
18. What do you tend to have the most difficulty with on the job?
19. What salary range are you looking for?
20. What type of work environment makes you feel the most at ease?
21. Are you planning to stay in social work?
22. (To BSWS) Are you planning to go to graduate school?
23. Have you ever done a job ineffectively?
24. Are you willing to work overtime?
25. Do you mind being on call?
26. How long do you think you would remain with this agency?
27. What type of decisions are most difficult for you?
28. What do you expect to be doing five years from now?
29. What do you know about our agency?
30. What personal characteristics do you think are important in social work?
31. Do you feel you did as well in college as you could have? Why or why not?
32. Have you ever had trouble getting along with people, such as other students or faculty?
33. How would you define the word *cooperation?*
34. What type of work interests you the most?
35. Do you think employers should consider grades important? Why or why not?
36. What have you done that demonstrates initiative?
37. Describe your time management skills.
38. How do you prioritize your workload?
39. What frustrates you the most?
40. In what ways has or hasn't a prior supervisor of yours assisted in your skill development?
41. How do you react to being evaluated?
42. Why should you be hired for this position instead of other candidates?
43. What do you think you could do positively for this agency?
44. What has been your worst difficulty with a prior supervisor? Explain.
45. Explain why you quit or were let go from prior jobs.

I needed more structured supervision than I do now. I don't feel he himself had the ability to help me the way I needed it."

Another response concerning a prior difficulty with a supervisor might concern that supervisor's lack of appropriate commitment to professional ethics which subsequently placed you in a precarious position. Or perhaps you feel you were not given sufficient credit for the work you did. Generally, it is best not to criticize former supervisors or employers severely. Rather, try to be honest, objective, and as specific as possible (Berk, 1990). Explain your side of the story in enough objective detail to make your perspective clear to the interviewer. Avoid negative emotional outbursts that make you sound resentful or whining. The most effective approach is to evaluate the supervisor's side of the story also. What factors influenced her to operate as she did? In this way you can show an interviewer that you are not only capable of analyzing such an agency situation, but have also learned from your experience and will probably handle a similar one better the next time.

An exceptionally difficult issue to confront during the interview is salary. If possible, research ahead of time what similar positions in that geographical location pay. Have some figures established in your mind (Berk, 1990). It is perfectly appropriate to address salary during the interview. Usually, if the interviewer does not bring it up, you should do so toward the end of the interview. If you bring it up too early, the interviewer may get the impression that money is all you're concerned about. If the interviewer indicates that the amount you expect is totally beyond reason, then perhaps this is not the job position for you. On the other hand, you may be willing to give up some salary for what you consider a super job. One other suggestion is to negotiate nonsalary benefits (Berk, 1990). How about two weeks of vacation the first year instead of one? Or is it possible to negotiate a raise after your six-month probationary period?

Note that it may be possible when offered a job to negotiate vacation. Often, you must work for some period (such as a year) before you can take any vacation time at all. You might consider negotiating for a week or two the first year without pay. A year without any vacation is pretty rough.

Participating in the Interview

Show up ahead of time for the interview. Allow yourself extra time for emergencies or for a quick rest stop. If you show up late, what does that tell an employer about your punctuality and planning ability? Spend the waiting time looking through any available brochures or other material placed in the lobby or waiting room.

"What should I wear to an interview?" is a common question. It's generally best to dress in a relatively conservative fashion, which may mean that it's probably better to overdress than to underdress (Berk, 1990). However, this still takes careful thought. What type of position are you interviewing for? If it's in a hospital, you'd best dress quite formally. Hospital social workers tend to enhance their credibility by dressing more formally because medical settings are inherently very professional and formal. However, if you are interviewing for a counseling position in group home for adolescents with behavior problems, how much should you dress

up? What if a lot of the job will involve recreational activities with the kids?

Two situations come to mind. Once an employer called for a reference for Carlene, a student. We were happy to provide a positive reference. However, one of the employer's questions struck us as strange. She asked, "Does Carlene always dress up so much?" We tried to think back. Yes, she always looked nice and often wore matching scarves, earrings, and other accessories. We didn't recall her ever coming to class in jeans. She always curled her long dark hair and wore attractive makeup. We remembered she was a little on the heavy side. We tried to empathize with the employer and what she meant by this comment. We responded to the employer that we felt this student took pride in her appearance, but always appropriately.

The point here is that Carlene apparently struck one of this employer's bias points. It appeared that this employer thought the student was inappropriately dressed. We surmised that the employer perceived informality as being more appropriate for that particular work setting.

On another occasion, we interviewed a candidate for an MSW position. The candidate appeared in an obviously expensive, tailored three-piece gray suit. The position was one of therapist for adolescents with serious behavioral problems in a day treatment center.[1] The job involved "getting one's hands dirty," so to speak, and jumping in to join a lot of adolescent activity. We looked at this candidate with his perfectly clipped beard and his perfectly matching gray socks. (Have you ever tried to match two different grays?) We thought that he would never fit into our informal, active agency environment. He later got a job as a hospital social worker where such attire was very appropriate. In essence, there is no perfect answer regarding what to wear. Dressing a little conservatively means you are probably less likely to strike someone's negative biases. Men can wear suits, or possibly sports jackets.

There still appears to be pressure for women to wear skirts instead of slacks. The term "conservative" might imply dark or dull colorless suits and boring hairstyles. If you're female, it's up to you. Do you think dowdy is more positive? Should women try to look as much like men as possible? In this context? Think of

---

1. This particular day treatment center provided both special education and therapy (individual, family, and group) to clients who continued to reside in their homes instead of being institutionalized.

HIGHLIGHT 16.9

WHAT IF THEY ASK ILLEGAL QUESTIONS?

Title VII of the Civil Rights Act of 1964 prohibits employers from discriminating on the basis of race, gender, age, national origin, religion, or pregnancy. Additionally, the Equal Pay Act of 1963 bars discrimination in pay because of gender.

To concur with these rights, a range of questions potentially asked by employers are illegal. They are considered too personal and are inappropriate for use in hiring decisions. Forbidden areas include questions about marital status, pregnancy, religion, skin color and its relationship to race, religion or religious participation, criminal records, credit history, ancestry, personal characteristics such as weight, organizational memberships, children, and whom you live with (Berk, 1990). What if the interviewer asks them anyway? You have the right to file a claim against the agency through the Federal Equal Opportunity Employment Commission or your state's Department of Human Rights. You can even file a civil suit if you want to. However, what do you think your chances are of that agency hiring you if it labels you a troublemaker?

What if an interviewer says, "I see you're wearing an engagement ring. Does that mean you'll be relocating with your fiancé if he gets a job elsewhere?" What are your options? Remember, legally you have the right to refuse to answer such a question. You might say any of the following:

"Excuse me—that question is illegal and I refuse to answer it."

"I'm happy to answer your questions, but I don't see that my personal life has anything to do with my potential job performance."

"I can understand that you would be concerned about whether getting married might affect my staying with the job. Believe me, my work and career are very important to both me and my fiancée. If I get this job, I am committed to staying with it."

How do you think an interviewer would respond to each statement? You have the right to make any of them. It is up to you. If you feel the question is so gross or rude that it is inexcusable, you really might want to tell the interviewer so. However, it is likely that if you offend the interviewer he will blackball you for the job. On the other hand, would you want to work for him or an agency that he works for? Note that the third response varies from the first two. This response answers the interviewer's question even though it is illegal. The response first empathizes with the interviewer's perspective ("I can understand that you would be concerned") and then emphasizes the job's importance, implying that the job supersedes the personal variable in question (namely, moving after getting married because of a spouse's job elsewhere).

Hillary Clinton and what she has worn in public interviews. Have you seen her wear a dark gray three-piece suit with her hair austerely pulled back in a bun? Observe the bright, attractive colors and variety of hair styles she wears. Consider what is important to you, what you think a potential employer might expect, and what attire will make you feel the most competent and comfortable.

When first meeting the interviewer, shake hands. Use a firm grip, but not a knuckle-crusher. Wait until you are asked to be seated. If asked whether you would like a cup of coffee, it's a good idea to accept the hospitality.

Use the micro skills you have acquired during the interview. Be warm, empathic, and genuine. Maintain good, appropriate eye contact. Respond straightforwardly and as succinctly as possible. Make certain you give adequate answers and explanations, but don't take forever to do so. If you don't understand a question or if you think you haven't given the information the interviewer desires, ask for clarification (NASW, Program Advancement Fund, undated).

Many agencies give prospective employees situation questions describing a case and ask the applicant to indicate what she or he would do in such a situation. These questions may be designed to test the applicant's values, knowledge base, or skills. In addition, some agencies will interview the applicant in front of a group of supervisors rather than in a one-on-one setting. This might be designed to test performance in stressful situations.

Expect the unexpected. In one interview the applicant was asked to describe the type of clients with whom he least liked to work. He replied that he did not like working with involuntary clients (those forced to come to see the social worker). A few minutes later he asked what the specific duties were of the position in question. "Juvenile probation agent" was the answer. He smiled sheepishly and said, "That's the type of client I just said I didn't like to work with, isn't it? Well, I'm flexible." His sense of humor in a difficult spot saved the interview. He was offered the position and became a highly respected social worker with juvenile offenders.

It is appropriate to ask an interviewer approximately when candidates will be notified about hiring decisions. It is also completely appropriate to ask questions about the agency and the position. You want to present yourself as a person who can communicate well in a dialogue instead of only responding dully and methodically to the interviewer's questions.

During the interview itself, let the interviewer know how motivated you are. A common reason given for not hiring someone is that he or she just didn't look all that excited about or interested in the job.

Bringing extra copies of your resumé to an interview makes you look prepared. If you're asked a specific question about some of your experience, both you and the interviewer can refer to the resumé's content.

At the interview's conclusion, remember to thank the interviewer for his or her time and interest. You might add that it was a pleasure to meet him or her and that you look forward to hearing about the decision.

Follow-Up

Write a brief thank-you letter following your interview. This will probably make you stand out as an exceptionally conscientious job candidate. For example, a candidate for a BSW case manager position was interviewed. She had a year of substantial social work experience and was articulate and bright. However, she didn't seem all that excited about the job prospect. The interviewer remained ambivalent regarding whether or not to hire

her. Suddenly, the agency received a mass of client referrals. State licensing requirements mandated that a social worker be hired immediately to meet client/social worker ratios. Ironically, the interviewer received a brief thank-you letter from that candidate the same day. He had neither the time nor the interest in doing more interviewing. He called her that day and asked if she could start the next. She, of course, responded that she had to give her current employer adequate notice.

As it turned out, she was an excellent worker. She was a dynamic, conscientious, ethical, hard-working person with a great sense of humor. As the interviewer later found out, the reason she presented such a sluggish initial impression was that she had strep throat during the interview and could hardly talk.

A question interviewees commonly ask is whether to call the interviewer or agency within a week or two of the interview if they haven't yet heard whether or not they got the job. It seems only right that you find out whether you have been hired or not, especially if the interviewer doesn't get back to you by the time he says he will. You might wait a few days or a week. You can then call and indicate that you would appreciate information regarding whether or not you were hired. You might add that you are in the midst of interviewing and deciding which job you will take. If the agency indicates no decision has yet been made, it is up to you whether you feel comfortable calling again after another week or two passes. Do not call the agency every day.

In the event that you are not hired, you can ask the interviewer for feedback about your performance during the interview.

Postscript

Getting your first position is enormously gratifying. It reinforces your sense of self-worth, though you may be nervous about starting your first "real" social work job. The suggestions discussed above are intended to increase your chances of getting that opportunity to be nervous.

Leaving a Job

Although at this point you are probably focusing on landing a job, leaving a position in a professional manner merits a brief note here. When applying for a new position, you do not have to let your employer know. Often,

---

HIGHLIGHT 16.10

ANSWERS YOU SHOULD NEVER GIVE

On a lighter note, while discussing this chapter's content, a group of students came up with some answers one should never give during a job interview. They include:

- I smoke too much.
- I never get my paperwork in.
- I really hate dealing with people.
- I only went into social work because my parents made me.

- I'm in social work for the money.
- I start things but I never finish them.
- I really don't have any weaknesses.
- I have a cocaine addiction.

The authors thank the Social Work Practice III, Section 2 students at the University of Wisconsin–Whitewater, spring semester, 1995, for providing these suggestions.

---

telling the employer creates a negative impression. She might think, "What's the matter? Doesn't he like working here? Doesn't he like me? What doesn't he like about me and my agency?" If you don't get another job right away, you'll have to live with hard feelings for quite a while.

It is appropriate and ethical to conduct a job search with correspondence and telephone communication directed to your home instead of to your work address. This prevents colleagues and administrative staff from knowing about your plans to leave the agency.

However, once you accept a new position, notify your current employer immediately. This allows her to begin looking for your replacement as soon as possible. It is also appropriate to provide your employer with some formal written notice of when you will be leaving. Some agencies specify the amount of time they prefer to have. Others leave it to your discretion. It might be two weeks or a month. But they do expect you to provide notice. Any notice less than two weeks can leave an agency "high and dry" for adequate service provision to your clients. If you do not give notice, you can potentially harm clients, and you can also smear your reputation in the professional community. Such action might be considered rude, selfish, or inconsiderate.

Chapter Summary

This chapter examines how to do a self-assessment in preparation for constructing resumés and participating in employment interviews. Assessment variables include competencies, accomplishments, job preferences, employment goals, and personal attributes. The investigation of potential employment possibilities is discussed. Strategies involved include using newspapers, state merit system lists, NASW publications, networking, technology, and college or university resources.

Ways to formulate and assess resumés are examined. Issues include content, length, spacing, using reverse chronological order, omitting reasons for leaving past jobs, using vibrant active verbs, adapting parallel structure, handling time gaps, number of resumés needed, choice of paper and printing, avoiding mistakes, and becoming outdated. Approaches for writing application cover letters are proposed.

The process of participating in job interviews is examined. Suggestions are offered concerning exploring the agency's context, preparing questions to ask, formulating responses to potential interview questions, and knowing how to act during the interview. Leaving a job is briefly addressed.

REFERENCES

Albercht, K. (1988). *At America's service.* New York: Warner Books.

Albercht, K. (1992). *The only thing that matters: Bringing the power of the customer into the center of your business.* New York: HarperCollins.

Albert, R. (1986). *Law and social work practice.* New York: Springer.

Alberti, R.E., & Emmons, M.L. (1976). *Assert yourself—It's your perfect right: A guide to assertive behavior.* San Luis Obispo, CA: Impact.

Alexander, R., Jr. (1993). The legal liability of social workers after DeShaney. *Social Work, 38* (1), 64–68.

Alter, C., & Evens, W. (1990). *Evaluating your practice: A guide to self-assessment.* New York: Springer.

American Psychological Association. (1968) Ethical standards of psychologists. *American Psychologist, 23* (23), 357–370.

Austin, D.M. (1995). Management overview. In R.L. Edwards (Editor-in-chief), *Encyclopedia of social work* (19th ed., Vol 2). Washington, DC: NASW Press.

Austin, M.J., Cox, G., Gottlieb, J., Hawkins, J.S., Kruzich, J.M., & Rauch, R. (1982). *Evaluating your agency's programs.* Newbury Park, CA: Sage.

Austin, M.J., Kopp, J., & Smith, P.L. (1986). *Delivering human services: A self-instructional approach* (2nd ed.). New York: Longman

Austin, M.J., & Lowe, J.I. (1994). *Controversial issues in communities and organizations.* Needham Heights, MA: Allyn and Bacon.

Baker, E., & Dees, J. (1978). How to prepare courtroom presentations. *Public Welfare, 36* (4): 30–35.

Barker, R.L. (1991). *The social work dictionary* (2nd ed.). Silver Spring, MD: National Association of Social Workers.

Barker, R.L. (1995). *The social work dictionary* (3rd ed.) Washington, DC: NASW Press.

Barker, R.L., & Branson, D.M. (1995). *Forensic social work: Legal aspects of professional practice.* New York: Haworth.

Barth, R.P., & Sullivan, R. (1985). Collecting competent evidence in behalf of children. *Social Work, 30* (2), 130–136.

Bartlett, H. (1970). *The common base of social work practice.* New York: National Association of Social Workers.

Bedwell, R.T., Jr. (1993). Total quality management: Making the decision. *Nonprofit World, 2* (3), 29–31.

Bell, A., & Hammersmith, S. (1981). *Sexual preference: Its development in men and women.* Bloomington: Indiana University Press.

Belle, D. (1991). Gender differences in the social moderators of stress. In A. Monat & R.S. Lazarus (Eds.), *Stress and coping* (pp. 258–274). New York: Columbia University Press.

Benjamin, A. (1974). *The helping interview.* Boston, MA: Houghton Mifflin.

Benjamin, M.P. (1994). Research frontiers in building a culturally competent organization. *Focal Point, 8* (2), 17–19.

Bennett, J.K., & O'Brien, M.J. (1994). The building blocks of the learning organization. *Training, 31* (6), 41–49.

Benson, H. (1975). *The Relaxation Response.* New York: Avon.

Berk, D. (1990). *Preparing for your interview.* Oakville, Ontario: Crisp.

Bernstein, B. (1991). Microcomputers in political campaigns—Lessons from the Jackson campaign in New York. In J. Downing, R. Fasano, P.A. Friedland, M.F. McCullough, T. Mizrahi, & J.J. Shapiro (Eds.), *Computers for social change and community organizing.* Binghamton, NY: Haworth.

Bernstein, B.E. (1977). Privileged communications to the social worker. *Social Work, 22* (4), 264–268.

Bernstein, B.E. (1979). Lawyer and therapist as an interdisciplinary team: Trial preparation. *Journal of Marriage and Family Therapy, 5* (4), 93–100.

Biegel, D.E. (1987). Neighborhoods. In A. Minahan (Editor-in-chief), *Encyclopedia of social work* (18th ed., Vol. 2, pp. 182–196). Silver Spring, MD: National Association of Social Workers.

Biegel, D.E., & Naparstek, A.J. (Eds.). (1982). *Community support systems and mental health: Practice, policy and research.* New York: Springer.

Biklen, D.P. (1983). *Community organizing: Theory and practice.* Englewood Cliffs, NJ: Prentice-Hall.

Bisno, H. (1988). *Managing conflict.* Newbury Park, CA: Sage.

Bloch, A. (1977). *Murphy's law and other reasons why things go wrong.* Los Angeles: Price/Stern/Sloan.

Bloch, D.P. (1991). *How to write a winning resumé.* Lincolnwood, IL: VGM Career Horizons.

Boehm, W.W. (1959). *Objectives of the social work curriculum of the future.* New York: Council on Social Work Education.

Brager, G., & Holloway, S. (1978). *Changing human service organizations: Politics and practice.* New York: Free Press.

Brager, G., & Holloway, S. (1983). A process model for changing organizations from within. In R.M. Kramer & H. Specht (Eds.), *Readings in community organization practice* (3rd ed., pp. 198–208). Englewood Cliffs, NJ: Prentice-Hall.

Brieland, D. (1995). Social work practice: History and evolution. In R.L. Edwards (Editor-in-chief), *Encyclopedia of social work* (19th ed., Vol. 2, pp. 2247–2258). Washington, DC: NASW Press.

Brieland, D., & Lemmon, J.A. (1985). *Social work and the law* (2nd ed.). St. Paul, MN: West.

Brill, N.I. (1990). *Working with people.* New York: Longman.

Brill, N.I. (1995). *Working with people: The helping process* (5th ed.). White Plains, NY: Longman.

Brodsky, S.L. (1988). The mental health professional on the witness stand: A survival guide. In B. D. Sales (Ed.), *Psychology in the legal process* (pp. 269–276). New York: Spectrum.

Brodsky, S.L., & Poythress, N.G. (1985). Expertise on the witness stand: A practitioner's guide. In C.P. Ewing (Ed.), *Psychology, psychiatry, and the law: A clinical and forensic handbook.* Sarasota, FL: Professional Resource Exchange, Inc.

Brown, B. (1977). *Stress and the art of biofeedback.* New York: Harper & Row.

Brown, C. (1965). *Manchild in the promised land.* New York: American Library.

Brown, E.J. (1991). *Jobology.* Pittsburgh, PA: Dorrance.

Brown, M.G., Hitchcock, D.E., & Willard, M.L. (1994). Why TQM fails and what to do about it. *Soundview Executive Book Summaries, 16* (5), 1–8.

Burghardt, S. (1982). *Organizing for community action.* Beverly Hills, CA: Sage.

Caulfield, B.A., & Horowitz, R.M. (1987). *Child abuse and the law: A legal primer for social workers* (2nd ed., pp. 1–61). Chicago, IL: National Committee for Prevention of Child Abuse.

Chess, W.A., & Norlin, J.M. (1988). *Human behavior and the social environment: A social systems model.* Boston: Allyn and Bacon.

Cheyne, I. (1987). KidsPlace: A kid's lobby for a vital Seattle. In J.E. Kyle (Ed.), *Children, families & cities* (pp. 13–16). Washington, DC: National League of Cities.

Children's Defense Fund. (1987). *A children's defense budget.* Washington, DC: Author.

Choldin, H.M. (1985). *Cities and suburbs.* New York: McGraw-Hill.

Church, D. (1981). *It's time to tell: A media handbook for human services personnel.* Washington, DC: U.S. Dept. of Health and Human Services.

Clifton, R.L., & Dahms, A.M. (1993). *Grassroots organizations* (2d ed.). Prospect Heights, IL: Waveland.

Cohen, M.D., & March, J.G. (1974). *Leadership and ambiguity.* New York: McGraw-Hill.

Cohen, M.D., March, J.G., & Olsen J.P. (1972). A garbage can model of organizational choice. *Administrative Service Quarterly, 17* (1), 1–25.

Cohen, M.I. (1987). Youth employment. In J.E. Kyle (Ed.), *Children, families and cities: Programs that work at the local level* (pp. 69–108). Washington, DC: National League of Cities.

Coley, S.M., & Scheinberg, C.A. (1990). *Proposal writing.* Newbury Park, CA: Sage.

Collier, H.V. (1982). *Counseling women: A guide for therapists.* New York: Free Press.

Collins, A.H., & Pancoast, D.L. (1976). *Natural helping networks.* Washington, DC: National Association of Social Workers.

Committee for Economic Development. (1987). *Children in need: Investment strategies for the educationally disadvantaged.* New York: Author.

Compton, B.R., & Galaway, B. (1984). *Social work processes* (3rd ed.). Homewood, IL: Dorsey.

Compton, B.R., & Galaway, B. (1989). *Social work processes.* Homewood, IL: Wadsworth.

Connaway, R.S., & Gentry, M.E. (1988). *Social work practice.* Englewood Cliffs, NJ: Prentice-Hall.

Cooper, G.L. (1981). *The stress check.* Englewood Cliffs, NJ: Prentice-Hall.

Cordero, A. (1991). Computers and community organizing: Issues and examples from New York City. In J. Downing, R. Fasano, P.A. Friedland, M.F. McCullough, T. Mizrahi, & J.J. Shapiro (Eds.), *Computers for social change and community organizing*. Binghamton, NY: Haworth.

Corey, G., Corey, M.S., & Callanan, P. (1993). *Issues and ethics in the helping professions* (4th ed.). Pacific Grove, CA: Brooks/Cole.

Cornell University Empowerment Group. (1989). *Networking Bulletin, 1*(2).

Council on Social Work Education. (1984). *Handbook of accreditation standards and procedures*. Alexandria, VA: Author.

Council on Social Work Education. (1992a). *Curriculum policy statement for the baccalaureate degree programs in social work education*. Alexandria, VA: Author.

Council on Social Work Education. (1992b). *Curriculum policy statement for the master's degree programs in social work education*. Alexandria, VA: Author.

Cournoyer, B. (1991). *The social work skills workbook*. Belmont, CA: Wadsworth.

Cox, F.M., Erlich, J.L., Rothman, J., & Tropman, J.E. (1984). *Tactics and techniques of community practice* (2nd ed.). Itasca, IL: Peacock.

Cox, F.M., Erlich, J.L., Rothman, J., & Tropman, J.E. (1987). *Strategies of community organization*. Itasca, IL: Peacock.

Crosby, P. (1980). *Quality is free*. New York: Mentor.

Cross, T., Bazron, B., Dennis, K., & Isaacs, M. (1989). *Towards a culturally competent system of care: A monograph on effective service for minority children who are severely emotionally disturbed* (Vol. 1). Washington, DC: CASSP Technical Assistance Center, Georgetown University Child Development Center.

Curtis, J.D., & Detert, R.A. (1981). *How to relax: A holistic approach to stress management*. Palo Alto, CA: Mayfield.

Daft, R.L. (1983). *Organization theory and design*. St. Paul, MN: West.

Daft, R. L. (1992). *Organization theory and design*. New York: West.

Deming, W.E. (1982). *Quality, productivity, and competitive position*. Cambridge, MA: MIT Center for Advanced Engineering Study.

Deming, W.E. (1986). *Out of the crisis*. Cambridge, MA: MIT Center for Advanced Engineering Study.

Department of Health, Education and Welfare. (1979). *Specialized training for child protective services workers: A curriculum on child abuse and neglect*. Washington, DC: DHEW. #79-30222.

Devore, W., & Schlesinger, E.G. (1987). *Ethnic-sensitive social work practice* (2nd ed.). Columbus, OH: Merrill.

Devore, W., & Schlesinger, E.G. (1991). *Ethnic-sensitive social work practice* (3rd ed.). Columbus, OH: Merrill.

Di Benedetto, M., & Pirie, V. (1989). Social work: New roles in computer information services. In W. LaMendola, B. Glastonbury, & S. Toole (Eds.), *A casebook of computer applications in the social and human services* (pp. 41–47). Binghamton, NY: Haworth.

Dluhy, M.J. (1981). *Changing the system: Political advocacy for disadvantaged groups*. Beverly Hills, CA: Sage.

Drolen, C.S. (1991). Teaching undergraduate community practice: An experiential approach. *Journal of Teaching in Social Work 5* (l), 35–47.

Drucker, P.F. (1990). *Managing the non-profit organization: Principles and practices*. New York: HarperCollins.

Edwards, R.L., & Yankey, J.A. (1991). *Skills for effective human services management*. Silver Spring, MD: National Association of Social Workers.

Emery, S.E., & Trist, E.L. The causal texture of organizational environments. *Human Relations, 18* (1), 21–32.

Emig, C. (1986). *Caring for America's children*. Chicago: Family Focus.

Entwistle, B. (1992). *Making cities work*. Pasadena, CA: Hope.

Epstein, L. (1985). *Talking and listening: A guide to the helping interview*. St. Louis, MO: Times Mirror/Mosby.

Etzioni, A. (1964). *Modern organizations*. Englewood Cliffs, NJ: Prentice-Hall.

Ewing, C.P. (Ed.). (1985). Mental health clinicians and the law: An overview of current law governing professional practice. *Psychology, psychiatry, and the law: A clinical and forensic handbook* (pp. 527–560). Sarasota, FL: Professional Resource Exchange, Inc..

Family Counseling Service. (1993). *JQS affinity group*. Ridgewood, NJ: Family Counseling Service.

Farmer, R.E., Monohan, L.H., & Hekeler, R.W. (1984). *Stress management for human services*. Beverly Hills, CA: Sage.

Federal Electric Corporation. (1963). *A programmed introduction to PERT*. New York: Wiley.

Feigenbaum, A. (1983). *Total quality control* (3rd ed.). New York: McGraw-Hill.

Fellin, P. (1987). *The community and the social worker*. Itasca, IL: Peacock.

Feutz, S.A. (1988). Testifying in legal action. *Journal of Nursing Administration, 18* (7, 8), 5–7, 42.

Filley, A.C. (1978). *The complete manager: What works when*. Champaign, IL: Research Press.

Finch, W.A., Jr. (1980). Social workers versus bureaucracy. In H. Resnick & R.J. Patti (Eds.), *Change from within: Humanizing social welfare organizations* (pp. 73–85). Philadelphia: Temple University Press.

Fisher, J., & Gochros, H.L. (1975). *Planned behavior change: Behavior modification in social work.* New York: Free Press.

Fisher, R. (1984). *Let the people decide: Neighborhood organizing in America.* Boston: Twayne Publishers.

Flanagan, J. (1980). *How to sell and how to ask for money.* Chicago, IL: National Committee for the Prevention of Child Abuse.

Freire, P. (1972). *Pedagogy of the oppressed.* New York: Seabury Press.

Fry, R. (1992). *Your first resumé* (3rd ed.). Hawthorne, NJ: Career Press.

Gambrill, E., & Stein, T.J. (1983). *Supervision.* Newbury Park, CA: Sage.

Garvin, C.D., & Cox, F.M. (1995). A history of community organizing since the Civil War with special reference to oppressed communities. In J. Rothman, J.L. Erlich, & J.E. Tropman (Eds.), *Strategies of community intervention* (pp. 64–99). Itasca, IL: Peacock.

Gary, L.E. (Ed.). (1978). *Mental health: A challenge to the black community.* Philadelphia: Dorrance.

Gerberg, R.J. (1990). *Robert Gerberg's job changing system: World's fastest way to get a better job.* Kansas City, MO: Andrews and McMeel.

Germain, C., & Gitterman, A. (1980). *The life model of social work practice.* New York: Columbia University Press.

Gibbs, L., & Gambrill, E. (1996). *Critical thinking for human service workers: A workbook.* Newbury Park, CA: Pine Forge/Sage.

Gibbs, L., Gambrill, E., Blakemore, J., Begun, A., Keniston, A., Peden, B., & Lefcowitz, J. (1994). A measure of critical thinking about practice. Unpublished paper presented at the fall Conference of the Wisconsin Council on Social Work Education, Stevens Point, WI.

Gilert, N., & Specht, H. (1974). *Dimensions of social welfare policy.* Englewood Cliffs, NJ: Prentice-Hall.

Ginsberg, L. (1992). *Social work almanac.* Silver Spring, MD: National Association of Social Workers.

Ginsberg, L., Khinduka, S., Hall, J.A., Ross-Sheriff, F., & Hartman, A. (Encyclopedia Supplement Committee). (1990). *Encyclopedia of social work.* (18th ed.). Silver Spring, MD: National Association of Social Workers.

Gordon, T.A., & Jones, N.L. (1978). Functions of social networks in the black community. In L.E. Gary, (Ed.), *Mental health: A challenge to the black community.* Philadelphia: Dorrance.

Gothard, S., (1989). Power in the court: The social worker as an expert witness. *Social Work, 34* (1), 65–67.

Gottlieb, B.H. (1983). *Social support strategies: Guidelines for mental health practice.* Beverly Hills, CA: Sage.

Gourash, N. (1978). Help seeking: A review of the literature. *American Journal of Community Psychology, 6* (5): 413–425.

Greenberg, H.M. (1980). *Coping with job stress: A guide for all employers and employees.* Englewood Cliffs, NJ: Prentice Hall.

Grisso, T. (1988). *Competency to stand trial evaluations: A manual for practice.* Sarasota, FL: Professional Resource Exchange.

Gummersson, E. (1991). Service quality: A holistic view. In S. Brown, E. Gummersson, B. Edvardsson, & B. Gustavsson (Eds.), *Service quality.* Lexington, MA: Lexington Books.

Gutierrez, L., GlenMaye, L., & Delois, K. (1995). The organizational context for empowerment practice: implications for social work administration. *Social Work, 40* (2), 249–258.

Hage, J., & Aiken, M. (1980). Program change and organizational properties. In H. Resnick & R.J. Patti (Eds.), *Change from within: Humanizing social welfare organizations* (pp. 159–182). Philadelphia: Temple University Press.

Hall, D.F., & Loftus, E.F. (1985). Recent advances in research on eyewitness testimony. *Psychology, psychiatry, and the law: A clinical and forensic handbook* (pp. 417–438). Sarasota, FL: Professional Resource Exchange, Inc.

Hall, E. (1969). *The hidden dimension.* Garden City, NY: Doubleday.

Halley, A.A., Kopp, J., & Austin, M.J. (1992). *Delivering human services: A learning approach to practice* (3rd ed.). New York: Longman.

Hallman, H.W. (1984). *Neighborhoods: Their place in urban life.* Beverly Hills, CA: Sage.

Hasenfeld, Y. (1983). *Human service organizations.* Englewood Cliffs, NJ: Prentice-Hall.

Hasenfeld, Y. (1984). Analyzing the human service agency. In F.M. Cox, J.L. Erlich, J. Rothman, & E. Tropman (Eds.), *Tactics and techniques of community practice* (pp. 14–26). Itasca, IL: Peacock.

Hasenfeld, Y. (1987). Program development. In F.M. Cox, J.L. Erlich, J. Rothman, & J.E. Tropman (Eds.), *Strategies of community organization* (4th ed., pp. 450–473). Itasca, IL: Peacock.

Hasenfeld, Y. (1992). *Human services as complex organizations.* Newbury Park, CA: Sage.

Haynes, K.S., & Mickelson, J.S. (1991). *Affecting change.* New York: Longman.

Hellenbrand, S.C. (1987). Termination in direct practice. In A. Minahan (Editor-in-chief), *Encyclopedia of social work* (18th ed., Vol. 1, pp. 765–770). Silver Spring, MD: National Association of Social Workers.

Hepworth, D.H., & Larsen, J. (1987). Interviewing. In A. Minihan (Editor-in-chief), *Encyclopedia of social work* (18th ed., Vol. 1, pp. 996–1008). Silver Spring, MD: National Association of Social Workers.

Hepworth, D.H., & Larsen, J. (1990). *Direct social work practice* (3rd ed.). Belmont, CA: Wadsworth.

Hepworth, D.H., & Larsen, J. (1993). *Direct social work practice: Theories and skills* (4th ed.). Pacific Grove, CA: Brooks/Cole.

Hetrick, E.S., & Martin, A.D. (1987). Developmental issues and their resolution for gay and lesbian adolescents. *Journal of Homosexuality, 14* (1/2), 25–42.

Hoffman, K.S., & Sallee, A.L. (1994). *Social work practice.* Needham Heights, MA: Allyn and Bacon.

Holland, T.P., & Petchers, M.K. Organizations: Context for Social Service Delivery. In A. Minahan (Editor-in-chief), *Encyclopedia of social work* (18th ed., Vol. 2, pp. 204–217). Silver Spring, MD: National Association of Social Workers.

Holloway, S.M. (1987). Staff-initiated change. In A. Minihan (Editor-in-chief), *Encyclopedia of social work* (18th ed., Vol 2, pp. 729–736). Silver Spring, MD: National Association of Social Workers.

Homan, M. (1994). *Promoting community change.* Belmont, CA: Brooks/Cole.

Hooyman, G. (1973). Team building in the human services. In B.R. Compton, & B. Galloway (Eds.), *Social work processes* (pp. 456–478). Homewood, IL: Dorsey.

Horsley, J.E., & Carlova, J. (1983). *Testifying in court.* Oradel, NY: Medical Economics Books.

Howard, J. (1982). *Basic issues in child welfare practice: A handbook for students and beginning workers* (pp. 31–32). Urbana, IL: Region V Child Welfare Training Center, University of Illinois at Champaign–Urbana.

Howing, P.T., & Wodarski, J.S. (1992). Legal requisites for social workers in child abuse and neglect situations. *Social Work, 37* (4), 330–336.

Huber, C.H., & Baruth, L.G. (1987). *Ethical, legal and professional issues in the practice of marriage and family therapy.* Columbus, OH: Merrill.

Hudson, W.W., & Thyer, B.A. (1987). Research measures and indexes in direct practice. In A. Minahan (Editor-in-chief), *Encyclopedia of social work* (18th ed., Vol.2, pp. 487–498). Silver Spring, MA: National Association of Social Workers.

Hull, G.H., Jr. (1990). Outcome study of UWEC social work graduate. Unpublished manuscript.

Hull, G.H., Ray, J.S., Rogers, J., & Smith, M. (1993). Revised BPD outcomes instrument findings: Initial report. *The BPD Forum,* 28–41.

Hunter, J., & Schaecher, R. (1987). Stresses on lesbian and gay adolescents in schools. *Social Work in Education, 9,* 180–184.

Hutchinson, E.D. (1993). Mandatory reporting laws: Child protective case finding gone awry? *Social Work, 38* (1), 56–63.

Isaacs-Shockley, M. (1994). Cultural competence and the juvenile system: Irreconcilable differences. *Focal Point, 8* (2), 19–20.

Jacobson, E. (1938). *Progressive relaxation* (2nd ed.). Chicago: University of Chicago Press.

Janis, I.L. (1982). *Groupthink.* Boston: Houghton Mifflin.

Jankovic, J., & Green, R.K. (1981). Teaching legal principles to social workers. *Journal of Education for Social Work, 17* (3), 28–35.

Johnson, D.W. (1986). *Reaching out: Intepersonal effectiveness and self-actualization* (3rd ed.). Englewood Cliffs, NJ: Prentice-Hall.

Johnson, L.C. (1989). *Social work practice: A generalist approach* (3rd ed.). Needham Heights, MA: Allyn and Bacon.

Johnson, L.C. (1992). *Social work practice: A generalist approach* (4th ed.). Needham Heights, MA: Allyn and Bacon.

Joiner, Brian, L., & Scholtes, P.R. (1985). *Total quality leadership vs. management by results* (pp. 1–9). Madison, WI: Joiner Associates, Inc.

Juran, J. (1989). *Juran on leadership for quality: An executive handbook* (4th ed.). New York: McGraw-Hill.

Kadushin, A. (1968). Games people play in supervision. *Social Work, 13* (3), 23–32.

Kadushin, A. (1977). *Consultation in social work.* New York: Columbia University Press.

Kadushin, A. (1995). Interviewing. In Richard L. Edwards (Editor-in-chief), *Encyclopedia of social work* (19th ed., Vol 2, pp. 1527–1537). Washington, DC: NASW Press.

Kanter, R.M. (1989). The new managerial work. *Harvard Business Review, 67* (6), 86–92.

Kettner, P.M., Daley, J.M., and Nichols, A.W. (1985). Initiating change in organizations and communities: A macro practice model. Monterey, CA: Brooks/Cole.

Keys, P.R. (1995). Quality management. In R.L. Edwards (Editor-in-chief), *Encyclopedia of social work* (19th ed., Vol. 3, pp. 2019–2025). Washington, DC: NASW Press.

Keys, P.R., & Ginsberg, L.H. (Eds.). (1988). *New management in human services.* Silver Spring, MD: National Association of Social Workers.

Kirst-Ashman, K.K., & Hull G.H., Jr. (1993). *Understanding generalist practice.* Chicago: Nelson-Hall.

Klein, D. (1980). Some notes on the dynamics of resistance to change: The defender role. In H. Resnick & R.J. Patti (Eds.), *Change from within: Humanizing social welfare organizations* (pp. 148–158). Philadelphia: Temple University Press.

Kleinkauf, C. (1981). A guide to giving legislative testimony. *Social Work, 26* (July), 297–303.

Knopf, R. (1979). *Surviving the BS (Bureaucratic System).* Wilmington, NC: Mandala Press.

Koestler, F.A. (Ed.). (1966). *The COMSTAC report: Standards for strengthened services* (mimeographed). New York: Commission on Standards and Accreditation of Services for the Blind.

Kramer, R.M. & Specht, H. (Eds.). (1975). *Readings in community organization practice* (2nd ed.). New York: Prentice-Hall.

Kramer, R.M., & Specht, H. (Eds.). (1983). *Readings in community organization practice* (3rd ed.). Englewood Cliffs, NJ: Prentice-Hall.

Kronenberg, P., & Loeffler, R. (1991). Quality management theory: Historical context and future prospect. *Journal of management Science & Policy Analysis, 8,* 203–221.

Kutchins, H. (1991). The fiduciary relationship: The legal basis for social workers' responsibilities to clients. *Social Work, 36* (2), 106–113.

Kyle, J.E. (Ed.). (1987). *Children, families, & cities: Programs that work at the local level.* Washington, DC: National League of Cities.

Lakein, A. (1973). *How to get control of your time and your life.* New York: Signet.

Landon, P.S. (1995). Generalist and advanced generalist practice. In R.L. Edwards (Editor-in-chief), *Encyclopedia of social work* (19th ed., Vol. 2, pp. 1101–1108). Washington, DC: NASW Press.

Larson, C.E., & LaFasto, F.M. (1989). *Teamwork.* Newbury Park, CA: Sage.

Lauffer, A. (1982). *Assessment tools for practitioners, managers, and trainers.* Beverly Hills, CA: Sage.

Lauffer, A., Nybell, L., Overberger, C., Reed, B., and Zeff, L. (1977). *Understanding your social agency.* Beverly Hills: Sage.

Lefferts, R. (1982). Getting a grant in the 1980s (2d ed.). Englewood Cliffs, NJ: Prentice-Hall.

Levy, C.S. (1982). *Guide to ethical decisions and actions for social service administrators: A handbook for managerial personnel.* New York: Haworth.

Levy, C.S. (1993). *Social work ethics on the line.* New York: Haworth.

Levy, P.A. (1991). Social work roles in law reform litigation. *Social Work, 36* (5), 434–439.

Lewinsohn, P.M., Munoz, M.A., Youngren, M.A., & Antonette, M.Z. (1978). *Control your depression.* Englewood Cliffs, NJ: Prentice-Hall.

Lewis, E.A., & Suarez, Z.E. (1995). Natural helping networks. In R.L. Edwards (Editor-in-chief), *Encyclopedia of social work* (19th ed., Vol. 2, pp. 1765–1772). Washington, DC: NASW Press.

Lewis, J.A., & Lewis, M.D. (1983). *Management of human service programs.* Monterey, CA: Brooks/Cole.

Lewis, J.A., Lewis, M.D., & Souflee, F., Jr. (1991). *Management of human service programs* (2nd ed.). Pacific Grove, CA: Brooks/Cole.

Lieberman, A.A., Hornby, H., & Russell, M. (1988). Analyzing the educational backgrounds and work experiences of child welfare personnel: A national study. *Social work, 33* (6), 485–489.

Lindsay, M. (1995). Understanding and enhancing adult learning. Unpublished paper prepared for presentation at the Spring Conference of the Wisconsin Council on Social Work Education, Wisconsin Dells, WI.

Lippitt, R., Watson, J., & Westley, B. (1958). *The dynamics of planned change.* New York: Harcourt, Brace & World.

Littlestone, R. (1973). Planning in mental health. In S. Feldman (Ed.), *The administration of mental health services.* Springfield, IL: Charles C. Thomas.

Loewenberg, F.M. (1987). *Fundamentals of social intervention* (2nd ed.). New York: Columbia University Press.

Loewenberg, F.M., & Dolgoff, R. (1985). *Ethical decisions for social work practice* (2nd ed.). Itasca, IL: Peacock.

Loewenberg, F.M., & Dolgoff, R. (1992). *Ethical decisions for social work practice* (4th ed.). Itasca, IL: Peacock.

Longres, J.F. (1990). *Human behavior in the social environment.* Itasca, IL: Peacock.

Lutheran Social Services of Wisconsin and Upper Michigan (LSS). (1993). *Getting started: TQS at LSS: A workbook on total quality service for employees.* Milwaukee, WI: LSS.

Macarov, D. (1991). *Certain change: Social work practice in the future.* Silver Spring, MD: National Association of Social Workers.

Mace, N.L., & Rabins, P.V. (1991). *The 36-hour day: A family guide to caring for persons with Alzheimer's disease, related dementing illness, and memory loss in later life.* Baltimore, MD: Johns Hopkins University Press.

Mackenzie, R.A. (1972). *The time trap: Managing your way out.* New York: AMACON.

Maguire, L. (1984). Networking for self-help: An empirically based guideline. In F.M. Cox, J.L. Erlich, J. Rothman, & J.E. Tropman, *Tactics and techniques of community practice* (pp. 198–208). Itasca, IL: Peacock.

Malcolm X. (1965). *The autobiography of Malcolm X.* New York: Grove.

Martin, L.L. (1993). *Total quality management in human service organizations.* Newbury Park, CA: Sage.

Mason, J.L. (1994). Developing culturally competent organizations. *Focal Point, 8* (2), 1–8.

Mason, M.A. (1992). Social workers as expert witnesses in child sexual abuse cases. *Social Work, 37* (1), 30–34.

Matthies, L.H., and Waalkes, A.K. (1974). *Essentials of project management.* Colorado Springs, CO: Systemation, Inc.

Matza, B.R. (1990). Empowerment: The key management skill of the 90s. *Retail Control, 58* (11), 20–23.

Maypole, D.E., & Skaine, R. (1983). Sexual harassment in the workplace. *Social work, 28* (5), 385–390.

Maypole, E. (1986). Sexual harassment of social workers at work: Injustice within. *Social work, 31* (1), 29–34.

McGoverns, J., & Peters, K. (1985). *Courtroom survival for expert witnesses* (tapes 1 and 2: L172–5 A and B). Seattle, WA: Author.

Meenaghan, T.M., Washington, R.O., & Ryan, R.M. (1982). *Macro practice in the human services.* New York: Free Press.

Miller, J. (1980). Teaching law and legal skills to social workers. *Journal of Education for Social Work, 16* (3), 87–95.

Mills, J.E. (1987). Juvenile Welfare Board: Pinellas County, Florida. In J.E. Kyle (Ed.), *Children, families & cities: Programs that work at the local level.* Washington, DC: National League of Cities.

Mizrahi, T., & Morrison, J.D. (1993). *Community organization and social administration.* New York: Haworth.

Mogil, H.B.M. (1989). Maximizing your courtroom testimony. *FBI Law Enforcement Bulletin* (May), 7–9.

Morris, R. (1987). Social welfare policy. In A. Minahan (Editor-in-chief), *Encyclopedia of social work* (18th ed., Vol. 2, pp. 664–681). Silver Spring, MD: National Association of Social Workers.

Morris, R., & Binstock, R.H. (1980). Organizational resistance to planning goals. In H. Resnick & R.J. Patti, *Change from within: Humanizing social welfare organizations* (pp. 132–147). Philadelphia: Temple University Press.

Morrow, C.A. (1987). Child and family homelessness. In J.E.Kyle (Ed.), *Children, families & cities: Programs that work at the local level* (pp. 109–156). Washington, DC: National League of Cities.

Morrow, D.F. (1993). Social work with gay and lesbian adolescents. *Social Work, 38* (6), 655–660.

Mossard, G.R. (1991). A TQM technical skills framework. *Journal of Management Science & Policy Analysis, 8* 223–246.

Motenko, A.K. (1989). The frustrations, gratifications, and well-being of dementia caregivers. *Gerontologist, 29* (2), 166–172.

Muckian, M. (1994). TQM bumps and bruises. In *Business* (June), 20–35, 39.

National Association of Social Workers. (1982). *NASW standards for the classification of social work practice.* Silver Spring, MD: Author.

National Association of Social Workers. (1993). *Code of ethics of national association of social workers.* Silver Spring, MD: Author.

National Association of Social Workers Program Advancement Fund. (Undated). *A step-by-step guide to the job search process.* Silver Spring, MD: Author.

National League of Cities. (1989). *Fighting poverty in cities.* Washington, DC: Author.

Netting, F.E., Kettner, P.M.,and McMurtry, S.L. (1993). *Social work macro practice.* White Plains, NY: Longman.

Neugeboren, B. (1991). *Organization, policy, and practice in the human services.* Binghamton, NY: Haworth.

North, C.S., & Smith, E.M. (1994). Comparison of white and nonwhite homeless men and women. *Social Work, 39* (6), 639–647.

Nunnally, E., & Moy, C. (1989). *Communication basics for human service professionals.* Newbury Park, CA: Sage.

Nurius, P. S., & Hudson, W.W. (1994). *Human services practice, evaluation, and computers.* Pacific Grove, CA: Brooks/Cole.

Obier, L. (1995). *The legal environment of social work* (rev. ed.). Washington, DC: NASW Press.

Okun, B.F. (1976). Effective helping: Interviewing and counseling techniques. Belmont, CA: Duxbury.

Osborne, D., & Gaebler, T. (1992). *Reinventing government: How the entrepreneurial spirit is transforming the public sector from schoolhouse to statehouse, city hall to the Pentagon.* Reading, MA: Addison-Wesley.

Pancoast, D.L., & Collins, A.H. (1987). Natural helping networks. In A. Minahan (Editor-in-chief) *Encyclopedia of social work* (18th ed., Vol. 2, pp. 177–182). Silver Spring, MD: National Association of Social Workers.

Parker, Y. (1989). *The damn good resumé guide.* Berkeley, CA: Ten Speed Press.

Patti, R.J. (1980a). Internal advocacy and human service practitioners: An exploratory study. In H. Resnick & R.J. Patti (Eds.), *Change from within: Humanizing social welfare organizations* (pp. 287–302). Philadelphia: Temple University Press.

Patti, R.J. (1980b). Organizational resistance and change: The view from below. In H. Resnick & R.J. Patti (Eds.), *Change from within, Humanizing social welfare organizations* (pp. 114–131). Philadelphia: Temple University Press.

Patti, R.J. (1980c). Social work practice: Organizational environment. In H. Resnick & R.J. Patti (Eds.), *Change from within: Humanizing social welfare organizations* (pp. 46–56). Philadelphia: Temple University Press.

Patti, R.J. (1983). Limitations and prospects of internal advocacy. In H. Weissman, I. Epstein, & A. Savage (Eds.), *Agency-based social work* (pp.214–223). Philadelphia: Temple University Press.

Patti, R.J., & Resnick, H. (1980). Changing the agency from within. In H. Resnick & R.J. Patti (Eds.), *Change from within: Humanizing social welfare organizations* (pp. 217–230). Philadelphia: Temple University Press.

Pawlak, E.J. (1980). Organizational tinkering. In H. Resnick & R.J. Patti (Eds.), *Change from within: Humanizing social welfare organizations* (pp. 264–274). Philadelphia: Temple University Press.

Pawlak, E.J. (1983). Organizational tinkering. In A. Weissman, I. Epstein, & A. Savage (Eds.), *Agency-based social work.* Philadelphia: Temple University Press.

Perlman, G.L. (1988). Mastering the law of privileged communication: A guide for social workers. *Social Work, 33* (5), 425–429.

Perlman, R., & Gurin, A. (1972). *Community organization and social planning.* New York: Wiley.

Perlmutter, F.D. (1990). *Changing hats from social work practice to administration.* Silver Spring, MD: National Association of Social Workers.

Perrow, C.A. (1961). The analysis of goals in complex organizations. *American Sociological Review, 26* (6), 856–866.

Peters, T. (1987). *Thriving on chaos: Handbook for a management revolution.* New York: HarperCollins.

Pincus, A., & Minahan, A. (1973). *Social work practice: Model and method.* Itasca, IL: Peacock.

Pittman, K.J., Adams-Taylor, S., & Morich, M. (1987). Adolescent pregnancy prevention. In J.E. Kyle (Ed.), *Children, families & cities: Programs that work at the local level* (pp. 157–194). Washington, DC: National League of Cities.

Popple, P.R. (1995). The Social work profession: History. In R.L. Edwards (Editor-in-chief), *Encyclopedia of social work* (19th ed., Vol. 3, pp. 2282–2292). Washington, DC: NASW Press.

Proctor, C.D., & Groze, V.K. (1994). Risk factors for suicide among gay, lesbian, and bisexual youths. *Social Work, 39* (5), 504–513.

Pruchno, R.A., & Resch, N.L. (1989). Husbands and wives as caregivers: Antecedents of depression and burden. *Gerontologist, 29* (2), 159–165.

Rapp, C.A. (1987). Information utilization for management decision making. *Encyclopedia of social work* (Vol. 1, pp. 937–944). Silver Spring, MD: NASW.

Rapp, C., & Poertner, J. (1992). *Social administration: A client-centered approach.* White Plains, NY: Longman.

Rappaport, J., Reischl, T.M., & Zimmerman, M.A. (1992). Mutual help mechanisms in the empowerment of former mental patients. In D. Saleebey (Ed.), *The strengths perspective in social work practice* (pp. 84–97). New York: Longman.

Reamer, F. G. (1983). Ethical dilemmas in social work practice. *Social Work, 28* (1), 31–35.

Reamer, F.G. (1987). Values and ethics. In A. Minahan (Editor-in-chief), *Encyclopedia of social work* (18th ed., Vol. 2, pp. 801–809). Silver Spring, MD: National Association of Social Workers.

Reamer, F.G. (1990). *Ethical dilemmas in social service* (2nd ed.). New York: Columbia University Press.

Reamer, F.G. (1995a) Ethics and values. In Richard L. Edwards (Editor-in-chief), *Encyclopedia of social work* (19th ed, Vol 1, pp. 893–902). Washington, DC: NASW Press.

Reamer, F.G. (1995b). *Social work values and ethics.* New York: Columbia University Press.

Reid, P.N., & Popple, P.R. (1992). *The moral purposes of social work.* Chicago: Nelson-Hall.

Reid, W.J. (1987). Research in social work. In A. Minahan (Editor-in-chief), *Encyclopedia of social work* (18th ed., Vol. 2, pp. 474–487). Silver Spring, MD: National Association of Social Workers.

Renzetti, C.M., & Currah, D.J. (1992). *Women, men and society.* Needham Heights, MA: Allyn and Bacon.

Resnick, H. (1980a). Appendix: A workshop on organizational change for supervisors and practitioners. In H. Resnick & R.J. Patti (Eds.), *Change from within: Humanizing social welfare organizations* (pp. 307–323). Philadelphia: Temple University Press.

Resnick, H. (1980b). Effecting internal change in human service organizations. In H. Resnick & R.J. Patti (Eds.), *Change from within: Humanizing social welfare organizations* (pp. 187–199). Philadelphia: Temple University Press.

Resnick, H. (1980c). Tasks in changing the organization from within. In H. Resnick & R.J. Patti (Eds.), *Change from within: Humanizing social welfare organizations* (pp. 200–216). Philadelphia: Temple University Press.

Resnick, H., & Patti, R.J. (Eds.). (1980). *Change from within: Humanizing social welfare institutions.* Philadelphia: Temple University Press.

Rivera, F.G., & Erlick, J.L. (1992). *Community organizing in a diverse society.* Boston: Allyn and Bacon.

Rompf, E.L., & Royse, D. (1994). Choice of social work as a career: Possible influences. *Journal of Social Work Education, 30* (2). 163–171.

Roskies, E. (1991). *Stress management: A new approach to treatment.* New York: Columbia University Press.

Ross, M.G. (1967). *Community organization.* New York: Harper & Row.

Rothman, J. (1980). Promoting an innovation. In H. Resnick & R.J. Patti (Eds.), *Change from within: Humanizing social welfare organizations* (pp. 231–263). Philadelphia: Temple University Press.

Rothman, J. (1984). Introduction. In F.M. Cox, J.L. Erlich, J. Rothman, & J.E. Tropman (Eds.), *Tactics and techniques of community practice.* Itasca, IL: Peacock.

Rothman, J., Erlich, J.L., & Teresa, J.G. (1981). *Changing organizations and community programs.* Beverly Hills: Sage.

Rothman, J., Erlich, J.L., & Tropman, E. (Eds.) (1995). *Strategies of community organization practice* (5th ed.). Itasca, IL: Peacock

Rubin, H.J., & Rubin, I.S. (1986). *Community organizing and development.* Columbus, OH: Merrill.

Rubin, H.J., & Rubin, I.S. (1992). *Community organizing and development* (2nd ed.). New York: Macmillan.

Russo, J.R. (1980). *Serving and surviving as a human-service worker.* Prospect Heights, IL: Waveland.

Russon, T. (1987). Conserve: the consortium for services to homeless families. J.E. Kyle (Ed.), *Children, families & cities: Programs that work at the local level.* Washington, DC: National League of Cities.

Saleebey, D. (Ed.). (1992). *The strengths perspective in social work practice.* New York: Longman.

Sapiro, V. (1990). *Women in American society.* Mountain View, CA: Mayfield.

Sarri, R. (1987). Administration in social welfare. In A. Minahan (Ed.), *Encyclopedia of social work* (18th ed., vol. 1, pp. 27–40). Silver Spring, MD: National Association of Social Workers.

Sashkin, M., & Kiser, K.J. (1993). *Putting total quality management to work: What TQM means, how to use it and how to sustain it over the long run.* San Francisco: Berrett–Koehler.

Schafer, W. (1978). *Stress, distress and growth.* David, CA: International Dialogue Press.

Schoech, D. (1987). Information systems: Agency. In A. Minahan (Editor-in-chief), *Encyclopedia of social work* (18th ed., vol. 1, pp. 920–931). Silver Spring, MD: National Association of Social Workers.

Schwab, A.J., & Wilson, S.S. (1989). The continuum of care system: Decision support for practitioners. In W. La-Mendola, B. Glastonbury, & S. Toole (Eds.), *A casebook of computer applications in the social and human services* (pp. 123–140). Binghamton, NY: Haworth.

Schwartz, S., & Dattolo, P. (1990). Factors affecting student selection of macro specializations. *Administration in Social Work, 14* (3), 83–96.

Segal, B. (1980). Planning and power in hospital social service. In H. Resnick & R.J. Patti (Eds.), *Change from within: Humanizing social welfare organizations* (pp. 275–286). Philadelphia: Temple University Press.

Segal, S.P. (1987). Deinstitutionalization. In A. Minahan (Editor-in-chief) *Encyclopedia of social work* (18th ed., Vol. 1, pp. 376–382). Silver Spring, MD: National Association of Social Workers.

Segal, S.P., Silverman, C., & Temkin, T. (1993). Empowerment and self-help agency practice for people with mental disabilities. *Social Work, 38* (6), 705–712.

Selye, H. (1956). *The stress of life.* New York: McGraw-Hill.

Sharwell, G.R. (1982). How to testify before a legislative committee. In M. Mahaffey & J. Hanks (Eds.), *Practical politics: Social workers and political responsibility.* Silver Spring, MD: National Association of Social Workers.

Sheafor, B.W., Horejsi, C.R., & Horejsi, G.A. (1988). *Techniques and guidelines for social work practice.* Boston: Allyn and Bacon.

Sheafor, B.W., Horejsi, C.R., & Horejsi, G.A. (1988). *Techniques and guidelines for social work practice* (2nd ed.). Boston: Allyn and Bacon.

Sheafor, B.W., & Landon, P.S. (1987). Generalist perspective. In A. Minahan (Editor-in-chief), *Encyclopedia of social work* (18th ed., Vol. 1, pp. 660–669). Silver Spring, MD: National Association of Social Workers.

Shulman, L. (1991). *International social work practice.* Itasca, IL: Peacock.

Simpson, C., & Simpson, D. (1992). *Exploring careers in social work.* New York: Rosen Publishing Group.

Sinclair, L. (1993). Making ethical decisions. In K.K. Kirst-Ashman and G.H. Hull, Jr. (Eds.), *Understanding Generalist Practice* (pp. 372–397). Chicago: Nelson-Hall.

Siporin, M. (1975). *Introduction to social work practice.* New York: Macmillan.

Slipman, S. (1986). *Helping ourselves to power.* New York: Pergamon.

Smith, M.K. (1987). Child care. In J.E. Kyle (Ed.), *Children, families & cities: Programs that work at the local level* (pp. 35–68). Washington, DC: National League of Cities.

Smith, R.F. (1995). Settlements and neighborhood centers. In R.L. Edwards (Editor-in-chief), *Encyclopedia of social work* (19th Ed., Vol. 3, pp. 2129–2135). Washington, DC: NASW Press.

Smith, T.W. (1987). *Public attitudes toward cities and urban problems.* Washington, DC: National League of Cities.

Specht, H. (1969). Disruptive tactics. *Social Work, 14* (2), 5–15.

Stern, P. (1991). Surviving in the courtroom: 10 rules on testifying as an expert witness. *APSAC Advisor, 4* (1), 3–4.

Sundel, S.S., & Sundel, M. (1980). *Be assertive: A practical guide for human service workers.* Beverly Hills, CA: Sage.

Taylor, E. (1987). *From issue to action: An advocacy program model.* Lancaster, PA: Author.

Telesford, M.C. (1994). Tips for accessing and involving families of color in a significant ways. *Focal Point, 8* (2), 11.

Thompson, J.J. (1994). Social workers and politics: Beyond the Hatch Act. *Social Work, 39* (4), 457–465.

Toseland, R.W., & Rivas, R. (1984). *An introduction to group work practice.* New York: Macmillan.

Townsend, P.L., & Gebhardt, J.E. (1992). *Quality in action: 93 lessons in leadership, participation, and measurement.* New York: Wiley.

Tracy, E.M. (1990). Identifying social support resources of at-risk families. *Social Work, 35* (3), 252–258.

Tropman, J.E. (1995). Value conflicts and decision making: analysis and resolution. In J.E. Tropman, J.L. Erlich, & J. Rothman (Eds.), *Tactics and techniques of community intervention* (3rd ed., pp. 66–74). Itasca, IL: Peacock.

Tropman, J.E. Erlich, J.L., & Rothman, R. (1995). *Tactics and techniques of community organization.* Itasca, IL: Peacock.

U.S. General Accounting Office (1977). *Returning the mentally disabled to the community: Government needs to do more.* Washington, DC: General Accounting Office.

Van Wormer, K. (1992). No wonder social workers feel uncomfortable in court. *Child and Adolescent Social Work Journal, 9* (2), 117–129.

Vayda, E., & Bogo, M. (1991). A teaching model to unite classroom and field. *Journal of Social Work Education, 27* (3), 271–278.

Verschelden, C. (1993). Social work values and practicum: Opportunities to work as a professional responsibility. *Social Work, 38* (6), 765–769.

Walton, M. (1986). *The Deming management method.* New York: Perigee Books.

Warren, R. (1978). *The community in America* (3rd. ed.). Chicago: Rand McNally.

Wasserman, H. (1980). The professional social worker in a bureaucracy. In H. Resnick & R.J. Patti (Eds.), *Change from within: Humanizing social welfare organizations* (pp. 86–95). Philadelphia: Temple University Press.

Watson, D.L., & Tharp, R.G. (1973). *Self-directed behavior.* Monterey, CA: Brooks/Cole.

Webster's Ninth New Collegiate Dictionary. (1991). Springfield, MA: Merriam-Webster.

Weil, M.O., & Gamble, D.N. (1995). Community practice models. In R.L. Edwards (Editor-in-chief), *Encyclopedia of social work* (19th ed., Vol. 1, pp. 577–593). Washington, DC: NASW Press.

Weissman, H., Epstein, I., & Savage, A. (1983). *Agency-based social work.* Philadelphia: Temple University Press.

White, V.P. (1975). *Grants.* New York: Plenum.

Whittaker, J.K., & Garbarino, J. (1983). *Social support networks: Informal helping in the human services.* New York: Aldine.

Whittacker, J.K., & Tracy, E.M. (1989). *Social treatment: An introduction to social work practice.* New York: Aldine.

Wilson, S.J. (1978). *Confidentiality in social work: Issues and principles* (pp. 1–274). New York: Free Press.

Wolk, J.L., Pray, J.E., Kalkbrenner, L., & Propp, J. (1986). Alzheimer's disease in rural areas: Can informal networks meet the needs? *Human Services in the Rural Environment, 10* (3), 8–13.

Wrightsman, L.S., Willis, C.E., & Kassin, S. (1987). *On the witness stand.* Newbury Park, CA: Sage.

Wyers, N.L. (1991). Policy practice in social work: Models and issues. *Journal of Social Work Education, 27* (3), 241–250.

Yessian, M.R., & Broskowski, A. (1983). Generalists in human service systems: Their problems and prospects. In R.M. Kramer & H. Specht (Eds.), *Readings in community organization practice* (pp. 180–198). Englewood Cliffs, NJ: Prentice-Hall.

Young, B. (1987). Comprehensive child care program. *Children, families & cities.* Washington, DC: National League of Cities.

Young, K.N. (1978). *The basic steps of planning.* Charlottesville, NC: Community Collaborators.

Ziesemer, C., Marcoux, L., & Marwell, B.E. (1994). Homeless children: Are they different from other low-income children? *Social Work, 39* (6), 658–668.

Zill, N., & Nord, C.W. (1994). *Running in place.* Washington, DC: Child Trends, Inc.

NAME INDEX

SUBJECT INDEX

PHOTO CREDITS